# BEYON

## ·THE·

# STORM

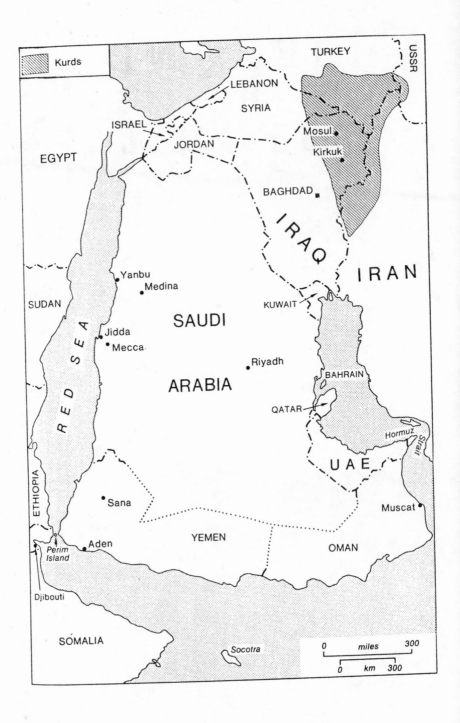

# BEYOND ·THE· STORM

## A GULF CRISIS READER

■EDITED BY■
**Phyllis Bennis and Michel Moushabeck**
Foreword by Edward W. Said
Introduction by Eqbal Ahmad

**CANONGATE**

This edition first published in Great Britain in 1992 by
**CANONGATE PRESS PLC**
14 Frederick Street, Edinburgh EH2 2HB
Originally published in the U.S.A. in 1991 by Olive Branch Press,
an imprint of Interlink Publishing Group, Inc.

The essay entitled "Thoughts on a War: Ignorant Armies Clash by Night" by Edward W.
Said appeared in the February 11, 1991, issue of *The Nation*. Copyright © 1991 by Edward
W. Said. Reprinted by permission. The essays entitled "The Warrior Culture" and "The Panama
Paradigm," (Original Title: "Who Wants Another Panama?") by Barbara
Ehrenreich appeared in the October 15, 1990 and January 21, 1991 issues of *Time*
Magazine. Copyright © 1990, 1991 by The Time, Inc. Magazine Company.
Reprinted by permission.

**British Library Cataloguing in Publication Data**

A complete record of Publication Data is available on request.
ISBN 0–86241–379–6

Printed and bound in the United States of America


9 8 7 6 5 4 3 2

# Contents

# Contributors

*Ibrahim Abu-Lughod* is Professor of Political Science at Northwestern University in Evanston, Illinois. He is a member of the Palestine National Council.

*Eqbal Ahmad* teaches social science at Hampshire College in Amherst, Massachusetts. He has been involved in peace and justice issues in the U.S., the Middle East and his native Pakistan for forty years.

*Naseer Aruri* is Professor of Political Science at University of Massachusetts, Dartmouth. He is on the board of directors of Middle East Watch, and is a former board member of Amnesty International, USA.

*Hanan Mikhail Ashrawi* teaches English at Bir Zeit University in the occupied West Bank and has been Dean of the Faculty of Arts for four years. She is an internationally known Palestinian leader who has participated in numerous meetings with U.S., European and other international officials.

*Bishara A. Bahbah* is a senior fellow at The Center for Policy Analysis on Palestine, and Adjunct Professor of Political Science at Brigham Young University. He is the author of *Israel and Latin America: The Military Connection*.

*Lyman Baker* teaches English at Kansas State University in Manhattan, Kansas. He is active in the Manhattan Coalition for Peace in the Middle East, and is on the steering committee of the Alliance on Central America.

*Mordechai Bar-On* is a reserve colonel in the Israeli Defense Forces. He is a founder member of Peace Now.

*Phyllis Bennis* covers the United Nations and the Middle East for Pacifica Radio, including WBAI's *Undercurrents* program in New York. She is the author of *From Stones to Statehood: The Palestinian Uprising*.

*Jeanne Butterfield* is Executive Director of the Palestine Solidarity Committee.

*Louise Cainkar* is Director of the Chicago-based Database Project on Palestinian Human Rights. She has initiated a project to assess the effects of the Gulf War on civilians in Iraq, Jordan and Kuwait. In April 1991 she spent several weeks conducting field work in Iraq.

*Noam Chomsky* is a noted author, lecturer and Institute Professor in the Department of Linguistics and Philosophy at the Massachusetts Institute of Technology (MIT). He is the author of numerous books and articles on linguistics, philosophy, intellectual history and contemporary issues, and has written extensively on U.S. foreign policy.

*Daniel Cirera* is the National Secretary of the Mouvement de la Paix. He is based in Paris, and is a regular contributor to *Temoignage Chrétien* and *La Pensée*. He is the author of *Why Missiles?*

*Stanley Cohen* is Professor of Criminology at the Hebrew University in Jerusalem. His most recent books include *Visions of Social Control* and *Against Criminology*. He has worked with organizations such as End the Occupation, and was a founding member of the Public Committee Against Torture in Israel.

*Barbara Ehrenreich* is a columnist for *Time* magazine, and author of several books, the most recent of which is *The Worst Years of Our Lives: Irreverent Notes on a Decade of Greed*.

*Max Elbaum* is a long-time anti-war activist based in Oakland, California. He is co-editor of *Crossroads* magazine.

*Hala Fattah* is Visiting Assistant Professor of History at Georgetown University in Washington, D.C. She writes frequently on the pre-oil history of Iraq, Arabia and the Gulf.

*Laura Flanders* is co-producer of the award-winning syndicated radio show *Undercurrents* on New York's WBAI radio. She also works with FAIR (Fairness and Accuracy in Reporting).

*Yvonne Yazbeck Haddad* is Professor of Islamic History at the University of Massachusetts in Amherst.

*Mustafa B. Hamarneh* is Assistant Professor of Modern Middle East History at the University of Jordan. He lives in Amman.

*Sherif Hetata* is a poet and novelist. He spent many years imprisoned by various governments of his native Egypt. After his release in 1964, he worked as a physician for Egypt's Ministry of Health and the United Nations. He is married to Nawal el-Saadawi.

**Samir Hulaileh** is a noted Palestinian economist. He lives in Ramallah in the occupied West Bank.

**Penny Kemp** is a former Co-chair of the British Green Party. She coordinated the international scientific symposium on the environmental effects of war in the Gulf, held in London during the first months of the crisis. She is author (with Derek Wall) of *A Green Manifesto*, and editor of *Europe's Green Alternative*.

**Clovis Maksoud** is the former Ambassador of the Arab League to the United Nations; he resigned in protest at the League's inability to resolve the Gulf crisis. He now teaches at the American University in Washington, D.C.

**Michel Moushabeck** is Middle East editor of Olive Branch Press, and publisher of Interlink Publishing Group in New York.

**Steve Niva** is in the doctoral program in Middle East Studies at Columbia University in New York City.

**Jack O'Dell** is Director of the International Department of the National Rainbow Coalition, based in Washington, D.C. He also serves on the board of the U.S. Peace Council, and is chair of the Pacifica Foundation.

**Talat Rahman** is Professor of Physics at Kansas State University. She is co-editor of *Pakistan Progressive*, and works with the Manhattan Coalition for Peace in the Middle East.

**Paul Rogers** teaches in the Department of Peace Studies at Bradford University in England, where he specializes in resource conflict and military force projection. During the Gulf crisis he wrote for *The Observer* and *The Guardian* in London.

**Sheila Ryan** is a freelance writer and a longstanding activist in the Middle East peace movement; most recently she founded the Network for Peace in the Middle East. She is a Middle East programmer for WBAI radio in New York.

**Edward W. Said** is Old Dominion Foundation Professor in the Humanities at Columbia University. He is a renowned Middle East scholar and critic, a member of the Palestine National Council, and the author of numerous books, including *Orientalism*, *The Question of Palestine*, *Covering Islam*, *After the Last Sky*, and *Culture and Imperialism*.

**Michael Tanzer** is president of Tanzer Economic Associates, Inc., a New York-based consulting firm specializing in energy and environmental economics. His most recent book is *Energy Update: Oil in the Late Twentieth Century*.

# Preface

Saddam Hussein, in forecasting "the mother of all battles" in the Gulf War, compared himself to Saladin. No doubt the response of the vast majority of people in the West was: Who? This lack of knowledge masks the vital need to respond to Saddam Hussein's posturing with the question "Why?" Why would this ambitious dictator, in seeking to justify his opportunistic invasion of a neighboring state, invoke the legendary figure of the twelfth century Muslim leader who fought back successfully against the European Crusaders?

A whole history has been rendered invisible if even such basic knowledge of the Middle East as the identity of Salah ad-Din al-Ayyubi is not accessible to those in the West. There is a long and tragic chronicle of Western involvement in the region known as the Middle East — from the Crusades through European colonialism and U.S. military and economic intervention. That history is what lies behind Saddam Hussein's self-aggrandizing pronouncements; equally it underlies the vehement opposition in most of the Arab world to U.S. and European intervention in the Gulf crisis. Little or no attempt was made by those in power in the West to address those sentiments; popular opposition only enters the minds of the strategic planners when it reaches the level of organized resistance. This wilful misunderstanding is what led us down the path to the seemingly casual slaughter of the Gulf War.

This book was conceived with the belief that it is only through the dissemination of information that the first steps towards peace can be made in the region. The essays in this anthology were mostly written at the height of the conflict or shortly afterwards, but this is in no way an instant book on the Gulf War. All of our contributors share the desire not only to oppose the war but to take the broader view: to place the crisis in its historical context, to widen the discussion to include other nations in the region (Jordan, Israel, Pakistan, Palestine), to lead the reader to the point where he or she feels the necessity of seeking further information.

The essays that follow all refuse the simplistic readings of the crisis which dominated the debate in the U.S. and Europe. Instead they address such interconnected issues as the history of U.S. foreign policy and the history of the various states in the region; domestic opposition in the U.S. and the difficulty of countering mainstream media constructions of the crisis; the impact of the conflict in Europe, in Jordan, in Egypt, in Pakistan; and the post-war catastrophe engulfing Iraq and Kuwait, both in terms of environmental damage, and in terms of the public health disaster experienced in Iraq in the wake of the twin destructive power of coalition bombs and UN sanctions.

One further thread runs through almost all of these essays: the question of Palestine. Saddam Hussein may have been merely the latest in a long line of Arab leaders who have sought to use the Palestinian issue and the Palestinian movement to further their own ends, but this does not alter the absolute necessity of finding a solution to the Arab-Israeli conflict if the Middle East is to be saved from the disaster of recurring wars. Indeed the Bush administration implicitly recognized this fact by sending Secretary of State Baker to the region immediately after hostilities had ended, to initiate another round of shuttle diplomacy. Although "linkage" was made a dirty word in U.S. policymaking during the crisis, nothing can erase the problem of Palestine. It is inextricably linked to all the other issues in the region, as our contributors consummately demonstrate.

*Beyond the Storm* does not pretend to exhaust all the levels of the Gulf crisis by any means, but it does hope to provoke critical thinking on the subject. The diversity of the writers contained in these pages — Palestinian, Jordanian, Israeli, British, French, Egyptian, Pakistani, American — reflects our desire to stretch the frontiers of the debate over the meaning and impact of the complex set of events of 1990–91 which were given the label "Gulf crisis."

The completion of this book owes a great deal to the many friends and acquaintances who gave us invaluable advice, assistance and critical support. Above all, a vast debt of gratitude is owed to the contributors who saw merit in our project and consented to devote their precious time to write in the midst of the crisis. Throughout the project we were fortunate to have the devoted support of our colleague Tim Watson, who cast a critical eye over our labors, and worked diligently and with unfailing insight and precision on the copyediting of the essays. His contribution and that of the staff of Olive Branch Press, who worked hard to get this timely book out quickly, is gratefully acknowledged. Special thanks are due to Connie Hogarth, Kathy Engel, Susan Sarandon, Ricardo Alarcon, Ruth Moushabeck, Riyad Khoury, Pete Seeger, Gus Newport, Robin Morgan and Douglas Foster for their encouragement, guidance and support for the project. We also profited immensely from the advice and invaluable assistance of Joe Stork, Martha Wenger and the staff of *Middle East Report*.

We owe a particular debt to our families, without whose patience, understanding and encouragement this book might never have been completed.

Lastly we would like to pay special tribute to all the victims of the war in the Gulf, civilian and military. In particular we note the words of Eqbal Ahmad in the introduction to this volume: "The history of our time is studded with unrecorded holocausts." It is our fervent wish that the people, both Iraqis and Kurds, living and dying in post-war Iraq, ravaged by malnutrition, poor sanitation, power blackouts and a chronic lack of medicines and healthcare facilities, will not become merely another item on that inglorious list.

—M.M. and P.B.
Brooklyn, New York
September 1991

# Foreword

## Thoughts on a War:
## Ignorant Armies Clash by Night

*Edward W. Said*

From the moment that George Bush invented Desert Shield, Desert Storm was all too logical, and Poppy turned himself into Captain Ahab. Saddam Hussein, a dictator of the kind the United States has typically found and supported, was almost invited into Kuwait, then almost immediately demonized and transformed into a worldwide metaphysical threat. Iraq's military capabilities were fantastically exaggerated, the country verbally obliterated except for its by now isolated leader, UN sanctions given a ludicrously short run, and then America began the war.

Since 1973 the United States has wanted a physical presence in the Persian Gulf: to control oil supply, to project power and above all, recently, to refurbish and refinance its military. With his crude brutality no match for U.S. and Israeli propaganda, Saddam Hussein became the perfect target, and the best excuse to move in. The United States will not soon leave the Middle East.

The electronic war to destroy Iraq as a lesson in retributive power went rapidly into full swing, the press managing patriotism, entertainment and disinformation without respite. As a topic, civilian "collateral damage" was avoided and unasked about; no one discussed how Baghdad, the old Abbasid capital, might survive the appalling rigors of technological warfare, or how the bombing of its water, fuel and electrical supplies, which sustain four million people, was necessary to this "surgical" war (a larger replay of Israel's destruction of Beirut). Few commentators questioned the disproportion of 200,000-plus air sorties against a country roughly the size of California.

It is curious, but profoundly symptomatic of the Gulf conflict, that the one word that was tediously pronounced and repronounced and yet left unanalyzed was "linkage," an ugly solecism that could have been invented only in late twentieth-century America. "Linkage" means not that there is

1

but that there is no connection. Things that belong together by common association, sense, geography, history, are sundered, left apart for convenience' sake and for the benefit of U.S. imperial strategists. Everyone his own carver, Jonathan Swift said. That the Middle East is linked by all sorts of ties, *that* is irrelevant. That Arabs might see a connection between Saddam Hussein in Kuwait and Israel in Lebanon, that too is futile. That U.S. policy itself is the linkage, this is a forbidden topic to broach.

Never in my experience have nouns designating the Arab world or its components been so bandied about: Saddam Hussein, Kuwait, Islam, fundamentalism. Never have they had so strangely abstract and diminished a meaning, and rarely did any regard or care seem to accompany them, even though the United States was not at war with all the Arabs but very well might have been, except for its pathetic clients such as Mubarak of Egypt and the various Gulf rulers.

In all the mainstream debate in the U.S. since August 2, 1990, much the smallest component in the discussion was Arab. During the Congressional hearings that went on for two weeks in December 1990, no significant Arab-American voice was heard. In Congress and in the press, "linkages" of all kinds went unexamined. Little was done to report oil-company profits, or the fact that the surge in gasoline prices had nothing to do with supply, which remained plentiful. The Iraqi case against Kuwait, or even the nature of Kuwait itself, liberal in some ways, illiberal in others, received next to no hearing; the point would not have been to exculpate Saddam Hussein but to perceive the longstanding complicity and hypocrisy of the Gulf states, the United States and Europe during the Iran-Iraq war. Efforts were made to grapple with Arab popular rallying to Saddam Hussein, despite the unattractive qualities of his rule, but these efforts were not integrated into, or allowed equal time with, the distortions in American Middle East policy. The central media failing has been an unquestioning acceptance of American power: its right to ignore dozens of United Nations resolutions on Palestine (or even to refuse to pay its UN dues), to attack Panama, Grenada, Libya, and also to proclaim the absolute morality of its Gulf position.

From prewar television reports of the crisis I cannot recall a single guest or program that raised the issue of what right "we" had to get Iraq out of Kuwait; nor any exploration of the enormous human, social and economic costs *to the Arabs* of an American strike. Yet on January 7, I heard a well-known "Middle East expert" say on TV that "war is the easy part; what to do afterward?" as if "we" might, in an afterthought, get around to picking up the pieces and rearranging the area. At the farthest extreme were the unmistakably racist prescriptions of William Safire and A.M. Rosenthal of *The New York Times* as well as Fouad Ajami of CBS, who routinely urged the most unrestrained military attacks against Iraq. The underlying fantasy strongly resembles the Israeli paradigm for dealing with the Arabs: Bomb them, humiliate them, lie about them.

From the beginning, when Arabs appeared on television they were the merest tokens: a journalist or two eager to show Arab failings and weaknesses (which were real and had to be pointed out); the Saudi or Kuwaiti Ambassador, more enthusiastic about war than most Americans; the Iraqi Ambassador, who defended the Husseinian view of the world with cautious amiability; the tiny group of Arab-Americans like myself whose position was neither with Iraq nor with the U.S.-Saudi coalition. Once, in the fifteen seconds I was given, when I began to elucidate an argument about the relationship between Iraqi aggression and American imperialism, I was cut off abruptly: "Yes, yes, we know all that."

Seen from the Arab point of view, the picture of America is just as constricted. There is still hardly any literature in Arabic that portrays Americans; the most interesting exception is Abdel Rahman Munif's massive trilogy *Cities of Salt*, but his books are banned in several countries, and his native Saudi Arabia has stripped him of his citizenship. To my knowledge there is still no institute or major academic department in the Arab world whose main purpose is the study of America, although the United States is by far the largest outside force in the Arab world. It is difficult to explain even to well-educated and experienced fellow Arabs that U.S. foreign policy is not in fact run by the C.I.A., or a conspiracy, or a shadowy network of key "contacts." Many Arabs I know believe the United States plans virtually every event of significance in the Middle East, including, in one mind-boggling suggestion made to me last year, the *intifada*!

This mix of long familiarity, hostility and ignorance pertains to both sides of a complex, variously uneven and quite old cultural encounter now engaging in very unmetaphorical warfare. From early on there was an overriding sense of inevitability, as if George Bush's apparent need to get down there and, in his own sporty argot, "kick ass" *had* to run up against Saddam Hussein's monstrous aggressiveness, now vindicating the Arab need to confront, talk back to, stand unblinkingly before the United States. The public rhetoric, in other words, is simply undeterred, uncomplicated by any considerations of detail, realism or cause and effect.

Perhaps the central unanalyzed link between the United States and the Arabs in this conflict is nationalism. The world can no longer afford so heady a mixture of patriotism, relative solipsism, social authority, unchecked aggressiveness and defensiveness toward others. Today the United States, triumphalist internationally, seems in a febrile way anxious to prove that it is Number One, perhaps to offset the recession; the endemic problems posed by the cities, poverty, health, education, production; and the Euro-Japanese challenge. On the other side, the Middle East is saturated with a sense that Arab nationalism is all-important, but also that it is an aggrieved and unfulfilled nationalism, beset with conspiracies, enemies both internal and external, obstacles to overcome for which no price is too high. This was especially true of the cultural framework in which I grew up. It is still true today, with the important difference that this nationalism has resolved itself into smaller and smaller units. In the colonial period as I was growing up, you could travel overland from Lebanon and Syria through Palestine to Egypt and points west. That is now impossible. Each country places formidable obstacles at its borders. For Palestinians, crossing is a horrible experience, since countries that make the loudest noises in support of Palestine treat Palestinians the worst.

Here, too, linkage comes last in the Arab setting. I do not want to suggest that the past was better; it wasn't. But it was more healthily interlinked, so to speak. People actually lived with each other, rather than denying each other from across fortified frontiers. In schools you could encounter Arabs from everywhere, Muslims and Christians, plus Armenians, Jews, Greeks, Italians, Indians and Iranians all mixed up, all under one or another colonial regime, interacting as if it were natural to do so. Today the state nationalisms have a tendency to fracture. Lebanon and Israel are perfect examples of what has happened. Apartheid of one form or another is present nearly everywhere as a group feeling if not as a practice, and it is subsidized by the state with its bureaucracies and secret police organizations. Rulers are clans, families and closed circles of aging oligarchs, almost mythologically immune to change.

Moreover, the attempt to homogenize and isolate populations has required colossal sacrifices. In most parts of the Arab world, civil society has been swallowed up by political society. One of the great achievements of the early post-war Arab nationalist governments was mass literacy; in countries such as Egypt the results were dramatic. Yet the combination of accelerated literacy and tub-thumping ideology, which was undoubtedly necessary at some point, has proved far too longstanding. My impression is that there is more effort spent in bolstering the idea that to be Syrian, Iraqi, Egyptian, Saudi, etc. is a quite sufficiently important end, rather than in thinking critically, perhaps even audaciously, about the national program itself. Identity, always identity, over and above knowing about others.

Because of this lopsided state of affairs, militarism assumed too privileged a place in the Arab world's moral economy. Much of it goes back to the sense of being unjustly treated, for which Palestine was not only a metaphor but a reality. But was the only answer military force — huge armies, brassy slogans, bloody promises and, alas, a long series of concrete instances, starting with wars and working down to such things as physical punishment and menacing gestures? I speak superficially and even irresponsibly here, since I cannot have all the facts. But I do not know a single Arab who would disagree with these impressions in private, or who would not readily agree that the monopoly on coercion given the state has almost completely eliminated democracy in the Arab world, introduced immense hostility between rulers and ruled, placed a much higher value on conformity, opportunism, flattery and getting along than on risking new ideas, criticism or dissent.

Taken far enough this produces an exterminism common to the Arabs and the United States, the notion that if something displeases you it is possible simply to blot it out. I do not doubt that this notion is behind Iraq's aggression against Kuwait. What sort of muddled and anachronistic idea of Bismarckian "integration" is this that wipes out an entire country and smashes its society with "Arab unity" as its goal? The most disheartening thing is that so many people, many of them victims of exactly the same brutal logic, appear to have identified with Iraq and not Kuwait. Even if one grants that Kuwaitis were unpopular (does one have to be popular not to be exterminated?) and even if Iraq claims to champion Palestine in standing up to Israel and the United States, surely the very idea that nations should be obliterated along the way is a murderous proposition, unfit for a great civilization like ours.

Then there is oil. While it brought development and prosperity to some, wherever it was associated with an atmosphere of violence, ideological refinement and political defensiveness, it created more rifts than it healed. It may be easy for someone like myself to say these things from a distance, but for anyone who cares about the Arab world, who thinks of it as possessing a plausible sort of internal cohesion, the general air of mediocrity and corruption that hangs over a part of the globe that is limitlessly wealthy, superbly endowed culturally and historically, and loaded with gifted individuals is a great puzzle, and of course a disappointment. We all *do* ask ourselves why we haven't done more of what other peoples have done — liberate ourselves, modernize, make a distinctive positive mark on the world. Where is excellence? How is it rewarded? There are first-rate novelists, poets, essayists, historians, yet all of them are not only unacknowledged legislators, they have been hounded into alienated opposition. For an author today to write is perforce to be careful, not to anger Syria or the Islamic authorities or a Gulf potentate or two.

What seems intellectually required now is the development of a combination discourse, one side of which is concretely critical and addresses the real power situation inside the Arab world, and another side that is mainly about affection, sympathy, association (rather than antagonism, resentment, harsh fundamentalism, vindictiveness). Many of the Arab thinkers of what the historian Albert Hourani calls the liberal age, the late eighteenth to the early twentieth century, were reformers eager to catch up with developments in the West. We've had too much since then of thinkers who want to start from scratch and zealously, not to say furiously, take things back to some pure, sacred origin. This has given all sorts of pathologies time and space enough to take hold in the middle distance, now, with their structures left unscrutinized, while intellectuals go off looking for what *would* have been better, what *would* have been just, and so on. We need to know what it is about the present that we should hold on to, and how. What is just, why is it just, why should we hold on to it? We need odes not to blood and mythology or uprooted, mourned or dead plants but to living creatures and actual situations. As the novelist Elias Khoury says, we need a language that allows one to write neither of a discredited past nor of an immensely distant future.

The supreme irony is that we Arabs are *of* this world, hooked into dependency and consumerism, cultural vassalage and technological secondariness, without much volition on our part. The time has come where we cannot simply accuse the West of Orientalism and racism — I realize that I am particularly vulnerable on this point — and go on doing little about providing an alternative. If our work isn't in the Western media often enough, for example, or isn't known well by Western writers and scholars, a good part of the blame lies with us. Hassanein Heykal, the great Egyptian journalist, has proposed a broadly focused pan-Arab cooperation authority for such things as development, coordinated industry, agriculture and the like. But we should also devote energy to an intellectual coordination effort that opens lines of communication among Arabs internally and externally with the rest of the world. The idea of equal dialogue, and rightful responsibility, needs to be pressed. The provincial and self-pitying posture that argues that a largely fictional and monolithic West disdains us ought to be replaced with the discovery that there are many Wests, some antagonistic, some not, with which to do business, and the choice of whom to talk to and how depends greatly on us. The converse is equally true, that there are many Arabs for Westerners and others to talk to. Only in this way, I think, will imperial America not be our only interlocutor.

If as Arabs we say correctly that we are different from the West, as well as different from its image of the Arabs, we have to be persuasive on this point. That takes a lot of work, and cannot be accomplished by a resort to clichés or myths. George Bush's idea that a new world order has to flow from an American baton is as unacceptable as the big idea that Arabs can muster a big army led by a big tough hero and at last win a few wars. That is dangerous nonsense. Americans, Arabs, Europeans, Africans — everyone — need to reorient education so that central to common awareness is not a paranoid sense of who is top or best but a map of this now tiny planet, its resources and environment nearly worn out, its inhabitants' demands for better lives nearly out of control. The competitive, coercive guidelines that have prevailed are simply no good anymore. To argue and persuade rather than to boast, preach and destroy, *that* is the change to be made.

The war was catastrophic and has only distorted the Arab world further. And there already are enough residual problems to start up another confrontation in the Middle East in a matter of seconds. We should be looking for political mechanisms with the Europeans and the nonaligned that would bring a lasting peace and send everyone — including Palestinians — home. It is good to be reminded of that phrase by Aimé Césaire which C.L.R. James, that great champion of liberation, liked to quote: "No race possesses the monopoly of beauty, of intelligence, of force, and there is a place for all at the rendezvous of victory." This may be utopian idealism, but as a way to think about an alternative to conflicts that go from cultural hostility to full-scale war, it is both more inventive and practical than shooting off missiles.

# Introduction

## Portent of a New Century

### *Eqbal Ahmad*

The twentieth has been a century most remarkable for its simultaneous capacity to promise hope and deliver disappointments. And as the end approaches, it seems to me that the century is ending in the same way in which it began: renewed hopes of a just and peaceable world order are being overwhelmed by politicians and warriors whose political minds remain rooted in the past.

For 300 years before the twentieth century dawned, the world had been transforming, a transformation brought about by modern science, technology, and imperialism. It was through this age of capitalist and European expansion that a world system came to be dominated by the West and the international market came to be controlled entirely for the West's benefit. That sounds rather benign, as though the free market was really free and worked merely to the advantage of the fittest. Far from it; Western domination was achieved by means of force so widespread, institutionalized, and legitimized by religion and morality that to date the epistemology of this universal violence still shapes relations between the Western and non-Western worlds.

The seventeenth, eighteenth and nineteenth centuries witnessed the genocidal destruction of grand civilizations: the great Mayas, Incas, Aztecs, and the Indian nations of North America; the conquest and subjugation of the rest of humanity. Eventually, even India was colonized; so was China, all of Africa, and ultimately the Middle East. These were the centuries that witnessed the transformation, forced and bloody, of land and labor into commodities in the capitalist sense of the word. Slavery was but one manifestation of this reality; the conversion of common land into individual estates, the wholesale dispossession of nations and peoples were the other manifestations. The history of our time is studded with unrecorded holocausts. Recording and remembrances were reserved only for occasions when the oppressed inflicted injury on the oppressor, when the colonized defeated the colonizer, when a Custer was killed, or a Gordon besieged.

Finally the wars of greed and expansion came home to roost. The colonial have-nots of the West took on the haves. Europeans fought a war among themselves, called it a World War, and gave it a number — One. It was a devastating conflict in which air and chemical warfare were introduced. You will remember that when World War I was over, a new time began, a time of hope. A time in which war in the Western world lost its appeal as an adventure, a Great Game to be played out in exotic, alien lands. A significant opinion in the West evinced revulsion from war and argued that peace was preferable. It was an environment which made possible the League of Nations and Woodrow Wilson's 14 Points. It was a time, in 1917–1918, when peace became a bestseller, when peace movements and peace associations were formed all over the world.

Then we saw the promises of the League of Nations betrayed systematically, first by dictated distortions of peace, then by reaction to them, then by the rise of fascism, and by the misuse of the League of Nations so that it became an instrument of power rather than of peacemaking. In the Middle East, where the Mandate of the League was twisted beyond recognition, the West's Arab allies were divided up as spoils, and Palestine was promised to Jewish fundamentalists whose mission was to create a biblical Israel where native people had dwelled for millennia. We are reaping still the harvest of those betrayals.

Then the West fought another World War, and gave it the next number: Two. This time many more millions died. Europe was wrecked, its cities and industrial infrastructure were destroyed and the confidence, I should say imperial confidences, of its elites and governments were undermined. Only one industrial nation emerged intact from this war. The United States alone was spared the devastations of modern warfare because no one crossed the oceans to strike at its vitals. On the contrary, war helped restore its economy and its self-image which had been so shaken by the Great Depression. As the leaders of this war-profiting giant of the Western hemisphere surveyed the ruins of Europe and East Asia, they had visions of world power and the illusion of imperial permanence. They called this time of ruination and tragedies "The American Century," promised to liberate the world, and to serve as the "watchman on the walls of world freedom."

What happened after World War II was very similar to what happened after World War I. Promises were renewed: it was the time when Winston Churchill and Franklin Roosevelt issued the Atlantic Charter; when the United Nations was founded, and new mechanisms were established to settle disputes collectively and without violence; the time when decolonization was considered a historic necessity, and the right to self-determination a cardinal principle of international politics; the time when nations were to be equal, aggression was forbidden; and conquests were outlawed. But these promises too were systematically betrayed. We were given instead the Cold War, the arms race, and superpower interventions.

The era of the Cold War and the arms race was really a time in which wars, big wars, came in from the cold. First, there was the war in which the

United States "lost China." Then there was the one in which it gained Greece and gave the world the Truman Doctrine. Then there was the Korean War; four and a half million people died in Korea, and Henry Kissinger called it a "limited war." There were so many "limited," "forgotten," and "invisible" wars in this period of "mutual deterrence" that one tends to lose count of the pain inflicted and damages done. None of the great powers kept promises and came clean in the post-war period of "peace." The Soviet Union intervened to suppress the democratic uprisings of Hungary and Czechoslovakia, and eventually invaded Afghanistan. In an attempt to define the parameters of colonialism, old and new, the British violated countries and peoples from Kenya to Malaysia. The French fought last ditch battles in Morocco, Tunisia, and finally in Algeria where in seven years of warfare one in every ten Algerians were killed.

But none equalled the United States in the frequency or violence of its interventions against the weak and vulnerable. It made covert war on Mohammed Mossadegh's constitutional government, which gifted Iran back to the corrupt Shah and murderous Savak. In Guatemala there was the assault on the elected government of Arbenz, which had nationalized the ill-begotten gains of the United Fruit Company. There was the war against revolutionary Cuba which eventually yielded the Cuban Missile Crisis and brought us very close to Armageddon. Another war against another elected government in the Dominican Republic; and yet another against the government of Salvador Allende in Chile, an intervention which destroyed the oldest and most stable constitutional democracy in Latin America.

Above all, the United States fought — this time the weak forced a fight — that most extraordinary of wars, the Vietnam War, properly called the Indochina wars. No one thought of counting the victims in this most computerized of wars. But there is little doubt that if the American leaders who conducted this war — including such luminaries as Robert Mac-Namara, Richard Nixon, and Henry Kissinger — were judged by the Nuremberg principles, they would most likely have been convicted of crimes against humanity and crimes of war. An estimated five million Vietnamese perished in this war. Add another three million Laotians and Cambodians who were killed in America's Indo-China war and its sequel — the criminal insanities of Pol Pot.

Vietnam was truly a landmark war. Its significance has not yet been fully understood, mainly because America's powerful propaganda machines — its media and its academic functionaries — have done their utmost, as Noam Chomsky has been painstakingly documenting, to deny this understanding. Even more than the Algerians did, the Vietnamese affirmed the superiority of people over machines, defeated the collective presumptions of modern technology, and inflicted upon the United States its first defeat in history. Vietnam also divided American society in a manner which brought out into the open its best instincts, and its anti-imperialist core. It is this latter reality which the American establishment has been at pains, since the 1970s, to suppress. George Bush may finally succeed in curing America of its splendid affliction — the Vietnam Syndrome — because Saddam Hussein was popularly regarded as a legitimate object of military intervention and because the Iraqi army, notwithstanding its build-up by the American government and media as the world's fourth largest, was defeated easily and at a low cost to the United States.

A new era apparently began in 1989, when one of the players in this Cold War punctuated with hot wars walked out on the deadly game, leaving the United States alone in the field. We are being told that this is the dawn of a "new world order." But what we are actually witnessing is the return of the old imperial order. George Bush and his associates have used the rhetoric of "new world order" most frequently in relation to Washington's stand against Iraq's occupation of Kuwait. They affirm that under this new order, acquisition of territory by force will be unacceptable; violations of the UN Charter shall not be permitted; UN Security Council resolutions affirming these `principles shall be enforced strictly and, if necessary, by military means. The fact that the permanent members of the Security Council agreed to impose sanctions against Iraq, authorized a deadline for the use of force against its occupation of Kuwait, and twenty-seven members joined the UN expeditionary force were cited as proof of a new international consensus behind international law.

We are being lied to; and we must not be deceived. What we are actually witnessing is a display of imperialism relieved of the limits imposed by superpower rivalry and nuclear deterrence. There is more continuity than change in American objectives in the Middle East, and that is why, since the end of World War II, America has discovered more Hitlers there than any other region. Mohammed Mossadegh, Iran's nationalist prime minister, was the first to be portrayed as Hitler. Then it was Gamal Abdel Nasser's turn. His book, *Philosophy of the Revolution*, was described by the U.S. media, including the *New York Times* and the *Washington Post*, as an Arab equivalent of *Mein Kampf*. Then Yasir Arafat was portrayed as Hitler. Most people do not recall that until he made his dramatic visit to Israel, concluded separate peace with Israel, and became a darling of American officials and the media, even Anwar Sadat was routinely portrayed as a fascist; allegations were dredged up of his links with the Nazis. And for the purposes of the Gulf War, of course, Saddam Hussein served as the new Hitler.

The special place that the Middle East has commanded in American demonology reflects the importance which the American establishment has accorded to this region and the challenges it has encountered in maintaining its hegemony there. In a series of studies on the global distribution of strategic resources which the United States government conducted after World War II, the Middle East leaps out as the key strategic area in the American calculus of post-war power politics. George Kennan, head of policy planning at the State Department in the late 1940s, was particularly prescient in identifying Middle Eastern oil as having a future leverage in defining America's relations with its Western allies.

In the early post-war years three objectives appeared central to U.S. policy in the Middle East. First, the Soviet Union was to be denied influence there. One of the earliest American challenges to Soviet power occurred in 1945 when Washington demanded that Moscow withdraw support from left-oriented movements in Iranian Azerbaijan and Kurdistan. Faced with the possibility of confrontation with the U.S., which had implicitly threatened a nuclear strike against the USSR, Moscow complied. Soon, the "sphere of containment" policy was extended to the Middle East. Within a year of the founding of NATO, U.S. policymakers had designed a detailed plan for what was to be called METO, the Middle East Treaty Organization. The scheme suffered setbacks because anti-imperialist, nationalist forces in the region resisted it. By 1953–54, Washington had, nevertheless, constructed bilateral defense agreements with several key "northern tier" countries – Pakistan, Turkey, Iran, Jordan and Iraq. Two years later, the Baghdad Pact was established.

Second, while the power to be projected in the Middle East was to be "the free world," American hegemony had to be affirmed in the region where British and French influence was still predominant. Hence, in the Middle East as well as elsewhere the allies had to be induced to take the position of junior partners. The intervention against Mossadegh in 1953 was ostensibly aimed at punishing his nationalization of the British-owned Anglo-Iranian Oil Company. As a result of the intervention, however, 40% of the share of Iranian oil passed into the hands of a consortium of American corporations. Britain followed as a mere junior partner, and eventually lost all influence in the country it had dominated for a century. There are many other instances of the United States cutting its French and British allies down to size in the Middle East.

Third, conservative monarchies, feudal land owners, bureaucratic and military oligarchies were viewed as being moderate and amenable to the West. They were to be reinforced against populist, nationalist, and democratic forces in the region. Thus, early allies of the U.S. were the monarchies in Iraq and Jordan, the Shah of Iran and the military oligarchy which supported him, and the bureaucrats and generals who proceeded to strangulate democracy in Pakistan. Some of these, such as the Saudi monarchy, the sheikhdoms of the Gulf, and the oligarchs of Pakistan have survived, with U.S. support, into our time.

Radicals, democrats, and nationalists, on the other hand, were America's *bêtes noir*; and they in turn tended to challenge the expansion of Western power and espouse non-alignment. The most powerful of these — the government of Abdel Nasser in Egypt — eventually suffered destruction from Israeli assault, American machinations, and its own miscalculations. In the 1980s, as a result of Egypt's defection to the American camp, exponential growth in Israel's military power, and hardening of the authoritarian arteries of the "nationalist" governments of Syria, Iraq, and Algeria, nationalist forces in the region were decisively weakened. The Soviet role in the Middle East was almost nullified; its defeat in Afghanistan by CIA-financed Islamic guerrillas merely climaxed the decline of Soviet influence. The only challenge to American domination came from Iran's Islamic revolution.

Presidential doctrines provide an indicator of the importance the Middle

East has had in American military and foreign policy planning. The Truman Doctrine had its origins in the American intervention in Greece. The Eisenhower Doctrine was first invoked to justify the 1958 intervention in Lebanon. With Israel and Iran serving as Kissinger's "regional influentials," the Middle East became the centerpiece of the Nixon Doctrine. The Carter Doctrine arrived in response to the Iranian revolution and the Soviet intervention in Afghanistan. Almost every post-World War II American president has had a doctrine on the Middle East, and has also seen his grand design challenged by Middle Eastern nationalists — Mossadegh in Iran, Abdel Nasser in Egypt, Qassem in Iraq. For example the Baghdad Pact, a seminal American scheme, was held at bay by Abdul Nasser, and rendered ineffectual by the 1958 nationalist uprising in Baghdad. The anti-imperialist component of Middle Eastern nationalism has frustrated U.S. designs on the region throughout the post-World War II period. In turn, it has been the prime target of American interventions, both covert and overt.

Within the framework of continuity, changes in American policy have occurred. Early in the seventies, the focus of the struggle for world power shifted from the Atlantic and the Pacific to the areas bounded by the Mediterranean and the Indian Ocean. Towards the end of the 1960s, the national security planners of the United States were beginning to perceive American power to be in serious decline. Washington began to concentrate intensively on the Middle East as the single most important instrument of maintaining America's position as the world's number one power. This perception caused a major shift in American policy in the region. Washington's posture in the Gulf in 1990–1991 will be better understood if we keep in view the evolution of its policy since 1969.

Between 1945 and 1968 the paramountcy of the United States had rested on four pillars. They were the following:

(i) **Strategic superiority over any other power or group of powers:** The U.S. alone had possessed strategic weapons and the global capability to deliver them. This superiority served as a leverage on allies and enemies alike. And the United States constantly put it to use; Dan Ellsberg has documented fourteen major instances of nuclear diplomacy.

(ii) **Economic and strategic domination of Western Europe and Japan:** While they were recovering from the ravages of war, the advanced capitalist countries remained America's junior partners, and under its nuclear umbrella. Its unquestioned leadership of the rich nations was a mainstay of its global status.

(iii) **Will and capacity to police the world:** Between 1945 and 1968, the United States intervened, by military or paramilitary means, once every sixteen months against a government or movement of which it did not approve. These interventions were the post-World War II equivalents of "showing the flag." They marked the global reach of the United States and its ability to protect its own and allied interests abroad.

(iv) **National consensus favoring a forward foreign policy:** It had sound economic and persuasive ideological bases. The post-war emergence of the U.S. as world power coincided with unparalleled affluence in the national and individual life of Americans. Imperialism struck a congenial chord in pragmatic Americans. But imperialism has not been a good word in American political culture. People do not identify with it. To become palatable, it has to draw on citizens' anxieties and their sense of mission. "You've got to scare the hell out of them," Senator Vandenberg is said to have told Harry Truman, who was looking for ways to increase defense spending. Anti-communism was a handy ideological tool; the threat was rendered credible by what Richard Hofstadter has called the paranoid streak in American culture. The mission was even easier to define. America always believed it was born to a mission, and manifest destiny. So it happily stood, in John Kennedy's ringing phrase, "watch on the walls of world freedom."

By the end of the sixties, however, all four pillars of American power were crumbling. The American Century had peaked in just twenty-five years. Vietnam stood at the finishing line. They loomed large in the American imagination, those humble men and women in black pajamas. So large in the minds of those in power in fact that the small big-men in Washington have not yet forgiven the Vietnamese their magnificent "crime" of having survived and defeated a pitiless and meddlesome super-power. Surely, they contributed to it, contributed significantly in fact, but the Vietnamese were not entirely responsible for the decline of American power. History takes its own course, and economics and technology shape it more decisively than deliberate human effort does.

The first pillar of American power lost much of its erstwhile significance in the international balance of power when the Soviet Union deployed its first fully operational ICBMs. The United States lost its strategic superiority, and parity was reached between the two powers. In strategic weaponry parity refers to qualitative, not quantitative equivalence. The U.S. retained the capacity to completely destroy the USSR, perhaps five times over; the Soviets could now annihilate the U.S. at least once with complete certainty. The doctrine of massive retaliation was not operational any more; the world had moved on to a state of MADness, Mutual Assured Destruction.

About the same time, in the late sixties, the United States was starting to confront a fundamental challenge within the capitalist bloc. Germany and Japan ceased to be junior partners; they became dangerous economic competitors whose growing influence was reducing America's leverage on Europe no less than on East and South East Asia. Furthermore, the attainment of strategic parity by the USSR had reduced the importance of the United States strategic umbrella over Europe and East Asia.

The war in Vietnam put into question American will and capacity for global intervention. These interventions rested on the doctrine of "limited wars," as Dr. Henry Kissinger had labeled them. Other academic experts, like Professor Samuel Huntington of Harvard and Zbigniew Brzezinski of Columbia University preferred other terms — forgotten wars, invisible wars. One might ask the question: limited for whom? The obvious answer is: only in its consequences for the intervening power. Forgotten by whom? Obviously, the American Congress, and the media. Invisible to whom? Always to citizens in the proudest of democracies; and never to the victims of intervention.

That 1953 intervention in Iran was limited indeed in its consequences for the United States; it cost no American lives, and less than five million dollars. It yielded 40% of Iranian oil to American companies, a client who did America's bidding, and opened the Iranian "market" to some $30 billion of American arms and luxuries. A more lucrative and limited intervention is hard to imagine. The U.S. Congress merely ignored the Executive power's aggression against a constitutional democracy. And the media portrayed Mohammed Mossadegh as an unstable and dangerous demagogue. It was only after its failure in the Bay of Pigs in 1961 that the CIA was compelled to disclose its "success" in Iran. The crime remained forgotten and un-atoned until the Shah finally fell, a forsaken victim of Iranian anger. They had reason to be angry, for the destruction of their hard-won democracy and their dreams of sovereignty, and for the terror the Shah inflicted on them. For the Iranians the CIA's covert war had unlimited consequences.

Vietnam destroyed the fundamental premise of the doctrine of interven-tion. The war that was supposed to be limited in its consequences for the intervening power cost it 57,000 dead, 225,000 wounded, and more than $2 billion. The war which was supposed to be invisible and forgotten loomed large before the American people, divided the nation, dominated the media, and was interminably debated in the Congress. Above all, the war in Vietnam decisively cracked the consensus on which America's Cold War aggressions had rested. The very elite universities which had supplied the cream of America's national security establishment began instead to produce anti-war draft resisters chosing prison over the foreign service and the CIA; nuns and priests were leaving their churches to confront the state; and even high-level government employees began to "blow the whistle" on their employer. Another, anti-interventionist America had emerged to challenge imperial presumptions and policies. This healthy development in civil society was named like a disease — the Vietnam Syndrome.

Just before he became Richard Nixon's adviser on national security, Henry Kissinger bemoaned the demise of the doctrine of limited wars. All our interventions in Latin America, he ruminated, had been "limited" and "successful"; but Vietnam has put an end to the efficacy of this doctrine as an instrument of policy. In power Dr. Kissinger managed, nevertheless, to get away with the secret bombings and intervention in Cambodia, and also the covert operation which yielded two decades of death, disappearances, torture, and imprisonments in Chile. But he did run into the Vietnam Syndrome when the American public and Congress balked at his plans to enlarge American involvement in Angola. That was in 1976, one year after American defeat in Vietnam had been formalized. Thus, by the sixties' end, all the pillars of post-war American paramountcy were collapsing, and a perception of decline pervaded the corridors of power.

When Senator J.W. Fulbright called the United States a "crippled giant," the phrase caught on with nearly the same rapidity as had the earlier strident announcement of the "A-Century" by Henry Luce. Decline became an obsession in America more than a decade before Paul Kennedy's book became a bestseller. By the early seventies mass circulation magazines — *Time, Newsweek, BusinessWeek* — had a cover story on America's Decline. In response to the perceived decline, President Nixon and Henry Kissinger developed a Grand Design which greatly affected the Middle East and which, *faut de mieux*, still defines American policies in that region. We ought to review it briefly in order to better comprehend the latest development in the Gulf.

When a country enters a period of perceived decline, its decision-making elite, and the intelligentsia in general, may respond in any of four ways. These may be labeled as restorationist, reformist, managerial, and radical responses. Restorationism involves an effort at restoring lost power and strengths. The reformist seeks renewal through change and adaptations. The managerial response is typically existential; it entails constant crisis management, and the expectation that cumulatively good management will resolve the larger crisis. Radicals tend to reject inherited structures and values, and seek to rebuild society anew.

The first fully articulated official response to the crisis of American power came during Richard Nixon's presidency. It may not be incidental that he chose as his national security advisor the United States' best known expert on the politics of restoration (Kissinger's first book on the post-Napoleonic diplomacy of Metternich and Castlereagh appeared under the title, *A World Restored*). Henry Kissinger's Grand Design revealed the singularity of his commitment to insuring the *status quo ante*, and his intellectual roots in the presumptions of international politics before the world wars.

He devised a restorationist blueprint par excellence. It included an attempt to regain the United States' strategic superiority by developing a first strike capability (counterforce; strategic defense initiative — star wars). More importantly, in order to overcome the stalemate inherent in MAD, it envisaged lowering the threshold on the use of nuclear weapons. Thus, the strategic doctrines of Massive Retaliation and Mutual Assured Destruction were now replaced by Flexible Targeting Options, and a variety of medium and small size nuclear weapons were introduced, ranging from cruise missiles to tactical nukes.

The quest for new leverages on old Western and Japanese allies involved the refocusing of American attention on the Middle East, which the United States had neglected during its protracted intervention in Indo-China. Both these centers of industrial power are sorely lacking in mineral resources. They depend on supplies of raw materials from abroad, and the Middle East is their primary source of energy. If the United States could attain unchallenged domination over that region it would acquire a powerful political and economic leverage over Western Europe and Japan.

In the Gulf area, where oil reserves are heavily concentrated, the United States was already the predominant power. Both Saudi Arabia, the world's largest oil producer, and Iran, the most populous country in the region, were its clients. So were the smaller Emirates of the Gulf. But the permanence of this influence was not assured. Abdel Nasser had been severely wounded by Israel in 1967, but he was still leading an Arab national movement which, despite the humiliating defeat of the Arab armies, had been buoyed by the strident emergence of the Palestine Liberation Organization. In the Gulf area, a guerrilla movement had persisted in Oman, and in South Yemen a Marxist group had taken power. Vietnam-conscious American policymakers expected nationalist and radical challenges to augment in the Middle East. It was at this crucial time that Britain decided to withdraw the bulk of its forces from the Gulf. The necessity to increase the United States' coercive capabilities was apparent; yet the Vietnam experience had drastically reduced the country's will to support further expansion of America's military power abroad.

This complex set of power relations persisted throughout the 1970s and 1980s, with U.S. military and economic influence in the Middle East offset by these two countervailing forces. Domestic pressure against overt U.S. intervention abroad remained strong, fueled by the Vietnam Syndrome; and populist and nationalist resistance to U.S. hegemony in the region continued to pose a considerable threat, starkly dramatized by the 1979 Islamic revolution in Iran, which gave the world a new phrase to add to its lexicon of conflict: the U.S. as the "Great Satan."

But as the 1980s ended, a perceptible shift in the balance of power was taking place. U.S. designs on Middle Eastern oil had intensified in response to a variety of challenges to U.S. hegemony. Secondly, the U.S. public had been successfully softened up for the renewed projection of U.S. military power by the invasions of Grenada and Panama. And thirdly, the gradual but persistent fragmentation of the Arab and Middle Eastern nations had rendered the nationalist and radical movements in the region weaker than they had ever been before.

These reasons underlie the U.S.'s aggressive response to the emergence of someone like Saddam Hussein as a Middle Eastern power. Instead of acting like a single state and limiting his ambition to Iraq alone, Saddam Hussein added to his regional appeal the call for Arab unity — and for the U.S. that was intolerable.

There was another common thread in U.S. policy at work here. It seems that the United Nations was used, in 1990 and 1991, in a manner very similar to the way it was used in 1950 to start the Korean war. That is to say, the U.S. used a multilateral mechanism to start and justify a unilateral war.

The American people thus were faced with a new "limited war." According to the *New York Times*, the Gulf War would be "very different from previous wars." Not only because it was to be short, they told us, but also because this time the "American people have had a debate of unusual length, seriousness and intensity."

This referred to the three-day debate in the Congress during January of 1991. Let us concede something: the debate was of unusual length for that Congress, which was previously not given to carrying out the functions for which it had been elected, namely to discuss matters of policy. And yes, there seemed to be some intensity in it. But where was the seriousness?

The Congresspeople failed to raise a number of serious questions. Each member of Congress, from both parties, denounced President Saddam Hussein as a Hitler, as a tyrant, as a murderer. Yet none of them asked a simple question: Where were we six months before? Where were we ten years ago when Saddam Hussein, a tyrant even then, invaded Iran? They would have had to answer: we were supporting him. And our government was supporting him.

More importantly, they didn't ask how, when Saddam Hussein had been effectively in power for 20 years and formally as president of Iraq for 12 years, did he become a Hitler only in August 1990? What fueled his extraordinary ambition? They didn't ask that question for one reason. If they had they would have had to answer: it was America's Middle East policy that enabled Saddam Hussein to emerge as a regional power, crystallized in the Camp David Accords.

Egypt, which for two centuries had been the regional power in the Arab world, was effectively isolated from its Arab milieu by the Camp David Accords, creating a power vacuum in the Middle East. When Anwar Sadat signed his separate peace with Israel, Egypt reposed its faith in $2 billion a year in U.S. aid, and in U.S. promises of a step-by-step, comprehensive settlement of the Israeli-Arab conflict. But the U.S. failed to keep its part of the bargain; instead of making peace, Israel continued to invade and conquer.

Arab states, including Egypt, watched helplessly as Israel tormented the Palestinians, colonizing their land and threatening to expel them from the last remnant of their ancient homeland. This is the historical backdrop that yields such bitter cynicism in Arab responses to U.S. claims of taking a "principled" stand against the Iraqi occupation.

After Egypt's alienation from the Arab world, popular hopes turned toward Saudi Arabia and its client states in the Gulf. The Saudis had glitter and gold. Multinational corporations sought their favors. Bankers relied on their investments. Even the U.S. dollar owed its hegemony to Saudi preference. It was reasonable to expect the Saudis to translate their economic power and strategic importance into political and diplomatic leverage to achieve Israel's withdrawal from occupied Palestinian, Syrian and Lebanese territories.

Indeed, Saudi Arabia responded to these hopes during the subsequent thirteen years with a military build-up and active diplomacy. The country entered the international arms bazaar as an extravagant buyer. In 1981, Saudi efforts led to a ceasefire between the PLO and Israel. But in 1982, the ceasefire was broken when Israel invaded Lebanon and devastated Beirut. An estimated 20,000 people died and 30,000 were wounded. The United Nations passed resolutions condemning the invasion, but the U.S. prevented the UN from enforcing its own actions. Israel occupied large parts of Lebanon for two years — and still occupies a portion of the south of that country.

The Gulf sheikhs pleaded with Washington to help save Arab face and protect their dynastic futures. But their efforts were bound to be in vain. They are prisoners of dependence, because they have acquired wealth without working, and make enormous profits without producing. Their economies are run by foreigners. They own billions but don't control their own capital. Their countries are littered with expensive machines but they have no indigenous technology. They rule over islands of affluence in a sea of poverty.

The sheikhs tied themselves symbiotically to the United States, but could not translate their wealth into power, or use their pro-American trade and investment practices successfully to pressure the U.S. for an even-handed policy in the Middle East. Their diplomacy was reduced to buying favors and pleading fairness. As popular expectations were disappointed, the sheikhs became objects of contempt. The power vacuum in the Arab world became palpable.

The first signal that Iraq might try to fill the power vacuum left by Egypt and the Saudis came in 1980, when Saddam Hussein invaded Iran. But instead of opposing his aggression, the U.S. quietly encouraged it as a way of preventing the consolidation of the Islamic revolution in Iran. In addition, Saudi Arabia and Kuwait supplied Iraq with an estimated $60 billion in aid during the Iran-Iraq war. The "monster" — if that is what Saddam Hussein was — was created by the same forces who now oppose him.

Then came another question Congress avoided. Everybody in Congress stated, accurately, that Iraq stood in violation of the United Nations Charter and UN resolutions. But not one Congressman or Congresswoman mentioned the potential relevance of the fact that in the 23 years before Iraq started violating the United Nations Charter, Israel had been violating it every month and every week and every day. No one mentioned the 42 United Nations resolutions on this subject. So while they were invoking the legitimacy of the United Nations, none in Congress had enough honor, enough self-respect, enough integrity, even to acknowledge that there was another country besides Iraq in the Middle East which at that moment stood in violation of the United Nations Charter.

Neither Congress nor the media seriously questioned the goals of the war. If they had looked beyond Bush's glib pronouncements about opposing aggression, they would have had to admit that this was at least partly a war designed to protect the conquests of Israel — not its security. The main reason why 46 of the 67 Democratic members of the Congress who crossed the floor to support the President's call to war did so was their strong support for Israel and their concomitant backing by the pro-Israeli lobby.

It also seems that U.S. policymakers significantly underestimated the power of the Arab street. They seemed to assume that the Arab street was not powerful, that there was no civil society functioning in the Arab world. They seemed to believe the Arab countries were not like Iran, not like Pakistan, where popular opposition overcame unpopular leaders; thus they believed that there would be no serious challenge to the U.S. alliance mounted in Egypt or Saudi Arabia, or elsewhere in the Arab world.

The good news, as the American people heard it, is that after paying lightly with the lives of just a few American men and women in the Gulf, and after paying with the uncounted lives of Iraqi and Kuwaiti people — estimates are running between 100,000 to 250,000 people killed — the U.S. had a victory. This is indeed quite different from 20 years ago when the U.S. lost militarily, politically and morally in Vietnam. This time one cannot say that America lost militarily in the Gulf; America has won. But the celebrations of victory herald their own nightmare. In order to understand that nightmare, the U.S. will have to understand the realities of Middle Eastern politics in a new way — from the point of view of the people of the Middle East. It is a vantage point far different from that of America itself, or of Israel, which Americans so often adopt.

Looking at the Middle East from a Middle Eastern vantage point, this is how the post-war period may begin to play out. First, Saudi Arabia and Egypt and Syria and all those craven sheikhs of the Persian Gulf who joined the American alliance in the war face a tremendous loss of credibility as they are seen to have the blood of hundreds of thousands of Arabs on their hands, having fought at the side of a foreign power.

Second, Iran is beginning to emerge as the major power in the region. Unlike Egypt and Saudi Arabia, which emerged from the Gulf War compromised by their alliance with Washington, Iran still carries the mantle of anti-imperialism. The Iranian posture reflects the popular consensus in the Middle East: oppose Iraq's aggression, but denounce U.S. intervention in the Gulf as a greater danger. Like Egypt, Iran is a large country, with a population estimated at 50 million and a history of exercising both power and cultural influence. But unlike Egypt, Iran is a rich, oil-producing country. While other nations became enmeshed directly in the Gulf War, Iran spent much of the crisis period rearming and reorganizing its military, while the Bush administration applauded Tehran for its responsible behavior.

Third, Iran also holds the banner of Islam. Following the defeat of Arab nationalism and the old forms of Arabism by the joint power of Israel, U.S.-backed Arab regimes, and the U.S. military itself, some in the region will turn to the old, tried and tested formula of Islamic solidarity. And Iran held that franchise in the period following the Gulf War.

Fourth, the people of the region are growing resentful of the Gulf's oil sheikhs, all of whom were installed in power by outsiders as recently as the 1960s. They reflect an extraordinary Middle Eastern anomaly. All the large countries of the Middle East have small reserves of oil; wherever there are lots of people, there is very little or no oil. Whenever there are no people, or very few people, there is a small sheikhdom — sitting atop a large oil reserve. Kuwait, with 500,000 citizens, is the second largest producer of oil in the world. The population of the oil-bloated United Arab Emirates is estimated at only 50,000 to 150,000. Americans don't ask the question, but Middle Eastern people ask: How did it happen that this wealth of the Middle East was de-coupled from its people? Who separated the wealth of the Middle East from the people of the Middle East? Why is it, in the same region, that Kuwait's per capita annual income is $16,000 a year, and

Egypt's is $650 a year? What explains this? People in the Middle East think the answer is "America," the answer is "Great Britain." Because it was these countries that separated the wealth of the Arab people from the Arab people themselves.

Therefore, now that this war is over, blood has been shed, reverberations from this kind of violence can be expected to spread inexorably through the aggrieved villages and cities of the Middle East. And it is this growing anger that the American people, as innocent as the Iraqi people, will reap in a bitter harvest. Everything about this environment suggests that this first Arab-American war will not be the last. Another, more protracted war could follow, making the Korean and Indo-Chinese wars look tame by comparison.

In the aftermath of the U.S. "victory" over Iraq, the following may emerge: Popular discontent in countries such as Saudi Arabia, Egypt, Morocco and Syria will grow exponentially. U.S. allies in the region, as well as U.S. personnel, corporations and installations, will become the targets of mass agitation throughout the Middle East. A power vacuum will emerge as the nationalist credibility of Egypt and Saudi Arabia plummets and the void is filled by forces influenced by Iran's Islamic government.

Additionally, there is a wide divergence between American and Arab points of view on Washington's motives. Did the United States go into the Middle East with such a large force to "oppose aggression?" President Bush said yes. Did they go to protect Kuwait's freedom? President Bush and the Congress said yes. Nobody in the Middle East believed it. Middle Eastern people saw the lie from U.S. history.

Take just one example. Israel invaded Lebanon in 1982; the United Nations reported, the United States government admitted, U.S. presidents and secretaries of state announced, that it was an unprovoked aggression. By official figures, the Israelis murdered 20,000 people in Lebanon; 30,000 people were maimed; a total of 50,000 casualties. But when the United Nations agreed all but unanimously to support sanctions against Israel, there was only one vote that broke the consensus, that opposed those sanctions. That vote was cast by the United States. The Arab people, Middle Eastern people, saw Lebanon then, and the Gulf now, as American-Israeli invasions to dominate the region.

A further point: the American people have lived in the shadow of nuclear weapons since the United States dropped them on Hiroshima and Nagasaki, and since the Soviets developed their own hydrogen bomb in the 1950s. But Americans at least had some satisfaction from living in the shadow of nuclear weapons — the assumption of deterrence. The Russians had the bomb, but America had it too. In fact America had a lot more than the Russians had.

In the Middle East today, no Arab country has nuclear weapons. America's best experts believe that Iraq was five to ten years away from nuclear weapons capability before the Gulf War. We were told that Pakistan was "close" to nuclear capability, and because Pakistan was believed to be close, the Congress in October 1990 stopped all aid to Pakistan. So Pakistan is denied all military or economic aid from the U.S., in spite of the fact that it's an old and faithful ally of Washington — because it is suspected of developing nuclear weapons.

In the whole region, only Israel is known to possess a nuclear arsenal — at least 200 high intensity nuclear bombs. The United States has supplied it not only with nuclear technology, but also the capacity to deliver them to any target — literally, *any* target — to which the Israelis want to deliver them.

Now the American people may love Israel; they may trust Israel as a Western-style democracy. But in the Middle East the image of Israel is that of a conquering power. In the Middle East people know that the Israeli parliament still refuses, after 44 years, to declare its own boundaries. So that Israel is the only country in the world today, the only member of the United Nations, that has no identified boundaries.

Some in the West may think that Middle Eastern fears of Israel are unjustified. But the truth is that those fears are reborn in the shadow of Israeli bombs. And they see those bombs as created by American power. In other words, these anxieties, the mistrust, the legacy of America's unbalanced, biased, one-sided relationships in the Middle East, will likely lead, after the American victory in the Gulf, to massive region-wide resistance to America and American interests.

In other words, welcome — not so much to World War III — but welcome to one, two, three or more Vietnams.

If the West fails to understand that, it must at least recognize that this time, in taking on the Middle East, it took on a people who have a history of having quite corrupt leadership, but who, when pushed to the wall, will fight back. They fought back against France in Algeria, and defeated it. They fought back against Israel in Lebanon, and beat it. And they fought back against the Soviet Union in Afghanistan, and defeated it.

Within the Muslim world, there is evidence of greater creativity than has been seen for the last 300 years. It can be seen now in Arabic literature, in Arab poetry, in Arab art. We are witnessing an Arab renaissance in creative activity. It reflects the yearning for democracy that began to be expressed in the last two-and-a-half or three years of the eighties — an expression as yet insufficient, but growing all the time. The Palestinian intifada is part of this quest for democracy. In the entire annals of the history of resistance there are very few examples like this, in which an essentially unarmed people managed to stand up and sustain resistance for years against an armed and ruthless occupying force whose aim is the exclusion and expulsion of that occupied population.

We are now coming to the end of the American century. And what we are witnessing is how hard it is for this American century to die. The ending of the Gulf War, with an unchallenged U.S. proclaiming victory over a ravaged Iraq, remains the portent of the new century to come.

# ■ PART ONE ■

## Before the Storm:

## An Historical Introduction

# 1

# Iraq: Years of Turbulence

*Michel Moushabeck*

Iraq's contemporary image provides few clues to the magnificence and power of her past. Certainly there is a distinction of sorts in being the pioneer recipient of the post-Cold War's fiercest aerial bombardment carried out in the name of enforcing George Bush's "new world order." But Iraq means many other things.

Known as Mesopotamia ("land between the two rivers"), Iraq, which lies between the Tigris and Euphrates rivers, was probably the earliest center of human civilization. Here the Sumerians flourished around the third millennium B.C., where the first city-states grew up and writing was invented; the Babylonians carried their great achievements in mathematics, astronomy and law far beyond their borders; and the Assyrians created a large empire and are credited with developing literary and art forms which were tremendously influential on future civilizations. The Code of Hammurabi (1792–1750 B.C.), ruler of Babylon, contained the world's earliest written laws.

In the words of C.W. Ceram:

> Whether or not it was here that Adam toiled and Eve spun and mankind had its cradle, it was very likely the cradle of human civilization. Here emerged the earliest scripts, the earliest architecture, and the earliest sciences. Here the Sumerians and their successors, the Babylonians and Assyrians, founded the first states. Egyptians and Persians invaded them, rarely did peace prevail in these lands, which nevertheless gave birth to the religion of peace and good will. Here the road traveled by Abraham still winds across the plain, and here the teachings of Muhammad took hold and spread. Here was the world of the Arabian Nights, the world of Harun al-Rashid. Here Greeks, Romans and Arabs ruled; and through this gateway passed all the trade and bustling commerce between Orient and Occident. Buffer land, occupied land, border land — Mesopotamia has always been in upheaval, down to the present day.[1]

## The Golden Age of Islam

After the Arab conquest of Iraq in 634 A.D. and the subsequent collapse of the Damascus-based Umayyad dynasty in 748 A.D., the Abbasid Caliphate moved the capital of the Islamic world from Damascus to Baghdad. For over five centuries, Baghdad grew into an international center of knowledge and trade, bringing enormous advances in literature, art and the sciences. This period witnessed the development of the *qasida* (Arabic poem); the first large library, known as *Bayt al-Hikma* (House of Wisdom) in Baghdad was established by the Caliph Ma'mun (813–833); the first geographical dictionary was composed by al-Yaqut (d. 1229); the principles of medicine were explained by Ibn Sina (Avicenna) in his book the *Qanun*, which would remain the main text for European medical studies until at least the sixteenth century.[2]

Basra, in southern Iraq, became one of the main trading centers: Arab ships sailed from Basra to the ports of western India and reached as far as China. Goods were also carried by river from Basra to Baghdad for transfer onward by camelback to Syria, Egypt, Anatolia and Constantinople.[3]

Known as the "Golden Age of Islam," this era came to an end in 1258 A.D., with the violent collapse of the Abbasid rule at the hands of Hulago and his Mongol armies, who captured Baghdad and destroyed what had taken five centuries to build.

It is a commonly held view among historians that it was during this period of influence and prestige of Islam, that cultural and ethnic identity sowed the first seeds of what would, many centuries later, take root as a strong pan-Arab movement.

## Iraq Under Ottoman Rule

From 1535 to the First World War, when it came under British occupation, Iraq was part of the Ottoman Empire — a period Arabs regard to some extent as characterized by abandonment and cultural stagnation. Arabic was downgraded as a language; political self-confidence and self-assertion declined; and what little was left of the splendor of the Abbasid period was allowed to fall into ruin. Nevertheless, the Ottomans, whose vital interests spread over three continents, always defended the frontiers of Islam and preserved Islamic religious and legal culture.

In 1623, Baghdad was captured by the Safavids of Persia (Iran) in a struggle which "gradually acquired religious overtones, for the Safavids proclaimed Shi'ism as the official religion of their dynasty, while the Ottomans became more strictly Sunni as their empire expanded to include the main centers of the high urban culture of Islam."[4] Sixteen years later, Baghdad was restored to the Ottoman Empire only to be lost again to the Mamluks who ruled Iraq from 1704 to 1821. In the mid-nineteenth century Iraqi and other Arab provinces began to be seriously integrated into the Ottoman Empire. Istanbul established Ottoman ruling groups in the provinces, and adopted new methods of organization and administration and legal codes. These *Tanzimat* or government reforms were later abolished by Abdulhamid II (1876–1909) in 1880, marking a period of absolutist rule and merciless exploitation. Prior to this, however, Iraq, then consisting of the three *vilayets* or provinces of Baghdad, Basra and Mosul, enjoyed "relative administrative, economic and fiscal autonomy."[5] The final year before the outbreak of the First World War saw a massive decline in Ottoman suzerainty, having lost all its remaining European territories as a result of the Balkan Wars of 1912–13.

## British Occupation

Britain's main strategic concern in the Middle East was protecting its vital links to India — the Suez Canal and the Gulf. Additionally, the British perceived a potential threat to their oil interests in Iran. Thus, when a British Royal Commission, after authorizing the acquisition of a 51% controlling interest in the Anglo-Persian Oil Company, declared in 1913 that "We must become the owners or at any rate the controllers at the source of at least a proportion of the oil which we require,"[6] there was little doubt left as to how far the British would go to protect these newly discovered oilfields.

Therefore, when the First World War broke out in November 1914 and Turkey formally allied itself with Germany against Britain and France, British Indian troops were immediately dispatched to the region. Facing little Turkish resistance (except in Baghdad itself which was not captured until 1917) the British invading forces took over from the retreating Turkish Army the whole of Turkish Arabia including the Iraqi provinces of Basra, Baghdad and Mosul.[7]

In the course of the war Britain, through a series of secret agreements to divide the spoils of the Ottoman Empire, secured Allied consent to its occupation of Iraq. The Sykes-Picot Agreement of 1916, which was later ratified by the League of Nations in April 1920 at the San Remo Conference, awarded Britain mandatory powers over the territory it had occupied. During the same period, however, growing resentment and opposition to British rule and the government's efforts to levy taxes, came to a head. In a bloody revolt in June 1920, "virtually the whole area rose against Britain."[8] The British suffered nearly 2,000 casualties, including 450 dead before putting down the revolt in February 1921.[9]

Six months later, the British installed Faisal, the son of Sherif Hussain of Mecca, as king of Iraq, and set up a "national" government while preserving for themselves supreme authority in both the internal and external affairs of the country. Subsequently, British-Iraqi relations were governed by a series of treaties "which maintained important exclusive British rights [air bases, oil concessions, etc.] in Iraq . . . [and were] approved only under heavy British pressure against the radical opposition which demanded unfettered independence."[10] In October 1932, Iraq was finally admitted to the League of Nations and became an independent state under British protection.

**From Monarchy to Republic**

Except for a small group of Sunni officials, and a few wealthy landowners and merchants, the end of the mandate mattered little to the majority of the people of Iraq. "It was widely believed by many Iraqis that they were not the true masters of their country."[11] The traditional conflict between the Shi'a and the Sunnis intensified after independence; and the Kurds in the north who constituted about 20% of the population even then, continued to demand an independent state of their own.

Iraq's internal stability was further threatened by King Faisal's premature death in September 1933. Until his death, Faisal and his inner circle of associates "were constantly involved in a delicate balancing act, having to satisfy the exigencies of British policy while at the same time trying to retain some degree of credibility with what may loosely be termed Iraqi national aspirations."[12] Faisal was succeeded by his son Ghazi, who lacked his father's authority and as a result the years that followed witnessed several *coups d'état*, and the emergence of the military as the leading power that would dominate Iraqi politics for years to come.

When King Ghazi died accidentally in 1939, Abd al-Ilah became regent for Ghazi's four-year-old son King Faisal II. He brought with him the pro-British General Nuri al-Said, who became the effective ruler of Iraq until the 1958 revolution. A brief attempt by the military to oust Nuri and the monarchy in 1941 was crushed by British military intervention.[13]

The end of the Second World War saw the consolidation of the strength of the anti-British and anti-monarchist opposition throughout Iraq. Communism, Nasserism, Ba'athism, and other forms of pan-Arab nationalism gained popularity as Nuri al-Said's repressive measures intensified against the Iraqi people. The widening socio-economic gap between the landowning classes and the vast majority of the population, and the frustration resulting from the denial of political power to the masses of peasants and urban workers, made matters worse.

Events outside Iraq further aroused strong anti-British sentiment. These included the 1948 war in Palestine and the expulsion of nearly 750,000 people from their homes, and the 1951 nationalization of Iranian oil by the nationalist government of Dr. Mohammad Mossadegh that encouraged similar demands by Iraq's nationalists. The regime's support for the U.S.-sponsored 1955 Baghdad Pact further divided the regime from the Iraqi population. The pact brought countries bordering the Soviet Union into an anti-communist military alliance with the West, and challenged directly the large-scale domestic support for the Iraqi Communist Party. Above all, Nasser's rise to power in Egypt in 1952 and his bold stand against Britain, France and Israel in 1956 helped to galvanize popular anti-British sentiment.[14] On July 14, 1958, discontent with the pro-Western monarchy and Nuri al-Said's regime reached a climax, and a bloody revolution, led by General Abd al-Karim Qasim and a secret group within the military known as the Free Officers, ensued.[15] The monarchy was overthrown, Iraq became a republic, and a Revolutionary Council and a Cabinet were established.

## From Revolution to Dictatorship

The year 1958 was of outstanding significance in Iraqi history. In the short term, the new government headed by Qasim as acting prime minister and defense minister, was met with unparalleled enthusiasm and support. Within a few months, substantial strides were made toward the fulfilment of many of the pre-Revolution demands of the opposition groups:

> withdrawal of Iraq from the Baghdad Pact and Sterling Area; evacuation of British bases; establishment of diplomatic and trading relations with socialist countries [mainly the Soviet Union and the People's Republic of China]; a program of land reform; negotiations with IPC [Iraq Petroleum Company] for a greater share of oil royalties; a housing program for the shanty-town dwellers on the outskirts of Baghdad; an amnesty for all political prisoners; a draft constitution; legal recognition for trade unions, peasant unions and similar democratic organizations; profits on consumer goods limited to 15%; rents reduced; and substantial cuts in the price of food and other necessities.[16]

In September 1958, the implementation of a progressive program of agrarian reform transferred large tracts of land from the wealthy landowners to the landless peasants. The enactment of Law 80 in 1961, under which the government took back from the foreign-controlled Iraq Petroleum Company (IPC) 99.5% of the unexploited concession area, had nationwide support.[17]

However, the instant popularity of Qasim's regime could not conceal the major political differences which were contained within it. Central to this power struggle was the issue of *wahda*, or union with Egypt and Syria. This concept was supported by the second in command, Colonel Aref, as well as the pan-Arab nationalists and Ba'athists; it was vehemently opposed by the communists. Qasim's own opposition to *wahda* and his bitter hatred of Nasser, put him in the same camp as the communists, although he never shared their political views and never allowed them to hold any position of power in the government.[18]

This conflict widened the rift between Qasim and the nationalist-Ba'athist alliance, who feared that Qasim could become a tool in the hands of the communists. The 1961 Kurdish revolt, and Qasim's inability to deliver on his promises of Kurdish autonomy, weakened the stability of his regime still further; his renewal in late 1961 of a longstanding Iraqi claim to Kuwait alienated Iraq's Arab neighbors. From then on, events in Iraq moved rapidly and Qassim became exceedingly distant from popular opinion, and especially from the views of army officers. He was ousted on February 8, 1963, in a coup led by a number of leading officers of both the nationalist and Ba'athist factions, brought together in a temporary alliance.

After the coup, armed with a list of names and addresses of Iraqi communists provided by the CIA, the Ba'ath Party set about to settle old scores.[19] The immediate task of their National Guard (the Ba'athist militia) was the physical elimination of their rivals; "thousands of communists and leftists were rounded up and arrested, and many were subsequently tortured to death or executed in prison."[20]

Nine months later, however, the Ba'athists were forced out of the alliance and full power was wrested by President Aref, who immediately announced his pro-Nasser sympathies. After a relatively uneventful reign by the Aref brothers, characterized largely by irresolution and lack of political direction, the Ba'ath seized power again on July 17, 1968 in a bloodless coup led by General Ahmad Hasan al-Bakr. Contributing factors to the regime's overthrow were: the continuing Kurdish unrest in the north, the failure to accelerate domestic improvements in people's lives, and especially the humiliating Arab defeat in the 1967 Arab-Israeli War. Iraq had sent a small contingent of troops to fight against Israel, but they had no clear direction from the leadership in Baghdad, and did not engage Israeli forces directly.

The Ba'ath's success in regaining power marked the opening of a new chapter in Iraq's history. Ba'athism, in brief, is a form of pan-Arabism which was founded in Syria in the mid-1940s by Michel Aflaq and two colleagues. Its main ideological focus centers on Arab unity and the formation of a single Arab nation throughout the Arab world. Although virulently anti-Marxist, Ba'athism has adopted a vague notion of socialism that includes the views that the economic wealth of a nation belongs to the people, land reform, and the provision of free social, educational and medical services. Secular in its sensibility, it adopted as its slogan "unity, freedom, socialism."

But despite the urban and potentially revolutionary character of Ba'athism, it has traditionally placed more emphasis on family and village ties, especially in the leadership structures, than on broader visions. In 1966, bitter personal rivalries caused the party to formally split into two branches: the Syrian Ba'ath Party and the Iraqi Ba'ath Party.

The day after the Ba'ath siezed power in Baghdad, Ahmad Hassan al-Bakr was proclaimed President of the Republic, and immediately a seven-man (later expanded to 22) Revolutionary Command Council (RCC) was elected by members of the Ba'ath Party Regional Command. Answerable only to the Ba'ath, the RCC under the new constitution maintained "an absolute monopoly of all judicial, legislative and executive authority,"[21] making it essentially the only functioning institution of government in Iraq. President al-Bakr was elected Chairman of the RCC. According to the constitution, in addition to being chief executive, the president becomes commander-in-chief of the armed forces and is empowered to nominate (and dismiss) a vice-president, cabinet ministers and judges.

Having learned in 1963 never to share power with non-Ba'athists, al-Bakr resorted to ruthless methods to crush the opposition and assert unchallenged Ba'athist rule.[22] This was largely achieved through the building of the president's personal security apparatus known as *maktab al-amn al-qawmi*, or National Security Bureau, headed by the young Saddam Hussein — a close relative of al-Bakr who also comes from the village of Tikrit. Hussein gradually took over control of *al-amn al-amm*, the "official" security service, and was placed in charge of the National Guard. With Saddam Hussein keeping a watchful eye on internal security and al-Bakr devoting his attention to the Ba'athization of the armed forces, the duo in a short period of time were able to maneuver all potential rivals out of the way.

After successfully ridding the armed forces of non-Ba'athist officers, the regime's main focus turned to broadening its social and political base. To enhance its image and win the support of the population, the government embarked on a number of major economic and political ventures. First it initiated relationships with a number of socialist countries. Most significantly, it secured a promise from the Soviet Union for assistance in the future development of the North Rumaila oilfield; and in 1972 a 15-year Iraqi-Soviet friendship treaty was signed.

Later that year, the newly exploited oilfield started generating revenue, thereby reducing the state's dependency on the (still foreign-owned) Iraq Petroleum Company (IPC). In June 1972, the government took the bold step of nationalizing IPC. That step "brought the country behind the Ba'ath Party as no other policy had done, and the regime made the fullest possible use of the new mood."[23]

The combined effect of IPC's nationalization and the phenomenal increase in oil prices following the October 1973 war, transformed Iraq's economic outlook. Between 1973 and 1978, Iraq's annual revenues from oil grew from $1.8 billion to $23.6 billion.[24] The sudden accumulation of income enabled the government to commence a series of ambitious development programs. First priority went to infrastructural projects. Enormous sums were also spent on education, health, housing and welfare: new employment opportunities were created, wages were increased, food subsidies were introduced; and living conditions dramatically improved for the population as a whole.[25]

Another major destabilizing element facing the regime was the continuing Kurdish rebellion in the north. Conscious of the need to find a lasting solution to the Kurdish problem, Saddam Hussein, then vice-chairman of the RCC, initiated autonomy talks with Kurdish leader Mulla Mustapha Barzani as early as 1969. By March 1970, negotiations ended, and President al-Bakr announced an agreement with the Kurdish Democratic Party that became known as the 1970 March Manifesto.

Initial reaction to the agreement was favorable. It provided for the creation of a Kurdish Autonomous Region in Iraqi Kurdistan, and promised Kurdish participation in the central government. It soon became evident, however, that the Kurds would not receive the degree of autonomy they sought and that they would not have any real decision-making power. Relations between Barzani and the Ba'ath rulers deteriorated further as a result of a dispute over the status of Kirkuk, an oil-rich area with a large Kurdish majority. According to the government, Kirkuk was to be excluded from the "autonomous region."

In March 1974, frustration over the lack of progress towards autonomy led the Kurds to rise in rebellion once again. This time, however, the Kurds conducted their fight with assistance from the Shah's government in Iran — who was spurred by U.S. Secretary of State Henry Kissinger to secretly funnel weapons and money to Kurdish rebels. The bitter fight which ensued at a time of growing territorial disputes between Iran and Iraq, and the serious threat it posed to his regime's survival, led Saddam Hussein to make a drastic move. With the mediation efforts of King Hussein of Jordan, Iraq and Iran signed the Algiers Agreement in March 1975. According to the terms of the agreement, Iraq accepted the median line of the Shatt al-Arab waterway as the Iran-Iraq frontier. In return, the Shah agreed to suspend his aid and close his borders to the Iraqi Kurds, whose resistance instantly collapsed. Barzani, now an old man, was forced into exile.

The "solution" of the Kurdish problem and the simultaneous settlement of the border dispute with Iran — another example of Saddam Hussein's pragmatism — gave the Ba'ath a greater feeling of security. For the Ba'ath, the agreement meant that they could now shift their resources towards crushing the remaining communist and underground Shi'a opposition. In May 1978, the regime carried out the execution of 31 communists who were allegedly involved in setting up cells in the army.[26] Two months later, in July 1978, non-Ba'athist political activity was banned for all former members of the armed forces (This actually meant all adult males, by virtue of compulsory enrollment in the army.) In 1979, the expulsion of "no fewer than 3,000 of the Communist Party's hardened members left the disadvantaged of the capital with no organized means of protest and produced a void in the underground which the Da'wah and Mujahidin hastened to fill."[27]

Al-Da'wah al-Islamiyya (the Islamic Cell) and al-Mujahidin (the Muslim Warriors) were the two main underground Shi'a opposition groups, and were also the target of the Ba'ath's ruthless repression campaigns in the late 1970s. The Shi'a — who represent more than half the Arab population in Iraq — have traditionally been excluded from active participation in the central government, which was largely dominated by Arab Sunnis. Both organizations — the older al-Da'wah, which was founded in the early 1960s in the holy city of Najaf, and al-Mujahidin, which emerged in 1979 and was strongly influenced by Iran's Islamic revolution — draw their inspiration from the thought of the late Sayyid Muhammad Baqir al-Sadr, "Iraq's most distinguished and most enlightened Shi'a legist."[28] While the main objective of both organizations was to combat the secularly oriented policies of the Ba'ath government, al-Mujahidin was more militant, and maintained a close association with the ruling clergy in Iran.

The growing threat the organizations meant for the Ba'ath led Saddam Hussein to warn of "stern punishment" under "the iron fist of the revolution" against anyone who participates in "the use of religion as a cover for politics."[29] In 1974 "he executed five members of the Da'wah party; in 1977 he sent eight other Shi'a to their death; in June of 1979 he ordered the arrest of the popular and widely respected Sayyid Muhammad Baqir al-Sadr," which triggered massive demonstrations and led to the violent arrest and deportation of many people.[30] The Ba'ath's harsh measures rapidly paid off in widespread intimidation, and no major protests took place after July 1979 when Saddam Hussein succeeded al-Bakr as president. A final blow was dealt to the Shi'a movements when al-Sadr was executed on April 8, 1980, and the al-Da'wah Party was banned by the ruling RCC.[31]

## The Iran-Iraq War

Two weeks after his takeover as president in July 1979, Saddam Hussein was personally involved in the execution of 22 top leaders who were allegedly conspiring with Syria to overthrow his regime.[32] With potential rivals eliminated, the opposition crushed and the armed forces thoroughly "Ba'athized," total power now rested in the hands of Saddam Hussein, a few close Tikriti relatives, and a handful of party loyalists.

The year 1979 also saw the departure into forced exile of the Shah of Iran and the triumph of the Islamic revolution. Since the overthrow of the Shah, Iraq, with its large Shi'a population with little share in political power, became highly suspicious of Iran's religious fervor. Furthermore, Ayatollah Khomeini and the new leadership in Tehran did not hide their ambitions to export the Islamic revolution. Khomeini proclaimed that all the regimes of Muslim countries in the region were corrupt and un-Islamic, and therefore deserved to be overthrown.

After four years of relative calm on the Iran-Iraq border, and cordial dealings between the two governments, their relationship deteriorated rapidly. By September 1980, after numerous border incidents and endless accusations by both sides that the other was trying to undermine its own authority, Saddam Hussein lost his patience. On September 17, in a dramatic speech broadcast on Iraqi television, he angrily tore up a copy of the Algiers Agreement of 1975 (that granted Iran sovereignty over its half of the Shatt al-Arab). A few days later he unleashed his *al-jaish al-aqaidi* ("the ideological army") against Iran in a massive invasion, which had Washington's tacit approval and support.

In invading Iran, the Ba'athist regime had multiple specific aims: regaining control over the Shatt al-Arab waterway; establishing control of Iran's oil-rich Khuzistan (Arabistan) province; breaking down Iraq's regional isolation; and most importantly, deterring Iran's revolutionary regime from its hostile actions and attempts to export its Islamic zealotry.

The U.S. shared Iraq's paranoia about Khomeini and the ruling mullahs in Iran, especially after their seizure of the U.S. embassy in Tehran on November 4, 1979, and the ensuing 444-day hostage crisis. Moreover, protection of the industrialized world's oil supplies was already an explicit aim of the U.S., which considered the Gulf a region of "vital interest" against which no challenge to the West's influence would be permitted (Carter Doctrine).

Therefore when the U.S. was robbed of its closest ally in the Gulf by the 1979 Iranian revolution, Saddam Hussein became a natural replacement. Five months before Iraq invaded Iran, Zbigniew Brzezinski, President Carter's national security adviser, declared on April 14, 1980 in a much publicized television interview that : "We see no fundamental incompatibility of interests between the United States and Iraq . . . We do not feel that American-Iraqi relations need to be frozen in antagonisms."[33]

The threat of an Iraqi collapse, especially after Iran's 1982 recapture of its own territory and shifting of the fighting to the Iraqi side of the border, prompted unusual international support for Baghdad. Soon after, despite its continuing human rights violations, the Reagan administration removed Iraq from the list of states supporting terrorism, giving it access to loans and credit guarantees. It also brought Iraq into a close intelligence-sharing relationship with the CIA and the Pentagon. In October 1984, the U.S. reestablished full diplomatic relations with Iraq, which Iraq originally broke after the 1967 Arab-Israeli War. This shift in U.S. policy towards Iraq was the subject of a May 1985 memorandum sent to then-CIA director William Casey which concludes: "Our tilt to Iraq was timely when Iraq was against the ropes and the Islamic revolution was on a roll."[34]

In the course of the eight-year Iran-Iraq war, Baghdad relied heavily on France and the Soviet Union for arms supplies. Iraq's war effort was also enthusiastically supported by the six Arab Gulf states — Saudi Arabia, Kuwait, Qatar, Bahrain, Oman and the United Arab Emirates. The largest proportion of Iraq's $80 billion war debt is owed to Kuwait and Saudi Arabia.[35] Egypt also supplied Iraq with weapons and ammunition, and Jordan became one of Iraq's firmest allies and the main route through which a substantial part of Iraq's imported weapons traveled. Of the remaining Arab states in the region, only Syria and Libya voiced support for Iran.

During the first few years of the war, Saddam Hussein was successful in insulating his people from the worst economic effects of the war. Ample food, relaxed restrictions on imports and growing expenditures in development and large industrial projects gave a "business as usual" impression to life in Iraq. But the endless war — instead of the rapid, crushing victory confidently anticipated by the Ba'ath — depleted Iraq's foreign reserves of $35 billion, and brought about a dramatic fall in its oil revenues.[36]

From 1982 to 1987, the war between Iran and Iraq was severely deadlocked. During this period both countries suffered heavy losses and the sporadic "War of the Cities," which began in early 1984, took its toll on the civilian populations. The prospect of achieving total victory by either Iran or Iraq looked dim until the middle of 1987 when a major shift in the war to the waters of the Gulf itself brought the U.S. into the war, solidly on the side of Iraq.

This change in direction had its beginnings in February 1986 when 85,000 Iranian troops crossed the Shatt al-Arab waterway and occupied the Iraqi port of Fao. Besides threatening Iraq's only access to the Gulf, the proximity of the Iranian forces to Kuwait increased the level of U.S. concern about the conflict. In 1987 the U.S. offered to reflag Kuwaiti tankers for protection, and rushed a 42-warship armada to the Gulf. "The general effect of this was to align the United States firmly on the Iraqi side, a tendency which was to gather momentum and to become a decisive factor in Iran's eventually losing the war."[37]

Far from safeguarding free navigation in the Gulf, the U.S. presence gave Iraq a boost and caused an intensification of the "Tanker War." Attacks on oil installations and commercial shipping increased; and by mid-year the U.S. was involved in a head-to-head naval confrontation with Iran. On July 20, 1987, the UN Security Council — six months after it was first introduced — passed Resolution 598 calling for an immediate cessation to all hostilities in the Gulf. Iraq accepted the resolution: Iran refused outright.

The war went on, despite the continuing efforts of UN Secretary General Javier Perez de Cuellar to bring about a ceasefire. In April 1988 — after six years on the military defensive — Iraq conducted a series of spectacular raids and recaptured the Fao Peninsula which Iraq had siezed in 1986. A few months later, a horrifying incident shocked the world: the USS *Vincennes* shot down a civilian plane belonging to Iran Air, killing all 290 passengers on board. Demoralized by this tragic loss and the latest military defeat, Khomeini was persuaded to accept the UN ceasefire resolution. In a statement read on Tehran radio, he said: "Taking this decision was more deadly than taking poison. I submitted myself to God's will and drank this drink for His satisfaction."[38] The ceasefire took effect on August 20, 1988.

After eight years of war and suffering, which left Iraq with nearly 750,000 dead and wounded, a ravaged economy and gigantic foreign debts, a jubilant Saddam Hussein declared that Iraq had won the war. He argued that this war was fought in the name of the "Arab nation" and that Iraq had acted as an "Arab shield" against Iran's Khomeinism. As for the people of Iraq, the end of this grim and terribly destructive war brought a glimmer of hope to their hearts, a vision of lasting peace and prosperity.

In a dramatic reversal, a few days after Iraq invaded Kuwait in August 1990, Saddam Hussein announced his decision to return to Iran all captured territory and restore the 1975 Algiers Agreement, thereby abdicating his last remaining claims of victory in the devastating eight-year war.

## Notes

1. C.W. Ceram, *The March of Archaeology* (New York: Alfred A. Knopf, 1978), p. 171.
2. For additional information on Arab achievements during the Abbasid period see Albert Hourani, *The History of the Arab Peoples* (Cambridge: Harvard University Press, 1991), pp. 189–205.
3. Hourani, *History of . . .*, p. 44.
4. Hourani, *History of . . .*, p. 221.
5. Marion Farouk-Sluglett and Peter Sluglett, *Iraq Since 1958: From Revolution to Dictatorship* (London: I.B. Tauris, 1990), p. 2.
6. Quoted by Sluglett, *Britain in Iraq: 1914–1932* (London: Ithaca Press, 1976), p. 104.
7. Sluglett, *Iraq Since 1958 . . .*, p. 9.
8. David Fromkin, *A Peace to End All Peace* (New York: Avon Books, 1990), p. 452.
9. For additional information on the June 1920 revolt see Fromkin, *A Peace . . .*, p. 453.
10. Peter Mansfield, *A History of the Middle East* (New York: Viking Penguin, 1991), p. 197.
11. Sluglett, *Iraq Since 1958 . . .*, p. 14.
12. Sluglett, *Iraq Since 1958 . . .*, p. 12.
13. For additional information on the coups d'etat of 1936–1941, see CARDRI, *Saddam's Iraq: Revolution or Reaction* (London: Zed Books, 1989), p. 10.
14. For additional information on the 1955 Baghdad Pact see Sluglett, *Iraq Since 1958 . . .*, p. 43.
15. For details on the coup d'etat of 1958 led by Qasim, see CARDRI, *Saddam's Iraq . . .*, pp. 24–25.
16. CARDRI, *Saddam's Iraq . . .*, p. 25.

17. For additional information on Law 80 see Sluglett, *Iraq Since 1958* . . ., p. 78.
18. For an explanation of the relationship between Qasim and the Iraqi Communist Party, see Sluglett, *Iraq Since 1958* . . ., pp. 62–66.
19. For evidence on the direct involvement of the CIA see CARDRI, *Saddam's Iraq* . . ., p. 32.
20. CARDRI, *Saddam's Iraq* . . ., p. 99.
21. Sluglett, *Iraq Since 1958* . . ., p. 118.
22. For additional information on the return of the Ba'ath Party to power in 1968 see CARDRI, *Saddam's Iraq* . . ., p. 100 and Sluglett, *Iraq Since 1958* . . ., p. 155.
23. Sluglett, *Iraq Since 1958* . . ., p. 155.
24. Hourani, *History of* . . ., p. 421.
25. For additional information on the Ba'ath economic policies after the sudden acquisition of wealth see Sluglett, *Iraq Since 1958* . . ., p. 173.
26. CARDRI, *Saddam's Iraq* . . ., p. 155.
27. Hanna Batatu, "Shi'i Organizations in Iraq: Al-Da'wah al-Islamiyah and al-Mujahidin" in Juan R.I. Cole and Nikki R. Keddie, eds., *Shi'ism and Social Protest* (New Haven: Yale University Press, 1986), p. 184.
28. Batatu, "Shi'i Organizations . . .," p. 194.
29. Saddam Hussein, "Nazrah fi al-Din wa al-Turath, " a talk given on August 11, 1977; in Saddam Hussein, *Al Turath al-Arabi wa al-Mu'asra* (Baghdad: al-Hurriyah Press, 1978), pp. 5–17.
30. Batatu, "Shi'i Organizations . . .," p. 195.
31. CARDRI, *Saddam's Iraq* . . ., p. 166.
32. Quoted by Sluglett in *Iraq Since 1958* . . ., p. 209.
33. Elaine Sciolino, *The Outlaw State* (New York: John Wiley & Sons, 1991), p. 162.
34. James Ridgeway, *The March to War* (New York: Four Walls Eight Windows, 1991), p. 13.
35. CARDRI, *Saddam's Iraq* . . ., p. 243.
36. Marion Farouk-Sluglett and Peter Sluglett, "Iraq Since 1986: The Strengthening of Saddam," *Middle East Report* No. 167 (November/December 1990), p. 21.
37. Sluglett, *Iraq Since 1958* . . ., p. 271.
38. Quoted by Sciolino in *The Outlaw State* . . ., p. 120.

# 2

# From Regionalism to Nation-State: A Short History of Kuwait

*Hala Fattah*

Historians of the Gulf region, Iraq and Saudi Arabia are just now begin-ning to grapple with issues of identity that underlie the foundation of Arab societies. The Gulf war has brought these differences to the fore in ways never before imagined. This is especially true with regard to the disparity, real or imagined, between the Arab East (*al-Mashriq al-Arabi*) and the Gulf region. One of the prevailing arguments in the Arab world has been that the Arabs of the Gulf are somehow different from the Arabs everywhere else; either by virtue of their being rich, or as a result of their enduring "tribal" loyalties, or even by the fact that they participated only in a very minor way in the struggle to create an Arab ideology in the sixties and seventies.[1] However acute these differences may be (and, more often than not, differences are a matter of perception), there is no doubt that these came about as a result of the various historical conditions that had a hand in shaping and influencing the Gulf from pre-modern times to the present.

Thus the differences in the economic resources, social structure, politi-cal control and, especially, the varying nature of the colonialist impact on the Gulf principalities (including, of course, Kuwait) and the Arabian peninsula played a part in shaping the development of political identity in this region. This combination of factors explains why Kuwait's attempts at carving out a specific socio-economic and political role based on its historic experience is different from that of Iraq or Syria. Kuwait's historic position as a port in trans-regional trade, its neutral stance throughout the eighteenth and nineteenth centuries with regard to regional conflicts and its smooth transition from British protectorate to statehood in 1961 gave it a different political orientation in the twentieth century. Therefore any analysis of the historical background to the Gulf War must begin with an examination of the similarities as well as the crucial differences in the formulation of identity and affiliation in Kuwait, Iraq, the Gulf and Arabia from the mid-eighteenth to early twentieth centuries. This article will tackle the issue with regard to Kuwait.

## A Regional World

Prior to the spread of the Wahhabi-Saudi alliance in 1745, a fluid, almost formless regionalism was the order of the day. A number of important commercial, social and political connections existed to bind the districts of southern Iraq, Arabistan/Khuzistan, central and eastern Arabia to the fledgling tribal/maritime principalities on the Gulf (Bahrain, Qatar and Kuwait). Of these connections, the most significant centered on long-distance trade. Kuwait, Qatar and Bahrain (all established circa 1740–66) were partly born out of regional necessity, and survived by functioning as ports of transit for the goods, capital and labor that circulated in the area. Pearls, horses, grain, dates, textiles, glass and Indian teakwood were distributed at strategic regional markets interspersed at different locations; overland merchants, shippers and livestock suppliers tied this regional network together and facilitated access to the region by means of a ready supply of revolving credit and a variety of local and international coin. Because of the vicissitudes of regional supply (which was often tied to the chronic instability of the market, caused by plagues, droughts and military adventures of tribal chieftains), borders were unnecessary and, in fact, counterproductive. Economic survival depended on open and easy access to a wide region in which secondary and tertiary markets made up for traditional trade centers which became inoperative over time. Thus regionalism was a practical ideology borne out by the conditions of the period.[2]

The regional world-view that permeated the districts of Iraq, Arabia and the Gulf in previous centuries grew out of a shared identity which tied the inhabitants of the wider region together, based on regional considerations that had little to do with an awareness of "Arabness" as such. Regional affiliations such as a person's birth-place, his or her adherence to a religious or legal interpretation (such as the Hanbali or Hanafi *madhab*) or even his or her occupation were much more important than his or her identity as a speaker of the Arabic language. In a sense, knowing Arabic as well as a number of other languages such as Persian and Turkish was good business (although, of course, Arabic was doubly important because it was the language of the Qur'an as well as of Arab civilization and culture): long-distance merchants living in the Gulf as well as in Basra, Iraq's seaport, realized that the transaction of regional trade necessitated an aptitude in the different languages of the region. In that sense, language or culture were not yet seen as symbols of national identity.

Another connection was through family networks. Other than Iraq, which in the eighteenth and early nineteenth centuries was under the rule of Georgian Mamluks initially brought in as slaves from the Caucasus, most districts in Arabia and on the Gulf coast were linked by family and tribal ties. Throughout this period Bahrain, Qatar and Kuwait were often ruled by sections of the same tribal confederation; at times, it seemed, almost interchangeably. For instance, the tribal sections that established Bahrain, Qatar and Kuwait were all from the Bani Khalid tribal confederation which itself was a branch of the powerful and all-important Anayza. The House of Saud which rose to power in 1745 and forged a large "state" under Wahhabi guidance was also originally from the Anayza.[3] In retrospect, the raids and counter-raids that provided the background to the historical formation of Bahrain, Qatar and Kuwait seem almost like petty family squabbles. Here, too, family ties delineated a wider region in which circulating elites migrated from one *imara* to another in search of stable bases of power and economic security.

As the nineteenth century wore on, regional historians began to document these developments. Historians sought to describe growing regional currents by delineating interlocking areas of trade, as well as movements of capital and labor. For instance, the Baghdad-based scholar Sheikh Ibrahim al-Haidari, who wrote a famous regional history of Baghdad, Basra, Kuwait and Najd in 1860, sought to recreate a regional world, tying southern Iraq to Kuwait, Arabistan/Khuzistan and central Arabia. For him, there were no frontiers in this widely-spread out region, and he took as much interest in the goings-on of merchants and landholders in Kuwait as he did in those of Basra.[4] In much the same vein, al-Ansari, a historian from Arabistan/ Khuzistan, wrote a history in the same period in which he referred to long-distance merchants as *al-afaqiyya* (perhaps loosely translated as those from far-away horizons). He also chronicled the transitory nature of regional merchants who, facing large-scale confiscations of their properties by the Ottoman governors of Basra, temporarily moved their commercial operations to Bahrain or even India.[5] Like al-Haidari, al-Ansari's concern was not the "Arabness" of districts of Iraq, Arabistan/Khuzistan or Kuwait but regional affinities and regional influences.

Finally, it is interesting to note that questions pertaining to regional identification and affiliation, and the concept of the fluctuating border were also recognized by imperial powers, such as Britain and the Ottoman empire. For instance, as a result of the Persian occupation of Basra in 1776–79, the British East India Company moved its headquarters from Ottoman Iraq to Kuwait. As Jacqueline Ismael explains:

> British records at the time generally identified Kuwait as a dependency of Basra. However, Kuwait's close relationship to Basra was based upon commercial, not political ties. Basra was Kuwait's main trading partner, even after the period of the Persian occupation of Basra and the subsequent rise of Kuwait's maritime power.[6]

More importantly, Ottoman governors of Baghdad and Basra were unable to interfere in the regional market that tied southern Iraq to Kuwait. British commercial firms also failed to make headway in capturing local trade. Regional merchants carried on a fierce competition for the goods, capital and markets of the area; and try as they might, British merchants were unable to make a dent in local markets until the 1860s. As late as 1852, British consular officials were noting that Kuwaiti merchants, unhampered by taxes (for the only Ottoman Customs House existed in Basra), regularly undercut their Iraqi competitors, and staved off British commercial intrusion in the bargain.[7]

## Kuwait's Changing Relationship with the Ottomans

It is important to note that, prior to the last decade of the nineteenth century, Kuwait had a fluid relationship with Ottoman Iraq. As noted above, it was considered to be a dependency of Basra, although only nominally so. As Ismael explains:

> During this early period, [throughout the eighteenth and early part of the nineteenth centuries] in fact, Ottoman authorities in Iraq had no Gulf policy *per se* and were not interested in asserting effective control over Kuwait. They were hard-pressed to maintain control over the tribes of Iraq and embroiled in continuous competition and intermittent wars with Persia. So long as Kuwait gave nominal recognition to Ottoman authority, then, and did not become allied to hostile powers, Kuwait was in fact not threatened by interference in its internal affairs.[8]

Following a largely autonomous policy with regard to its interests in overland (desert) trade as well as in overseas commerce with India, the sheikhdom of Kuwait was known to diverge only occasionally from its autonomous stance. For the most part, this had to do with Kuwait's perception of its relationship to Ottoman Iraq. While technically autonomous, Kuwait found it prudent to lend a helping hand to Ottoman authorities in their continous battles to "pacify" Iraqi tribes or other local rulers. For instance, in 1827, at the request of the Ottoman authorities in southern Iraq, Kuwait's naval fleet came to the assistance of Basra when it was under attack by the Bani Kaab Arabs; in 1836, Kuwait helped Ottoman forces quell an uprising in southern Iraq; in 1837, it again offered its services to assist the Ottomans in their attack against Muhammara; and in 1845, Kuwait assisted in the defense of Basra.[9] Probably as a recompense, the al-Sabah family, the rulers of Kuwait, were given large amounts of land in Fao and Sufiyeh (southern Iraq); interestingly enough, these lands were offered as gifts to the Sabah family by the sheikh of the Muntafiq tribal confederation of southern Iraq, an off-and-on Ottoman ally.[10] According to Ismael, by the end of Sheikh Jabir al-Sabah's reign in 1859, "these date groves constituted the Sabah family's principal source of income."[11]

In 1871, as a result of the increasingly active Ottoman role in eastern and central Arabia, the al-Sabah family abandoned their traditional reserve and moved so closely within the Ottoman orbit that the then-ruler, Sheikh Abdullah accepted the Ottoman title of *Qaim-maqam* (district governor) and Kuwait formally became an administrative unit of the Ottoman empire. The alliance between Ottoman Iraq and Kuwait seemed so watertight that by 1893, there was nothing left for the British Ambassador to Istanbul to do but to officially acknowledge Ottoman sovereignty along the coast from Basra to Qatif, including Kuwait.[12] However, by 1899, Kuwait's relationship with the Ottoman government had changed once more, this time radically and perhaps finally, although at first, appearances belied that change. The transformation of Kuwait's role, and its ensuing abandonment of local/regional alliances, was brought about by two reasons. In order to understand these, we must focus on Kuwait's growing importance in the international arena.

## Kuwait's Changing Relationship with the British

According to Abdul-Aziz al-Rashid, one of the early historians of Kuwait, Sheikh Mubarak, the younger brother of the reigning sheikh of Kuwait, was a hot-tempered, quarrelsome man who was only interested in raiding and plundering the tribes on the Najdi-Kuwaiti frontier.[13] Kept on a short leash by his brothers, Mubarak plotted to overthrow them and make himself the ruler of Kuwait. In 1896, he did just that, by assassinating his two brothers and proclaiming himself sheikh. As a result of this move, Mubarak found himself at odds with the rest of his extended family (in particular his nephews) and the Ottoman governors of Basra, who sided with Mubarak's relatives. In order to thwart his enemies, as well as to forge a more independent stance, Mubarak drew closer to Britain. Thus emerged a new constellation of forces in the Gulf: for although the Mubarak-British alliance was to take time to congeal into a permanent friendship, Mubarak had initiated the first step towards separation from the Ottoman empire. Eventually his partnership with Britain would lead his sheikhdom into independence.

For their part, the British saw Kuwait as a necessary adjunct of their imperial policy in the Gulf. By the last quarter of the nineteenth century, the protection of the routes to India had taken on a dynamic of its own; the British felt that no precaution should be spared to secure their unrivalled control of all the sea-lanes leading into the Indian subcontinent. Kuwait's strategic position at the tip of Shatt al-Arab made it a coveted prize, and a source of constant inter-European friction (especially between the Germans and the British). Thus Mubarak's desire for more independence from the Ottomans and British designs on Kuwait colluded at a propitious time in the sheikhdom's history. Mubarak's repeated entreaties to the British to sign a treaty with him were finally crowned with success; in 1899 Britain entered into a secret agreement with the ruler of Kuwait not to cede, sell or lease any territory to any other power without British consent. Moreover, in an accompanying letter, Britain assured Mubarak of its good offices towards him and his heirs and agreed to pay him 15,000 rupees on the condition that he adhere to the treaty and keep it secret. Naturally, the lid was soon blown wide open and, in the words of Jill Crystal:

in the course of [several] attacks and threats [from the Ottomans as well as local Arab rivals], from the sea and the desert, Britain became increasingly drawn into protecting the sheikhdom. The secret treaty soon became a standing obligation.[14]

But what had happened to the regional ties that earlier al-Sabah rulers had cultivated so assiduously? In the wake of Mubarak's unilateral decision to seek protection from the British, a number of important events took place that changed the region's fortunes drastically. In the eighteenth and nineteenth centuries, a regional market had grown up around the buying, selling and shipping of local goods. From Zubara (Qatar) to Bombay, a steady stream of overland and sea-going merchants traded, exchanged and bartered foodstuffs, livestock and textiles over long distances. These regional merchants breathed life into Kuwait's economy. During the Persian siege of Basra in 1776–79, Iraqi merchants took refuge in Kuwait and were partly instrumental in the expansion of the sheikhdom's boat-building and trading activities.[15] As a result, Kuwait's maritime commerce boomed. From that moment on, Kuwait became an important link in the ever-expanding regional market.

By the 1860s, however, the regional market was reeling under the blows of competition from European capital. As a result of the introduction of British steamships on the twin rivers of Iraq, the laying of telegraph cables, the opening of the Suez canal and the expansion in agriculture, European merchants became more competitive. Regional merchants increasingly found themselves cut out of transit trade, and everywhere they were on the defensive. In Kuwait, Mubarak's transition from Ottoman to British ally sowed the seeds for a new breed of merchant. Ismael calls them the Utbi merchants (to differentiate them from the more traditional regional merchants) and sees their emergence as being at the expense of the regional merchants.[16] The Utbi merchants became wholehearted supporters of British-led trade and took on the role of intermediaries for European centers of production.

In other words, Mubarak's accession led to the fracturing of the regional market, in which Kuwait once played an important role. In its place, Mubarak and his merchant allies actively courted international trade. Although a subsequent merchant-led rebellion broke out against Mubarak's attempt to raise taxes in 1909, the al-Sabah rulers realized that they needed the merchant elite, and strove actively to enlist them on their side. According to Crystal:

> With Mubarak's support, the Bani Utub [or Utbi] merchants became increasingly separated from their regional ties and dependent on the Sabahs and, through them, Britain. Mubarak's policies were thus a crucial link in the integration of Kuwait's economy into Britain's economy. After Mubarak, Britain gradually came to dominate both long-distance trade to India and Africa and local trade to Basra, relying on steam power and fire power. Bani Utub trade was relegated to subsistence goods for the city, desert trade and limited shipping. Mubarak weakened regional . . . merchants, through customs and supported Bani Utub merchants by transferring taxes to them through liberal loans.[17]

### The Sabah family and the Merchant Elite

It is important to realize that regional currents did not disappear overnight in Kuwait, and that the formulation of a Kuwaiti identity and the shaping of

Kuwaiti allegiances did not immediately entail the exclusion of other influences, especially those emanating from contiguous Arab states. This is especially true with regard to the embryonic Kuwaiti opposition of the 1920s and 30s; for even though Mubarak's agreement with Britain in 1899 forbade Kuwait from entering into a political agreement with any other state or alienating any Kuwaiti territory without Britain's express permission, Britain's treaty obligations to Kuwait did not muffle regional demands, but may have indeed spurred them on. In order to understand how this regional world-view collided with the more state-centered ideology of the al-Sabah family, we must discuss the development of Kuwait's merchant opposition.

Prior to World War II, the merchants of Kuwait were divided into at least two categories: those "big" merchants who had made their fortunes in pearling and were now investing their capital in Iraqi date plantations, and the smaller entrepreneurs who had far less capital and therefore took more risks. The former had been cultivated assiduously by Mubarak but had had their differences with him; in 1909, as mentioned above, the "big" merchants refused to pay the extraordinary taxes imposed on them by Mubarak's government and promptly organized the departure from Kuwait of several leading members of the community, forcing Mubarak to plead for their return.[18] In the constant struggle for power between the merchant community and members of the al-Sabah family, the former often held the advantage; because of their financial independence, they had a pronounced influence over the al-Sabah family, who often had to defer to their wishes. In 1921, when Sheikh Salim al-Sabah died, a group of merchant notables headed by the influential Hamad al-Saqr organized themselves into a council and demanded to have a say in government matters, including matters relating to the succession. They succeeded in drawing up a list of three contenders from the al-Sabah family, from whom family members selected Ahmad Jabir al-Sabah, who would rule until his death in 1950. Although this organized merchant opposition failed to have a continous impact on the al-Sabah, it did provide the precedent for later reform movements, specifically the movement for the establishment of the Legislative Assembly of 1938.

The struggle for power between the merchant community and the al-Sabah family was capped with the discovery of oil, which could not have come too soon for the government. Oil negotiations had begun in 1923, but the first well was not drilled until 1936. In the meantime, the al-Sabah family was coming under increased political pressure, made worse by the fact that the pearl market had suffered a ruinous eclipse in the 1930s due to the introduction of Japanese cultured pearls. Although the smaller merchants of Kuwait suffered a tremendous blow to their livelihoods, at least eleven of the "big" merchant houses were able to withstand the decline of the pearling industry, due to the diversification of their holdings.[19] Nonetheless, the crash of the pearl market had a pronounced effect on the merchants' economic as well as political power, aggravated all the more by the discovery of oil, which strengthened the al-Sabahs' hand.

In 1938, a combination of governmental inaction, official corruption and lack of popular participation in the affairs of the emirate led to a vociferous demand for reform. A number of merchant notables banded together to press for improvements in basic services: when the initial meeting was disrupted by the government, the opposition met a second time and elected a Legislative Assembly of fourteen members and, following the election, Kuwait's first political party was established, the National Bloc (al-Kutla al-Wataniyya). After pressure had been placed on the government, Sheikh Ahmed al-Sabah consented to the Assembly. Although the Assembly only lasted six months (Sheikh Ahmed found a pretext to dissolve it), it gave Kuwaiti notables a first taste of popular participation in government affairs, and heralded the beginning of Kuwaiti self-determination. It must be noted that all of this popular upheaval was influenced by external as well as internal factors, for Iraqi support — especially that of Ghazi, the intensely nationalistic king of Iraq — was deemed crucial by the Kuwaiti opposition. Indeed, one of the rebels who was tried, convicted and executed by the Kuwaiti government was accused of "handing out leaflets declaring the ruling family deposed and calling on Kuwaitis to resist, assuring them of the Iraqi army's imminent arrival."[20] Meanwhile, another member of the opposition, Suleiman al-Adasani was found in possession of a letter, signed by other Assembly members and addressed to King Ghazi, requesting Kuwait's immediate incorporation into Iraq.[21] Finally, after all hopes for the uprising were dashed, one of the leading opposition members, Abdullah al-Saqr, fled to Iraq.

Crystal believes that the 1938 movement left an enduring legacy in Kuwait's history, According to her:

> [The legacy of the 1938 movement] was that it left Kuwait's merchant community at a peak of political organization just at the moment when the historical economic base of its political influence was about to be removed by a new, outside revenue: oil. . . . . The interaction in 1938 was a harbinger of political changes to come: the merchants demanded a say in the distribution of the new revenues; the rulers, realizing the merchants could no longer compel such input, refused. The merchants, however, fought back politically. It was fortunate for them that they did because, after oil, when the rulers no longer needed the merchants at all economically, it was the rulers' memory of the merchants oppositional potential that persuaded them to buy the merchants out of politics rather than simply drive them out. . . . The act of defiance [i.e the 1938 movement] also streamlined and homogenized the community, turning it into the most coherent and organized political force in Kuwaiti society . . . As a result, legitimate opposition to the ruling family became identified with, and more or less the sole preserve of, a small segment of Kuwaiti society.[22]

Although many opposition figures were to emerge in the fifties, sixties and seventies, carrying forward the call for progressive reforms in Kuwait, the 1938 *Majlis* movement has gone down in Kuwaiti history as the precursor of the movement for democracy in the country. While it is true that it was fueled by merchant concerns, and that it primarily called for less autocratic rule in Kuwait, it can also be seen to have promoted a legacy of another sort. For one thing, it was very much a regional movement, in which opposition leaders made common cause with Iraqi nationalists resisting British designs. Many Kuwaitis called for the dissolution of the Kuwaiti state and union with Iraq. Regional ideals — such as the abolition of colonial-era borders — were among the principal issues raised by the *Majlis* movement. Moreover, as Arab nationalism reached heady proportions in the late fifties and sixties, Kuwaiti nationalists again demanded union, this time with Iraq, Syria and Egypt.[23] While it is true that union was seen by many opposition leaders as a tactical, not strategic move, designed to put pressure on the al-Sabah government for more reforms, it is necessary to reiterate that at least throughout the sixties, a strong regional current still held sway in Kuwait.

## The Frontier Problem

Regional realities were also fractured by the creation of new borders in the Mandate period. Some material is available to detail the political, economic, demographic and social repercussions on Kuwait, Iraq and Saudi Arabia of the establishment of the new "lines in the sand"; interestingly enough, most of it comes from the memoirs of colonial observers. One of the most widely-quoted is Lieutenant-Colonel Harold Dickson, at one time the Political Agent in Kuwait. Dickson was present at the conference held in Uqair (then a modest port in eastern Arabia) in November 1922 when Sir Percy Cox, British High Commissioner in Iraq, took out his famous red pencil and re-drew the map of the Middle East, in the presence of Abdul-Aziz ibn Saud, later first King of Saudi Arabia, Sabih Beg (the Iraqi Minister of Communication and Works), Major J.C. More, the Political Agent in Kuwait (who was ostensibly there to represent the sheikh of Kuwait) and various British and Arab officers. Although Cox gave Ibn Saud and Sabih Beg five days to propose how and where the boundary lines should be fixed between Iraq, Kuwait and Saudi Arabia, in the end he lost his patience and, according to Dickson:

> reprimanded [Ibn Saud] like a schoolboy. . . . . [telling him] that he, Sir Percy Cox, would himself decide on the type and general line of the frontier. Thus ended the impasse. Ibn Saud almost broke down, and pathetically remarked that Sir Percy was his father and mother, who had made him and raised him from nothing to the position he held, and that he would surrender half his kingdom, nay the whole, if Sir Percy ordered . . .[24]

After that episode, Ibn Saud threw in the towel, and Cox had a free hand in drawing the frontiers, giving Iraq a large part of the territory claimed by Najd and, to placate Ibn Saud, depriving Kuwait of nearly two-thirds of her territory by also giving it to Najd. Cox further carved out two Neutral Zones, one in Iraq and the other in Kuwait because, as he candidly told the Iraqi representative, the British suspected that oil was to be found there and he wanted both Iraq and Kuwait to have a half-share of the resources. According to Dickson, when Ibn Saud realized what had transpired, he challenged Cox in his tent and then burst into tears at the great injustice dealt him by the British. Cox, too, was seized by the emotions of the moment and, abandoning his traditional British reserve, also broke down in tears. Nonetheless, after the emotion had dissipated, matters remained where they had been before the altercation in Ibn Saud's tent and "Sir Percy's boundary line stood."[25]

When the news of the boundary agreement was broken to the sheikh of Kuwait, he was shocked and dismayed. Major More, who was supposed to be representing the sheikh's interests and who, according to Dickson, had barely uttered a word throughout the whole conference, had the unpleasant task of explaining to Sheikh Ahmad why it had been considered necessary to lop off two-thirds of Kuwait's territory. Assuaging Ibn Saud was deemed more significant than protecting Kuwait's traditional interests. As a result, finding his hands tied, the sheikh was forced to assent to the agreement.

Although the new borders eventually gained some legitimacy, regional influences remained strong in the area for quite some time. A simple boundary line was not enough to keep tribes away from their traditional grazing lands, and raids and counter-raids launched from Saudi Arabia continued to plague the southerly districts of Iraq and Kuwait until 1930 when, the Ikhwan rebellion broken, peace finally descended upon the area.

## Oil, Governmental Centralization and the Growth of a New Class

In June 1946, the first barrel of oil was exported from Kuwait. Sheikh Ahmad al-Sabah, the then-ruler of Kuwait, opened a valve to load the first tanker with a cargo of crude oil to Britain. The rest, as they say, is history. Since 1946, oil has been the dominant feature of Kuwait's economy; and according to some estimates, it provides almost 93% of the government's revenue today.[26] As has been pointed out, oil gave the state the independence and the necessary leverage to out-distance and out-maneuver the merchant elite. Oil revenues also allowed the state to coopt the merchant class by creating new opportunities for speculation in real estate, construction and services. As a result, many merchant families became heavily involved in contracting. Moreover, substantial state income funneled to under-represented interests in Kuwaiti society created new alliances between the state and Islamic parties, (both Sunni and Shi'a), tribal groups (especially deputies in the Assembly) and some elements of the progressive opposition. Finally, the government's control of oil revenues widened the al-Sabah family's hold over ministries and government departments. Thus it has been calculated that "overall, one-quarter of Kuwait's seventy-five ministers have been Sabahs [and] Sabah representation has never fallen below one-quarter."[27]

Because Kuwaitis were, for the most part, unprepared to rise to the challenges of the spectacular economic, infrastructural and technological changes brought about by massive oil earnings, (partly because a local cadre of Kuwaiti technocrats, managers and teachers had yet to emerge in the fifties and sixties), the state was obliged to contract out for Arab, Asian and European workers to help in Kuwaiti development. In less than twenty years — i.e from 1965 to 1985 — expatriate labor had risen to 77% of the total labor force employed in Kuwait.[28] By 1985, "foreigners" (including Arab Palestinians, Jordanians and Egyptians) constituted 63% of the total population, or 1.6 million.[29] Finding itself swamped by expatriate labor, and sensing a threat to its still-nebulous political identity, Kuwait began to follow a two-tiered policy. First, the state began to award Kuwaiti nationals (who had become a minority in their own country) greater economic privileges to differentiate them from the mass of expatriate labor, and second, the government instituted an array of exclusionary, largely artificial, political distinctions between Kuwaitis and non-Kuwaitis, some of them Arabs born in Kuwait. According to Salih:

> In order to analyze these tendencies which result from the influx of foreign skills into the country, it is necessary to examine the defensive measures undertaken by the government on behalf of its citizens. The most important of these was the Naturalization Decree of December 1959 which restricted Kuwaiti citizenship to those residents, and their heirs, who had lived in the state continuously since 1920. The decree was subjected to amendment in 1960 to permit the naturalization of 50 aliens each year, after ten years residence if they were Arab nationals and after fifteen years, if they were non-Arab. [However] the impact of the naturalization act was reinforced by the electoral law of 1962 which denied the non-native born citizens who had been naturalized since 1952 the right of participating in national elections. The right to vote was restricted to only 50,000 citizens.[30]

The same sort of defensive mentality was exhibited in government regulations that "reserved all senior civil posts, civil service tenure and exemptions from civil service examinations to citizens. And the purchase and exchange of land as well as commercial dealings were officially restricted to Kuwaiti citizens alone."[31] While it is true that many of these tendencies were resisted by the nationalist opposition, it is important to realize that the government's defensive mentality soon became so pervasive that it began to challenge the Kuwaiti opposition's call for a wider, and more equitable participation in government. In fact, the state had become so powerful in the 1980s that it began to suppress the democratic freedoms of Kuwaitis and non-Kuwaitis alike.

Interviewed by the *Washington Post* from his hospital bed (where he was recuperating after having been shot by unknown assailants hours after the entry of Allied forces in Kuwait at the end of the Gulf war), Hamed al-Ju'an, "a prominent Kuwaiti lawyer and active campaigner for democratic rule in Kuwait,"[32] remembers the government's transformation in this manner:

> I was elected to Parliament in 1985. In that election, 60,000 Kuwaiti citizens, all of them male and representing 10% of the population, were eligible to vote. We had no political parties. In 1986, we [i.e the Democracy Movement, of which Ju'an was a member] demanded the implementation of the constitution of 1962, which gives parliament a share of power. But the royal family refused to share power, and the emir suspended parliament, banned free newspapers and refused to listen to our calls for democracy. We formed the Constitutional Movement for Democracy which had 30 of the 50 members of parliament. We organized small meetings to explain our views, and those quickly became large meetings

that attracted thousands. But the police began breaking up the meetings, even using tear gas and arresting some of the leaders. This confrontation reached its peak in the weeks before the Iraqi invasion. . . . .[33]

## Conclusion

Regional influences in Kuwait, Iraq and Saudi Arabia remained strong long after the creation of nation-states in the Arab world. In Kuwait, however, a greater sense of national identity brought on by mass education, broader social programs and more widespread public employment promoted allegiance to the nation-state of Kuwait from about the end of the sixties onwards. Oil undoubtedly fueled that change, allowing the patrimonial state to redistribute oil income selectively, thus creating a new basis for state support. And because the nation-state — *any* nation-state — promotes a more exclusive identity, a new generation of Kuwaitis began to shift their allegiances from the broader concept of Arabism to the narrower one of the Kuwaiti nation. Time will only tell if the Gulf War will deepen the exclusionary nature of Kuwaiti nationalism or broaden it by retrieving and refashioning its long and vibrant regional tradition to suit the present needs of Kuwait.

## Notes

1. For an excellent article dealing with the issue of identity, regional and otherwise, see Ghassan Salame, "Perceived Threats and Perceived Loyalties" in B.R. Pridham, ed. *The Arab Gulf and the Arab World*. London: Croom Helm, 1988.
2. For a more detailed analysis of this question, see Hala Mundhir Fattah, "The Development of the Regional Market in Iraq and the Gulf, 1800–1900," Ph.D dissertation, U.C.L.A., 1986, pp. 1–62.
3. Ahmad Mustafa Abu-Hakima, "The Development of the Gulf States" in Derek Hopwood, ed, *The Arabian Peninsula: Society and Politics*. London: George Allen and Unwin, 1972, p. 32.
4. Ibrahim Fasih ibn Sabghatullah Al-Haidari, *Kitab Inwan al-Majd fi Bayan Ahwal Baghdad, Basra wa Najd*. Basra: Dar Manshurat al-Basri, n.d, pp. 178–183.
5. Ahmad Nur al-Din al-Ansari, "Al-Nasra fi Akhbar al-Basra," Parts I-II, edited by Yusif Izzidin, *Majallat al-Majma' al-Ilmi*, vols. 17–18, 1969, pp. 299–300.
6. Jacqueline Ismael, *Kuwait: Social Change in Historical Perspective*. Syracuse: Syracuse University Press, 1982, p. 42.
7. F.O 78/907, Taylor to the Foreign Office, Basra, May 1, 1852.
8. Ismael, *Kuwait*. . . . ., p. 42.
9. Ismael, *Kuwait*. . . . ., p. 45.
10. Al-Haidari, *Kitab Inwan al-Majd*. . . . ., pp. 174–178, p. 185.
11. Ismael, *Kuwait*. . . . . ., pp. 45–46.
12. Ismael, *Kuwait*. . . ., p. 46.
13. Abdul-Aziz al-Rashid, *Tarikh al-Kuwait*. Beirut: Hayat Press, n.d, p. 138.
14. Jill Crystal, *Oil and Politics in the Gulf: Rulers and Merchants in Kuwait and Qatar*. Cambridge: Cambridge University Press, 1990, p. 24.
15. Ahmad Mustafa Abu-Hakima, *The Modern History of Kuwait. 1750–1965*. London: Luzac and Co., 1983, pp. 24–25.
16. Ismael, *Kuwait*. . . . ., p. 47.
17. Crystal, *Oil and Politics*. . . ., pp. 25–26.
18. Peter Lienhardt, "The Authority of Shaykhs in the Gulf: An Essay in Nineteenth Century History," in *Arabian Studies*, vol. II, London: C. Hurst and Co., 1975, pp. 72–73.
19. Ismael, *Kuwait*. . . ., p. 68.
20. Crystal, *Oil and Politics*. . . ., pp. 49–50.
21. Crystal, *Oil and Politics*. . ., p. 50.
22. Crystal, *Oil and Politics*. . . ., p. 57.

23. Crystal, *Oil and Politics*. . . ., p. 86.
24. H.R.P. Dickson, *Kuwait and her Neighbours*. London: George Allen and Unwin Ltd., 1956, p. 274.
25. Dickson, *Kuwait*. . . ., p. 275.
26. Kamal Osman Salih, "Kuwait: Political Consequences of Modernization" in *Middle Eastern Studies*, vol. 27, no. 1, January 1991, p. 48.
27. Crystal, *Oil and Politics*. . . . ., p. 110.
28. Salih, "Kuwait. . .," p. 49.
29. Salih, "Kuwait. . . . .," p. 49.
30. Salih, "Kuwait. . . .," p. 50.
31. Salih, "Kuwait. . . .," pp. 50–51.
32. *The Washington Post*, April 10, 1991.
33. *The Washington Post*, April 10, 1991.

# 3

# The Crisis in the Gulf—Why Iraq Invaded Kuwait

*Bishara A. Bahbah*

$S$addam Hussein's decision to invade Kuwait on August 2, 1990 took friend and foe by surprise. One can explain Iraq's decision to invade Kuwait by outlining and reviewing the list of grievances Iraq had against Kuwait. These included: historical and territorial claims that Iraq had over Kuwait; Kuwait's refusal to lease two strategic islands to Iraq; Iraq's anger over Kuwait's pumping of huge quantities of oil from the Rumaila field which lies underneath both countries; Kuwait's refusal to forgive Iraq's debt incurred during the Iran-Iraq war; and Iraq's accusations that Kuwait had waged economic warfare against it.

Nevertheless, it can be argued that Saddam Hussein's personality played a key role in his decision to embark on such a disastrous venture. Moreover, Saddam Hussein seriously and persistently miscalculated and failed to predict other countries' reaction to his invasion of Kuwait. And, when the invasion did occur, he failed to realize that the coalition of forces amassed against him would soundly defeat his forces in a very short period of time.

## Historical and Territorial Claims

The borders of present day Iraq and Kuwait are the product of the colonial powers. Under the terms of the San Remo conference in 1920, most of the territories of the Arab Middle East, formerly part of the Ottoman Empire, were divided between Britain and France, which received mandates from the League of Nations to establish and supervise national governments in these territories. In 1921, Britain established the kingdom of Iraq made up of the three former provinces of Mosul, Baghdad, and Basra (which had included the Ottoman district of Kuwait).

In 1922, the British High Commissioner for Iraq, Sir Percy Cox, delineated the modern borders of Iraq, Kuwait and Saudi Arabia. He gave Kuwait a coastline of 310 miles, leaving Iraq a mere 36 miles. Although this angered the Iraqis, they did little to alter that reality because Iraq was under varying degrees of British influence.

However, two developments led to a drastic change in Iraq's relative silence. In 1958, the pro-Western monarch in Iraq was overthrown in a military coup led by Major General Abdul-Karim Qasim. And, in 1961, Britain and Kuwait terminated the 1899 agreement which had allowed the Sabah family to run internal affairs in Kuwait but made Britain responsible for Kuwait's defense and external relations.

When, in June 1961, Kuwait declared its independence, General Qasim laid claim to Kuwait and threatened to annex it by force. British forces rushed to Kuwait deterred an Iraqi invasion. On February 8, 1963, Qasim was overthrown and the Ba'ath party, Iraq's current ruling party, subsequently recognized Kuwait's independence on October 4, 1963 in exchange for a large payment from Kuwait.

Notwithstanding this agreement, Iraqi regimes continued to raise questions over border issues. In 1973, a contingent of Iraqi troops briefly occupied a Kuwaiti border post.

In a somewhat unusual but interesting twist, and on the eve of Iraq's invasion of Kuwait, Iraq accused Kuwait of violating its territorial integrity. In a letter sent to the Secretary General of the League of Arab States dated July 16, 1990, Iraqi Foreign Minister Tariq Aziz complained that the Kuwaiti government had " . . . implemented a plot to escalate the pace of the gradual, systematic advance toward Iraqi territory. The Kuwaiti government set up military establishments, police posts, oil installations, and farms on Iraqi territory."

## Access to the Gulf: Kuwait's Refusal to Lease Two Islands to Iraq

In its quest for a deep sea port in the Gulf, Iraq requested from Kuwait, in the early 1970s, control over the two islands of Warbah and Bubiyan. These islands overlook the approaches to Umm Qasr, one of Iraq's two ports on the Gulf. In 1975, Kuwait rejected an Iraqi proposal to cede Warbah island and lease half of Bubiyan island to Iraq for 99 years. Shortly after the outbreak of the Iran-Iraq war in 1980, Kuwait refused a similar Iraqi request. And, in 1989, after the end of the Iran-Iraq war, Kuwait refused another request to lease the two islands.

Given that one of the main reasons for the Iran-Iraq war was the issue of who controls the Shatt al-Arab waterway which separates Iran and Iraq and which provides Iraq with its only access to the Gulf, Iraq viewed Kuwait's refusal to accommodate its needs with regard to a deep sea port as unfriendly. Thus, the issue of the two islands has been a major irritant in Iraqi-Kuwaiti ties.

## The Dispute over the Rumaila Oilfield

Despite Iraq's recognition of Kuwait's independence in October 1963, the two governments did not settle their dispute over ownership of the huge,

50-mile-long Rumaila oilfield, which lies beneath the Iraq-Kuwait border. About 90% of the banana-shaped field, which is estimated to contain 30 billion barrels of oil, is in Iraq. Nevertheless, Iraq claimed that during the 1980s Kuwait pumped over $10 billion worth of oil from the field that should have gone to Iraq, without any agreement between the two countries.

The significance of this Iraqi gripe against Kuwait becomes even more serious when considering the huge debt that Iraq found itself saddled with as a result of the Iran-Iraq war. More importantly, a significant portion of Iraq's debt was owed to Kuwait.

## Kuwait's Refusal to Forgive Iraq's Debt

Saddam Hussein viewed Iraq's war with Iran as having been fought on behalf of all Arabs, helping to protect them from Khomeini's Islamic revolution. He, therefore, expected Arab countries, particularly those in the Gulf region, to be grateful for his role in checking the spread of Khomeini's Islamic revolution.

Iraq's war with Iran, by most estimates, cost Iraq about $500 billion. Iraq emerged from the conflict with debts exceeding $80 billion—about one and a half times its gross national product—including at least $30 billion in short-term debt that had to be repaid to Europe, Japan, and the United States in dollars or other hard currencies. About half of Iraq's debt was owed to Saudi Arabia, Kuwait, and the United Arab Emirates.

In February and July 1990, Iraq demanded money from the Arab states in the Gulf, and both times, it was turned down.

## Economic Warfare

Kuwait not only refused to forgive the debt, it deliberately, according to Iraq, flooded the oil market in violation of OPEC production quotas agreed to by the major oil producers. This Kuwaiti overproduction depressed the price of oil and, in turn, hurt Iraq, which was already short on funds.

During the Baghdad Arab summit which was held at the end of May 1990, Iraqi President Saddam Hussein claimed that every one dollar drop in the price of a barrel of oil meant a loss of $1 billion a year for Iraq. He then added, in no uncertain terms, that in Iraq's present economic state of affairs, this overproduction amounted to "an act of war."

Iraq badly needed funds to rebuild its shattered economy, devastated by years of war with Iran. One of the ways that Saddam Hussein had maintained internal support for his policies was by spending generously on goods and services even through the bleakest moments of the war. Now that the war with Iran had ended, the Iraqi population's expectations for a better standard of living were on the rise. The rulers of Iraq were aware of that and strived to cope with these rising expectations. This created tremendous pressures to try and get Iraq's debt forgiven and to increase the income generated from the sale of oil.

In a memorandum dated July 15, 1990, addressed to the Secretary

General of the United Nations, Iraqi Foreign Minister Tariq Aziz explicitly named Kuwait and the United Arab Emirates as the two "culprits" in overproduction.

## Saddam Hussein's Personality and Miscalculations

Saddam Hussein's personality, compounded by the fact that he exercised absolute control in Iraq, played a key role in the unfolding of events in the Gulf. He views himself as one of the great leaders of history, ranking himself with Nasser, Castro, Tito, Ho Chi Minh, and Mao Zedong. He has been consumed by dreams of glory, and he identifies himself with Nebuchadnezzar, the King of Babylonia who conquered Jerusalem in 586 B.C., and Salah ad-Din who regained Jerusalem in 1187 by defeating the Crusaders. He believed (it is not clear if he persists in those beliefs) that there' could be only one supreme Arab nationalist leader, and he was the one. He was driven by what he perceived as his mission to lead the Arab world.

Nevertheless, based on his actions and statements, Saddam Hussein is a pragmatic man. When he deemed certain "unthinkable" actions to have been in his favor or better than the existing alternatives, he carried out the "unthinkable."

In March 1975, he signed an agreement with the Shah of Iran, stipulating joint sovereignty with Iran over the disputed Shatt al-Arab waterway in return for Iran ceasing to supply aid to the Kurdish rebellion. Then, in June 1982, Hussein reversed his earlier militant attitude toward Iran and Khomeini and attempted to terminate hostilities by offering a unilateral ceasefire. And, on August 15, 1990, Hussein agreed to meet Iranian conditions for a permanent ceasefire by promising to withdraw from Iranian territory, agreeing to an exchange of prisoners, and, most importantly, agreeing to share the disputed Shatt al-Arab waterway — one of the main reasons for initiating the Iran-Iraq war in 1980 — all because he desperately needed the 500,000 Iraqi troops who were tied up along the Iran-Iraq border.

Given his pragmatism, why then did Saddam Hussein occupy Kuwait and refuse to withdraw when it was obvious that a majority of the world community led by the United States supported UN Security Council resolutions that condemned Iraq's invasion of Kuwait, and subsequently authorized the use of force to evict Iraqi troops and liberate Kuwait?

Saddam Hussein's actions were based on serious miscalculations and misperceptions.

First, given Saudi Arabia's long-standing sensitivity to the presence of foreign troops on its soil, Saddam Hussein assumed that the Saudis would not ask, or be convinced, to accept U.S. and other foreign, particularly non-Muslim, troops to help defend their country and liberate Kuwait. He was wrong.

Second, Saddam Hussein overestimated the level of support he would have in the Arab world. He assumed that the have-nots in the Arab world would be happy with the demise of oil-rich Kuwait. He was surprised by the opposition to his occupation of Kuwait by even those who were closest to him, such as Jordan and the Palestine Liberation Organization.

Third, Saddam Hussein believed that the United States would not interfere militarily if he were to occupy Kuwait. When the United States
decided to send troops to defend Saudi Arabia and liberate Kuwait, he
thought that the U.S. was bluffing and would not wage a war against Iraq
because of the former's Vietnam complex — the fear of being entangled in
a long drawn-out war in a distant land. He felt that, even if the United States
did attack Iraqi troops, the low tolerance of the American public to U.S.
casualties would force the United States to end the war and negotiate an
acceptable agreement with Iraq.

Fourth, Saddam Hussein was determined to attack Israel if a war erupted.
He believed that Israel would then retaliate, leading to the collapse of the
Arab, and hence, the international alliance against Iraq. When attacked,
Israel opted not to retaliate and reaped enormous benefits for its restraint.

Fifth, Iraq's victory over Iran, albeit at an outrageous cost, and the end of
the Iran-Iraq war, unleashed an unrealistic level of confidence in the Iraqi
military's capabilities. Iraq emerged as the fourth largest army in the world
— an army that was well-equipped, and battle-hardened. Where Saddam
Hussein miscalculated was by assuming that this army would or could put up
a fight against the U.S. and other Western armies. More importantly, the
Iraqi leader miscalculated when he assumed that his troops were committed
to fighting for the sake of retaining Kuwait.

## Conclusion

Iraq's invasion of Kuwait will go down in history as one of those tragic
events that precipitated as a result of one man's miscalculations. Whether
Iraq had justifiable grievances against Kuwait no longer is the issue. These
grievances were quickly overshadowed by the tremendous destruction
caused by Kuwait's invasion, and during the battle for its subsequent
liberation.

Many have argued that Saddam Hussein could have settled his grievances
with Kuwait without having to physically occupy the country. Nonetheless
what Saddam Hussein could or could not have done is in the realm of
speculation. What is unshakably clear is that Iraq's invasion of Kuwait led to
a chain of events which threaten not only Saddam Hussein's career, but
also Iraq's ambition to be the dominant power in the Gulf and the Arab
world.

# 4

## The Battle is Joined

*Steve Niva*

When Iraqi tanks and troops rumbled down the road between Basra and Kuwait City in the early hours of August 2, 1990, few would have guessed that within eight months this same road would become the "highway of death" during the merciless U.S. bombing of battered and fleeing Iraqi forces in the hours after their leaders had agreed to withdraw from Kuwait. Estimates put the number of Iraqi soldiers killed in the last days of the American-orchestrated ground offensive in the tens of thousands, though the exact numbers remain concealed in the mass graves that litter the desert alongside the road. Although many people, equiped with their new "Gulf Crisis Maps," learnt during the conflict how to locate this site and the contentious borders that demarcate the "target areas" of Iraq and Kuwait, the cartography involved in tracing the road between August 1990 and March 1991 is of an altogether different sort. The military hostilities began and ended near the shores of the Persian Gulf; the bulk of the conflict played out in the networks of power and influence far removed from the actual combat sites.

Although the possibility of armed conflict between Iraq and Kuwait had reached its boiling point on August 1, the Kuwaiti Emir and members of the ruling family were apparently surprised by the Iraqi invasion and barely escaped in helicopters to Saudi Arabia minutes ahead of Iraqi attack choppers and ground troops. With an estimated 100,000 Iraqi troops on the Kuwaiti border, talks with Iraq had broken down two days earlier, when Iraqi officials stormed out of their meeting with Kuwaiti negotiators in Saudi Arabia, angry that Kuwait had offered them only a fraction of their demands. Iraq accused Kuwait of intentionally over-producing oil to damage the Iraqi economy and slant-drilling into what is largely Iraq's Rumaila oilfield, and demanded forgiveness on the bulk of Iraq's $17 billion Iraq-Iran war debt to Kuwait. The Iraqis also demanded an arrangement with Kuwait that would have allowed them shipping access to the Gulf near the Kuwaiti controlled islands of Bubiyan and Warbah. The Kuwaiti officials reportedly refused to comply and offered only a nominal sum.

The war of words between Baghdad and Kuwait throughout 1990 had heated up in June as Iraq's economy deteriorated and social discontent intensified. On July 23, Iraqi troops mobilized at Kuwait's border. In this context the U.S. sent contradictory signals: U.S. Navy warships began to hold exercises in the Gulf to reassure the Kuwaitis but U.S. officials, including the U.S. Ambassador to Iraq (April Glaspie) and the U.S. undersecretary for Middle East affairs, distanced themselves from taking any position on a possible Iraqi-Kuwaiti conflict. On July 31, the Kuwait-Iraq talks lasted two hours and two days later the Iraqi army rolled.

As interpretations of the invasion began to proliferate over global wire services from its epicenter in Kuwait, Baghdad radio began broadcasting its version: Iraq's armed forces had liberated Kuwait from the ruling al-Sabah family at the request of Kuwaiti revolutionaries who had established a "Provisional Free Kuwait Government." Within seven hours of crossing the Kuwaiti border, Iraq's Republican Guards and up to 350 tanks occupied Kuwait City. Iraq's President Saddam Hussein threatened he would turn Kuwait into a "graveyard" if any outside powers intervened.

Almost immediately, the U.S. activated diplomatic channels in Britain and France to arrange an official joint condemnation of the Iraqi invasion and a demand for immediate Iraqi withdrawal, and then moved to freeze Iraqi and Kuwaiti assets, ban Iraqi trade and halt all arms deliveries to Iraq. The USSR then suspended military shipments to Iraq, while the 12-member European Community condemned Iraq, though it refrained from adopting economic sanctions or freezing Iraqi assets. The price of crude oil jumped 15%, amidst speculation about Iraq's control of the world's fourth largest proven reserves of crude. Late in the day, in an emergency meeting hastily called by the U.S., the UN Security Council passed Resolution 660 unanimously condemning Iraq's invasion and demanding immediate withdrawal. Whatever its ambiguity before the invasion, the Bush administration wasted little time in utilizing its resources to internationalize the conflict.

The official posture in the Middle East differed dramatically from the aggressive U.S. reaction. Kuwaiti officials appealed to the Arab League council meeting in Cairo to organize a joint force to counter the Iraqi invasion and called on Arab governments to condemn Iraq. But the meeting adjourned without a proclamation and Arab capitals withheld official declarations, reportedly to discourage foreign intervention and to give time for an Arab diplomatic solution to the crisis. Throughout the day, Jordan's King Hussein had been attempting to arrange a mini-summit, hosted by the Saudis in Jeddah, which would officially negotiate the terms of an Iraqi withdrawal from Kuwait. President Saddam Hussein had warned that an Arab League condemnation would be counterproductive and King Hussein believed he had convinced Egypt's President Mubarak to withhold condemnation of Iraq in order to give the mini-summit a chance to work. While meeting with Mubarak, King Hussein spoke with President Bush and reportedly told Bush that he was working on an Arab solution to end the crisis. President Bush issued the first of what would be many similar deadlines: King Hussein had only 48 hours to find a solution.

On the morning of August 3 King Hussein met with Saddam Hussein in Iraq who, on the King's account, was receptive to the initiative and agreed to begin initial troop withdrawals as the mini-summit began on August 5. Baghdad radio announced the planned withdrawal and King Hussein returned to Jordan. Later that day, however, the plan collapsed; 14 of 21 Arab League foreign ministers voted, under heavy Egyptian pressure, to condemn Iraq's invasion of Kuwait and demanded an immediate Iraqi withdrawal, although they cautioned against foreign intervention. Jordan, Sudan, Yemen, Mauritania and the PLO abstained, although spurious reports in some Egyptian papers claimed the PLO had sided with Iraq. Observers close to the session said that many believed the U.S. and the British were behind Egyptian actions. King Hussein later said he felt he had been betrayed. The Syrians and the Saudis had also pushed the resolution.

The unyielding response in Washington cast a shadow over regional attempts to negotiate an end to the conflict. PLO chairman Arafat shuttled a peace proposal between Cairo and Baghdad between August 4 and August 6 and Yemen's President Ali Abdullah Saleh embarked on a mediation tour of Arab capitals. However, President Bush asserted that the U.S. would accept nothing less than a total Iraqi withdrawal from Kuwait and warned Arab leaders not to moderate their stance against Iraq. There could be no compromise in the face of Iraq's "naked aggression." In addition, the Pentagon and U.S. officials began to circulate reports that Iraq was reinforcing its troops in Kuwait and was poised to strike Saudi Arabia, eventhough King Hussein and Iraqi officials vehemently denied that Iraq had any intention to invading Saudi Arabia.

On August 6, the U.S. and Britain pushed through UN Security Council Resolution 661 that imposed a sweeping economic boycott of Iraq, and President Bush called for full and total enforcement, threatening a naval blockade. The U.S. continued its efforts to secure maximum involvement by those countries nearest the conflict. U.S. Secretary of State Baker met in Ankara with Turkish leaders and promised them military and economic favors for strict boycott compliance against Iraq and for closing Iraq's oil pipeline, to which they responded favorably. Reports circulated that U.S. officials had even made overtures to Syria and Iran to participate in the *cordon sanitaire* it was organizing around Iraq.

The official Saudi "invitation" for U.S. military intervention came on August 7. Defense Secretary Cheney, armed with U.S. intelligence reports on Iraqi troop strength and force posture (the *New York Times* reported that some Saudi officials doubted reports of Iraqi invasion plans) met with King Fahd, who reportedly submitted to nearly all of Washington's requests. President Bush immediately ordered U.S. forces to Saudi Arabia, although reports later surfaced that British Prime Minister Thatcher had told King Hussein that U.S. forces "were halfway to their destination before the request came for them to come." The immediate U.S. goal was to effect a "multinational" look to the deployment. Secretary Cheney worked his way around the region with carrots and sticks in efforts to arrange an Arab component to the military force in Saudi Arabia, but Egypt and Morocco turned down his initial attempt. U.S. diplomats in Europe and elsewhere began to solicit cooperation for the U.S. deployment and sought to convince NATO allies to join its forces in Saudi Arabia. In sum, the U.S. desired and obtained to no small measure a "multinational" appearance which would become the mantle of legitimacy for its distinctly unilateral plans. Before long, Britain, Canada, France, Australia and others began to supply naval vessels and equipment to the contingent assembling in the Gulf.

As U.S. troops dug in on the Saudi border on August 8, the Iraqi government proclaimed its annexation of Kuwait, which was immediately followed by UN Security Council Resolution 662 declaring the Iraqi annexation "null and void." Diplomacy in the Arab world continued, however; this round of diplomacy was aimed at giving Arab League legitimacy to Arab troop deployments in Saudi Arabia. This culminated in the hotly contested August 10 resolution to support Arab forces in Saudi Arabia. Only 12 of the 21 Arab League members supported the resolution (five of the twelve were the tiny Gulf monarchies of Qatar, UAE, Bahrain, Kuwait, and Oman) and the alternative resolution presented by the PLO calling for a negotiated settlement was kept from the table. Soon after, 3,000 Egyptian troops were dispatched to "defend" Saudi Arabia. Then, on August 12, Saddam Hussein issued his terms for an Iraqi withdrawal: Iraq would withdraw from Kuwait if Syria pulled out of Lebanon and Israel ended its occupation of the West Bank and Gaza and the Golan Heights.

The Iraqi proposal was immediately rejected by U.S. officials and the proposed solution was labeled unacceptable, due to its "linkage" of regional issues. With President Bush racing his power boat and "recreating" in Maine, the major media played down the Iraqi offer as it would the others that followed; the *New York Times* managed to dismiss it with one line of news copy. Iraq issued several more proposals during the month. The first was a general proposal by President Saddam Hussein on August 19 that the U.S. be replaced by UN troops and the issue of Kuwait be dealt with in a regional context. The second of these, however, was a high level proposal delivered to National Security Advisor Scowcroft on August 23 which offered a complete Iraqi withdrawal from Kuwait in return for a cessation of sanctions, full Iraqi control of the Rumaila oil field and guaranteed access to the Gulf. Some senior U.S. officials reportedly said the offer was "serious" and "negotiable." The Bush administration did not officially announce the Iraqi proposal (it was revealed in the press days later) and certainly there was no attempt to consider it a first step toward de-escalating the conflict.

However, the U.S. acted quickly to establish its terms for the embargo and expand its military capabilities in the Gulf. On August 12, President Bush unilaterally ordered naval forces to interdict Iraqi oil exports and all imports, acting before the U.S. could bring the issue of military force to a UN vote. It was widely reported that a number of UN Security Council members, including the USSR, France and China, were resisting the U.S. plan. The first offensive U.S. move against Iraq came on August 16, when the Pentagon directed the U.S. Navy to implement the President's order. Within two days, U.S. warships fired the first shots across the bows of two Iraqi oil tankers bound for Iraq. The recalcitrant Council members soon fell into line with Washington's wishes. Washington made a number of concessions in order to obtain more than a simple majority on the vote, which it felt was essential for the appearance of UN legitimacy. The UN Security Council passed a diluted Resolution 665 on August 25 which did not explicitly authorize force but gave the U.S. room to use force if needed.

At the same time, U.S. officials, including Defense Secretary Cheney on August 17, were leaking word to the press that the U.S. was preparing for a "long commitment" in the Gulf. The Pentagon exponentially inflated troop projections needed to "defend" Saudi Arabia against an Iraqi attack (estimates went from 100,000 to 250,000 in a week). The public relations effort kicked into overdrive to mobilize support for the build-up; on August 15 the president told a group of Pentagon employees that U.S. actions were necessary to protect "our jobs, our way of life, our own freedom and the freedom of friendly countries around the world." A key component of U.S. plans for a "long commitment," and a hitherto unrealizable prize for U.S. planning during the past decade, was achieved when the United Arab Emirates put its military bases at the disposal of U.S., British, and French forces on August 19. Qatar followed suit eight days later.

The incorporation of Gulf military facilities into U.S. planning was secondary in the media spotlight to what became known as the "hostage issue." On August 9, the Iraqi government announced that foreigners would not be allowed to leave Kuwait or Iraq. Americans were numbered at over 3,000, with British numbers slightly higher; a lesser known fact was that an estimated 2 million expatriate workers — 1 million Egyptians and hundreds of thousands of Indians, Filipinos, Thais, Bangladeshis and Pakistanis — were still in Iraq and Kuwait. The issue took on prominence when Iraq ordered specifically "Western" foreigners in Kuwait to assemble in hotels, and on the following day, August 18, announced that citizens of "aggressive nations" were being moved to strategic civilian and military installations to serve as "human shields" to prevent a foreign attack. On August 19, President Saddam Hussein offered to release the foreigners if the U.S. agreed to withdraw its forces from the area under UN supervision, promised not to attack and allowed Kuwait to be treated as a regional issue. President Bush soon added the resolution of the "hostage issue" to the growing U.S. list of non-negotiable demands.

The U.S. build-up quietly but rapidly acquired a less than defensive hue; on August 22 the president called up an initial 40,000 members of military reserve units – the first reserve mobilization since the 1968 Tet Offensive – and by September 6 the number of troops in Saudi Arabia had reached 100,000. On September 15 U.S. officials announced they had established a credible defense and were now building up their offensive capability.

Military hardware and massive arms transfers followed the troops into the region. The Pentagon had announced earlier on August 15 that it was expediting previously negotiated arms sales to Egypt and Saudi Arabia and giving Arab requests highest priority. On August 28 Bush administration officials acknowledged their decision to sell and deliver to Saudi Arabia 24 F-15s along with M-60 tanks and stinger missiles that were part of a $6-8 billion package, and revealed a Saudi letter of intent to buy 315 M-1 tanks at a cost of $3 billion. Then in response to Israeli protests over the Arab arms sales, on August 31 U.S. officials revealed their plans to transfer $1 billion worth of weaponry to Israel to offset the Saudi deliveries.

The emerging "coalition" was hardly unified on all points and the administration had to move quickly on a number of occasions to keep the facade of unity from cracking. The USSR seemed uncomfortable with the one-track U.S. military escalation, and on September 4 Soviet Foreign Minister Scheverdnadze proposed convening an international peace conference which would address the "several complex interlocking problems" in the region. In response to heavy U.S. pressure, he amended the proposal three days later by emphasizing the need to deal with the Gulf crisis before any other regional issues, and on September 9 when President Bush met with President Gorbachev to issue a joint statement on the crisis, the proposal was not mentioned. But the Soviets had held out a second track that would continue to shadow the administration's trajectory towards armed conflict.

At some points the U.S. almost left its "coalition" behind. The administration almost forgot that its "solid support" in the Arab world rested upon dictatorial thrones and regimes whose tiny political base had the least to fear from U.S. designs in the Gulf. On September 5 Secretary Baker announced a plan for a long-term U.S.-led "regional security structure" in the Middle East similar to NATO. However, the NATO analogy elicited a sharp response from the U.S.'s Arab partners, who did not publicly share the long term U.S. vision. The next day Secretary Baker had to amend the proposal so as to "fit the realities" of the Middle East. "Coalition" sensitivities were again stretched on September 17, when Secretary Cheney had to move quickly to fire U.S. Air Force Chief of Staff Dugan for revealing U.S. planning for a massive bombing campaign against Baghdad and plans to target President Saddam Hussein.

There was also a less than unanimous outlook on one of the most significant issues of U.S. strategy: funding the expedition. The U.S. had been pressuring the Japanese and West Germans for contributions on terms that put the bulk of the funds at the disposal of the Americans. On August 22 Japan offered to help Egypt directly and later suggested that funds should be distributed through an international consortium of industrialized nations under UN auspices. The plan met with approval from European nations but was quickly derailed by the U.S., which quickly formulated a plan of its own and launched a public campaign to push it on its hedging allies. On August 30 it was reported that the Bush administration planned to underwrite the cost of deployment with contributions from its wealthy allies in the sum of $23 billion in aid for the first year, with half going to the U.S. Then on September 4, Treasury Secretary Brady embarked on an international mission to implement the plan. At the same time Secretary Baker paid his respects to the Gulf royal families; by September 10 Baker reported that Gulf states had pledged $12 billion, half of which would cover U.S. military costs and the other half going to countries financially affected by the crisis.

Secretary Brady's efforts were less immediately successful. The European Community refused to contribute directly to the U.S., choosing to give billions in aid to the nations financially strained by the crisis. A West German official leaked that Bonn would not donate funds to the U.S. build-up because it was seen as an essentially bilateral arrangement between the U.S. and Saudi Arabia. But on September 14, Japan agreed to contribute $4 billion to what it termed "multinational efforts" in the Gulf, including soft loans worth another $2 billion to Turkey, Jordan and Egypt. It insisted its decision was not made in response to administration pressures. The next day West Germany announced a similar $2 billion pledge. The Bush administration, still far from reaching its financial goals, moved to circumvent an alternative financial network by announcing plans on September 25 to set up the "Gulf Crisis Financial Coordination Group" to direct aid distribution. Arms sales also took their place at the fund-raising table. The most stunning example of the lengths the Bush administration would go was its announcement of plans for a $20 billion sale of sophisticated weaponry to Saudi Arabia. This plan had to meet with Congressional approval, which was not forthcoming due to pressure from pro-Israel members of Congress. A scaled back $7.5 billion sale was announced on September 26.

The administration did its best to conceal its plans for the "Gulf Crisis" but a pattern began to emerge which contrasted bland and even hopeful public statements with behind the scenes preparation for conflict. The 45th session of the UN General Assembly opened on September 24, precipitating a burst of diplomatic posturing and public pronouncements. French President Mitterand announced a 4-stage proposal to solve the conflicts in the region, and the USSR announced a visit to Iraq by its special mediator Yevgeny Primakov. These moves turned up the volume for a diplomatic settlement, forcing President Bush to moderate his remarks at the UN General Assembly by hinting that Iraqi withdrawal could open the way to Israeli-Palestinian peace. Away from the international media on October 5, however, Bush initiated private discussions with members of Congress on the possible use of force against Iraq. Reports began to circulate that the Bush administration might have to secure Congressional approval for any military action.

The Bush administration faced its most severe public relations challenge following the October 8 massacre at the Haram al-Sharif compound in Jerusalem, where Israeli border guards shot and killed 21 Palestinians and wounded more than 100, after a group of Palestinians had gathered to defend the Islamic holy site from rumored extremist Israeli provocations.

Bush strongly, and transparently, rebuked Israel for not acting "with more restraint." The major media ignored the film footage and testimony that revealed the Israeli attempt to cover up the killings and pin the blame on the Palestinians and instead focused on the President's anguish over keeping the "coalition" together. On the surface it seemed that the U.S. might have finally overplayed its hand.

Non-aligned members circulated a resolution that called for a UN Security Council fact-finding mission to investigate conditions in the occupied West Bank and Gaza and suggest ways for the Security Council to protect Palestinians, a suggestion which met with widespread support. The U.S. threatened to use its veto, delayed the vote and then submitted its own resolution that ambiguously condemned the "violence" and "particularly the Israeli response." The key issue for the U.S. (and Israel) was to keep the Security Council from setting a precedent by assuming responsibility for Palestinians under Israeli occupation. The UN Security Council finally passed a U.S. orchestrated resolution on October 12 that allowed for the Secretary-General to send a representative who would report back to the Security Council, and dropped any mention of proposals for the Security Council to protect Palestinians.

But the Israelis quickly undercut what appeared to be a successful U.S. maneuver by rejecting UN intervention and refusing to cooperate with the Secretary-General's delegation. The Israeli move set off a string of UN battles that forced the U.S. time and again to intervene on Israel's behalf, exposing a chief contradiction at the heart of U.S. regional strategy and weakening its dubious claim to UN legitimacy against Iraq, as well as deepening popular resentment against the Arab regimes who had sided with Washington. On October 24 the UN Security Council unanimously voted to condemn Israel for its refusal to cooperate with the UN investigation. Israel finally agreed to accept a visit from UN representative Jean Claude Aimé with reported U.S. assurances that it would block future attempts to implement proposals for the UN to assume responsibility for Palestinians.

Fortunately for Washington, its Arab allies, including its new found partner and recipient of Saudi Arabian financial largesse, Syrian President Hafez al-Assad, had their own issues to attend to. The Syrian army demonstrated the rewards of rapprochement with the U.S. by storming East Beirut and assuming full control of the Lebanese capital on October 15 without fear of Israeli or American retribution. Egypt secured a measure of its pay-off when Saudi Arabia, Kuwait and the United Arab Emirates cancelled its collective $6 billion debt on October 24. Things were more complicated in Saudi Arabia, however. On October 13 Kuwait's Crown Prince, under heavy pressure from much of the exiled Kuwaiti community in Saudi Arabia, was pressured into offering to hold free elections and revive the parliament if Kuwait was liberated. And internal differences within the Saudi royal family surfaced on October 21 when Saudi Defense Minister Sultan hinted to the press that Saudi Arabia might not oppose an Iraqi withdrawal from Kuwait in exchange for some territorial concessions. The royal family quickly retracted the minister's words after Bush administration public relations efforts scrambled to erase the offer from the books; President Bush had to reiterate the U.S. position against anything less than a total and unconditional withdrawal.

The ambiguous signals from Saudi Arabia about exploring alternatives to what appeared to be impending conflict were amplified in clear statements from Gorbachev and Mitterand on October 28 that there was still room for diplomatic accommodation with Iraq. Gorbachev declared, "It is unacceptable to have a military solution to this question," and on November 4 Mitterand insisted that the embargo be given more time because it was working. French and Soviet limitations were made quite apparent on this question, however, with the *Los Angeles Times* report on October 29 that the Bush administration was secretly discussing its timetable for an attack on Iraq; a timetable for launching an air war in January arranged at this time was confirmed on March 3, 1991 by the *New York Times*. The administration set its plan in motion on November 3 when Secretary Baker departed Washington on the first leg of his quest for a UN authorization to use force against Iraq.

The administration waited for the U.S. Congressional elections to pass before it unveiled its strategy. Two days after the elections President Bush authorized a troop increase of 200,000 to insure the "offensive military option" and the next day Secretary Cheney announced that the troops in the Gulf would be there for the duration. Congress reacted sharply, demanding President Bush concede to Congress any authorization for the use military force, though Bush reminded them that on October 2 they had given him what many considered was a "blank check" in support of administration actions in the Gulf. October polls indicated that although most Americans supported the administration's goals in the region, the overwhelming majority did not support a U.S. war in the region. An additional factor in the domestic equation was the increasing number of groups opposed to U.S. intervention in the region. Demonstrations, teach-ins and town meetings throughout the country condemned the administration's escalation of the crisis. Major demonstrations were held October 20 in New York, San Francisco, Los Angeles, Seattle, Cleveland, Minneapolis and other cities.

With one eye on the polls, the Bush administration searched for justifications to garner public support for war. On November 2 administration officials admitted that "it remains important that people not see this as a battle over oil." Secretary Baker's September 4 statements that "We seek a region . . . in which energy supplies flow freely" and a "more durable order" was not generating public support and proved to be a liability as opposition forces played on the public misapprehension of fighting a war for oil supplies. Administration justifications changed with the pressing needs of the moment, ranging from the defense of Saudi Arabia to the restoration of Kuwaiti sovereignty, from not rewarding aggression to equating Saddam Hussein with Hitler. But with polls showing less support for the president than previous months and a majority opposed to the use of force before sanctions were given a chance to work, the administration played on the public demonization of Saddam Hussein and connected it to security at home.

On November 14, in a widely publicized speech, Secretary Baker warned that Saddam Hussein threatened the "economic lifeline" of the West and that U.S. military deployment was justified to protect American jobs. Baker's comments were met with public skepticism. Later in the week, however, a major *New York Times* poll indicated that 54% of respondents thought one reason was good enough for the U.S. to take action against Iraq: the need to prevent Iraq from obtaining nuclear weapons. Speechwriters quickly inserted this nugget into Bush's speech in Germany and two days later, in a Thanksgiving holiday trip to Saudi Arabia, President Bush hammered away at the need to prevent Saddam Hussein from obtaining a nuclear capability saying that Saddam Hussein has "never possessed a weapon he hasn't used." The threat of Iraqi nuclear weapons dovetailed with the widely publicized Iraqi chemical weapons threat, and the following weekend the nuclear weapons issue was pushed by National Security Advisor Scowcroft and Defense Secretary Cheney on the Sunday morning TV circuit.

Persuasion of another sort enabled the U.S. to obtain the major prize to keep the administration strategy "on schedule": a near unanimous UN resolution authorizing military force on November 29. Secretary Baker's global tour secured European cooperation, but more importantly he offered the Soviets a deal they could not refuse; a day after the UN vote the Gulf states pledged $6 billion in financial aid to the USSR in consideration for its support. The administration was more than generous in its offers to developing countries on the Council. In separate deals, Columbia, Ethiopia and Zaire were offered new aid packages, access to World Bank credits or IMF loans in return for their vote. The Chinese proved more intractable but administration promises for a high level White House meeting with the Chinese ambassador, thus ending China's post-Tienanmen isolation, and a promise to push withheld World Bank credits secured the Chinese abstention on the vote. On the eve of the vote the U.S. was still scrambling to ensure an overwhelming victory, going so far as to arrange a meeting between Secretary Baker and the Cuban foreign minister which brought only a defiant rebuttal from the Cubans. Yemen also held out against U.S. pressure and voted against the resolution; within minutes the Yemeni ambassador was told by a U.S. diplomat that it was the "most expensive 'no' vote you ever cast" and within days Yemen's $70 million in U.S. aid and vital financial aid from the Gulf states was terminated.

With crucial UN cover secured, the administration lowered the decibels on its march to war. On December 1, President Bush called for talks with Iraq as part of fulfilling administration promises to a number of countries that had voted for the UN resolution. Iraq accepted immediately and announced its plans to bring all the issues in the region — including the issue of Palestine — to the table, which met with a predictably negative U.S. response. The strong preference for sanctions over armed conflict was aired in an unlikely place — the House Armed Services Committee hearings. Two retired chairs of the Joint Chiefs of Staff and seven former secretaries of defense broke with the administration and supported the continuation of sanctions. Their comments appeared to be buttressed by CIA Director Webster's December 5 report that the trade embargo had dealt a "serious blow" to the Iraqi economy. But when Saddam Hussein announced Iraq's release of the hostages on December 6, President Bush publicly responded to the release by saying that it only made it easier for the U.S. to attack Iraq. Despite this statement, in a glaring display of corporate media deference to the administration agenda, ABC cancelled its December 7 *Nightline* "town-meeting" on the Gulf crisis that was to feature anti-war voices, on the grounds that administration plans for peace talks with Iraq made it unnecessary.

Massive public demonstrations against U.S. intervention and the apparent march towards war in Tunisia, Algeria, Jordan and elsewhere pressured renewed Arab efforts to find diplomatic alternatives to war. Algeria and Jordan launched a last-ditch effort on December 9 designed to bring Saddam Hussein and King Fahd together for negotiations. Algerian President Benjedid met with Saddam Hussein on December 13 but any hopes for progress were squelched on December 14, when King Fahd, reportedly under heavy U.S. pressure not to open himself to diplomatic accommodation with Iraq, cancelled Benjedid's visit while his plane was in mid-air, in a public humiliation of his efforts. King Hussein unveiled a plan the next day for an international conference, but the U.S. ignored it. In February, former Defense Secretary Zbigniew Brzezinski insisted that war could have been avoided if the administration had not sabotaged this Algerian peace initiative.

In the last days of December, U.S. officials leaked word to the press of the administration's fear of a "nightmare scenario" — that Iraq would begin pulling its troops out of Kuwait and force the remaining issues to the negotiating table. Public haggling over U.S. talks with Iraq continued through December with no agreement. On December 24 Iraq recalled its ambassadors from foreign capitals for a strategy session in Baghdad, and on December 26, Saddam Hussein announced that he would be willing to participate in a serious and constructive dialogue with the U.S. On January 2, U.S. officials disclosed that Iraq had made a number of offers, including an offer that was relayed to the White House through Yugoslav emissaries in the nonaligned movement that Iraq would withdraw from Kuwait as long as the U.S. pledged not to attack, removed its troops from the region and agreed to an international conference on the Palestine question. U.S. officials even admitted that it was "interesting" that the Iraqi offer dropped any claims to the Gulf islands or the Rumaila oil field. A day later, PLO Chairman Yasir Arafat met with Saddam Hussein; Arafat said that neither of them insisted that the Palestinian problem be solved before Iraqi troops withdrew from Kuwait, saying instead that all that was necessary was a public link to be guaranteed by the permanent members of the Security Council to deal with the other pressing issues in the region, including the Palestinian question.

With less than two weeks to go before the UN deadline authorizing the use of force, on January 3 President Bush offered that Secretary Baker meet with Iraq's Foreign Minister Aziz in Geneva, a move largely interpreted as a bid to win Congressional authorization for military force on the grounds that the administration had exhausted its diplomatic options. But with the official administration position insisting on nothing less than unconditional Iraqi withdrawal, and President Bush's persistent statements that he doubted whether Saddam Hussein had really "got the message that we are serious," the outcome of the January 9 meeting in Geneva was a foregone conclusion. Negotiation was reduced to dictation. The "talks" did, however, secure the administration Congressional authorization of military force over those who pressed for the continuation of sanctions. With the crucial backing of the pro-Israel lobby and its Congressional leaders, the Solarz-Michael resolution passed in the House by a vote 250–183 and the Senate passed a similar resolution by the narrow margin of 52–47.

The frantic last days before the January 15 deadline produced little to halt the trajectory towards war. UN Secretary-General Perez de Cuellar, bound by UN resolutions to insist on total Iraqi compliance embarked upon a largely ceremonial trip to Baghdad on January 13. The transcripts of the meeting were suppressed; when they surfaced a month later they revealed Perez de Cuellar's deep frustration with U.S. dictation at the UN, and an Iraqi willingness to negotiate provided it was given political cover to withdraw. On January 14, France proposed a plan, with the support of a large number of countries, for rapid Iraqi withdrawal, with the incentive for Iraq being that the UN would convene an international peace conference on the Middle East within a year. The plan predictably met with immediate U.S. and British rejection; the U.S.'s UN Ambassador Pickering stated that the proposal was unacceptable because it went beyond previous UN resolutions.

The January 15 deadline passed with no Iraqi movement. On January 16, the U.S. unleashed massive air attacks on Baghdad and other major cities in Iraq, and against Iraqi military emplacements in southern Iraq and Kuwait. An immediate target was the civilian infrastructure of Iraq's major cities, including water, electrical and communications facilities. High altitude bombers unloaded tons of charged high explosive weaponry on the soldiers clinging to the desert floor below. The attack was quick and devastating and Iraqi air defenses were immediately overwhelmed. President Bush addressed the U.S. two hours later to announce what most people already knew. The unrelenting bombing campaign continued until the very last day of the ground offensive; among the early targets was the Iraqi nuclear facility at Tuwaitha near Baghdad, in direct contravention of UN resolution 45/58 J forbidding destruction of nuclear facilities near civilian areas.

Saddam Hussein kept his frequent promises to target Israel first if attacked. Iraqi scud missiles hit Israel on January 17 and 18, damaging neighborhoods on the outskirts of Tel Aviv. While Israeli citizens huddled nightly in sealed rooms to protect them from possible chemical attacks, the Israeli army placed a total 24-hour curfew on the entire occupied territories. Palestinians were denied gas masks by the army, who defied a court order on January 15 to distribute masks by claiming only to have enough for a small portion of the Palestinian population. The military shot those who tried to evade the curfew.

With great media fanfare, the U.S. rushed Patriot missiles to Israel — which Prime Minister Shamir had refused in the week prior to the war — but reportedly refused to provide Israel's air force with the codes necessary to avoid hostile encounters with U.S. aircraft in Iraqi airspace, which contributed to the "restraint" shown on Israel's part. On January 21, after meeting with U.S. envoy Eagleburger, who had become a permanent fixture on the Israeli landscape, Prime Minister Shamir announced Israel would respond "at a suitable time." On January 28, Israeli Peace Now members and others announced support for the war against Iraq claiming, in Yael Dayan's words that it was "necessary in order to attain peace" and criticized peace movements outside of Israel for not supporting the war.

By January 23, Pentagon officials announced they had flown nearly 12,000 bombing missions over Iraq and Kuwait. The administration media strategy followed closely the outline signaled by a *Los Angeles Times* article on December 28: administration officials said that "Bush assumes that the American public will be mainly concerned about the number of U.S. casualties, not the tens of thousands of Iraqis who stand to die or be maimed in a massive air assault, and that even the killing of thousands of civilians — including women and children — probably would not undermine American support for the war effort." The media had been rendered serviceable to administration efforts on a number of levels; most importantly Pentagon restrictions in the Arabian peninsula kept selected reporters tightly monitored in a "pool system," daily Pentagon briefings and White House photo opportunities set the print and visual media agenda and a proliferating number of retired or semi-active military and government officials — including convicted Iran-Contra liar Richard Secord who appeared on CNN as an air war expert — reduced commentary to tactical military observations and patriotic advice. News features predictably reflected the Pentagon's image of a sterile "surgical" war, made a fetish of advanced U.S. weapons technology and framed issues in terms of U.S. strategy.

As the air war droned on, Bush administration public relations efforts began to prepare the public for the ground war. On January 24 White House spokesperson Fitzwater echoed Cheney and Powell's public hints the day before that the American public should be prepared for "unpredictable" changes in U.S. military strategy. The hints were confirmed in a calculated leak to the *New York Times* on January 27 that administration officials had told key members of Congress that air strikes alone might not be enough to dislodge Iraq from Kuwait. Administration officials also hinted at plans to go beyond the UN mandate by taking out Iraqi President Saddam Hussein. However, many already believed the UN mandate to be in jeopardy because of the destruction being visited upon Iraq. Soviet officials warned that the U.S. was exceeding its mandate on January 26, followed by

Egyptian warnings on January 27. On January 29, French Defense Minister Chevenment resigned from his post, citing his refusal to go along with the U.S. escalation beyond UN goals.

An increasing chorus of international public dissent, including massive demonstrations in the U.S., Europe and Middle East — among them a 300,000 strong march on February 3 marred by government violence in Morocco — raised voices against the destruction of Iraq and the wanton civilian casualties. Still, a virtual blackout existed on the details of the destruction in Iraq until Iraqi officials finally announced on February 6 that civilian casualties exceeded 7,000. The major American media outlets ignored a trip to Iraq from February 2–8 by former U.S. attorney general Ramsey Clark who reported massive destruction of neighborhoods, businesses, schools, roads and vehicles with "no evidence of any military aspect." On February 9, Gorbachev signaled that he might make an independent move to try to end the destruction by personally warning that the U.S. was clearly in danger of exceeding the UN mandate; he would wait three days before acting.

British and U.S. pressure silenced the UN Security Council in what was ostensibly its jurisdiction; efforts to bring the Council into session on January 31 had to be withdrawn under this pressure. On February 9, the UN Security Council finally announced it would meet. But so as not to "send mixed signals" the Council was ushered into a special closed-door meeting, only the fourth in UN history. The U.S. bombing of the Ameriyeh bomb shelter in Baghdad, killing over 1,500 Iraqi civilians, precipitated a heated debate in the Council on February 14 that included a Cuban draft resolution calling for a halt to the U.S. bombing, which the U.S. and British ambassadors termed "unacceptable" and "unnecessary." Little came of the muted session.

At this point, Soviet leader Gorbachev, whose support had been instrumental to U.S. intervention plans since August, revealed both his diplomatic skills and the Soviet Union's "new world order" limitations by initiating action designed to get Iraq moving out of Kuwait before the U.S. launched a ground offensive. On February 12, Gorbachev sent his envoy Yevgeny Primakov to Baghdad; by February 15 Iraq's Revolutionary Command Council announced that Iraq might be ready to accept Resolution 660 for a complete withdrawal from Kuwait. Three days later, Iraqi Foreign Minister Aziz was in Moscow studying the Gorbachev plan, which the Soviet leader had communicated to Washington and European capitals. Gorbachev could not have known that the Bush administration had already set February 21 as the date for the ground war, according to later reports in *Time* magazine, though Soviet activity forced the administration to move the date back to February 23.

Bush and Scowcroft were reportedly irritated with the Soviet interruption of their scheduled plans, but withheld an outright rejection in the belief that Gorbachev would not bring relations with the U.S. to the breaking point and that it would be too risky publicly to denounce Gorbachev's efforts. Iraq's February 15 announcement, however was met with scorn and incitement; Bush declared it a "cruel hoax" and publicly called on the Iraqi people to overthrow Saddam Hussein in order to avoid a U.S. assault, reportedly angering a broad spectrum of U.S. allies. With each Soviet-Iraqi announcement, the administration produced further impediments, including a time-table designed to force the Iraqis to leave most of their equipment behind in Kuwait. The shuttle between Baghdad and Moscow continued until February 21 when Gorbachev announced the revised plan: Iraq would withdraw from Kuwait City in four days, the entire country in twenty-one. At this point, recalled a top Bush strategist to *Time*, "we were determined we would end this war when we wanted to, not a damn day sooner." On Friday, February 22, with the majority of his coalition lined up behind him, President Bush delivered his ultimatum: Iraq had twenty-four hours to accept the U.S. terms of one week for total evacuation of Kuwait or the U.S. would launch its assault. With little hope of preventing the ground war, Gorbachev continued his efforts right up to its announcement, personally pleading with Bush to put the decision off by a day or two in order to strike a compromise between the two proposals. The deadline passed at noon on February 23 and within hours General Schwarzkopf plunged ahead, "on schedule."

The U.S. coalition ground assault overwhelmed the Iraqi forces who had endured two months of daily terror, including B-52 carpet bombing and the horrifying fuel air explosive bombs condemned by the Geneva conventions. Iraqi troops were quickly defeated or surrendered in large numbers to the advancing U.S. coalition troops. Though it meant little change in the coverage, the Pentagon imposed a 48-hour news blackout. After a day, an American Brigadier General reported, "We're deep in Indian country" — which was later revealed to mean that the U.S.-led coalition forces had established dominion over southern Iraq. An entire battalion was directed to secure Rumaila oil field to preposition for post-war negotiations. American rockets and artillery were directed by satellite readings input through computer, attack helicopters unleashed furious attacks on Iraqi forces that dared to move from dug-in positions, and Iraqi escape routes and communications networks for the most part were destroyed. U.S. and French airborne troops destroyed the bridges to Basra and Iraqi troops were trapped. On February 25, Baghdad radio announced Iraq's unconditional surrender and called on its troops to withdraw, but the news did less to deter the U.S. coalition onslaught than the rainy weather system that had moved over southern Iraq. Bush cited the need for Iraqi compliance with all twelve UN resolutions, including the provisions for reparations and a war crimes trial for Saddam Hussein, as a pretext for pursuing the ground war and bombing campaign to their grisly conclusion.

The skies cleared on February 26 to reveal the snarling traffic jam of Iraqi vehicles and troops desperately scrambling to get out of Kuwait, and the most horrific slaughter of the war thus far commenced. U.S. and coalition attack helicopters, missile launchers, fighter-bombers and B-52s rained explosives and bursting shrapnel on the stricken Iraqi withdrawal, resulting in total carnage. A report from the USS Ranger carrier contended that air strikes were being launched so feverishly that planes were loaded with whatever bombs happened to be closest to the flight deck; one U.S. pilot complained in a *Washington Post* interview that the mad rush prevented many planes from loading up with the preferred cluster bombs. Many U.S. commanders and soldiers were reportedly gleeful about the "turkey shoot." Estimates of the Iraqi slaughter ranged in the tens of thousands, though the Bush administration refused to make public its tally of the number of Iraqi soldiers later buried in mass graves along the Iraq-Kuwait border area.

News of the mounting Iraqi death toll reached the UN and members of the UN Security Council tried in vain to broach a discussion of a ceasefire. The administration would stop when it wanted, and no sooner. President Bush announced the suspension of hostilities as of midnight February 27. With U.S. troops securing their hold on the southern third of Iraq, the administration pushed through a March 2 UN resolution setting ceasefire terms that underwrote a continued U.S. military presence, delayed a UN observer force until all U.S. conditions were met and maintained the food embargo and threat of renewed war against Iraq. The terms, which would take weeks to implement, seemed designed to give the U.S. time to shape Iraq's post-war future.

On March 3, with General Schwarzkopf dictating terms to Iraqi generals in southern Iraq, it was reported that the U.S. and Saudi Arabia had worked out an agreement for a permanent U.S. presence in the Gulf. U.S. contractors were promised 70% of the post-war reconstruction bonanza. But reports from Saudi Arabia suggested a less than rosy future: the Saudis claimed war-related costs of $64 billion and questioned whether they would be able to cover the $13.5 billion originally promised to the U.S. in addition to arms sales already in the pipeline. Kuwait was placed under marshal law by decree on February 26. Kuwait's Interior Minister on February 14 had announced that the Sabah family had already formed a "comprehensive security plan" for the first three months after liberation, which stressed the need for the "cleansing of Kuwait"; this process began with wholesale detentions and interrogations of Palestinians who had remained in Kuwait.

On all counts Iraq had been devastated. With water lines destroyed and no fuel to boil polluted drinking water from the Tigris River, sanitation systems destroyed and raw sewage flooding in many areas, meat costing $17/pound, rationing, electricity out in most places in the country, health conditions and survival were reaching breaking point. The UN mission to Iraq to assess post-war damage issued its report on March 20: "Nothing that we had seen or read had quite prepared us for the particular form of devastation which has befallen the country . . . Iraq has, for some time to come, been relegated to a pre-industrial age, but with all the disabilities of post-industrial dependency on an intensive use of energy and technology."

Whether instigated by CIA clandestine radio broadcasts urging rebellion or simply the inevitable result of the massive destruction wrought by U.S. bombing, Kurds in the north and Shi'a in the south began to rise up against the Ba'ath regime in Iraq. On March 6 reports suggested that Shi'a groups had taken over Basra and the rebellion had spread throughout the south. With U.S. forces within a mile in some cases, under orders not to act, Saddam Hussein's forces leveled upstart towns and massacred resistance forces. In the north, a short-lived Kurdish revolt was overwhelmed by Republican Guards who stormed Kirkuk taking few prisoners. The Bush administration turned a deaf ear to members of the Iraqi opposition's Joint Action Committee who spent two weeks in March trying to get a hearing with even lowly State Department officials. Apparently, U.S. strategic plans did not include anti-Ba'athist resistance; the administration was working with the Saudis in Riyadh putting together the pro-U.S. and Saudi Free Iraqi Council as an alternative to the indigenously organized Iraqi opposition.

Although the official war had ended, conflict continued to take its deadly toll on those who survived the UN-sanctioned round of fighting. Peace was not a term that could be used to describe the post-Gulf War Middle East. The map of the region was permanently altered in ways that would not easily be redressed. The seemingly inexorable march to war, that began with the Iraqi invasion of Kuwait, and took on an entirely new complexion after the Bush administration decided that the regional status quo could not remain as it was, was never the only option. Yet when the decisions had been made and the logic of actions played out, the conflict returned to the place it had started — on the road between Bastra and Kuwait City, amidst the sounds of gunfire and explosions, rumbling machines and human tragedy.

# ■PART TWO■

## Behind The Storm:

## U.S. Foreign Policy in the Middle East

# 5

## After the Cold War: U.S. Middle East Policy*

### *Noam Chomsky*

U.S. policy towards the Middle East has been framed within a certain strategic conception of world order that is widely shared, though there are tactical disagreements. There are also important changes in the world, to which this strategic conception must be adapted.

There has been much recent talk about a "new world order." Implicit in it is the assumption that there was an "old world order" that is changing. That system of world order was established after World War II. At the time, the U.S. was in a position of power without historical precedent. It had about 50% of the world's wealth, and a position of remarkable security. Political and economic elites were well aware of these facts, and, not surprisingly, set about to organize a world system favorable to their interests — although they also recognized, quite explicitly, that more noble rhetoric would be useful for propaganda purposes.

Basic elements of a new world order were coming into focus 20 years ago, with the emergence of a "tripolar world" as economic power diffused within the domains of post-World War II U.S. power. The U.S. remains the dominant military power, but its economic superiority, though still manifest, has declined, and may well decline further as the costs of the Reagan-Bush party for the rich fall due. The collapse of Soviet tyranny adds several new dimensions. First, new pretexts are needed for Third World intervention, a serious challenge for the educated classes. Second, there are now prospects for the "Latin Americanization" of much of the former Soviet empire, that is, for its reversion to a quasi-colonial status, providing resources, cheap labor, markets, investment opportunities, and other standard Third World amenities. But the U.S. and Britain are not in the lead in this endeavor. A third important consequence is that the U.S. is more free than

* This article is excerpted from a talk with the same title given in London, Jan. 20, 1991, and published in the *Jewish Quarterly* (London), and from *Z magazine*, February 1991, with a few modifications.

before to use force, the Soviet deterrent having disappeared. These changes in the international system have implications for the Middle East, as for every other region of the world.

During World War II, representatives of U.S. corporations and government carried out far-ranging studies on what they called a "Grand Area," a world system in which the interests they represented would be expected to flourish. The plans extended to all major areas and issues, and were to a large extent implemented in the early post-war years. In fact, there is a very close similarity between these studies and top-level government planning documents of later years.

Within the Grand Area, the industrial powers were to reconstruct, under the leadership of the "great workshops," Japan and Germany, now under U.S. control. It was necessary to restore traditional conservative rule, including Nazi and fascist collaborators, to destroy and disperse the anti-fascist resistance, and to weaken the labor movement. This was a worldwide project, conducted in various ways depending on local circumstances and needs. It constitutes chapter one of post-war history, and generally proceeded on course.

With respect to the Soviet Union, policy divided along two basic lines, both aiming to incorporate the USSR within the Grand Area — which, for most of the region, meant returning it to its pre-1917 status as part of the Third World, in effect. The hard-line "roll back" approach was given its basic formulation in NSC 68 of 1950, written by Paul Nitze, who succeeded George Kennan as head of the State Department Policy Planning Staff. The softer Kennan policy of "containment" proposed reliance on the overwhelming economic advantages of the U.S. and its allies to achieve more or less the same ends. Note that these goals have basically been achieved, with the collapse of the Soviet system in the 1980s.

Few anticipated a Russian military attack. The general assumption was that "it is not Russian military power which is threatening us, it is Russian political power" (Kennan, October 1947).

The Third World also had its role in the Grand Area: to be "exploited" for the needs of the industrial societies and to "fulfill its major function as a source of raw materials and a market." I am quoting from documents of George Kennan and his Policy Planning Staff. Kennan was one of the most influential of the post-war planners, representing generally the "softer" extreme of the spectrum. He emphasized that a major concern was "the protection of our resources" — *our* resources, which happen, by geological accident, to lie in other lands. Since the main threat to our interests is indigenous, we must, he explained in secret, accept the need for "police repression by the local government." "Harsh government measures of repression" should cause us no qualms as long as "the results are on balance favorable to our purposes." In general, "it is better to have a strong regime in power than a liberal government if it is indulgent and relaxed and penetrated by Communists." The term "Communist" refers in practice to labor leaders, peasant organizers, priests organizing self-help groups, and others with the wrong priorities.

The right priorities are outlined in the highest level secret documents. They stress that the major threat to U.S. interests is "nationalistic regimes" that are responsive to popular pressures for "immediate improvement in the low living standards of the masses" and diversification of their economies for domestic needs. Such initiatives interfere with the protection of our resources and our efforts to encourage "a climate conducive to private investment," which will allow foreign capital "to repatriate a reasonable return." The threat of Communism, as explained by a prestigious conservative study group, is the economic transformation of the Communist powers "in ways that reduce their willingness and ability to complement the industrial economies of the West," and thus to fulfill the Third World function. This is the real basis for the intense hostility to the Soviet Union and its imperial system from 1917, and the reason why independent nationalism in the Third World, whatever its political cast, has been seen as a "virus" that must be eradicated.

Plans for the Middle East developed within this context. The major concern was (and remains) the incomparable energy reserves of the region. These were to be incorporated within the U.S.-dominated system. As in Latin America, it was necessary to displace traditional French and British interests and to establish U.S. control over what the State Department described as "a stupendous source of strategic power, and one of the greatest material prizes in world history," "probably the richest economic prize in the world in the field of foreign investment." President Eisenhower described the Middle East as the most "strategically important area in the world."

France was quickly excluded by legal legerdemain, leaving a U.S.-British condominium. There was conflict for a time, but it was soon resolved within the framework of U.S. power. U.S. corporations gained the leading role in Middle East oil production, while dominating the Western hemisphere, which remained the major producer until 1968. The U.S. did not then need Middle East oil for itself. Rather, the goal was to dominate the world system, ensuring that others would not strike an independent course. There was, at the time, general contempt for the Japanese, and few anticipated that they would ever be a serious economic competitor. But some were more farsighted. In 1948, Kennan observed that U.S. control over Japanese oil imports would help to provide "veto power" over Japan's military and industrial policies. His advice was followed. Japan was helped to industrialize, but the U.S. maintained control over its energy supplies and oil-refining facilities. As late as 1973, the U.S. controlled about 90% of Japanese oil. After the oil crisis of the early 1970s, Japan sought more diverse energy sources and undertook conservation measures. These moves reduced the power of the veto considerably, but influence over oil pricing and production, within the range set by market forces, remains a factor in world affairs.

As elsewhere, the major policy imperative is to block indigenous nationalist forces. A large-scale counterinsurgency operation in Greece from 1947 was partially motivated by the concern that the "rot" of independent nationalism there might "infect" the Middle East. A CIA study held that if the rebels were victorious, the U.S. would face "the possible loss of the petroleum resources of the Middle East." A Soviet threat was concocted in the usual manner, but the real threat was indigenous nationalism, with its feared demonstration effects elsewhere.

Similar factors led to the CIA coup restoring the Shah in Iran in 1953. Nasser became an enemy for similar reasons. Later, Khomeini was perceived as posing another such threat, leading the U.S. to support Iraq in the Iran-Iraq war. The Iraqi dictator Saddam Hussein then took over the mantle, shifting status overnight from moderate friend to a new Hitler when he invaded Kuwait, displacing U.S.-British clients. The primary fear throughout has been that nationalist forces not under U.S. influence and control might come to have substantial influence over the oil-producing regions of the Arabian peninsula. Saudi Arabian elites, in contrast, are considered appropriate partners, managing their resources in conformity to basic U.S. interests, and assisting U.S. terror and subversion throughout the Third World.

The basic points are fairly clear in the secret planning record, and often in the public government record as well. Thus, in early 1990, the White House presented Congress with its annual National Security Strategy Report, calling — as always — for a bigger military budget to protect us from the threat of destruction by enemies of unimaginable power and bestiality. For the last few years, it has been hard to portray the Russians as the Great Satan, so other enemies have had to be conjured up. By now, it is conceded that the enemy is Third World nationalism. This Report therefore explains that we have to build up a powerful high tech military because of the "technological sophistication" of Third World powers, intent on pursuing their own course. We must ensure the means to move forces "to reinforce our units forward deployed or to project power into areas where we have no permanent presence," particularly in the Middle East, where the "threats to our interests" that have required direct military engagement "could not be laid at the Kremlin's door" — a fact finally admitted. "In the future, we expect that non-Soviet threats to these interests will command even greater attention." In reality, the "threat to our interests" had always been indigenous nationalism, a fact sometimes acknowledged, as when the architect of President Carter's Rapid Deployment Force, aimed primarily at the Middle East, testified before Congress in 1980 that its most likely use was not to resist a (highly implausible) Soviet attack, but to deal with indigenous and regional unrest (called "radical nationalism" or "ultranationalism"). Notice that the Bush administration plans were presented at a time when Saddam Hussein was still George Bush's amiable friend and favored trading partner.

The Anglo-American condominium in the Gulf region received its first major challenge in 1958, when the nationalist military coup in Iraq overthrew a dependent regime. In his history of the oil industry, Christopher Rand describes the 1958 coup as "America's biggest setback in the region since the war," "a shocking experience for the United States" that "undoubtedly provok[ed] an agonizing reappraisal of our nation's entire approach to the Persian Gulf." Recently released British and American documents help flesh out earlier surmises.

In 1958, Kuwait was the particular concern. The "new Hitler" of the day was Gamal Abdel Nasser, and it was feared that his pan-Arab nationalism might spread to Iraq, Kuwait, and beyond. One reaction was a U.S. Marine landing in Lebanon to prop up the regime; another, apparent authorization of nuclear weapons by President Eisenhower "to prevent any unfriendly forces from moving into Kuwait." To deflect the nationalist threat, Britain decided to grant Kuwait nominal independence, following the prescriptions designed after World War I when the imperial managers realized that British rule would be more cost-effective behind an "Arab facade," so that "absorption" of the colonies should be "veiled by constitutional fictions as a protectorate, a sphere of influence, a buffer state, and so on" (Lord Curzon). Britain reserved the right of forceful intervention to protect its interests, with the agreement of the U.S. which reserved the same right for itself elsewhere in the region. The U.S. and Britain also agreed on the need to keep the oilfields in their hands. Foreign Secretary Selwyn Lloyd had already summarized the major concerns, including free access to Gulf oil production "on favourable terms and for sterling," and "suitable arrangements for the investment of the surplus revenues of Kuwait" in Britain.

Declassified U.S. documents reiterate that Britain's "financial stability would be seriously threatened if the petroleum from Kuwait and the Persian Gulf area were not available to the U.K. on reasonable terms, if the U.K. were deprived of the large investments made by that area in the U.K. and if sterling were deprived of the support provided by Persian Gulf oil." These factors and others provide reasons for the U.S. "to support, or if necessary assist, the British in using force to retain control of Kuwait and the Persian Gulf." In November 1958, the National Security Council recommended that the U.S. "be prepared to use force, but only as a last resort, either alone or in support of the United Kingdom," if these interests were threatened. The documentary record is not available beyond that point, but there is little reason to suspect that guiding doctrines, which had been stable over a long period, have undergone more than tactical change.

At the time, a main concern was that Gulf oil and riches be available to support the ailing British economy. That concern was extended by the early 1970s to the U.S. economy, which was visibly declining relative to Japan and German-led Europe. As the U.S. and Britain lose their former economic dominance, privileged access to the rich profits of Gulf oil production is a matter of serious concern. The point was captured in a current Wall Street witticism. Question: Why do the U.S. and Kuwait need each other? Answer: Kuwait is a banking system without a country, and the U.S. is a country without a banking system. Like many jokes, it is not a joke.

Capital flow from Saudi Arabia, Kuwait, and the other Gulf principalities to the U.S. and Britain has provided a good deal of support for their economies, corporations, and financial institutions. These are among the reasons why the U.S. and Britain have often not been averse to increases in oil price — and why the U.S. would follow essentially the same policies if it were 100% on solar energy, just as it followed the same policies pre-1970, when it had little need for Middle East oil. The sharp price escalation in 1973 was in many ways beneficial to the U.S.-U.K. economies, as was widely noted in the business press and scholarly journals; the U.S. trade balance with the oil producers actually improved, and became favorable to the U.S., as the oil price rose, enriching U.S. energy, manufacturing, and construction corporations and allowing the U.S. and Britain to profit from their own high-priced oil in Alaska and the North Sea. The issues are too intricate to explore here, but these factors surely remain operative.

When we consider these factors, it should come as no great surprise that the two states that established the imperial settlement and have been its main beneficiaries followed their own course in the Gulf crisis, moving at once to undercut sanctions and block any diplomatic track, thus narrowing the options to the threat and use of force. In this course they were largely isolated, apart from the family dictatorships that rule the Gulf oil producers as an "Arab facade." Though it was clear from August that sanctions and diplomacy had unusually high prospects of reversing Iraq's aggression peaceably, the Administration policy of narrowing the options to capitulation or war has a certain chilling logic: it is the right policy choice if the goals are to firm up the mercenary-enforcer role and establish the rule of force, the dimension of power in which the U.S. reigns supreme. Adopting that role, the U.S. must continue to enforce obedience (called "order" or "stability" in the doctrinal system), with the support of other industrial powers. Riches funneled by the oil-producing monarchies will help prop up the troubled economies of the guardians of order. To be sure, force is only a last resort. It is more cost-effective to use the IMF than the Marines or the CIA if possible; but it is not always possible.

One major U.S. concern in the Middle East has been, and remains, the "stupendous source of strategic power." A second has been the relationship with Israel. There is considerable debate over whether that special relationship derives from the role of Israel in U.S. strategic planning, or from the influence of a "Jewish lobby." My own view, for what it is worth, is that the former factor is by far the more significant, and that the so-called "Jewish lobby" is actually one component of a much broader group, including liberal intellectuals who were deeply impressed by Israel's military victory in 1967, for reasons that had a good deal to do with the domestic scene. In this judgment, I disagree with many commentators, including the leadership of the lobby, which publicly claims vast influence. But we needn't try to settle this issue. However one weights the factors, both are there. I'll keep here to the first, which in my view is the more important. I would expect, frankly, that the U.S. would ditch Israel in a moment if U.S. planners found this in their interest. In that case, the Jewish lobby would be as ineffective as it was in 1956, when Eisenhower and Dulles, on the eve of a presidential election, ordered Israel out of the Sinai.

One can trace the thinking behind the "special relationship" back to

Israel's early days. In 1948, Israel's military successes led the Joint Chiefs of Staff to describe it as the major regional military power after Turkey, offering the U.S. means to "gain strategic advantage in the Middle East that would offset the effects of the decline of British power in that area" (Avi Shlaim). Historian Abram Sachar, whose interpretation is particularly interesting because he is custodian of the archives of Truman's influential associate David Niles, alleges that Truman's ultimate decision to support Israeli expansion was based upon the Israeli military victory, which showed that Israel "could become a strategic asset — a kind of stationary aircraft carrier to protect American interests in the Mediterranean and the Middle East."

As for the Palestinians, U.S. planners had no reason to doubt the assessment of Israeli government specialists in 1948 that the refugees would either assimilate elsewhere or "would be crushed": "some of them would die and most of them would turn into human dust and the waste of society, and join the most impoverished classes in the Arab countries" (Moshe Sharett's Middle East section). Accordingly, there was no need to trouble oneself about them. U.S. assessments of Israel and the Palestinians have hardly changed since that time.

Shortly after the Iraqi coup in July 1958, the National Security Council concluded that a "logical corollary" of opposition to radical Arab nationalism "would be to support Israel as the only strong pro-Western power left in the Middle East." That understanding was extended in the 1960s. U.S. intelligence regarded Israeli power as a barrier to Nasserite pressures on Saudi Arabia and other oil producing clients. That role was firmed up with Israel's smashing victory in 1967, destroying the nationalist threat; and again in 1970, when Israeli threats played some role — a major role, according to Kissinger's rather dubious account — in protecting Jordan from a possible Syrian effort to support Palestinians who were being slaughtered by King Hussein's army. U.S. aid to Israel sharply increased at that point.

These moves were in the context of the new Nixon doctrine, according to which other powers must deal with regional problems within the "overall framework of order" maintained by the United States, as Kissinger put it, admonishing Europe to put aside any ideas about striking out on its own. A few years later, Kissinger pointed out in private talks with American Jewish leaders, later released, that one of his prime concerns was "to ensure that the Europeans and Japanese did not get involved in the diplomacy" of the Middle East — a commitment that persists, and helps explain U.S. opposition to any international conference. In the Middle East Iran and Israel were to be the "cops on the beat" (in the phrase of Defense Secretary Melvin Laird), safeguarding order. Police headquarters, of course, remained in Washington.

More serious analysts have been clear about these matters. In May 1973, the Senate's ranking oil expert, Senator Henry Jackson, emphasized "the strength and Western orientation of Israel on the Mediterranean and Iran on the Persian Gulf," two "reliable friends of the United States," with powerful military forces, who work together with Saudi Arabia "to inhibit and contain those irresponsible and radical elements in certain Arab States . . . who, were they free to do so, would pose a grave threat indeed to our principal sources of petroleum in the Persian Gulf"; in reality, also to U.S. control over riches that flow from these sources.

The relationship deepened as Israel became, in effect, a mercenary state, beginning in the 1960s, when the CIA provided Israel with large subsidies to penetrate Black Africa in the U.S. interest, later in Asia and particularly Latin America. As one high official put it during the Iran-contra affair, Israel is "just another federal agency, one that's convenient to use when you want something done quietly." Other relationships also developed, including intelligence sharing, weapons development, and testing of new advanced weapons in live battlefield conditions.

The relations between Israel and Iran were intimate, as later revealed (in Israel) after the Shah fell. The relations of Israel and Iran to Saudi Arabia are more subtle and sensitive, and direct evidence is slight. Saudi Arabia was virtually at war with both Israel and Iran, which had conquered Arab islands in the Gulf. But as Senator Jackson indicated, there appears to have been at least a tacit alliance; more, we may learn some day, if the documentary record is ever revealed. That tripartite relationship continued after the fall of the Shah, when the U.S. began, virtually at once, to send arms to Iran via Israel, later (and perhaps then) financed by Saudi Arabia. High Israeli officials involved in these transactions revealed that the purpose was to inspire an anti-Khomeini coup and restore the traditional alliance. This was, incidentally, long before there were any hostages. It is one of the many features of the Iran-contra affair suppressed in the Congressional-media damage control operation. The same model of overthrowing an unwanted civilian government had been pursued successfully in Indonesia, Chile, and other cases, and is, in fact, fairly standard statecraft: if you want to overthrow some government, support its military, hoping to find elements who will do the job for you from inside.

Notice that in accord with this strategic conception, a peaceful political settlement of the Israel-Arab conflict is not of any great importance, and might even be detrimental to U.S. interests. And not surprisingly, we find that the U.S. has blocked a political settlement of the Arab-Israeli conflict for 20 years.

The depth of this rejectionist stance was dramatically revealed on January 14, 1991, when France made a last minute proposal at the UN calling for immediate Iraqi withdrawal from Kuwait in return for a Security Council commitment to deal with the Israel-Palestine problem "at some appropriate moment," which remains unspecified. The U.S. with Britain tagging along, announced at once that it would veto any such resolution. The French proposal reiterated the basic content of a Security Council statement in which members expressed their view that "an international conference, at an appropriate time, properly structured," might help to "achieve a negotiated settlement and lasting peace in the Arab-Israeli conflict." The statement was a codicil to Security Council Resolution 681 of December 20, calling on Israel to observe the Geneva Conventions. It was excluded from the resolution itself to avoid a U.S. veto. Note that there was no "linkage" to the Iraqi invasion, which was unmentioned. The U.S. was determined to go to war rather than allow even a hint that there might someday be an international effort to deal with the Israel-Palestine problem. The pretexts advanced need not detain us.

It is worth noting that the U.S. has also been firmly opposed to a diplomatic settlement of the second major issue that has been raised during the Gulf crisis: Iraq's very dangerous military capacities. Here the U.S. rejection of "linkage" is particularly remarkable, since it is beyond dispute that disarmament questions must be addressed in a regional context. Iraq has raised the issue several times since August, but all proposals have been rejected or ignored, on the pretext that the U.S. cannot accept "linkage" — in this unique case. Again, we know perfectly well that "linkage" and "rewarding the aggressor" have nothing to do with it. In fact, Saddam Hussein had made a similar proposal in April 1990, when he was still George Bush's friend and ally. He then offered to destroy his chemical and biological weapons if Israel agreed to destroy *its* nonconventional weapons. The State Department rejected the link "to other issues or weapons systems." Note that these remain unspecified. Acknowledgement of the existence of Israeli nuclear weapons would raise the question why all U.S. aid to Israel is not illegal under Congressional legislation of the 1970s that bars aid to any country engaged in nuclear weapons development.

These matters are of enormous significance for understanding the current crisis, and for speculating about the future. The U.S. and U.K. were quite supportive of Saddam Hussein prior to August 1990. A decade earlier, they had helped prevent any UN reaction to Iraq's attack on Iran. At the time, Iraq was a Soviet client, but Reagan, Thatcher and Bush recognized Saddam Hussein as "their kind of guy" and moved to change that status; within a few years, Iraq was largely Western-oriented. Iraq was removed from the list of states that sponsor terror, permitting it to receive substantial credits from the U.S. and become a major trading partner, exporting its oil to the U.S. and receiving U.S. agricultural and other exports. Western corporations took an active role in building up Iraq's military strength, including its weapons of mass destruction. The Reagan and Bush administrations intervened forcefully to prevent any meaningful Congressional censure of their friend's atrocious human rights record, crucially barring any sanctions that might have interfered with profits for U.S. corporations or with Iraq's growing strength. In July 1990, the State Department indicated to Saddam Hussein that it had no serious objection to his rectifying border disputes with Kuwait, or intimidating other oil producers to raise the price of oil to perhaps $25 a barrel. There was no doubt in anyone's mind that he was a murderous gangster, but, it was assumed, he was "our gangster." Saddam's record was already so sordid that conquest of Kuwait added little to it, but that action was a crime that matters: the crime of independence. Torture, tyranny, aggression, slaughter of civilians are all acceptable by U.S.-U.K. standards, but no stepping on our toes, whether the guilty party is a committed Third World democrat or a brutal thug.

According to sources in the Iraqi democratic opposition, which had long courageously opposed Bush's old friend, they were rebuffed by the White House in February 1990 when they sought support for a call for parliamentary democracy in Iraq. It is a very revealing fact that the Iraqi democratic opposition was also scrupulously excluded from the media after the crisis erupted in August — naturally enough, since their positions were hardly distinguishable from those of the mainstream of the U.S. and European peace movements. Unlike Bush and Reagan, the peace movement and Iraqi democratic opposition had always opposed Saddam Hussein, but also opposed the quick resort to violence to undercut the danger that sanctions and diplomacy would lead to a peaceful resolution of the conflict. Such an outcome would have avoided the slaughter of tens of thousands of people, an environmental catastrophe, chaos in Iraq and the likely emergence of another tyranny — but, crucially, it would not have established the lesson that the world is to be run by force, the U.S. comparative advantage.

There had been diplomatic possibilities for resolving the crisis since August, including Iraqi offers described by high U.S. officials as "serious" and "negotiable." All were rejected out of hand by Washington. The last made public before the bombing started was disclosed by U.S. officials on January 2: an Iraqi offer "to withdraw from Kuwait if the United States pledges not to attack as soldiers are pulled out, if foreign troops leave the region, and if there is agreement on the Palestinian problem and on the banning of all weapons of mass destruction in the region" (Knut Royce, *Newsday*, Jan. 3, 1991). U.S. officials described the offer as "interesting" because it dropped any border claims, and "signals Iraqi interest in a negotiated settlement." A State Department Mideast expert described the proposal as a "serious prenegotiation position." The U.S. "immediately dismissed the proposal," Royce continues.

The next day the *New York Times* reported that Yasser Arafat, after consultations with Saddam Hussein, indicated that neither of them "insisted that the Palestinian problem be solved before Iraqi troops get out of Kuwait." According to Arafat, "Mr. Hussein's statement August 12, linking an Iraqi withdrawal to an Israeli withdrawal from the West Bank and Gaza Strip, was no longer operative as a negotiating demand." All that is necessary is "a strong link to be guaranteed by the five permanent members of the Security Council that we have to solve all the problems in the Gulf, in the Middle East and especially the Palestinian cause."

Two weeks before the deadline for Iraqi withdrawal, then, the possible contours of a diplomatic settlement appeared to be these: Iraq would withdraw completely from Kuwait with a U.S. pledge not to attack withdrawing forces; foreign troops leave the region; the Security Council indicates a serious commitment to settle two major regional problems: the Arab-Israeli conflict, and the problem of weapons of mass destruction. Disputed border issues would be left for later consideration. We cannot evaluate the prospects for settlement along these lines, because the offers were flatly rejected, and scarcely entered the media or public awareness.

The United States and Britain maintained their commitment to force alone.

The claim that the U.S. was unwilling to "reward the aggressor" by allowing future consideration of these two regional issues is undeserving of a moment's attention. The U.S. commonly rewards aggressors and insists upon "linkage," even in cases much worse than Saddam Hussein's latest crimes. It follows that the reasons presented are not the real ones, and, furthermore, that no reason at all was presented for going to war; none whatsoever. That seems obvious enough, if one is willing to think the matter through.

The real reasons, again, are not obscure. The U.S. opposes a diplomatic settlement of all the "linked" issues. Therefore, it opposes "linkage," that is, diplomacy. If that means a devastating war, so be it. Further withdrawal offers in February were contemptuously dismissed, on grounds too absurd even to discuss, outside the commissar culture.

From the outset, the President was clear and unambiguous that *"there will be no negotiations."* "Diplomacy" will be limited to delivery of an ultimatum: capitulate or die. It took willful blindness to misunderstand these facts. The reasons had nothing to do with "rewarding aggressors" or "linkage," nor with "annexation" (the U.S. dismissed at once offers that would have terminated the annexation), or with the severity of Saddam Hussein's crimes, which were monstrous before, but of no account. His latest crimes, furthermore, do not compare with others that the U.S. and U.K. cheerfully supported, and continue to support today, including the near-genocidal Indonesian invasion and annexation of East Timor, successful thanks to the decisive support of the U.S. and U.K., which continues today. U.S.-U.K. posturing on this matter has descended to a level of cynicism that is extraordinary even by the standards of statecraft, and it is an astonishing commentary on our intellectual culture that it does not merely inspire ridicule, and is even parroted.

These considerations direct us towards the future. I see little reason to expect the U.S. to modify its goals with regard to oil production and profits, or to abandon its rejectionism on the Israel-Arab conflict.

Since 1917, the pretext offered for U.S. intervention has been defense against the Russians. Before the Bolshevik revolution, intervention was justified in defense against the Huns, the British, "base Canadian fiends," or the "merciless Indian savages" of the Declaration of Independence. For the last several years, the Russians have not been available as a pretext. The U.S. invasion of Panama kept to the normal pattern, but was historic in that it was the first post-Cold War act of aggression, and appeals to the Russian threat were beyond the reach of even the most fevered imagination. So the U.S. was defending itself from narcoterrorism. Little has changed apart from rhetoric.

As noted earlier, there are real changes in the world system, with a number of important consequences: (1) at the rhetorical level, new pretexts are needed for intervention; (2) the "end of the Cold War" opens the way to the "Latin Americanization" of large parts of the former Soviet empire; (3) the elimination of the Soviet deterrent leaves the U.S. more free than before to use military force.

In the new world order, the Third World domains must still be controlled, sometimes by force. This task has been the responsibility of the United States, but with its relative economic decline, the burden becomes harder to shoulder. One reaction is that the U.S. must persist in its historic task, while others pay the bills. Deputy Secretary of State Lawrence Eagleburger explained that the emerging new world order will be based on "a kind of new invention in the practice of diplomacy": others will finance U.S. intervention to keep order. In the London *Financial Times*, a respected commentator on international economic affairs described the Gulf crisis as a "watershed event in U.S. international relations," which will be seen in history as having "turned the U.S. military into an internationally financed public good." In the 1990s, he continues, "there is no realistic alternative [to] the US military assuming a more explicitly mercenary role than it has played in the past" (David Hale, *FT*, Nov. 21, 1990).

The financial editor of a leading U.S. conservative daily puts the point less delicately: we must exploit our "virtual monopoly in the security market ... as a lever to gain funds and economic concessions" from Germany and Japan (William Neikirk, *Chicago Tribune*, Sept. 9, 1990). The U.S. has "cornered the West's security market" and will therefore be "the world's rent-a-cops"; the phrase "rent-a-thug" might be more accurate, if less appealing. Some will call us "Hessians," he continues, but "that's a terribly demeaning phrase for a proud, well-trained, well-financed and well-respected military"; and whatever anyone may say, "we should be able to pound our fists on a few desks" in Japan and Europe, and "extract a fair price for our considerable services," demanding that our rivals "buy our bonds at cheap rates, or keep the dollar propped up, or better yet, pay cash directly into our Treasury." "We could change this role" of enforcer, he concludes, "but with it would go much of our control over the world economic system."

How, then, can we expect U.S. policy towards the Middle East to adapt to these changed circumstance? There is no reason to expect changes in the principles that guide policy. There are no significant public pressures for policy change. In polls, about two thirds of the public regularly express support for the international consensus on a two-state settlement, but few have the slightest awareness of U.S. isolation in blocking the peace process, and even such elementary facts as the official U.S. position and the record of diplomacy are rigidly excluded from the media and public discussion. There is, then, little reason to anticipate a shift in U.S. rejectionism.

This is, of course, not a certainty. The tactical divide of 20 years ago still exists in elite circles, and might lead to internal pressures for the U.S. to join the world community on this matter. If this radical policy shift takes place, hard problems quickly arise.

More likely, in my view, is continued support for the position articulated in February 1989 by Yitzhak Rabin, then Defense Secretary, when he told a group of Peace Now leaders of his general satisfaction with the U.S.-PLO dialogue, low-level discussions without meaning that would divert attention while Israel used forceful means to crush the intifada. The Palestinians "will be broken," Rabin promised his interlocuters, and he may be right. There is a limit to what flesh and blood can endure. If so, then the U.S. and Israel can continue to assume, as they did 40 years ago, that the Palestinians will "turn into human dust and the waste of society," while Russian Jews, now effectively barred from the U.S. by legislation designed to deny them a free choice, flock to an expanded Israel with U.S. financial support, leaving the diplomatic issues moot. With U.S. support, Israel had long blocked any opportunities for economic development in the occupied territories. Palestinians had been permitted to serve as virtual slave labor for the Israeli economy, but those options are being sharply reduced. The curfew during the Gulf War administered a further blow to the remaining shreds of a Palestinian economy. In the natural course of events, there will be only marginal opportunities for survival, and "invisible transfer" of those who are able to leave may remove the remaining obstacles to a full Israeli takeover.

There is every reason to expect the U.S. to persist in its traditional rejectionist stand, most recently elaborated in the 1989 Baker-Shamir-Peres plan, which bans an "additional Palestinian state" (Jordan already being one); bars any "change in the status of Judea, Samaria and Gaza other than in accordance with the basic guidelines of the [Israeli] government," which preclude any meaningful Palestinian self-determination; rejects negotiations with the PLO, thus denying Palestinians the right to choose their own political representation; and calls for "free elections" under Israeli military rule with much of the Palestinian leadership in prison camps. Palestinians, with representatives chosen for them in effect by Israel and the U.S. will be permitted to collect garbage in Nablus and set tax rates in Ramallah, and those who can, will leave. The media and educated communities will then have the task of finding new pretexts for old policies, and extolling the high ideals and noble purposes of the U.S. government, which, unfortunately, could not be fully realized because of the intransigence of the Palestinians and the fears of the Israelis — which we so easily understand, for they are human beings like us, not Third World degenerates.

The political leaderships in Washington and London have created economic and social catastrophes at home, and have no idea how to deal with them, except to exploit their military power. Following the advice of the business press, they may try to turn their countries into mercenary states, serving as the global mafia, selling "protection" to the rich, defending them against "third world threats" and demanding proper payment for the service. Riches funneled from the Gulf oil producers are to prop up the two failing economies. The rest of the Third World will be controlled by economic pressures if possible, by force if necessary.

There are some of the contours of the planned new world order that come into view as the beguiling rhetoric is lifted away.

# 6

## The Panama Paradigm

### Barbara Ehrenreich

We don't want another Vietnam, everyone says, squinting into the desert sun. We want something swift and decisive, short and sweet — a Panama perhaps. For these are the two poles of our collective military memory: on the one hand, the quicksand of Vietnam; on the other, the "brilliant success" of Panama, or so it was heralded at the time — a military action so flawless, so perfectly executed that, as one of the generals responsible for carrying out the invasion boasted shortly afterward, "There were no lessons learned."

On December 20, 1989, you will recall, the U.S. Army invaded the nation of Panama and soon thereafer arrested its de facto head of state. The UN General Assembly swiftly denounced the invasion as a "flagrant violation of international law," but never mind — for most Americans, the lofty ends justified the brutal and lawless means. We had to stop the drug traffic. We had to restore stability and, as usual where guns and flag waving are involved, democracy.

Now, more than a year after the arrest of the loathsome dictator, it's fair to ask: What *did* we accomplish in Panama? Because if Panama is to be our standard for success and the yardstick by which any action in the Persian Gulf may be measured, we ought to know what "success" looks like — after the smoke clears, that is, and the dead have all been laid to rest.

First, there's the matter of drugs. In August 1990 *The New York Times* reported that according to Panamanian pilots and dockworkers, the cocaine traffic was back to pre-invasion levels and, if anything, "more open and abundant than before." American officials believe that the Panamanian banking industry still serves as a laundromat for the hemisphere's cocaine profits, but the U.S.-installed government of Guillermo Endara is resisting a pact that would help catch drug-money depositors.

Democracy is a little harder to assess, but by all accounts most of the gains have accrued to Panama's tiny, white-skinned elite of wealth. In the wake of the invasion, labor unions have been repressed and nonwhites shut out of high-ranking government positions. With unemployment running at more than twenty-five percent, crime is rampant, and angry protest marches are once again in a common sight. President Endara, who is notoriously indifferent to the nation's low-income majority, has so far refused to legitimate his apparent pre-invasion victory with new elections — a tactless omission for a man who was sworn in, with few Panamanians even present, on a U.S. military base.

Then there's the dictator. When Manuel Noriega was apprehended, some commentators wondered whether he would ever really be brought to trial, given what he might reveal about his long association with former CIA Director George Bush. They were right to wonder. With the revelation — mysteriously leaked to CNN — that the U.S. government has been eavesdropping on Noriega's conversations with his lawyers, the prosecution may have opened the door for Noriega to walk, untried, to a relaxing life in exile.

So that's the sordid aftermath of Operation Just Cause, as the invasion was called. And the human cost? Twenty-three American service members' lives — which is not bad unless one of them happened to be your husband, son, sweetheart, or father — and the lives of somewhere between 202 (the U.S. estimate) and 4,000 Panamanian civilians. That may not sound so bad either, until you recall that the number of Kuwaiti deaths in the Iraqi invasion was in the same general range: between "hundreds" (Amnesty International's estimate) and 7,000 (according to exiled Kuwaitis).

If this was "success," one shudders to think what failure might look like. And one shudders with particular horror because the same tape is now on instant replay: a cruel thug and former U.S. ally, who just happened to be sitting on a key resource (oil this time, the canal in Noriega's case), was singled out as the president's personal nemesis and *casus belli* — only that the outcome, this time around, was infinitely bloodier. With all due respect to the general cited above, Panama may, after all, hold a lesson or two to be learned.

The first, it seems to me, has to do with the limits of official foresight. Conservative ideologues talk about a "law of unintended consequences," which means, roughly, that the effort to fix things sometimes worsens the damage. Of course, the ideologues apply the "law" selectively, as an argument against anti-poverty efforts, not military ventures abroad.

But if anything illustrates the pitfalls of well-intended meddling, it's Panama, not the much-maligned War on Poverty. Clearly, the aim was not to promote the cocaine trade or reduce Panama from a mere banana republic to the status of international basket case, yet that's what we seem to have accomplished. Before pulling the trigger on Saddam Hussein, shouldn't we have reflected, as true conservatives surely would want us to, on the dangerous arrogance of all human schemes and designs? Shouldn't we have tallied up the entirely possible and thoroughly unintended consequences of a war in the Gulf? An ever deeper recession, for example, a wave of anti-American terrorism, a devastating attack on Israel?

The second lesson is that however noble the ends, the use of force always entails one tragic and, realistically speaking, *intended* consequence, and that is the loss of lives. Maybe, if President Bush ever overcomes his obsession with Saddam, he might think about how to repay the estimated $1 billion in damage caused by his invasion of Panama. But the dead, whether they number in the thousands or "only" hundreds, will not wake up to see that happy day. Nor will the tens of thousands who died in the Gulf War — Americans, Iraqis, and others — ever stir again now the tanks have rolled away across the sand.

Before he ordered another shot fired, George Bush ought to have stopped and counted very slowly to ten because we might have been wading into another Vietnam. Or — what may well prove in the long term just about as bad — another Panama.

# 7

# Countdown for a Decade: The U.S. Build-Up for War in the Gulf

*Sheila Ryan*

One of the aspects of the Gulf War of 1991 which seemed to amaze many Americans was the efficiency with which the U.S. military carried out the enterprise. Within six months of the Iraqi invasion of Kuwait, the United States had deployed half a million military personnel to the region, and had all their supplies and equipment on hand: television viewers in the United States watched the process transfixed, for many of them experienced great difficulty in being deployed about their daily routines over bridges rusting out for lack of maintenance, pothole scarred roads and public transportation systems characterized by delay and discomfort. People marveled as targets were sought out and destroyed by smart bombs produced by the very country whose declining educational system seems to be producing a dumb generation.

The question of why this slaughter in the desert was accomplished with such ghoulish skill requires examination. After all, it was perpetrated by the same U.S. military which forgot to bring the maps when it invaded Grenada. Leaving aside the issues of ethics and questions of political consequence, why was the project so "successful" on a technical level?

The success can be traced to years of planning and generous funding for preparation (as well as to the serendipitous element of choosing an enemy whose regime, with hindsight, appears to have been so unpopular that it was unable to rally popular support for the kind of protracted conflict which could have inflicted significant casualties on troops of the anti-Iraq coalition and perhaps have precipitated a political decision on the part of the United States to withdraw). Let us examine those preparatory processes and the strategic context within which they developed.

## Strategic Overview

Ironically, the political context for the massive deployment of U.S. troops in Operation Desert Storm began to be sketched with an announcement by President Richard Nixon in 1969 that the United States would no longer be willing to dispatch U.S. personnel for intervention in the Third World. With the United States tied down in a losing war in Indochina and with domestic opposition mounting as increasing numbers of American soldiers returned home in bodybags, President Nixon told reporters in Guam that in the future U.S. allies would have to deal with problems of "internal security" and "military defense" without U.S. troops, although the United States would supply the weaponry for the task.[1]

The Israeli victory two years earlier in the June War had humiliated two states defined, however inappropriately, by the United States as Soviet clients in the region; this geopolitical boon had been accomplished without a single drop of American blood, and had created a climate of enthusiasm in Washington for vicarious victory in the Middle East. The region was to become the center of gravity for the Nixon Doctrine, the concept that the United States could achieve a favorable stasis through armament of regional powers. In the Middle East, those powers formed a somewhat wobbly tripod: Israel, Iran and Saudi Arabia.

Under the Nixon Doctrine, U.S. arms transfer abroad underwent not only a quantitative but a qualitative change. No longer did "arms aid" connote shipping obsolete U.S. equipment and second hand uniforms and boots to a Third World regime: now new and sophisticated weapons systems were exported. Israel, which had received no substantial U.S. military assistance before its victory in 1967, soon became the leading U.S. "security assistance" recipient in the world. The proportions of U.S. military aid allocated to the Middle East and Asia indicate the shifting locus of U.S. intervention: between 1950 and 1963, while Asia was receiving 31.4% of all U.S. military aid, the Middle East received a mere 3%. While the Middle East's share rose to 9.5% between 1963 and 1970, it was dwarfed by the 75% flowing into Asia. In the 1971–75 period, the Middle East's portion leapt to 60.2%, remaining at 58.1% until 1980, while the Asian measures fell to 23.3% in 1971–75, trailing off to a small fraction during the rest of the decade.[2] Two major regional clients for U.S. military industries were paying customers, not aid recipients: Saudi Arabia and Iran. The new wealth and economic power of these states, attributable to the rise of OPEC, the oil cartel, and the increase in oil prices, made them prime markets for U.S. military contractors, who might otherwise have suffered declining demand with the end of the Vietnam War.

The massive infusion of U.S. military goods, services and aid into the Middle East during the 1970s had diverse significant effects on the state systems of the region. In Israel, the combined effect of subsidy for the occupation of Arab lands and the expansion of the social role of the military was to create hothouse conditions for the growth of the right, and indeed in 1976, the Labor Party lost to the Likud for the first time since the establishment of the state. In Iran, the staggering military imports from the United States may have constituted one of the factors leading to the erosion of the stability of the Shah's regime.

The armament programs helped to provide the United States with the image of ascendant superpower in the region. Under President Sadat, Egypt came to accept the premise that only the United Sates could end the continued Israeli occupation of the Sinai and the enormous burden on Egypt of military hostility, the combined effects of which were placing an intolerable political and economic strain on the Egyptian regime. The Camp David Agreement brokered by President Carter, while couched in the diction of peace, actually heralded the entry of Egypt into the American military alliance in the region, and was accompanied by huge military aid packages for both Israel and Egypt. In order to sweeten the deal for Israel, and as part of the process of negotiations, President Carter agreed to ask Congress for an extraordinary $3 billion in military assistance to subsidize the transfer of Israeli military bases from the Sinai to Israeli territory,[3] and $1.5 billion in arms aid over three years to Egypt.[4] Egypt quickly assumed second place only to Israel as a recipient of U.S. arms assistance.

The growing internal political problems of the Shah of Iran cast a shadow over the discussions of peace and military procurement at Camp David, a shadow Israeli Prime Minister Begin and Egyptian President Sadat were very aware of during their talks at the presidential retreat. When the Shah's regime collapsed in the face of massive Iranian demonstrations and when the Islamic Republic came to power, it was clear that the old Nixon Doctrine concept of imposing U.S. dominance over strategic parts of the region by remote control had suffered a serious defeat. President Carter announced in his State of the Union address in 1980 that henceforth: "An attempt by any outside force to gain control of the Persian Gulf region will be regarded as an assault on the vital interests of the United States of America, and such an assault will be repelled by any means necessary, including military force."[5]

The Carter administration had actually turned toward a direct interventionist posture in the Gulf even earlier. Its first two years in office were marked by vacillation in strategic planning: some voices within and around the administration argued for an extension of the kind of military stance which had concentrated U.S. efforts in Europe in the post-Vietnam War period, while accepting a sharp decline in troop strength and limited prospects for U.S. military adventure abroad. Others demurred, among them Samuel P. Huntington of Harvard, who early in the Carter era wrote a memorandum suggesting that, contrary to the wisdom prevailing in Washington, the Gulf, not the NATO region, was to become a prime arena of U.S.—Soviet confrontation.

Huntington addressed his memorandum to Carter's national security adviser, Zbigniew Brzezinski, who responded by refurbishing the old concept of a "fire brigade," a military unit especially equipped for quick response to "brushfire war" in the Third World. This counterinsurgent formation came to be called the Rapid Deployment Force, and Carter officially inaugurated it in August 1977, in Presidential Directive 8. This marked a turning point in U.S. strategic contemplation of its options in the area. While the U.S. had had an established naval presence in the Gulf since the Second World War, late in the Carter administration U.S. policymakers not only expanded the naval presence, but also considered seriously for the first time landing ground troops in the Gulf.

The preferred formulation of the "threat" the United States confronted in Southwest Asia continued to be the prospect of the Soviet Union "taking advantage" of regional instability to intrude. Indeed, in the immediate aftermath of the toppling of the Shah the Pentagon produced contingency papers examining the possibility of resorting to theater nuclear weapons to block Soviet troops streaming through the mountain passes of an internally unstable Iran towards the Gulf oil resources. During the Carter administration, however, U.S. officials began to recognize the possibility of "threats" other than the Soviets. For example, Harold Brown, Secretary of Defense under President Carter, told Congress:

> Not all of the challenges confronting us are of Soviet origin. While the Soviets no doubt will continue to exploit situations when and where they can, were we to view all challenges and all problems through a Soviet prism, we would seriously handicap our ability to come to grips with them.
> [Of the other challenges] the most obvious and important example is oil . . . Our dependence and the even greater dependence of our allies and friends in both the industrialized and the developing worlds threatens our standard of living, our economy and our security . . . Despite their new-found wealth and influence, many oil-exporting nations are militarily weak and highly vulnerable. They are thus potentially tempting targets for aggressive powers who may be driven by their own energy needs or by a desire to control the energy that others need. The potential of external aggression that would cut off access to oil, especially in the Persian Gulf, is a severe and by now well-recognized challenge.[6]

As soon as the Reagan administration came in, the terms of official discussion of threat reverted to a nearly exclusive emphasis on the Soviet Union or its regional "surrogates." The countries classified as surrogates shifted over time, but the category survived. The stated goal of the Reagan administration in the region was to array its allies in a "strategic consensus" against the Soviet Union. This was a formulation essentially uncongenial to the area, where the Arab-Israeli conflict seemed to take precedence in the minds of both Arab and Israeli leaders, and where Iraqi-Syrian, Iraqi-Iranian, or Saudi-Iranian tensions were much more significant to those involved than the far-fetched scenario of Soviet encroachment marketed by the Reagan administration. Nevertheless, a number of states desirous of U.S. weapons found a way to merchandise their claims in the anti-Soviet lexicon.

The pattern of a strong emphasis on the Middle East region as a locus for U.S. security assistance which emerged in the mid-1970s continued through the Carter and Reagan administrations. Of the ten largest recipients of U.S. military assistance between 1977 and 1989, the top three, Israel, Egypt and Turkey, are Middle Eastern states, as are Pakistan and Jordan, both of which rank lower on the list. Greece, Spain and Portugal, three others of this big ten, are given military assistance primarily to obtain U.S. base rights in these countries, bases which are important to the United States especially because they support deployment capability to the Middle East/North Africa region. Only two states on the top ten list, South Korea and the Philippines, are neither in the Middle East or primarily on the list because they are vital to U.S. access to the region.[7]

## The U.S. Military Build-Up

The United States was at a great logistical disadvantage as Pentagon planners contemplated military operations in the Gulf. The region is 7,000 air miles or 12,000 sea miles from the east coast of the United States, while all but adjacent to the Soviet Union. The planning throughout the 1970s had been to deal with regional problems through indigenous forces. Suddenly the premises of the planning were transformed, and major changes had to take place in strategic thinking, force organization, procurement programs and base construction projections.

Preparations for deployment to the Gulf were a strong determinant of conventional U.S. military strategic planning and procurement policies during the 1980s. On a strategic conceptual level, the concept of low-intensity warfare was developed to supplement the inter-superpower conflict which had dominated much of U.S. military thinking previously. In the context of the Middle East, the low-intensity concept began to segue into the notion of "mid-intensity conflict," that is, major conventional war against a well-armed regional power.

The Reagan administration developed the Rapid Deployment Force established by President Carter into a far more powerful military capability. In January 1983, it was renamed the Central Command; as Secretary of Defense Caspar Weinberger declared: "This marks the first geographic unified command created in over 35 years and highlights the importance we have placed on Southwest Asia and our ability to deter or oppose Soviet aggression in the region."[8] By the mid-1980s the Central Command could mobilize well over 300,000 troops.

Along with the organization of the troops to be deployed went expensive programs to procure the air- and sealift capability for their efficient transportation to the region. The most complicated part of the planning involved land facilities which would have to be prepared for the troops en route and within the region. The question of base rights within the region proved to be a very sensitive issue. The historical memory of the humiliation of the colonial powers' foreign bases in the region, Arab popular anger at the U.S. for its massive support to Israel, and the special religious and cultural problems foreign military presence posed for Saudi Arabia all militated against formal acquisition of bases in the region, and indeed, governments firmly opposed such a notion. The U.S. was forced into flexibility, after Secretary Brown's initial efforts to find bases in the region proved unavailing. The concept of a "facility" was developed as a sanitized version of a "foreign military base." Rather than the U.S. flag flying over installations in the Middle East, the U.S. would plan and in some cases finance development of air and naval facilities, which would remain under their national flags but would be available for use by the United States as necessary. "In no case are we seeking to create a new U.S. base, per se, in Southwest Asia. Rather, the purpose is to improve facilities we might use in crises or exercises and to arrange for prompt access when needed," Secretary of Defense Brown told Congress.[9] An exception to the need for discretion was the tiny islet of Diego Garcia in the Indian Ocean. Little more than a rock outcropping, it had no large indigenous population to express outrage, and its British owners were amenable to arranging for the United States to greatly enlarge its naval and airbase capacity. The construction program for the new or expanded bases was extremely ambitious and expensive. Between 1980 and 1983, Congress appropriated $435 million for the Diego Garcia project, $91 million for Egyptian bases at Ras Banas, $255 million for facilities in Oman, $58 million for Kenya, $54 million for Somalia and $647 million for the Lajes base in the Azores, an important stop off point on the long trip to the Gulf.[10] The total came to nearly a billion dollars, and did not include even more extensive construction in Saudi Arabia, being carried out at Saudi expense.

The Pentagon also embarked on a program of "prepositioning" in the region much of the materiel which would be required in the event of a troop deployment to the Middle East/Gulf region. By the beginning of 1983, 18 chartered ships full of equipment and supplies were afloat in the region as the Near Term Prepositioning Force.

### The Saudi Case

The particular forms of U.S. military preparation vis-a-vis Saudi Arabia are worth examining in some detail both because of their relatively important weight in overall efforts and because the Saudi connection was of such essential significance in the Operation Desert Shield/Desert Storm episode.

The United States government has had a long and close relationship with the Saudi monarchy for several decades, extending back to the contacts between President Franklin Roosevelt and the Saudi king during World War II. During the early years, much of the threat perceived by the U.S. government in relation to Saudi Arabia was from Britain, and the priority of U.S. policy was exclusion of competing external powers, especially the British. Throughout the 1950s and 60s, the kingdom served as a source of great corporate prosperity for American multinational energy corporations, but it remained quite underdeveloped itself. In the mid-sixties, Saudi Arabia was still rather poor, with much of its income being derived from sources other than oil, such as the *hajj*, the annual Muslim pilgrimage to Mecca.[11] The notion that Saudi Arabia could be an important regional military or political force would have seemed ludicrous during this period.

Even in the early 1970s, when a democratic nationalist insurgency broke out against the Sultan of Oman in the western province of Dhofar, although the location was virtually adjacent to Saudi Arabia, Iranian troops were deployed to suppress the rebellion; a Nixon Doctrine exercise par excellence, and a general acknowledgement that the Saudis were too weak militarily to be called upon for such a role. Although it did not like the presence of Persians on the Arab side of the Gulf, the Saudi regime lacked the military stature to be taken seriously.

U.S. military sales to Saudi Arabia began to skyrocket when oil prices did. Between 1950–70, the United States had sold Saudi Arabia some $176 million in military equipment and services. Between 1971 and 1975, the figure rose astronomically to $2.5 billion.[12] The sales simultaneously "recycled petrodollars," bringing a share of the income that Saudi Arabia was now receiving for its oil back into U.S. corporate coffers, and moved Saudi Arabia into a position of increasing regional influence.

These massive purchases were striking at the outset in light of two salient characteristics of the Saudi situation. The first is the Saudis' relatively small military, the low number of men under arms being attributable to the sparse population of the country, believed to have a native-born population of only 7 to 9 million (more precise estimates are not released by the Saudi government). To some extent the dearth of native-born Saudis is offset by the use of foreign personnel under contract; Pakistanis and Jordanians, as well as Westerners supporting purchased weapons systems. By the late 80s, the Saudis still had fewer than 75,000 in the regular armed forces, perhaps 10–15,000 more in the paramilitary Royal Guard and National Guard.[13] The second relevant factor is that, aside from some tension along the Yemeni border, Saudi Arabia throughout the 1970s had been untouched by any external military friction. Certainly there was never any real prospect of Saudi-Israeli clashes, and while there was some level of tension at times between the Shah and the Saudi monarchy, actual military hostilities between the two U.S. allies were unthinkable. It was not until the 1980s, when the Saudis would have had some basis for fearing Iranian ambitions in the region, that initiation of a real armament program would have made sense: by then, the Saudis were well on their way to a truly impressive arsenal.

The Saudi government has in some sense compensated for its relatively small number of military personnel by massive investment in equipment and other Saudi expenditure per soldier. The Saudi expenditure per soldier has reached the staggering figure of $223,592 annually, compared with $66,000 for the United States or $6,960 for Iraq.[14]

One role the United States took on during the 1970s was assistance with internal security. In 1975, an American corporation, Vinnell, contracted with the Saudi government to supply military advisors to train four mechanized infantry battalions and an artillery battalion for the National Guard, the Saudi internal security force, for a price of at least $77 million. The U.S. Agency for International Development's Office of Public Safety conducted a study of internal security and other matters for the Saudi police.[15] In 1979, when a radical Islamic grouping led by Juhayam al-Utaybi (ironically an ex-noncommissioned officer in the Saudi National Guard) seized the Grand Mosque in Mecca, the U.S. Army Corps of Engineers advised the government on recapture of the Islamic holy place. The close surveillance which the CIA has implemented has provided it not only with the capacity to alert the monarchy to impending threat but also with an entree to observe the monarch's personal peccadillos: Kind Fahd is said to indulge considerably in alcohol, although it is forbidden to Muslims and he derives much of his prestige from his role of guardian of the Islamic holy places.

A crucial element in U.S. cooperation in the building of a Saudi military infrastructure was the role of the U.S. Army Corps of Engineers in the planning and supervision of Saudi bases, many of which were then constructed by U.S. contractors. By 1976, the U.S. Army Corps of Engineers was overseeing nearly $20 billion of military construction in Saudi Arabia, including three entire "military cities" — al-Batin, in the east near the Iraqi border, Tabuq in the north-west, and Khamis Mishayt in the south-west.[16] The Army Engineers moved their foreign headquarters from Germany to Saudi Arabia, an indication of the relative importance of these Saudi projects. Operation Desert Shield would have been virtually inconceivable without the sophisticated military infrastructure the Saudis developed in the closest collaboration with the United States. The relative importance of construction and other "nonhardware" items on the U.S. sales lists to Saudi Arabia is suggested by the fact that of $50 billion in U.S. military equipment and services purchased since the 1950s, only 15% has gone for weapons systems, with the rest expended on construction, infrastructure, nonlethal supplies and other support.[17]

After the fall of the Shah, Saudi Arabia began to appear far more vulnerable in the eyes of military planners in Riyadh and in Washington. The United States had also become vulnerable in a sense, for the spectacle of the powerlessness of the United States to maintain the Shah in power, an exhibition of powerlessness made all the more humiliating by the prolonged hostage crisis, had severely eroded U.S. credibility with the regimes dependent upon U.S. armament and security support. Even before the 1980 election a study team in Washington had formulated a plan for the enhancement of Saudi air defenses by the sale of AWACS, a highly sophisticated airborne electronic intelligence system with an advanced communication, control and command capacity. The AWACS sale seems to have been accepted in Washington prior to 1980 election, but public announcement or submission of the deal to Congress was postponed for fear that opposition of the pro-Israel lobby would kill the deal in an election year. Congress approved the $8.5 billion deal in 1982, after an intense battle, pitting the influence of President Reagan and the considerable lobbying power of many energy corporations and military contractors against the previously undefeated American-Israel Public Affairs Committee. The huge sale was the largest single arms deal in U.S. history.

There are several elements of the package which are important to examine in some detail, since they suggest important factors in the pattern of U.S.-Saudi military relations. First, the program was specifically designed to provide Saudi Arabia with no advantages in any future military conflict with Israel, but to deal with possible hostilities in the Red Sea and Gulf areas only. The training and software support were focused on potential conflict with Yemen, Iraq or Iran, not with Israel. The computer software was configured to reduce the effectiveness of the Saudi system against the type of U.S.-manufactured jet fighters used by the Israeli Air Force. Secondly, the Saudi system was made heavily dependent upon the United States. The aircraft cannot be flown for more than a month unless U.S. support personnel in Saudi Arabia cooperate, and key equipment on the AWACS requires U.S. support after operating for a few days.[18] Crucial maintenance procedures must be performed in the United States. Thirdly, the AWACS included a "digital look down link" to permit the United States to draw upon the electronic intelligence data gathered by the Saudi AWACS and in fact by their entire air defense system. Fourthly, and most importantly for the present consideration, the AWACS deal would create within Saudi Arabia a potential to host a deployment of U.S. aircraft without any of the political disadvantages of creating an overt U.S. airbase in Saudi Arabia. Anthony Cordesman explains:

[The package] gave the U.S. the ability to deploy up to two wings, roughly 140 USAF fighters, to support Saudi Arabia and the conservative Gulf states in an emergency. In fact, each main Saudi air base had the basic support equipment for 70 U.S. F-15 fighters in addition to supplies for its own F-15s. The package meant that Saudi Arabia would have all the necessary basing, service facilities, refueling capability, parts and key munitions in place to accept over-the-horizon reinforcement from USAF F-15 fighters. No conceivable improvement in U.S. airlift or USAF rapid deployment and 'base basing' capability could come close to giving the U.S. this rapid and effective reinforcement capability . . .
The facilities that would become part of the Saudi system would also help to strengthen U.S. ability to deploy forces from the eastern Mediterranean and project them as far east as Pakistan in those contingencies that threatened both U.S. and Saudi interests. No conceivable build-up of U.S. strategic mobility, or of U.S. staging bases in Egypt, Turkey, Oman, Somalia or Kenya could act as a substitute for such facilities in Saudi Arabia. The closest other U.S. facility in the region was in Diego Garcia, which is as far from the western Gulf as is Dublin, Ireland.[19]

These military advantages would accrue to the United States, moreover, on the basis of Saudi expenditure alone: the U.S. would pay nothing, while the U.S. military contractors would benefit from the huge deal, the true cost of which was projected at $15 billion over a ten year span.

Shortly after President Reagan's re-election, his administration planned to announce a new proposal for a major arms sale to Saudi Arabia during a visit to Washington by King Fahd in February 1985. The projected deal incorporated many of the elements of "interoperability" with U.S. forces and construction of facilities which would assist U.S. troops deployment to the region: the proposed deal featured the sale of F-15s, but included other weapons systems as well. Before the proposal was announced, however, the administration recalculated the political costs in the United States. The internal debate within the administration appears to have pitted the geo-strategists with a global perspective on strengthening the U.S. position vis-a-vis the purported Soviet threat and the domestic architects of a right wing coalition, whose important pro-Israel components included not only lobbies based in the Jewish community but Christian fundamentalist and neoconservative ideologues as well. Instead of announcing the proposal during the King's visit, the administration opted to announce that it would delay proposals for arms sales to the Middle East pending completion of a study. A series of postponements ensued, until the Saudis finally asked President Reagan for a letter stating that the United States did not contemplate making the deal, and would understand a Saudi decision to look for another supplier. The Saudis then made a $9 billion deal with the British to purchase Tornado jets, and the British became the major Saudi arms supplier in the late 1980s.[20]

These twists and turns in the arms pipeline to the Gulf were infuriating to the Saudis and other conservative weapons consumers in the region, and extremely frustrating to those charged with implementing U.S. military policies in the region. General Norman Schwarzkopf told a Congressional committee in the spring of 1989 that: "The Central Command Security Assistance Chief in our country recently told me that one of his European counterparts expressed it this way: 'Because of its security assistance practices, the United States is Britain's best marketeer.'"[21] The general estimated that the United States had lost $43 billion in arms sales over a four year period. Moreover, he argued, restriction on sales, and Congressionally imposed reductions in security assistance to smaller Gulf states like Oman and Yemen detracted from the U.S. strategic position in the Gulf:

> In order for the United States to exercise an effective leadership within a cooperative regional framework, a credible security assistance program for the Central Command region is necessary. Security assistance is an essential instrument in the implementation and integration of the twin pillars of our national security program — deterrence and forward defense ... Program reductions since 1985 and restrictive arms transfer policies have damaged our credibility as a reliable security assistance partner and threatened our regional access and overall military to military relationships.[22]

There are also indications that the U.S. administration was relieved in the Saudi case by the decision to seek sophisticated weapons systems elsewhere and obviate the need for bloody political battles within the United States. Since the 1985–86 Saudi arms sale imbroglio, the Reagan administration generally chose to avoid major efforts to gain Congressional support for arms sales to the Saudis. It submitted a proposal for sale of missiles in 1986, which Congress turned down without any intense lobbying effort on the scale of the 1982 campaign for the AWACS sale.

## From Military Exercises to Military Operations

The first attempt by the United States to try out the new strategies of rapid deployment was Operation Bright Star in 1981, which involved joint training exercises in Egypt, Somalia, Sudan and Oman. The biannual regional joint exercises became important not only for military purposes but for political ones: to accustom people in the region to the presence and maneuvers of U.S. troops. In general there has been no significant regional or domestic U.S. opposition to the exercises.

The advent of the Iraq-Iran war also functioned as a kind of practice run for Operations Desert Shield and Desert Storm, although the alignments were quite different. The United States appears to have provided electronic intelligence to Iraq about Iranian targets at least since 1982: this process provided opportunities for testing the "interoperability" of Saudi and U.S. systems and for actual combat testing of the system. The reflagging operation in 1987–88, when the largest U.S. naval armada assembled since World War II operated in the Gulf region, provided experience in operation in the very special environment of the Gulf, with its space constraints in waterways and harsh climatic conditions.[23] It facilitated an expanded accord with the Saudis for U.S. operations: as the Iraq-Iran war intensified and appeared to threaten tankers, administration officials persuaded the Saudis to agree to the stationing of a KC10 aerial tanker in Saudi Arabia to allow U.S. fighter-bombers to target Iranian assets in the northern Gulf.

More intangibly, but of great significance, was the opportunity for the administration to test the political climate in the United States, and to find it accepting of U.S. military operations in the Gulf. During this "forward deployment of the U.S. Navy," as Secretary of Defense Weinberger called it, U.S. forces were engaged in actual hostilities. In two dramatic "accidents" the Iraqi Air Force, with which the United States was tacitly allied, attacked the U.S.S. *Stark*, causing more than 40 deaths among the U.S. sailors; not long after that the U.S.S. *Vincennes* mistook an Iranian civilian airliner for a military jet and shot it out of the sky, with a consequent toll of 291 Iranian lives. Even these untoward events did not create an effective opposition to the enterprise in the United States.

Nor was collective wincing at the cynicism of policy sufficient to create an obstacle to its implementation. Until the toppling of the Shah, Iraq had been depicted by successful U.S. administrations as a Soviet client (indeed, although the Ba'ath government was ruthless in its suppression of the Iraqi Communist Party, it received large amounts of Soviet arms). The official American description of Iraq was rapidly transformed to permit support to Saddam Hussein in his war against Iran, which came to be construed as the principal U.S. regional enemy. In fact, Iraq was removed from the U.S. list of "terrorist states" in order to facilitate that support. It was while the U.S. was its tactical ally that Iraq used chemical weaponry with savage effect against poorly trained and ill equipped Iranian troops, and even against Iraqi Kurdish citizens in March 1988. During the Iran-contra scandal, information came to light about U.S. transfers to Iran in the "arms for hostages" affair, but not even data about a U.S. regional approach which involved military assistance to both combatants simultaneously provoked sufficient moral outrage to force a reassessment of the U.S. military role in the Gulf.

In restrospect the seeming marvel of the rapid and efficient U.S.

deployment and assault against Iraq is amazing essentially not for happening as it did but for not having been foreseen more broadly during the decade of costly and extensive U.S. preparations for such an eventuality.

## Notes

1. Statement of President Nixon to reporters in Guam, July 25, 1969.
2. *Background Materials on Foreign Assistance: Report of the Task Force on Foreign Assistance to the Committee on Foreign Affairs*, U.S. House of Representatives, February 1989. Calculated from materials on p. 288.
3. Letter of Secretary of Defense Harold Brown to Israeli Defense Minister Ezer Weizman, March 1979.
4. Letter of Secretary of Defense Harold Brown to General Kamal Hassan Ali, Egyptian Minister of Defense and War Production, March 23, 1979.
5. President Jimmy Carter, State of the Union Address, January 1980.
6. *Report of Secretary of Defense Harold Brown to the Congress*, January 19, 1981.
7. *Report of the Task Force on Foreign Assistance* to the Committee on Foreign Affairs of the U.S. House of Representatives, U.S. Congress, February 1989, p. 23. On the role of Portugal, Greece and Turkey as providers of base rights crucial to U.S. access to the Middle East, see *Hearings and Markup* before the Subcommittee on Europe and the Middle East of the Committee on Foreign Affairs, U.S. House of Representatives, U.S. Congress, March and April 1989, pp. 187–188 and 193–197.
8. *Report of the Secretary of Defense*, 1983, p. 194.
9. *Report of the Secretary of Defense*, 1981, p. 193.
10. *Report of the Secretary of Defense*, 1983, p. 203.
11. See, for example, Mark Heller and Nadav Safran, *The New Middle Class and Regime Stability in Saudi Arabia*, Cambridge, MA: Harvard University, Center for Middle East Studies, 1985, p. 11.
12. Helen Lackner, *A House Built on Sand: A Political Economy of Saudi Arabia*, London: Ithaca Press, 1978, p. 131.
13. Anthony H. Cordesman, *The Gulf and the West: Strategic Relations and Military Realities*, Boulder: Westview Press, 1988, p. 199.
14. International Institute for Strategic Studies, cited in *Proposed Sales and Upgrades of Major Defense Equipment to Saudi Arabia*, Hearing Before the Subcommittees on Arms Control, International Security and Science and on Europe and the Middle East of the Committee on Foreign Affairs, June 19, 1990, p. 28.
15. See, for example, Lackner, *op. cit.*, p. 133.
16. *United States Arms Policies in the Persian Gulf and Red Sea Areas: Past, Present and Future*, Committee on Foreign Relations, U.S. House of Representatives, 1977, pp. 28ff. See also Fred Halliday, "A Curious and Close Liaison: Saudi Arabia's Relations with the United States," *State, Society and Economy in Saudi Arabia*, Tim Niblock, ed., London: Croom Helm, 1982, p. 137.
17. Testimony of William F. Rope, Principal Deputy Assistant Secretary, Bureau of Politico-Military Affairs, Department of State in *Proposed Sales and Upgrades of Major Defense Equipment to Saudi Arabia*, Hearing Before the Subcommittees on Arms Control, International Security and Science, and on Europe and the Middle East of the Committee on Foreign Affairs of the U.S. House of Representatives, June 19, 1990, pp. 11–12.
18. Cordesman, *op. cit.*, p. 259. Articles by Cordesman in *Aviation Week and Space Technology* during the controversy over the AWACS sale provide abundant detail on these issues.
19. Cordesman, *op. cit.*, Table 8.3, pp. 265–266.
20. Sanjiv Prakash, "The New Saudi Era," *Defense and Foreign Affairs*, January 1989, p. 17.
21. *International Security Environment (Strategy) Hearings* before the Committee on Armed Services of the United States Senate, U.S. Congress, April–June 1989, p. 703.
22. *Ibid.*, p. 742.
23. For an excellent review of this episode, see Joe Stork, "Reagan Reflags the Gulf," *Middle East Report*, September–October 1987, pp. 4–5.

# 8

## U.S. Aid to Israel: Funding Occupation in the Aftermath of the Gulf War

### Jeanne Butterfield

$P$rior to the Gulf War, U.S. relations with Israel were perhaps at the lowest point they had been for ten years. The Palestinian peace initiative of November 1988 had issued a bold challenge to U.S. policy in the region. With the Palestinian people firmly on record as being in favor of UN Resolutions 242 and 338, and ready to accept an historic compromise that would result in a two-state solution to the conflict, the U.S. had opened a dialogue with the Palestine Liberation Organization. The Israeli government had responded in the spring of 1989 with Prime Minister Shamir's election proposal. Widely portrayed in the U.S. as a genuine plan for democratic elections in the occupied territories, the Shamir proposal was seen throughout the Middle East and the rest of the world as little more than a subterfuge, designed by Shamir to stall and further delay any real attempt to make peace with the Palestinians.

Shamir's "elections" would have allowed Palestinians in the West Bank and Gaza (but not East Jerusalem) to elect representatives who would then begin a "dialogue" with Israel to determine what form, if any, possible peace negotiations would take. After modifications and clarifications by Egypt's President Mubarak and by U.S. Secretary of State Baker, Shamir's bluff was called when the Palestinians in fact agreed to discuss the proposal. It was ultimately Shamir, after months of U.S. diplomacy, who rejected his own plan. By the time the Gulf conflict began, another round of U.S. diplomacy had crashed on the rocks of Israeli intransigence and Baker had publicly stated that if Shamir was ever serious about peace, he could call the White House.

In the aftermath of this failed attempt, Israel was further rebuffed when the U.S. administration refused to release $400 million in housing loan guarantees that Congress had voted for Israel in early 1990. There had even been unprecedented discussion in the halls of Congress about reshaping

U.S. foreign aid in light of the dramatic changes in Eastern Europe. Senator Robert Dole's proposal to cut aid by 5% to the top five U.S. foreign aid recipients made no exception for Israel.[1] Though Israel remained the largest single recipient of U.S. aid (over $3 billion in 1990) there was a sense that U.S. aid to Israel was no longer sacrosanct.[2] Reducing aid to Israel actually began to be discussed, especially as Israel remained obstinate and continued its harsh and violent repression of the 1.7 million Palestinians living under military occupation.[3]

Perhaps the most dramatic consequence of the Gulf War was the speedy reversal of many of these difficulties. U.S.-Israeli relations warmed once again, though not without underlying contradictions. While the Gulf War exposed some of these limitations of Israel as a strategic asset to the U.S., it also exacted a price in terms of "payback" for Israeli cooperation during the course of the war.

The Gulf War revealed very dramatically the limitations of Israel as a strategic and military asset to the U.S. in the Middle East region. In the Gulf conflict, on Arab soil and with Arab nations pitted against one another, the U.S.-Israeli alliance was a liability. If Israel had entered the war, the coalition would have broken apart. If the U.S. was seen to be fighting a war that served the interests of Israel, the coalition could have faltered. And in its weakened economic state, the U.S. needed the Arab alliance not only to provide political cover, but also to pay the bill. If the U.S. was to reach its own objectives in the Gulf, it simply could not have Israel enter the war.

The U.S. administration had signaled its Arab partners about a further distancing of its relations with Israel in two critical ways. First, the U.S. administration continued throughout the war to withhold the housing loan guarantees that Congress had voted for Israel. Second, for the first time in decades, the U.S. refrained from vetoing three key UN Security Council resolutions which criticized Israeli actions against Palestinians in the West Bank and Gaza, and which called for protection for the Palestinians living under occupation.[4]

In the long term, the fact that Israel stayed out of the war may raise deeper questions about Israel's value as a U.S. military partner in the region. In addition, the administration's need to satisfy its Arab coalition partners by resolving the Israeli-Palestinian conflict raises questions about Israel's value to the U.S. in strategic terms. In the short term, however, Israel's grudging agreement to stay out of the Gulf War, and its "restraint" in the face of Iraqi scud missile attacks, was an unprecedented act that earned a high pay-off in terms of U.S. aid.

Congress has long been a compliant partner when it comes to voting aid for Israel. Israel's lobby in the U.S., the American-Israel Public Affairs Committee (AIPAC), has been extraordinarily effective in seeing that pro-Israel candidates are elected to Congress.[5] And it is widely acknowledged that several key Congressional races have been determined by the strength of AIPAC support. In the weeks just after the Gulf War ceasefire, AIPAC held its annual dinner in Washington D.C.. No less than 48 Senators and 100 Congresspeople attended, in a massive show of support. AIPAC's acknowledged political clout cannot be denied in an election year. The timing could not be better, as Israel put Congress on notice that the price tag for its "restraint" during the Gulf War would be an additional $13 billion in U.S. aid and loan guarantees.

The contradiction that this poses in terms of U.S. policy is clear. While the U.S. administration clearly must satisfy its Arab coalition partners and at least give the appearance of moving to resolve the Israeli-Palestinian conflict in the aftermath of the Gulf War, it finds that across the street in Washington D.C., Congress is intent on providing the funds that will enable Israel to maintain a hard-line stance in opposition to any "land for peace" formula.

### Gulf War "Payback": More Aid for Settlements

The first instance of a Gulf War payback was increased U.S. aid to Israel in the form of housing loan guarantees to assist the resettlement of Soviet Jewish immigrants. Congress had already granted Israel $400 million in housing loan guarantees by the time the conflict began. The funds had been withheld because the U.S. administration demanded assurances from the Israeli government that the monies would not be used to settle the new immigrants in the occupied territories, including East Jerusalem. Although no change in Israeli settlement policy was apparent, and no assurances were given, the funds were suddenly released as the Gulf War ended.

Soviet Jewish immigration to Israel resumed in the wake of the Gulf War. Four hundred thousand new immigrants were expected to arrive in 1991 alone. The price tag on this new immigration has not yet been calculated, but Israel estimated that it needed over $1 billion to settle the new immigrants in 1991 alone. In the wake of the war, Israel announced that it would request an additional $10 billion in housing loan guarantees from the U.S. for the years 1991–1995.

### New Economic and Military Aid as a Result of the Gulf War

The Gulf crisis provided yet another basis on which Israel could demand more aid from the U.S.. As part of its Gulf coalition strategy, the U.S. promised to forgive a portion of Egypt's military debt. Israel demanded the same. The U.S. Congress took steps to satisfy Israel, if not completely acceding to every demand.

First, Congress took the step of authorizing Israel to redirect up to $200 million of its economic aid to "defense purposes."[6] Then it authorized another $700 million minimum of additional military aid in the form of advanced weapons systems, which supposedly would buttress Israeli defenses against Iraq and offset recent arms sales to Saudi Arabia.[7] This $700 million worth of weapons was supposed to come from U.S. stockpiles in Europe, on the theory that such a "drawdown" transfer would not cost the U.S. any additional money.[8] These Congressional votes came after the Israeli massacre of Palestinians at al-Aqsa Mosque in early October 1990, proving once again that human rights violations and occupation do not seem to matter to Congress when it comes to the question of aid for Israel.[9]

A mere six days after the bombing of Baghdad had begun, Israel presented the U.S. with the bill for its "restraint" in the Gulf War — $13 billion.[10] Of this amount, $400 million was compensation for keeping the military at its highest level of alert, another $1 billion was for losses to the economy caused when the nation shut down for four days during the first week of the air war, another $1 billion was for losses to the tourism industry. The remaining $10 billion would be for additional housing loan guarantees needed to resettle the expected Soviet Jewish immigrants.[11]

The U.S. Congress began the payback in earnest in early March, when it voted an additional $650 million for Israel to help cover "war related costs."[12] Israel promised it wouldn't make any new requests until after September 2, 1991, 28 days before the end of the fiscal year. However, as AIPAC Director Thomas A. Dine testified before the House Appropriations Committee on Foreign Operations, Israel's supporters in the U.S. do not recall that this promise was ever made.[13] Israel has recently indicated that it will formally request more funding just after the September 2nd deadline.[14] In the meantime, the administration's fiscal 1992 budget request included a renewed $3.1 billion in economic and military aid for Israel.

### U.S. Aid to Israeli Occupation

Israel continues to be the single largest recipient of U.S. economic and military aid. U.S. aid to Israel presently totals $3.1 billion per year.[15] This figure is supplemented by a total of $1 billion more in the form of various grants, loans, joint research and development projects, and interest.[16] U.S. aid to Israel totals nearly 20% of the entire Israeli national budget and nearly 25% of the entire U.S. foreign aid budget of $13.7 billion for fiscal year 1991.[17] In terms of military aid, Israel receives 36% of the worldwide U.S. allotment. U.S. aid is also equivalent to the annual Israeli budget deficit in each of the past several years. Not only has the U.S. consistently maintained this level of funding over the past decade, but it has often increased funding with supplemental grants totalling $1.5 billion in 1982 (covering the cost of the invasion of Lebanon) and totalling $750 million in 1985 and again in 1986 when the Israeli economy was in crisis. Of course these figures do not include private U.S. funds or donations from individual U.S. citizens.[18]

The next largest recipient of U.S. aid is Egypt, which receives $2.2 billion. But Israel, with a total population of 4.3 million and a per capita output of $6,810, receives a total of $720 per person in U.S. aid. Egypt, with a population of 53 million and a per capita output of only $670, receives only $42 per person. Pakistan and Turkey, the next largest recipients, each receives $0.6 billion in U.S. aid. They have populations of 100 million and 50 million respectively, and U.S. aid per person amounts to $6 for Pakistan and $11 for Turkey. U.S. aid to the entire continent of Africa adds up to a mere $1 per capita.[19]

## Israel's Special Treatment: No Strings Attached

U.S. aid to Israel is not only unique in its sheer amount. It is also unique in the way that it is given. U.S. aid to Israel includes $1.3 billion in economic aid and $1.8 billion in military aid.[20]

The economic aid is unique in that it is an outright cash transfer, with no strings attached. Of Egypt's economic aid of $815 million only $115 million is in cash. Israel receives the cash up-front, on or before October 30 of each year. What does it do with this cash? Israel deposits it in the Federal Reserve Bank of New York, where it immediately starts earning nearly 8% interest. This interest, which totalled $76.7 million in 1989, is in effect additional aid.[21]

Other examples of Israel's special foreign aid treatment abound.[22] Other countries, including Egypt, lose all U.S. aid except food assistance if they are more than a year behind on their payments to the U.S. for military and economic loans. This was mandated in 1975 by the Brooke-Alexander amendment to the U.S. Foreign Assistance Act. But again, Israel has a special deal. In 1984, Congress stated as a matter of policy that Israel's economic aid will always amount to at least as much as its annual debt payments to the United States.[23] Israel is therefore guaranteed that it can pay its debt because it will receive enough aid to make the payments. Moreover, Israel's debt is lower than that of most nations, because so much U.S. aid to Israel is in the form of actual grants rather than loans. Israel's current "debt" is $4.5 billion, and the cash it receives from the U.S. economic aid package is more than enough to cover its annual military debt payments.[24]

Military aid to Israel is also given without the close supervision by the Pentagon that oversees any other U.S. military aid.[25] Military aid of $1.8 billion funds Israel's fighter plane upgrade program, naval modernization, upgrades and improvements for attack and utility helicopters, and armor and artillery development. The military aid figure is supplemented by another $600 million in offsets and purchases, joint research and development projects and subsidies for Israeli purchases of U.S. weapons and fighter planes. In addition, Israel is allowed to spend $400 million of its military assistance in Israel itself, while other countries must spend their military aid funds in the U.S..[26] Not only can Israel use U.S. money to pay for its own weapons, but the U.S. itself has become a purchaser of Israeli weapons. Fifty four percent of the entire U.S. foreign weapons evaluation budget is spent evaluating Israeli products, and the U.S. currently spends over $250 million purchasing Israeli-made weapons.[27] The key R & D projects currently underway are the joint development of an anti-tactical ballistic missile system, a helicopter night-targeting system, and "counter-obstacle vehicles." A pact signed in September of 1989 by Israeli Defense Minister Rabin and U.S. Secretary of Defense Cheney allows the U.S. for the first time to *lend* materials, supplies and equipment to Israel for military research and development.[28]

What is the purpose of this massive infusion of military aid? According to former Israeli General Matti Peled, "This money gives Israelis a false sense of security. It is fueling the arms race in the Middle East and subsidizing American arms manufacturers. The one thing it does not do is make us more secure."[29] The one thing U.S. aid to Israel does do is make Israel the fourth largest military power in the world today, a power which has nuclear weapons, and a power which continues a brutal occupation of Palestinian land and people.

### U.S. Law and Aid to Israel

U.S. law, specifically the U.S. Foreign Assistance Act of 1961 (Sections 502B and 116(a)), sets out important guidelines for the use of U.S. funds abroad. The Act provides that no U.S. aid shall be provided "to the government of any country which engages in a consistent pattern of gross violations of internationally recognized human rights, including torture or cruel, inhuman, or degrading treatment or punishment, prolonged detention without charges, or other flagrant denial of the right to life, liberty and the security of person . . ."

In addition to this law, the U.S. has often threatened to condition aid on other countries observance of other international standards and treaties, including the nuclear non-proliferation treaty and the Comprehensive Anti-Apartheid Act.

It is difficult to determine exactly how much U.S. aid goes to maintain and fund Israeli activities which are illegal under both U.S. and international law (settlements in the occupied territories, house demolitions, expulsions, killings of unarmed civilians, Iran-contragate, arms sales and transfers to South Africa and El Salvador). U.S. aid to Israel is an actual cash transfer with no accountability, earmarking, or oversight. But it is clear that Israeli human rights violations are gross and consistent.[30] It is also clear that the occupation could not continue if Israel did not receive this massive infusion of U.S. aid each year.

The mere costs of suppressing the intifada bring this into stark relief.[31] The Israeli Ministry of Defense asked its own government for an extra $200 million for 1990 as reimbursement for uprising-related costs. Brig. Gen. Michael Navon, director of the Defense Ministry's Budget Department, stated that the cost of fighting the uprising had reached about $500 million by March 1990. This is only the cost to the defense establishment, and doesn't include losses to the civilian economy, estimated by the Bank of Israel as $650 million in 1988 alone.[32]

### U.S. Policy and Aid to Israel

U.S. policy continues to oppose the establishment or expansion of Israeli settlements in the occupied Palestinian West Bank and Gaza Strip, including East Jerusalem. Such settlements are illegal under international law according to the terms of the Fourth Geneva Convention. The U.S. regards the settlements as an obstacle to peace under any "land for peace" formula. In his May 22nd statement before Congress, Secretary of State Baker said that "the new settlements were the largest obstacle to his mission." Israel continues to seize Arab land and Israeli settlements in the occupied territories are rapidly expanding. In the first few months of 1991 Israel seized an additional 7,500 acres of formerly Arab land in the West Bank "giving the state possession of more than half the territory in the West Bank . . . Much of the seized land is used for settlements."[33]

In addition to its regular aid allotment, the U.S. provides housing loan guarantees which are explicitly for the purpose of building housing for Soviet Jewish immigrants. Even though Israel continues to maintain that it has no "official policy" of "requiring" Soviet Jews to settle in the occupied territories, the facts contradict this assertion.[34] Approximately 200,000 Soviet Jewish immigrants arrived in Israel in 1990. According to the U.S. State Department, 4% of these new immigrants, approximately 8,000 people, were settled in occupied Palestinian territory. Three thousand new settlers went to the West Bank and Golan Heights, and 5,830 settled in East Jerusalem. Israel reports only 1%, since it refuses to consider East Jerusalem or the Golan Heights as "occupied territory." The State Department report indicates that Jewish settlers now make up about 13% of the total population of the territories, numbering just over 200,000 in 200 settlements. These figures can be broken down approximately as follows: 90,000 settlers in the West Bank, 110,000 in East Jerusalem, and about 3,000 in the Gaza Strip. West Bank settlers increased by 10,000 in 1990 alone, and by 40,000 from 1984 to 1990.[35]

Israeli Housing Minister Ariel Sharon announced that at least 10,000 new housing units would be built in the occupied territories in 1991; 7,100 units in the West Bank and Gaza, 1,100 units in the Golan Heights, and 2,000 units in East Jerusalem.[36]

While no official policy exists to force new immigrants to settle in the West Bank, Gaza, or East Jerusalem, the severe housing shortage in Israel propels people to these areas.[37] Settlers who "choose" the West Bank and Gaza settlements get direct housing subsidies of up to $21,000, and those building their own homes are given land at 5% of its assessed value. Interest-free mortgages are given to settlers for 65% of the loan's value, with reduced interest rates for an additional 25% of the loan. Costs of utility hookups are absorbed by the government and government-subsidized transportation is provided to bus settler children to schools in Israel.[38]

## U.S. Policy and U.S. Aid: After the Gulf War

The Gulf War has resulted in a dynamic in which the U.S. administration is compelled to address its seeming double standard and make fresh attempts to resolve the Israeli/Palestinian conflict. At the same time, the U.S. Congress, with the acquiescence of the Bush administration, continues to provide funding which allows Israel to continue its occupation of Palestinian territory. The contradiction does not bode well for a peaceful or speedy resolution of the conflict. The payback that Israel demanded in the wake of the war would not only strengthen the Israeli military, long the strongest in the region; it would also allow Israel to expand dramatically its illegal settlements in the West Bank and Gaza, presenting a further obstacle to peace.

If U.S. goals in the Gulf crisis were taken at face value, the U.S. should be held in this instance as well to ending occupation, upholding international law and enforcing UN resolutions. Instead, the U.S. continues to fund occupation, accede to Israeli violations of international law, and fail to enforce UN resolutions which clearly call for the withdrawal of Israeli forces from the occupied territories. Continued U.S. funding of occupation is contrary to stated U.S. policy in the region. It is also contrary to U.S. and international law. U.S. actions during the Gulf crisis suggest another path: stop funding, impose sanctions, and implement UN resolutions that provide for the convening of an international peace conference to resolve the Israeli-Palestinian conflict on a just and peaceful basis.

## Notes

1. *New York Times*, op-ed, January 16, 1990.
2. "Lean times are seen for foreign aid," *Boston Globe*, February 20, 1989.
3. Congressmen Hamilton and Obey actually ordered the U.S. Agency for International Development to withdraw a $1.5 million grant intended for an Israeli school that trains Orthodox rabbis. The rabbis would teach in settlements in the occupied territories, a goal at odds with U.S. policy which opposes Israel's settlement policy in the West Bank, Gaza and East Jerusalem. *Washington Post*, October 10, 1989.
4. UN Security Council Resolution 672, October 12, 1990.
   UN Security Council Resolution 673, October 24, 1990.
   UN Security Council Resolution 681, December 20, 1990.
5. See *Stealth PACs: How Israel's American Lobby Seeks to Control U.S. Middle East Policy*, Richard H. Curtiss, (American Educational Trust, Washington D.C., 1990).
6. *Washington Post*, October 3, 1990.
7. *Washington Post*, October 16, 1990.
8. *Washington Post*, August 30, 1990.
9. See "U.S. Aid: Subsidizing Collective Punishment of Palestinians," Joe Lockard, *American Arab Affairs*, 29, Summer 1989.
10. *New York Times*, January 23, 1991.
11. *New York Times*, January 21, 1991.
12. *Washington Post*, March 6, 1991.
13. In testimony before the Committee, chaired by Congressman David Obey, on April 17, 1991.
14. *Washington Post*, May 6, 1991.
15. U.S. aid to Israel has totalled $50 billion since 1949, $30 billion of this in the past decade.
16. The total for fiscal year 1989 was $3,742,100,000, according to the Congressional Record, March 7, 1990.
17. For comparisons, see "Report of the Task Force on Foreign Assistance to the Committee on Foreign Affairs," U.S. House of Representatives, February 1989.
18. Adding private corporate and individual donations brings the total money flow from the U.S. to Israel to about $6.2 billion a year, or $1,377 per Israeli. See "The Money Tree: U.S. Aid to Israel," by Martha Wenger, *Middle East Report*, #164/5, May–August 1990.
19. "Dear Colleague" letter, dated February 5, 1990, circulated by Congressman George Crockett and signed by 9 other members of the Congressional Black Caucus.
20. Congressional Record, May 1, 1990. "Scorecard on the Israeli Economy: A Review of 1989."
21. *New York Times*, September 21, 1990.
22. The Congressional Research Service report on U.S. Aid to Israel, reported in the Congressional Record of May 1, 1990, lists 43 special laws pertaining to U.S. aid to Israel. See "American Aid to Israel: The Facts," Donald Neff, *Middle East International*, June 8, 1990.
23. *New York Times*, September 21, 1990.
24. *Manchester Guardian Weekly*, March 26, 1989.
25. In fact, this lack of oversight resulted in what Israeli officials described as the biggest scandal

ever uncovered involving the misuse of U.S. aid to Israel. U.S. defense contractors and an Israeli air force general allegedly diverted millions of dollars in aid to their own personal bank accounts. *Washington Post*, March 19, 1991.

26. National Association of Arab Americans, *Action Alert*, January 1990.
27. Statement by Edward W. Gnehn, Deputy Assistant Secretary of Defense, Near East and South Asian Affairs, before the House Foreign Affairs Committee, Subcommittee on Europe and the Middle East, March 1, 1989.
28. *Boston Globe*, September 27, 1989.
29. "Too Much Aid," by Major General (ret.) Matti Peled, *The Other Israel*, No. 39, Nov.–Dec. 1989.
30. See the U.S. State Department annual report on Human Rights and Country Conditions, which documents many Israeli human rights violations. See also annual reports by Amnesty International, Middle East Watch, and the Palestine Human Rights Information Center.
31. See Pinchas Landau, "Potential Effects of the Disturbances in the West Bank and Gaza on the Israeli Economy," distributed by the World Zionist Press Service, May 2, 1990.
32. Reported in *Palestine Perspectives*, Sept./Oct. 1989.
33. "Israel Angered by Baker's Remarks on Settlements," Joel Brinkley, *New York Times*, May 24, 1991.
34. See NAAA Issue Brief, May 1990, "Status of Aid to Israel for Resettling Soviet Jews."
35. *Washington Post*, March 22, 1991.
36. *Washington Post*, March 11, 1991.
37. "Jewish Settlements Grow in Occupied Territories," Jackson Diehl, *Washington Post*, June 23, 1990.
38. "West Bank's 'Garden Views' and 'Special Loans' Are Luring Jewish Settlers," Joel Brinkley, *New York Times*, March 4, 1990.

# 9

# False Consensus: George Bush's United Nations

*Phyllis Bennis*

From the beginning of the Gulf crisis, it seemed the United Nations was at the center of the whirlwind. Meetings went on around the clock, decisions were made, and the international organization took the world to war. From the first Security Council vote on resolution 660, condemning the invasion and laying the groundwork for comprehensive anti-Iraq sanctions, through the precedent-setting Resolution 678 authorizing the use of force against Iraq, to the harshly punitive ceasefire terms set out in Resolution 687, it was the United Nations at the center of decision-making. It was the Security Council that imposed deadlines, and refused to delimit the Pentagon's jurisdiction to carry out the battle however and wherever it saw fit. It was the United Nation's war. Or so it seemed.

But by the end of the first stage of the crisis, by the spring of 1991, the international organization was already being viewed as one of the key victims of the Gulf War. UN independence, UN integrity, and the UN's peace-making identity all were undermined by Bush administration coercion.

UN involvement in the crisis began the first day, on August 2, 1990. Within hours of the Iraqi invasion of Kuwait, U.S. Ambassador to the United Nations Thomas Pickering called for an emergency session of the Security Council. The sudden urgency of the U.S. response raised a few eyebrows around UN headquarters — after all, it was public knowledge that Iraq had enjoyed Washington's backing through much of the eight-year Iran-Iraq war, and U.S. Ambassador to Iraq April Glaspie had told President Saddam Hussein only five days earlier that Washington did not have a defense treaty with Kuwait and had little interest in inter-Arab border disputes. Nevertheless, Baghdad's invasion clearly represented a violation of international law and the Charter of the United Nations. Ambassador Pickering had no difficulty orchestrating a 14–0 Security Council vote of condemnation (Yemen, the sole Arab country on the Council, declined to participate in the vote).

The U.S. ambassador's high-profile role in directing the Security Council, and the incessant campaign for unanimity in Council decisions regarding the Gulf, were to become hallmarks of Bush administration strategy throughout the crisis. And the imprimatur of the United Nations on Washington's military build-up in the Gulf quickly emerged as a critical component of George Bush's "new world order."

There was the rhetoric and appearance of an international organization mobilizing the world to confront and punish an international outlaw. But the reality was far different; Middle East scholar Eqbal Ahmad called it "the use of a multilateral instrument to carry out a unilateral war." It was, ultimately, a clear U.S. exercise of what one United Nations official privately called "raw power."

## Soviet Decline Brings Unipolarity

Washington's selection of the UN as its instrument of choice to legitimate its war against Iraq did not reflect a new-found respect for international law and multilateral diplomacy. Of far greater influence in that choice was the demise of the Soviet Union as a superpower capable of challenging U.S. intervention around the world.

In this newly uni-polar world, without the ideological justification of "the Soviet threat," the U.S. had to create a new public relations framework to validate its international hegemony. White House and State Department spin-masters went to work, and the PR campaign was created. It would rely not on the outmoded image of the superpower U.S. battling its Soviet counterpart, but instead on the vision of the U.S. as the leader of a brave new free world coalition, even including the Soviet Union, operating against tyranny in the name of all the nations of the world. New legitimacy and importance for — matched by enhanced U.S. control of — the United Nations would be a critical tool.

For Washington, the stakes were high. Bush insisted that his military build-up in the Gulf was on behalf of a grand international coalition, of the "whole world against Saddam Hussein." And gaining the support of the Security Council was crucial to carrying out his strategic agenda. He needed the vote on Resolution 678, authorizing the use of force against Iraq, to counter potential resistance both from uneasy allies, especially in the Middle East, and from a nascent domestic unease.

Internationally, the Arab regimes allied with Washington all faced varying degrees of instability. The Arab component of the anti-Iraq coalition was composed of non-democratic, often military regimes, or autocratic near-feudal monarchies. It was not surprising that those governments were nervous about joining an alliance that could exacerbate challenges to their continued rule.

Egypt's impoverished 50 million people, for example, largely opposed sending troops to the Gulf, and the resulting street confrontations further destabilized President Mubarak's government. Syrian President Hafez al-Assad found his legitimacy undermined, with his historic role of leader of the so-called "confrontation states" arrayed against Israel fading as his troops moved into the desert to join those of Israel's superpower sponsor. Even the wealthy and pliant citizens of Saudi Arabia and the oil-bloated Gulf statelets began to whisper a few concerns about how long the alien troops would be present to pollute the soil of the sacred lands of Islam. In some areas, most notably in Saudi Arabia itself, nascent movements for democracy emerged with embarrassing questions for the heretofore unchallenged princes of the royal family. For all of these governments, broad multilateralism was a requisite cover factor in joining the U.S.

Further incentive for the U.S. to turn to UN endorsement as a legitimating factor centered on changes in the Soviet Union. Throughout the Cold War, Washington and Moscow had faced off in the Security Council. The threat of each other's veto often left the Council paralyzed. But economic and political crisis now faced Soviet President Mikhail Gorbachev, and Moscow's European allies had undergone massive transformations and new alienation from their one-time ally. The resulting collapse in Soviet global reach meant that the threat of a Security Council veto against U.S. plans had become an impossibility. The Soviets were now too dependent on U.S. and Western economic aid, and too committed to a strategy of superpower cooperation, for the Soviet Union's power of veto to have much clout.

In just two or three years, the world had become unipolar. So, for the first time, U.S. strategic power in the Security Council remained unopposed. On January 16, 1991, during the first hours of the U.S. bombardment of Baghdad, a few journalists caught up with Soviet Ambassador Yuli Vorontsov as he headed up a UN escalator. Since the Soviet Union has no troops in the Gulf, he was asked, aren't you concerned about the Pentagon alone making all the decisions for a war being waged in your name? "Who are we," he answered, "to say they should not?"

## The U.S. Turns to the United Nations

So it was not surprising that Washington turned to the UN as a strategic lever, for almost the first time in over a quarter of a century. The Reagan administration's highly publicized disdain for the UN reflected a long history of right-wing opposition to the world body. With a short-lived shift during the Carter years, Washington had continued to view the organization as irrelevant at best, and a dangerous forum of radical Third World bombast at worst. George Bush's own years as U.S. ambassador to the world body seemed to have brought only an incremental, rather than qualitative, gain in acceptance of the value of the UN.

The United Nations' early post-World War II years reflected the heady idealism of the allied victory over fascism. But with the emergence of the Cold War and the break-up of Europe's colonial empires, the organization's credibility and usefulness for the U.S. took a sharp dive. During the post-war years in which U.S. economic and political domination of the underdeveloped countries of Asia and Africa was replacing outmoded forms of European colonialism, the U.S. had little interest in supporting true independence in the former colonies. Washington's disavowal of the UN as a vehicle for international conflict resolution began early in the 1960s, in the tumultuous era of decolonization.

As the newly independent countries, especially in Africa and Asia, took their seats in the General Assembly hall, the UN began to lose its early image of the post-World War II allied victors' club — overwhelmingly white, and dominated by the U.S. and Europe. As the 50 or so post-war member states climbed to over 150, the Assembly's new members brought changes in color, wealth, and level of development. Since democratic rules still ensured each country one vote, regardless of gross national product or size of army, the result was a UN General Assembly controlled by a large Third World majority.

Not so the Security Council. The Council holds the actual power (that is, the power to wage war or enforce peace) of the UN. Only Council resolutions, not those of the General Assembly, are binding on member states. And the Council remains the bastion of the "Perm Five," the veto-wielding permanent members: the U.S., Britain, France, the Soviet Union and China.

Over the years the U.S. has used its Council veto with a vengeance — most notably and consistently to prevent passage of resolutions criticizing Israel. Since 1967 alone, the U.S. has vetoed over 40 such resolutions. And in the UN generally throughout those years, Washington remained a grudging and half-hearted participant in multilateral diplomacy.

The Bush administration's 1990 decision to revitalize the UN as a crucial part of U.S. diplomacy can best be viewed in the context of changes in international power as a whole. The Security Council of the 1990s reflects less the West's domination of the East, than the sharply polarizing Northern domination of the South. With the Soviet Union, at least in the early years of the 1990s, unable to challenge U.S. interventionist aspirations and willing to tacitly back them in the name of superpower cooperation, at least four of the five permanent Council members function within the U.S.-led Northern power alliance.

Only China remained a question mark. However, Beijing's need for economic assistance and its desire to establish a more decisive role in international diplomatic circles make it unlikely to stand against U.S. interests; its Third World development challenges, however, ensure that it remains objectively part of the South.

When the August 2 emergency session of the Security Council convened, there was little disagreement over condemning Iraq's invasion and demanding its withdrawal from Kuwait. Yemen's refusal to participate, however, marked an early challenge to the U.S. search for unanimity by reminding the Council that the United Nations Charter requires that regional solutions be relied on first, before looking to international intervention to solve regional crises.

At the time of Iraq's invasion, the Arab world viewed the problem largely as an Arab, regional, containable crisis; it was not until Bush's announcement of massive U.S. troop deployment that the crisis was transformed into a global conflagration. When Iraqi tanks rolled into Kuwait, an Arab League meeting in Cairo was about to go into session. Jordan's King Hussein, a long-time friend of President Bush from the period when Bush headed the CIA and Hussein was an asset of the agency, called the White House. He pleaded for time for the Arab League to find an Arab solution, a regional solution. Bush replied: You've got 48 hours.

It surprised no one that the Arab League, an often uneasy coalescence of widely diverse governments, could not resolve the crisis in two days. King Hussein contacted Bush again, this time bolstered by a plea from President Mubarak. They pleaded for more time. No dice, came the White House answer; we're sending the troops.

By August 6 the U.S. had pushed through Resolution 661, imposing harsh economic sanctions against Iraq. Yemen and Cuba abstained, concerned about the legal implications of imposing such sanctions (often viewed as an act of war under international law) and about the impact of the sanctions on civilians in Iraq.

Other resolutions followed in rapid succession. Resolutions 662 (August 9) rejecting Iraq's claimed annexation of Kuwait, and 664 (August 18) calling for the release of third-country nationals held in Iraq and Kuwait, were both adopted unanimously. Resolution 665 (August 25), tightened the economic embargo with a naval blockade; it passed with Yemen and Cuba again abstaining. Resolution 666 (September 13) tightened the embargo again with greater restrictions on food and medical supplies imported to Iraq; Yemen and Cuba opposed. Resolutions 667 (September 16) and 669 (September 24), both passed unanimously, called on Iraq to restore protection to embassies and diplomatic personnel, and took responsibility for the increasing requests for financial assistance from countries impacted by the anti-Iraq embargo. Resolution 670 (September 25) expanded the blockade to aircraft; only Cuba voted against. Resolution 674 condemned Iraq's treatment of foreign nationals, claimed other instances of violations of prior resolutions, and called on the Secretary General to use his good offices to help resolve the conflict; Yemen and Cuba abstained. Resolution 677 (September 28) condemned Iraq's effort to change the demographic composition of Kuwait; it passed unanimously.

### Linkage Joins the New World Order's Vocabulary

Throughout the autumn, Bush's efforts to construct strong majority support in the Council for his anti-Iraq build-up seemed to be working. There was only one major glitch in the operation: the question of Palestine.

The U.S. need to maintain the loyalty of its (sometimes new) Arab allies in its anti-Iraq build-up meant that it could no longer routinely veto resolutions criticizing or condemning Israel for actions against Palestinians in the occupied territories. But that new set of relationships did not mean that Israeli treatment of Palestinians improved, or that efforts to stop the repression through UN action would be halted.

On October 8, the killing of at least 19 Palestinians by Israeli military authorities on the steps of the Haram al-Sharif in Jerusalem called into question the smooth running of the UN front of Washington's Gulf build-up.

Within hours of the killings, the seven non-aligned members of the Security Council introduced a resolution backed by the PLO. The cooperation among the widely disparate non-aligned Council members was particularly significant. Among them, several (Zaire, Colombia, Cote d'Ivoire, and Malaysia) had long histories of strong U.S. ties. But in this instance they moved as one to challenge the might of Washington's key Middle East ally. In fact, it was the pro-U.S. and Islamic Malaysia, incensed by the murder of Muslims at the Dome of the Rock, that led the non-aligned effort.

The non-aligned resolution won immediate support, with varying degrees of enthusiasm, from 14 of the 15 Council members, including Britain, whose ambassador, Sir David Hannay, was that month's President of the Council. The U.S. was the one hold-out.

The resolution initially did not use the word "condemn." It "deplored" the killings. But it called on the Council to send its own mission to Jerusalem to investigate the killings and to return with recommendations for how Palestinians living under occupation could be protected.

The debate was sharp, with speaker after speaker expressing their nation's outrage at the carnage in al-Aqsa Mosque. The Malaysian ambassador, despite his government's close ties to the U.S., was among the strongest voices. He called Israel's policy "truly a bloody one." He cautioned that Israel and its friends "must not be allowed to . . . masquerade behind what the Israeli representative described as 'the international coalition mustered against Iraqi aggression.'" He mentioned possible sanctions against Israel, stating that "the Council could not ignore those serious Israeli violations in the light of recent developments in the region. To do so would mean that the Council was allowing double standards to prevail over justice and moral considerations."

U.S. diplomats forced a delay in the vote. By the next afternoon, Washington had submitted its own resolution, which became, for the U.S. press, the only one under discussion. The U.S. draft used the word "condemn" for the first time. But the real sticking point was the nature of the investigation team to be sent to Jerusalem. Washington's proposal left the Security Council out of the picture, calling instead for the Secretary General to send his own representative. While SG missions had traveled to Jerusalem and the occupied territories before, they had never had an impact on continuing Israeli violations of international law and human rights. They would go, look, and return without the influence, prestige, and ultimately power of the Security Council, the UN's highest body.

Palestine's Permanent Observer to the UN at the time, Ambassador Zehdi Labib Terzi, made clear his delegation's priorities. On October 9, he said "we are not interested in semantics; what we want is for the Council to take action. The U.S. draft does not call on the Council to do anything."

The immutable U.S. rejection of a Council role was rooted in the recognition that it would finally place the Council in a position of assuming responsibility for the Palestinians living under Israeli occupation. That, for the U.S., represented the first step down the slippery slope towards a UN-sponsored international peace conference. Resistance to such a conference, of course, remained a cornerstone of the U.S.-Israeli alliance, and not even the new set of commitments to new Arab allies would change Washington's position.

What was different this time around was the consequences of a U.S. veto. In past incidents of Israeli atrocities, a routine U.S. veto on the grounds that a resolution critical of Israeli policies was "one-sided," or that it "did not advance the peace process" would be roundly condemned, but then set aside. This time, Washington's carefully constructed Arab legitimacy for its military build-up in the Gulf could not afford the political fall-out of a U.S. veto of a Council resolution condemning Israel's bloodbath at the doors of two of Islam's holiest shrines.

The governments of Saudi Arabia and Egypt, in particular, as well as Syria, were uneasy about the consequences of a U.S. veto. They stood to lose even more popular support if they continued backing U.S. troops against Saddam Hussein in the face of Washington's veto of Palestinian rights. Non-aligned diplomatic sources indicated that Saudi and Egyptian pressure on the PLO to give the U.S. a compromise way out was fierce. Palestine's diplomats did not agree, however, hoping that the commitments of other Council members to support a Council-mandated mission would remain strong. A Soviet diplomat indicated in the early morning hours of October 10 that his government would not back down "unless the Palestinians agreed." The French and the Canadians refused early U.S. efforts to persuade them to abandon the non-aligned resolution.

By the night of October 10, the British had engineered a compromise, calling for the Secretary General to send a representative, but asking that he report back to the Council. The observer's mandate did not include proposals to the Council for ways to protect the Palestinians living under occupation.

Throughout the days and nights of October 11 and 12, the U.S. noose tightened. Washington pressured its Western allies, while alternately cajoling and threatening the non-aligned members of the Council. Late in the night of October 12 the vote was taken, and Resolution 672, calling for only an SG representative to investigate, was unanimously accepted.

The fragile consensus had been preserved. But the reluctance of the U.S. to accept a resolution targeting Israel's 23-year occupation of the West Bank and Gaza, after its enthusiastic challenge to Iraq's only hours-old occupation of Kuwait, brought the question of U.S. double standards to center stage. U.S. credibility among the developing countries, and some of its Western allies, plummeted.

The Secretary General's special representative ultimately made a brief trip and reported back to the Council. But over the next two months, while the military build-up in the Gulf continued at breakneck speed, the U.S.

continued its efforts to strip the proposed resolution of anything likely to offend Israel.

The U.S. was determined that the enforceable sections of the resolution exclude anything the Israelis would be likely to refuse (which included virtually all of the proposals for protection of Palestinians) to avoid the possibility of Council members proposing sanctions against Tel Aviv to force its compliance with the Council decision — relying on the anti-Iraq sanctions as precedent.

The breathtaking double standard of Washington's UN responses to the Gulf crisis and the occupation of Palestine did not receive much attention in the mainstream U.S. media. In an especially cynical example, *New York Times* reporter Paul Lewis described Washington's effort at gutting the already-weakened fourth draft resolution in an article headlined "U.S. Backs UN Bid Criticizing Israel."

## The United Nations Goes to War

But the long and painful debate over the Palestine resolution also served to divert international attention from the fundamental goal of Washington's UN strategy during that fateful autumn.

With the military build-up well under way, the Bush administration turned to diplomatic weapons in its Gulf arsenal, and the UN became the venue of battle. While UN-watchers' eyes were on the Palestine debate, U.S. eyes remained focused on the Gulf. The goal was a resolution authorizing Bush's war-in-the-making against Iraq, and allowing him to wage that war in the name of the United Nations. The vote was planned for the end of November, the month in which the U.S. held the Council presidency.

It would not be enough, in these circumstances, to win a minimum nine-vote majority on the Council; that would look embarrassingly equivocal. So to ensure a vote that could be spin-mastered to look like an overwhelming endorsement, U.S. diplomats went to work with every economic and political weapon in their considerable arsenal.

Virtually every developing country on the Security Council was offered new economic perks in return for a vote in favor of the U.S. war: Colombia, impoverished Ethiopia, and Zaire (already fully in thrall to the U.S.) were all offered new aid packages, access to World Bank credits or rearrangements of International Monetary Fund grants or loans.

Military deals were cut as well. Ethiopia's government was given access to new military aid after a long denial of arms to that civil war-wracked nation. Colombia was also offered a new package of military assistance.

China was the sole member of the Perm Five not toeing the U.S. line. It was common knowledge among UN-based journalists that China was looking for two major concessions in return for not opposing the U.S. resolution. One was Washington's support for Beijing's return to international diplomatic legitimacy after 18 months of isolation after the Tienanmen Square massacre. The second was economic development aid. On November

28, the day before the vote authorizing the use of force against Iraq, the White House announced a high-profile meeting between President Bush and Chinese Foreign Minister Qian Qichen, the first since Tienanmen Square, to be held the day after the vote. It was designed officially to welcome Beijing back into the international diplomatic fold. China abstained on the resolution. And less than one week later, the World Bank announced that China would be given access to $114 million in economic aid.

As far as Cuba was concerned the U.S. had few options. Washington's 30-year-long diplomatic and economic blockade against Havana meant that the State Department had few diplomatic or economic weapons available to it. But in an interesting example of just how far the U.S. was willing to go to gain support for its resolution, Washington agreed to its first foreign minister-level meeting with Cuba in over 30 years. The brief meeting between Secretary of State James Baker and Foreign Minister Isidoro Malmierca was held at an East Side hotel in Manhattan on the eve of the November 29 vote on the use-of-force resolution. The encounter received little publicity, and officially was deprecated by U.S. diplomats as nothing more than an ordinary meeting between the Council president and a Council member. (The U.S. held the Council presidency in November, and Baker had come to New York to preside personally over the session. He had asked all other Council foreign ministers to attend as well.) But the unprecedented meeting was likely designed to assess the possibility of convincing Cuba to stop its efforts to win other countries away from Washington's war. To no one's surprise, the effort failed.

The operative language of Security Council Resolution 678 "authorizes Member States cooperating with the Government of Kuwait . . . to use all necessary means" to implement prior resolutions "and to restore international peace and security in the area." The resolution passed with a vote of 12 to 2, with one abstention. It was introduced and sponsored by the U.S., the Soviet Union, Great Britain and Canada. The negative votes were cast by Cuba and Yemen; China abstained.

The resolution was designed to give Washington a free hand in beginning hostilities against Iraq. Resolution 678 did not make even a pretense of requiring further UN consultation, let alone UN or multilateral control, in the launching of a war in the Gulf.

And even as the war moves escalated, the U.S. continued deploying its diplomatic weapons. The one Arab member of the Council had voted against Resolution 678. Since its unification in the late 1980s, Yemen had maintained cordial ties with Washington. But now the small and impoverished country was to be made the example to the world of the consequences of violating a U.S.-ordered consensus. Within minutes of the Council vote, Yemen's Ambassador Abdallah Saleh al-Ashtal was informed by a U.S. diplomat in full earshot of the world via the UN broadcasting system, that "that will be the most expensive 'no' vote you ever cast." Three days later the U.S. cut its $70 million aid package to Yemen, one of the poorest countries in the region.

But beyond the pay-offs and threats to the developing countries, the crucial new relationship the U.S. had to forge in the Council was with the Soviets. If the Bush-Baker strategy of using the Security Council to create the appearance of an international consensus was going to work, the world would have to see Moscow fall into line as part of the U.S.-orchestrated new world order. And the strategic weakness rooted in the escalating political and economic crises facing Mikhail Gorbachev and the Soviet leadership made it possible. The arrangement was sweetened with a $4 billion aid package the U.S. negotiated for the Saudi government to pay to Moscow, but it was the Soviet collapse as a superpower capable of influencing events around the world, or at least able to check U.S. ambitions, that set the new conditions.

## Deadline for War

After the passage of Resolution 678, authorizing the use of force against Iraq after January 15, activity quieted down around the United Nations. A majority of the Council had agreed not to meet formally again until after the deadline, to avoid giving Iraq the appearance of weakness.

In the last weeks before the deadline, several other diplomatic initiatives were explored. Iran attempted a negotiated solution, supported by the Soviet Union, and another was proposed by a group of non-aligned leaders led by Daniel Ortega and Rajiv Gandhi. Some approaches seemed to have a plausible chance of averting war; the Iraqi response to several was relatively forthcoming. But each time there seemed to be a potential way out, Washington played a new round of "move the goal-posts," insuring that each new diplomatic effort would fail. It was clear that nothing would be allowed to divert the U.S. march towards war.

On the eve of the January 15 deadline, UN Secretary General Javier Perez de Cuellar made a high-profile last-minute trip to Baghdad to meet with the Iraqi president. When he returned, he closeted himself with the Security Council to report that he had failed to bring peace, that Saddam Hussein had refused to withdraw from Kuwait. The minutes of the SG's hours-long meeting with Saddam Hussein were not released.

But through private diplomatic channels a copy of the secret transcript was obtained, and it shed some light on the SG's reluctance to go public. In a crucial section of the Perez de Cuellar-Hussein meeting, the Iraqi president discussed U.S. influence in the Security Council. The following exchange took place:

> Hussein: We have said and still assert that we seek peace and that we are prepared to shoulder our responsibilities as part of the universal family of the United Nations. But are the others ready to shoulder their responsibilities on the same basis? . . . Note what the President of the United States said: He is talking about procedural matters which do not touch the substance. The substance is of interest to us because we are a vanquished nation. He is talking about the possibility of withdrawing "ground forces" once the "crisis is over." He did not mention anything about withdrawing air or naval forces. He is talking about the

possibility of easing "some" economic measures, and did not talk about the economic measures, all of them.

Perez de Cuellar: These were not my decisions, but the resolutions of the Security Council.

Hussein: These are American resolutions. This is an American age. *What the United States wants at present is the thing that is passed*; and not what the Security Council wants.

Perez de Cuellar: *I agree with you* as much as the matter involves me. (Emphasis added)

That acknowledgement by the Secretary General, that "what the U.S. wants" is what gets passed in the Council, would likely be a source of embarrassment for Perez de Cuellar. But of even more significance is the general tone of the conversation as a whole, and especially the remarks of Saddam Hussein. The Iraqi leader's statements, while not making explicit promises, do not reflect a rejection of diplomatic possibilities. There is a certain amount of flexibility, an apparent willingness to consider diplomatic alternatives based on an Iraqi withdrawal from Kuwait, possibly linked with a broader regional settlement. Whether these possibilities might have become realities will never be known; all that is certain is that the unequivocal "no" indicated in the Secretary General's report to the Security Council is not reflected in the meeting's unauthorized transcript.

### Moving Towards War

The January 15 deadline passed quietly. The following evening, the Security Council was again in session late, again debating a resolution focused on Israeli actions against the Palestinians. Word came to the waiting journalists outside the Council chamber that the Council intended to adjourn for a few hours, and reconvene at 10:00 p.m. that night; the rumor was that a reception was scheduled at the Canadian Mission. It was almost 6:30.

Someone came down and told the cluster of journalists that they had seen "something" on television upstairs. "Something" seemed to be going on in the skies above Baghdad. A few diplomats began to trickle out of the Council chamber, and they too heard the news. News was scant, but responses were quick, and identical for journalists and diplomats alike. All scattered to offices throughout the Secretariat building, in search of televisions.

The UN was taking the world to war, but the UN had nothing to say about it. The thousand points of light in Baghdad's sky were from U.S. planes flown by U.S. pilots dropping U.S. bombs. The United Nations was out of the loop.

During the weeks of the air war, some diplomatic efforts continued. The Soviet Union and Iran attempted to forge a settlement before the ground war began. But the U.S. and Great Britain remained locked in a no-ceasefire, no-withdrawal, nothing-less-than-surrender scenario. And within the U.S.-led coalition among some members of the Security Council, particularly the Soviet Union, opposition to the Washington-London no-compromise axis was growing.

Moscow was willing to accept Iraq's agreement to withdraw from Kuwait under the terms set by Resolution 660. The U.S.-British position at the time was that that wasn't good enough, that Baghdad must accept and implement all resolutions simultaneously. Soviet Ambassador Yuli Voront-sov stated that while he was "in favor of Iraq accepting all 12 UN resolutions, 660 is the one we started with."

When Moscow indicated an openness to accept Iraq's withdrawal, the U.S. added new terms, dashing any hope of avoiding a ground war. Bush demanded that the statement regarding withdrawal be made personally by President Saddam Hussein, that the statement simultaneously accept all relevant UN resolutions, and, significantly, that withdrawing Iraqi troops must leave their weapons behind. Otherwise, Bush stated, there would be no ceasefire and retreating soldiers would continue to be targeted by U.S. and allied forces.

Saddam Hussein answered with a speech calling on his forces to withdraw from Kuwait, but throughout the day Iraqi soldiers trying to retreat were bombarded with U.S. cluster-bombs.

In a closed-door all-night Security Council meeting on February 28, some discussions apparently focused on the question of a ceasefire. Soviet officials in Moscow at the highest level went on record in support an immediate ceasefire. Deputy Foreign Minister Alexander Belonogov stated that "we would like to hope such a declaration of the Security Council would be unanimous and that it would facilitate the speediest possible end to bloodshed and an end to hostilities." Gorbachev's spokesman, Vitaly Ignatenko, supported the ceasefire idea, saying that "it is in everyone's interest that the war end today; Saddam Hussein has practically thrown out the white flag, he has capitulated." Gorbachev himself suggested that superpower relations were "still very fragile," and hinted that U.S.-Soviet relations might be at stake in the settlement of the Gulf War.

This apparent Soviet commitment to a ceasefire revived talk at the UN about the possibility of splits within the U.S.-led anti-Iraq coalition. Western diplomats, including several usually genial press attachés, were aggressively outspoken throughout the day in defending the no-ceasefire position. Sir David Hannay, Britain's ambassador, described the situation as one in which the "good news is that Iraq accepts 660; the bad news is that it only accepts 660."

As had become the norm in the Security Council, U.S. wishes carried the day, diplomacy was left behind, and the air war took to the ground. Yemen's ambassador Abdallah Saleh al-Ashtal, dismayed with the UN failure to reach a political solution, noted, "this is the only time the Security Council has been reluctant to facilitate the withdrawal of an occupying force in compliance with its own resolution."

### The Non-Ceasefire Halt in Hostilities

The UN war came and went, with the UN having very little to say about it. The center of gravity remained in Washington. Resolution 678 had been designed to give Washington a UN credential but a free hand in its war against Iraq. The use of military force was unlimited by UN oversight of duration or destructiveness.

In early March, the U.S. introduced Resolution 686, calling for a temporary halt in hostilities. But it explicitly did not call for a ceasefire, and there were rumors of some discontent among Council members. A now-familiar pressure campaign swung into action.

The vote had been expected throughout the late afternoon hours of March 3, and as the meeting stretched into the early evening, journalists and diplomats alike were growing impatient. It appeared that the ambassadors of both Zimbabwe and Ecuador, two important non-aligned members of the Council, were late.

When they finally showed up, the vote took place quickly. Both Zimbabwe and Ecuador voted with the U.S. According to knowledgeable diplomatic sources, both ambassadors were late because they had been closeted at their respective missions, getting last minute instructions on how to respond to Washington's latest pressure tactics: unspecified yet classic threats to Ecuador, and irresistible offers of cheap Kuwaiti oil to impoverished Zimbabwe. The pressure worked. The resolution passed.

Finally, Resolution 687, calling for a stringently regulated ceasefire, was put on the table on April 3. The resolution did not hold out much of a promise for peace, however. As Yemen's Ambassador al-Ashtal described it, "We want a situation of peace — with this ceasefire we are still in a state of war. We need peace."

The resolution imposed drastic controls on post-war Iraq. Along with the expected destruction of Iraq's chemical and biological weapons, it continued indefinitely an absolute international embargo against *any* arms sales to Iraq.

Opposition to the resolution centered on its failure to place arms control in a regional context. While the preamble refers to "the objective of the establishment of a nuclear weapons free zone in the region of the Middle East," the resolution's binding terms refer only to Iraq's weapons. No mention was made of the 200 high-density nuclear bombs possessed by Israel, the only nuclear power in the region.

Significantly, economic sanctions remained in place, ensuring that Iraq remain financially dependent. The resolution allowed Iraq to begin oil production but not its export. When exporting oil was finally to be allowed, an unstated percentage of the income was designated to pay compensation for Iraq's war-generated debts. While easing the controls on food and medicine, the resolution did not allow Iraqi access to vitally needed consumer goods and the equipment needed to rebuild the country's devastated infrastructure. Further, by denying Iraq the right to sell its oil, the resolution ensured its inability to purchase food and medical supplies.

One of the most hotly contested portions of the U.S. draft, of special concern to the non-aligned caucus within the Security Council, was the question of the Iraq-Kuwait border. Resolution 687 demanded that the two countries accept the border indicated in the minutes of a bilateral meeting in 1963, which had never been ratified and remained in dispute. Iraqi diplomatic sources, as well as non-aligned members of the Council, stated the view that the appropriate venue for resolving such conflicts must be the International Court of Justice, not the Security Council.

There was a great deal of unease in the Council about the precedent the resolution would set. Never had the UN been put in the position of guaranteeing a disputed border not accepted by the two parties.

The overall impact of the resolution was to keep Iraq economically dependent and militarily vulnerable. And by leaving economic sanctions in place, the U.S.-drafted resolution virtually ensured continued instability inside Iraq, as the population struggled to rebuild shattered lives.

But despite its unpopularity with the Council, the vote supporting the U.S. was strong. Only Cuba voted no. Even Yemen was only able to abstain, along with Ecuador. The rest of the Council voted yes.

## The Post-War United Nations

The passage and implementation of the ceasefire resolution embodied the end of the UN's center-stage role in the Gulf crisis. While it would remain engaged in the post-war chaos engulfing the region, trying to orchestrate relief for the Kurds and verification of Iraq's weapon destruction, there was no longer the illusion of UN decision-making power.

Much of the future of the United Nations still lies with the United States. Washington's high-profile projection of the UN as a part of its global strategy in the Gulf was a new, almost experimental, approach. It is likely to be some time before U.S. policymakers come to a consensus assessment on the strategic value of the UN.

In the immediate post-Gulf war period, the question of the UN's role in the world is on the front burner. Debates regarding selection of the next secretary general, the composition of the Security Council, and other issues remain unresolved. A challenge to Washington's double standard selectivity on enforcement of UN resolutions remains high on the non-aligned agenda.

The Bush administration succeeded during the Gulf crisis in holding the UN hostage to its drive towards war. In doing so, however, it also opened up the Pandora's box of UN potential — in a post-new world order world of true multilateralism and a return of the UN to the goals most, at least, of its founders envisioned: an instrument to prevent war and preserve the peace.

# PART THREE

# Weathering the Storm:

# Reaction in the U.S.

# 10

## The Warrior Culture

*Barbara Ehrenreich*

In what we like to think of as "primitive" warrior cultures, the passage to manhood requires the blooding of a spear, the taking of a scalp or head. Among the Masai of eastern Africa, the North American Plains Indians and dozens of other pretechnological peoples, a man could not marry until he had demonstrated his capacity to kill in battle. Leadership too in a warrior culture is typically contingent on military prowess and wrapped in the mystique of death. In the Solomon Islands a chief's importance could be reckoned by the number of skulls posted around his door, and it was the duty of the Aztec kings to nourish the gods with the hearts of human captives.

All warrior peoples have fought for the same high-sounding reasons: honor, glory or revenge. The nature of their real and perhaps not conscious motivations is a subject of much debate. Some anthropologists postulate a murderous instinct, almost unique among living species, in human males. Others discern a materialistic motive behind every fray: a need for slaves, grazing land or even human flesh to eat. Still others point to the similarities between war and other male pastimes — the hunt and outdoor sports — and suggest that it is boredom, ultimately, that stirs men to fight.

But in a warrior culture it hardly matters which motive is most basic. Aggressive behavior is rewarded whether or not it is innate to the human psyche. Shortages of resources are habitually taken as occasions for armed offensives, rather than for hard thought and innovation. And war, to a warrior people, is of course the highest adventure, the surest antidote to malaise, the endlessly repeated theme of legend, song, religious myth and personal quest for meaning. It is how men die and what they find to live for.

"You must understand that Americans are a warrior nation," Senator Daniel Patrick Moynihan told a group of Arab leaders in early September, one month into the Middle East crisis. He said this proudly, and he may, without thinking through the ugly implications, have told the truth. In many ways, in outlook and behavior the U.S. has begun to act like a primitive warrior culture.

We seem to believe that leadership is expressed, in no small part, by a willingness to cause the deaths of others. After the U.S. invasion of Panama, President Bush exulted that no one could call him "timid"; he was at last a "macho man." The press, in even more primal language, hailed him for succeeding in an "initiation rite" by demonstrating his "willingness to shed blood."

For lesser offices too we apply the standards of a warrior culture. Female candidates are routinely advised to overcome the handicap of their gender by talking "tough." Thus, for example, Dianne Feinstein, gubernatorial candidate in California, embraced capital punishment, while Colorado senatorial candidate Josie Heath found it necessary to announce that although she is the mother of an 18-year-old son, she was prepared to vote for war. Male candidates in some of the fall 1991 contests found their military records under scrutiny. No one expected them, as elected officials in a civilian government, to pick up a spear or a sling and fight. But they must state, at least, their willingness to have another human killed.

More tellingly, we are unnerved by peace and seem to find it boring. When the cold war ended, we found no reason to celebrate. Instead we heated up the "war on drugs." What should have been a public-health campaign, focused on the persistent shame of poverty, became a new occasion for martial rhetoric and muscle flexing. Months later, when the Berlin Wall fell and communism collapsed throughout Europe, we Americans did not dance in the streets. What we did, according to the networks, was change the channel to avoid the news. Nonviolent revolutions do not uplift us, and the loss of mortal enemies only seems to leave us empty and bereft.

Our collective fantasies center on mayhem, cruelty and violent death. Loving images of the human body — especially of bodies seeking pleasure or expressing love — inspire us with the urge to censor. Our preference is for warrior themes: the lone fighting man, bandoliers across his naked chest, mowing down lesser men in gusts of automatic-weapon fire. Only a real war seems to revive our interest in real events. With the Iraqi crisis, the networks report, ratings for news shows rose again — even higher than they were for Panama.

And as in any primitive warrior culture, our warrior elite takes pride of place. Social crises multiply numbingly — homelessness, illiteracy, epidemic disease — and our leaders tell us solemnly that nothing can be done. There is no money. We are poor, not rich, a debtor nation. Meanwhile, nearly a third of the federal budget flows, even in moments of peace, to the warriors and their weaponmakers. When those priorities are questioned, some new "crisis" dutifully arises to serve as another occasion for armed and often unilateral intervention.

Then, with Operation Desert Shield-Desert Storm, our leaders were reduced to begging foreign powers for the means to support our warrior class. It did not seem to occur to us that the other great northern powers —

Japan, Germany, the Soviet Union — might not have found the stakes so high or the crisis quite so threatening. It did not penetrate our imagination that in a world where the powerful, industrialized nation-states are at last at peace, there might be other ways to face down a pint-size Third World warrior state than with massive force of arms. Nor have we begun to see what an anachronism we are in danger of becoming: a warrior nation in a world that pines for peace, a high-tech state with the values of a warrior band.

A leftist might blame "imperialism"; a right-winger would call our problem "internationalism." But an anthropologist, taking the long view, might say this is just what warriors do. Intoxicated by their own drumbeats and war songs, fascinated by the glint of steel and the prospect of blood, they will go forth, time and again, to war.

# 11

## Peacetime Militarism: An Epidemic Disorder

*Jack O'Dell*

"Though this be madness, yet there's method in it."
— Hamlet

When the American war in the Persian Gulf ended, at least in its initial phase, a sense of relief emerged among the people of the United States. The military authorities prepared to implement a delayed ceasefire, the exchange of prisoners of war took place and other activities confirmed the termination of certain military hostilities. But by early spring of 1991, it was a "peace" whose reality was far less substantial than hopes would justify.

It was a war that was criminally wasteful as measured both by the cost in human lives and precious resources, not to mention the spending of a billion dollars a day by the American government. To be sure, U.S. families were relieved that the number of deaths and casualties sustained by U.S. forces was much lower than anticipated. This should not, however, obscure the painful fact that thousands of Iraqi civilians were killed by American saturation bombing of their cities and villages, and tens of thousands have died from disease and starvation since the ceasefire, due to the devastation the bombing wrought on the Iraqi civilian infrastructure. This unconscionable slaughter stands in the lineage of Hiroshima, Mylai in Vietnam, and Panama. The legacy of bitterness, pain and disillusionment it has created in the Middle East towards U.S. policy, will undoubtedly bear bitter fruit for years to come.

Yet this international tragedy holds some important lessons for the American people as well, and the impact will inevitably prove to be profound. The Gulf crisis brought the Middle East into the center of the American national consciousness. This community of nations is no longer a mere footnote to the agenda of the peace and justice movement, or its efforts at fundamentally changing U.S. policy of intervention. Political awareness of the Middle East and the aspirations of its peoples has been qualitatively expanded, in the course of the events following August 1990. Primarily through the efforts of the peace movement, millions have acquired a more solid understanding of the larger geo-political objectives that are the motor of U.S. foreign policy.

There is no deeper commitment held by the people of the United States than their concern with maintaining the norms of a civilized society and steadily improving its democratic quality as a legacy to future generations. To accept the Gulf War as the great American success story that shapes the politics and culture of the U.S. for the decade of the nineties would be both deceptive and dangerous. It also runs directly contrary to those democratic commitments and hopes. It would invite a government policy based upon more-of-the-same: a prescription for the American people to be given a new "foreign enemy" every other year, in preparation for endless military adventures. This has nothing whatsoever to do with genuine requirements for the military defense of the country.

Recognizing that all too often the first casualty of war is truth itself, the peace movement accepted responsibility for activating a public debate of the issues involved. Through teach-ins on campuses, town hall meetings in the community, participating in radio broadcasts and organizing mass demonstrations, peace activists initiated a campaign to inform public opinion and encourage public debate on the Bush administration's policy. The churches, student groups and community organizations that had been involved in efforts to secure the peace dividend, and existing "solidarity" organizations, all these served as vehicles for reaching constituencies all across the country. Newly formed groups that emerged, like the Military Families Support Network and others, added strength and capability. All this gave people who had reservations about the policy a sense of strength, coming from the knowledge that they were not alone. This conviction was reinforced by the realization that people were also marching and engaging in similar activities in Paris, London, Morocco, Stockholm, Tokyo and many other countries across the world.

The peace movement's basic objective was to prevent the military build-up which the Bush administration had ordered from escalating into a full scale war with all the potential tragedy that held. It obviously did not succeed in meeting that objective. Nevertheless, during the course of organizing, public opinion was steadily shifting to the side of peace and an insistence on a political solution to the problems. In the face of this trend, the administration decided to go to war anyway. Rational debate, in which informed opinion was being molded and motivating responsible citizens to insist upon government accountability, was viewed as a dangerous trend that had to be scrapped, and replaced by jingoism.

There was never any doubt that the U.S., with the largest arsenal of weapons of mass destruction in the history of the world, could score a military victory over Iraq, a nation of 18 million people the size of California. Quickly, that which was never in doubt was achieved. But this should hardly have been cause for the triumphal spirit of jingoism that was then introduced into the political atmosphere.

The war was unnecessary. It resulted from the fact that all peaceful diplomatic efforts at resolving the crisis arising from Iraq's invasion, military occupation, and annexation of Kuwait, were rejected by the Bush administration, in its determination to pursue a military solution. History will judge this adventure as an unjust military aggression by the United States against yet another small nation — this time 7,000 miles away in western Asia. When the full truth is known to the world, it may reveal that the U.S. was a party to one of the great war crimes of the twentieth century.

The assumption that the use of military force was right because it accomplished the objective, at a cost *to Americans* that was lower than expected, is a negative contribution to morality in international relations between countries. It remains a major responsibility of the peace movement to challenge this assumption, especially because it is intended, for all practical purposes, to become one of the philosophical pillars of the Bush administration's "new world order." Martin Luther King, Jr., nearly a quarter of a century ago, touched this problem in his cogent observation: "America is a society whose technology has outstripped its civilization. We have guided missiles and misguided men."

The movement, from the very beginning of the crisis, condemned Iraq's invasion of Kuwait as unjustified and a violation of international law. Majority opinion gave full support to UN resolutions calling for the immediate withdrawal of Iraqi troops from Kuwait and the beginning of negotiations between the two countries to resolve the differences.

A diplomacy of peace would have been guided by acknowledging the reality that the dispute between Iraq and Kuwait was rooted in a colonial past. The seeds were planted in an era when the Western powers were carving up the Middle East as they had done Africa; as a means of securing their respective spheres of influence at the expense of the inhabitants of those lands. In this context, Britain carved out Iraq, the land of ancient Mesopotamia, from three provinces of the Ottoman Empire after the latter's defeat in the First World War. Then it carved Kuwait out of southern Iraq and installed King Faisal in Iraq as an absolute monarch. The borders between these two states were not formalized until 1961. France carved out Lebanon from Syria in the same period. The Western powers who recently joined in a grand alliance in the Gulf War are themselves, then, a primary source of the problem.

What the Bush administration was defending in the Middle East during the Gulf crisis were the values and symbols of absolutist monarchy, wealth, corporate greed, and the racist traditions of Western colonialism. The act of verbally drawing lines in the sand, accompanied by official bellicose rhetoric, serves to underscore one of the most striking realities of the modern age: rampant militarism and racism have become inseparable. As "the greatest purveyor of violence in the world today" the American government is counting on its ability to maintain an atmosphere of triumphant chauvinism, as a way of diverting public attention away from the urgent need to address this reality.

The economic and cultural impact of the Gulf War on the United States will be far-reaching. Billions of dollars have been added to the deficit of a country that was already three trillion dollars in debt before August 1990.

Family life in many areas has been disrupted due to the call-up of many reservists. In some cases, children were left without either parent to take care of them. A Defense Department official, interviewed by CBS' Garrick Utley, admitted during the war that the Pentagon had no contingency plans to deal with the issue of the children of servicepeople sent overseas.

The Gulf War has aggravated an already dismal picture of layoffs, declining real income of wage earners, and a farm crisis, all of which had been developing since the early years of the Reagan/Bush administration. More than 1.5 million Americans lost their jobs between June 1990 and February 1991.[1] This will inevitably result in many of these working people losing their health insurance. Some will be vulnerable to any serious illness, and that could further push them into the growing ranks of the homeless. This poorest stratum of our working class communities is reduced to living a hand-to-mouth existence on the streets of our urban centers, sleeping under bridges or in subway or railway stations. In rural America some are living in abandoned farm houses or caves. Social services in many small towns, as well as in some urban centers, have been stripped of personnel in hospitals, fire departments, and other areas to meet the needs of this emergency.

The Gulf crisis has been a big blow to the living standards of the farmers in the Midwest states. The rise in the prices of gasoline and propane have increased the cost of production. U.S. farmers are caught between the GATT* agricultural policy of reducing farm prices, which the Bush administration is pushing, and the Gulf military build-up which led to war. Our farm communities probably will be feeling the economic effects of this for the remainder of the decade.

Small business bankruptcies, now at the highest rate in seven years, have escalated in cities and towns whose local economies have become addicted to military spending. Sending troops to the Persian Gulf stripped them of their customers. The Gulf War has contributed to the downward spiral to ruin among all strata of the working population, including sections of the middle-class.


## One, Two, Three, Four, Kill Hussein![2]

Recruits in Fort Benning, Georgia, took up this chant as part of their military training from the beginning of the Gulf crisis. Identifying all Iraqis with Saddam Hussein is just one example of the climate of racist violence that was stimulated and activated by the government and media through the propaganda that demonizes Arabs. Arab-Americans were subjected to FBI harassment on the grounds that they were "suspected terrorists."[3] Mob violence against them in their neighborhoods, bombing businesses they own — these were among the experiences to which they were being exposed during this period. In some areas of the country with substantial Arab-American populations, even the public school classroom became an

* General Agreement on Trade and Tariffs

area of tension as slander and poisonous stereotypes were propagated. As in the case of our nation's previous involvement in the Vietnam and Korean Wars, the Gulf War served to introduce into the American English language, already overcrowded with racist obscenities, yet another set of derogatory terms, this time applied to the Arab community.

The seeds for these epithets are ever present in the soil of institutional racism and the history of economic plunder and deprivation it has served. Nevertheless, in a period when nationalistic jingoism accompanies a reckless military adventure abroad, strengthened racism provides the fuel for the war machine. It is as vital to the cultivation of the instinct to kill and destroy other people and their achievements as the fuel for the tanks and other mobile military hardware.[4]

We are reminded that when U.S. troops returned home from World War II, Black servicemen often faced lynch mobs in the South. When U.S. troops were sent to Korea, another invasion organized through the manipulation of the UN Security Council, they found Confederate flags, the emblem of slavery, flying from U.S. battleships alongside the Stars and Stripes. And they returned home to the repressive era of McCarthyism. In the 1990s, rampant police brutality, as epitomized in the recently recorded beating of Rodney King in Los Angeles, gang warfare in the neighborhoods frequently related to the flourishing drug traffic, violence experienced by women students on college campuses, these are everyday occurences in our nation's life. This climate of dehumanization is fed and encouraged by the organized violence of the state, as implemented by its war machine. To separate the random violence and chaos of daily life at home from the organized, systematized violence of the war machine, as it functions abroad, is to overlook the real life organic connection between them.

The plight of Vietnam veterans is well-known. Many are today among the jobless and homeless in our cities and small towns. After years of therapy and medical rehabilitation treatment that had helped them to heal their lives, some Vietnam vets were reportedly going back to the hospitals during the Gulf crisis because they began experiencing a recurrence of post-traumatic stress syndrome when the news of the aerial/ground war was announced.

The troops coming home from the Gulf War discovered the V.A. hospitals were already overcrowded, understaffed, and facing further financial cutbacks proposed by the Commander-in-Chief. After the ticker tape carnival was over and the balloons and yellow ribbons faded away, sober reality began to reassert itself. All the problems they left behind when sent to the Persian Gulf were still there, and in some areas conditions grew worse, due to the neglect imposed by the military priority.

### An Official Campaign of Public Deception

One of the most serious developments in U.S. national life that accompanied the military build-up and war in the Persian Gulf is the campaign of disinformation that consistently encouraged us to believe one thing, when in fact another was really happening. For our democracy to function, one of the cornerstone requisites is the right of the public to know what the government is doing, as the basis for its accountability to the people. Yet the people of the United States have seen over the course of two wars in the last two years — Panama and the Persian Gulf — a carefully orchestrated effort to deceive the public by half-truths, disinformation, and outright falsehoods presented as truth. Sometimes the media are muzzled by the military, a process which began as early as the invasion of Grenada. Sometimes their access to information and their mobility to acquire it are restricted, as in the case of the invasion of Panama. And sometimes it appears the media have become willing accomplices to government policy of keeping the truth from the people.

Early on, in preparations for the Gulf War, we were told that the deployment of 200,000 troops to Saudi Arabia was for the defense of that country, when in fact it is now clear that it was part of the preparation for an offensive military thrust against Iraq. The public was told the troops were being sent to defend the freedom of Kuwait while the public was told nothing of the actual lack of freedom in pre-invasion Kuwait, such as the fact that its parliament had been abolished by the Emir in 1986.

President Mitterand of France suggested, in his speech to the United Nations in September, that the objective of the international community should be to restore the sovereignty of Kuwait, but also to give the Kuwaiti people the opportunity to decide what kind of government they wanted to live under, through UN-supervised free elections. The Bush administration rejected that proposal out of hand. U.S. policy has always stood behind the restoration of the Emir and the al-Sabah family.

We were told the Bush administration was using the military build-up to enforce all the resolutions of the United Nations relating to the Gulf crisis. In point of fact, the very first resolution passed by the UN Security Council (UN Resolution 660) has as one of its three points the emphasis on negotiations between Iraq and Kuwait to settle their differences. It is clear that the policy pursued by the Bush administration was to reject and at all times discourage negotiations at any level, out of fear that such negotiations would ultimately make the military option unnecessary.

The Bush administration consistently described the coalition of countries it led as "the world against Saddam Hussein." This coalition is made up of some 28 other countries at the most. The UN General Assembly has 160 member states, and this international body has never voted on a resolution to support a military invasion of Iraq.

The government spent a billion dollars a day of taxpayers' money on Operation Desert Storm, but when Manuel Rivera was killed in the Gulf by "friendly fire," the government refused his parents' request for air travel arrangements that would allow them to be flown from the South Bronx to the funeral at his home in Los Angeles. Examples of official bureaucratic callousness towards the families of servicemen and women who have died in the Gulf War are in plentiful supply.

Thousands of young men and women from the apartheid-style Black townships, Hispanic barrios, and rural poverty areas across the country have voluntarily enlisted in the armed forces of the nation in search of hope and opportunity that were not present in their communities. Enticed by the Pentagon's public relations slogan, "Be All You Can Be in the Army," they set for themselves limited goals, such as earning enough money for college tuition and getting some specialized training. Once inducted, they found themselves serving under a President and Commander-in-Chief who vetoed the Civil Rights Bill of 1990 and whose Department of Education recently took preliminary steps towards abolishing minority college scholarships.

Troops recruited from the African-American community today are the sons and daughters of men and women who, along with their compatriots, fought to protect the U.S. from Nazi fascism during the Second World War. Unlike their white compatriots, they faced the daily insult and humiliation of segregation in the Armed Forces. Now, two generations later, their children and grandchildren face the same dilemma. The form of the dilemma has changed, but the substance has not.

One-third of the African-American community in the U.S. lives in poverty, and nearly half of the children under age 15 are trapped in that condition.[5] An unemployment rate that is double the national average has plagued the community for so long it has become an accepted feature of American life that neither government nor private industry addresses with any seriousness. What did the Gulf War, with whatever sacrifices it entailed, contribute to the solving of these longstanding and urgent problems? The search for an answer to this question was undoubtedly a factor in the clearsighted "Open Letter" addressed to President Bush by the National Emergency Summit of African-American Leadership. This meeting was convened by a number of prominent religious leaders representing several denominations at the historic Abyssinian Baptist Church in Harlem early in 1991. The following is a quote from the first few paragraphs:

Dear President Bush:

We, . . . do herewith declare our opposition to the war in the Gulf on moral, spiritual, humanitarian, economic and political grounds. Further, we are outraged that you allowed the use of January 15th, the birthday of one of the world's foremost peacemakers and apostles of nonviolence, as the deadline for declaring war in the Middle East.

Let us, first, be very clear and forthright. We affirm that we have a moral imperative to speak out and take action against the war in the Gulf. This war is not a clean, sanitized, high-tech display of allied superior military power . . . We are outraged at the countless number of innocent civilians who have been killed as a result of wanton military action. This is not a "just war."

. . . The United States should take the initiative for peace not war. The problems of the Middle East are complex and interrelated. There is no military solution to these problems. It is senseless to continue to waste human life in such futile effort. We respect and value the lives of all U.S. and allied troops deployed in the Persian Gulf region. We also respect and value the lives of all of the peoples of the Middle East. Our opposition to this war, therefore, is not a question of "supporting the troops." We do question and oppose the brutal immorality of the war in the Gulf.

We urge the convening of an international conference that brings all the parties in the region to the conference table. Our primary objective must be peace with justice for all the people in the region . . . including Iraqis, Kuwaitis, Egyptians, Jordanians, Palestinians and Israelis. There will be no peace in the Middle East until there is justice for all parties, and the issue of poverty amidst affluence is addressed . . .

The reference in this document to the January 15th birthdate of Dr King reminds us that, to add insult to injury, the ground war phase of this allied invasion was ordered by President Bush on February 23, the birthdate of W.E.B. DuBois.

## Turning a Minus Into a Plus

Racism, militarism, and poverty, in their collective impact, remain the incorrigible pathology stalking the present and clouding the future of the U.S. They are systemic ills and will certainly not yield to an exhibition of waving flags and yellow ribbons. These deep seated problems have plagued American society, in varying degrees of intensity, for most of the twentieth century. We are reminded this has been a century which was ushered in with the racist/colonial doctrine of "manifest destiny." In the modern evolution of this multiple scourge, militarism is the spearhead, or warhead, depending upon which metaphor one prefers. Racism is the fuel, and poverty, both material and spiritual, the inevitable consequence. These are the signposts to the new world order.

As Americans welcome their relatives, neighbors, and friends home from the Persian Gulf, the peace movement also seeks to enlist them and the valuable experiences they embody in the struggle for a better America, a just society, and a peaceful world. President Dwight Eisenhower warned the U.S. of the growing power and centralized authority of the military-industrial complex in the country, more than 30 years ago. The Bush administration, as a faithful servant of this formidable center of power, is basking in a contrived moment of glory that will prove to be short-lived. The people of the United States have an agenda of hopes and dreams that require peace and development as a prerequisite for their fulfillment.

The administration had high stakes in and preferred a military victory in the Persian Gulf, because the administration wanted to send a message to the world that the U.S. must be accepted as the world's policeman. This is the centerpiece in the proposed new world order. Yet this latter proposal is an illusion; a mirage in the Desert Storm. It is not new since it rests upon the old assumptions of Western arrogance and "white supremacy." It is not the world. It is a deal between a couple dozen countries and their respective elites to control the resources and human capital of the rest of the world. It is not order but a prescription for chaos and instability abroad and an acceleration of the pattern of social ruin here at home.

Knowing the awesome destructive capacity of the military machine the U.S. has built up over 40 years of the Cold War, we recognize the stakes are high for the peace movement as well. The movement is guided by a world outlook that recognizes peace as more than merely the absence of war; it is the presence of justice. That indivisible connection between peace and justice engages the movement in a struggle for a different national morality that will free the U.S. from its obsession with militarism. The struggle to meet this challenge and resolve the moral-spiritual crisis which confronts the nation will allow the U.S. to make a giant leap toward fulfilling the revolutionary promise of the Declaration of Independence.

## The Crisis of National Leadership

The debate on the use of force finally held in Congress was useful as an assist in educating the public. These discussions acknowledged that the administration had shifted into high-gear by escalating the military build-up immediately after the elections in early November. In light of this, the decision by the Democratic Party leadership to delay holding these Congressional debates until *after* the administration had secured the November 29th vote in the UN "authorizing the use of force" is, to say the least, a default in leadership. Given the urgency of the situation, a vigorous debate in Congress in mid-November (rather than in January) would have strengthened the public effort at guaranteeing the political solution was chosen.

The people of the United States have witnessed a succession of Democrat administrations, supported by Republican conservatives, lead the nation into military invasions of Vietnam, the Dominican Republic and Korea, over a period of twenty years. We have also experienced a succession of Republican administrations, supported by conservative Democrats, that have led us into military invasions of Cambodia, Grenada, Panama and Iraq over a period of twenty years, in addition to financing the military destruction of Beirut and southern Lebanon by Israel. Military aggression as public policy is truly a bipartisan enterprise and it is in the highest national interest that the American people break this reactionary monopoly of the nation's political life.

This confrontation with militarism, in all of its aspects, is of central importance to mobilizing the national will required to address the profound problems and needs of the human rights agenda. Having recently had the Pentagon admit that the U.S. military dropped 88,500 tons of explosives on Iraq,[6] we hold as a self-evident truth, that this is a sickness, not a source of national glory.

The people of the United States embody an enormous reservoir of human potential in talent and creativity, and the country also has the material means to solve the problems of homelessness, to provide health care for all, to clean up and protect the environment, to end racism and the daily violence against women in our society, and to rescue American children from the crude, many-sided forms of destruction that haunt their daily existence.

The Gulf War is one more clearly definable lesson in the function of racism and its alter-ego, national chauvinism, in the political culture of the U.S. Its role is to mask and obscure reality as a means of confusing and disorienting millions of people so that they are uncertain about their real interest, and are led to embrace false symbols rather than true substance. In some countries this has led to the national tragedy of fascism. Only deep awareness and the unbreakable will to resist can prevent this tragedy from repeating itself.

As we stand on the threshold of a new millennium in the world this is indeed a defining moment in American national history as well. What we do beyond this moment of crisis coming out of the Gulf War will define American morality and the national character in a clear and unmistakable way. It was Martin Luther King who cautioned us in his Riverside Church speech, "The world expects of America a maturity we may not be able to achieve." The peace and justice movement, in all its diverse organizational and community constituencies, is the primary vehicle of struggle for the long overdue achievement of that maturity. In its growing strength and unlimited expansive possibilities it can become the historical replacement of the military-industrial-media complex. As such, it is the custodian of the world's expectations that the people of the U.S. will join the international community as a partner in peace and world development.

## Notes

1. Figures on unemployment are those announced by the U.S. Commerce Department. Comments on the farm crisis are from the North American Farm Alliance in Nebraska.
2. The Fort Benning chant as viewed on CNN.
3. The Center for Constitutional Rights in New York is handling cases of Arab-Americans' harassment.
4. On the historical development of racism and militarism, see *Beyond Survival*, published by South End Press, Boston.
5. See reports of the Children's Defense Fund for a picture of the African-American situation.
6. The bombing figure cited is from the report given by the U.S. Air Force General at the news briefing in Riyadh, following announcement of the temporary ceasefire in early April 1991.

*This article is an edited version of a larger work.

# 12

## The Storm at Home

### Max Elbaum

From the onset of the 1990–91 Gulf crisis, George Bush's administration waged political and ideological war at home just as methodically as it prepared for military action against Iraq. Winning domestic support for the use of force was crucial not only for achieving Washington's goals in the Middle East. At stake was Bush's fundamental strategy of relying on military power to secure U.S. hegemony in the "new world order." That strategy would be impossible if the ability to employ massive violence was checked by domestic political considerations. So the United States' 20-year-old Vietnam Syndrome had to be crushed as thoroughly as Saddam Hussein.

Setting such an objective required the administration to take on formidable opponents. For starters, Bush had to contend with major sections of the country's political and economic elite who held an alternative vision of the U.S. role in the post-Cold War world. In contrast to Bush and his "geo-strategists," these "geo-economists"* saw maintaining U.S. superpower status as principally dependent upon rebuilding economic dynamism relative to Japan and Western Europe. They feared the political consequences of waging war and worried that bloated sums poured into the military-industrial complex would weaken U.S. capacity to compete with its capitalist rivals. These establishment critics had steadily gained influence during the latter half of the 1980s, as confrontation with the Soviet Union receded, competition with Japan and Western Europe intensified, and deterioration of the U.S. social and physical infrastructure accelerated.

Bush was also up against broad-based popular reluctance to go to war. The invasions of Grenada and Panama had proved that the public would support military interventions that were short and not costly in U.S. lives. But opposition to U.S. ground troops engaging in what might prove a lengthy war, and skepticism about official rationales for such adventures,

---

* The terms are Michael Klare's, from his excellent article in *The Nation*, October 15, 1990.

retained a powerful grip. A decade of jingoism under Reagan and Bush had chipped away at this legacy of Vietnam, but had far from eliminated it.

Of course Bush and his inner circle also remembered Vietnam. The administration's entire campaign for hearts and minds at home was based on the lessons it drew from the failures of Lyndon Johnson and Richard Nixon. For Bush, Colin Powell, James Baker and company, the prime lesson was that more sophisticated use of military power, media manipulation, demagogy and anti-Arab racism could make war palatable once again.

## The Anti-War Movement

Bush's most determined opponent in the battle to affect popular sentiment and influence policy debate was the grassroots-based anti-war movement. In less than seven months — from Bush's early-August troop deployment to the February 27, 1991 ceasefire — this movement generated a whirlwind of activism. At its peak in January it brought over half a million people onto the streets and influenced the thinking of millions of others. The anti-war movement made numerous misassessments and had a number of serious weaknesses. But under difficult circumstances it mounted a powerful challenge to Bush's drive towards war.

The movement was politically heterogeneous. Its bottom-line unity was opposition to U.S. military action in the Gulf. A measure of consensus was achieved: war would be immensely destructive in human terms; it would solve none of the longstanding political problems in the Middle East; it would divert resources from pressing social needs at home; it would exacerbate racism towards the Arab world, the Third World generally, and people of color at home; it would be an ecological disaster. But different parts of the movement gave these points drastically different weights, and on key questions — especially the link between the Gulf crisis and Israel's continuing occupation of Palestinian land — certain sections conciliated the administration line.

Like the Bush administration, the anti-war movement drew many lessons from Vietnam. Thousands of veterans of the earlier movement threw themselves into protests. The anti-Gulf War movement got off to a faster start and was, by and large, more politically sophisticated than its 1960s predecessor. But this was a movement rooted in the conditions of 1990–91 — with economic, demographic, cultural and political realities very different from 25 years earlier.

## Bush's Victory

The war's outcome changed those realities again. The post-war world was a different place than before the Gulf War, and so was the terrain of U.S. politics. Bush largely achieved his goal of winning a decisive domestic victory over the Vietnam Syndrome. On March 1, the day Bush officially proclaimed that Syndrome dead, his approval rating reached 91%, the highest any president has attained since the week of the Nazi surrender in

World War II. Even as newspapers began to report that Iraqi dead might number up to 200,000, the country experienced an orgy of victory fervor complete with hosannas about "how few people" were killed in the war. The spectacle reflected Bush's ability to manipulate popular opinion — but it was also a sobering reminder of the profound racism and immorality embedded in U.S. political culture.

Still, all the flag-waving could not turn the clock back to 1950. The Third World was not about to retreat quietly to colonial status, nor was it likely that the U.S. economy would again enjoy a 20-year boom. The Middle East was not "pacified," and soon all the regional problems exacerbated by Bush's war began to reemerge. The multi-billion dollar war bill came due, adding more problems to a society already scarred by widespread poverty and social crisis. With the fading of the immediate euphoria of "victory," it began to seem likely that the many individuals caught in the "patriotic" tide would have second thoughts as the horrific human, physical and ecological carnage wrought by U.S. firepower became clearer.

It will take time to summarize such a rich and complex experience. But a useful starting point is to trace the main stages and characteristics of the anti-war movement's development and work. The first period began when Bush dispatched troops to the Gulf in early August 1990, and the President and the movement staked out their basic positions. A new stage opened up November 8 when the administration doubled its deployment and made offensive action imminent; this period saw an unprecedented public disagreement within the elite and a growing grassroots-based movement.

The third period, which started January 16, 1991 when Bush went to war, was characterized by a mass upsurge of grassroots opposition, and the elite closing ranks behind Bush. The first expressions of pro-war grassroots sentiment also began to appear and Bush — able to hold his international coalition together and minimize U.S. combat losses — succeeded in gaining and holding substantial majority support. The final stage, a virtual walkover for Bush, began with Iraq's first diplomatic moves toward surrender in late February.

## I. The Battle Lines Are Drawn; Early August to Early November

Iraqi troops entered Kuwait on August 2, 1990. By August 7 Bush had sabotaged efforts for an Arab solution to the crisis and manipulated an "invitation" to send U.S. troops to Saudi Arabia. Declaring that "Iraq's action will not stand," the President made it crystal clear that U.S. military action was a definite option. Immediately, a number of figures within the U.S. elite voiced anxiety over that prospect. But in this period the polarization between Bush and his elite opponents was somewhat muted.

With Bush emphasizing defense of Saudi Arabia rather than immediate action against Iraq, there was little disagreement within the policy establishment with the need to protect this oil-rich client state. Bush also limited elite opposition by going to the UN and winning overwhelming support — the Soviets included — for resolutions condemning Iraq's takeover. The liberal establishment was delighted, seeing this approach as a move away from U.S. unilateralism and a step toward strengthening international law.

Planning ahead, Bush also moved quickly to establish the main themes of his ideological campaign to prime the public for war. At this stage two objectives were primary: creating a demonic enemy whose image would stay in the public mind; and convincing the populace that this enemy could be defeated quickly and with minimal U.S. losses. Tackling the Vietnam Syndrome head-on, Bush hammered the media day after day with his summation that "in Vietnam we fought with one hand tied behind our back." He set out to create a more suitable enemy for the new "war at home." As with Willie Horton and Manuel Noriega, the Bush high command, using every hypocritical and racist trick in its vast arsenal, began its campaign to turn Saddam Hussein — a petty dictator once favored by Washington — into another Hitler.

Even sections of the progressive movement failed to confront Bush's policy at this stage. Jesse Jackson and SANE/Freeze president William Sloane Coffin initially supported U.S. deployment of troops for "deterrence," though not for offensive military action. The peace movement paid a high price for its longstanding neglect of the Middle East and vacillation on the justice of the Palestinian cause. The argument that U.S. intervention was justified by the need to "defend Israel" prevented many activists, most but not all progressive Jews, from forthrightly opposing U.S. military moves.

But in the main, peace and progressive activists responded to Bush's policy with a burst of anti-war initiative. Before August was over dozens of protests had been held and local anti-war committees and coalitions had formed in dozens of cities. The impetus for starting such formations most often came from Middle East groups such as the Palestine Solidarity Committee or the International Jewish Peace Union; other sectors of the anti-intervention movement, especially Central America activists; or from various socialist organizations. But an outstanding characteristic of the initial wave of organizing was the degree to which it was not limited to these forces. On the contrary, activists rooted in other social movements and a flood of people new to political protest stepped forward to assume prominent roles.

### Military Families Speak Out

Families of people in the military — as well as military personnel and veterans of previous wars — were right at the forefront of the burgeoning anti-war movement. Their involvement received national attention with the *New York Times* August 23 publication of an "open letter" to Bush from Alex Molnar. Entitled "If My Marine Son Is Killed," the letter declared: "Now that we face the prospect of war I intend to support my son and his fellow soldiers by doing everything I can to oppose any offensive American military action in the Persian Gulf. The troops I met deserve far better than the politicians and policies that hold them hostage." Molnar and others established the Military Families Support Network, which quickly grew to over 3,000 members united in opposition to launching a war. The class-biased and racist nature of an "all volunteer" military whose ranks were filled by victims of the poverty draft was underscored time and again in anti-war agitation. Simultaneously, resistance took shape within the military as men and women declared themselves conscientious objectors and/or refused to be mobilized to the Gulf. Refusals accelerated after Bush's major call-up of reserve units in November.

A lot of misinformation has been promoted about the 1960s movement being anti-soldier. Overwhelmingly, the Vietnam-era movement was sympathetic to GIs, made extensive efforts to organize and defend the rights of servicepeople, and offered far more support to returning veterans than mainstream institutions or the general population. It is true, however, that the movement against the Gulf War was far more aggressive about linking opposition to Bush's policy with explicit support for people in the military, and gave far more attention to reaching the mainstream with this message. This approach enabled the movement to gain an extremely broad hearing during the build-up to hostilities. But the shade of difference between "Support Our Troops — Bring Them Home Alive" and "Support Our Troops — Win The War" can widen into a chasm once actual fighting begins, and some of the pitfalls of the movement's heavy emphasis on "support our troops" began to hit home once Bush went to war.

### People of Color Shape the Movement

A second determining characteristic of the anti-war movement established from the outset was the central role of organizations and activists of color. Prominent figures in the African-American, Latino, Asian-American, Arab-American and Native American communities were among the first to denounce Bush's preparations for war and to emphasize its inherently racist nature. The direct connection between pouring money into the military and cutbacks in social programs, as well as the disproportionate number of African-Americans, Latinos and Native Americans in combat units, propelled the full range of community leaders and elected officials into action. A striking indication of the breadth of opposition in the African-American community in particular came in early September when Rev. T.J. Jemison, president of the National Baptist Convention USA — the largest organization of Blacks in the world with 7.8 million members — denounced Bush's action in the strongest terms at his organization's annual convention. Throughout the crisis polls showed African-Americans more opposed to war than any other group.

Additionally, a surge of direct anti-war organizing by activists of color rooted in community organizations, social service agencies, colleges and high schools began in August and accelerated after November. This grassroots activity had a qualitative impact on the racial politics and composition of the anti-Gulf War movement. Identification of the racist character of the war was established early on as an integral theme in almost all anti-war organizing. And the extensive participation of people of color challenged white activists, especially those who have long predominated in the "traditional peace movement," to grapple in a concrete, up-close way with issues of racial/cultural bias and the distribution of power and leadership in coalitions.

### All Sectors Come Out

Other constituencies also lent their strength to anti-war activism early on. Opposition was voiced at every level of the labor movement, in contrast to Vietnam when it took years of rank-and-file mobilization to squeeze anti-war endorsements out of the bulk of union officialdom. The Church sector added its moral authority, almost every major religious denomination going on record against offensive military action. A wave of student activism — building on several years of organizing around the issues of apartheid, Central America, campus racism, sexism and homophobia — swept colleges and universities. Many activists rooted in the lesbian and gay community — one of the most dynamic sectors over the last ten years, especially because of the AIDS crisis — took up anti-war organizing. The main organizations of the women's movement denounced the looming war; feminists took the lead in pointing out the playground-style male posturing of both Bush and Saddam and the link between U.S. male socialization and resort to violence. A gender gap showing women more opposed to the war than men persisted throughout the crisis. The 1990–91 anti-war movement was also distinguished by its stress on the ecological dangers of war and the participation of important sections of the environmental movement. Relations between these diverse sectors were not always harmonious. Struggles over racism, sexism, homophobia and class bias were frequent. But overall the movement seriously grappled with its internal conflicts and was able to build significant cooperation across sectoral lines.

A striking feature of the initial period of anti-war agitation was the extent of outspoken opposition from institutions and individuals focused on domestic issues. These voices made the direct link between Bush's foreign adventure and funds drying up for social needs at home.

In the mid-sixties, the U.S. economy was hegemonic in the capitalist world and was still riding the crest of its long post-World War II expansion. But by the summer of 1990 the U.S. faced major economic challenges from Japan and a rapidly unifying Western Europe, and average real wages had been falling for over a decade, Reaganomics had gutted spending on social programs, and growing layers of the population, especially in communities of color, were falling right through the social safety net. These conditions necessarily shaped the perspective of the anti-Gulf War movement and significantly determined the constituencies that would be most supportive of it.

The U.S. socialist left brought dedication and experience to the anti-war upsurge. U.S. socialists and Marxists brought important skills to particular organizing efforts, and the left also projected valuable political analysis and historical perspective into the mobilizations. (Special credit for this latter contribution should be given to the small and overworked community of left intellectuals who focus on the Middle East, and to publications like *Middle East Report*.)

### National Coalitions Form

This early period also saw the formation of two coalitions that would attempt to call nationwide actions and coordinate national anti-war activity. The Coalition to Stop U.S. Intervention in the Middle East was formed in early August, with former attorney general Ramsey Clark providing an important voice within it.

The National Campaign for Peace in the Middle East was formed in September by a broad range of peace and anti-intervention organizations, Middle East groups, community and student organizations and prominent figures from the Rainbow Coalition and various left tendencies. The National Campaign, after considerable debate, voted to include condemnation of Iraq's invasion of Kuwait in its perspective; it also left room for a wide variety of views on the validity of economic sanctions against Iraq, the role of the UN, etc. The Coalition, in contrast, abstained from any criticism of the takeover of Kuwait and took the position that sanctions were an act of aggression against Iraq.

Demonstrations in this initial period were frequent but not yet on a mass scale. Larger demonstrations took place on October 20, a national day of protest endorsed by both national coalitions: simultaneous protests also occurred in Europe and Japan, and from here on the U.S. movement would draw strength from and try to publicize the existence of an international anti-war movement.

Gulf policy was not a main issue in the fall Congressional elections. This underscored the extent to which the Democratic Party mainstream was united behind Bush's initial steps towards war. Public opinion polls showed support for military action dropping a few points each week from its early August peak. By October public opinion was split right down the middle, and this may have contributed to Republican unease about making support for the war an issue.

### II. The Elite Argues and the Movement Grows; November 8 to January 15

Two days after the November 6 mid-term elections, Bush announced that he was sending another 200,000 military personnel to the Gulf, nearly doubling the U.S. deployment there. This dramatic escalation made it clear that offensive action was now on the administration's agenda.

Showing the Vietnam Syndrome's continuing strength, public support for Bush immediately dropped. A November 19 *New York Times*/CBS poll showed only 21% favoring rapid military action; 51% said that Bush had not offered a convincing explanation of the reasons for the U.S. military presence in the Gulf.*

The administration immediately sought a better set of arguments to win the public to its predetermined course. The public relations scramble took place in full public view. After a month or so of monitoring public opinion polls, the administration decided that campaigning against Iraq's alleged capacity to develop nuclear weapons was the winning ticket.

### Unprecedented Ruling Class Dissent

Bush, however, was facing far more than a reluctant public that could be softened up by a month of air-wave bombardment. The most striking feature of the weeks following November 8 was the sharp and public opposition coming from people with impeccable establishment credentials. "Sanctions-not-war" dissent was not limited to Democratic liberals such as Senators Ted Kennedy of Massachusetts or Paul Simon of Illinois. (In fact, many traditional liberals — such as Representatives Stephen Solarz of New York, Mel Levine of California and others closely tied to the powerful pro-Israel lobby — were in Bush's camp on this one.) Bush's policy was raked over the coals by powerful pro-military Democrats like Senator Sam Nunn of Georgia, hawkish ideologists like Zbigniew Brzezinski and conservative business leaders like H. Ross Perot.

These figures did not challenge the administration's goals of "liberating" Kuwait and strengthening U.S. influence in the Middle East. But they saw the risks of going to war to achieve those goals as immense: negative reaction in the Arab world, danger to the economy, potential upheaval at home. A particularly dramatic moment was the "beware-of-war" Congressional testimony by two retired chairs of the Joint Chiefs of Staff and seven former secretaries of defense at the end of November. (This was the same week that the UN Security Council authorized the use of force unless Iraq pulled out of Kuwait by January 15.) Daniel Ellsberg called such public dissent on the part of retired military brass "absolutely unprecedented" and argued that "they would not have done so unless they knew the Pentagon was filled with admirals and generals who believed George Bush's rush to war in the Gulf was a mad course of action."

### Leap in Grassroots Activity

Such conspicuous establishment dissent had a complex impact. On the one hand, it opened a broad terrain for anti-war activism to reach out to a wider public. Opportunities presented themselves to stretch the usual boundaries of dissent in the media. The empowering idea took hold that it might

---

* What would the public have thought if they knew Bush had already decided on war? Months later, at the height of the post-war euphoria, when the revelation brought praise instead of probing questions, the *New York Times* reported that the President had approved his timetable for military action in October. Ronald Reagan may have been a "Great Communicator" on camera, but Bush is second to none when it comes to timing presidential "leaks."

actually be possible to marshall a national and international coalition sufficiently strong to prevent a war. All these were major pluses for the grassroots anti-war movement.

On the other hand, the prominence given to elite opposition voices served to limit the national debate to "what will the cost be *to the U.S.* in terms of money, international reaction and casualties?" This narrow framework even affected the anti-war movement, exerting pressure to emphasize arguments about potential U.S. casualties rather than stressing concern for all victims of war. The problem of anchoring anti-war sentiment in the potential cost to "us" became brutally clear, however, when it turned out the U.S. military had the ability to slaughter Iraqis in huge numbers without thousands of U.S. soldiers coming home in bodybags.

But in the period before the war, the space for anti-war activism opened by the deep split in the ruling class was vital. Every anti-war constituency experienced a leap in activity. In the military, filings for conscientious objection increased, especially among reservists being called to the Gulf. Steps were taken to develop the National African American Network Against U.S. Intervention in the Gulf. Four major Latino organizations — the League of United Latin American Citizens, the Mexican American Political Association, the Latino Issues Forum and the American G.I. Forum — ran full-page ads in the *New York Times*, focusing on the negative impact war would have on the Latino community.

Anti-war positions were taken by numerous labor councils and individual unions, and an open letter to President Bush signed by the presidents of nine national unions was published as a full page ad in the *New York Times*. The Arab-American community made its voice heard more strongly, and the ideological and material rise in anti-Arab racism (FBI harassment, hate crimes) became an issue for the entire anti-war movement. Jesse Jackson, William Sloane Coffin and other well-known individuals who had vacillated in August began to speak out against the threat of war.

Demonstrations increased in size and frequency in hundreds of communities. Large teach-ins took place on numerous campuses, as faculty as well as student opposition swelled. Local alternative newspapers and community radio (especially the Pacifica network, which did an outstanding job) began to devote more attention to anti-war coverage. Simultaneously media activists began to mobilize grassroots protest against the bias of mainstream news coverage.

### The Week Before the Deadline

Protest reached fever pitch in the week immediately preceding the deadline for war. The long-awaited meeting between Secretary of State James Baker and Iraqi Foreign Minister Tariq Aziz took place January 9 but produced no results. From that moment, through the January 12 Congressional vote right up to midnight on the 15th, the country (and the world) was immersed in the war/anti-war polarization. In a supreme irony, the January 15 date itself symbolized the two approaches to humanity's problems that were locked in conflict: Bush's deadline for war was also Dr. Martin Luther King's birthday.

The extent, and the limits, of the differences within the ruling class were highlighted most sharply in Congress. Throughout the fall, Bush had refused to take his case to Capitol Hill; he only proposed a vote when his calculations showed almost certain victory. And the Democratic alternative was not a forthright opposition to war; it was a plan calling for more time for economic sanctions, which acknowledged the eventual "legitimacy" of initiating hostilities.

But despite these limits, the House and Senate debates were tremendously significant and extremely sharp. Dozens of Democrats pilloried Bush's policy on nationwide TV. References to Vietnam were constant, and more than a few Congresspeople denounced the race and class bias of the military. Bush's margin of victory was quite narrow — 250 to 183 in the House and only 52 to 47 in the Senate. No comparable establishment split on going to war had taken place since the Civil War.

Meanwhile grassroots mobilization became constant. In the days before the Congressional vote anti-war letters and telegrams flooded onto the Hill and activists launched a mass lobbying campaign. (This effort did not involve all sectors of the anti-war movement, however, due to complacency or alienation from lobby-Congress tactics. After the war was over, Ron Dellums said he thought the anti-war movement failed to go all-out at this juncture and targeted this as the movement's biggest mistake.)

Popular activism reached such proportions that the mainstream media was forced to take notice: the *New York Times* carried a page one story January 11 headlined, "Drawing on Vietnam Legacy, Antiwar Effort Buds Quickly." On the weekend of January 12–13, vigils, rallies, town meetings and civil disobedience actions took place across the country. Actions continued January 14, and that evening saw the biggest single protest of the pre-war period when upwards of 30,000 marched in Seattle. On January 15, annual Martin Luther King birthday commemorations in dozens of cities were punctuated by anti-war messages; one of the largest was in Atlanta where several thousand people marched. In the ideological battle of symbols and images, projection of Dr. King's vision and personal example of non-violent resistance to oppression and opposition to the Vietnam War was one of the most powerful weapons the anti-war movement had. January 15 saw round-the-clock actions, with many vigils and protests, at the United Nations and elsewhere, continuing right up to and past the midnight deadline.

The movement was gaining momentum with each passing hour. Public opinion polls showed the country still split down the middle. Anti-war protests were spreading in Japan, Europe and the Muslim world where government figures were expressing last-minute anxieties about the prospect of war and calling for a midnight-hour diplomatic solution. Bush had his UN and Congressional authorizations for war, but all these pressures seemed to be placing him in a tight, use-it-or-lose-it-spot.

### III. Bush Goes to War, the Elite Closes Ranks, and the Movement Surges into the Streets; January 16 to Late February

Bush used it — and by this time almost no one was surprised. Less than 24 hours after the war deadline, the air attacks against Iraq began.

So did a heightened propaganda campaign at home. Bush got off to a fast start by claiming near-complete destruction of the Iraqi air force and "decimation" of the Iraqi Republican Guard within the first 24 hours. These claims turned out to be wildly exaggerated. But they were useful in establishing the idea that the war would be quick and U.S. losses light. This impression, combined with the surge of "rally round the flag" sentiment which has accompanied the first days of every U.S. war, gave Bush the political initiative.

The administration gave prime attention to censoring and manipulating the press, to avoid images of the war's carnage becoming regular features of the evening news. Control was accomplished through an unprecedented censorship in which — with a few muted exceptions — the major media collaborated absolutely.

At the sound of the first shot, Washington closed ranks, and almost every elite voice which had been shouting "Wait!" just a week earlier quickly signed on. When Congress voted a resolution to "support the commander-in-chief and the troops," only 12 representatives — ten members of the Congressional Black Caucus (all Democrats), Democrat Henry Gonzalez of Texas and independent socialist Bernie Sanders of Vermont — refused to vote in favor.

#### Popular Movement on Its Own

This rapid shift in posture of the ruling class left the popular movement on its own. Building on the momentum it had been gaining in the weeks before the war, horrified and angry at the violence underway, the movement responded with its most intense and large-scale activity yet. Emergency demonstrations following the outbreak of war drew thousands.

There was an immediate expansion of organizing aimed at particular communities and sectors. A flurry of walkouts took place at high schools and junior high schools. An outburst of protest against censorship and one-sided coverage was directed at the major media.

The first two weekends following the outbreak of war saw huge national mobilizations in Washington, D.C. and San Francisco. January 19 saw 80–100,000 turn out in San Francisco and 40–60,000 in the nation's capital (plus 10,000 in Los Angeles and thousands more in other cities). On January 26, 150–200,000 marched in Washington, 100–125,000 in San Francisco, 25,000 in Los Angeles and many more in other places.

This zenith of anti-war mobilization unleashed tremendous energy. But it also spotlighted all the complexities of building and sustaining a broad-based movement.

One such complication involved the "Support Our Troops" slogan once fighting had begun. Logically, it was still true that the best way to protect the lives of U.S. military personnel was to stop shooting and bring them home. But in terms of conveying an ideological message, the beginning of combat gave every advantage to those who emphasized the "Our" in "Support Our Troops" and who wrapped into one package supporting the soldiers and defeating the "enemy" who was shooting at them. The administration succeeded in weaving defeat of Saddam Hussein, support for the country and support for the troops into a single message. And this message was attached to symbols with tremendous emotional appeal: the flag and the yellow ribbon.

The main tendency in the anti-war movement was an attempt to deny the pro-war forces sole claim to these symbols. Arguing that "peace is patriotic," most of the movement fought to get across its stop-the-war interpretation of "Support the Troops." Significant sections of the movement tried to appropriate the flag and the yellow ribbon, displaying these symbols combined with the peace sign or some other emblem indicating dissent.

Some positive results were achieved with this approach, in that it attracted a number of people who might otherwise have shunned the protest movement. On the other hand, this tactic tended to push exposure of the havoc being wreaked upon the Iraqi people to the background. As it became clear that Bush's war involved a lot more mass murder by air than combat between armies, more and more anti-war activists felt uncomfortable with the effort to appropriate patriotic symbols, or openly criticized it as a negative ideological concession to a government slaughtering civilians.

### Israel and Palestine

Another controversy within the movement revolved around Israel and the Israeli-Palestinian conflict. From the beginning of the crisis, some Jewish peace activists strongly resisted any criticism of Israel as part of anti-war agitation. By way of justification, they offered convoluted explanations about why Israel's illegal occupation of the West Bank and Gaza was "different" from Iraq's illegal occupation of Kuwait, or why sympathy for Iraq expressed by a desperate Palestinian population justified the Israeli government's longstanding rejection of an independent Palestinian state, or the 24-hour-a-day curfew clamped on Gaza and the West Bank. Those who might bring up the issue of Palestinian rights without simultaneously pledging respect for Israeli "security," were accused of "Israel-bashing," or anti-Semitism. Meanwhile the peace movement as a whole was publicly criticized by some Jewish activists for adopting a "knee-jerk" anti-Israel stance. All this intensified after Iraqi scud missiles landed in Tel Aviv in the first week of the war.

This tendency came into sharp conflict with the activists of all backgrounds (including Jews) who were committed to Palestinian rights and knowledgeable about the expansionist and aggressive role Israel has played in Middle East politics for decades. Challenging anti-Arab racism, they pointed out how Israel was using the crisis as an excuse to step up repression in the occupied territories and stressed that only a settlement of the Palestinian-Israeli conflict that protected the national sovereignty of both sides could bring lasting peace.

### The Flashpoint of Race

Race was another flashpoint of struggle within the anti-war movement. The disproportionate impact of the war on communities of color was so inescapable that virtually every sector of the movement incorporated that point into its perspective. But more than a few voices argued that the only way to build a broad movement was to keep the focus narrowly on the war and de-emphasize "secondary issues." There was a none-too-subtle color code in the type of "breadth" that was envisioned in such an approach. The real issue beneath many a fight over how strongly to link the war to domestic issues was what importance to attach to fighting racism and to ensuring the central participation of people of color in the anti-war movement.

Controversy also swirled around giving appropriate recognition to anti-war leaders in communities of color as leaders of the movement as a whole. Even among anti-war activists there were many whites who could not imagine, or feel comfortable in, a movement where people of color held the levers of power.

An all-too-familiar pattern saw mainly white peace formations set up a coalition, establish its political perspective and a certain style and tone, and then begin "outreach" to organizations and activists of color. At times there was genuine dialogue across racial lines and a real overhaul in the leadership structure and method of organizing. But at other times whites in authority simply got defensive and continued operating as before, thus weakening the movement. This pattern, however, was not universal. Where anti-war organizing began with a strong multiracial core, the movement developed on a sounder basis.

### Bush Holds the Initiative

While these internal debates sharpened once the war began, the movement's main character in this period was intense, outward-looking activity. Tens of thousands of people poured their energy into anti-war organizing. The main problems they faced were not internal; they lay in the Bush administration's power to manipulate public opinion and, even more than that, in the way the war was proceeding in the Middle East.

Immediately following the initiation of hostilities, Bush's approval rating went up to roughly 80%. As the air war proceeded, with few U.S. aircraft losses, no defections from the U.S.-orchestrated international coalition and little or no media reporting about the extent of Iraqi civilian casualties, his support stayed at that level. The first significant demonstrations in support of Operation Desert Storm began to take place. These were never as large as anti-war protests, but they received extensive media coverage and became more widespread through the month of February. Only among African-Americans did a bare majority register continue opposition to the war during this period.

By mid-February, Bush held the near-complete political initiative. The public was apprehensive about the looming ground war, but this anxiety was not translating into stop-the-war sentiment. Even the first major exposé of the air war's toll on civilians — the February 13 revelation that two U.S. "smart" missiles had killed hundreds of men, women and children in a Baghdad shelter — didn't have much impact. Inability to dent Bush's support was taking its toll on the anti-war movement. Nationally coordinated protests called for the weekend of February 16–17 were still substantial in size and breadth, but there was a definite drop in momentum relative to the peak of activity in January.

## IV. The Final Week: Bush Kills and the Movement Reels

On February 15, Iraq offered a new peace proposal which again stated its willingness to withdraw from Kuwait; it also called for the withdrawal of foreign troops from the region and an Israeli withdrawal from the occupied territories. But it was far too late for such a plan to have any impact in the U.S.. The President's harsh rejection of it won support from all members of his international coalition and from public opinion at home.

But the Soviet Union and Iran saw an opening to end the war and within a few days presented the first of what would be billed as "Soviet" peace initiatives. Each version provided for Iraqi withdrawal from Kuwait, with the only "conditions" involving the details of the pullout and terms for lifting sanctions against Iraq. Iraq dropped all reference to its own plan and accepted the first Soviet proposal February 19.

But there was no way Bush was going to settle for anything less than complete capitulation and humilitation of Iraq. Washington's "new world order" required a military juggernaut and casualties be damned. And for once Bush's imagery matched his actions: while one U.S. commander talked of sending troops into "Indian country," and another gloated over the "turkey shoot" of Iraqi troops attempting to flee the bombing, the President took a leaf out of the Wild West gunslinger tradition and issued a "High Noon" ultimatum to Iraq February 22, threatening a ground assault within 24 hours. Bush won over 70% approval for his decision to launch the ground war.

What followed was a literal slaughter. Iraqi troops offered little resistance, with thousands surrendering or killed trying to flee. After two days Saddam Hussein ordered his army to withdraw but Bush still would not let up. Wounded Knee style kill-fever soon swept the military, as described in a front page story February 27 in the *Los Angeles Times*: "Again and again on Tuesday, loudspeakers on the carrier *Ranger* blared Rossini's William Tell Overture — the rousing theme song for the carrier pilots aboard, as well as for the Lone Ranger. Each time — instead of a 'Hiyo, Silver, awaaay!' —

another strike force of A-6 Intruder jets roared off the flight deck to bomb what one pilot called 'The Jackpot' — the roads north of Kuwait City, clogged with retreating Iraqi trucks/armored vehicles. 'This morning it was bumper to bumper,' said Lt. Brian Kasperbauer, 30. 'It was the road to Daytona Beach at spring break.'"

As the U.S. military moved from one "success" like this to another, Bush's support from the ruling class and his standing in the polls just kept going up. Anti-war activity was now overshadowed by a blitz of pro-war demonstrations.

### Movement Stands its Ground

Though overmatched, the anti-war movement mobilized what resistance it could. When the Soviet-Iranian peace initiative was proposed demonstrations were organized demanding that Bush move toward peace. Efforts were made to get the "Negotiate — Stop the Killing" message into the mainstream media. After Bush's ultimatum, there were emergency vigils and protests. Other actions took place within hours of the announcement that a U.S. ground offensive had begun. Five thousand turned out at the largest action in the Bay Area, several thousand in New York. Activists scrambled to get out up-to-date press statements and agitational material.

Anti-war organizations worked right through the war's final days and after. There was no impulse to fold up activity: quite the contrary, discussions were initiated about how to refocus the movement for the post-war period. Groups readjusted their plans for demonstrations. An immediate impulse was to turn attention to campaigns for enforcing UN resolutions demanding Israel's withdrawal from the occupied territories. Demands were raised to bring all U.S. forces home immediately — no permanent military presence in the Middle East.

The ground war, and the U.S. victory, happened so fast that anti-war activists had huge political, emotional and psychological readjustments to make. It was not easy to confront directly the human costs of the war, the degree of support given to Bush by the U.S. population, or the political and ideological initiative now in the President's hands. But by and large early March saw anti-war activists forthrightly examining these issues — some in despair, but many more determined to learn lessons for how to carry on the fight.

### Conclusion: The Balance Sheet and the Lessons

In the face of such a bitter outcome, a balance sheet of the anti-war movement has to begin by asking: Was there another way to build the movement that would have prevented Bush's victory?

The answer is undoubtedly no. Overwhelmingly, Bush's gamble paid off because of factors far beyond the anti-war movement's control. The most important of these were: (1) the overriding stake the U.S. military-industrial complex had in winning total victory over Iraq; (2) the deep crisis in — and politically disastrous stance of — the Soviet Union, which kept that country from its longstanding role of checking U.S. militarism abroad; (3) the unwillingness of key governments in Western Europe — in particular the Socialist government of Francois Mitterand — to break with Washington; (4) the overwhelming military superiority the U.S. held over Iraq; and not least, (5) the thoroughly backward nature of Saddam Hussein's regime and the catastrophic policy he pursued.

Within the historical limits set by these factors, the U.S. anti-war movement did quite well. It brought its message to broad layers of the population, galvanized a new generation of activists, built a new set of relationships between different sectors of the popular movement. It served as a supportive community of conscience for people horrified by the war. These achievements stand despite Bush's victory. But a critical reflection on the movement's shortcomings, and the lessons from its experience, is also required.

### Destructiveness of Modern War

A prime question to address is the anti-war movement's apparent misassessment of the relative military strength of the U.S. and Iraq. While everyone knew that the U.S. would eventually win any shooting war, virtually no one predicted that the U.S. would prevail with so few losses. It is clearly necessary for peace activists to take a hard look at U.S. technological and military capacity; and to make exposure of the inhuman destructive power of U.S. weaponry more central to all future anti-intervention efforts.*

This is connected to a broader point about the devastating character of modern war generally. The peace movement has targeted the genocidal/ suicidal character of nuclear war for several decades. As many proponents of "new thinking" especially have pointed out, it is time to take a new look at "conventional" war as well. The scientific and technological revolution in weaponry has accelerated dramatically in the last 20 years, and such "innovations" as fuel air bombs, laser-guidance systems, cruise missiles and 12,000 pound "blockbusters" have blurred the boundary between "weapons of mass destruction" and the "conventional" arsenal.

---

* At the same time, this war was a profound example of the continuing interconnection between political and military struggle. The one-sidedness of Iraq's defeat cannot be separated from the fact that the country was led by an anti-popular regime pursuing political aims that were as unjust — though hardly as ambitious or world-threatening — as Bush's. No international front could be assembled to defend Iraq's illegal takeover of Kuwait. It was impossible for Iraq's regime to forge strategic alliances even with others opposed to U.S. intervention in the Middle East. A host of Iraqi actions were designed to ensure Saddam's political survival after a lost war rather than to defend the Iraqi people against allied butchery (from sending his air force to Iran early in the war to diplomatic posturing even after the decision had been made to leave Kuwait). All of these factors affected every aspect of the military struggle, from how long the U.S. could go on bombing without its coalition falling apart to the motivation any Iraqi soldier had to fight instead of surrender.

*Empires in Decline*

The public's response to the war spotlighted the depth of chauvinism, racism and immorality in the dominant U.S. political culture. This can't all be chalked up to Bush's sophisticated propaganda campaign; it has a long history in the U.S. And now there is a new factor: typically, empires in decline turn toward militarism and seek popularity through foreign wars that promise to avert the loss of "number one" status. In the 1980s, Britain's war to keep the Falklands engendered a surge of racism and patriotism as large sections of the English working class cheered the military pummeling of Argentina and engaged in a flurry of physical attacks on Asians and Blacks at home. This ideological regression was a major element in the rise of Thatcherism. In the U.S., the last decade's surge of "national pride" over military "triumphs" in Grenada, Panama and now the Gulf, the retrenchment of racism, the rise in mean-spiritedness toward the poor and homeless — these indicate a similar dynamic has taken hold in the U.S.

Combating such sentiment is a difficult task. The warmakers are most vulnerable when arguments are raised about worsening domestic conditions and the economic cost of foreign adventures. Less than a week after the war, for example, when Bush's approval rating on foreign policy remained upwards of 80%, a *New York Times*/CBS poll showed only 42% approval of how the President was handling the economy. But unless agitation on this point is accompanied by a straightforward ideological challenge to racism and jingoistic patriotism, the result may well be racist populism rather than a stronger progressive movement.

Especially in this context, the prospects for appropriating symbols of U.S. patriotism to the anti-war cause seem extremely dubious. We should not concede to the right the idea that advocating peace is unpatriotic. But the experience of the anti-Gulf War movement shows the pitfalls of attempting to lend a progressive connotation to the symbols of a mercenary empire in decline. A better approach is to find images that have national recognition but carry a very different ideological message. For the anti-Gulf War movement, the most effective strategy was projecting Martin Luther King as the symbol of what the country should be striving for in both foreign and domestic policy.

*A Class Perspective*

Another instructive aspect of the Gulf War concerned the nature of divisions within the ruling class. Given the balance of forces in the U.S. today, no major political aim can be achieved without the tactical support of some section of the ruling class. Any perspective that trivializes the importance of splits in the elite is left-wing posturing, not serious politics. Efforts to widen such divisions must be an integral component of any anti-war strategy.

This necessarily means giving careful attention to tactics that directly influence votes in Congress. Letter-writing and lobbying campaigns are crucial at pivotal moments. But in a more ongoing way, so is electoral work to defend the seats of representatives who do hold themselves accountable to a peace agenda.

Simultaneously, the war provided an unmistakable example of the limits of ruling class dissent and the importance of a popular movement independent of it. Because of this, the question of class remains at the core of movement-building strategy. Narrow conceptions of who constitutes the "real working class" or dogmatic assertions that class position is necessarily the main determinant of an individual's politics, must be rejected. But the importance of building an independent popular movement — and in the U.S. the popular sectors are overwhelmingly working class — cannot be stressed enough.

### New Ways to Communicate

Likewise, the last seven months contain valuable lessons about tactics. Mass mobilizations once again showed their value for calling public attention to the existence of dissent as well as fostering a sense of community and empowerment within the movement. But their limits were visible as well. The movement is less skilled at conducting an all-sided public relations battle than at organizing demonstrations. Peace activists have lagged in mastering new communication technologies and the most up-to-date ways of making their message attractive and accessible. Without a sustained and professional effort to overcome this problem, the anti-war movement will find itself fighting 1990s ideological battles with 1960s weapons.

\* \* \* \* \*

The movement against the Gulf War developed with a speed and breadth unprecedented in U.S. history. It mobilized the energy and imagination of thousands of people. The first full-scale political flow of the 1990s, the movement taught activists a great deal about what peace-and-justice politics would look like in the new decade. Clearly, anti-war and progressive forces in the U.S. face some very tough going over the next while. Drawing every lesson possible from the intense experience of resisting Bush's war will be one ingredient in making it through.

# 13

## Restricting Reality: Media Mind-Games and the War

*Laura Flanders*

In the wake of Washington's military victory in "Desert Storm," the U.S. media trumpeted the President's glee, and according to headline news the "specter of Vietnam" was once and for all banished from the U.S. dream. It is hard to remember that just months earlier, a crisis was just beginning in a far off region of the world about which the U.S. public knew very little, cared even less, and was confused by what little it knew.

In July 1990, the public mind was focused on the so-called peace dividend and the disaster of the "Savings and Loans" collapse. The case against Manuel Noriega seemed to be floundering and world attention was slowly waking up to the death toll of the U.S. invasion of Panama. An economic debacle was gripping post-socialist Central Europe and tip-toeing up Capitol Hill was a delicately-framed discussion of cutting military aid to Israel. Ron Kovic's *Born on the Fourth of July* was playing across the country, stirring emotions with its anti-war message.

The transformation of that doubt and suspicion of August 1990 into the officially-celebrated confidence of March 1991, is a testament to the U.S. establishment's ability to mold public opinion through the mainstream media. From the beginning of the Gulf crisis, the U.S. Constitution, the legitimacy of free speech, international law and even the concept of right and wrong were thrown into question. A period of vigorous public protest and profound division was recast as a revival of U.S. consensus, and mainstream anti-war activists were told that their reality not only did not matter, but with respect to the official record, did not exist. Given that the war against Iraq achieved none of its various declared goals — nothing in the way of defending democracy, destroying monsters, protecting oil reserves, or building stability, this unstated war aim — the further erosion of the U.S. political and social conscience may prove to have been the most successful goal of all.

Traveling in the United States with a group of Arab women from the Gulf during the height of the Gulf War, I picked up a copy of *Newsweek* (March 11, 1991). An article buried deep inside the magazine described the allies' assault on thousands of Iraqis caught fleeing Kuwait City in the last days of the ground war.

"As we drove slowly through the wreckage, our armored personnel carrier's tracks splashed through great pools of bloody water," wrote *Newsweek's* Tony Clifton, who witnessed the result of what was essentially the carpet bombing of a traffic jam.

"We passed dead soldiers lying, as if resting, without a mark on them. We found others cut up so badly, a pair of legs in its trousers would be 50 yards from the top half of the body. Four soldiers had died under a truck where they had sought protection . . . Most grotesque of all was the charred corpse of an Iraqi tank crewman, his blackened arms stretched upward in a sort of supplication . . ."

None of this made it to the front cover of *Newsweek*. That week's magazine bore the flushed, grinning face of General H. Norman Schwarz-kopf beneath a bold white headline "Victory!" The emphasis even of Clifton's story was not on the carnage but rather the bravery of the U.S. Tiger Brigade that had been instructed to "cut off Iraqi forces fleeing to their homeland." His essay was part of a "Desert Victory" special entitled "A hellish, hundred-hour ground war destroys Saddam's fighting machine."

Turning *Newsweek's* glossy pages, the Arab women with me peered into photographs of wreckage, looking for signs of anyone they knew. Several Iraqi families living abroad have seen their relatives, imprisoned, dead or injured, for the first time on the nightly news. Unfamiliar with U.S. popular culture, my friends were shocked by the magazine's cheering cover and the reporters' uncritical tone, and outraged that the soldiers of Iraq should be referred to not as humans, but as hardware. Was this something new, they asked, a victim press, carried away by what the President was calling "euphoria?" Or was this what we were used to? The answer is that no, the press was hardly victimized, but yes, the coverage of the war was something we have unhappily come to expect.

Far from exposing new and exciting media failings, the presentation of the Gulf War repeated all-too familiar patterns. In the first month of the crisis, when broad public discussion should have reflected the uncertainty that was seizing the country, the United States' two most influential, in-depth news programs, *Nightline* and the *MacNeil/Lehrer Newshour* contained no parallel debate. According to the media watch group, FAIR (Fairness and Accuracy in Reporting), not a single U.S. guest on *Nightline*, argued against U.S. military intervention in that month. Only once on *McNeil/Lehrer*, when a panel of Arab-Americans was invited, did criticism of the U.S. administration's policy get aired. At the same time, nearly half the U.S. guests on both programs were current or former government officials and when non-U.S. guests appeared, they were even more likely to be government representatives.

"Expert" commentators came overwhelmingly from conservative think tanks like the American Enterprise Institute and the Center for Strategic and International Studies. As FAIR's researchers point out: "Analysts from the centrist Brookings Institution provid[ed] the 'left' boundary of debate" (*EXTRA!*, Nov/Dec '90).

On television's nightly news, which is the single most important information source for the majority of people in the United States, constituencies that consistently opposed military action had a feeble showing. Guest lists that were overwhelmingly pro-Pentagon and pro-war were also predominantly white and male (Caucasians made up 98% of *Nightline*'s guests and 87% of *MacNeil/Lehrer*'s; the proportion of women was the same as the proportion of people of color). From the commitment of (disproportionately non-white) troops (August 8, 1990) until January 3rd 1991, FAIR found that ABC devoted only 0.7% of its total Gulf coverage to the war's opponents, CBS just a tenth of a percent more. The one-time appearance of critics Noam Chomsky, Edward Said and Erwin Knoll on *Newshour* did not redress the balance.

Media marginalization complicated but did not stop public mobilization. The call-up of additional troops in November and December resulted in dwindling public support for deployment — let alone war. This surfaced slightly in the press, more than on television, even if couched in articles like Jason DeParle's November 17th *New York Times* story, which began "What if they had a war and no protest movement came?" DeParle's "On the Left, Voices Amid Confusion" appeared just as massive demonstrations were being organized by two national campaigns and local groups were holding protests across the country. Meanwhile, in the Saudi desert, U.S. soldiers were disarmed by their superior officers before they could attend Thanksgiving with President Bush, and a few articles, like one in the *Washington Post*, (12/9/90), interviewed servicepeople who were seriously questioning their mission in the sand.

During this period of mounting public doubt, certain opinion polls received more attention than others. One of the favorite and most often cited surveys was a *Los Angeles Times* poll that was reported to prove that 67% of Americans supported the maintenance of U.S. troops in the Gulf even if Iraqi forces withdrew from Kuwait with 26% opposed. Taking a closer look at the poll, however, one finds that the respondants were replying to a question phrased as follows: "If Hussein pulls his troops out of all Kuwait, should the U.S. keep a military presence in the Persian Gulf to maintain stability in the region, or not?" Given the options, a vote against a U.S. presence was a vote against stability. More broadly worded questionnaires showed that opinion in the country was deeply divided, with significant sections of the population voting en bloc against the war. Women, for example, in a Harris poll taken at the end of November, voted 73% against war with Iraq, as opposed to 48% of men. African-Americans too, consistently voted more strongly than whites against military action.

By January, a 47 to 52 vote in the Senate showed that the country was split down the middle. A Doonesbury cartoon pillorying Bush's henchmen was getting laughs across the country. Certainly there was no consensus driving the U.S. into war. If it was fear of the growing opposition that gave Washington the impetus for the early deadline, and for the bombing and more bombing that followed, the action worked. Once the aerial assault was underway, mainstream anti-war opinion was quickly edged back out of the public forum.

Like victims of assault who are told their experience never happened, activists who felt the war was wrong, unnecessary or too hurried, could find nowhere on their nightly news or in their morning paper any adequate reflection or discussion of their fears or doubts. A tide of yellow ribbon jingoism was rising everywhere and, all subtleties eliminated, the choice became the choice to cheer or disappear.

Two countries full of people were reduced to two media celebrities: one good guy against one bad. The *New York Times* had dubbed George Bush the "leader of all countries," back in August (editorial, 8/12/90). President Saddam Hussein was long since elevated to a demon. Having ignored for more than a decade well documented abuse and torture by government forces in Iraq, highbrow journals and tabloids alike regurgitated the administration line that President Saddam Hussein was a "beast" (Mary McGrory, *Washington Post*, 8/7/90), or a "monster" (*Newsweek*, 8/20/90) and on January 19th, The *New York Times* published prominently on its opinion page a David Levine cartoon called "The Descent of Man." In the style of innumerable cartoonists of empire, Levine looked for chuckles by showing Clark Gable (man) transforming into gorilla, ape, through snake, to "Saddam," a dark looking, shrimp-size Arab, surrounded by a swarm of flies.

Hussein as Hitler was such a popular theme that *New Republic* editor Hendrick Herzberg thought it was a "joke" to doctor a photograph of Hussein so that his moustache looked more like the Nazi leader's (see *EXTRA!* 11/90). It is possible that this metaphor was targeted specifically at European nations (Germany and France) who were resisting the fully-fledged enthusiasm of their British and U.S. colleagues.

With a deft turn of Hitler-era phrase, the policy of successive Republican administrations to support Iraq even when Iraqi missiles had killed 37 sailors on the U.S. frigate *Stark*, was either conveniently forgotten, or, for some Democrats, represented as "appeasement"—underlining the need to act against the duplicitous villain. The paper that had editorialized "Why the Invasion [of Panama] was Justified" on December 21, 1989, chimed on August 3rd "Iraq's Naked Aggression" (*New York Times*). With memories of Panama expunged, no mainstream journalist derided President Bush's cry that his war was an act of "right against wrong."

Once bombs began to fly, every TV channel unabashedly cheered the allied troops and their mission, and newscasters proved their loyalty to their flag by using the ubiquitous "we" to mean U.S. and allied military forces.

"It was spectacular news," said Robert Bazell to the *Today* show's host, Bryant Gumbel the day after the first aerial assault. "We've only lost one casualty." "We were winning everything," said NBC's George Lewis two days later. "Let's say we've knocked out half the Iraqi air force," CBS's Bob

Schiefer suggested, in a discussion with a military analyst standing in front of the network's map of the war zone, January 18.

Thus was the TV audience wedded, willingly or not, to the allied assault and its architects, at the same time that anti-war opinion was being misrepresented or blatantly ignored. At one extreme was CBS's Ed Bradley who proclaimed it "eerie" that "there's no one on the streets of New York," on the night that thousands of protestors marched the miles from New York's Times Square to the United Nations to Washington Square Park to demand an end to the bombardment of Baghdad (1/16/91).

Ted Koppel on ABC's *Nightline* asserted that "the good news led to a rather unique feeling of euphoria throughout the country." This, the day after the first night of bombing, when sizeable portions of the U.S. public, even according to mainstream opinion polls, were resisting the adulation of what the television pundits were calling the "picture perfect" bombing raids and the "marvel(ous)" missile attacks. A *New York Times* poll taken in the first week of the air war found that 42% of those questioned still approved peace talks to bring the war to a quicker end. This was down from 56% in favor of a Mideast peace conference in a poll taken on the eve of the war.

According to source studies of the first weeks after the bombing of Iraq and Kuwait began, no fewer than 47% of all those interviewed on nightly news programs were representatives of the governments — U.S. or allied — that were ordering the air raids. Three out of ten sources were members or retired members of the U.S. military. As for the anti-war movement, protestors were asked about the war about as often as people in airports were asked about their travel plans. Between January 17th and January 30th, seven times as many Super Bowl players as peace organization leaders were asked to comment on the conflict.

Those who voiced opposition to the allied assault were rapidly dismissed, even if they were heads of previously friendly states. Jordan's King Hussein strongly opposed the Iraqi invasion of Kuwait and endorsed legal UN sanctions against Jordan's neighbor and prime trading partner, but when the Jordanian head of state condemned the U.S. bombing of Iraqi territory, CBS's favorite Arab, Fouad Ajami said the King was merely trying to placate the "Palestinian mob in Amman."

Interviewed by Leslie Stahl on *America Tonight* (2/14/91), Ajami laid out possible opinions on the war. A caller asking if people who "opposed this war" were being adequately covered by the media was translated by Stahl into: "Do you believe that pro-Arab views are not getting enough of a hearing on television?"

Arab expert Fouad Ajami replied: "I think everyone is being heard." Who did he define as everyone? "The people who favor this war, the people who think it's a just war are being heard, the people who think it's just barely a just war are being heard, the people who believe Saddam is a hero are getting their airtime from Amman and from the West Bank and so on."

Anyone looking to television for information about the anti-war movement must have been powerfully alienated by what they saw. The seemingly compulsory contrast that every network drew between protests said to be "against the war" and those described as "supporting the troops," made invisible all those who wanted to support the soldiers by bringing them home. As for those who feared violence at the protests, the long-standing love-affair that exists between TV editors and images of burning flags or massed, helmeted police, did its bit to misrepresent what were overwhelmingly non-violent demonstrations. Repeated comparisons be-tween the anti-war movement of the 90s and that of the Vietnam era imposed a frame of reference on a movement whose constituencies, political agenda, and international perspective were far from a simple revival of the 1960s and 70s. Finally, tapping Western culture's vast reservoir of anti-Arab racism, mainstream media reports associated anti-war feeling with support for Muslim fundamentalism in a conflation that must have provided powerful discouragement to many wavering on whether to voice their opposition to the war.

Violent-looking anti-war demonstrations in Jordan and the West Bank attracted television attention that pro-negotiation demonstrations in the United States did not. One memorable CNN story that aired repeatedly on February 9, showed an auction in Amman at which aggressive seeming men were said to be bidding for pieces of a U.S. missile. The anger of the crowd was palpable as narrators explained that chants in Arabic were hailing "Saddam" and calling for the downfall of the United States.

What the CNN announcers failed to mention was that auctions were taking place regularly in Amman and all over Jordan at that time. In a country starved of resources because the U.S. embargo on Iraq had not coincidentally cut off Jordan's ports as well, Jordanians were selling off jewelry, paintings and sculptures along with, on this unusual occasion, plane wreckage, to raise money for medicine and food for the people of Iraq. No television crew filmed the bake sales in Jordanian primary schools that were held to send food to children in Baghdad, whose homes were bombed by U.S. fighters.

Sheryl McCarthy, in her *New York Newsday* column, was one of the few strong voices challenging the racism that was emerging in the media's portrayal of anti-war feeling. She reminded readers (2/6/91) that anti-Arab violence was surging in the so-called "civilized" world.

> In this country we bash the Arabs because they thwart our political and economic goals in the Middle East: they are in conflict with Israel, our major ally in that region, and they thwart our desire to exploit their oil reserves. We despise them because they are non-European, non-Christian, and we can't boss them around.

Columns like McCarthy's "Bashing Arabs to Silence Debate" did make it into the pages of *New York Newsday* (Feb. 6, 1991), along with strongly critical columns by Jimmy Breslin, Sidney Schanburg and consistently challenging investigations and exposés of the Bush administration from Knut Royce. The *Village Voice* featured damning media criticism from Doug Ireland and James Ledbetter, and delving reports from James Ridgeway and his colleagues. A roster of prominent progressives — Barbara Ehren-reich, Alexander Cockburn, Christopher Hitchens, Noam Chomsky, Edward Said and others published occasional opinion pieces in mainstream dailies as well as progressive periodicals. But on-the-scene-reports from Saudi Arabia suggest that the same strategy was in place with respect to reporters as was functioning to discourage public debate at home.

As far as possible, "pool" journalists were shielded from any awareness that they could be doing something different than toeing the administration line, and freer thinkers quickly found themselves cast out of the accepted fold.

The "press pool" system was announced by the Pentagon in October 1984 in the wake of criticism about the exclusion of journalists from the island of Grenada during the U.S. invasion a year before. The three-day lockout of journalists covering that attack had successfully stalled the exposure of Reagan administration lies (like those about the massive number of Cubans in Grenada, the state of their arms supplies and the alleged threat posed to U.S. students), but the blanket ban had upset the public. Media management through selection rather than exclusion was the essence of the "press pool" system and although it was not activated in Panama, it was announced early in the fall of 1990 that "pooling" would be the process of choice for the war of '91. A small number of reporters chosen by the military from mainstream media organizations were to be chaperoned into battle and instructed to share their information with their sidelined colleagues.

One award-winning journalist who did not dive into the sanctioned "pool," *The Independent*'s Robert Fisk, described the situation as follows:

> Most of the journalists with the military now wear uniforms. They rely upon the soldiers around them for advice and protection . . . They are dependent on the troops and their officers for communications and perhaps, for their lives. And there is thus the profound desire to fit in, to "work the system," a frequent absence of critical faculties.

According to Fisk, a colonel commanding a U.S. air base in Saudi Arabia during the first week of bombing distributed small U.S. flags to the "pool" reporters stationed with his squadron. The flags had been carried in the cockpits of the very first U.S. jets to attack Baghdad, said the colonel, but the journalists deserved them because "you are warriors too." And they were.

Fisk, a 15-year veteran of the Middle East with experience in Beirut and the Lebanon war, ran into trouble covering the battle of Khafji, where Iraqi troops clashed with allied soldiers in what was to be the only competi-tive land conflict of the war. Whereas pool reporters were kept up to 15 miles from the fighting and were told by their military "minders" that the town had been recaptured, Fisk trekked independently up to the scene and reported that the fighting was continuing despite allied government claims to the contrary. An incensed Brad Willis of NBC told Fisk "You asshole. You'll prevent us from working. You're not allowed here. Get out," and alerted a Marine public affairs officer to Fisk's presence.

Other journalists who filmed the officially non-existent fighting in Khafji were forced at gunpoint to hand their videotape over to a U.S. marine, not because the French crew's tape contravened security guidelines, but because they were not part of the pool. In the same period in another part of the desert, a London *Sunday Times* writer was told by a British major that he could not file independent stories on a local regiment because he would "ruin it" for the pool. Three days later, Fred Bayles of the Associated Press and Laurent Rebourg, a photographer, were detained for six hours by the First Cavalry because, they were told, they were working outside the pool system (See "Moving Target", *Village Voice*, 3/26/91. ) During all this time, CNN's Peter Arnett was the target of exceptional and often highly personal abuse for having elected to remain in Baghdad and file stories from beneath the bombing. Wyoming's Republican Senator Alan K. Simpson, went so far as to call Arnett a "sympathizer" and repeat libellous charges about Arnett's wife's supposed relationship to the Vietnamese "Viet Cong."

After thousands of tons of bombs had been dropped on Iraq and Kuwait and hundreds of hours of extended television news reports had repeated the same impenetrable Pentagon videotape and tedious desert briefings, journalists and editors realized that the government's press restrictions were losing them the exciting new audiences of the first days of war. It was only then that the "censorship" story hit the mainstream headlines, invoking public memory of the 1990 scandals involving the National Endowment for the Arts, Robert Mapplethorpe, et al.

Significant though it is that the question of the government's right to restrict press access became prime news for both television and print reporters, uncomfortable mainstream institutions were not concerned enough to challenge officially the Pentagon's policies. None of the country's papers of record (*The New York Times, The Washington Post, The Los Angeles Times, The Wall Street Journal, The Boston Globe*) or television producers joined the lawsuit filed by the Center for Constitutional Rights on behalf of a number of small, progressive media outlets, to overturn the pool system. When the *New York Times* liberal, Tom Wicker complained: "Perhaps worse, press and public largely acquiesced in this disclosure of only selected information" (3/19/91), one has to wonder why he did not join Sidney Schanburg, E.L. Doctorow, Michael Klare and eleven news organizations in suing the federal government — or at least, why he did not pressure his editors to cover the New York case in full (They never did.)

A negative aspect of the focus on official restrictions was that once the "censorship" bell was tolled, the issue came to attract more attention overall than the supposedly "censored" stories themselves. Debate about the morality of telling the truth about the war came to supplant debate about the morality of waging it.

The Pentagon refused in January to allow journalists to report allied attacks on Iraqi nuclear laboratories, but those restrictions could not forbid discussion of the repercussions of such action. U.S. military officers confirmed that Iraqi nuclear installations had been "taken out" in a briefing the following week, but no mainstream front page devoted even a column to a full consideration of the ecological or political ramifications of actions that were clearly outlawed under international law. The lack of coverage was especially significant in light of the passage on December 4 of a United Nations General Assembly resolution expressly forbidding any attack on a nuclear facility that had been certified as being for peaceful purposes by the International Atomic Energy Agency. Iraq's two small nuclear research reactors had been so certified. The Assembly vote was close to unanimous: Washington cast the only negative vote.

Nor did Pentagon censors intervene and forbid ABC television to investigate Soviet satellite photographs, acquired by the network, that seemed to contradict President Bush's claim in early September that "half a million" Iraqi troops were massing on the Saudi Arabian border. The network established that satellite surveillance accurate to five meters did not seem to show a troop presence of the type that Bush was using to justify international "defensive" action, but according to Jean Heller of the *St Petersburg Times* (which did eventually run the story, with copies of the pictures), the network considered their pictures insufficient evidence. They did not return to the issue after Heller pursued and published her own investigation.

Presumably individual loyalty, not Pentagon restrictions, led Andrew Rosenthal on February 21 (*New York Times*) to omit from his biography of Brent Scowcroft, any discussion of his subject's employment by a Kuwaiti-owned and directed oil company.

Rosenthal quoted one unnamed White House official's opinion that, "It was Brent's presentation at one of the meetings on August 3, that Friday after the invasion, that made clear what the stakes were, crystallized people's thinking and galvanized support for a very strong response." But he censored himself the fact that in 1984, 1985 and 1986, according to *Standard and Poor's Register of Corporations*, Brent Scowcroft was hired by the government of Kuwait [Kuwait Incorporated's Kuwait Petroleum Corporation (KPC)] to sit alongside Ali Jabar al-Ali al-Sabah on the board of directors of KPC's U.S. subsidiary, Santa Fe International; the same oil company responsible for the controversial slant drilling that enabled Kuwait illegally to extract oil from under Iraq's Rumaila oilfield.

Individual decision, rather than Pentagon restraint, allowed allied assertions regarding "smart bombs" to go unchallenged. One did not need to be on the front line to question where 20% of bombs had landed if the sorties had an 80% "success" rate, or what the accuracy was of the majority of explosives if only 7% of bombs were "smart." Yet no mainstream editorial writers challenged Defense Department enthusiasm for high technology. Reporting like that of Lamis Andoni, or Patrick Cockburn, describing the craters along the road from Amman to Baghdad, gave eyewitness reality to the video-game fiction, yet most common sense reporting was submerged somewhere in the breathless rush to be in the right place at the right time (with the victors, not the victims).

Comments like that of NBC anchor Tom Brokaw in a discussion of the possibility of ground war, capture forever the warped humanity of the influential mediamen (and some women) of this war. "So far," said Brokaw, "the U.S. has fought this war at arm's length, with long-range missiles, high-tech weapons. This is to keep casualties down." No one appeared to state the obvious — that the technology relied on to limit U.S. casualties was destroying thousands of lives a week in a country that had done nothing but be ruled by a dictator — a dictator built into a regional force by U.S. policymakers and their arms-selling associates.

"The media coverage of the war confirmed what we've been saying all along, that there is no real debate on network TV," says Jim Naureckas, editor of the media group FAIR's journal, *EXTRA!* "Television news doesn't adhere to even the most basic journalistic standards."

Traditional complaints took on additional significance as soon as expanded news reports brought war-boosterism into the homes of viewers across the U.S., and courtesy of Cable News Network, U.S. reporting and analysis became the staple diet of TV audiences — and journalists — around the world. On one occasion, radio reporters on New York's WBAI were heard telling their Israeli correspondents in Jerusalem what was happening in the occupied territories, transmitting information from West Bank journalists to commentators starved for anything other than CNN.

Another new factor was the public attention paid to what became known as "media issues," and the integration of those concerns into the broad, progressive platform of opposition to the war. Demonstration organizers invited media critics to address their crowds; activists took protests to the steps of the news empires themselves and when high school students walked out of class in Brooklyn, New York, it was to their local television station that they marched.

The abuse by mainstream media organs of hours of prime time television and reams of newspaper print became so obvious that dozens of "media watch" organizations sprang into action in the United States and Europe, and existing groups expanded. "We've seen a massive upsurge of attention to media issues" says Renu Nahata, activist director of the media watch group, FAIR. "Suddenly people are flocking to FAIR to find ways to combat war-mongering in the media."

At the same time, a bevy of independent video-makers, radio producers and anti-mainstream journalists sprang into action and some successively mobilized public pressure to get their work wide distribution.(The Gulf Crisis Video Project was seen on public television in the U.S. and internationally and close to 500 cable channels played the tapes. The radio show *Undercurrents* was picked up by shortwave broadcasters and relayed around the world. C-Span was convinced to cover the anti-war rally of January 26, live in full from Washington D.C.)

An opening exists to build an alternative media model — consolidating the work of the anti-war activists. This would involve acknowledging the facts: that the mainstream media, fed and watered by the individuals and the corporations that support the agenda of the political establishment, are rarely going to act against their own interests. Criticism is indispensible, but so is creativity — to develop a media alternative that would reflect, not reshape, public debate, and challenge, not champion the government perspective.

Until then, it is a mixed blessing that so many new activists have come to see the media as the enemy. From a brief survey of audiences gathered to address the war in the winter and spring of 1990–1991, it seems that the crimes of the media provoke a more palpable and immediate response than the crimes the media is supposed to cover. It is as if what *Lies Of Our Times* calls the media's "Minefields of Disinformation" are the only assault the U.S. public recognizes. While this has positive implications for organizing purposes, it is also disturbing.

In the week that allied airplanes began to drop bombs on Iraq, *The Nation* columnist Alexander Cockburn wrote of the "tragicomedy" of television news. "The reporters — actors in fact — [have] mostly as little relationship to reality as the Greek chorus in the Agamemnon debating what Clytemnestra is up to ('Is that a noise I hear?') as she hacks the King to death." The challenge is not to let the chorus of media criticism become such a noise that it drowns out the murderers themselves.

# PART FOUR

# The Eye of the Storm:

# Regional Perspectives and

# Repercussions

# 14

## The Arab World in the "New World Order"

*Clovis Maksoud*

What is being described as a "new world order" is a consequence of developments that have taken place in the Northern part of the globe. The Southern part of the world — of which the Arabs are the geopolitical vanguard — has been largely unaffected, but when events have touched the South the results have been negative, adverse and tragic. Recent events and conflict in the Gulf region testify to this conclusion.

In fact, the Southern part of the globe has neither been consulted nor involved in defining or determining the nature and direction of this "new world order." The rights, aspirations, pain, problems and interests of the peoples of the South — otherwise known as the Third World — are not solicited, let alone factored into the process of shaping this "order."

The question that arises is how to render the "new world order" new and worldly by being inclusive and orderly.

To become new, the world order must improve existing conditions and not solely be different. It must introduce globalism into the governance. This means that global authority on certain levels must be ascertained and rendered preponderant over sovereign prerogatives of states. This is necessitated by emerging global problems and challenges, many of which are endemic and becoming more dangerous and pressing. These include problems related to the environment, migration of labor, AIDS, drugs and the transfer of technology in addition to the interaction of capital transfer, multinational corporations, famine, disasters, water resources, etc. All have a global dimension and invariably require a highly coordinated intergovernmental approach and a keen awareness and instant readiness to forgo insistence on individual national initiatives. The term "new," therefore, must signal a profound change in the concepts of state sovereignty, international commitments and the changing meaning of government, state management and diplomatic action.

For the "new world order" to become worldly, the meaning of the word must be inclusive and its proponents sensitive rather than patronizing, egalitarian not hegemonic, inclusive not exclusive, and believers in as well as being advocates of the world order. To remain North-centric will render this last decade of the nineties the same as the last decade of the preceding century.

The "global order" is an outcome of changes that have taken place in the Soviet Union and Eastern Europe, as well as the democratizing process that ensued. It is also the result of the unification of Germany and the growing thrust towards political and economic union in Europe. The equation of power between the two superpowers ultimately led towards what is fast becoming a unipolar system.

All the changes that have taken place during the last two years, and even before, have been changes within the Northern part of the globe. The South was not affected, except as a spillover. Nor was there any particular sensitivity towards the aspirations, hopes, problems, agonies and pains of the Arabs and of the peoples of the Third World in general. Permit me to call the Third World the "southern part of the globe," because the growing tension between North and South is beginning to replace the earlier tensions between the East and West.

The "new world order" must be orderly. The word "order" implies a determination of the way in which matters are disposed with an end in view and whereby the functions of each component are so arranged that the world and individual countries begin to have a notion of what developments, consequences and results are all about. It implies a conceptual scheme in which the world becomes easily adaptable to change, equipped to anticipate transformations and capable of absorbing the unexpected and cushioning mutations so as to minimize their adverse consequences and maximize the usefulness of opportunities they might provide. Order, in this context, provides the world system with the mechanisms to adapt to the vicissitudes that the scientific, technological and communication revolutions have introduced.

The growing perception in the South is that stability, desirable as it might be, may mean for many peoples intolerable stagnation, continued disfranchisement and perpetual economic deprivation and social dislocation. It is, in this respect, that the new world order remains one where the South has at best, a minimal say, and whereby any acquiescence to its present thrust constitutes an abdication from control of its destiny.

We in the South must not allow ourselves to become intellectually atrophied in the name of stability. "Stability," if it means stagnation — as it does in our part of the world — is a concept which we reject.

We reject the stabilizing facets of social stagnation, economic inequality, and political disfranchisement. Instead, we want the stability which will enable us to evolve, to contribute to the process of evolution, and to be the recipients of the benefits of the scientific, technological, and industrial revolution.

Since the Camp David Accords, vertical relations between individual Arab countries and the Northern part of the globe — especially the northwest part of the globe, namely the United States and Western Europe — have taken precedence and become more significant than the horizontal relations among Arabs themselves.

This was further accentuated by the emergence of the Gulf Cooperation Council. This led to a strategic dependence on the United States in particular, reinforcing the vertical relations at the expense of inter-Arab horizontal relations. This is crucial, because it did create cracks in the Arab body politic, which rendered it vulnerable to the dislocations and distortions that occurred prior to, and since, the Gulf crisis. This dependency gave a legitimacy — an Arab cover — for the hastened internationalization of the Gulf crisis. We were then faced with a situation which, as President Bush correctly stated, constituted the first test for the post-Cold War period.

The question arises as to whether the end of the Cold War was positive or negative. The question itself carries with it the weight of a North-centric agenda. The Cold War was waged between two superpowers and their clients. The South indicated its alienation from the Cold War by pursuing the policy of non-alignment. This was the South's way of exercising its independent judgement and mobility in the midst of a bipolar world. With the end of the Cold War and the emergence of what is virtually a unipolar world, the South finds the need to adjust to this new situation by moving towards a world where a North-South discourse — with all its tensions, impediments and opportunities, would replace the non-aligned course which relied on counterbalance to negotiate and ascertain its role and interests during the Cold War.

Of course, the end of the Cold War is positive to the extent that it removes the threat of nuclear war and promises to transfer funds allocated to the arms race to development and the improvement of the quality of life. The anxiety that was generated by the Cold War suspended many projects aimed at correcting the economic imbalance, and rendered long-range planning vulnerable and susceptible to sudden reversals and derailment.

It is clear therefore, that the end of the Cold War carries with it the opening of opportunities unavailable at the peak of superpower confrontation. One of the prime objectives of the policy of non-alignment was to contribute to the ending of the Cold War.

While the positive aspects of the end of the Cold War are readily admitted and welcomed, the potential for negative consequences cannot be ruled out. They lie more in the dual assymetry of an emerging unipolar system in superpower relations and the continued discrepancy and functional indifference in the North-South relationship.

Perhaps one of the glaring consequences of the Gulf War lies in the excessive projection of military power without a commensurate clarity of purpose and policy. As a result, we witness the restoration of legitimacy in Kuwait constituting the restoration of order while concomitantly releasing regional anarchy, as we witness in a torn Iraq and a frozen peace process in the Arab-Israeli conflict.

It is from this perspective that an Arab assessment can be discerned, and an Arab judgement can be tentatively rendered.

With the invasion of Kuwait by Iraq on August 2, 1990, the U.S. energized the UN Security Council and pursued the implementation of its resolutions to the bitter end. Kuwait was liberated and Iraq was bombed "into the pre-industrial age" as the UN reported. We have seen the attack on Iraq, brilliantly performed in military terms, but brilliance divested of policy vision. We have seen how this military success, that has generated a fascination with technological performance, has also brought home to the Arabs their sense of vulnerability. This inflicts deep wounds on the collective Arab psyche; the threat of famine and epidemic among the Iraqi population and the pathetic transfer of population compound the sense of shame that such a disaster was not diverted through Arab collective efforts.

Arabs have been further traumatized by what happened to the Kuwaitis — the unbelievable brutality they experienced at the hands of their Iraqi occupiers, as well as the treatment suffered by many Palestinians, Sudanese and others at the hands of some Kuwaitis.

The dehumanizing process on all sides is staggering and mind boggling. For this reason, the lifting of economic sanctions on Iraq is necessary, because their continued imposition could become an act of sheer vengeance rather than what they were intended to be — a corrective and an incentive to comply. Reconstruction of both Kuwait and Iraq is necessary.

Those measures do not in themselves constitute the "peace option," but are the obvious remedies needed to initiate a rational approach to deconstruct the cycle of reckless and ruthless behavior and policies practiced both by the Iraqis and against the Iraqis; and by Iraqis against Iraqis; and by Kuwaitis in the same manner they were practiced against the Kuwaitis.

There are two simultaneous developments that appear to be contradictory: a sharpening of divisions among Arab governments and states, and a new consciousness of the unity of Arab destiny among the people. As to the governments, the invasion was a violation of the Arab state system, but the speedy invitation to international forces, preventing the Arab League from resolving its own disputes, was equally a violation.

But the Arabs as a people, with fringe exceptions, are rediscovering the fact that they are targeted as Arabs, and so are beginning to respond as Arabs. This feeling manifested itself in the places where there was a small opening for democratic expression: North Africa, Jordan, Yemen. It even manifested itself in those North African countries with which the U.S. has had the longest and friendliest relations: Tunisia and Morocco. Because of the memory of previous Arab disfranchisement, the current crisis struck a raw nerve in their collective psyche.

This popular feeling has now been emboldened. It will try to elicit an unprecedented level of accountability from the governments as to all the "whys" that are emerging: Why did a leader in Iraq unilaterally undertake policies that proved detrimental to the lives of millions of people? Why was there the level of extreme dependence on the West that tended to pre-empt the inter-Arab system? Why the discrepancy of private wealth and public poverty? Why was the UN Security Council so energized on the

Gulf issue — rightly so — but so paralyzed by Israel's defiance of other UN resolutions?

It is now clear that there has always been a linkage between the crisis in the Gulf region and the Arab-Israeli conflict, despite the fact that linkage during the military operations was treated as taboo.

While Secretary Baker's contention that Iraq did not invade Kuwait in order to liberate Palestine was in itself correct, equally true is the fact that Israel's continued defiance of all UN resolutions, and the United States' persistent shielding of Israel from sanctions and condemnation, created enough cracks in the Arab body politic to render it amenable to adventurist pursuits such as Iraq's invasion of Kuwait, and predisposed it to accommodate U.S. permissiveness towards Israel without cost, as the Camp David agreements have shown.

With Egypt no longer an active deterrent to Israel's aggression, with Iraq militarily humbled, with Syria once again targeted, and with the Gulf states recoiling, dependent and self-contained, a glaring assymetry is emerging in the Middle East, reinforcing Israel's intransigence and its ability to stonewall and to sustain its obduracy.

We are faced, also, with the reality that we in the Arab world are always excluded from global decision-making. We have reached a stage in the twentieth century where our oil wealth has not been used to address our areas of poverty. We are a rich nation, of poor people. We have not corrected this. We have not used our capacities to harness and rebuild our institutional infrastructure. We have seen how, while the Arabs were being exposed, rendered vulnerable, while they were reacting by tribalistic reflexes, and avoiding the elements of their national cohesion, Israel was completing its objectives of bringing forward the largest single wave of immigration since 1948. For this reason, it is important to refocus again on the central issue, the Palestinian question, which keeps being interrupted by all those diversionary elements in our midst (and which makes it vulnerable to intervention from outside).

To deal with this dangerous situation, it is necessary to bring about a two-pronged strategy. One, to restore a proper "Arab order" which insures a credible balance with Israel. This will insure that negotiations are purposeful and consequential. A strategic imbalance will enable Israel to render negotiations a purpose in and of itself if they further Israel's annexationist and hegemonic objectives.

The Arab order implies a revitalized Arab League. It should be stated as clearly as possible that the Arab League, in its summit meeting in Cairo in August 1990, was pre-empted from undertaking its own functions in attempting to resolve a basically inter-Arab dispute.

I must mention why I think that the Arab League was pre-empted. Because, since the Camp David agreements, an increased level of Arab dependency has emerged. The Camp David agreements, and the peace treaty which was undertaken unilaterally by Egypt and Israel, led to a situation where the Arab world lost, to some extent, its compass.

In a way, the crisis provided the opportunity for the Arabs to articulate the questioning process. They realized that questions without answers are a prescription for disaster. In this respect, also, one should point out that before the crisis, there were the beginnings of a blending process between Arab nationalism (which had been marginalized for too long), and Islamic fundamentalism (which had been on the rise). For the first time in modern history, Arab nationalists and Islamic fundamentalists, by rediscovering the spiritual, intellectual and cultural context of their identity, were realizing that Islam and Arabity cannot be decoupled from each other. It is in this blending process that Islamic fundamentalism began to shy away from its obscurantist social and intellectual features, and Arab nationalism began to shy away from its strict interpretation of secularism as divested of its spiritual and cultural roots. The convergence that was taking place — particularly in Jordan and among the Palestinians, as well as in North Africa — constitutes in my judgement one of the most important historical developments in the Arab world. It is this potentiality for a healthy evolution in the Arab psyche which constitutes one of the most promising intellectual developments that, if nursed, could be the basis of the corrective for various imbalances and distortions that we find in the Arab world.

Along with the construction of an Arab order, the second prong of the strategy must involve the UN. The Security Council must be actively involved in insuring compliance with the resolutions relevant to the Arab-Israeli conflict, and insisting that all parties — including the PLO — are involved in achieving a comprehensive and durable peace.

The present attempt at removing the PLO from the negotiating process is tantamount to ratification of Israel's conquests. The claim that the PLO endorsed Iraq's invasion of Kuwait is a deliberate distortion of the record. That the Palestinian people felt a profound sense of solidarity with the Iraqi people remains a valid demonstration of Arab popular sympathy with the suffering of both the peoples of Kuwait and Iraq, in exactly the same way that instant solidarity was felt by all Arabs with the peoples of Palestine, Lebanon, Sudan and Somalia.

For Israel to claim that the PLO is disqualified *now*, is to fly in the face of its well-established contempt; as if prior to Iraq's invasion, Israel was on record as being even *willing* to recognize the PLO, let alone the right of the Palestinian people to self-determination.

Never in the history of diplomacy has an adversary sought to dictate who will represent his enemy. Of course, the Palestinians and the Arabs would prefer to negotiate with the constituency of conscience within Israel, with Peace Now. But unfortunately, Peace Now cannot deliver on the outcome of negotiations. And perhaps Israel would like to negotiate with some Palestinians — who still remain fictional — who Israel designates; but they cannot deliver, either. If one is serious about negotiation, one negotiates with those who can deliver on the outcome.

In that respect the PLO is the framework of Palestinian peoplehood. The Palestinians of the diaspora, the Palestinians of the refugee camps, the Palestinians under occupation: they are a people; they are not demographic additions in Lebanon, in Syria, in Egypt, in Iraq. They are a people entitled to self-determination. The PLO is not Yasir Arafat, nor is it George Habash. The PLO is a state of mind for the Palestinian people in the absence of their state. The PLO is their sense of identity in the absence of their citizenship. That is why any attempt to circumvent, or delay, or marginalize the PLO is an exercise in futility, and indicates the degeneration of the usage of the term "negotiations."

There must be negotiations. These have to be done with the PLO. The PLO can deliver the Palestinian people to a commitment to a historical reconciliation, a reconciliation which they might accept grudgingly, but to the realization of which they will commit themselves.

The entire UN General Assembly went to Geneva in November 1988 because the PLO was not allowed to come to the U.S. at the appropriate diplomatic level. At that time, Arafat indicated that a historical act of reconciliation would be made. The PLO was persuaded to make this act of reconciliation by many Arab countries. These Arab countries promised the PLO that significant steps towards an independent Palestinian state would be made.

At that time and now, the term "Arab moderate" is used to refer to the Arab who is willing and eager to accommodate America's accommodation of Israel, rather than an Arab who is rational and reasonable and committed to his or her own people. That definition and distortion of the term "moderate" has led to a great deal of dislocation of the priorities of American policy towards the Arab world, particularly in its permissiveness towards the Israeli propensity for territorial annexation.

Movement towards a comprehensive peace in the Middle East is possible but difficult. After the UN Security Council energized itself on the Gulf crisis, it can no longer afford to remain paralyzed on the Israeli-Arab conflict. Otherwise, a "new world order" as envisaged by the U.S. will become the license for regional instability and the clock of history will again have been set back in the Middle East.

The UN was called upon to reassert its credibility and effectiveness as the proper vehicle for building a new global order. The harshness of the measures it authorized to enforce its resolutions on Iraq set in motion expectations that similar measures will become applicable to all those who continue deliberately to defy its authority and consistently violate its resolutions.

If these expectations are dashed by a recurring permissiveness towards Israel, then the peace that has long eluded the Middle East will continue to highlight the flaws in the alleged commitment to the new world order and further accentuate the deep sense of grievance and frustration prevalent throughout the Arab and Third World.

A bold step towards self-determination for the Palestinian people, including their right to an independent state, will enable the Arab order to begin to heal the many wounds, whether self-inflicted or inflicted by others. It will enable the Arab order to address the problems of a rich nation of poor people. It will restore the self-confidence necessary to insulate the Arabs from being coopted by the West and free them from the propensity to confront it. In as much as the Arabs are the geopolitical vanguard of the South, their order can usher an orderly discourse and dialogue with the North.

Questions arose in the Arab world during the Gulf crisis about issues which were never mentioned before. How come there is so much concentration of wealth in the hands of the very few, and so much widespread poverty? Why has it been possible for families — the ruling families of Kuwait and other Gulf countries — to have private wealth which equals the sum total of the national debts of both Egypt and the Sudan? Why were the Security Council resolutions so eagerly pursued and implemented when it came to Iraq, when so many other resolutions pertaining to southern Lebanon, the occupation of the Golan Heights, and the rights of the Palestinians to self-determination, have remained for so long on the books of the Security Council without pursuit or implementation? How come the decision-making processes are concentrated in the hands of the very few elites, and popular ability to participate in the decision-making process has been ruled out? How, also, can unilateral decision-making on the part of one person — anywhere in the Arab world — affect the destinies of hundreds of thousands, millions of people, without being answerable to anyone? All these questions led to a ferment, an intellectual, political, and psychological ferment.

The consequences of such an Arab discourse will inevitably help to shape an internationalist and genuinely "new global order." At that juncture the "new world order" will cease to trigger memories of an "old imperial order" and will instead prepare humankind jointly to render the 21st century an era in which the ideal and the real blend in creative accommodation and co-discovery.

# 15

# The Kurds: An Old Crisis at a New Moment

*Clovis Maksoud*

To the Arabs the Kurdish situation in Iraq is viewed less as a problem and more as a challenge. Constituting nearly eighteen percent of the Iraqi population, the Kurds live predominantly in the northern area of the country. They are all citizens of Iraq; they also have a rich cultural heritage and a separate language. They perceive themselves to be part of a "Kurdish nation" which exists principally in three other countries — Iran, Turkey and the Soviet Union. In these respective countries, they enjoy different degrees of autonomy — and suffer varied levels of discrimination. That the Kurdistan nation desires to become a Kurdistan state is undeniable as an aspiration. It is readily admitted, however, even by the most vigorous nationalists among the Kurds, that this wish — or dream — cannot be an achievable objective at this historical juncture. In many ways the Kurds have reconciled their political and legal dispersion across four countries with the legitimacy of their sense of cultural unity.

This Kurdish dilemma has posed for the Arab nationalist a profound intellectual and political, as well as moral, challenge. On the one hand, this challenge has impelled the Arab nationalist to broaden the concept of Arabism to transcend ethnic or linguistic criteria as exclusive or even dominant components in determining Arab identity.

The problem that a prevailing culture engenders among its ethnic and religious minorities cannot be glossed over, dismissed or ignored. In Iraq, the situation has been consistently mishandled, and often exacerbated by Iraq's overall human rights problems. While coercion and the denial of human rights in Iraq was non-discriminating, the sense of grievance was accentuated among Iraq's disempowered Kurdish minority.

The Kurdish leadership, including Massoud Barzani and Jalal Talabani, led the post-war insurrection and encouraged an interventionist policy by the U.S. and allied forces, only to negotiate an apparently satisfactory "autonomy" agreement whereby their cultural identity would be recognized and their political rights guaranteed. It was inevitable that these negotiations with the Iraqi leadership were painstakingly undertaken and conducted amidst a profound crisis of confidence. Earlier broken promises as well as the rescinding of the 1970 autonomy agreement rendered the Kurds suspicious of new relations with the Iraqi regime. Assurances in themselves were insufficient unless backed by some form of international cover. On the other hand, the Iraqi state has been wary of the genuineness of the sense of belonging that Kurds felt as citizens of Iraq. Previous association with U.S. and Israeli intelligence by certain Kurdish leaders exacerbated suspicions of Kurdish loyalty, especially when significant elements of the Kurdish population helped and were helped by successive regimes in Iran.

The aftermath of the Gulf War led to two apparently contradictory considerations. A weakened Iraqi regime, exhausted by the devastation wreaked upon it, became more disposed to adopt an accommodating response to the historical and genuine grievances of the Kurdish population. This was the moment, Kurdish leaders must have felt, which was propitious to secure objectives long held in abeyance, and unrealized.

A further consideration that entered into the Kurdish leadership's calculations was that the alternative to accommodation with the Iraqi regime would mean a structured dependency on outside forces who are reluctant to provide aid, either because of their own restive Kurdish populations (i.e., Turkey and Iran) or, as is the case with those more distant forces (i.e., the U.S., UK and France), because they would use the dependency of the Kurds more as a means to achieve hegemonic intrusion into the region rather than seeking their humanitarian protection.

These factors were all important considerations for the Kurdish leadership, as was the awareness that extracting an administrative and cultural autonomy from a weakened Iraqi regime would be an example for the Kurds in Turkey and Iran to become emboldened in seeking to redress their own similar grievances. Besides, an underlying awareness on the part of the Kurdish leadership that realization of their national aspirations would lead to a geopolitical explosion in the region, helped lower their sights and bring about what, at the time of writing (May 17, 1991), seemed to be a workable agreement that could be viable and uphold the political rights of the Kurdish people.

Barring a last minute hitch, this agreement has significance beyond the parameters of the Kurdish problem. It can, if properly executed, carry within it the seeds of democratization for the entire Iraqi population and help structure new constitutional forms that could bring about national unity in Iraq through spontaneous cohesion rather than forceful coercion.

It seems to me that this agreement should expedite the process of lifting the economic sanctions and enable a democratic Iraq to rebuild and reenter the community of nations with confidence and dignity, after the trauma and tragedy that it and the other Arab nations have experienced.

# 16

## The Politics of Linkage:
## The Arab-Israeli Conflict in the Gulf War

*Ibrahim Abu-Lughod*

Had the Bush administration been less opposed to the Palestinian right to self-determination and more sensitive to the general body of opinion in the Arab world, it would have responded less defensively to Iraq's endeavor to play the "linkage" issue in the politics of the Gulf conflict. Its adamant denial of either an objective or a subjective linkage between the Palestine/ Israeli/Arab conflicts and that of the Gulf remained singular throughout the crisis and appeared inauthentic. Even before the termination of the military conflict both President Bush and Secretary of State Baker saw fit to address themselves to the issues without admitting the linkage. And as soon as Iraq was defeated, the Bush administration "resumed" what it has described as the "peace process" in the Middle East, affirming if not a linkage certainly an important connection between the two issues.

Whereas the linkage issue was both advocated and denied, the precise understanding of what constituted linkage was not made clear by the protagonists. It will be recalled that the term linkage emerged in the politics of the Cold War, and on various occasions referred to the strategic interest of a power in one region where it was anxious to resolve a particular conflict and thus was prepared to compromise in favor of its competitor in another region in which its own interests were not viewed as critical. But linkage could emerge from more objective and substantive norms and interests. The first notion of linkage would have called for a settlement of the Gulf conflict by an acceptance of the principle of Iraq's withdrawal from Kuwait — a critical objective of American policy — in return for an American commitment to bring about a settlement of the Palestine/Israel/Arab conflicts, presumably an important objective of Iraq's foreign policy. The Bush administration ridiculed Iraq's allegation that its invasion of Kuwait was in any way related to its commitment to the rights and interests of either the occupied Arab states or to the Palestinians. The U.S. rejection of Iraq's assertion, in that specific sense, was clearly based on Iraq's own public statements. For it is now evident that Iraq justified its invasion and occupation of Kuwait on the basis of either historical claims, or territorial/economic issues. But Iraq, especially after the occupation of Kuwait, referred to a connection between the two issues but more often than not addressed the linkage in terms of the principles and norms of international relations and law. As far as can be determined from the public record and other pronouncements, Iraq did not commit itself to withdraw unconditionally from Kuwait if a settlement of the Palestine/Israeli/Arab conflict was achieved either through the initiative of the U.S. or that of the UN. Both in the Arab world and elsewhere the linkage continued to be viewed as one stemming from historical/political factors or normative values. I shall therefore address myself to the issue of linkage between the two conflicts as it played itself out in that part of the Arab world that did not endorse the American-inspired military solution to the Gulf conflict, and more particularly among the Palestinians.

## II.

Iraq's invasion of Kuwait on August 2, 1990, produced two different reactions in the Arab world. The first reaction, and the overarching policy that logically followed from that reaction, questioned the legitimacy of Iraq's action on the grounds that all the Arab states have long adhered to and accepted the validity of the principle of self-determination of people and respect for the territorial integrity and sovereignty of the states of the region. Although Iraq justified its invasion with historical claims relating to the administrative and political system of the region prior to its fragmentation by European imperialism, the Arab states recognized the moral basis of the historical/territorial claim without accepting its policy implication in the way Iraq did.

There was no doubt in 1990, any more than there was in 1961 when Kuwait acquired its full sovereignty and independence, that Iraq and Kuwait, and of course much of the rest of the Arab world, constituted a different and more broadly-based geopolitical unit prior to the First World War. The process of state formation that has characterized Arab political development from the nineteenth century on, and the intervention of European imperialism contributed significantly to the emergence of the contemporary state system. Whether the "people" of the region accepted the legitimacy of the system as it emerged is immaterial to our present consideration. The fact remains that the Arab state system emerged, and each Arab state acquired a particular territorial frontier, often drawn by the European powers — in the case of Iraq, Kuwait and Saudia Arabia by Britain in 1922 — and collectively gave rise to a territorially-based national identity.

Two values were held simultaneously with the emergence of the state system. On the one hand the states collectively accepted their own national identity as Arab states (frequently mentioned in their constitutional documents), thus affirming a degree of cultural ethnic cohesion that could contribute to the achievement of a wider political system. When the Arab states began to formalize their political kinship by organizing the League of Arab States they committed themselves to advance their coordination and cooperation, to respect each other's independence and sovereignty, and to settle their disputes, of whatever type, by peaceful means. This collective Arab commitment, reflected by their adherence to the Charter of the Arab League, did not prevent any member from seeking closer association or unity with other members. It has been clearly understood that such bilateral or multilateral attempts at unification and integration are consistent with the broad principles of Arab cooperation and unification and meet an important national Arab aspiration; successful achievement of such unification, however, must be based on the free will of such states.

Iraq's invasion of Kuwait, irrespective of the historical, economic or territorial justification advanced by Iraq, in fact violated a principle long respected by the Arab state system. It was viewed as violating the right of the state to its independence and sovereignty, but also was a violation of the right to self-determination of the people of Kuwait. At the Arab summit conference held in Cairo on August 10 no member of the League of Arab States endorsed Iraq's military action. Clearly what disagreement existed was occasioned by the resolution endorsing the use of the U.S. military to reverse Iraq's act.

Three major issues then appeared that suggested strong and evident linkage with the Palestine/Israel/Arab conflicts. Those are: self-determination, occupation of territory of another state and means of settlement of inter-state conflict.

The collective Arab position on the need for acceptance of the principle of self-determination, in this case the people of Kuwait, was clearly consistent with the historic drive of the Arab people in general and the Palestinian people in particular to exercise their self-determination. The Palestinians' right to self-determination has been universally endorsed and voted upon by the United Nations but their exercise of that right has been violently negated by Israel; needless to say the United States has consistently opposed the Palestinian right to self-determination. When the Bush administration justified its impending military operations against Iraq on the basis of Kuwait's national right to self-determination it made the linkage evident. But more importantly the reaction of the people of region was clear from the outset of the conflict. The Arab states that cooperated with the U.S. in its military operations subordinated their assessment of the reality of the linkage to the need to dislodge Iraq's army. But it should be evident that historically all the Arab states, those who cooperated with the U.S. and those who opposed the military operations, have consistently supported the Palestinian people's right to self-determination. What became evident in the course of public discussion of the issue of linkage was the degree to which the U.S. and its European allies were motivated in their pursuits by their concern with the principle of self-determination. For if the principle is valid in one case it must clearly be valid in all similar cases. As the conflict unfolded it became clear that while the linkage issue was not openly productive of a change in American policy, the Bush administration began to pay some attention to Palestinian Arab assertions of equivalence.

Irrespective of the validity of Iraq's historical/national claims on Kuwait, Iraq's military attack constituted both a violation of Kuwait's sovereignty and of both the provisions of the Charters of the Arab League and the United Nations. The issue is clearly two-fold: can a state, even on the basis of a territorial claim based on national identity, alter the status and acquire that territory by force? The collective Arab response to the issue was clear: the frontiers of the Arab states may not be changed by military means. Status of states could be changed peacefully and as long it is accomplished voluntarily by the agreement of the states concerned, the Arab state system (and others) have been prepared to respect such changes. In the pursuit of Arab unity, both Egypt and Syria achieved a voluntary unification of their states in 1958. The resulting United Arab Republic was accorded Arab and international recognition immediately. More recently the Arab Republic of Yemen and the Peoples Democratic Republic of Yemen, again in an attempt to undo the effect of European imperialism and to realize their own national aspirations, agreed to merge their sovereignties and produced the new Republic of Yemen. Again the new state received immediate recognition regionally and internationally.

Clearly the differing reaction of the regional and international communities to the UAR, Yemen and Iraq's absorption of Kuwait related to the means and not to the idea or the aspiration for greater unification. The Bush administration's rejection of Iraq's action which theoretically was premised on the Charter of the United Nations and the principles of international law was of course correct. But regionally it gave rise to the question of why the U.S. had acquiesced in Israel's military invasion of Palestinian and other territories of the adjacent states, when in fact Israel has even less of a national/historical claim on those territories than Iraq has advanced regarding Kuwait. The linkage in the nature of the act is too clear to ignore.

The third issue that links the two conflicts is clearly the United Nations context of the resolution of the issue. The U.S. assumed a crucial role in mobilizing the UN Security Council, not only to pass the appropriate resolutions condemning Iraq's act but also in imposing sanctions and eventually obtaining authorization to use military force to dislodge Iraq. Of course the U.S. utilized all its leverage to obtain the appropriate resolutions enabling it to act and justifying the fierce military attack that followed. But the UN and its Security Council have probably passed more resolutions and recommendations on the Palestine/Israel/Arab conflicts than on the Gulf crisis. The UN has condemned Israel for its continued occupation and annexation of the Syrian Golan Heights and Jerusalem, and for violating Palestinian political and human rights. Israel has been severely censored for its violation of the Geneva Convention and other human rights charters. Whether the U.S. obstructed or supported the passage of such resolutions is not important for this issue; what is important to note is that such resolutions have been passed by the General Assembly and the Security Council, yet the situation on the ground has become worse as time has gone on. Certainly the U.S. has not seen fit to use any means of pressure either to compel Israel to rescind its legislation of annexation of territory (the Golan Heights and Jerusalem) or to halt the colonization which is changing the demographic composition of the occupied Palestinian territories. If occupation is illegal in both places, if invasions are condemned in both areas and if annexation violates both international law and UN resolutions then clearly those measures pursued with such alacrity in the Gulf War ought to be pursued in the Palestine/Israel and Arab conflicts.

The fourth principle of linkage as advanced in the Arab region but most forcefully advanced by the Palestinians relates to the mode of settling the dispute in the Gulf. Of course the Arab heads of state who attended the Arab summit conference in Cairo wished a settlement of the conflict. But whereas a slim majority went along with the proposal to use force, the other Arab states and more particularly the PLO emphasized the need to settle the conflict peacefully through a process of negotiation. This mode of settling inter-state conflicts is clearly consistent with the UN Charter and international law. The peaceful settlement of international disputes is of immeasurable value. The Palestinians have upheld that value and gave it open expression in the Declaration of Independence at Algiers (1988), and then used that commitment to launch a major policy initiative that called for a negotiated political settlement of their conflict with Israel under international auspices. A negotiated settlement of the Palestine/Israel/Arab conflicts has been an important policy objective of the U.S. for quite some time, which achieved partial success in the Camp David Accords. Hence the Palestinian/Arab endeavor to demonstrate that the linkage between the two conflicts is not only related to values, norms of international politics and law and UN resolutions but subjectively to the mode of resolving international conflict. If the Palestinians, the Arab states of Syria and Lebanon are prepared to resolve their conflict with Israel in a process of negotiation under international auspices why could the same goal not be pursued with regards to the Iraq-Kuwait conflict? If negotiation and peaceful measures fail, should the international community utilize force in all similar situations to halt invasions, occupation, annexation of territories and violation of human and political national rights?

## III.

A cursory examination of statements that expressed the views of both the proponents and opponents of linkage between the Gulf crisis and Palestine/Israel/Arab conflicts would reveal that the issues discussed above constituted the "core" of the linkage issue. Rarely did such statements reflect an understanding of historical links between Iraq and Palestine and of course the negative encounter between Israel and Iraq. Probably it would be fair to suggest that those who opposed linking the two conflicts viewed Iraq's assertion as opportunistic behavior intended to mobilize Arab opinion against the U.S. and/or to embarrass those Arab states that accepted American leadership in resolving the Gulf conflict. The reverse is true. The Arabs who called attention to the linkage wished of course to unmask the "real" intentions of the U.S.: far from being concerned with principles of self-determination, international law and enforcement of UN resolutions the U.S., in their perspective, intended variously to control the oil re-sources of the Arab region in its entirety, to cripple any potential Arab power that could be used to advance Arab welfare and so forth. The fact that the U.S. had behaved in imperialist fashion toward Grenada and Panama and other parts of Central America demonstrated its true standards of international behavior; but closer to the region not only did the U.S. condone Israel's repeated violations, and even sustained it by various forms of economic and military assistance, but in fact endorsed the act of conquest by its ally the Shah of Iran when, in November 1971, his forces invaded and annexed three islands that had been part of the United Arab Emirates. Even earlier the U.S. looked with favor, even if it did not encourage, Jordan's annexation and incorporation of the West Bank.

The Arab view of American political and military behavior is rooted in the historical encounter of the Arabs with the West in general and Israel in particular. Israel is in Palestine and is engaged in the systematic violation of Palestinian rights, not only as a consequence of Britain's previous commit-ment and support but more importantly through the recent support of the U.S. Iraq's position of support was clear even before Saddam Hussein became president: it opposed the displacement of the Palestinians and sought peaceful ways of persuading Britain to accommodate both peoples in Palestine without committing an act of injustice against the Palestinians. When the Palestinians engaged in the general strike of 1936 and in their major revolution in the Mandate period, Iraq's policy was to render direct support (financial and paramilitary) to the Palestinians and to use its diplo-matic machinery and good offices with Britain to bring about a fair solution to the Palestinian Arab/Jewish conflict. Iraq participated in the 1939 round table conference on Palestine in London, and its views were helpful in the issuing of the White Paper on the future of Palestine. Certainly Iraq was very supportive of the Palestinians in the first years of the UN. After May 1948 some of its forces crossed the Palestinian/Jordanian frontier in a hopeless effort to prevent Israel from acquiring more territory than it did. It is a matter of some significance to point out that despite the fact that the Iraqi army was in Palestine in 1949, withdrawing only in the context of international negotiations, Iraq is one of the Arab states that did not sign the armistice agreement with Israel. It should be clear then that Iraq's support for the Palestinians is historically consistent and certainly did not originate with either the Ba'ath party or President Saddam Hussein. After the overthrow of the Iraqi monarchy in 1958, President Qasim called for the liberation of Palestine by inviting the Palestinians to undertake the initiative in the process of liberation and committed Iraq to provide the necessary training and support. That historic support was affirmed when the Ba'ath party consolidated its power in Iraq after 1968 and continued to play an active Arab role in promoting Palestinian rights.

Iraq's historic support for the Palestinians, and opposition to Zionism/Israel is clearly related to Arab nationalism as an idea, and to the Arab identity of both peoples. The Palestinians not only affirm their own Arab identity but, equally importantly, consider Palestine to be part of the Arab national homeland. Their view of Palestine as an Arab territory and Iraq's adherence to the principle of Arab unity produce a policy that clearly links the struggle for Palestinian liberation with other Arabs committed to the freedom and independence of the Arab world. It is this historic, national link that makes Iraq an antagonist in the Palestine/Israel/Arab conflict.

Not only did Iraq play that active role in Palestine itself but additionally it tried to provide assistance to the Arab states when the latter were involved in conflicts with Israel in 1967 and 1973. Parts of Iraq's army were dispatched to both Syria and Jordan during those two conflicts.

Perhaps of equal significance (and this might have been an important factor in the eruption of the Gulf conflict) was the political leadership role that Iraq played in the wake of the Camp David Accords of 1978. It will be recalled that the peace treaty resulted essentially in removing Egypt from the Arab side of the Arab-Israeli conflict. That removal meant that Egypt was no longer able to assume the hegemonic role in the Arab world; on the contrary, it was even expelled from the Arab League. Iraq's emergence to a position of modest leadership goes back to that period; it was Iraq that coordinated Arab policies of isolating Egypt, of coordinating Arab policies on the resolution of the Palestine/Israel conflict and in providing the political support for opposition to American peace initiatives more supportive of Israel's interests. It would not be an exaggeration to suggest that Iraq aspired to fill the vacuum that developed with Egypt's demise. In that sense whatever Iraq did had an important reference to the Palestine/Israel/Arab conflict.

## IV.

Our discussion of the linkage would be incomplete if we did not take into account Israel's perception of Iraq's identity, role and aspirations. Of course Israel dealt with the monarchy of Iraq in its successful endeavor to persuade Iraqi Jews to migrate to Palestine. Israel also encountered Iraq's army in the field, and as Iraq acquired greater regional power it confronted Israel indirectly through its Palestinian proxies. Israel was fully conscious of Iraq's commitment to the Palestinians. While Iraq acquired modern weapons and gained military experience in the course of its war with Iran, Israel had played a most important role, not only in supporting the Shah and providing the imperial army with weapons and other forms of support, but also in pursuing similar policies during the reign of Ayatollah Khomeini. Israel's perception that Iraq constituted a strategic danger to Israel was epitomized by Israel's destruction of Iraq's nuclear reactor in 1981 and in many of its public relations campaigns warning of Iraq's acquisition of modern weapons. There was no doubt in Israel's thinking that Iraq was and perhaps remains a very important power in the Arab coalition against it. Whether the scud missiles launched against Israel confirmed Israel's perception or not is immaterial. But the constant allusions to the potential Iraqi threat to Israel suggest that Israel prepared itself for the mutually antagonistic roles of both, stemming from the Palestine/Israel/Arab conflicts.

## V.

In the aftermath of the Gulf War, the question of whether Iraq will recover its territorial integrity and what role it will play as a consequence cannot yet be assessed. But there seems to be no doubt that the U.S. has concluded that Iraq's power is no longer a factor in the settlement of the Arab-Israeli conflict. The ability of the U.S. to exercise unchallenged and immediate political hegemony throughout the Arab world is no longer in doubt. It is clear that the U.S. is now more ready to acknowledge the linkage between the Gulf crisis and the Arab-Israeli conflict. President Bush stated in his fall 1990 address to the UN and his subsequent speech to Congress that the Arabs and Israel will find it easier to deal with their conflict after Iraq's eviction from Kuwait and that there should be a settlement of the Palestinian issue. Secretary of State Baker was equally clear in his Congressional testimony on the connection between President Hussein's appeal to the Arabs and the chronic Arab-Israeli conflict, and thus the imperative of resolving that conflict. What becomes evident now that the Gulf War is over is that the antagonists clearly understood that the linkage exists; they differed on how to deal with it. Those Arabs who were sympathetic to the idea of linkage hoped for an outcome consistent with universally accepted principles of self-determination, equality of states, respect for international law and enforcement of UN resolutions. For the U.S. linkage may mean a freer hand in resolving the Palestine/Israel/Arab conflict in accordance with a design more supportive of Israel and detrimental to the Palestinians. The initiative undertaken by Secretary Baker so soon after Iraq's defeat not only confirms the existence of linkage but also assures that any solution to this bitter conflict will have to be approved by the U.S., in their position as the unchallenged hegemonic power in the region.

# 17

## The Other Occupation: The Palestinian Response

*Hanan Mikhail Ashrawi**

An honest presentation of what Palestinians feel and how they reacted to the Gulf crisis must start with a review of the region, of the objective factors affecting Palestinians during the crisis. This is crucial not for the purpose of indulging in hindsight or retrospection or recriminations, but because it is important that we have a clear understanding of these factors, since they continue to exist. Failure to deal with the factors underlying the Palestinians' longstanding grievances runs the risk of creating an artificial peace, leaving the real causes of insecurity and instability intact and liable to erupt again and again.

During the Gulf crisis certain misconceptions distorted the Palestinian position, even though Palestinians themselves remained consistent to their principles, including their opposition to occupation. Not a single Palestinian, whether from the PLO or the occupied territories, ever condoned the occupation of Kuwait by Iraq. We actively wrote statements condemning the occupation and asking for Iraqi withdrawal; but at the same time we said that one cannot correct an error by committing a larger one. We opposed the presence of foreign troops on Arab soil and felt that adopting the military option without giving political and diplomatic options a chance was not only immoral and unjust, but was also counterproductive and would only create further problems.

Throughout the crisis, the Palestinian position was against war, against the military option. We have been consistent with our principles in proposing a peaceful settlement of the Palestinian-Israeli conflict; we could not in all conscience turn round and change our position in favor of military intervention in the Gulf. Our society is not monolithic, and many differences of opinion exist, for example over such decisions as whether or not to meet with Secretary of State Baker; but at the same time there is a

* This article is adapted from a speech given by the author in San Francisco in March 1991.

191

unity of purpose. There is a fierce determination among Palestinians to achieve our goals — principally the goal of national rights — and although disagreements on tactics and procedures exist, Palestinians are united in our national/political program.

## The Background to the Palestinian Position

The first factor made the Palestinians adopt their position in the Gulf crisis was Israel's escalation of repression, its "iron fist" policy, in occupied Paletine, and the unchecked excesses and prolongation of the occupation in which Palestinians felt, and continue to feel, victimized. But nobody cared about the brutalization of Palestinians; international attention was concerned only with Israel's "security."

The second issue was Israel's policy of creating facts on the ground, of presenting the world with a *fait accompli*, especially with regard to the immigration of Soviet Jews and the settlement policy in the occupied territories. We felt, literally, that the very ground on which we live, the very land which is the source of our self-definition, the very resources we need to survive, were being stolen from us. While Secretary Baker talked gently about Israeli settlements as an obstacle to peace, Palestinians felt that the settlements were completely illegal and a form of theft of Palestinian-Arab land.

A third factor was the political stalemate in the peace process. In this regard Palestinians felt that Israel had been given a free hand to undermine and actually block the peace process. This became even more apparent with the dissolution of the previous Labor-Likud coalition in Israel and the formation of a right-wing government. This new government has very clearly been shifting the parameters of political discourse to the right, for example by the incorporation of parties like Molodet, an avowedly racist organization, into the government. The limits of political orthodoxy are shifting from the political extremism of Herut or Prime Minister Shamir, to the even more fanatic extremism of Moledet, with its stated policy of "transfer," a euphemism for the expulsion of Palestinians from the occupied territories.

The failure of the Arab regimes was the fourth factor. Historically the Arab states have failed, both politically and militarily, to bring about any sort of equitable solution to the Palestinian question. This has created a sense of bitterness and frustration among Palestinians, and a deep distrust of the existing Arab regimes, who have consistently manipulated the issue of Palestine in order to gain popular credibility or legitimacy, or even economic well-being. Additionally Palestinians in the West Bank and Gaza felt that the intifada had been let down by Arab governments, that no support was forthcoming. It appeared that these regimes understand only too well that the intifada is a breath of fresh air, of democracy, of popular resistance and empowerment in a region where they are in desperately short supply, and perhaps deep down they are afraid that this might be either exportable to their countries or contagious. Such an effect could well threaten the foundations of many, if not all, Arab regimes.

The final issue that needs to be understood in any analysis of the Palestinian position during the Gulf crisis is the grossly unequal distribution of wealth in the region. There exists on the one hand an ostentatious display of wealth — conspicuous consumption, to borrow Thorstein Veblen's phrase — in the Gulf states. And yet elsewhere in the Middle East, and not only among Palestinians, one sees real deprivation. In the Sudan people are facing famine yet again; in Jordan, Yemen, and other Arab countries you see immense poverty. What made matters worse was that during the Gulf crisis billions of dollars were found to support the war effort, when these billions could have been put to far better use in raising the standard of living for millions of people in the region. This display of inequity is something that further embittered Palestinians.

The treatment of Palestinians, and of other non-citizens and foreigners in the Gulf states added fuel to the fire. No security has ever been provided to Palestinians working abroad; they have been denied citizenship and any sense of financial or even human security, as evidenced in post-war Kuwait by the treatment of Palestinians accused of "collaboration" with the Iraqis. Such discriminatory policies practiced by the Gulf states led Palestinians to say in the wake of Iraq's invasion of Kuwait: perhaps now the whole region will be shaken up, perhaps now people will understand that the multi-tiered victimization of the Palestinians must be brought to an end.

## U.S. Aid to Israel

In terms of U.S. policy, people felt that the U.S. had not been even-handed. There is an understandable mistrust, a lack of faith in U.S. policy, because it has been shown consistently to be on the side of Israel, and has actually shielded Israel in many cases from the consequences of its mistakes. Palestinians see the U.S. as actually subsidizing Israel's occupation.

Palestinians cannot accept that $3.5 billion has to go to Israel every year, along with the unlimited invisible benefits that come with the financial aid. But beyond that longstanding concern, several major elements increased the Palestinians' sense of hostility towards the U.S.. The American veto in the UN Security Council of the June 1990 resolution calling for protection of the Palestinians in the occupied territories was the most painful example. At that time a group of us were on hunger strike. It took tremendous will and self-control, following the Reshon Letzion massacre (in which seven Palestinian workers were killed and dozens more wounded by an Israeli ex-soldier) to say that we did not want to respond to violence with more violence; that we wanted instead to use the highest form of civil disobedience to make a human, non-violent statement. The hunger strike lasted for nearly two weeks, and our only demand was for international protection. We asked the UN for accountability to its own resolutions regarding the rights of peoples living under occupation, and for the dispatch of UN observers to look at Israeli practices in the territories with the same standard as those used to judge other occupations. The U.S. vetoed that resolution. This action further deepened the chasm of distrust caused by the Bush administration's suspension of the U.S.-PLO dialogue the same month.

What further strengthened that feeling of insecurity was the emergence of a unipolar world, as the Cold War came to an end, and the U.S. stood unchallenged as the pre-eminent world power. Palestinians felt that there had to be a more impartial approach to the issue of Palestine, and they feared that the thaw in the Cold War would give rise to all sorts of regional problems.

In August of 1990 they were to be proved right. To their intense shock, the Palestinians — who had put their faith in the United Nations as a means of achieving international legitimacy for their struggle — saw the UN mobilized not to make peace but to sanction war; in the new unipolar world, Palestinians were given a lesson in *realpolitik*, in the politics of pragmatism and power, as the U.S. manipulated the world body with ease to serve the interests of the world's one remaining superpower.

To Palestinians suffering under Israeli occupation, this display of American double standards was breathtaking. How could Washington have allowed all the UN resolutions on Palestine to remain unimplemented for all those years, and then have mobilized the UN in a few short months to legitimize the destruction of an Arab country, the taking of so many human lives? The Bush administration called it a moral war; Palestinians did not see how this, or indeed any war could be moral, or just.

Internationally there is a recognition of the PLO, and of the Palestinian people as a whole, as representing a national liberation movement, committed to freedom and human rights. As such, the Palestinian people could not accept the presence of foreign troops on Arab soil. We felt that we were being consistent, that our position with respect to a political settlement to the Palestinian-Israeli conflict had to be applied equally to the crisis in the Gulf.

As stated before, the intifada is a movement of empowerment, a popular statement of the will of the people. Through the intifada Palestinians have said that it is the will of the people that brings liberation, and not a decision by a foreign government, whether it is by force of arms or diplomacy, whether it is an Arab government or any other, whether it is based on patronage or manipulation.

However, during the Gulf crisis we witnessed a serious regression into what we might call the "messianic approach" to the Palestinian issue. This approach ran counter to the ethos of the intifada and affected Palestinians in particular. One of the significant accomplishments of the intifada has been the reinforcement and implementation of the spirit of self-reliance, of taking initiatives, and maintaining a sense of creativity and versatility in resisting the cruelty and oppression of the occupation. The days are over when the Palestinians looked to salvation from outside or relied on a *deus ex machina* savior from above. We have grasped the reins of our own destiny and we cannot — must not — relinquish our will or fate to any external forces.

In recent years, the region has witnessed the emergence of super-nationalism, a revival of pan-Arab nationalism, and increased radicalization; it showed these forces were still there under the surface. Palestinians asked of other Arab peoples: are they simply hibernating, are they going to wake up from the stupor they appear to have fallen into? Or is this the stupor of death? After so many years of living with suppression, repression, and the lack of basic freedoms, have the Arabs lapsed into a kind of paralyzed silence? Still, Palestinians kept their faith that this is a temporary state of affairs, that one day the Arab people would wake up.

In addition, the region saw a resurgence of religious fervor which tended to support the anti-nationalist movement, Hamas, in Palestine. However, the phenomenon seemed short-lived because the religious organizations were not capable of presenting a complete or popular approach to the problems in our region; only the nationalist movement could offer that.

The Palestinians also were victims of guilt by association, in which the Iraqi issue was superimposed on the Palestinian issue. It seemed there was an effort to erase the differences between the Palestinian issue, which has its own sense of internal legitimacy and justice, and the issue of the military defeat of Iraq.

## Double Meanings

After the Gulf crisis, Palestinians need a period for healing wounds, for taking stock and assessing. There are many subjective factors involved, having to do with perceptions and perspectives; our view of the West as ethnocentric, understanding only images and discourse that are produced by the West, and not trying to make the imaginative leap necessary to understand the images, the discourse and the symbols of the Arab or the Palestinian. We felt there were double standards. We felt that in the cultural dimension there remained a serious lack of understanding of emotive terms, like dignity and pride and honor. We felt there was a lack of understanding of all our myths and symbols and even questions of ritual and decorum, having to do with preserving the pride and the respect of people who are representatives of our culture.

One can give many examples of these different definitions. Secretary Baker talks about "new thinking," we talk about a "new vision of the future." He talks about a "twin-track approach" and we talk about a "comprehensive approach." So this linguistic dimension emerges, in which things work both ways. There is a lack of understanding of our rhetorical devices, sometimes in the form of metaphor, hyperbole, or formulae; at other times, what were misunderstood were literal statements of policy or politics. The tone, to Palestinians, is an essential element of such statements, a subtlety often ignored by those in the West who view us through an Orientalist lens.

Language, for us, is an expression of national identity, and not just a tool for communication. I am going to suggest here a dictionary of alternative appropriate definitions.

We view the term "moderate" as applicable to one who has abandoned the Palestinian substance and who has adopted the American or Israeli logic.

"Alternative leadership," as used in the West, to us means quislings or collaborators, or anti-PLO forces.

The "new world order" to us means American hegemony; our alternative is international legitimacy.

"Realpolitik" or "realism" or "pragmatism" to us mean more concessions are needed fron the Palestinians.

"Security considerations" to us mean that Israel calls the shots.

A "properly structured international conference at the appropriate time" to us means never.

"New thinking among Arab leadership," as Mr. Baker has said, to us means a willingness on the part of Arab leaders to bypass the PLO and to make a separate peace with Israel.

"New thinking in Israel" means to us: "We will give up not one inch, but deliver the Arabs to us."

"Legitimate political rights," is another example. We talk about legitimate national rights. National rights are not legitimized, they exist.

When we hear about "domestic political considerations in the U.S.," we immediately think about AIPAC.

The "Jordanian option," "Egyptian option," and so on, are all terms with double meanings. In our linguistic discourse we must be very careful in choosing what terms we use. The semantic level is not just formalistic. In a way, it tends to define substance, it defines our rights, and the way in which the peace process is going to move.

Because much of our history has been shaped by forces and voices outside our control, we have become particularly wary of any attempts at confiscating Palestinian rights, the Palestinian voice, or Palestinian representation. Therefore we will not surrender Palestinian representation regardless of the pressures.

The Palestinian issue is not an internal Israeli issue; it is an issue of a people and a nation, and has to be addressed as such. The peace process must not be bogged down in semantics and technicalities and artificial obstacles, whether they are concerned with representation, whether people are from East Jerusalem or the West Bank, or whether the agenda is open or closed. These are terms imposed by Israel, and must not be allowed to impede a peace process.

We do not need new UN resolutions on Palestine; we do not need new Security Council meetings, except to state, very clearly and simply, that the resolutions that exist now have to be implemented. That is all we need.

If Israeli retrenchment and rejectionism are allowed to continue, they will feed the direct relationship between Israeli rejectionism, hardline politics, and the emergence of rejectionism on the other side. Entrenchment feeds entrenchment, intransigence feeds intransigence.

## Winning the Peace

Immediately after the Gulf War, a new surge of vitality and versatility was felt in Palestinian political discourse. There was a very vibrant atmosphere in occupied Palestine, in which everybody was discussing these issues, trying to plot courses. It is this type of awareness and commitment to a peace process, a commitment based on real rights and real legitimacy, that has to be taken into account. There is a willingness, a predisposition among the Palestinians to make peace, but there was not and is not a willingness to give up our basic rights. One must not confuse these two issues.

The pressure to obtain further concessions from the Palestinians is not just an exercise in futility, but one that can be counterproductive and will eventually backfire. The West does not need a Palestinian leadership that has lost its popular base. The Palestinians have made as many compromises and concessions as are possible, taking into account the highly politicized constituency that holds its leadership accountable. A Palestinian friend of mine speaks of our "maximum-minimum" political program. These are our minimal demands, and these are our maximum demands. We are not going to claim any irredentist position, but at the same time we are not going to give up any of our basic rights.

It must be understood that the Palestinian political program is not shaped by Israeli or Western priorities. It is shaped according to the internal realities, and the authentic needs and rights of the Palestinians.

"Confidence-building measures" was another very popular term in the post-Gulf War period. Or: "confidence and security building measures." But Palestinians did not accept that these could be used to reward Israel for its aggression. We did not understand why Israel has to go to one regional conference on security, and then to another regional conference on development, and then perhaps, if the Palestinians or the Arabs behave themselves, then Israel will agree to go to a narrowly-delimited peace conference.

We need to go straight to a peace conference, without further delay. The status quo is extremely painful for Palestinians, and completely untenable, and it is being used to undermine the possibilities of peace in the region. It is being used in an attempt to make the occupation irreversible, so Israel must be prevented from buying more time.

Occupation must not be rewarded. The west cannot accept Israel's stranglehold on lands which it illegally occupies, and at the same time tell Israel that we "understand your security concerns." The U.S. and the West have to "understand the concerns" of others as well.

The new realities that have emerged as a result of the Gulf War include the recognition that security cannot be achieved through geography, which President Bush alluded to in a speech to Congress. Therefore the illegal acquisition of land cannot provide a source of security. Israel was perceived not as a strategic ally during Gulf War, but as a liability, because it needed to be protected. Only a real, genuine peace will provide a source of security not just for Israel but for everybody in the region.

In order to bring about a real peace process to address all the fears of the Arabs in the region, and to stem the tide of radicalization and popular resentment, there will have to be a withdrawal of foreign troops. Any settlement will have to be comprehensive, without sidestepping the real issues and representatives, including Palestinian representatives, and will have to tackle long-standing grievances and problems that are endemic to our region. Some of these include the absence of democracy, human rights and accountability, the inequitable distribution of wealth and resources, and so on.

Finally, the West in the flush of victory over Iraq must not continue to punish the victims, the countries like Jordan, Yemen, the Sudan. Jordan is embarking on a new process of democratization, Yemen has embarked on a process of unification. The Sudan suffers from a famine. Palestinians are in the midst of an intifada. These people have been punished doubly by the Gulf crisis and by the political decisions that are being taken in the West, by the Gulf states, and elsewhere.

In the future we will need real regional disarmament, real regional cooperation, and real regional development based on a genuine commitment to address the sources of grievances and the sources of instability. Some have spoken of "winning the peace." But peace is much more difficult to win than war. A lasting peace in the region must be an exercise in saving lives and resources, and arriving at real solutions that would guarantee justice and national rights, not merely further exercises in cosmetic surgery.

# 18

# The Gulf Crisis and the Economy in the Occupied Territories

*Samir Hulaileh*

Following August 2, 1990, the Gulf crisis brought about the reformulation of economic relations between the occupied territories and neighboring Arab countries, Israel, and even internally between north and south sectors, between Gaza and the West Bank. This crisis was a turning point in the economic history of the region which is certain to leave its mark on the next phase. This transformation was not the result of the Gulf crisis alone, but was the cumulative result of the conditions of Palestinian political and economic reality through years of occupation, including those of the Palestinian uprising.

The Palestinian economy has been a subject of heated discussion for the past twenty years. The concentration of the Palestinian national struggle in the occupied territories after 1973 (the formation of the National Front), with municipal elections, and the formation of a number of youth, women's, agricultural and medical grassroots organizations, posed a number of important questions concerning what was required of the national movement.

Following the Arab summit in Baghdad and the ratification of the Joint Palestinian-Jordanian Committee's budget in Amman in 1978, the PLO was confronted with a number of practical questions about how to spend hundreds of millions of dollars on development in the West Bank and the Gaza Strip. The response was spontaneous, void of any long term planning, and not linked to a specific strategy for development. This was consistent for the PLO which did not, at that point, identify as one of its main tasks the responsibility for the Palestinians living under occupation, before their liberation.

The theory that everything would become possible after liberation was still dominant, with Israeli occupation seen as a passing phenomenon soon to disappear. Therefore efforts should not be wasted, it was thought, on economic development under the harsh conditions of occupation. And despite comprehensive discussions by a number of Palestinian economists in the early 1980s on funding priorities and possibilities for development in the occupied territories, the prevailing theory that development under occupation was not on the agenda precluded any possibility for developing resources in the occupied territories.

But the seeds of a new outlook were planted, and they germinated in the growth of grassroots organizations in various development areas. The end of the 1980s witnessed a polarization and crystallization of specific outlooks on development which were adopted by political and grassroots organizations in their dialogue with various funding institutions.

The Palestinian intifada emerged to pick the fruits of the previous phases, and to turn the focus to the Palestinian people inside the occupied territories, leading their struggle beneath the banner of the PLO. The intifada was a historical chance for Palestinians inside the occupied territories and their leadership to identify the core of their vision and priorities in the interests of their day-to-day struggle under occupation, based on the dynamic interaction between economic and political decision-making. The intifada terminated the debate on the question of whether there could be development under occupation. The Palestinian leadership found itself, for the first time, facing a new challenge. It was no longer only the political leadership of the Palestinian people in their struggle for political independence, but also, by necessity, their leadership in everyday activities on the path towards building the infrastructure of the coming state.

The economic slogans of the intifada — boycotting Israeli products, reducing rents, stabilizing the exchange rate of the Jordanian dinar, returning to agriculture and home economy, new agreements between factory owners and labor unions — crystallized a pioneering economic role for the PLO without any form of imposition of will, but through popular initiatives. In this context, the possibility of real development even under occupation began to materialize. There were many views on how that development process should emerge. But regardless of the practical results, one can say that the best aspect of this experience has been its multiplicity and its democracy.

So, when the Gulf crisis occurred, the local Palestinian economic base was still in an experimental phase, trying to survive despite difficulties and measures imposed by the occupation. In addition to the negative impact on economic growth of the great number of general strike days, there were the military orders in March 1988 limiting money transfers to the occupied territories from Jordan. These orders had a great impact, decreasing the amount of remittances from Palestinians in the Gulf and Jordan by half — to only $200 million. By the end of 1988 the Jordanian dinar began to suffer a marked decrease in value and by early 1989 it had declined to a level of only 50% of its previous value compared to foreign currencies (especially the dollar).

Since most savings were held in dinars, the occupied territories lost $300 million in currency value in savings alone. Also in early 1989, the Jordan valley and the north suffered the West Bank's worst-ever period of frost, leading to agricultural losses of $50 million.

In 1989 economic activity began to stabilize, with fewer days of general strikes and increased industrial production. The economic boycott against Israeli goods began to have an impact in terms of higher levels of investment in Palestinian industry and animal husbandry. There was also marked improvement in the construction and tourism sectors. In 1990, economic growth and investment activities continued to expand the practical base for self-sufficiency and tightening up the boycott.

However, in 1990 large-scale Jewish immigration to Israel from the Soviet Union began unexpectedly and in unprecedented numbers. Due to this immigration, coupled with the increasing political tension in the occupied territories following the al-Aqsa massacre (in which 19 Palestinians were killed by Israeli military authorities on October 8) and the increasing attacks by Palestinian workers, especially towards the end of 1990, a state of restlessness surfaced in Israeli circles. The Israeli authorities used political criteria to prohibit the entry of 12,000 Palestinian workers to Israel. In addition, a one-year plan was implemented aimed at reducing the total number of Palestinian workers in Israel by half.

So the Gulf crisis occurred at a time when these pressures and new conditions were at their height. All of this aggravated the impact of the crisis to a level that the young economy of the occupied territories could not bear. It even threatened to undermine political gains in the economic sphere.

Following the Iraqi occupation of Kuwait on August 2, new variables began to affect the economic situation in the occupied territories, and some began quickly to take effect. The first was the decrease in remittances from Kuwait and other Gulf countries to the occupied territories, including Palestinian, official, and non-governmental Gulf remittances, as well as indirect remittances via the PLO.

Estimates indicate that there were 800,000 Palestinians living in the Gulf countries; about half in Kuwait, 300,000 in Saudi Arabia, and the rest in the smaller Gulf states. Of the 400,000 in Kuwait, the total number of Palestinians with the right of return, according to Israeli law, is about 63,000. Of those, 19,000 are workers, and represent 7% of the Palestinian labor force in the occupied territories. Thus their return could raise the present unemployment rates by more than a third.

There was also a decrease, or even a total halt, in some Palestinian exports to some Gulf countries and Jordan, and tourism came to a complete halt in the occupied territories. Some thousands of now-unemployed Palestinians returned to the territories, placing a new burden on the narrow labor market.

Direct aid from non-governmental Gulf institutions was temporarily suspended, in particular the Arab Fund in Kuwait, the Islamic Bank in Jedda, OPEC, and the Gulf Fund. Since the beginning of the intifada these institutions had provided up to $35 million annually to the health and education sectors in the occupied territories.

What was worrying to Palestinians about the donations provided by those Arab funds was the direct control the Saudi and Kuwaiti governments had on financing and setting priorities for the funds. Despite consistent assurances from the funds' administrators and some Gulf states that direct and indirect aid to the Palestinians would not decrease, it seemed certain that inter-Arab politics would decide the fate of these donations.

Many Gulf countries, Saudi Arabia in particular, have given donations to the Palestinians by financing a number of medical, educational and religious institutions. The PLO has also received official donations from these countries, in addition to the deductions from the salaries of Palestinians working in the Gulf countries which are paid into the budget of the Palestine National Fund. It was clear in the aftermath of the war that the PLO's stand in the Gulf crisis was going directly to affect the sum of money provided to Palestinian institutions.

The losses of the Palestinian tourism sector in the twelve months following August 2, 1990 amounted to $90 million, which equaled the usual annual profit of this sector. This loss also added thousands of unemployed to the labor market in the occupied territories.

In summary, one can say that the occupied territories experienced a decrease in gross national income of 20% compared to 1987, equivalent to a loss of more than $400 million for the year following August 2, 1990.

But this was only a part of the devastation of the Palestinian economy. The Israeli authorities sealed off the occupied territories and imposed a 24-hour curfew beginning January 17, 1991, at the beginning of the Gulf War. The total curfew lasted for 40 days, and subsequently was somewhat relaxed, although restrictions continued on travel between cities, between villages and cities, between the West Bank and Jerusalem, and between the West Bank and Gaza. The direct effect of the curfew was that 304,000 Palestinian workers lost their sources of income. The total additional losses for that period can be estimated at $200 million.

At the same time, the Israeli authorities used this opportunity to begin the implementation of their previously declared program of forbidding Palestinian workers from returning to work in Israel. These measures were like a death blow to the possibility of growth in the Palestinian economy. The new restrictions led to economic stagnation for months after the curfew. The actual number of unemployed in various sectors rose to no less than half the entire Palestinian work force, a catastrophic percentage for a small and developing economy. The Israeli occupation authorities also continued tax-collection raids, forceful collection of police tickets, and insisting on payment of water and electricity bills under threat of terminating those services.

In a field survey conducted in the fifth week of the war, in two villages north of Ramallah, a tremendous decrease in the nutritional value of the food being eaten was noted due to the deteriorating economic situation. Consumption of dairy products fell by 70%, red meat by 80%, chicken and fish by 40%, and fresh fruits and vegetables by 60%. There was a notable increase in the consumption of rice, wheat, sugar, eggs and potatoes, with relatively lower nutritional value, raising the possibility of malnutrition in children after a few months. In one village 102 of 160 families were in debt to the grocer, and 12 families were near starvation (with no food at all except for olives, olive oil and thyme).

In this context, we must consider post-war Israeli policies towards the Palestinians in the occupied territories, and the role they play in the formulation of economic priorities and tasks. At the center of these policies lie the various measures aimed at controlling the movement of Palestinians in the occupied territories and into Israel.

The increased expulsion of Palestinian workers from Israel came as a result of three simultaneous measures by the Israeli government: first, the decision of the Israeli Defense Ministry to distribute special ID cards prohibiting entry to Israel to some 12,000 Palestinians in the West Bank, and new magnetic-coded ID cards for the Gaza Strip workers. Second was the expulsion of workers from the private sector in Israel — for so-called "security reasons" — under pressures from the right wing, the general tense atmosphere caused by the Gulf War, and the rush to employ new Jewish immigrants from the Soviet Union in light of the special incentives provided for that by the government. The third factor was the new restrictive measures introduced by the government controlling the work and stay of those Palestinian workers allowed into Israel, especially in the field of the semi-clandestine "undocumented labor." It is clear that under this multifaceted cover the government was intent on beginning the process of replacing Arab workers with Soviet Jewish immigrants.

These measures gained momentum during the war when the occupied territories were completely sealed off from Israel for more than a month. At the same time, Israeli authorities began reorganizing Palestinian labor requirements in Israel. Gradually, Palestinian workers were allowed back to work in Israel, but only on condition that the employer and worker both submit a request and guarantees from the employer to transport the worker to and from the place of work; approval was subject to security checks. Naturally, these complicated procedures for employing Arab workers in Israel reduced the demand for them by Israeli employers, especially in conjunction with the incentives provided by the state for the employment of new immigrants from the Soviet Union.

However, the most damaging consequence of this "permit" system was the division of the occupied territories into four separate areas with restrictions on travel between them. Although this policy might result in the revival of small local businesses and home economy, it destroyed with an iron fist economic growth on the national level. Agricultural production based on the specialization of certain areas in producing vegetables and others in producing fruits began gradually to be destroyed. Medium and large-size industries, the pillar of the industrial sector in its contribution to the national income, as well as the seeds for future industrial growth, were in great distress. As for the transport and service sectors, they were jeopardized by the decrease in the number of commercial transports to and from Israel, the Gaza Strip, etc. And naturally a major part of the economic, cultural, religious and health services in Jerusalem were no longer accessible to residents of the occupied territories.

On the economic level, employing only 40–50% of Palestinian workers in Israel, weakening the mechanisms of the local market and preventing investment in productive sectors, placing obstacles to economic relationships with the Israeli market in the absence of economic alternatives, all mean that the local economy is subject to the dangers of reversal and collapse, and a long state of economic stagnation.

All of these new conditions confront us with a real economic crisis, and a unique case in the history of the Palestinian-Israeli struggle since 1967. What faced Palestinians was a case of almost total disappearance of work opportunities in the Gulf, Jordan and Israel, besides wide-scale restrictions on the perseverance and expansion of production sectors in the occupied territories.

The Palestinian response to the new needs and dangers was quick. A number of local Palestinian institutions initiated studies of the crisis and drew up a plan of action based on Palestinian self-reliance, in order to coordinate efforts on the local and international levels to serve the local vision and needs. These institutions fought a difficult struggle against the distribution of the restrictive green ID cards, the control of movement of workers into Israel, the curfew and its effects during and after the war, new tougher requirements for licensing businesses, directing emergency aid from international channels, etc.

The features of the most important Palestinian economic achievement become more clear. It is not the creation of a development plan under occupation, nor is it the marked progress in the productivity of some economic sectors during the intifada, nor is it the partial separation from the Israeli market. It is in fact the Palestinian human and institutional economic build-up, linked to the dynamics of Palestinian political resistance in the occupied territories. It is the linked texture of institutions with various visions and directions, that are coordinated and working at paving their way in the economic field towards one unified aim. That aim is serving the current Palestinian struggle, prioritizing the maintenance and development aspects of the Palestinian individual and collectivity under occupation, and preparing the infrastructure of the coming state, its institutions and its expertise in the economic development field.

# 19

## From the Sealed Room:
## Israel's Peace Movement During the Gulf War

*Stanley Cohen*

Peace Now, liberals from the "left Zionist" parties, Jewish-Arab dialogue groups, Women in Black, socialist feminists, anti-Zionist or non-Zionist or post-Zionist Marxists, human rights activists, religious doves, old-style Communists, moral witnesses against the Occupation, pacifists, soldiers who refuse to serve in the occupied territories, supporters of PLO factions . . . these and other fragments make up what is known as the "Israeli peace movement." It is less a unified social movement than a shared assembly point and a common ideological base flexible enough to allow the Revolutionary Communist League and Rabbis for Peace to work together.

Given this ideological diversity, it is difficult to find a common reaction to the complex moral and political issues raised by the Gulf War. At the risk of caricature — these forces overlap and shift in unpredictable ways — let me distinguish between the mainstream liberal forces and those on the more radical or leftist wing. I will freeze the story as it stood at the end of the war.

### The Mainstream

In the international media as well as Israeli public discourse, the peace movement is identified with Peace Now, the "left Zionist" parties (Mapam and the Citizens' Rights Movement), a number of highly visible politicians such as Yossi Sarid and literary doves such as Amos Oz and A.B. Yehoshua.

These forces were the subject of the public story that emerged within weeks of the beginning of the Gulf crisis in August 1990: the apparent collapse of the Israeli peace movement. The initial PLO support for Saddam Hussein (qualified as it was by token opposition to the invasion of Kuwait) touched a primeval nerve here. Prominent doves appeared in every public forum to express their deep disenchantment with the Palestinian

205

position. The dominant tone was despair and frustration. After all these years of dialogue, all these attempts to persuade public opinion that the Palestinians were indeed ready for a historic compromise — now they betray us. "We were wrong about you," one politician wrote, "if you want to talk peace go find yourself another partner." "Let them come looking for me," was Yossi Sarid's notorious phrase.

This news, of course, was just what the Right wanted to hear, and these liberals were gleefully welcomed back to the national consensus. This resonant narrative — trusting the enemy, betrayal, the return home — was replayed even more dramatically when the war actually began. Now the threat was immediate: the missiles falling on Tel Aviv, the damage and casualties, the sealed rooms and gas masks, the anxiety about a chemical attack. The official PLO leadership continued its support for Saddam Hussein and although some prominent Palestinians from the occupied territories condemned the attacks on civilians, the most vivid image became the local Palestinians "dancing on the roof tops," cheering as the missiles landed on Tel Aviv. This image has become a permanent part of Israeli public discourse. It is repeated in every conceivable political argument.

Two messages now emerged: not just an admission that the Palestinian position had set back the prospects of resolving the Israeli-Palestinian conflict, but a total lack of sympathy with the European and American anti-war protests. Many who were against the war right up till January 15, now took the position that once the full extent of Iraq's military capability had been revealed, there was no option other than supporting the coalition's maximalist war aims. Given the immediate threat to Israel, the "Stop the War" slogan was dismissed as merely sentimental or the product of a reflexive and anachronistic anti-Americanism. Far from calling on the Yankees to go home, we should welcome their protection. There might be a blessing in disguise: post-war pressure on the Israeli government to reach some deal with the Palestinians.

At the level of public discourse at least, this is where the mainstream peace forces remained. Not everybody joined in the national sport of military glorification, but the consensus was that even if the initiation of the war was not absolutely "just," its conclusion was now absolutely necessary for Israel's security. The story, though, of the "collapse of the peace movement" needs some understanding and qualification.

The main point to understand, is that these sectors of the peace movement have always taken care to operate within the national consensus on Zionism and state security. They have never seen themselves as a protest movement on the edges of society. In this sense, the description "back to the consensus" is misleading; these groups never left the consensus. As Michael Warshawsky noted, the sense of relief at being welcomed back into the fold — the pleasure in rallying around yet another "unavoidable war" — allows you to show that you are not outside the consensus, you do not belong to the alienated left.[1]

In truth, it is a little too easy for those of us who do come from more leftist and internationalist traditions to repeat the standard theoretical critiques of the mainstream peace movement. We are easily infuriated by its strategy: the isolationism; the spurious symmetry in which the Palestinian-Israeli conflict is presented; the singing of *Hativka* (the national anthem) after each demonstration; the resolute opposition to selective army refusal to take part in repressing the intifada. But we speak from the margins of the margins of Israeli society. Our criticism is self-indulgent unless we accept our dependence on these forces — and therefore, the need to understand their social base.

We know that the Palestinian betrayal story is somewhat mythical. The notion of betrayal assumes a prior deep relationship of mutual trust. Despite encouraging Israeli-Palestinian contacts built up over the last few years, there has been little genuine collaboration based on shared political values. This was an unlikely prospect precisely because the mainstream peace forces had to remain within the consensus. In these terms, a politics based on guilty conscience emerged. The assumptions of Zionism remained unexamined, but the occupation began to be seen as a historic tragedy. This allowed real sympathy to be expressed for the Palestinians' plight — but not solidarity with their aspirations. It would have been political suicide for these groups to declare their "solidarity" with the uprising.

The historical analogy is by no means perfect, but these groups fit Albert Memmi's classic portrait of the "benevolent colonizer" — whose choice is not between good and evil, but between evil and uneasiness. When their uneasiness was translated into cautious support for the "Two State Solution," this appeal came to rest on three different perceived Israeli interests. The morally best of these pointed to the corrosive effects of the occupation on Israeli society; the morally neutral drew on the pragmatic need to end all the cost and trouble; the morally most repugnant rested on the "demographic problem": the need for a hermetic separation to preserve a Jewish majority.

It is both inevitable and understandable that the Palestinian support for Iraq has exposed the fragility of this ideological base. If sympathy becomes patronizing and condescending, the sympathizers demand that its object must behave only in the image they need. The Palestinians turned out to be neither graceful nor grateful. They refused to behave like suitable victims. And even the "separation" impulse — so morally objectionable because it went beyond liberal pragmatism to appeal to a barely disguised racism — now collapses because the Palestinians are not even to be trusted as a neighbor in their own state. Their true face has now been exposed, the mask of moderation unveiled.

As to the war itself, again the consensual character of the mainstream peace movement explains its current position. This is the only peace movement in the world which has always been pro-American. It has reflected rather than questioned the deep Israeli dependency — economic, military, cultural — on the United States. Even though there are no illusions about American interests in the Gulf — every schoolchild understands that oil and power count more than the liberation of freedom-loving Kuwait — there is a basic faith that American pragmatism will eventually impose its will on the Shamir government. And, indeed, Soviet policy in the Middle East — at first mischievous and now non-interventionist — might leave little alternative.

I have said that this picture needs some qualification. From the beginning, there have been real disagreements within the mainstream peace movement. Some embarrassment was expressed about the offensive demand that the Palestinians change their leadership and forget their history in order to become eligible as "partners." There appeared to be a little more understanding of the gut support for Iraq. Many realized that the tone of the attack on the Palestinians would play into the hands of the right. This fear was justified by Shamir's cabinet appointment of Rahamin Ze'evi, the leader of the pro-transfer Moledet party and a fascist in everything but name. No one was ready to abandon the Palestinians — whatever that means. Everyone — including the "betrayed" — understood that after the war, the Palestinians would still be there (although many are still preaching at them to find a more "responsible" leadership than the PLO).

The war itself, however, allowed fewer nuances and differences of opinion. Here, the boundaries of the national consensus have been drawn again for those who appeared to have strayed beyond them. There have been some quite extraordinary expressions of this national mobilization. On February 14, a well known literary liberal, Professor Dan Meron, expressed the sentiment that if Israel, did not actively retaliate against Iraq, this would be a sign of *Galut* (diaspora) mentality. In the same week, the leading Peace Now spokesman, Tsali Reshef — while denying that the war had embarrassed the peace camp and arguing that only Israeli intransigence had allowed Saddam Hussein the pretext of "linkage" — simply took for granted that "it is a good thing that the world is destroying Saddam's threat." The range ran from enthusiastic support for destroying Saddam Hussein to an acceptance that it would be in Israel's interest for the war to take its course.

The fissures in Israeli public opinion exposed by the Lebanon War appeared covered up. The middle class relapsed into the profound narcissism that so characterizes Israeli culture. The question became: how is the war affecting *us*? The media were totally preoccupied with what was called "the home front" and an army of psychologists — the high priests of Israeli secular society — was drafted to deal with "war-stress." There was somewhat less attention paid to the Palestinians — weeks under strict curfew (shot on sight for curfew violation) and for most without gas-mask protection. The Massada myth was being replaced by the image of the sealed room.

Some of this threat, of course, was real and it faded away as the war ended. My sense at this point was that despite the permanent presence of the iconography of "dancing on the roof tops," the much heralded *pax Americana* would once again expose the fundamental inflexibility of the Shamir government. This, and the increased desperation of the far right at the prospect of any compromise even remotely acceptable to the Palestinians (or even to the international community) would allow the liberal peace forces to emerge from the sealed room.

In summary: any understanding of the Israeli peace forces and the effect of the war on Israeli society as a whole, should make it obvious why an anti-war movement here was literally inconceivable. Since the political challenges limiting the effect of anti-war forces elsewhere in the West were even stronger in Israel, how could there have been a peace movement in the country which (whatever the historical dialectic) was now the imminent victim? The barrier that defined any anti-war protest as anti-Israel was insurmountable. This barrier still exists even for those who well understand that the dangers "revealed" over this half-year — the imbalance of power, the militarization of the whole region, the proliferation of unconventional weapons, cannot be eradicated by unilateral victory over Iraq — but only by a comprehensive settlement that includes the Palestinian question.

No "peace movement" in the sense of a broad multi-tendency coalition appeared on the scene. But in the special Israeli context, the movement did not "collapse" in the sense of losing its motivation to find some peaceful and acceptable resolution of the Palestinian issue.

## The Left

What about the more radical and leftist forces? Here — not for the first time — the apparent sophistication of our theoretical discourse was (and is) matched only by our numerical weakness and our detachment from the immediate concerns of ordinary people. Our anti-war arguments themselves looked no different from those of our natural political friends in Europe and the United States. These included thus: deep distrust of American interests; cynicism about the selective and hypocritical standards applied to *some* occupations and *some* UN resolutions; a critique of the emerging global power structure which the war sought to ratify; belief that sanctions were not given a real chance; skepticism about the moral legitimacy of the war and revulsion at its human costs. Versions of these arguments appeared here as elsewhere.

The most extreme version derived from an identification with the Palestinian cause that explained the war as yet another episode in the familiar script of American imperialism. This explanation was the same invoked by the anti-war movement outside Israel. "No Blood for Oil," "Iraq Will Not Be Panama" were the standard slogans. Added to this was the call to keep Israel out of the war (not a particularly radical demand, as only the lunatic right was against the government's "restraint").

The sounder parts of this argument emphasized the massive militarization of the Middle East and its transformation into a market for selling and a laboratory for testing this arsenal of mass destruction. How could we possibly support this grotesque project? The weaker part of the argument asserted (to quote from one leaflet) that the "immense popular support which Iraq has gained in all the Arab countries . . . heralds a deep social and political change towards democratization in our region." This seems to me nonsense. It ignores those realities of the Iraqi regime which, as Fred Halliday and others argued well before the war,[2] render bogus every single one of its claims: the unification of the Arab world, the redistribution of oil wealth, the liberation of Palestine or resistance to imperialism. If the liberal peace movement should be ashamed by its emotional attacks on the Palestinians, so was it unedifying to see parts of the Israeli left taking up apparently pro-Saddam positions solely on the grounds of "solidarity" with the Palestinians.

The Arab masses — whether from deep class resentment at the oil sheikhs, dormant pan-Arab aspirations or simple hatred of Zionism and the United States — might indeed have seen Saddam Hussein as their savior. But it is one matter to understand this sentiment; it is a cruel self-indulgence for Western (or Israeli) radicals to nourish it. In this type of Third World romanticism, every twist of Palestinian nationalistic rhetoric is accepted as gospel truth. And Israel is judged by moral standards (universal notions of human rights) that are suspended elsewhere on the grounds that military dictatorship, theocracy and totalitarianism are the "inevitable" legacies of colonialism — and therefore beyond condemnation.

It is possible of course, to avoid these excesses. An intellectual position, however, that comprehends the Israeli-Palestinian conflict, the Middle East as a whole *and* the new international order, almost defies imagination. But even if this formula emerged, it would hardly solve the immediate problem of the Israeli left. It is not enough to stay faithful to our two commitments: first, to social justice for the Palestinians and second, to internationalism and our natural anti-war impulse. We also cannot be psychotically out of touch with Israeli society. Whatever our criticisms about the patriotic kitsch (American Jewish solidarity missions standing around Patriot launchers singing "God Bless America" or women employed by the VIP Escort Agency distributing "We Are All Patriots" stickers) and the faked nature of the Israeli "restraint," the truth was that missiles fell and people were frightened.

Yes, the loss of life was minor, property damage restricted, the actual time spent in sealed rooms measurable in mere hours. Yes, this was nothing like our bombing of Beirut in 1982. Yes, Israel was not a random target. But none of this knowledge removed the threat. Critical discourse, by refusing to go along with common sense, must pay a price. Our position is analogous to someone who knows the social causes of and solutions to street crime, but is about to be mugged.

In this situation, our first commitment (that is, to the Palestinians) was far easier to sustain because it is based on universal values of social justice. These are the values we share — however asymmetrical the power relations — with our Palestinian counterparts. They are less fragile than either liberal sympathy or a vague desire for "peace" because they are not dependent on the Other — victim or enemy — behaving nicely. From this position, we can oppose Palestinian support for Iraq as a mistake — but also understand its historical causes in the experience of exile and occupation. In the three years of the uprising, the average Palestinian has been exposed to a level of violence and humiliation worse than suffered by Blacks in South Africa. Only the shortest memory can erase this record. The old battles remain, with the same tactics of human rights work, education, army refusal, solidarity work and cooperation with the mainstream movement.

The second of our commitments (to our theoretical internationalism and anti-war impulse) was much harder to sustain. I'm afraid that I did not share my friends' sense that here too, business could be as usual. Progressives could not ignore what was happening in the Israeli street, nor could they be indifferent to Iraq's attempts to export its regime of state terror to its Arab neighbors. To our fellow citizens (and ourselves) with genuine fears about chemical attacks (derived from German-supplied substances), it was hardly sufficient to point out that the technology was probably inadequate or that more Iraqi civilians were being killed. And the fact that the same global military-industrial complex that created Saddam Hussein was now demonizing him, was historically correct but politically ambiguous.

To be honest, I don't think that anyone here resolved these contradictions. In the second week of the war, a petition was drawn up by an ad hoc radical group (which had changed its name from "One Minute Before the War" to "An End to the War"). This drew attention to the cynical interests behind the war and the terrible price it would exert on all. It then called for a mutual ceasefire, increased pressure on Iraq to withdraw from Kuwait, followed by a withdrawal of the allied forces and an international conference to discuss regional conflicts (including the Israeli-Palestinian) and a ban on chemical, biological and nuclear weapons. I signed this petition — but couldn't help feeling that it sounded a little quixotic.

In the third week of the war, various radical groups began working on the issue of the prolonged curfew on Palestinians in the occupied territories. Real suffering — the effects of the curfew and continual harassment by the army, problems of access to food and medical care and, above all, lack of salaries because workers were not allowed into Israel — became known to Israeli human rights organizations[3] and other groups with Palestinian contacts. This knowledge was blocked by the media and most of the public; little sympathy could be found for a petition to end the curfew.

The overall contradictions within the Israeli peace movement and the liberal-radical differences, showed up clearly in its most durable and visible wing, the womens' movement. The more mainstream group, Reshet, was most dismayed and confused. Their sense of betrayal by perceived Palestinian indifference to the dangers of the war, was deeply felt. Women in Black — a loose network which includes veteran leftist and feminist activists as well as women drawn into this one commitment by the intifada — suspended their weekly vigils for three weeks. This was a reflexive reaction (as well as conforming to civil defense regulations). After intense debate, the vigils were resumed, though (in Jerusalem, the largest group) only with the traditional single "End the Occupation" signs. No other slogan could be agreed upon that conveyed the nuances of political opinion. Meantime, the smaller more radical groups — Shani (Women Against the Occupation) and the Women and Peace Coalition, stayed with their established commitments and searched for a moderate anti-war position. At the beginning of March, the Coalition organized a convoy (stopped by the Army) to deliver food to a refugee camp and distribute a leaflet of solidarity addressed to their "Palestinian sisters."

The immediate uncertainties in the Israeli peace movement and the somewhat different contradictions that the Gulf crisis have created for progressives elsewhere, will be with us for a long time. We are in the middle not just of a momentous shift in the Middle East, as fateful as the dismantling of the Ottoman Empire after the First World War and the establishment of the state of Israel in 1948. This is not the end of history, but the beginning of another history: the first serious crisis since the Second World War which is not being fought between the West and international communism. It is too facile however, to present this simply as a clash between the privileged North and the deprived South. Progressives and anti-war forces everywhere must sense that this morality play has been made a little ambiguous by casting Saddam Hussein as the savior of the wretched of the earth. For the few Israelis and Palestinians working together, the ambiguities are even more painful.

## Postscript

The above comments are drawn from an article I wrote (for *Il Manifesto*) on February 17. Now, three weeks after the official end of the war, these impressions might need a further gloss.

In the mainstream peace movement and even extending up to the dovish center of the Labor Party, there is a perceptible mood of optimism. I would characterize this mood as dependent, pragmatic and passive.

The mood is *dependent* in the sense — as always — of relying totally on American benevolence. The international post-war assumption is ritually invoked: a weak and divided Arab world confronted with a demonstrable United States hegemony, is the best guarantee of peace. The hope is that some permutation of economic crisis (caused particularly by the Soviet immigration), international isolation and real American pressure will push even the Shamir government to some meaningful negotiations. A few centrists in the Labor Party have even publicly recognized the prospect of a Palestinian state. But the decision about exactly what form of settlement to support — whether or not a Palestinian state lies down the line and whether or not the PLO is wholly in the picture — will take its cue from whatever the State Department announces.

This mood is *pragmatic* in the sense — even more than before the war — that there is no principled acknowledgement of the justice of the Palestinian cause. Indeed, any grudging respect that the Palestinians gained by the sheer persistence of the intifada, has been eroded by their support for Saddam Hussein. The PLO has been discredited once again and the images of the "Oriental mind" (as cruelly indifferent to human life and prone to mass fantasies) have been revived. There will likely be further terrorist murders in Israel to confirm this pattern. Yossi Sarid's sentiment that the Palestinians should get their state even if they don't "deserve" it, is widely shared. Out of sheer exasperation, we have to get rid of this unpleasant burden. Another pragmatic argument has emerged: the demolition by the scud missiles of the security case for retaining those extra miles of territory.

Finally, the mood is *passive* in the sense that there is no sign of liberals being mobilized into active political work. I argued a year ago[4] that although the intifada had achieved a genuine cognitive victory in placing the two-state solution on the political map, there was a vast gap between this perception and the willingness to work towards realizing it. This gap seems to me even larger now: the sealed room mentality survives beyond the war. Although the organized part of the movement — especially Peace Now — will recover its momentum and will soon be able to appeal to dormant anti-occupation and humanitarian sentiments, a large part of its constituency has decided to just sit and wait.

Meantime — while these volatile ideological currents are finding some form — the government is taking full advantage of its international credit rating to further humiliate the Palestinians and try again to break the back of the intifada. The immediate post-war weeks in the occupied territories have seen full or partial curfews continued, other forms of collective punishments imposed, selective banning of labor into Israel, renewed school closures and arrests of middle-level political cadres. My more optimistic friends see this as a desperate flurry before the American pro consul arrives. My sense, however, is that these are signals of a firm political stance, entrenchment for a long war of attrition. There is no evidence of an imminent fragmentation in the ruling elite — along similar lines, for example, as the split in the Nationalist Party in South Africa between the fundamentalists and the victorious pragmatists.

If there is an Israeli de Klerk waiting in the wings of history, he or she is keeping very quiet. This scenario assumes anyway, that there will be real American pressure rather than another round of public relations rhetoric about the "peace process." The political elite then responding to any such pressure, will look not at the 20% of the Israeli Jewish population prepared for compromise but at the 60% that extends over the Labor-Likud consensus and the further 20% in the religious camp or the crazy right.

As this story unfolds, the Palestinians can do little more than stand firm. They have again become an absent presence. "If you believe Iraq invaded Kuwait for the sake of the Palestinians, then you can believe anything," said Crown Prince Hassan of Jordan. It is just as unbelievable that the United States and more unbelievable that Israel will do much for the sake of the Palestinians. As the "new Middle Eastern order" begins to reveal itself to be just another form of disorder, the radical agenda remains as it was before the war.

## Notes

1. Michael Warshawsky "An Open Letter to a Friend on the Zionist Left," *News from Within*, October 3, 1990.
2. Fred Halliday. "The Crisis of the Arab World: The False Answers of Saddam Hussein," *New Left Review*, 178 (December 1990).
3. See "Human Rights in the Occupied Territories During the Gulf War," *B'Tselem*, Information Sheet, January–February 1991.
4. Stanley Cohen, "The Intifada in Israel," *Middle East Report*, May–August 1990.

# 20

## Israel and the Gulf War:
## A View from the Israeli Peace Movement

*Mordechai Bar-On*

This essay was written a full month after the opening of hostilities in the Persian Gulf, which resulted from the Iraqi invasion of Kuwait, and the first Iraqi scud missile attack on Israel. Anybody who tries to predict the future of such complex and volatile phenomena risks being refuted even before his or her writings go to print, yet one of the lessons twentieth century history has taught us is that nations who do not consider the necessities of post-war arrangements before the actual end of a war, may win the combat but lose at the same time the purpose for which they were fighting. Therefore, it seems that the risk of considering the new order of the post-Gulf War Middle East is not only worth taking but vital at this stage.

This paper does not aspire to cover the entire parameters of a new Middle East order. It will try to examine those aspects that have a direct bearing on Israel and its place and role in such an order. Let me state right at the outset my banal conviction that the Middle East will have no order, stability or tranquility if Israel is not part of it and if a genuine process to solve the Palestinian problem is not a central part of it.

### The Israeli War Experience

Whether fully justified of not, the Israeli public underwent a traumatic experience as a result of the Iraqi missile attacks on civilian population centers. The recurrent expressions of hatred and of joy at the pain suffered by the Israelis among the Palestinians in the occupied territories and in the East Bank, carried daily by the Israeli media, fortified the deep sense of suspicion which Israelis have entertained against the Arabs for a long time, and may well harden public opinion in Israel against taking any security risks in the framework of a peace process. On the other hand it may also help Israelis realize what security risks they may confront in the future if the conflict persists without any satisfactory solution.

It seems also that the wrong-headed Palestinian political gamble, and the reappearance of a crude Palestinian itch for vengeance and hope for violent redemption, tended to harden the ideological barriers that the Israeli ruling elite has been putting up for quite some time in order to block any serious effort at reaching a compromise on the basis of exchange of "land for peace." The Shamir government has already begun to use these themes, whether cynically or out of honest conviction, to pre-empt international pressures to start a peace process with the Palestinians soon after the war is over.

## Diminished Iraqi Threat

Whether the "Israelis in the street" fully realize it or not, in the short and medium term the Gulf War has greatly diminished the danger of an anti-Israeli aggression on its eastern frontiers. The ability of Iraq to move significant forces through Jordan or Syria to engage the Israeli army has dramatically diminished, for both military and political reasons. This fact may help Israeli strategists and decision-makers be more ready to take risks in their diplomatic calculations.

## The Role of Egypt and Syria

The continued involvement of Syria and Egypt in the anti-Saddam coalition, in spite of grave internal and external pressures, will entitle them not only to a seat in international forums but also to a leading role in any Mideast forums which will decide the future of the region. Moreover, their rejection of the "simultaneous linkage" that Saddam advocated between Kuwait and the Palestinian issue necessitated strong adherence to a "deferred linkage" posture on their part. It is quite clear that these two nations will apply heavy pressures on the UN, U.S. and other coalition members to resolve the Palestinian issue forthwith. Their coalition colleagues will find it very difficult to ignore such a pressure or to sidestep it.

## What Has Not Changed?

Wars may change political and economic configurations, but they seldom change underlying demographic, geographic and even social conditions. Three determining factors will remain unchanged by any of the vicissitudes of the Gulf crisis:

## The Palestinian People and Their Aspirations

Neither the miscalculated attachment of Arafat and the PLO to the cause of Iraq, nor the more understandable yet unfortunate pro-Saddam enthusiasm of the frustrated and angry Palestinian masses could change the basic facts of Palestinian national existence and the reality of their plight and suffering. The Iraqi invasion of Kuwait on August 2, 1990 reminded the world that there are indeed rivalries and conflicts in the Middle East other then the 70 year-old Israeli-Palestinian struggle, but the relative success of Saddam in cynically linking his egotistic conquest of Kuwait with the plight of the Palestinians, at least in the eyes of those victims of another nation's shortsighted egotism, reminded us also that this last one is a sore wound to the whole of the Middle East which must be healed if enlightenment and peace are to be found in this embattled region.

## The Israeli Occupation

Some observers claim that Saddam Hussein killed the Palestinian intifada with his invasion of Kuwait, and squandered its erstwhile achievements. We do not share this view. The five week-long curfew and blockade in the West Bank and the Gaza Strip managed to suppress temporarily many of the resistance activities which have become a common part of Israel's political landscape during the last three years. The sympathy the Western world felt towards Israel in the wake of Saddam's wanton and senseless missile attacks has indeed rescued the image of Israel, so heavily tarnished during these years by its clumsy attempts to contain the intifada. Yet these seem to give Israel only a temporary respite. The tendency of many Israeli employers to lay off workers from the occupied territories over the last quarter of 1990, as a reaction to the wave of stabbings which took place after the tragic events on the Temple Mount (in which 19 Palestinians were killed and scores wounded by Israeli troops), gained a new momentum during the curfew, and a growing number of Palestinian bread earners found themselves deprived of even a subsistence level of income. The events in the Gulf further curtailed sources of income for many Palestinian families in the occupied territories, who customarily drew some of their income from family members who were employed in the Gulf area. These added socio-economic hardships will no doubt refuel the already deep frustration of the Palestinians and add new explosives of desperation to the intifada. The inevitable harsh reaction of the Israeli security forces will soon reactivate world public criticism, and the sympathy Israel gained during the war will dissipate and will be soon replaced by a growing clamor to end the strife and find a just solution to the Palestinian problem.

## Israeli Security Concerns

The relatively successful use Saddam made of the Arab enmity to Israel — exemplified dramatically by his missile attacks on Haifa and Tel Aviv and the deplorable regression of the Palestinian masses to a belligerent anti-Israel posture — gave again a clear proof that Israel has a real, not only imagined, security problem. Moreover, it became obvious once again that only the realization by the Arabs generally and the Palestinians in particular, that

Israel is too strong to be defeated, will enable them, in spite of their grievances and deep hatred, to come to terms with a compromise solution. There has always been a trade-off between security and the peace process in the Israeli mind; the missile trauma and the blatant Palestinian hatred will most likely make the post-Gulf War Israeli even more concerned with security issues and suspicious of compromise solutions.

## Jordanian Instability

The relatively stable Hashemite regime in Jordan has been considered by Israel as an important strategic asset for many decades. It was considered that King Hussein had a common interest with Israel in containing aggressive Palestinian schemes as well as serving in future Mideast conflagrations as a buffer against Iraqi intervention westward and against southward flanking operations against Israel by Syria. It has always been doubtful that the King would be able to resist Palestinian and Iraqi-Syrian pressures to join in a crucial attempt to defeat Israel. Yet Dr. Dore Gold of the Jaffe Center for Strategic Studies justly points out the obvious weakening of Hashemite control over Jordan and the growing internal instability of this state, as a result of the Gulf crisis (along with the strengthening, one might add, of Islamic fundamentalism, which was growing in Jordan even before the crisis).

Israel remains, more then ever before, interested in a stable Jordanian state which will be committed to ensuring that its territory does not become the main arena of the next Mideast war. The longevity and legitimacy King Hussein has acquired over the last forty years and the loyalty of his armed forces make this combination the best assurance for the stability of Jordan, but this is not necessarily the only possibility. What is important is not the ideological or social nature of the regime, but its commitment to the independence and sovereignty of the Jordanian state. The rise of Muslim fundamentalism in Jordan may replace a pragmatic regime with strong irrational elements which will have more commitment to their religious zeal than to the sovereignty of their state and its independence. In any case, Israel should certainly be interested in assuring this independence and demanding that Jordan remains free of any foreign military intervention as part of a new order in the Middle East. Yet, again, Israel will be able to forward such claims only if it is an honest partner in the attempt to solve other Mideast problems.

## The Missiles Factor

It is not the first time in Israeli war history that traumas have not produced new opinions and conceptions but fortified old ones. Both Israeli "hawks" and "doves" use the Iraqi missile attacks on Israeli population centers as the ultimate proof of the correctness of their preconceived perceptions of Israeli vital security requirements. In our view the missile attacks prove nothing except that wars in general become more and more nasty. Firstly, the fact that an Arab state has the capacity to hurt Israel from a distance of 500 miles does not make the capacity of another Arab state or irregular Arab forces to hurt Israel from much shorter distances any more or any less problematic; it can neither prove nor disprove the significance of holding on to the high ground in the West Bank for security reasons. Secondly, the Iraqi missile terror was launched against Israel under very special circumstances. The fact that it was done in the context of massive air strikes by the American-led coalition on Iraq's heartland and the strong pressure put on Israel by the U.S. not to react, deprived Israel of the capacity to hit back either as a means of denial or of deterrence through retaliation. Thirdly, these circumstances proved that while the personal sense of private security of many Israeli citizens was gravely affected, such missile attacks are nothing more then wanton and cruel acts of terror and have no real bearing on the strategic balance. It also seems that either through the improvement of the Patriot or the completion of the new "Hetz" anti-missile missile, much of the potential danger of the scuds may be soon obviated. One also has to remember that Israel may well have the capacity to retaliate in kind, even without using its nuclear arsenal.

It is true that the Iraqi missile attacks made it clear that a "missile war of attrition" may cause both sides a lot of damage and pain and that the Israeli air force may have to engage a significant part of its power to deal with this menace at a time when it will be most needed to stop the advance of enemy ground forces, but this possibility was not created nor aggraveted by recent events. This indeed was the main difficulty the Israeli army faced in 1973. Nevertheless, surface-to-surface missiles cannot decide the survivability of Israel; they only add to the amount of pain and cost of such a survival. It certainly fortifies the logic of war prevention relative to strategies for military victory.

## The Strategic Value of the West Bank

No strategic expert will argue that the military occupation of the West Bank by the Israeli army gives Israel an important strategic advantage. But is not this very occupation also the main strategic Israeli liability due to the fact that it, in and of itself, feeds the main motivation for the Arabs to wage war against Israel in the first place; and the presence of one and a half million Palestinians in these areas compounds a major strategic problem for Israeli forces in times of war as well as in times of peace. The problem of the West Bank was never strategically speaking a matter of choice between bad and good, but rather between bad and worse.

Therefore, there has always been a wide consensus in Israel that a peace settlement must be based on proper security arrangements which will minimize the dangers involved in any breakdown of peace. It was rather on the "dovish" side of the Israeli "Grand Debate" that much thinking was done about the exact nature of these security arrangements. The Israeli peace movement, much more than supporters of "Greater Israel," felt obliged to delineate the different parameters of the security arrangements required in any territorial compromise struck with the Palestinians. The Israeli right wing has had little use for such considerations since it did not want to give up the occupied territories anyhow. Dr. Gold lists skillfully in his study all the points and aspects of such an arrangement, such as the need to demilitarize the territories west of the Jordan which will have to be evacuated by Israeli forces when peace comes; the need to maintain early warning devices on the high ground along the central mountain ridge running north to south west of the Jordan River; the need to give the Israeli forces clear access to the area along the Jordan in case of an imminent attack from across the river; freedom of the entire airspace west of the Jordan for the Israeli air force and the complete denial of this space to any other air force.

The main point of Dr. Gold's study is that the Gulf crisis necessitates the expansion of these security requirements (which I suspect were never acceptable to Dr. Gold anyhow) to a degree which would make an Israeli retreat from the occupied territories, let alone the creation of a Palestinian state, impossible. Yet his arguments are not very convincing since, as we have seen in our previous sections, the overall strategic situation of Israel has improved as a result of the war, and there is no need to expand the security margins Israel will have to demand in a settlement of its conflict with the Palestinians; on the contrery, the capacity of Israel to take risks has increased.

Ever since the October War in 1973, some military observers and many peace movement activists in Israel have maintained that war ceased to be an option for Israeli Mideast policy since even a victorious war may be too painful and costly for Israel to sustain. The Gulf War underlines these conclusions. The acquiring of military technology is only a matter of time and money. Arab states will sooner or later get their hands on those "smart" bombs and may then bleed the Israelis white even without winning a pitched battle on the ground. The sights of the damage caused by the scud missiles in Ramat-Gun and elsewhere may become a powerful reminder for many Israelis that security in modern times may not be a military term any more, but rather a game of motivations which should be handled not by generals but by compassionate and wise politicians.

## A New Middle East Order?

Much of the notion of a post-war Middle East is totally dependent on the possibility of establishing peace in the entire region as a precondition for economic prosperity and civilized life opportunities for the people of the region. The war in the Gulf has proved that the Palestinian problem is not the only unsettling factor in the region. Nevertheless, it is no less clear now that without a proper solution to the Palestinian problem no stability or peace and prosperity may ever be gained in the region. The dispersion of millions of Palestinians throughout the area, the strong emotional and ideological attachment of other Arab people and regimes to the Palestinian issue, and the continued restiveness of the Palestinian body politic are powerful unsettling factors, strong enough to prevent the success of any new order for the Middle East. This is the reason why even those who rejected out of hand the simultaneous linkage Saddam Hussein was advocating between the Kuwait affair and the Palestinian problem, accepted willingly the idea of "consecutive linkage," namely the conviction that the Palestinian issue will have to be attended to as soon as the war is over and Saddam gets out or is driven out of Kuwait.

## Regional Security Arrangements

The new order of the Middle East will have to include certain "security arrangements" in which Israel has a vital interest. The effective neutralization of Jordan, the assurances which will prohibit the rebuilding of Iraq's massive military machine and its aggressive capabilities in the future, deployment of UN or other international forces in the area, and some controls on further proliferation of non-conventional weapons — in all of these Israel will have a very keen interest and certainly would want to influence their exact formulation. However, the opportunity to voice effectively its position in such consultations will be available to Israel only within the framework of a genuine peace process, in which Israel will be called upon to facilitate the solution of the Palestinian problem. Otherwise, Israel and its strategic concerns may be completely left out and neglected. If the Israeli government continues to put up an essentially rejectionist position, such as it has espoused since January of 1990, it may incur very rapidly the anger and antagonism of the U.S. administration and certainly of Europe and the Soviet Union. Electoral considerations may mitigate overt expressions of U.S. animosity, but an American posture of "benevolent negligence" may not be any less dangerous for Israel. Thus, for example, the US administration may decide to interpret its "new world order" as being limited to problems of the Gulf itself, to the exclusion of security issues much closer to the frontiers of Israel, such as the internal situation in Jordan or Syrian rearmament and the role Syria will play in the Middle East over the next few years. This, and a reduction in financial and military assistance from the U.S. in real terms, or even the refusal on the part of the U.S. to increase its financial support and assist Israel in its efforts to absorb the hundreds of thousands of new immigrants from the USSR, may spell disaster to the Israeli economy and its security.

In addition a very sensitive issue is certain to arise when the future of non-conventional weapons in the area is considered. While overall disarmament and prohibition of chemical and biological weapons may by acceptable to Israel if it includes all Arab states, dismantling of nuclear weapons will be seen by Israel as unilateral in practice and too big a prize to be given to Saddam after his defeat. The preservation of Israel's twenty year-old nuclear option of "the bomb in the drawer" may also necessitate the active participation of Israel in future Middle East consultations and a credible Israeli peace-seeking posture.

In any case, some sort of arms control in the Middle East will become a prime Israeli interest since the cost of the next round of the Middle East arms race, in both conventional and non-conventional weapons, may become prohibitive, especially in light of the gigantic budgets Israel will need to absorb the flood of immigrants from the Soviet Union.

## The Syrian Option

It seems quite likely that massive pressures will be put on Israel, as soon as the war in the Gulf is over, to facilitate a genuine peace process, which will be minimally acceptable to the Arabs. The Israeli government too is conscious of this and shows clear signs of nervousness about it. Some early attempts to pre-empt this pressure and devise initiatives which may minimize its damage are being sought. The more radical wing on the Israeli right seems to be suggesting the idea that Israel should ask the U.S. to push the Saudis to conclude a peace treaty with Israel, since this, so they say, will not necessitate territorial concession on the part of Israel. The more moderate elements in the coalition government are ready to accept the need to open negotiations with Syria. This may imply some concessions on the Golan Hights, since this, so they believe, may let Israel off the hook as far as the West Bank and the Gaza Strip are concerned.

The Israeli government may also try to play for time, on the assumption the the American administration will soon plunge into the 1992 election campaign and that President Bush will have to turn his main attention to domestic problems as soon as the Gulf crisis ends. Once of the ideas which some parts of the Israeli establishment is playing with is to offer "unconditional" negotiations with some Arab states, especially with Syria, as a way to obviate the need to deal with the Palestinians and the need to offer them concessions. Similar assessments of the decline in the putative role of the PLO as a negotiation partner were made by many political observers in the U.S.

Some central members of the Israeli peace movement have indeed maintained that the tragic mistake the Palestinian leadership made by joining Saddam's bandwagon will disqualify them in the eyes of the West, as well as in the eyes of the Arab participants in the anti-Saddam coalition, from participating in a meaningful way in the diplomatic process that will shape the future of the region. Therefore, while not giving up their convictions as to the political rights of the Palestinian people, these members of the Israeli left now also advocate what one may call the "Syrian Option." While in the past these exponents of the Israeli peace initiative maintained that the way to peace with Syria runs through the Palestinians, they now maintain that the road to peace with the Palestinians runs through Damascus.

The mainstream of the Israeli peace movement, however, does not share these assessments, yet is not ready to discard any option for peacemaking which may come our way. If anybody can bring the Syrians to the negotiating table under any circumstances, their efforts should be welcome. What is important at this stage is not the question of who should be the first partner for peace negotiations, but rather what the partners negotiate and reach a compromise about.

The little we have so far heard from Israeli officials about the possibility of negotiations with Syria was rather discouraging. Foreign Minister David Levy and Deputy Foreign Minister Benjamin Netanyahu recently invited the Syrian government to come forward and open negotiations with Israel "without any preconditions." This is obviously a non-starter. No negotiations to end a conflict, certainly such a bitter and prolonged conflict, ever started "without preconditions," whether explicit or implied. President Anwar Sadat would have never come to Israel unless he had been given proper assurances that the basis of the coming peace talks was the return of the Sinai to Egyptian sovereignty. The situation between Israel and Syria is symmetrical in many ways. It would be misleading to think that the Syrians will ever approach the table of peace negotiations if the principle of their sovereignty over the Golan Hights and their security interests in the Bekaa Valley in particular and Lebanon in general, are not recognized in advance. Israel, for its part, will never come to the negotiating table if its security concerns are not accepted in advance as legitimate. To advance pre-negotiation negotiations Israel must signal to the Syrians, publicly or secretly, its readiness to make some concession which will make negotiations attractive to them.

### Palestinian Autonomy or Phased Independence?

In Israeli circles much talk is spent on the possibilities of "interim arrangements." There is a wide agreement that any solution devised will need to be implemented gradually to allow Israel to be convinced that the Palestinians are indeed committed to full conciliation and that security arrangements are credible and safe. Even the Israeli peace movement thinks of a "phased" peace settlement. Interim arrangements, however, will be acceptable to the Palestinians only if they are convinced that they will lead at the end of the road to total independence from Israeli rule and the practice of their own "right of self-determination."

The Israeli Likud government keeps harping on the theme of "autonomy" as included in the Camp David Accords and the Israeli-Egyptian peace treaty. But "autonomy" became, in the eyes of the Palestinians and in the eyes of many critics of Likud policies, a code word for immobility. It is clear that Likud strategists refuse to consider "autonomy" as a phase in a process leading to the evacuation by Israel of the occupied territories. At best they consider it as an open-ended step which would not commit Israel to any further step. This too is a non-starter. It is clear that no peace process will ever start unless the minimal principle of "territories for peace" is at its base, neither with the Palestinians nor with Syria or any other Arab state.

**Palestinian Representation**

The decline of the PLO's standing should have been considered by Israelis, who aspire honestly to ending the 70 year-old strife with the Palestinians, as truly regrettable. Peace for Israel will never be complete and credible unless the Palestinians as a nation accept in practice its provisions. This cannot be achieved by personal persuasion of the Palestinian masses. The hatred and grievances, even the hope for the eventual destruction of Israel, will continue to simmer in the wide Palestinian consciousness for many years after a peace settlement between the two bodies politic becomes a reality. The only way to bring the collective will of the Palestinians to accept a compromise and maintain faithfully its provisions is through the establishment of a political authority which will have the power to lead the Palestinian people and to discipline them into accepting the immense pain they will have to sustain as a result of such a conciliation.

Syria has only very limited influence on the bulk of the Palestinian population; it has none whatsoever in the occupied territories and Jordan and very little in the refugee camps in Lebanon. The King of Jordan is another matter, since the majority of his population are Palestinians. He may indeed still play an important role in the process of peacemaking and the idea of a joint Jordanian-Palestinian delegation to any peace negotiations may still be revived, but this can only happen with the consent of the Palestinian leadership. This of course brings us back to the question of Palestinian representation.

The PLO has succeeded over the years in establishing itself as the internationally recognized "sole representative of the Palestinian people." This is true also as far as the majority of the Palestinian people are concerned. The only serious challenge to this leadership position has come during the last few years from the Muslim fundamentalists of the Hamas movement, who according to different estimates may command the loyalty of some 20–30% of the Palestinians in the occupied territories. Yasir Arafat lost much of his standing in the eyes of the West and in the eyes of the anti-Saddam Arab governments, but he did not lose the loyalty of his own people. On the contrary, his attachment to the cause of Saddam may have made him even more popular with them. Yet the struggle over the Palestinian leadership goes on. The more frustrated the Palestinian people become the greater chance there is that Hamas will win their loyalty. There is no third group that has the possibility of achieving a serious leadership position, and between the fanatic and intransigent Hamas and the relatively more moderate and rational PLO leadership, Israel should pray for the success of the PLO in wining the upper hand.

**Do the Palestinians Want Peace? Are the Israelis Ready for It?**

Unless there is total surrender, a compromise peace is normally achieved between enemies when two circumstances exist: firstly, the two sides must desire peace above any other strategic interests they may aspire to.

Excepting the basic values of existence, sovereignty and security they must put peace as the most important value. Secondly, they must have the capability to deliver their nations and commit them to whatever peace compromise may be arrived at. We have already dealt with the second condition. We shall now turn to the first: have Israel and the Palestinians arrived at the point where they are willing to compromise and even risk other important assets and interests for the sake of peace?

The answer to this question touches on problems of perception: the Palestinians' perception of their own identity and the Israelis' perception of the minimal requirements of their security. Over the last thirty years, since the founding of Fatah by Arafat and his young colleagues in 1958 and the establishment of the Palestine Liberation Organization in 1964, the Palestinian mind has undergone a very intricate and painful evolution from a total link between the definition of their own identity and the complete denial of any rights for Jews in the land of Palestine in the sixties; through the concept of a "democratic secular state of Palestine" in the seventies, which allowed for personal religious rights for the Jews; then to the "stages theory" in the early eighties which accepted the possibility of a Jewish state alongside Palestine as an interim concession which would eventually lead to the destruction of Israel. Only the self-assertion and newly found dignity which the intifada brought to the Palestinian masses, and the realization that these assets might be lost if they were not transformed into political achievements, brought the Palestinian leadership to the last phase, which crystallized at the Palestine National Council in Algiers in October 1988. The acceptance of UN Resolutions 242 and 338, the recognition of Israel, though oblique, the strong adherence to the two states formula and the denunciation of terror, were the expressions of a new phase not only in the tactics of the Palestinians but, more importantly, in their self-perception. These transformations were naturally still only shallow and could not at that stage go far beyond the upper level of part of the political elite.

The failure of the Israelis to reward the PLO for its moderation, which came to a head with the failure of Shimon Peres to establish a "narrow coalition" committed to the peace process, and the advent of a right wing rejectionist government in Jerusalem; the continuation of the harsh suppression of the intifada in 1989 and 1990 and the severance of the Palestinian-U.S. dialogue prepared the ground for a massive regression of the Palestinian mind. When Saddam Hussein began to rattle his missiles in April 1990 and forged for himself the image of a violent savior of the Palestinians, most of them reverted to a belief in violence as the only avenue to their redemption. They also lapsed back to pan-Arab dreams which were very prevalent among them in the days of Gamal Abdel Nasser in the fifties and early sixties.

The Israelis on their part too were prisoners of their own fears and security concerns. From a crude concept of the Jordan River as the only credible line of defense, some of them moved to the Allon Plan, which allowed for the retreat of Israel from most of the occupied territories provided a strip of land along the Jordan was left under Israeli control; then on to the Dayan plan of the "functional compromise" which was ready to give the Palestinians almost full sovereignty over the entire territories occupied by Israel since 1967, saving necessary defense holdings in limited areas on the upper ground of Judea and Samaria; and then on to the idea of a demilitarized Palestinian state with limited security arrangements. The Gulf War and the Palestinian regression to a violent and pan-Arab posture threw most Israelis back to a more defensive posture and made many of them doubt the possibility of reaching any credible compromise with the Palestinians. The margins of security have been widened by the Iraqi missiles and the popular image of Palestinians dancing on the rooftops at the sight of those missiles flying over their heads on their way to Tel Aviv and Haifa. The perceptual gap has been widened again. The large task of healing this breach will have to be set in motion after the war, but images in the Middle East are always volatile and shifting rapidly and the fact that both the Palestinians and the Israelis do not have any other options may give some ground for renewed optimism.

## Conclusions

### *The Palestinian-Israeli Peace Process*

Whether the PLO will be party to the shaping of the new Middle East or not will not depend on Israel. This will be decided by Egypt, Syria, Saudi Arabia and the international community. It would have made little practical sense for Israel to open negotiations with the PLO when the rest of the world disqualified that organization, though it might have been to the advantage of Israel. But as soon as the PLO becomes a party to any Middle East consultations, and this is very likely to happen sooner rather than later, Israel must open channels of communication with the only body which in spite of all its vicissitudes continues to command the loyalty of the vast majority of Palestinians.

Simultaneously or alternatively, elections in the occupied territories should be held soon, according to the Five Baker Points, and on the basis of the principle of "territories for peace" and eventual fulfillment of the right of self-determination of the Palestinian people. The immediate release of recognized Palestinian leaders from administrative detention should be agreed upon immediately.

### *The Modality of Negotiation*

An international conference to deal with Middle East problems and with the Arab-Israeli conflict is a rather cumbersome and ineffective mechanism to sort out these highly complex issues. To quote Leslie Gelb on this: "It would produce only endless haggling over its own power and guarantee Israel's isolation and intransigence." Bilateral, trilateral and ad hoc forums to address the different subject matters would be preferable. "Baskets of issues" pertaining to the particular conflicts should be negotiated by the relevant parties. Yet an international umbrella for all these complex sets of negotiations may be needed and should not be rejected out of hand. It may assure the parties of international sanctions against any betrayal of solemn undertakings, it will assure the full and active participation of the USSR in any settlement arrived at, and it may assure international financing of regional and national economic rehabilitation plans, which will be much needed in any peace formula. It is, however, essential that no single modality should be adhered to, to the exclusion of other possible configurations. Thus, for example, the Israeli government should not be allowed to excuse itself from opening the peace process with the Palestinians just because negotiations with Syria fail to get off the ground. The approach that a comprehensive settlement with all Arab states should be a precondition for a settlement of the Palestinian issue should be dismissed as a rejectionist and obstructive posture.

### Halt to Further Settlements in the Occupied Territories

Settlement in the West Bank, the Gaza Strip and the Golan Heights are an obstacle to peace. Further settling of Jews in these areas are a pure waste, send a rejectionist signal to the Palestinians and endanger foreign financial assistance for the absorption of Soviet immigrants. Further increases in the population of the existing settlements, not to mention new settlements, should be stopped forthwith.

### Soviet Jewish Immigration and the Palestinian Right of Return

The right of Soviet Jews to immigrate to Israel should be recognized by the international community as a basic human and national right, as much as the right of Palestinian refugees to return to Palestine. Both undertakings will require large amounts of international finance and investment. These can in no way be accomplished at the same time as large military investment is still going on. In this respect war and human rehabilitation are incompatible. Israel cannot raise any longer the two flags of territorial expansion and human expansion simultaneously. The prolongation of the occupation cannot be accomplished without heavy investment in military hardware and human resources. To keep the national social welfare level and absorb another million immigrants from the Soviet Union cannot be done under the conditions of continued strife with the Arabs. The moment of truth has arrived and Israel will be forced to choose between the immigration of another million Jews and the suppression of two million Palestinians.

# 21

## Jordan Responds to the Gulf Crisis

*Mustafa B. Hamarneh**

Nowhere in the Arab world are pan-Arab patriotic feelings as strong as in the countries that compose the fertile crescent. For seventy years, in this area comprised of modern Iraq, Syria, Lebanon, Palestine/Israel, and Jordan, generation after generation of schoolchildren have been taught that Western imperialism is to blame for the area's political divisions and the establishment of the state of Israel. From among these Arab states, Jordan has been the most affected by the Palestinian issue. The reasons for this are its particular historic objective conditions, chief among them its geographic proximity to Palestine, and its demographic composition. As a result, pan-Arab nationalist ideology has been historically appealing to the masses in Jordan. The post World War I Arab nationalist ideology was based, for the most part, on the rejection of existing Arab political fragmentation, the struggle to liberate Palestine, and putting an end to foreign intervention. Consequently, the pro-Western policies implemented by the monarchy have put Jordan, for most of its seventy year history, on a collision course with the forces of Arab nationalism within Jordan and in the region as a whole. There were brief periods, however, when the monarchy took political stands that seemed consistent with those of the Arab nationalists and therefore were interpreted as a departure from its traditional pro-Western policies. During the Suez crisis of the 1950s, King Hussein backed Egypt against foreign invasion, and in 1990–1991 he condemned the allied war against Iraq.

In general, Arab modern history has been a series of defeats. Ever since World War I, the peoples of these lands have been politically frustrated.

* This brief essay is an attempt at explaining the Jordanian response to the Iraq-Kuwait crisis that erupted on August 2, 1990. It is based, for the most part, on personal interaction and involvement in the crisis in Jordan, and on interviews with politicians of different ideological orientations, government officials, and academics. Most of the government officials interviewed preferred to remain anonymous. The essay was begun right after the war ended and was completed at the end of March 1991. It is intended to generate more discussion and study, rather than immediate conclusions.

Despite their war effort alongside the allies during World War I, their aspirations for unity and progress were thwarted. Their wartime allies had become their conquerors and colonizers. Britain and France, having carved up most of Arab North Africa in the previous century to suit their own interests, now divided the fertile crescent. Then there was the 1920 overthrow of the Faisal government in Damascus by the French, the defeat in Palestine of 1948 and the establishment of the state of Israel, Israel's decisive victory over Egypt, Syria and Jordan in the 1967 War and its subsequent occupation of Arab lands, including Jerusalem. To further compound the sense of defeat there was the 1982 Israeli bombing and subsequent occupation of an Arab capital, Beirut, and finally the Palestine Liberation Organization's (PLO) inability to achieve its declared objectives.

Still there have been periods in contemporary Arab history when breaking the cycle of defeat seemed a possibility. In the mid-1950s, President Gamal Abdel Nasser of Egypt implemented a series of policies that were highly popular in Jordan and the rest of the Arab world. He nationalized the Suez Canal Company, bought arms from the socialist countries, and with the help of the Soviets began building the Aswan Dam. Although Egypt lost militarily in its fight against Britain, France and Israel to uphold its nationalization of the Suez, it scored a major political victory. Because of the anti-Western nature of these measures, Nasser's ability to proceed forward, and Egypt's quest to develop its own weapons system capable of striking Israel, Nasser became the center and living embodiment of Arab nationalist ideals. For the first time since the war against the Ottomans, the Arabs began to think that the possibility of correcting injustices inflicted upon them by outside forces was now a likelihood. Nasser had strong mass support in the Arab world. In Jordan, his stand against the Baghdad Pact was sufficient to block the Jordanian government's attempt to join the Pact. For a short period, King Hussein departed from his traditional pro-Western stand and supported Egypt against foreign aggression. During these months of the Suez crisis, Jordan lived through a short yet exciting democratic period.

But the hopes that Nasser represented were again shattered in the defeat of 1967. The humiliation suffered at the hands of the Israelis brought forth the then small, clandestine Palestinian resistance organizations. Soon, these groups gained legitimacy and claimed leadership of the Arab nationalist coalition. Their assertion was that through "revolutionary" armed struggle, carried out by the masses, the Arabs could achieve their goals of defeating Israel and achieving unity. Jordan became the largest base for the Palestinian movement and the center of Arab political activity. In September 1970, the Palestinian movement and its allies suffered a major military defeat in Jordan when it collided with the regime. Subsequently the government banned all political parties (except for the Muslim Brotherhood). Their military defeat in Jordan, their inability to score major military victories elsewhere, the consequences of the Israeli occupation of Beirut, and since then their continuous losses on the political front, as well as the internal conflicts within the Arab nationalist coalition itself (Syria, Iraq,

PLO, and Libya, etc.), has led to a slow but gradual diminution of their position as leaders of the pan-Arab nationalist coalition. As the ongoing Gulf crisis clearly revealed, the current popular support for these groups in Jordan (where they are strongest, possibly with the exception of the occupied territories) has declined to its lowest level since their emergence.

To the Arab masses, the eighties represented a decade of total collapse. They had neither the political nor the military power to achieve their goals. Instead, Egypt had signed a separate peace treaty with Israel, Iraq was engaged in a war with Iran, Syria became entangled in Lebanon's internal affairs, and any hope that Libya represented proved hollow. In the meantime, Israel reigned supreme: it bombed Iraq's nuclear reactor, openly established more and more settlements on the West Bank, further occupied a strip of land in south Lebanon, and bombed PLO headquarters in Tunisia. With the battles of the last months of the eight-year Iran-Iraq war, the Iraqi army scored major breakthroughs and it appeared that these military successes brought the war to an end. The speedy process of reconstruction of Iraq and its attempt at developing into a modern state, the revelation that Iraq possessed chemical weapons as a deterrent to Israel's nuclear capability, and President Saddam Hussein's forceful restatement of the Palestinian issue in February and May 1990 gave the Iraqi leadership credibility among the Palestinian and Jordanian masses.

When the Iraqi army marched into and took over Kuwait in but a few hours, the masses in Jordan saw this as the beginning of a new and genuine process of decolonization. For them, this process meant unity, control over Arab destiny and wealth, hope of overthrowing the rest of the other highly unpopular dynasties of the Gulf, and ultimately shortening the road to Jerusalem.

Unlike his predecessors, leaders of the Arab nationalist movement, Saddam Hussein delivered. In Jordan, his image was enhanced and he gained credibility and respect.

### The Development of the Hashemite-Ba'athist Relationship

Until the 1978 Baghdad Arab Summit conference, the relationship between the Jordanian regime and the Ba'ath regime of Iraq was one of mutual distrust. Although Iraq (despite the rhetoric) was a non-revolutionary regime, it was internally implementing non-capitalist methods and its foreign policy placed it in the forefront of the anti-Zionist camp. The Ba'ath regime regularly characterized the monarchy in Jordan as pro-Western and reactionary.

In the late seventies Jordan came under strong pressure from the Carter administration; the Americans were compelling Jordan to join the Camp David peace process. Unwilling to accept the Carter formula, the king and his government insisted on the return to the international conference plan to prevent Israel from concluding separate peace treaties with the Arab states. King Hussein was well aware that Jordan's geographic position, its meager resources and reserves, and the demographic composition of its population made him vulnerable. Alone, it was unlikely that Jordan could withstand the pressure.

The objective of the 1978 Baghdad Summit conference was to devise an Arab strategy to counter President Anwar Sadat of Egypt and his drive to conclude a separate peace treaty with Israel. Angry at what he took as a betrayal by Sadat, King Hussein hoped that the Arabs in Baghdad would unify their stand and, according to one of his chief advisers, behave in a "responsible" and "rational" manner, avoiding angry and negative reactions. The king and his advisers hoped that the summit would adopt measures that would strengthen inter-Arab relations and use Arab resources more effectively. The Jordanians maintained that if peace was to be achieved, the Arabs needed to strengthen themselves not only militarily but in all spheres.[1]

The results of the conference satisfied the king. Jordan was promised large amounts of capital to procure arms for defense purposes. It was believed that the diversity of the sources of aid pledged would help Jordan withstand political pressure. The king was also impressed by Saddam Hussein (the second man then). According to a source close to him, the king saw in Saddam Hussein a new Nasser, a force that had the capability to devise a politically unified Arab stand to counter Sadat's strategy. With the start of the Iran-Iraq war, the king feared that an Iranian victory over Iraq might result in the establishment of an order in the Arab world similar to the one that existed on the eve of World War I. Again, in the name of Islam, a non-Arab power would rule the Arab world putting an end to his hope of setting up a "moderate" Arab order.[2] Therefore, at the outset of the war King Hussein supported Iraq openly and forcefully, a stand that surprised even the Iraqi leadership.

It is important to note, however, that when the Iran-Iraq war began, the majority of the population blamed Saddam Hussein for starting a war that they believed was aimed at thwarting the Iranian Revolution: a revolution which implemented anti-Western measures and adopted a position that was identical to the original Arab stand vis-a-vis Israel, i.e., the rejection of the existence of the Zionist entity. However, as the war with Iran continued, the central assertion of his statements on the Palestinian issue, Israel, the U.S. and the new Arab world was interpreted by the masses in Jordan as a forceful attempt to restate the Palestinian problem, but more importantly, a convincing argument that Iraq had the military might to back up and implement these statements.

The 1978 Arab Summit conference and the Iran-Iraq war laid the foundations for a pragmatic relationship between the Hashemite rulers of Jordan and the Ba'athist regime in Iraq, hitherto ideological foes. This new marriage of convenience included Iraq's acceptance of Jordan's limited maneuverability. For Jordan, oil-rich Iraq made a powerful ally. In a public show of support for Iraq, the king fired an artillery shot at Iran on one of his visits to the front and visited Baghdad over 40 times during the war. His relationship with Saddam on the personal level grew more intimate.

Jordanian-Iraqi economic ties grew stronger between 1980–1989 on all levels. During this period, exports to Iraq averaged about 22% of all Jordanian exports. These exports included agricultural produce, eggs, clothing, some industrial products, cigarettes, etc.[3]

During this period Iraqi foreign relations in general became less ideological. Egypt, Jordan, Yemen and Iraq formed the Arab Cooperation Council, which was to be the nucleus for a more unified Arab world. This signified that the vision was more conservative than the visions of the 50s, 60s, and 70s.

As the war with Iran came to an end in 1988, King Hussein felt vindicated and he hoped that Iraq's victory would lead to a strengthening of the order he and Saddam Hussein were trying to build. With the ceasefire, Jordanian officials believed that the country would witness an economic boom similar to the one of the seventies. Officials in Jordan also believed that the rulers of the Gulf states would be even more grateful to Iraq for stopping the Khomeini "menace," and therefore a more unified Arab world would indeed emerge with positive implications for Jordan. Instead, in his dealings with the Gulf rulers, King Hussein was receiving disturbing messages concerning Iraq.

The Gulf rulers viewed Iraq as a threat to their regimes. Furthermore, what appeared to be sudden and augmented revelations in the Western press about Iraq's military build-up, its possession and use of chemical weapons, the Iraqi supergun, and the Western media's treatment of the Basoft case (the execution of an alleged British spy) confirmed the suspicions that psychological warfare was being waged against Iraq. It was sensed in Jordan that there was something amiss and that Iraq was being targeted. According to a source close to the government, with the eruption of the Iraq-Kuwait crisis, the king's suspicions were confirmed and he moved quickly in an attempt to solve it and avoid foreign intervention which he believed would escalate the crisis, and to maintain the order that he and Saddam Hussein were trying to build.

### The Crisis

In early 1990, a series of events contributed to Saddam Hussein's popularity and credibility in Jordan. At the end of February 1990, the Iraqi president delivered a speech at the opening session of the conference of the Arab Cooperation Council in Amman. In it, he expressed his views on Arab cooperation and the need for a unified Arab stand vis-a-vis the U.S. and Israel. The speech was interpreted as a reminder that the U.S. was responsible for Israel's arrogant belligerence. The Americans, said Saddam Hussein, were supporting Soviet Jewish immigration to Palestine. They were also supporting Israel with its stockpiling of strategic weapons. The Arabs are weak, and their weakness, he noted, was the result of the lack of trust among the Arab regimes. Arab strength is to be based on Arab solidarity. Furthermore, he pointed out that the Arabs want peace and justice, and they desire to set up relationships with others based on mutual respect and on an equal basis.[4]

Then in a meeting with Iraqi officers (parts of which were televised on Jordanian television), Saddam Hussein revealed that Iraq possessed chemical weapons and warned Israel that if it attacked Iraq, Iraq would retaliate by "burning half of Israel." In May, an Arab Summit conference, coined the Arab National Security Summit conference, was convened in Baghdad. Saddam Hussein delivered the opening address. He reiterated some of his earlier statements. The U.S., he declared, was the source of Israel's strength. He placed the culpability for Israel's aggression and expansionist plans on the American government. He warned that if Israel attacked an Arab country, Iraq would retaliate "forcefuly."

Historically, many other Arab leaders have expressed similar views on Arab solidarity, unity and the Palestinian question. In Jordan, Saddam Hussein's declarations were received with more enthusiasm than the earlier speeches of his counterparts. They were popular speeches and pronouncements, and increased Saddam Hussein's standing among the people. These two speeches, with the disclosure that Iraq possessed a modern arsenal of weaponry including chemical weapons, led the masses in Jordan to believe that finally someone in the Arab world could put an end to Israel's arrogance and expansionism, and eventually help achieve Arab rights in Palestine. They became convinced that Israel, with its massive military machine and vast nuclear arsenal, was no longer the only power in the region. In Jordan, people began to assume that Iraq, with Saddam Hussein at the helm, would put an end to the Arab cycle of humiliation and defeat.

After eight years of war with Iran, and the decrease of oil prices, Iraq needed large amounts of capital for its reconstruction and development plans. It supported OPEC's production quota system, hoping to increase the price of oil to $20/barrel. But Kuwait and the United Arab Emirates increased their oil production above their quota limitations. This led to a decrease in the price of oil which directly affected Iraq. Kuwait was producing 2 million barrels of oil per day; about half a million above its quota. This caused Iraq to lose about $1 billion annually. Iraq's total debt was about $80 billion; of that, $40 billion was owed to oil producing countries. At the May 1990 Arab Summit conference, Saddam Hussein complained bitterly of the practice of producing more oil than the OPEC quotas allowed. The effect of such practices on Arab wealth in general, and on Iraq's economy in particular, strengthened the existing opinion that Iraq was being targeted by the U.S. and Israel. And the Kuwaiti ruling family was seen as the tool used by the Americans to weaken Iraq and thus further Israeli interests.[5]

Soon after the May 1990 Summit conference, Iraq and Kuwait began negotiations to reach an agreement on the Rumaila oilfield, border disputes and production quotas. But these negotiations collapsed. Iraq blamed Kuwaiti arrogance and intransigence. Subsequently Iraq took the extreme measure of invading Kuwait.

The Iraqi annexation of Kuwait once again rekindled Arab nationalist hopes. As the opposition to the Iraqi action crystallized and foreign troops amassed in Saudi Arabia, support for Iraq and Saddam Hussein escalated in Jordan. To the masses, the belligerent statements from Western capitals, along with the swift passing of twelve Security Council resolutions against Iraq, signaled the destruction of Iraq's military and economic capabilities. In gatherings, conferences and rallies in Jordan, the U.S.-led action was interpreted as further evidence that the Arabs would again be denied control of their destiny. Jordanian support for Iraq cut across class, gender, religious and regional barriers in the country. Iraq was not to be defeated.

### Reaction to the Crisis at the Official Level

Although the declared position of the government was the upholding of the principle of the inadmissibility of the annexation of territories by force, the impression in the country was that the king favored the Iraqi move. At the emergency Arab Summit conference held in Cairo on August 13, 1990, the king did not condone the Iraqi action, but rather, he described what happened as a tragedy. According to the king, Jordan's position was to try to solve the crisis within the Arab League. He maintained that Saudi Arabia was in no danger of being invaded by Iraq and he rejected the initial argument to send foreign troops to defend it. Jordan was pressured to condemn Iraq's action, but the king believed that this was an attempt to put an end to his role as a mediator, so as to facilitate foreign intervention. In fact, Jordanian newspapers accused Egypt, Saudi Arabia, and other Gulf states of complicity with the U.S., and stated that the Cairo conference served only as a pretense.[6]

These declarations, issued by a traditionally pro-Western monarch in the area, fixed the fears of the masses that Iraq was being targeted for destruction, and helped to strengthen the Iraqi stand in Jordan.

The government continued to follow this line publicly throughout the crisis, but when the war broke out, the relationship between Jordan and Iraq grew even stronger. In a speech on February 6, 1991, the king condemned the U.S.-led aggression in strong terms and the official mass media served as Iraq's outlet to the Arab world. Public officials (government functionaries) continued to support Iraq, and their attempts to collect donations went unhampered. Even in the armed forces, an institution which has traditionally been kept "politics-free," support for Iraq was expressed publicly and fervently. It was widely claimed that some technicians from the Jordan armed forces were granted early retirement and "allowed" to go to Iraq and train Iraqi technicians in manning the American Hawk batteries confiscated in Kuwait.

King Hussein and Crown Prince Hassan made themselves quite accessible to Western media, attempting to clarify Iraq's and Jordan's position without condemning the Iraqi action. In the early days of the crisis, Prince Hassan's repeated statements of Jordan's non-acceptance of the annexation of Kuwait drew criticism from various sectors of the population. As the crisis progressed, however, the Prince's sophisticated handling of the press turned the criticism into admiration of his role.

## At the Popular Level

On August 2, 1990, a "neutral" announcement in Jordanian media, that the Iraqi army had taken Kuwait, touched off widespread spontaneous support for the Iraqi action. The term "invasion," to describe the Iraqi move into Kuwait, was avoided by the media and supporters of the Iraqi action. The use of the term "invasion" in Jordan implied condemnation of the Iraqi move. Initially, the mass response to the move was swifter and less guarded than that of the existing political organizations, except perhaps for the pan-Arab groups.

At the outset of the crisis, the Muslim Brotherhood, the largest political organization in Jordan, issued no statement in support of the Iraqi move. Mr. Abdallah Akaileh, a Muslim Brotherhood member of Parliament, reiterated his party's stand on Arab and Muslim unity, and hoped that differences between "brothers" would be solved through dialogue. Although he avoided taking a clear position on the issue of Iraq's takeover of Kuwait, he did come out against the presence of foreign troops in the holy land of Islam.[7] As the crisis went on the position of the masses exerted pressure on the Muslim Brotherhood leadership and gradually edged them into backing Iraq. Furthermore, as it was perceived that the monarchy supported Iraq, the traditionally pro-Hashemite Muslim Brotherhood party followed suit. This might help explain, in part, the unique support of the Muslim Brotherhood in Jordan for Iraq, which put it at odds with other Muslim Brotherhood organizations in the Middle East and in the world.

Mr. Yacoub Zayadeen, Secretary General of the Jordanian Communist Party, was the only politician in the country to openly oppose the Iraqi move. In an interview in *Ad-Dustour*, Mr. Zayadeen said that he "saw no justification" for what he termed an invasion of a neighboring country. He believed that the Kuwaitis ought to be left alone to manage their own affairs.[8] However, Mr. Zayadeen represented the minority stand within the Communist Party. The majority of the cadre supported Iraq.

The balance of other political organizations in the country gradually followed the masses and backed Iraq. But the strongest initial support came from pan-Arab groups, the remaining Nasserites and the Ba'athists, including a majority of the Ba'ath party organization of Syrian President Hafez al-Assad in Jordan.

Increasingly, public expressions were beginning to take on strong anti-American, anti-Western and anti-Gulf Arab tones. As the crisis proceeded with massive deployment of American and other allied troops and equipment into Saudi Arabia, the Iraqi position remained "confident" and adamant, and their attempt at linking the Iraqi withdrawal from Kuwait to Israel withdrawal from occupied Arab lands contributed to the Iraqi leadership's new image of statesmanship.

Throughout the crisis, many neighborhoods, villages, mosques, churches, students, academics, school children, housewives, government employees and trade unionists organized the largest grassroots voluntary aid campaign in Jordanian history. These groups carried out fundraising drives, food-collection drives, etc. Donations of cash and kind were either taken to the Iraqi embassy, or to headquarters of charitable organizations and trade unions. Hundreds of vehicles loaded with foodstuffs and medical supplies (collected from homes in villages and towns throughout Jordan) were sent independently to Iraq. The allied forces' bombing of the Baghdad-Amman highway posed no deterrent to these efforts by the public. The amount of food, money and blood donations by far surpassed that collected for the intifada. With the start of the war and what appeared to be Iraq's steadfast-ness and ability to withstand the onslaught, the collection drives and the level of donations increased.

However, unlike the struggle in the 50s, 60s, and 70s, what began as support for a pan-Arab cause increasingly took on Islamist connotations. The Muslim Brotherhood was riding the mass wave of support for Iraq by condemning foreign intervention and holding rallies in the early weeks of the crisis in support of the intifada. This almost always guaranteed large attendances at their rallies. The leadership was careful not to condemn the Saudi king for his role in facilitating the foreign intervention. There was also the impression, and this was encouraged by different fundamentalist groups, that the Islamic Republic of Iran would soon join the anti-Western camp. And perhaps most important was Saddam Hussein's declaration of a *jihad* against the infidels. Iraqi official public discourse was becoming increasingly religious and Islamic, and the "mother of all battles" was cast in terms of believers fighting infidels, and the forces of good against the forces of evil. By invading the ideological camp of the fundamentalists, and borrowing slogans and concepts, the Iraqi leadership substantiated fun-damentalist beliefs that Iraq was moving closer to their own ideology and further away from the traditional Arab nationalist formulations. Although the Muslim Brotherhood standing in Jordan prior to the Gulf crisis had somewhat diminished, the Gulf crisis, up until Iraq's withdrawal from Kuwait at the end of February, made them the strongest political party in the country.

## The Effects of the Crisis on Jordan

Although Jordan was going through an economic crisis long before Iraq invaded Kuwait, the government maintained that Jordan suffered most behind Iraq and Kuwait. The loss of the Kuwaiti market was significant to Jordan. Kuwait used to absorb about 30% of Jordan's agricultural exports. Remittances from Jordanians and Palestinians living in Kuwait came to a halt. The magnitude of the Iraqi-Jordanian economic relationship varies according to the source. According to one estimate, over 70% of Jordan's industrial capability was produced for Iraq.[9] Transit trade with Iraq stopped as a result of the UN sanctions. The tourist and transport industries suffered heavily as well. All this is believed to have cost Jordan up to $3 billion and an increase in unemployment from 20–40%.[10] Saudi Arabia ceased oil shipments to Jordan and many of Jordan's goods were no longer allowed to be sold in Saudi Arabia. The situation was further aggravated when hundreds of thousands of third country refugees fled Kuwait via Jordan. Yet, despite the hardships that were felt by all segments of the population, support for Iraq kept growing and the people were determined to maintain their political stand. It was strongly believed that Iraq must win and the U.S. must be defeated.

Apart from the immediate economic hardships on Jordan, not all the effects have been negative. Ever since the elections of November 1989, Jordan has been living through the longest, most open and democratic period of its history. The Iraq-Kuwait crisis had helped strengthen the democratic process. Conferences, rallies and demonstrations were held around the country with few incidents. Dr. George Habash and Mr. Nayef Hawatmeh, two Marxist leaders of the Palestinian movement, who were previously banned from entering Jordan, came to Amman in September 1990 to participate in a conference of representatives of over a hundred political parties gathered from throughout the Arab world. These leaders visited their respective party headquarters in Amman, were interviewed by local journalists and reporters, and socialized with relatives, friends and comrades in Jordan. Dr. Habash gave a public lecture at the Royal Cultural Center. The king met with both men separately, and the atmosphere, according to the statements issued by their parties, was warm and courteous. The U.S. condemnation of Jordan for allowing these two men to enter the country and the holding of the conference in Amman further verified the U.S.'s double standards.

In addition, impeded by strict censorship in other Middle East countries involved in or affected by the Gulf crisis, hundreds of international correspondents and reporters from all sectors of the news media arrived in Jordan, where they encountered no such obstacles. Public officials and private citizens were free to speak out. And no government escorts accompanied the foreign media.

However, despite the open political atmosphere in Jordan, a peoples' delegation of Kuwaiti exiles was unable, for days, to find a forum from which to explain Kuwait's position, until the Royal Cultural Center gave them the only opportunity to address the public. The Kuwaiti delegation was unfortunately received with hostility and belligerence by leading columnists and commentators in the media, and during their public appearances.

The king and the crown prince continued to declare Jordan's position of neutrality. Officially the country declared that it abided by the UN sanctions, upheld the inadmissibility of the acquisition of land by force, and recognized the Kuwaiti emir's regime in exile. The population ignored all of these declared positions of the government, yet there was no tension and no chaos in the country. The prevalent sense in the country was that the king's genuine position differed from his public position. Alleged minutes of the king's meetings with various groups in the country circulated widely among the population. These indicated that the king was anti-Sabah (the

Kuwaiti ruling family), had a low opinion of President Mubarak and King Fahd, and was against American intervention. As with the Suez crisis, this departure from his traditional pro-Western policies contributed to the king's increased popularity and to the atmosphere of political openness.

Another positive effect of the crisis was that the groundwork was prepared for a genuine rebuilding of Jordanian-Palestinian relationships in the country. It is maintained here that tensions in the Jordanian-Palestinian communities have been the result of political factors. For decades, the majority of the Palestinians were under the impression that the Hashemite policies concerning the Arab-Israeli conflict were in collusion with the Zionists. The king's stand during the crisis has been the most important factor in contributing to better relations between the two communities. The king's popularity reached unprecedented levels. Although he always enjoyed a high level of popular support among the Jordanian majority, during the crisis he made sizeable inroads among the Palestinian portion of the population. This led to a considerable lessening of tensions between the two segments of the population.

However, the Jordanian government, which was noticeably ineffective and parochial during the crisis, had faltered on two issues which had a negative impact in the country. First, the king, his government, and leading politicians in the country had warned from the start that if war broke out, Israel might attack Jordan. Left-wing and nationalist politicians and organizations, as well as Muslim fundamentalists demanded that the population be armed immediately in preparation for a possible Israeli attack. But the government insisted on lengthy, voluntary military and civil defense training programs. The second issue was the government's objection to issuing permits for demonstrations outside the U.S. embassy in Amman for fear of violent outbreaks. After the American bombing of the Ameriyeh shelter in Baghdad, Jordanian police stopped a spontaneous demonstration from reaching the American embassy. Although police opted for dialogue with the mostly women demonstrators, the sight of riot police in full gear, with a large number of police cars blocking the roads, brought back old images of animosities and confrontations between the people and the regime. The Friday following the Ameriyeh bombing, riot police used force to break up a demonstration attempting to reach the U.S. embassy. The government's stand on these two issues has revived old conspiracy theories in some opposition circles that the Hashemites' actual position was not on Iraq's side.

Despite these incidents, the democratic process which began in 1989 survived its first major crisis.

## Conclusion

The expected Iraqi victory never materialized and instead Iraq suffered a major military defeat. The sudden announcement that Iraq accepted the conditions set by the U.S.-led coalition to withdraw from Kuwait sent a shock wave through Jordan. Disbelief, confusion, anger and despair set in.

Although the population in Jordan had access to a wide range of news coverage of the events in the Gulf, they believed only the Iraqi news releases carried by the Jordanian media. Several factors have contributed to this.

For the masses, the U.S. displayed an arrogance of power and lack of civility in dealing with the Iraqis. Comparisons of Saddam Hussein to Hitler, and the Republican Guard to the Nazi SS were taken as ideological and propagandistic. To them, nothing could be further from the truth. In contrast, Iraq's military communiques were viewed as dignified and defiant, though not bombastic, and signified a high level of military preparedness. Allied euphoria after their first air strikes over Iraq was crushing news in Jordan. But within twenty-four hours Iraq fired a missile at Israel. This was an indication that Iraq employed modern technology and was able to absorb the initial attacks, and the people believed that Iraq could withstand the aerial attacks and ultimately defeat the allies in the ground war.

Soon the allies began issuing contradictory statements on Iraqi military losses, and tightening up allied censorship of the media covering allied military operations. Therefore, the Western media began gradually but decisively to lose credibility with the masses in Jordan. Furthermore, the allies were unable to destroy the mobile missile launchers that continued to strike at Israel. The Iraqi attack on Khafji and their ability to hold on to the town and then fight their way out over allied lines was an important factor in lifting the morale of the people and their expectation of victory. The little information coming out of Iraq on the military operation and the conflicting reports of the allies, in part, contributed to the widespread rumors of Iraqi victories by "eyewitness" accounts coming from Iraq. Thus the eventual ground war, as far as "public opinion" in Jordan was concerned, would lead to the crushing of the allied forces by the formidable and entrenched Iraqi army and seal Iraqi victory.

Anti-government violence in the north and south of Iraq gradually diminished beliefs that Iraq had been victorious. The uprising and subsequent repression of the Shi'a and the Kurds in Iraq showed that the situation remained volatile. Although some of the Iraqi opposition's grievances were legitimate, i.e., democratization, political participation, human rights, the opposition's links with the West doomed them in the wake of a U.S.-initiated war.

As for Jordan, criticism of what was perceived as serious miscalculation by the Iraqi leadership was aired in public without fear of intimidation. Yet support for Iraq and its territorial integrity remained high. Cessation of hostilities and the confusion that ensued did, however, have a negative impact on the process of fundraising for Iraq in Jordan. Along with the preoccupation with Iraq, Jordanians and Palestinians began once again to debate internal issues. A national congress will soon be held to ratify the National Charter. At the writing of this essay, a genuine process of reevaluation has not yet begun. Unlike the 1967 War, where Arab defeat was total, in this crisis the rich and conservative Arab regimes financed, backed and participated along with foreign troops in a military attack against an Arab country. Therefore, as far as these regimes are concerned they scored a major military and political victory. This represents a major obstacle for the unfolding of a process of reevaluation. In the meantime, hopes for unity, progress, and the liberation of Palestine will not disappear.

## Notes

1. *Ad-Dustour*, November 3, 1978. (Jordanian daily newspaper). An interview with Abdel Hameed Sharaf, then chief of the Hashemite Royal Court.
2. The king expressed this view at the beginning of the Iran-Iraq war to several of his advisers. On this issue, as well as others in this essay, I have benefited from discussions with one of the king's advisers. Although there were no conditions set as to what I was permitted to use from the interview, he preferred to remain anonymous.
3. An unpublished study by Dr. Ahmad Qassem El-Ahmad, Director of the Research Center of the Royal Scientific Society, Amman, 1989.
4. *Al Ra'i*, February 25, 1990 (Jordanian daily newspaper).
5. See statements of Dr. Jawad Anani (economist) in *Ad Dustour*, August 13, 1990.
6. See headlines and commentaries on the Cairo Summit conference of August 13, 1990, as well as King Hussein's statements, in *Al Ra'i* and *Ad Dustour*, August 12 and 13, 1990 issues.
7. *Ad Dustour*, August 3, 1990. Interview with Dr. Abdallah Akaileh, a Muslim Brotherhood Member of Parliament.
8. See *Ad Dustour*, August 3, 1990.
9. Walter Robinson, *Boston Globe*, dispatch from Amman, August 19, 1990.
10. These are Jordanian government figures, regularly published in Jordanian print media.

# 22

## What Choice Did Egypt Have?

*Sherif Hetata*

When the Gulf crisis erupted many people in Egypt found it difficult to accept that Egypt should choose to be on the side of Israel and the West against Iraq, that the Egyptian army should fight side by side with the allied forces. They knew that the war had not really been launched to liberate Kuwait, or uphold international law, or establish a new international order where peace and justice would prevail, but to keep control of the Middle East, especially the Gulf oil reserves, and to ensure oil money stayed in the banks. They knew it would lead to more profits on arms sold by the military-industrial complex, and let the multinationals rush in to reconstruct what has been destroyed by allied bombs, and above all to the destruction not of Saddam Hussein so much as of an Iraq which could be a threat to American interests in the Gulf and to the heavily militarized state of Israel which has been so effective in helping to thwart many legitimate Arab aspirations.

Amongst the Muslim political tendencies the more radical fundamentalist groups openly supported Saddam Hussein against the "Allies" and the Egyptian government, but their ranks had been weakened by massive arrests, especially after the assassination of the previous president of the People's Assembly Rifaat el-Mahgoub. The more moderate "Muslim Brotherhood" condemned Saddam Hussein's invasion of Kuwait but strongly opposed the massive military punitive war inflicted on Iraq, and saw in it another example of Western intervention in the affairs of the Arab countries to the advantage of Israel. Official Islam as represented by Al Azhar and the sheikhs supported the government; as did the majority of the Egyptian people burdened by economic problems of everyday life, strongly influenced by the official media, tired of Arab difficulties and conflicts in a country which historically has nurtured less Arab feeling than the other states in the region, inclined towards the peace and stability of a river civilization which has witnessed less upheavals than other Arab peoples and hoping that the Gulf region could still remain a market for Egyptian labor and hard currency revenues.

The right wing Wafd party was even more a supporter of the allies than the government itself and went as far as to attack the Soviet Union for its attempts to mediate in the conflict, firstly to bring about a postponement of military operations and later on for its ceasefire proposal once the "blitzkrieg" or "desert storm" had been launched against Iraq.

The left wing was also divided. The more extremist tendencies sided with Saddam Hussein and Iraq while the more moderate tendencies condemned the Iraqi invasion of Kuwait but opposed the massive allied intervention as another manifestation of Western policies aimed at maintaining the exploitation of Arab resources and control over the Arab region.

The Nasserist groups in general were sympathetic towards Iraq and Saddam Hussein except for a small minority of leaders.

On the whole most Egyptians felt that the Kuwaiti state was not worth all the destruction and sacrifices its defense imposed on the region. They saw in it a regime built on glaring social injustice, riddled with corruption, high handed in its dealings with other Arab nations and cringing before its Western masters. They believed in a peaceful solution, were upset by the crippling of the Iraqi nation, but did not sympathize with Saddam Hussein. However as the allied raids on Iraq were intensified anti-Western feeling kept slowly gaining ground in the public opinion.

It was a complex situation. Many people probably had mixed feelings, sometimes forgetting what Saddam Hussein had done, as the savage enormity of the Western retaliation was revealed, and it became clear that the Arabs in general were being taught a lesson, particularly when they were told that they were to remain obedient, and accept an order of things which would be ruled solely by Western interests to the advantage of the Shamir fundamentalist state now ruling in Israel.

For many politically oriented people in the country the position of the Egyptian administration was humiliating. The official media went as far as to gloat over the destruction and punishment meted out not only to Saddam Hussein and the ruling clique but also the Iraqi people. It was difficult for them to sympathize with Mubarak as a leader and with the official policies he appeared to have initiated. And yet one is reminded here of the experience of many Third World leaders and what happens to them when they are trapped in the net of Western (especially American) domination euphemistically described as "development aid." Such aid rapidly becomes a stranglehold from which it is increasingly difficult to break out, and which leaves little room for any maneuvering. The position of Egypt in the Gulf War is a vivid illustration of such a situation.

When the Arab Summit meeting was held in Cairo immediately after the Iraqi invasion of Kuwait, Mubarak tried to press for an Arab solution. It is now well known that he engaged in discussions over a peace proposal to separate the two states involved in the conflict with Arab troops, possibly under UN supervision. However, this proposal came under heavy and threatening pressure from Bush and Saudi Arabia, and was pre-empted by other Gulf state resolutions which endorsed immediate U.S. intervention and by a rapid deployment of American troops to "protect" Saudi Arabia. In fact the Mubarak administration found itself facing what was to all intents and purposes almost a *fait accompli*. To attempt to turn back at this point despite American admonitions would have meant for Mubarak a sudden break with policies of the Sadat era, followed substantively throughout the last two decades, with all the implications of such a break in the areas of foreign and domestic policies.

Egypt, burdened with a foreign debt usually calculated at around $50 billion, waiting desperately for World Bank approval in order to receive new foreign loan injections or obtain some form of respite on existing obligations, suffering from a yearly foreign trade deficit of $7 billion, was hardly in a position allowing it outspoken rebellion. If we add to this the offer to cancel the military debt owed to the United States as a part of the carrot and stick diplomacy of the Bush administration, the economic relations of Egypt with the Gulf states as sources of funding and as markets for its surplus labor, generating a yearly income of $4–5 billion in hard currency earnings, Mubarak was understandably hesitant to take the plunge of arbitration, mediation or neutrality, especially as he knew that Bush was eager for an Arab and especially Egyptian cover for his retaliation operation.

If we add to all this the absence of the Soviet Union as a possible counterweight, and the fact that being a military man he was convinced that the U.S. military build up meant a very strong likelihood of a large scale war operation against Iraq, it is quite clear that he and his collaborators balked at the idea of confronting an American administration which was quickly swinging in favor of massive retaliation, egged on by a president who felt that his own image and future were at stake. Mubarak had suggested postponement of military operations against Iraq for three months after the Security Council Resolution 678 to use force was passed, but his proposal fell on deaf ears.

Last and perhaps not least, the internal situation inherited from the Sadat period continued to give economic and political circles closely linked to the United States the upper hand. Mubarak has had some differences with these circles before and lost. He had resisted World Bank policies for sometime and again lost. With the hysteria raised over the Iraqi invasion of Kuwait it was hardly likely that a cautious and slow moving man like Mubarak would take a leap which could only appear suicidal. The balance of international and national forces was very far from favorable to the taking of any such risks.

Many people in Egypt therefore ask themselves if the policy followed by Mubarak in the Gulf War was not dictated by over-riding considerations related to the stability and peace of the country, and the real dangers involved in a confrontation with Western interests at a moment of explosive tension.

Certainly that balancing act between the national needs of Egypt and the involvement of foreign powers inside the country was nothing new for

Egypt. Its origins lie at the root of the emergence of the post-monarchy Egyptian state.

## The Free Officers' Movement

The revolution initiated by "The Free Officers' Movement" on the night of July 23, 1952 had started out as a patriotic movement against colonial exploitation and occupation by the British. Its only social dimensions, therefore, were those intrinsic to a movement which seeks to break out of the circle of foreign oppression. For apart from this its political aims did not go beyond the restoration of liberal democracy through free elections. This necessitated a limitation of the powers exercised by King Farouk, his family, and the feudal capitalist landlords who constituted the mainstay of the previous regime, and the internal support agency for British rule which continued to be exercised despite the Anglo-Egyptian Treaty of Independence signed in 1936. We may also add to these aims a declared intention to fight against corruption in high quarters.

This simple platform was the result of an interplay between conflicting right, intermediate, and left wing forces in the "Free Officers Movement." Nasser and those who collaborated with him soon emerged as the "middle liners" struggling to force their way against both the right and the left wing forces in the revolutionary movement.

## True Independence: Linking the Political to the Economic and the Social

However since the central aim of the revolution was to achieve independence, the "Free Officers" soon realized that they had to break the power of the dominant forces within the country upon which the British had continued to depend in order to maintain their economic interests and their rule.

This led to the formulation of the first "Agrarian Reform" law[1] issued on September 9, 1952, which was also an attempt to release land-locked capital into entrepreneurial circulation, followed in July 1953 by a decision to abolish the monarchy and declare Egypt a republic with Naguib as president instead of Farouk as king.

Both these measures were directed against the feudal landlord capitalist class but also served to create the beginnings of social support mainly among the middle classes and petit bourgeoisie of the cities, towns and villages of Egypt, but also in the population as a whole.

Naguib, a general with liberal leanings, did not last long. The "Free Officers" and Nasser, who quickly emerged as their acknowledged leader came mainly from middle class and petit bourgeois families. They had little political experience and no fixed ideology. Their political progression and the lines of action which they took were the combined result of their anti-colonialism, their social origin, the power struggle and empirical experience. As time passed they moved from one step to the other, and this movement gradually led to a clearer definition of the aims of the new regime. Their policies were the result of practice rather than of a preconceived theory. This emerges clearly when we follow the development of the revolution in its successive phases.

After 1954 political independence was achieved and the British occupation forces, apart from a few military experts, were evacuated from the Canal Zone. But now there were other problems which had to be faced, such as the threat constituted by declared Israeli expansionist policies and incursions. The "Free Officers" who had fought in the 1948 Arab-Israeli war were very conscious of this threat. Arms therefore had to be sought, preferably from the West. But when the West maneuvered, Nasser went East.

Besides this, with a rapidly growing population and limited land resources, agricultural and industrial expansion became a pressing necessity. Economic aid was again sought in the West, particularly from the United States. Later the World Bank was solicited for a loan to build the Aswan High Dam. So an old dream relegated to the archives came to life. This was a transitional period pregnant with change, lasting from 1954 to 1956. The doors of Egypt were opened to foreign capital by new laws. But neither the Americans nor anyone else from the West really tried to help or invest, and even when the United States played with the idea of a loan from the World Bank the conditions inspired by John Foster Dulles and conveyed by Eugene Black were too reminiscent of colonial days to be accepted by people with a real patriotic bent.

Capital had therefore to come from other sources. In 1956 the Suez Canal was nationalized. The British, the French and the Israelis attacked. When the war ended foreign enterprises which held the economy of Egypt in their grip were nationalized, and the first nucleus of a public sector created to ensure that their capital would be utilized for national development instead of passing into the eager hands of Egyptian capitalists for whom developmental projects in a Third World country meant less profit and too much of a risk.

In 1961, when Nasser issued Egypt's widespread nationalization decrees, he was continuing along the path he had been pushed into by the United States and other Western countries. Banks, insurance companies, and commercial and industrial enterprises owned by Egyptian capitalists were taken over by the public sector, since all attempts to draw big and middle Egyptian capital into the national development process had been met with unyielding resistance. In 1964 the Aswan High Dam was inaugurated after it had been built with Soviet help, who were also involved in sixty-five other industrial establishments. Egypt was now launched on the path of real independence.

## The Tide Turns Back

In 1967 the disastrous June war broke Egypt's and Nasser's back. The opportunity long awaited by international and local capital was now in sight.

But it had to wait for Nasser's death. With his will, his charisma, his record as a man who maneuvered but refused to yield to the stick, he could still keep things going despite his faults. He could still rebuild the army, maintain popular support, and keep the multinationals in check.

When he died the lid that held them down in the cauldron came off. On May 15, 1971 Sadat took over complete power from a failing Nasserite clique. In 1974 the "open door policy" consummated Egypt's return to the economic fold of the West. The road to independence had been blocked. For some time already post-war history had been turning back and Egypt was part of the process. The multinationals had learnt their lesson, had learnt to adapt. The tree of independence could not lift its head without vital economic sap, and on the other side of the world "socialist support" was getting ready to collapse.

### Art, Politics and Human Rights

I was one of the moderate left elements who opposed intervention by the allied armies and the punishment inflicted on the Iraqi regime and people. I had seen the United States and other countries of the West so patient in conflicts where the agressor like Israel was its friend.

It was not because I supported the Iraqi invasion of Kuwait, or felt the slightest sympathy for Saddam Hussein, but because I hoped against hope for a peaceful solution which would avoid a terrible war for the Kuwaiti and Iraqi peoples, a war which would also undermine the strength of the Arab nations, reinforce Israeli aggression against Palestinian rights, and permit the United States to reinforce its grip on the Middle East and drain its resources more effectively.

But I am a writer, not a politician in power, and my role is to uphold peace, justice and human rights until the day when there will no longer be such deep contradictions between politics, art, morality and human rights. Until then, like many others I will have to live with the dilemma which faces all those who can understand what politicians do, or are forced to do sometimes, and who know that there are considerations of expediency and yet must protest when human beings are being crushed.

So, maybe Mubarak was not as wrong as some people thought and the readers of this article will not protest at such a seemingly paradoxical view. He kept Egypt out of a confrontation in which it could only have lost. To act differently would have required a different man, a different political and economic context and the kind of choices which lead from the start to real independence, greater freedom, and more justice. Even if Mubarak thinks sometimes in those terms, the path that Egypt has followed since Sadat made it too late for him to try his hand.

We are in a new era very different from the one which Nasser helped to forge, and the road to true independence will remain blocked until new internal and international forces gather their strength. People can say after all Mubarak avoided a collapse. Compare our situation to the catastrophe Saddam Hussein has imposed on Iraq. They will say thank God or Allah is

Great, even though America will ride heavy handed over our backs, continue to work the oil pumps vigorously, drain petrodollars into Western banks, keep planes and warships ready for attack from bases located in the Middle East, try to impose a masked Israeli annexation of the Gaza Strip and West Bank, and try to bury the conflict which will only burst out at some other point of time, instead of giving the Palestinians their chance to have a state in which they can live, and work, and build, and forget.

People will say America is strong and has taught us that the language of bombs has paved the way for a "new American era" launched by Mr. Bush, and for a new international order where cooperation will be cemented by material force rather than by human rights.

But in the long run America will have lost because "desert storms" can destroy but not build. Americans will learn that in Egypt as elsewhere they have gained the Kingdom of hatred and lost the Kingdom of God.

The people of Egypt can say Mubarak's policies will help once more to send our laborers and peasants and technicians to the Gulf where we can earn money and send it back home. Egypt has not been isolated from an important part of the Arab world with which we have ties, and may be able to play a role in paving the way for an independent Palestine. The Egyptian army has come out of the war intact, and still remains an asset to the Arab world. Egypt has upheld UN resolutions, now it is time to do the same elsewhere, to end Israeli occupation of Arab lands, establish a lasting peace, and banish nuclear, chemical and other weapons from all countries in the Middle East.

People can say Egypt will remain a moderating force despite the fact that the Gulf War waged by the West against Iraq has helped to strengthen the Islamic fundamentalist movement, and deepen an economic crisis which drives many of our youth to fanatic versions of Islam.

Nevertheless, for a writer like myself it is difficult to see these aspects and forget that the return road of Kuwaiti sheikhs and of American oil derricks to Kuwait has once more been paved with Arab lives and Arab blood.

## Notes

1. The second "Agrarian Reform Law" limiting agricultural landowning to 50 hectares was issued in January 1961

# 23

## Operation Desert Shield/Desert Storm:
## The Islamist Perspective

*Yvonne Yazbeck Haddad*

Operation Desert Shield/Desert Storm has left much wreckage in its wake. The economic havoc it has brought to the area is only now being assessed: the billions of dollars spent on the armed forces by both sides to the conflict; the loss of livelihood by hundreds of thousands of people; the wanton and vindictive destruction of two countries, Kuwait and Iraq, who for decades had applied their resources in the effort to modernize; the ecological disaster of millions of barrels of oil burning in the sand and the potential harm that it will have on the food chains of India and Iran. Also being assessed is the damage done in the political sphere: Who really won the war, and what was its influence on the intricate web of inter-Arab and inter-Islamic relations that existed prior to August 2, 1990? What effect will all of this have on a possible resolution of the Arab-Israeli conflict?

Allied forces, both American and those from the "moderate" Arab nations (seen by Islamists as those subservient to American interests), along with the Zionist leadership, have been quick to determine who is to be rewarded and who punished in terms of the degree of their support for the war effort. The Islamists (generally called Muslim fundamentalists by the Western press), meanwhile, have been producing their own version of the events. Some Muslim intellectuals, along with the Islamists, have dubbed the war "Operation Desert Trap."[1] They see that it was designed neither to "shield" Saudi Arabia nor to "storm" Kuwait in order to liberate it, but rather to trap Saddam Hussein into an expedition he did not have the means to win.[2]

From this perspective Desert Shield/Desert Storm cannot be seen as a direct response to the Iraqi invasion of Kuwait. Rather it was a consequence of a well laid-out scheme by which the United States not only coordinated and instigated the conflict as part of its long range plan to control the area, but actually set the trap into which Saddam Hussein

248

walked. The aim from the beginning was the destruction of the Iraqi forces for the express purpose of maintaining Israeli military domination of the area.[3]

Many feel that the haste to condemn and punish Iraq was both unnecessary and indecent, that the United States did not give diplomacy a chance because it was committed to the destruction of the Iraqi military-industrial complex.

> The way that America rushed to call for a meeting of the United Nations and pushed with dispatch for a decision and a world coalition against a nation, such as was formed against Iraq, is unprecedented in United Nations history. Initially they claimed that they came to defend the Arabian Peninsula and the Gulf (to our knowledge no one had threatened these nations). The goal was later redefined as forcing Iraq to withdraw from Kuwait and restoring the emir to power. It then became evident that the intention, as articulated by Western leaders, was the destruction of the power of Iraq.[4]

The Gulf crisis precipitated some deep rifts in Arab ranks. There was mutual fear and distrust between citizens of Jordan, Palestine, Sudan, Yemen and North Africa on the one hand and of the Gulf states on the other. There was unprecedented division among the Islamists, with those in the Peninsula and the Gulf taking one position and most of those in the Sudan, Tunisia and the West Bank taking another. In Egypt it split the Islamic movement into two camps (the majority in sympathy with the Iraqi people) with no general consensus as to what policy to pursue vis-a-vis the occupation and no means of dealing with it.[5] While many Egyptians strongly opposed the war, those in support of Mubarak's policy felt American intervention was justified. Sheikh al-Tantawi[6] issued a *fatwa* in support of it, and some of the Egyptian *ulama* rejected an invitation to attend the conference of religious leaders convened by Saddam Hussein to discuss the peril facing the Muslim nation, saying: "We refuse to join Saddam in a conspiracy against Islam and the Muslims."[7] Other Egyptian intellectuals and *ulama* who wanted to attend pro-Iraqi meetings were banned from doing so by the Egyptian authorities, while still others managed to attend conferences condemning protection by foreign troops.[8]

The split was also apparent within the Tunisian Islamic movement, the Nahda Party. Rashed al-Ghannoushi came out with a statement explaining what he understood to be the motives behind the American intervention.[9] Far from being a reaction to the immediate causes, he said, it is part of the struggle for a new world order in which the conflict is no longer between East and West but between North and South in which the North (now including the Soviet Union) represents Christianity and the South represents Islam. He condemned Western intervention as the "occupation of the Holy Places [of Islam] by imperialist forces . . . a battle between the North, arrogant with its power, and the oppressed South armed with faith and dignity."[10] Al-Ghannoushi felt that behind all of the Gulf events is an American plan developed since 1973. This plan deals with the sensitive area of the Muslim world which is denied the means of industrialization or military strength so that Israeli domination can be maintained without competition. One had only to follow the reports of the Western press in seeing how the U.S. dealt with Iraq at the end of the Iraq-Iran war, he said, to see how they raised the specter of the highly-armed Iraqi army, laying the groundwork for the need to destroy it. The story of Iraq's giant gun, Western rage at the execution of the alleged British spy, Israeli destruction of the Iraqi nuclear plant, and the oil policy of the Gulf countries geared to decrease Iraqi income were all part of this overall scenario.[11] The Nahda Party Shura Council initially issued a statement condemning what it termed the American "Crusader" attack and the Arab regimes that joined the coalition, and calling for solidarity with the Iraqi people.[12]

As the crisis dragged on, several Tunisian leaders moderated their response to fault the Iraqi regime for instigating the confrontation.[13] Disagreeing with al-Ghannoushi, who under no circumstances saw justification for intervention by American forces, was Hawadi al-Jebayli of the political bureau of the Nahda movement. Once the Malta agreement replaced Yalta, he said, the Arab region came under the direct domination of the U.S. with no competition from the USSR. He therefore felt that it was inevitable that Iraqi action would precipitate the American response that it did, and that Saddam Hussein was very foolish to have invaded Kuwait. Saudi Arabia then had no choice but to seek foreign intervention because of the danger inherent in the situation. "If I feared a danger threatening me," said al-Jebayli, "I might seek aid even from Satan."[14] 'Abd al-Fatah Moro refused to participate in the Iraqi-sponsored Muslim Conference on the grounds that Iraq is a secular regime whose members do not believe in heaven, do not wear Islamic dress, and do not participate in the various religious responsibilities incumbent on Muslims. He also found Islamic legal sources both in support of and denying the legitimacy of seeking help from polytheists, and said that therefore people are free to choose. Thus, although he initially signed the Declaration of August 17 denouncing such a move, by the end of August he apparently had no qualms about Saudi Arabia seeking aid from the West.[15]

Al-Ghannoushi's ideas on the matter also were attacked by people outside Tunisia. Fahmi al-Huwaydi, a Muslim intellectual writing for a Saudi magazine, took him to task for his concern that American troops once in the area would be retained under the guise of security arrangements. That is irrelevant, al-Huwaydi said, in light of the immediate issue of Iraqi aggression against Kuwait. "Why ignore the present danger in order to focus on a potential one?" he asked. Of the two threats, American occupation and Iraqi invasion, he saw the latter as significantly more serious and called Iraq a menace that places citizens of the Gulf countries in mortal danger that cannot be ignored.[16]

The issue of foreign troops was thus debated on several levels. Some Muslims questioned the wisdom of allowing an alien presence on Arab land given the history of the Muslim experience of the Crusades, of the expulsion of Muslims from Spain in the 15th century,[17] and more recently, of Western colonialism. How could a Muslim country "invite" foreign troops? they asked. Who, in the end, would determine when their task was done and when they were to leave?

The Saudi invitation to American and European troops to protect Saudi territory also raised a second, more serious issue of whether the protection of the holiest sanctuaries of Islam by non-Muslims constituted defilement. Some argued that the protection of the holy places should not be deemed more important than the protection of the wealth of individual (Kuwaiti) Muslims. Others saw that the protection of the domain of Islam as a whole from foreign intervention is more important than the issue of inter-Arab or inter-Muslim conflict.

The third issue raised was whether it is Islamically acceptable to seek the patronage of non-Muslims against Muslims. Abd al-'Aziz bin Baz of Saudi Arabia issued a *fatwa* legitimating such protection. A similar opinion was declared by an international group of *ulama* convened in Saudi Arabia (September 10–12) by the Muslim World League to debate the topic.[18] A number of Islamic conferences were held, some subsidized by the Saudi and the Iraqi governments respectively to provide justification for their positions and others organized by different international Islamist groups.[19] Prominent Muslim leaders from all over the world met and issued conflicting declarations about what they saw as the primary issues and which is the highest Islamic principle to be upheld. Debate was enveloped in religious discourse, well documented by quotations from the Qur'an and the Sunna.

To justify the Saudi position, Bin Baz quoted Qur'anic verses enjoining the believers to provide force and to seek protection against impending attack. "O ye who believe, take protection" (S. 4:71); and "Make ready for them all you can of force" (S. 8:60). Opponents of the presence of American troops quoted other verses as more appropriate for the situation. The Qur'an rejects the right of non-Muslims to kill Muslims, they said. "God will not give the disbelievers any [success] against the believers" (S. 4:141). They also argued that there is a Qur'anic injunction against using non-Muslims for protection. "O ye who believe! Choose not my enemy and your enemy as patrons" (S. 60:1); "O ye who believe! Take not the Jews and Christians for patrons. They are patrons to one another. He among you who takes them for friend is [one] of them. Lo! God guideth not those who do wrong" (S. 5:51).

In Britain the Muslim Youth League held a conference entitled "The Gulf Crisis: The Islamic View." Participants said that Muslims who defended Iraq were incapable of understanding the truth about Saddam Hussein and his "crusader" regime, accusing Saddam of having fought Islam yesterday and pretending now to be the defender of the faith.[20] The Islamic Council of Europe, on the other hand, ruled that Iraq's occupation of Kuwait was an internal Islamic matter to be resolved by Muslims themselves. The American and Western forces "are loyal to the nations that sent them and no one — whether Muslim or non-Muslim — can claim that its allegiance has now shifted towards Islam."[21]

The Islamic Movement of Iraq issued a statement arguing that Saddam Hussein's regime was responsible for the killing of millions of people in

Iran and the expulsion of half a million Muslims of Iranian origin, the destruction of Iranian resources that would have been able to withstand the international Crusader-Zionist threat, the use of chemical weapons killing 10,000 Kurds, cooperating with the Crusader Maronite regime in Lebanon allied with the Israelis against the Muslims, banning the circulation of Islamic books, and the execution of religious leaders both in Iraq and overseas. His efforts to organize a conference of religious leaders to withstand the threat of foreign forces should not fool Muslims, they said; it is he who is responsible for bringing these foreign forces into the area.[22]

There is no question that Operation Desert Shield/Desert Storm dealt a major blow to the myth of Arab nationalism, Arab brotherhood and Arab unity. While Arab nations supporting American intervention argued that it is the impotence of the Arabs that necessitated the invitation of the allied forces to the region, the Islamists saw the failure in a larger perspective. Islamists have agreed with the secularists that Iraq's occupation of Kuwait and the American intervention in the area were a proof of the failure of regional organizations such as the Arab League to provide solutions to inter-Arab conflict, but they have differed from them as to the efficacy of maintaining a nation-state system which was imposed by the West in the beginning. While Arab nations supporting American intervention have argued that it is the impotence of the Arabs that necessitated the invitation of the allied forces to the region, the Islamists see that it is the nation-state system itself that is to blame. Had there been Islamic unity, and had Islamic principles been applied in the various nations, the conflict would not have taken place.[23]

Regional conferences revealed the deep dissatisfaction of a number of Islamist leaders in various countries with the Saudi action.[24] The Muslim World League, established by the Saudi government in the 1960s as an instrument for garnering international Islamic consensus, failed to win the approval and support of many of the organizations around the world that it had actually subsidized for over two decades.

> The spirit of battle and confrontation was predominant over dialogue and discussion of solutions. It is as though the *ulama*, the intellectuals and the popular movements lined up in the opposing trenches of war instead of each having an independent voice and stance that was above the sides of the opposing rulers. They had not been consulted either prior to or following the policies that governed the official and governmental decisions nor about the consequences these decisions may lead to. Their role was marginal. They were asked to deliver *fatwas* after the fact, then other *fatwas* after other events.[25]

Distressing to some in the rank and file of the Islamist movement is not only the marginalization of the *ulama* and their dependence on government hierarchies, but also their collusion with the various regimes.[26] It became evident in the course of these debates that many of the *ulama* are accountable to the governments that support them and that in responding to the crisis they found religious justification for whatever position they were expected to take. "There was no independent opinion based on *shari'a*, rather the *shari'a* was used to justify whatever the ruler wanted."[27] They were criticized for what was seen as their duplicity — in some cases *ulama* that had previously attended Iraqi-sponsored conferences and had lavished praise on the regime now were forced to denounce Iraq for its present actions.[28]

During the seven months of the Gulf crisis George Bush acquired several epithets that show clearly how Islamists perceived the war and the role of both America and Saudi Arabia in it. During early August, when Saudi Arabia authorized American intervention in the Gulf and therefore its ability to defend Mecca and Medina was called into question, Bush came to be referred to by many Jordanians as "Hami al-Haramayn," Protector of the Holy Places (of Mecca and Medina). This was a reference to the assumed title by King Fahd of Saudi Arabia of "Khadim al-Haramayn," Servant of the Holy Places, the implication being his failure to live up to such an exalted title and a sharp critique of his apparent surrender of the most holy places of Islam to the protection of foreign forces.(It was at this time that King Hussein asked the Jordanian Parliament to refer to him as al-Sharif Hussein, the title held by his great grandfather, who was the ruler of the Hijaz area which includes Mecca and Medina until the Saudis invaded and annexed it with the complicity of the British.)

Questions have been raised as to what it was that George Bush was trying to protect. One Muslim student in the United States, taking off on the "Hami al-Haramayn" label for the American president, said that he might better be called "Hami al-Haramiyyin," Protector of the Thieves, those who have robbed the Muslim masses of their rightful heritage. For several decades Muslim authors have explained that according to Islamic jurisprudence natural resources are the property of the Muslim people as a whole, not of private companies or individuals. Rulers of Kuwait and Saudi Arabia have been faulted not only because they have not shared the resources so as to promote the development of the poorer Arab nations,[29] but because they have squandered their wealth for personal pleasure on gambling tables and women in Europe and the United States. These policies, and what is perceived as the arrogance of the "Gulfies," are considered responsible for the lack of development in Muslim countries. As a consequence many of the best scientists have emigrated, part of the brain drain of those who left the Arab world in order to preserve their dignity and "avoid the arrogance of the sons of 'the families' who strut with power."[30]

Another of the names given to George Bush is St. George on the Eleventh Crusade. At first glance the title appears fitting, since St. George is an important figure for both Christians and Muslims in the Middle East. (He is always depicted as slaying a dragon, which some would see as appropriate given Bush's demonization of Saddam Hussein.) It is actually representative of the perception in Muslim countries, articulated over the last four decades, that "American neo-colonial imperialist" interests in the Middle East are a continuation of the Crusades, fired by Christian hatred of Islam. The establishment of the state of Israel in Palestine, an area fought over and coveted by the Crusaders, has led to the depiction of Western intervention in Middle Eastern affairs as a "Crusader-Zionist conspiracy" against Muslim lands and Islamic peoples.

In mobilizing the country for war in the Gulf, President Bush evoked some unfortunate Christian imagery which reinforced the image of Crusader. On January 17, he went to church with Billy Graham, who had spent the evening at the White House. Graham had been one of the many leaders of the Christian "right" who endorsed the war, even though most of the mainstream denominations (including Bush's own Episcopalians) had spoken out against it. Bush later appeared before Christian audiences to claim that he was waging a just war, a war declared against the forces of evil. To Muslim listeners, the message was one of a Holy Crusade with the United States standing on the side of righteousness, a war wrapped in and justified by the rhetoric of Christian moralism and Western values.[31]

Another name that George Bush acquired as a consequence of his Middle East adventure is that of the *Dajjal*, the Deceiver, one who misleads and tells lies. It is a designation used by some of the Muslim students on American campuses in reference to his misleading the American people about the real reasons why the war was being waged. There appears to be a consensus among Islamists that the United States did not go into the war to save "poor Kuwait from aggression," but rather that there were strategic as well as economic reasons for American involvement. Iraq's punishment was a consequence of its insolence, its refusal to downsize its army after its role in controlling the spread of Islamic revival in Iran was completed. By continuing its economic, military and industrial development and by acquiring military hardware proscribed for non-industrialized countries it crossed what one source called the "red line" laid down for it by Kissinger's Center for International and Strategic Studies. Its real sin therefore was not the invasion of Kuwait as such but its refusal to reduce its army to the point where it would not be able to threaten Israel's security, which is seen as the cornerstone of American foreign policy in the Middle East.[32]

One traditional Islamic understanding of the *Dajjal* is that it is the name for the Anti-Christ who will sow discord prior to the return of the Messiah at the end of time. It is important to see, however, that none of the references to George Bush as the *Dajjal* appear to be tapping into Islamic religious expectations of the millennium. Unlike some Christian fundamentalists who saw in Operation Desert Storm the unfolding of the last days before the Rapture, Islamist literature has been down to earth, analyzing issues in their political, economic and social contexts rather than from an apocalyptic perspective.

Popular Arab and Muslim reaction against American intervention in the area thus has been deeply influenced by their bitter memories, many very recent, of different kinds of Western colonialism. It is also an expression of hurt and anger at what is seen as the double standard of the international community in dealing with issues of conflict in the world. Several authors have contrasted world reaction to the massacre of Palestinians in October by the Israeli police at the al-Aqsa mosque in Jerusalem with reaction to the situation in Iraq. In the words of one,

And when the United Nations met to discuss the massacre, they spent five days and were unable to come out with any meaningful decision because the U.S. rejected any resolution that might give legitimacy to international protection of the Palestinians. The American ambassador said clearly, "Let us presume that the United Nations takes a resolution that is not acceptable to Israel. What is the use? What can we do?" Strange!!! The whole world cannot do anything to halt Israeli aggression and is incapacitated for fear of its anger, while [the ambassador] confronts all the Arab and Islamic world and does not care whether they are pleased or angered. He forces a boycott of a whole people with no concern that their children may die of hunger.[33]

While the United States government insisted that the occupation of Kuwait and the occupation of the West Bank and Gaza must not be linked, they could not convince most people in the Arab-Muslim world that the two situations were not parallel. The very fact that the United States has supported persistent Israeli violations of United Nations resolutions (by casting over 40 vetoes to circumvent international condemnation) has persuaded many of the duplicity and hypocrisy of American involvement in Desert Shield/Desert Storm. That President Bush professed to be nauseated by pictures of mangled Kuwaiti children and destroyed Kuwaiti property no one doubts; questions are raised, however, as to why he seems to suffer from "selective nausea" in being offended by these atrocities while turning a deaf ear to the suffering and pain of Palestinians under Israeli occupation and a blind eye to the destruction of property and human life in the occupied territories.

The concern displayed by the American administration and the press for the few Israeli victims of scud attacks alongside the cavalier reports about the Iraqi victims being reduced to inanimate "collateral damage," as well as comments from members of the U.S. military that firing on retreating Iraqi soldiers was like a "turkey shoot," reconfirmed feelings that Americans do not value Muslim life. "Like the bloodthirsty crowds of ancient times who gathered to watch in sport the sickening murder of human beings by animals or by each other," said one Muslim observer, "the leaders of the United States reduced war to the seriousness of a video game."[34] This sense of Western callousness toward Arabs has grown over four decades of Western reports about events in the Middle East where the death of a few Jews makes headlines, but the killing of scores of Arabs by Israelis is relegated to the back pages, if it is reported at all.

Whatever their feelings about the Gulf War, Arabs are in general agreement that selective implementation of United Nations resolutions and an apparent double standard on the part of the United States lends little credibility to the moral stance on which George Bush tried to predicate American action in the Gulf. Where was the world, asks al-Shihabi, when Britain occupied the Falkland Islands or when America invaded Grenada or Panama? Or when the Shah of Iran occupied and annexed the Arab islands of Greater Tanb, Lesser Tanb and Abu Musa? And where was it during the eight years of fighting between Iraq and Iran? The truth is that the world was arming both sides, forestalling making any decisive resolutions such as those formulated against Iraq, with the purpose of extending the war and destroying the strength of both sides. Where was the world, he asks, when America occupied Vietnam or when the Soviets occupied Afghanistan? And where was it when the Lebanese civil war bled Syria and Lebanon, or when Israel occupied the West Bank, Gaza, Sinai, Golan and south Lebanon (most of which it still occupies)?[35]

Muslims see that one of the reasons why the idea of American intervention in the Gulf sold well to the American public as a kind of "crusade" was because of the biased image that the West has of Islam as a religion of war and violence. They believe that the Islamic concept of *jihad* is deliberately misinterpreted and misused by the enemies of Islam in order to elicit fear and hatred of Muslims. Western critics either fail or refuse to understand that there are several meanings to the term. The higher struggle, the real *jihad*, is that waged against the tendency of the soul to veer toward evil, the struggle of the self to effect righteousness through obedience to God. According to Islamic principles, *jihad* as war is sanctioned only when Muslims are not allowed to practice their faith. The association of Islam with holy war, and of Muslims with the propagation of violence, seems to be endemic to Western awareness of Muslim faith. This is deeply disturbing to Muslims. When a member of the American military was interviewed on television and said that if they want to get to their Allah he didn't mind speeding up the process, he was heard by Muslims to be both condescending and derogatory, expressing an overt lack of reverence for Muslim life and Islamic faith.

There is concern in Muslim circles that this kind of misunderstanding and bigotry has been generated by such Zionist scholars as Bernard Lewis (in his post-1967 writings) and Daniel Pipes, both of whom write for the popular press, as well as by novelists and commentators. It is clear that it has been propagated by members of the American administration since 1980. There is a perception that by the end of the Reagan administration and the advent of perestroika, the "Evil Empire" he felt called upon to destroy had shifted from Communism to Islam.[36] Many Muslims believe that it would have been impossible for the Bush administration to rally such support for the "massacre" of over 100,000 Iraqis were it not for the climate of fear and hate generated by the American press. Such a climate can only be fostered by the kind of remark made by Vice President Dan Quayle to the graduating class at the May 30, 1990 commencement ceremony of the U.S. Naval Academy. Citing the remarkable changes that have taken place with the passing of the totalitarian era, he said that "the world is still a dangerous place. . . . We have been surprised this past century by the rise of Communism, the rise of Nazism, and the rise of Islamic radical fundamentalism . . ."

For at least two decades there has been discussion among the Islamists concerning the kind of Islam that can deliver a better future for the Muslim people and that can restore the *umma* to its former potency and dignity as a standard of righteousness in the world. As Islamists have begun to survey the ruins that Operation Desert Shield/Desert Storm has left in its wake they are more eager than ever to establish a stronger and more accountable Islamic unity in the face of the evil that seems to threaten their lives.

This unity is to supersede regional attempts by various governments and regimes to offset local threats, attempts that have fostered such ineffective organizations as the Arab League, the Maghreb Federation, and the Arab Cooperation Council. The nation-state system put in place by the West in this century is unacceptable to most. As Mukhtar 'Aziz says, it was created in a "mutilated and crippled [form] by the will and fiat of the victorious nations of the Second World War. It is a system that in its framework, structures and instrumentalities is incapable of [bringing about] the progressive development or the vision that can [effectively] respond to the needs of the region."[37]

Muslims who share this perspective perceive that they have no say in determining their destiny. Arab governments are rendered weak *mustad'a-fun*, oppressed by those in the West who seek to dominate the area, to rob it of its wealth and resources, and to take advantage of its strategic importance for its own purposes. Or as one author puts it: "It is clear that Arab oil is not for Arabs, nor Arab wealth for Arabs, nor Arab land for Arabs."[38] It is also clear to them that the West is bent on the destruction of the Islamic movement, the only popular force that continues to say "No" to occupation and domination by foreigners. The West is perceived as eager to deny to Muslims either self-determination or democracy because it knows that while it is in the survival interests of some governments not to resist Western hegemony, the people will continue to vote against foreign intervention.[39] Consequently the appeal of the Islamists is that they refuse to acquiesce in having Arab people denied the right to make decisions concerning their own destiny.

> The momentous decisions concerning the affairs of the *umma*, the gravest choices, are outlined for the nation. But it is held accountable for the responsibilities and for the consequences [of these choices]. At the moment of decision, [the *umma*] is deemed "immature," incapable of making such choices, and thus the big powers scheme and negotiate its [territory] as spheres of influence. In times of prosperity, [the *umma*] is expected to become a domesticated rabbit to be devoured by the "lion," if the latter deems it necessary. In times of trouble, it is judged as responsible for its own "choices," choices it never had any say in making.[40]

It is clear from the Islamist literature that the Muslim world feels itself to be in a state of heightened jeopardy, keenly aware of the possibility that it may suffer even deeper losses. Muslims find themselves oppressed by foreign armies that want to dictate the future and destiny of their nation, surrounded by enemies that seek the eradication of Islamic awakening and a war against Islam whose purpose is the humiliation of the Muslim *umma*. What they can least afford is division. Unity is critical for safeguarding the faith. For the purpose of promoting this unity a great deal of emphasis is put on the importance of dialogue among various Muslim groups based on Islamic principles of conflict management and consensus building.[41]

The critical discourse that is taking place in various parts of the Arab world as a direct result of the Gulf War shows that the lessons learned are very different from that America thinks that it has "taught." Important topics often ignored in the name of respect for Arab brotherhood have been openly discussed. Issues such as the violation of human rights and free speech in Arab countries are not only being analyzed but are also being placed on the agenda for continuing conversation. There is a growing consensus that reform and democratization must take place within the Arab political system. Social and political oppression long tolerated for fear that outside enemies would manipulate the opposition to foster divisions among Arab Muslims can no longer be tolerated. The call is for genuine unity among the popular forces that can transcend and transform illegitimate regimes maintained in power by dependence on foreign governments. What the West may find hard to understand, however, is that Islamists see that reform and democratization must be based not on a relinquishing of Islamic principles but on their reaffirmation. As one Islamic newsletter put it: "There is no hope for the Islamic world, or indeed for the entire world, without democracy in the Islamic world, without Islam."[42]

Some Islamist writers have been defiant in refusing to be mired in self pity. They see the Muslim people rising from the ashes of destruction to build a better future.

> The navies bent on destroying our renaissance will be the impetus to hasten it. The destructive bombs dropped on our cities and children to intimidate and terrorize will cause [new] identities to burst forth and will empower our men and women to discard the remnant of retardation and enter the new world order as strong, powerful, and victorious and not as America wants them to be. From the strategy of destruction the *umma* will create a strategy for change. And from the plan for the American century, a plan [will come] for the centuries of Islam.[43]

As one Muslim leader in the U.S. said in confidence, Muslims are taught by the Qur'an that we must trust in God. We should not see this defeat in any sense as the end. It may be that God has special plans that we do not now understand. Remember that the last destruction of Baghdad came in 1258 by the Mongol hordes under Hulagu. From that came an eventual triumph for Islam as they converted to the faith. "God's ways are inscrutable," he said, "and He only knows what He holds for the future of America."

## Notes

1. Sayyid Syeed, editor of the *American Journal of Islamic Social Sciences* in an interview with Michael MacManus, *The Paducah Sun* (February 8, 1991).
2. "Editorial" *Anba' Tunisiyya*, # 26 (February 12, 1991) p. 1; c.f. in the same issue a statement by the Shura Council of the Nahda Party of Tunisia, "Labbayka 'Iraqa al-'Uruba wa al-Islam;" c.f. in the same issue an appeal signed by the Islamists Rashed al-Ghannoushi, Hasan al-Turabi, 'Isam

'Attar, Munir Shafiq, Layth Shbeylat, 'Adel Hussein and Ibrahim Shukri, "Nida' ila al-Umma al-Islamiyya," p. 6. C.f. "Harb Masiriyya", *al-Sabil* 21 (February 1991), p. 1.

3. Mukhtar 'Aziz described America's role as "leading and coercing the concerned parties into the trap of conflict." See "Al-'Ajil wa'al-Ajil fi Azmat al-Khalij," *Risalat al-Jihad* 9/96 (February 1991), p. 6. C.f. The leaders of the Islamic Movements of Egypt, Jordan, Syria, Yemen, Algeria, Pakistan, Turkey and Malaysia met in Jordan and formed a delegation to seek an Islamic solution to the crisis since they perceived it as a consequence of a Crusader Imperialist-Zionist conspiracy. "Bayan 'An al-Liqa' al-Islami," *Anba' Tunisiyya*, 13 (September 22, 1990) p. 4.

4. Ibrahim Yahya al-Shihabi, "Izdiwajiyyat al-Ma'ayir al-Duwaliyya bayn Majzarat al-Aqsa wa-Azmat al-Khalij", *Risalat al-Jihad* 9/95 (January 1991), p. 36.

5. Fahmi al-Huwaydi, "Al-Jard Qabl al-Akhir", *Al-Majalla* 11/572 (January 23–29, 1991), p. 27.

6. *The Washington Post* (September 14, 1990).

7. "'Ulama' al-Islam fi Misr Yarfudun Da'wat Saddam," *Al-Majalla* 11/571 (January 16–22, 1991), p. 9.

8. Several Egyptian Islamists were part of the delegation that visited Muslim countries in search of an Islamic solution. They included Ibrahim Shukri, 'Adel Husayn and Ahmad 'Izz al-Din. For the record of their efforts, see: "Al-Bayan al-Sahafi li al-Wafd al-Islami Athar Jawlatihi al-Khassa bi Azmat al-Khalij," *Al-Insan* 1, 3, (December 1990) p. 13.

9. For a complete text of his reflections, see Rashed al-Ghannoushi, "Ay Hawl Akbar mi Hadha . . . al-Salibiyyun Yahtallun Bilad al-Haramayn al-Sharifayn," Typescript. C.f. Rashed al-Ghannoushi, "Hal ma Yahduth fi al-Khalij Mu'amara?" *Anba' Tunisiyya* 21 (December 1, 1990), pp. 2–3.

10. Fahmi al-Huwaydi, "Hiwar Ma' al-Ghannoushi," *al-Majallah* 11/556 (October 2–9, 1990), p. 30.

11. Rashed al-Ghannoushi, "Ma Yahduth fi al-Khalij Mu'amara," *al-Fajr* 19 (November 24, 1990), p. 2.

12. *Anba' Tunisiyya* 26 (February 12, 1991), pp. 5–6.

13. "Kayf Ta'amalat al-Harakat al-Islamiyya ma' al-Hadath," *Al-Maghreb* 214 (August 31, 1990), p. 11.

14. "Al-Sa'udiyya laysat bi al-Darura Mu'adiya li al-Masalih al-'Arabiyya," *al-Maghreb* 213 (August 24, 1990), p. 5.

15. *Realite* 262 (August 31-September 6, 1990), p. 11. For a text of a statement denying the possibility of seeking aid from non-Muslims see Mustafa bin Muhammad al-Wardani, "Al-Nahi 'an al-Instinsar fi 'Umur al-Muslimin bi al- Kuffar", edited by Taha Jabir Fayyad al-'Alwani, *al-Far* 12 (October 6, 1990), p. 16.

16. Huwaydi, "Hiwar", p. 31. Cf. Al-Majlis al-Islami al-Urubi, "Ru'ya Islamiyya li Azmat al-Khalij," *Al-Insan* 1/3 (December 1990), p. 21: "Which is the greater evil, the fall of one regime here or there or the consigning of a whole *umma* to a destiny placed in the hands of an enemy?"

17. The Islamic Council called attention to the memory of the Muslim experience in Spain when the rulers of al-Andalus lost the land when they sought protection from Christian kings against other Muslim rulers. Al-Majlis al-Islami, "Al-Andalus Da'at Hina Ista'ana Muluk al-Tawa'if bi 'Aduwwihim," *Al-Badil*, 6 (October 1, 1990) p. 14.

18. For a full text of their deliberations and declaration, see, "Al-Mu'tamar al-Islami al-'Alami li-Munaqashat al-Awda' al-Hadira fi al-Khalij," *Al-Insan*, 1/3 (December 1990) pp. 8–12.

19. A conference in Lahore, Pakistan called on Muslims all over the world to put pressure on the United Nations to lift its embargo against the Iraqi people, demanded the withdrawal of all foreign forces, condemned Israeli aggression against Palestinians and expressed support for the Muslim people of Kashmir, Afghanistan and all those struggling for self-determination. Present at the conference were the following movements: Jamaati Islami of Pakistan, Muslim Brotherhood of Egypt, Islamic Movement of the Sudan, The Nahda Movement of Tunisia, Muslim Brotherhood of Jordan, Islamic Movement of Turkey, Islamic Movement of Malaysia, Islamic Movement of Lebanon, Islamic Party of Afghanistan, Islamic Front of Afghanistan, Islamic Federation of Afghanistan, Muslim Brotherhood of Syria, Hamas of Palestine, and the Islamic Movements of the Gulf, United States and Europe. See "al-Tatawwurat al-Siyasiyya: al-Bayan al-Thani li al-Harakat al-Islamiyya Hawl Harb al-Khalij," Flyer.

20. *Al-Majalla* 11/571 (January 16–22, 1991), p. 26.

21. Al-Majlis al-Islami al-Urubi, "Ru'ya Islamiyya li Azmat al-Khalij," *al-Insan* 1/3 (December 1990), p. 19.

22. "Radd al-Mu'arada al-Islamiyya al-'Iraqiyya 'Ala al-Mu'tamar al-Sha'bi al-Islami Alladhi Da'a Ilayhi Saddam," *Al-Majalla* 22/571 (January 1991), p. 11.

23. "The Tahrir Party announced that it was in support of the union between Kuwait and Iraq because of its commitment to Islamic unity regardless of its form or shape." "Kayf Ta'amalat al-Harakat al-Islamiyya ma' al-Hadath," *Al-Maghreb* # 214 (August 21, 1990), p. 11.

24. For a variety of statements, declarations and resolutions by Islamic groups in various Muslim countries see *Anba' Tunisiyya*, 11 (September 1, 1990), p. 1.

25. "Malhuzat 'Ala Hamish Azmat al-Khalij," *Al-Insan* 1/3 (December, 1990), pp. 3–4.

26. Al-Ghannoushi in a lecture for Islamic missionaries, *du'at*, in Morocco called for a reconciliation between the *ulama* and the *du'at*, the former being "hostages of the enemy." "Kalimat

Du'at 'Ulama' al-Maghreb al-'Arabi," *Anba' Tunisiyya* 13 (December 22, 1990), p. 4. To the dismay of many of his supporters, Yusuf al-Qaradawi in an interview with the Saudi *National Guard Magazine* expressed the opinion that seeking the help of foreigners is permissible. Reprinted in *Al-Insan* 1/3 (December 1990), p. 23.

27. "Those who issue *fatwa* legitimating the aid of non-Muslims at such times have not one single evidence from the Qur'an or Sunna to support their *fatwa*." Al-Majlis al-Islami, p. 20.

28. "Malhuzat," p. 5.

29. King Hussein reported that in a meeting with Emir Jaber al-Sabah of Kuwait shortly before August he discussed the economic condition in Jordan. The emir is said to have told him, "Since you are not an oil-producing country, why did you build roads and establish telephone communications?" The king reportedly responded, "We were wrong, it is our fault, we did not request your permission in the matter." "Liga' al-Malik Hussein Ma' al-Muhallilin al-Urduniyyin," *Anba' Tunisiyya* 13 (September 22, 1990), p. 6.

30. 'Abd al-Subur Marzuq, "Al-Ab'ad al-Gha'iba fi Azmat al-Khalij," *Risalat al-Jihad* 9/96 (February 1991), p. 8.

31. It is important to note that while many Muslims in general and Islamists in particular saw Operation Desert Storm as waged for the ultimate purposes of the "Zionist Crusaders," they did not seem to buy into the claim of Saddam Hussein that he was the new Salah ad-Din (Saladin), the Muslim leader who was victorious over the crusading forces of Christendom in the 12th century.

32. Mukhtar, "Al-'Ajil," p. 7.

33. Al-Shihabi, p. 37. Other statements of similar nature include: "The United States justified its invasion by saying that altering borders is illegitimate. Where was it on the day of the occupation of Jerusalem, Golan [Heights] and Sinai; did it not finance and encourage the occupation." *Al-Islam wa-Filastin* (September 1990) p. 24. C.f. "While the United States government was massing forces in the Gulf to force Iraq out of Kuwait, Moshe Arens, Defense Minister of Israel announced on August 11, 1990 that Israel will not allow the Lebanese government to regain control of the South. What is the difference between Israeli affirmations and the Iraqi declaration that Kuwait became Province 19?" Marzuq, p. 30.

34. "The Great Betrayal", *al-Mashriq* (January-February 1991), p. 8.

35. Al-Shihabi, p. 37.

36. Yvonne Haddad, *The Muslims of America* (New York: Oxford University Press, 1991), pp. 217–235.

37. Mukhtar, 'Al-'Ajil," p. 7.

38. Al-Shihabi, p. 37.

39. Declaration signed by Egyptian Islamists, *Al-Islam wa-Filastin* (September 3, 1990), p. 27.

40. Mukhtar, "Al-'Ajil," p. 7.

41. "Malhuzat," p. 6.

42. *North African News* 2/1 (January-February 1991), p. 5. C.f. "After the War, Is Peace Possible?" *North African News* 2/1 (January-February 1991), p. 1.

43. Editorial in *Anba' Tunisiyya* 26 (February 12, 1991), p. 1.

# PART FIVE

The Global Storm:

International Perspectives and

Repercussions

# 24

## Oil and the Gulf Crisis

*Michael Tanzer*

The purpose of this article is to analyze oil's role in U.S. foreign policy in the current Persian Gulf crisis. Historically, it has always been a U.S. goal to have as much control as possible over non-renewable resources, especially oil. And for most of the twentieth century, this control was exerted by a combination of high domestic production and the U.S. oil companies' ownership of foreign crude oil. This in turn was buttressed by U.S. economic and military power.

In this latter regard, by now most people are familiar with the CIA-led overthrow of the Mossadegh government in Iran after it replaced the Shah in 1951 and then dared to nationalize the oil industry. Less well known is that when, in the summer of 1958, a military group overthrew the feudal monarchy in Iraq, and the entire Middle East was in ferment, in its first post-Korean War intervention U.S. troops landed in Lebanon, while British paratroopers landed in Jordan. That Iraq was the real target was indicated by a report from the New York *Herald Tribune* that initially the U.S. government gave "strong consideration" to "military intervention to undo the coup in Iraq." According to the *New York Times*, the U.S. and British leaders jointly decided that: "Intervention will not be extended to Iraq as long as the revolutionary government in Iraq respects Western oil interests." The continuity of this policy can be seen from the fact that the new Iraqi government of Colonel Qasim was overthrown in 1963 by another coup, which followed the formation of a state oil company to exploit oil lands seized from the companies in 1961; the Paris weekly *L'Express* stated flatly that: "The Iraqi coup was inspired by the CIA."

Within the last twenty years, however, what was once a monopolistic industry *par excellence* has seen very serious fragmentation, basically paralleling the decline of U.S. hegemony in the late 1960s and early 1970s. U.S. oil production has dropped significantly and at the same time imports have increased sharply. In 1970, the U.S. produced about 20% of the world's oil supply, and imported only about 12% of its domestic consumption. Today, it produces only about 10% of the world's oil and imports about half of the oil it consumes.

The decisive upheaval stemmed from the events of the 1970–1973 period, culminating in the 1973 Arab-Israeli War. It needs to be recalled that the Organization of Petroleum Exporting Countries (OPEC) was created in 1960, and in its first decade accomplished relatively little, except for stabilizing the per barrel revenues of its governments in a period of declining oil prices caused by intensifying competition among the companies.

Contrastingly, in the early 1970s the OPEC countries effectively achieved goals that had been the dreams of oil nationalists throughout the twentieth century. They wrested away from the companies the historic pillars of control of the industry: effective ownership of the countries' crude oil, and the right to determine the price of the oil and the amount to be produced. From the producing countries' viewpoint, it appeared as if the millennium had arrived, and twenty-five years early no less.

Now, however, some fifteen years after the great OPEC revolution, it is clear that while much was accomplished, much more was not. The international oil companies and their home governments, with their vast financial resources, control of refining and distribution facilities in oil importing countries as well as of crude oil production in non-OPEC countries, have been shown again to be cats with ninety-nine lives.

Another factor which has changed in the last twenty years is the rise of Japan and Europe as economic rivals of the United States. At the same time, since these countries have very few natural resources, particularly oil, they have also become major importers of oil. Further, we have the rise of the U.S. as the world's overwhelming military power, marked by the apparent abdication of the Soviet Union as a military competitor. And finally, one other important underlying situation, which hasn't changed, is the continuing and heightened dependency of the U.S. economy on oil; there has been a virtually complete failure in the last two decades either to reduce demand sharply by energy conservation or to expand production of renewable energy resources such as solar power as an alternative to oil.

Turning now to the current Persian Gulf crisis, it seems clear that oil politics was the key factor which precipitated the Iraqi invasion of Kuwait. As the London-based *Petroleum Economist*, which has no sympathy for Iraq, noted in September 1990:

> Although debt compiled during its war with Iran has done much to devastate the Iraqi economy, the slackness of world oil prices — in no small part due to the perpetual problem of OPEC over-production — has contributed to the persistence of Iraq's economic problem. The current Iraqi government budget is characterized by its open austerity measures, import substitutions and an order to all government departments to cut their numbers of staff of 50%. In 1988 alone, Iraq's gross domestic product fell by some 10% . . .
> In stark contrast, the Kuwaiti economic picture in the past year has been particularly comfortable. Kuwaiti oil revenues in the first three quarters of 1989 were up some 60% over the same period in 1988 . . . [T]his income has been

accrued on the ability consistently to produce and market oil greatly in excess of its OPEC quota, without redress from other member nations.

While the oil situation may have been the underlying cause of the Iraqi invasion, there has also been a lot of discussion of whether U.S. diplomacy "bumbled" by sending out the wrong signals to the Iraqi government that Washington would not oppose any invasion of Kuwait. Without being privy to U.S. ruling circles it is not possible definitively to know whether or not Iraq was "lured into" this invasion. But if we look at oil events, it is interesting to see what actions the president took either to avoid or to force war. After the Iraqi invasion, but prior to the U.S. bombardment of Iraq, in a period when the oil markets were panicked, the president refused to take any actions to calm them. Most significant was his refusal to release crude oil supplies from the Strategic Petroleum Reserve which had been stockpiled for just such a contingency. And even the *Petroleum Economist* admitted in September 1990 that "had governments and the IEA [International Energy Agency] quickly insisted that stocks should not be kept topped up, and released a few hundred thousand b/d [barrels per day] of their own reserves, the crude spike would soon have been blunted."

In stark contrast to this, the day after the U.S. bombed Iraq, the president announced that he would release emergency stockpiles to calm the situation in the oil markets, and overnight the price of oil fell by a third. Thus, looking at actions rather than words, in the earlier period the effect of the administration's lack of action was to keep oil prices high and volatile and the oil market in a panicky state. But immediately after U.S. military action began, the administration made a major and successful effort to calm oil markets. Thus, the administration's actions were exactly the reverse of what one would except if the aim was to calm oil markets before a war began, but totally consistent with an attempt to keep them volatile as a sign that sanctions were not working, while in an Orwellian way, war could be associated with peaceful oil markets.

Furthermore, even before the U.S. bombardment began, there was no real justification for the inflated and volatile current oil prices. Here the real villain seems to be the key role which is now played by speculative commodity markets for oil, which were previously negligible or non-existent. Historically, virtually all of the crude oil traded was between and among oil companies and prices were based on long term supply contracts. In the early 1970s the spot market, which covers one-time shipments of oil, accounted for less than 5% of world oil trade, and futures markets for later delivery of oil did not even exist. Now, by contrast, daily spot and futures trading can amount to as much as eight times total world oil consumption. Little wonder then that a long-time oil industry operator, Leon Hess, chairman of Amerada Hess, testified to a Congressional committee investigating the skyrocketing oil prices that "there is not a supply problem on crude oil," and concluded, "I'm an old man, but I'd bet my life that if the Merc [Mercantile Exchange] were not in operation, there'd be ample oil at reasonable prices all over the world without this [price] volatility."

Moreover if we examine the data on futures prices for the medium term, we find that before the U.S. bombing began, the market was pricing oil for delivery six months later and beyond at a relatively low level: at $23–25 per barrel compared to the wildly fluctuating current price of $30–$40 per barrel. This strongly suggests that the consensus of market participants was that either there would be no war or that any war would not have a serious disruptive effect on supply/demand in the medium term. And this assumption of the market undoubtedly rested partly on the clear ability of industrial countries to release the emergency stockpiles in case of a truly supply-disruptive war.

In conclusion, it seems to me that the administration's actions in the current crisis are understandable in the light of the underlying long term objectives we sketched out in the beginning. The administration moved hundreds of thousands of troops into the Persian Gulf, first with the ostensible goal of blocking an Iraqi invasion of Saudi Arabia, and then with the goal of forcing Iraq out of Kuwait. Thus, it achieved a longstanding goal of obtaining a military presence in Saudi Arabia and turning that country into a virtual U.S. protectorate. By destroying Iraq, the administration may have hoped to become the military arbiter for the whole region, and even turn this to a profit in the growing rivalries and struggles with continental Europe and Japan.

In this latter connection, continued Anglo-American control of "petro-dollars" is of major significance. These moneys — the revenues received by petroleum exporting countries which are surplus to their trade needs — thanks to OPEC's power rose to the hundreds of billions of dollars in the last two decades. "Recycling" of these vast sums into the dollar and sterling banking systems has been a major source of profits for Anglo-American banks. In addition, the petrodollar system shored up the dollar internationally by making it the key currency for OPEC producers and their customers. This in turn allowed the U.S. government in particular to run large external deficits in financing the defense of its empire.

Such a reassertion of the old Anglo-American oil imperialism which prevailed in the Gulf region for many years seems to be in line with the goals of the largest international oil companies, for which the *Petroleum Economist* is a good spokesperson:

> The Iraqi invasion of Kuwait on August 2, and the political ramifications of the landmark Western military involvement on Saudi territory, have changed the course of Middle East politics in the most significant manner since the creation of the state of Israel. Moreover, the end of Kuwaiti independence has called into question the efficacy of the entire OPEC system, if not its very existence, and radically altered the political disposition of Middle East oil. . . .
>
> The effects of the Western military response to the current situation in the Gulf has been directly to internationalize the political disposition of world oil production from OPEC's most important members. Additionally, it has placed the West in the role of primary regional military power in the northern part of the Gulf. (September 1990)

Interestingly, a somewhat contrary position is taken in an *Oil and Gas Journal* editorial, "War and change in the oil world" (January 21, 1991).

Although the editorial starts out with the same kind of ringing statement: "For the international petroleum industry, war in the Middle East means the world will never be the same," it then goes on to caution:

> But there are huge questions beyond those involving the conflict itself. The petroleum industry must now wonder what happens once the shooting stops. . . .
>
> For industry, the dangers are obvious. What may be less obvious is the rapidly diminishing degree to which companies in the future will be able to rely on stability enforced from abroad. The petroleum world — and that includes consumers — has played its Western military ace. If this fight lives up to its bloody expectations who will lead the next defense of the world's economic sustenance?
>
> Not the U.S. A loud minority didn't want to fight to defend petroleum interests this time. Next time it won't be a minority. And this war, coming as it does at the beginning of a recession and well into a period of fiscal distress, will be costly. If the next crisis comes any time soon, the U.S. won't possess the military and financial resources necessary to respond. And if the world's single biggest oil consuming country doesn't respond, no one will.

By way of footnote, in my view the reason for the cautious approach is that the *Oil and Gas Journal* tends to reflect the views of the smaller independent U.S. oil companies, which focus on U.S. production. Such an ideological split also took place during the Vietnam War, when oil was the key lure in the Nixon administration's strategy to try and shore up South Vietnam's crumbling economy by attracting U.S. investment there. While major international companies like Shell and Mobil were successfully drawn in (indeed Mobil was busily drilling offshore on the last day of the war), by that point *Oil and Gas Journal* was urging U.S. companies to get out because their presence was giving the industry a bad name.

For those who are opposed to continuing U.S. intervention in the Middle East, this history of the differential strategies within the U.S. oil industry is of considerable significance. Since the region is likely to be in turmoil for a long time to come, there will tend to be a continuing impulse by oil imperialists to play the role of local policeman. For those who will oppose such a role, it is important to keep in mind that the politically powerful oil industry is not a monolith, and that strange bedfellows can be enlisted on their side — particularly if the anti-war movement can make the link in the public mind of the necessity of reducing dependence on foreign oil in order to reduce the impulse for oil interventionism.

# 25

## Bushbacking: Britain Goes to War

*Paul Rogers*

In March 1982, Argentina invaded and over-ran the Falkland Islands, a British possession in the South Atlantic. Britain responded by sending a major naval task force and, after a brief but brutal war lasting six weeks, defeated the Argentine forces and recaptured the islands. While there was an anti-war movement in Britain during the conflict, it had relatively little effect among the population at large, and the victory in the south Atlantic and the subsequent return of the troops and warships to Britain were occasions for euphoria.

In the three years prior to the war, Britain's Conservative government under Margaret Thatcher had plumbed the depths of political unpopularity. By early 1982 it was over the worst of this, but was still a deeply unpopular administration. During the course of the Falklands War, however, Thatcher was increasingly seen as a strong and decisive leader and the popularity of her government improved rapidly. Its confidence also increased and she went on to score a landslide victory in the general election of 1983. Britain, it seemed, had re-asserted itself on the world stage. Its defeat of the Argentine junta showed that it was, once more, a force to be reckoned with.

It did not matter that Britain had been maintaining close business links with that same military junta just before the war. Nor did it matter that most European countries regarded the war as an event located somewhere between farce and tragedy. Even the huge post-war costs of building a major air-base and defense system for the islands, to protect barely 1,800 islanders, were questioned by no more than a handful of politicians.

All this was put aside by most of the politicians and populace — the self-image in Britain was of a country re-asserting itself. This re-assertion was not as a response to any specific event such as the effects of some previous Vietnam-style military disaster, but rather to a long period of

268

relative economic decline and progressive loss of international political status.

As well as providing an immediate and substantial boost to the political fortunes of Margaret Thatcher, the Falklands victory encouraged the more forceful and dogmatic aspects of her own political character and that of her government. It brought to the fore stronger right-wing opposition to European unity which was to contribute to her downfall in 1990. It also contributed to her innate determination to respond forcefully to Iraq's invasion of Kuwait.

Mrs. Thatcher was on a visit to Aspen, Colorado, in early August 1990 when the invasion took place. Within hours, she had met President Bush and had urged him to be strong in his response to the Iraqi action. She committed Britain to supporting the early build-up of military force, expanding Britain's long-standing naval presence in the Persian Gulf and ordering the deployment of several squadrons of planes and an armored brigade.

Even as the forces were being expanded in the Middle East, Mrs. Thatcher's own political position worsened in Britain and in the autumn of 1990 she was forced to resign as a result of an internal revolt in the Conservative Party. Even so, the party, under her successor John Major, continued to support a strong military response to the crisis.

When war came in mid-January, British forces were heavily committed to the conflict, with Tornado strike aircraft taking a major role in the air assault. After six weeks, Kuwait was liberated and Iraq defeated, yet there was little evidence of any euphoria in Britain.

Contrary to the post-Falklands mood, the Gulf War as a political issue failed to have much positive effect on the Conservative goverment's standing. Barely a week after the end of the war, a parliamentary by-election in Ribble Valley in Lancashire resulted in the shock defeat of the Conservative candidate by a centrist Liberal Democrat in one of the biggest swings for a decade.

Britain had been a promiment member of the coalition forces, there was blanket media coverage of the crisis, the war and the subsequent victory, yet there was little euphoria in that victory. This contrasts strongly with the response in Britain to the Falklands victory and in the United States to the Gulf War where the course of war proved hugely popular.

A number of factors may explain these differences. They are worth examining because they throw light, not just on differences in perception between the countries but also on the future roles of the United States and the European Community in matters of global security, especially in the Middle East.

## Britain in the Gulf

Until the Second World War, Britain and France had shared political power in much of the Middle East, often uneasily and with constant competition for influence. In some areas, as in Palestine, power was exercised through a

League of Nations mandate, and elsewhere usually took the form of protectorates and agencies rather than straightforward colonies.

Prior to 1945, the Middle East was of relatively limited economic value to Europe but of great strategic importance. Central to this was its position in relation to South and Southeast Asia, with control of the Suez Canal being of dominant strategic significance. Furthermore, countries such as Iraq and Iran were important in helping to limit Soviet influence.

Britain's long-term involvement with Middle East politics was represented in popular culture as something akin to a love affair with the Arab world — Kitchener of Khartoum and Lawrence of Arabia being the most notable representatives. During the Second World War, the defense of Egypt and the Suez Canal against the Italians and the Germans was crucial in the early war years. The victory of General Montgomery and his troops, the "Desert Rats," against Rommel's German forces in the Battle of El Alamein, was a much-needed boost to national morale at a particularly difficult period in the war, and this, too, reinforced the British self-perception of prowess in the desert.

The reality of the early post-war years, though, was of Britain and France being steadily replaced by the United States as the leading Western influence in the Middle East. While British oil companies were instrumental in the early exploitation of oil in Iran, Iraq and Kuwait, they were, by the 1970s, overshadowed by the much more substantial U.S. oil interests.

As if to accentuate the growing power of the United States, the Suez crisis of 1956 ended in a clear demonstration of increasing U.S. political capabilities in the region. The Egyptian leader, Nasser, had nationalized the Suez Canal and had been opposed by the British and the French, both countries colluding with Israel to force Egypt from the Canal Zone. The crisis ultimately led to Anglo-French military intervention against Egypt, pushed through by the strong personal commitment of the British Prime Minister, Anthony Eden. This late-colonial endeavor was intolerable to the Eisenhower administration in Washington and strong U.S. political pressure forced the British and French into an ignominious withdrawal.

The crisis left Britain with diminished political influence throughout the region, and was instrumental in speeding up Britain's commitment to decolonization, as the pre-crisis attitudes of the Eden government were replaced by the foreign policy pragmatism of his successor, Harold Macmillan.

In the Gulf region, though, some British influence remained, especially among the small coastal states. Prior to the discovery of oil, most of these sheikhdoms had been "town states" rather than city states, living mainly by pearl fishing and coastal trading, and mostly under British tutelage.

During the 1960s and early 1970s, many newly-rich Gulf states gained their full independence and, in the case of Oman, required continuing British military assistance to survive internal revolt. A combination of direct military aid, extensive assistance with military training and a continuing, if small, naval presence, ensured that Britain still retained some military influence in the Gulf region even after the general military withdrawal from "East of Suez" at the end of the 1960s.

In common with other Western powers, Britain regarded the Iranian revolution in 1979 as a threat to regional security, since it was considered to represent a form of Islamic fundamentalism which was inimical to Western political and economic interests. While the United States, especially with its embassy hostage experience, was strongest in its opposition to Iran, Britain was happy to strengthen its naval forces in the early 1980s as a means of expressing commitment to pro-Western Gulf states such as Kuwait, Qatar and the United Arab Emirates.

Britain, like the United States, maintained an embargo on arms sales to both Iraq and Iran during their long war. In practice, though, it was willing to offer Iraq much more assistance in other ways, including export credits and considerable aid with industrial projects, many of which could be used for military purposes.

Over the same period, Britain was successful in increasing its arms exports to states of the Arabian peninsula, its greatest success coming with a major contract with Saudi Arabia to equip its air force with advanced interceptors and strike aircraft.

With the ending of the Iran-Iraq war in 1988 and the access to power of the more pragmatic government led by President Rafsanjani, Britain looked to the opening up of new trade and development links with Iran. It still sought to develop further links with Iraq, though, and in early 1990 there was controversy in Britain over claims that several British engineering companies had been involved in supplying components for a massive Iraqi artillery project, the so-called "supergun."

Thus, by July 1990, Britain was maintaining good military and economic links with pro-Western Gulf states. It was developing its trading relationship with Iraq; and it was hopeful of closer contact with Iran. Thus it was within this context that, for Britain, the invasion of Kuwait presented considerable political difficulties.

## The Invasion and Its Immediate Aftermath

The Iraqi invasion of Kuwait on August 2 was unwelcome to Britain for several reasons. It was clearly an outrage and in obvious contravention of international law, yet Britain had close and profitable economic links with Iraq. Furthermore, Iraq was a heavily armed state and would not be easy to evict from Kuwait. There were also several thousand British nationals working in Kuwait and Iraq and they could well be at risk.

Against this, Iraq was perceived to be threatening a key strategic area. Britain was self-sufficient in oil, thanks to the North Sea oil deposits, but much of this oil production was re-exported and Britain's refining capacity was designed to process crude oil imported from the Gulf. Iraq's invasion of Kuwait already gave it control over about a quarter of the world's oil reserves, and any threat to Saudi Arabia and the Emirates meant that 54% of world oil reserves were at risk of slipping away from Western influence.

The potential threat of further Iraqi action was thus serious, the more so as Britain maintained valuable economic relations with many of the other Gulf states. Balancing these factors, one would have expected Britain to have acted quite firmly, at least going as far as accepting the need for economic sanctions.

In any event the Thatcher response was much stronger. In part this was due to a concern over the invasion itself and the claimed threat to other Gulf states, but also important were Mrs. Thatcher's personal style and her desire for closer relations with the United States.

Over the previous couple of years, Anglo-American relations, as perceived by London, had deteriorated. Thatcher had been opposed to German reunification and felt that its implementation would lead to a united Germany which would overshadow Britain's relationship with the United States. Coupled with Thatcher's more general fear of the increasing power of the European Community, this made her even more anxious to improve relations with Washington. The end result was her decision to offer considerable support to George Bush backed up with an immediate commitment of military forces.

Within two weeks of the invasion of Kuwait, Britain announced that it would reinforce its naval presence in the Gulf and would station strike aircraft and interceptors in Saudi Arabia, Oman and Bahrain. The stated object of these deployments was to offer protection to Saudi Arabia and other states, but the deployment of "deep-strike" Tornado bombers indicated that an offensive capability was being organized.

During August and September, Britain was, among all the allies of the United States, the most dominant in supporting Bush, in demanding the fullest sanctions and in commencing military deployments. By mid-September it was apparent that the United States was deploying massive air, ground and naval forces, sufficient to take a war to Kuwait and even Iraq. Britain followed suit in announcing further increases in its military deployments to the region. The most significant was the commitment of a reinforced armored brigade to Saudi Arabia.

During the early autumn an anti-war movement began to develop in Britain, usually taking the form of local committees in towns and cities which proceeded to arrange public meetings and organize demonstrations. Nationally, the most significant organization was the Campaign for Nuclear Disarmament, still a well-resourced group although campaigning at a much lower level than during the height of the peace movement in the early 1980s.

In some parts of Britain, especially in London, there were major arguments within the anti-war movement between a majority of campaigners who were concerned just with the war, and a small but vociferous segment of doctrinaire socialists who saw it as an opportunity for more general anti-American political activism. At times, this diverted much energy from the process of campaigning.

At the national political level, the Labor Party adopted a broadly bipartisan approach, supporting Conservative government policy but emphasizing the importance of the United Nations and the use of sanctions to force Iraq from Kuwait.

The Labor Party was not prepared to criticize the deployment of British military forces and its leadership privately believed that war was highly unlikely and that a diplomatic solution could be found.

At the same time, there were notable exceptions to this bipartisan approach. These included a substantial minority of left-wing Labor members of parliament, but, in terms of the national debate, two leading figures of an earlier generation were far more significant. From the start of the crisis, the former Conservative Prime Minister, Edward Heath, took the view that any war against Iraq would be folly and that a process of sanctions and naval blockade was far preferable to the massive military build-up then in progress. During the autumn of 1990, Heath travelled to Baghdad, met Saddam Hussein and persuaded him to release some of the British hostages, a process which attracted considerable media attention.

Even more effective than Heath, especially as a media debater, was the former Labor cabinet minister, Denis Healey. He took a similar view to Heath, regarding the prospect of war as being fraught with huge risks, and argued persuasively on many television and radio programs in favor of using the sanctions route.

The significance of the actions of Heath and Healey lay in the fact that they prevented opposition to a possible war from being seen purely as a left-wing phenomenon. While the bipartisan approach held for the leadership of the main political parties, Heath and Healey gave weight to the view that early recourse to war would be highly dangerous and that this was a reasonable, mainstream political view.

**Prelude to War**

During October and November, substantial British army units were deployed in Saudi Arabia, and Thatcher continued to characterize Saddam Hussein as a brutal dictator who must be evicted from Kuwait, whatever Britain's previous relations with the regime. There was general support for this stance, although opinion polls showed an almost equal split between those advocating early military action and those supporting longer term use of sanctions.

In early November, the United States sought and obtained UN approval for a January 15 deadline for the Iraqi withdrawal from Kuwait and also announced a decision to increase massively the U.S. army, air force and naval units assigned to the area. The prospect of war loomed suddenly larger. In Britain, though, this heightening of tension in the Gulf was overshadowed by a major domestic political crisis which led, by the end of the month, to the resignation of Thatcher herself.

For much of the previous year, the Thatcher government had been deeply unpopular, mainly because of the replacement of local property taxes with a flat-rate community charge or "poll tax." Although there was a rebate system for people in poverty, the poll tax was widely regarded as unfair and resulted in a series of bad by-election and local election results for the government, coupled with opinion polls which were amongst the worst on record.

A further problem was the political style of Thatcher herself, with her hectoring and authoritarian manner becoming increasingly unpopular. She also occasioned opposition by her increasing antagonism to political unity within Europe and her constant undermining of the position of more moderate cabinet ministers within her administration.

A long-time critic of her style and substance was Michael Heseltine, a former cabinet minister who had resigned his post four years previously while retaining his parliamentary seat. Under the Conservative Party constitution, the party leader could be challenged in an election by members of parliament each autumn, and, by late October, it was looking increasingly likely that Heseltine would be persuaded to stand against Thatcher.

Three factors determined this outcome, a particularly bad by-election in Eastbourne, a normally loyal Conservative area in southern England, the resignation of the Foreign Secretary, Sir Geoffrey Howe, over Thatcher's opposition to Europe, and opinion polls which showed that the Conservative Party would do substantially better under another leader.

With an election barely eighteen months away, this was enough to ensure Thatcher's downfall and in a fortnight of high political drama at the end of November, she was forced to resign and was then replaced by the more centrist John Major.

In a little-noticed decision at her final cabinet meeting, Mrs. Thatcher ordered a substantial increase in Britain's military commitment to the Gulf resulting in the deployment of a reinforced armored division as well as further planes and ships. This would take Britain's force levels in the Gulf to around 40,000, comprising the cream of the army and well over 10% of Britain's entire armed forces.

### Fears of the Consequences of War

During December and early January, the domestic political climate in Britain began to settle down, to be replaced, once more, by the Gulf as the main focus of attention. As the coalition military build-up continued it became increasingly apparent that war was possible, although polls continued to show an almost equal split between those favoring early military action and the continued use of sanctions.

The Labor Party continued to support the government, even to the extent of supporting the troop reinforcements, but there were serious differences within the party and a minority of members of parliament were prepared to break ranks and insist that sanctions should be given much more time.

There were also increasing fears in the country as a whole over the consequences of a war, with a number of analysts forecasting high casualties among troops and considerable media attention being given to the extensive preparation of medical facilities to treat such casualties.

In early January, considerable publicity was given to reports that Iraq had mined a substantial proportion of Kuwait's oil wells, and activists were quick to point out the potentially catastrophic environmental consequences of a war, should these be ignited.

As the deadline of January 15 approached, the attitude to a potential war could be characterized as a mixture of excitement and apprehension, the former built up largely by the tabloid press which campaigned hard for early military action. Given the bipartisan political approach of the opposition parties, and the almost total press support for military action, it is surprising that there was so much concern over the possible damaging consequences of war.

## War and its Effects

Once the war started, polls indicated a considerable majority in support of government policy, but much of this was based on supporting the troops now that they were in combat. The devastating impact of the onset of the air war on January 16 soon convinced people that the war would be over in a matter of days. Within a few days, though, it was apparent that there had been considerable military over-confidence and that the war would last some weeks, involving a more protracted bombing assault followed by a potentially bloody period of ground combat.

There was blanket coverage of the war in the media, although the great majority of the information came from coalition sources. The overwhelming impression was given of a war fought against "real estate" rather than people, and great use was made of combat footage showing precision-guided bombs destroying bridges, missile sites and the like rather than people.

Reports of Iraqi casualties were initially sparse, and little attention was given to the extensive use by the coalition of cluster bombs, fuel-air explosives and other anti-personnel weapons on the Iraqi forces.

After four weeks of intensive air bombardment, some news began to filter out about the destruction of Iraq's civil infrastructure and the high civilian casualties being suffered, and this was given a boost by the graphic film of the bombing of the Baghdad bunker. Even though this was balanced by extensive coverage of persistent Iraqi atrocities in Kuwait, many Conservative politicians were deeply critical of the media for even reporting from within Iraq.

A national debate on the advisability of going to war was limited mainly because of the bipartisan approach of the main political parties. Furthermore, the main political opponents to the war, Edward Heath and Denis Healey, refrained from voicing their opposition once British troops had been committed.

There were numerous local demonstrations and public meetings, but only a few columnists and politicians spoke out against the early use of military force rather than the continued use of the blockade and sanctions. There was thus no major national focus for dissent.

Most of the media's analysis of the course of the war utilized retired military officers who were generally optimistic about an early victory, but there were a number of opportunities for independent analysts to present more cautious views, certainly more so than during the Falklands War.

A few newspapers provided column space for anti-war views, but these tended to be the "quality" papers such as the *Guardian*, rather than mass-circulation tabloids. The left-wing weekly, *New Statesman and Society*, provided a major channel for alternative views, and became increasingly influential during the course of the war.

As a separate endeavor, a group of journalists started an independent weekly news journal, *War Report*, which endeavored to cover the conduct of the war from a critical perspective. This grew rapidly in circulation to over 10,000 during the six weeks of war, but its real significance was that it was widely read by journalists.

By the fifth week of the war, it was apparent that a ground assault against Kuwait was likely, but the attempts of the Soviet Union and others to forestall this by seeking a last-minute Iraqi withdrawal from Kuwait seemed to hold some promise of avoiding such a conflict.

It was generally recognized in Britain that a ground war might prove very costly and there was real apprehension among many people at its possible consequences. One national opinion poll taken on February 16–18, a few days before the ground war started, showed 40% in favor of a land campaign against 46% favoring a ceasefire and negotiations.

Once the ground war started, there was something akin to a collective holding of breath, followed by a sense of relief that the end came so quickly. There was very little celebrating, in spite of the best attempts of the tabloid press.

In part, this was due to the early realization of the extent of the chaos and disorder which was following the war. The pictures of the destruction in Kuwait City, the massive Iraqi casualties on the roads north to Basra, and the effects of the huge oil well fires all combined to cool any tendency to euphoria.

Another factor was the unfortunate incident, in the closing stages of the ground assault, when nine young British soldiers were killed, by accident, as a result of an attack by an USAF A-10 aircraft. This was reported widely in the UK media just hours before the ceasefire. It did not give rise to any anti-American feeling but rather served to remind people of the human costs of any war.

Shortly after the end of the war, some sectors of the media made attempts to decry those "Jeremiahs" who had predicted a longer and more costly war, but the most surprising aspect of the immediate aftermath was the way in which the war receded from the headlines within days.

This was clearly quite different from the situation in the United States and appears to have a number of causes. One was the relatively quiet style of the Prime Minister, John Major, compared with his predecessor Margaret Thatcher. If Mrs. Thatcher had been in charge during the war, the entire tone of the government would have been far more belligerent and there would have been great insistence on celebrating the eventual victory.

The entire operation would have been presented as proving the value of the Anglo-American relationship, and would have provided her with a much-needed counter to the growing influence of Europe.

A second factor was that the war was not seen as Britain's war, but rather a war led by the United States with Britain playing a subsidiary role. Even though the media accentuated Britain's involvement, it was a very different conflict to the Falklands War where Britain had been the sole actor.

Furthermore, there was genuine apprehension as to the consequences of war, and it was this which led to the feeling of relief rather than euphoria at its end. This, together with a rapidly deepening recession and continued problems with the poll tax, combined to return the British political scene to "business as usual" in a remarkably short space of time.

In the Ribble Valley parliamentary by-election, which took place barely a week after the end of the war, pollsters were hard-put to detect any "Gulf factor" in voting intentions; the poll tax was the dominant issue. The remarkable victory of the Liberal candidate in a previously rock-hard Conservative seat was the first serious blow to John Major's political fortunes in 100 days in office. A June general election was still possible, but it seemed likely that it would be won or lost on domestic issues. Talk of the government riding to victory on the back of a military success, as in 1983 after the Falklands War, was widely discounted.

## Aftermath

At the height of the war, a U.S. correspondent for the London *Observer* newspaper, Andrew Stephen, returned to Britain for a brief visit and was struck by the national self-delusion over Britain's role in the Gulf, at least as expressed in the media. With the country slipping into deep recession, the transport system in mid-winter chaos and the National Health Service near to collapse, he found the news media almost totally preoccupied with the war, and representing it as primarily a British operation, even though the country's contribution was less than 6% of the total coalition forces.

Stephens reflected on what seemed to him:

> a kind of vicarious imperialism. Britain is no longer in a position to fight a major military conflict, but is, nonetheless, basking in nostalgic war rhetoric made possible by American military munificence (*Observer*, February 17, 1991).

It was an accurate assessment of the media, five weeks into the war, which makes it all the more surprising that it did not long outlast the war. What appears to have happened is that the national news media was not accurately reflecting the mood of the country.

While opinion polls may have shown a majority support for the war, they did not indicate the strength with which that majority supported the war. The reality was of support mixed with apprehension and it was this apprehension which dictated the relief rather than euphoria which was felt at the end of the war.

In the United States, much of the public mood was generated by a need to lay the ghost of Vietnam to rest and demonstrate to the world at large that the U.S. could take forceful and effective military action against a Third World dictator. In the immediate post-war weeks, this led to a huge surge in popularity for President Bush and a feeling that the United States was clearly the world's sole superpower.

In Britain, on the other hand, the first month after the war provided people with a picture of undiluted devastation. This started with the reports of the carnage involved in the destruction of the fleeing Iraqi armies on the roads to Basra and Umm Qasr. TV news footage of U.S. soldiers preparing mass graves was shown widely in Britain, as was horrifying film of the effects of the cluster bombs against trucks, buses and cars.

As Iraq degenerated into a bitter three-way civil war, reports emerged of the devastation of the country's economy. Lack of electricity supplies, drinking water, fuel and food, destruction of bridges, irrigation dams, roads, railroads, civil administration offices and factories all indicated that the war had gone far beyond attacks on military targets and had involved the systematic dismemberment of Iraq's economic and administrative infrastructure.

During the war, the impression had been given of an air assault involving precision-guided bombs and missiles, whereas Pentagon statistics released later showed that 93% of the bombs dropped were unguided free-fall bombs and 75% of these missed their targets. It was hardly surprising that reports of thousands of civilians dead and injured seemed only too believable.

Moreover, it slowly became clear that there had been systematic and large-scale use of dedicated anti-personnel munitions including napalm, fuel-air explosives, cluster bombs and multiple rocket launch systems fitted with fragmentation sub-munitions.

Within a fortnight of the war's end, there were indications from a number of sources that Iraqi casualties exceeded 100,000 killed and at least a similar number injured, making this one of the most intensive periods of killing since 1945.

In Kuwait, the failure of the government to restore order was accompanied by the kidnapping, torture and murder of Palestinians accused, often on the most flimsy evidence, of collaborating with Iraqi occupying forces. The preoccupation of the Kuwaiti royal family with refurbishing their palace, while the city remained in chaos, was not well received, and the consolidation of U.S. ground forces in Kuwait and south-east Iraq seemed to indicate a long-term U.S. involvement in the area, rather than a quick victory followed by an early withdrawal.

The most visual representation of the aftermath of war was the holocaust caused by the mining and firing of the Kuwaiti oil wells. With the Burgan oilfield, the world's second largest, on fire and out of control, it appeared that the end result of the war was to produce a catastrophe of quite remarkable proportions. These fires had a particular effect in Britain because of a spectacular and costly oil rig disaster in the North Sea four years previously, when the Piper Alpha rig exploded and caught fire, killing over 100 oil-workers.

Much of this information seeped into the British media through specialist routes such as low-circulation newspapers or some of the more specialized current affairs programs on TV and radio. Even so, their effect was cumulative and added to the feeling that the war looked likely to cause as many problems as it appeared to solve.

In all, the war ended with two countries in ruins, Iraq in a state of civil war, at least 200,000 people killed and injured, a massive and escalating refugee problem, food shortages and a regional environmental disaster. This hardly augered well for the achievement of a peaceful new world order, even if it was not a view likely to gather much support in the United States.

By the end of March, domestic issues once again dominated British politics, although most sectors of the media were still documenting the continuing chaos in the Gulf. The Conservative government of John Major was quietly ditching the more extreme and unpopular policies of the Thatcher era, and was looking once more to Europe as the natural context for Britain's political future.

In the final analysis, Britain is torn between trying to maintain its perceived status as a major international actor, while having to face the reality that its economic and political future lies with Europe. During the seven months of the Gulf crisis, British politics passed a turning-point. Thus the crisis started with Thatcher in control and seeking a future not entirely in Europe. Strong support for the U.S. in the Gulf presented a grand opportunity to re-build the transatlantic alliance.

By a great irony, though, Thatcher and many of her policies were cast aside just half-way through the crisis, and it ended without the great trumpeting of victory which her presence might otherwise have ensured. Following the experience of the Falklands War, one would have expected the Gulf War to have produced a similar mood of national self-confidence. That it did not do so may be an indication that Britain is slowly facing up to political realities.

The Gulf War seemed, initially, to be proof positive that the "special relationship" between Washington and London was alive and well. In reality, it may prove to have been the final fling.

# 26

## Lost Illusions: Europe's Peace Movement

### Daniel Cirera

It is often said that "Europe was absent from the Gulf War." It all depends on the meaning given to the word Europe.

Obviously, the various European governments did not speak with one voice. There were numerous contacts between leaders. The European Community did make proposals towards a negotiated peace, but only belatedly and timidly. The most striking fact is on the whole a European alignment with the United States. A close analysis shows that the forces most favorable to European integration were also the keenest advocates of war, and the staunchest supporters of the Bush administration. This applies to France, but also to Belgium, Italy and Spain (Britain, with its longstanding opposition to closer links within Europe and its strong support for the use of force, is the outstanding exception to this pattern). The new regimes in central Europe, such as Czechoslovakia, Hungary and Poland, did not voice any objections to the coalition's military intervention. As for the Soviet Union, its role is well-known, both in the United Nations, and in its various attempts to promote a diplomatic solution before the start of hostilities in January and just before the ground war began in February. In November 1990, at the Paris summit of the Council for Security and Cooperation in Europe (CSCE), pan-European consultations mainly served to pave the way for acceptance of Resolution 678.

However, if diplomatically Europeans did not play an independent role likely to have an influence on U.S. policy, they were directly involved, and at several levels:

— direct military involvement within the coalition, particularly France and Britain;

— activity and voting in the UN Security Council;

— activities within the Western European Union (a military alliance of nine Western European countries, all members of the EEC and NATO:

Germany, Belgium, Spain, Britain, France, Italy, Luxemburg, Holland and Portugal);
— the part played by NATO, including the use of military bases in Turkey, and other facilities in Britain, Italy and even France, the latter for the refueling of B-52 bombers;
— financial support on the part of Germany and other countries such as Denmark;
— the fact that a sizeable part of the U.S. deployment of troops and equipment was made direct from Europe to Saudi Arabia;
— finally, the part in which most of us were directly involved, Europeans were active for the whole duration of the crisis and the war, in the development and demonstrations of the anti-war movement.

The phrase "European peace movement" must be used with qualifications. Its use is justified if it means that in every country in Western Europe, even in Turkey, there were anti-war actions and mobilizations. This movement, however, is characterized by great diversity, corresponding to different political situations, and to each country's position in the economic, political and strategic structures of Europe. Having said this, it is possible to try to find common trends, starting with the similar problems that public opinion and movements were confronted with across Europe, and also with the similar objectives given to the struggle. We must also take into account the common experience gained during the struggles against the siting of nuclear missiles in Europe in the eighties. Contacts between movements were quickly re-established, information networks were set up and coordinated. After the fighting stopped, common challenges confronted peace activists, although realities differed from country to country.

In Europe, as elsewhere, the movement was characterized both by new dimensions and by continuity with the nuclear disarmament campaigns of the eighties (just as the American anti-war movement was strengthened by its links with the mobilizations against the Vietnam War, against U.S. intervention in Central America, and against the nuclear arms race).

The rekindling of a powerful peace movement which reflects anti-war public opinion has been an obsessive fear of Western governments. They have all drawn lessons from the Vietnam War and the anti-nuclear struggles of the last decade or so. "In the Gulf War, everything will no doubt hinge on world public opinion," explained Admiral Lacoste, former head of the French information agency, in *Le Figaro* (February 13, 1991). Thierry de Montbrial, director of the French Institute of International Relations, and a member of the Trilateral Commission, stressed that "President Bush's unwavering determination, the efficiency of American diplomacy and of its armed forces, *the evolution of public opinion*, and the situation in the Soviet Union, are the major factors explaining why today the U.S. is free to complete under its own conditions, the war of liberation of Kuwait" (*Le Figaro*, February 26, 1991). Implicit here is an admission that political leaders have permanently had to take into account the resistance of public opinion, and the influence of peace movements, in their options and their arguments. They gauge the state of public opinion every day. Witness the efforts made, at the highest level, by Presidents Bush and Mitterand, and by the British prime minister, to justify the deployment of forces, the massive bombing campaign, and then the ground war. Official positions were constantly adapted to fit the evolution of public opinion.

Special efforts were made to legitimize the use of armed forces, and then of war itself. What was at stake was the uprooting of an idea deeply embedded in European minds, namely that war cannot be a proper means of settling international disputes. So the war has been legitimized through both moral arguments (the need to stand against "aggression") and legal ones (invoking international law), while at the same time the true goals of military intervention have been perceived, although often unclearly.

It is true that in this respect, as Thierry de Montbrial points out: "The conviction that the liberation of Kuwait was a moral cause has kept on spreading, an evolution that was far from obvious at the start of the crisis, a conviction that the Iraqi dictator's atrocities did much to contribute to . . . Yet it is rare to find cases in which moral precepts (the respect due to international rights) coincide so perfectly with those of realpolitik (oil, Israel), with financial and geopolitical interests" (*Le Figaro*, February 26, 1991).

In circumstances profoundly different from those of the Korean War, by putting the intervention under the banner of the United Nations — or, rather, that of the Security Council — the United States placed a veil over its true ambitions: to assert its hegemony in the face of the Third World, and also of the USSR and its own allies; to highlight the fact that the U.S. has the capacity to intervene militarily in any part of the world against anything that might jeopardize its interests — what Bush calls the "new world order." By ensuring a lasting presence in the Middle East, the U.S. gains a privileged situation in a highly strategic zone, economically, politically and militarily, at the crossroads of three continents, and close to the borders of the Soviet Union. By controlling the oil reserves in the region, the U.S. has achieved the means to exert major pressure on its economic competitors, particularly Germany and Japan. These real war goals, however, had to be veiled in moral and legal rhetoric because they were not acceptable to large sections of public opinion, either morally or politically.

So, as is now well-known, the invasion and annexation of Kuwait by Iraq was only a pretext for broader U.S. goals. And all the efforts of the peace movement have been to show that the choice did not lie between Saddam Hussein "the bad guy" and Bush "the hand of justice," between "crime" and "right," but between a negotiated solution, political and economic pressure — and war.

Arguments to counter those of the peace movement were developed in several directions, corresponding to events and shifts in public opinion:
— the invasion of Kuwait is unacceptable. International law must be respected. War is legitimate;
— it is not only an American war, since the coalition contains 29 countries; it is supported by the UN, and, in that framework, by the Soviet Union;

— it is not a war against the Third World, or against Arab countries, since the coalition comprises nations from the region, and military forces from countries such as Bangladesh;
— war is inevitable due to Saddam Hussein's obstinacy;
— Saddam Hussein is a dangerous dictator, a "new Hitler" who, with his military, chemical, and future nuclear potential represents a grave threat to peace and world security;
— the war will be short and "clean." It will not be another Vietnam;
— the peace movement plays into Saddam Hussein's hands.

Considerable resources, at the political and media levels, were used to counter the objections and concern of the public, to counter the arguments put forward by the peace movement, and to divide and discredit that movement. To this end, in Europe, much was made of the Munich agreement, comparing the anti-war movement to those who, in 1938, had left the field clear to Hitler for his invasion of Czechoslovakia. Ultimately, however, this argument had little impact, due to the diversity of opposition to the war. Police actions and repressive measures were also used against peace activists, and in industry against those trade unionists who were campaigning against the war. From December 1990 onwards demonstrations were banned in Paris. In each case the government was compelled to authorize them at the last moment, because of the numbers of people who assembled. Nevertheless these bans created a climate of tension in France. In other places demonstrations were more severely repressed, especially in Spain and Turkey; clashes in the latter country led to the death of a female demonstrator.

The major media, and particularly television, submitted totally to the Pentagon's war propaganda: there was a complete absence of real information, and the Pentagon, via CNN, had a monopoly on visual images of the war. The truth of the war, with its hundreds of thousands of victims, its horrors and its destruction, was totally hidden. The news media did their best to minimize all demonstrations, mentioning pacifism and peace activists only in terms of "decline" and "waning strength." The representatives of the peace movement were practically banned from the media.

These official interventions, such as the censorship exercised on the major media, with complete silence on the victims of the bombings, and the development of media campaigns against the peace movement, were all the more necessary because, from the beginning of the crisis to the end one could measure the difficulty of making the war acceptable.

Doubtless public opinion could not remain unaffected by the media bombardment. From September 1990 to January 1991 the movement kept getting stronger, culminating around January 12, just before the final deadline set by the Security Council for Iraq's withdrawal from Kuwait. All the polls showed that the predominate feeling was against the war; the central motto of demonstrations was "No to the war" with a demand for the withdrawal of Western troops. In France the proportion of people opposed to the war was above 70%. However, on the day after the war began the mood changed; the number of demonstrations decreased, although it still remained high. The reasoning behind this was probably that people felt that nothing could be done any more; now the war had started it had to be finished quickly, with as few casualties as possible — on the allied side.

And yet, there was no clear support for the war. People saw things in a highly contradictory way. In the same public opinion polls a majority would express its support for U.S. policy, and for the intervention of French troops, while simultaneously supporting the proposal for renewed negotiations with Iraq, or expressing a favorable appreciation of the actions of the peace movement. Hence the need for leaders of countries involved in the war to insist on Saddam Hussein's responsibility, and on their desire to prevent war to the last; they felt that support for their policies was very fragile. "The war has given a new impetus to the peace movement," pointed out a journalist in *La Croix*, February 14, 1991. "The line argued by the peace activists when we get beyond the oversimplified caricature (that they are the heirs of the appeasers of Munich, defeatists, or that they are manipulated by communists) may eventually shake public opinion."

Indeed, what characterized the movements in Europe was the swiftness of their reactions, and the persistence of the pressure they exerted on European governments right up until the end of the war, even if the actions were not of the same intensity towards the end. Demonstrations were organized as early as August in Spain, and they followed in most European countries, often coinciding with the departure of troops. Great surprise was expressed at the scale and scope of these demonstrations: 30,000 in Paris on October 20, on the same day as large demonstrations took place in New York and Tokyo. The movement kept developing from then on, until it included all European countries by mid-November. On January 12, 200,000 people marched in Paris; similar numbers were seen in capitals and major cities across Europe.

All analysts describe this massive popular mobilization as exceptional, unprecedented, coming as it did before the opening of hostilities, before public opinion could measure the consequences of the war in terms of bodybags or mass destruction, and before the social and economic costs were known. A partial explanation for this phenomenon is that the memory of previous peace campaigns was still fresh in people's minds, and the organizations and coordination between them were still active. In the eyes of these activists, this was a new stage in the struggle for peace.

Yet what gave the movement its strength was the deeply felt rejection of war in European public opinion. It was manifested not only in the scope of the demonstrations, but also in the diversity of forms of action. Within a few weeks hundreds of thousands of people signed petitions, and numerous personalities and organizations launched their own appeals. The involvement of women as an organized constituency has marked the movement from the start. French polls showed that, whatever their political opinions, women always outnumbered men in their opposition of the war. Associations of soldiers' mothers were set up, and their public declarations had a strong emotional impact on public opinion.

In several countries the trade unions took a clear stand against the war.

In France, Italy and Spain calls for work stoppages contributed to the mobilization of working people, linking opposition to the war to struggles against austerity measures taken under the pretext of the economic cost of the conflict. Youth organizations — Christian, communist, socialist — were initiated in high schools and universities. The rejection of the war manifested itself notably in the increasing numbers of conscientious objectors, and of soldiers refusing to leave for the Gulf. In Spain, for instance, the number of conscientious objections rose from 13,000 in 1989 to 19,000 in 1990.

Finally, the stand taken by the churches, and in particular by Pope John Paul II when he spoke of the war as "an adventure with no return," contributed to giving a moral sanction to the movement. At the climax of the campaign to justify the war in the media, the editorial writer of *La Croix*, the daily expressing the opinion of the French Catholic establishment, generally viewed as conservative, wrote: "Should morality exercise its right only in times of peace? Must the voice of conscience keep silent when everywhere the urge mounts to play the great western? Is it not necessary to introduce a grain of sand of reason into the system of passions and the logic of war? . . . In the ethical debate, the major reference is that of Pope John XXIII: 'It is becoming humanly impossible to consider war, in our nuclear age, as the adequate means of re-establishing justice after a violation of rights'" (*La Croix*, August 28, 1990).

Even from within the parties of the government, and in conservative circles, some voices were raised against the war. This was the case with the Socialist Party in France. If the Communists and the Greens were the only parties, as such, which committed themselves to the peace movement, in parliament a number of socialist and right-wing members voted against France's involvement in the war on January 16, saying: "This war is not our war." Former ministers of de Gaulle refused to associate themselves with what they saw as an American war, in which France had nothing to gain, and everything to lose, in particular its privileged relationship with Arab countries. A well-known commentator wrote in a financial paper: "Among the ruins left behind by the Gulf War will be the ashes of French foreign policy" (Albert du Roy in *La Tribune de l'Economie*, February 14, 1991).

The French government's agreement to allow B-52s to fly over French territory, and to station U.S. refueling planes on French bases provoked grave concern. A demonstration organized in front of these bases in the south of France drew more than 5,000 people. Since France's withdrawal from NATO's military structure, under de Gaulle, public opinion remains highly sensitive to whatever may put into question France's independence as regards the U.S.

One of the most spectacular manifestations of this feeling was the resignation of the Minister of Defense, J. Pierre Chevenement, in the middle of the war. He resigned in opposition to the decision in Paris for French troops to participate in the U.S.-backed allied military build-up in Saudi Arabia.

The European parliament was another body where opposition to American plans was visible. During a vote, three quarters of the members favored a diplomatic solution.

On February 13, a group of 150 people from fifteen countries and 80 organizations — a diverse group of socialists, greens, communists, and others — met and drafted an appeal to the peoples of Europe condemning the military intervention, and putting forward proposals for a negotiated solution. Another meeting was scheduled for March 22, 1991.

All these examples demonstrated that the motivations for opposition to the war were extremely varied — ethical, political, religious, ecological, social, economic, and expressions of solidarity with the Third World.

The development of the anti-war movement, its scope and diversity, may be accounted for by the shock experienced by the public when it discovered that war had become possible again. Europeans have experienced, directly or through the history of their families, war, bombings, destruction, deprivation, exile. Many were able to imagine the impact of the dropping of tens of thousands of bombs on the populations of Iraq and Kuwait. Most Europeans have been living in peace for 40 years. For the French the end of the Algerian war of liberation dates back 30 years. The period of detente during the 1970s, then the U.S.-Soviet disarmament agreements, the vanishing of the Soviet threat, have all left their imprint on people's minds. For decades the justification of the possession of weapons, in particular nuclear weapons, has been to prevent war through "deterrence."

The so-called "end of the Cold War," symbolized by the fall of the Berlin wall in November 1989, had created the illusion that an era of peace had started for good. And then, a few months later, almost overnight, soldiers were going to risk getting killed in a war of which no one knew the consequences, and the reasons for which seemed uncertain. In a way, public opinion, from the way it perceived the balance of forces in the world, was not prepared for such a war. And so Western leaders had to place the military intervention under the rhetorical auspices of international law and the defense of peace.

At the same time, the Gulf crisis launched a debate in all European countries about its significance, about the real balance of forces in the world, about U.S. military power and interventions; of those states committed to a military solution, for many this was the moment of lost illusions, and of a difficult return to reality.

When they discovered to their amazement that war was again possible, many people in Europe began to wonder how things had reached such a point. Many issues that had seemed foreign to them, issues reserved for experts and diplomats, became everyday issues. This was reminiscent of a similar phenomenon during the crisis over the siting of nuclear missiles in Europe in the 1980s, when millions of people became interested in and involved in issues of strategy, in the real stakes in the arms race.

Many people were deeply concerned by the part played by the UN, or more precisely by the Security Council; particularly the fact that it could be used to justify Desert Storm. Many aspects of the positive role of the UN, which had previously been taken for granted, were now called brutally into question: it now seemed naive in the extreme to see the United Nations as a forum where all states, in particular Third World nations through the non-aligned movement, could have their say on world events.

Washington's seizure of the UN, turning it into a tool for the sole benefit of a superpower, appeared in much of Europe to be totally alien to the spirit and goals laid down in the UN Charter. The mightiest nation could lay down the law without meeting any serious obstacle; the most obvious example of which being the bribery and manipulation which went on around the passing of Resolution 678, which gave the green light for the war.

The use of the right of veto was seen in Europe as scandalous, since a single nation could have the final say on war or peace, regardless of the majority or the near-unanimity of the international community. Another shock was the new meaning given to the concept of the "new world order," totally emptied of its original content. This "new order," which was to ensure peace and stability, became the instrument of justification for the law of the jungle in international affairs; of the preservation — and aggravation — of the former order of domination.

The use to which international law was put also raised new questions. Many realized that in this case the law had merely served to legitimate the policy of the powerful, and that the result was far from justice. Compared to the massive troop deployment and the use of force to implement the resolutions concerning the invasion and occupation of Kuwait, the non-implementation of the many Security Council resolutions on Palestine, on Israel's need to withdraw from the territories it occupies, on Cyprus, and other issues, clearly revealed that there was a double standard operating.

It could be seen, then, that even if the principles of the UN were profoundly right, their implementation depended on a certain balance of forces. In this case the balance had shifted completely, to the sole benefit of the United States and the Western powers. The attitude of the Soviet Union during the crisis was a matter of grave concern to those who, whatever their opinion of the Soviet regime, believed they could rely on Gorbachev to assist them in their struggles. So, for a while, peace activists felt isolated: the U.S. seemed to be absolutely free to act as it pleased. Rapidly, however, the development of the anti-war campaign, and its influence on governments, rekindled hope, and led people to understand that the determining factor would be the movement's ability to mobilize public opinion, independently of the position taken by any particular government, beyond the unpredictability of diplomatic moves.

In southern European countries, which have traditionally had close ties to the Arab states, the war took on another dimension. In France, for instance, the presence of a very strong community of North African immigrant workers, and of their children, could have proved a source of great tension. Fortunately the solidarity links established between the peace movement and immigrants' associations probably forstalled a split between the two communities. These links were further strengthened by the initiatives of the trade unions, and the common declaration by representatives of the Catholic and Protestant churches, and the Jewish and Muslim communities.

Still, with the experience of war, the question of North-South relations was directly raised — what is at stake in the concept of "development?" What meaning should be given to the phrase "new world order?" The contrast between the resources available for war and the ever-worsening problems in Third World countries (during the war, for instance, an epidemic of cholera in Peru claimed thousands of victims but went largely unnoticed) underlined the scandal of present world disorder.

The debate on peace and the arms race has also taken a new turn, since the "enemy" is now no longer perceived to be a major developed power, close at hand, which for half a century or more has been presented as a threat to liberty in Europe and the rest of the world. In a way the debate has now moved beyond ideology, beyond the traditional political prejudices and *a priorisms* often superimposed on internal, national debates.

So the trauma caused by a previously unthinkable war has led to a reappraisal of such fundamental issues as the consequences of the arms race and the arms trade, the urgency of meeting the needs of developing countries, and the role of people in setting up a new, truly international order.

Despite all efforts to stop it, the war took place. As could have been foreseen, the U.S.-led coalition won decisively on the battlefield. With this fact, European peace movements are confronted with several major new challenges:
— the risk of considering war a legitimate means of solving problems;
— the desire of the Western powers to use the experience gained in the Gulf War to pursue and accelerate a new phase in the arms race.

Peace movements are only too painfully aware that they were unable to prevent the war; that, in spite of the pressure exerted on them, Western governments had enough freedom to maneuver, which they will no doubt want to use to justify future wars. Those in the anti-war movement must now reflect on the political effectiveness of their struggle.

Until January 16, the overwhelming majority thought the war impossible. Now that it is over, great efforts are being made to demonstrate that the cost in human lives has been minimal — which explains why there is a deafening silence regarding the tens, if not hundreds of thousands of casualties in Iraq and Kuwait. As for the destruction of property, it is being marketed as a means of boosting Europe's economy when Western firms pick up the contracts for the major reconstruction which must now take place. There is a real danger of seeing the use of force become the post-Gulf War common denominator in relations between states.

The war will also be used to justify rearmament and military reinforcement in Europe. In the U.S., the Pentagon's success gives ammunition to those in favor of SDI. Likewise in Europe governments will use the coalition's military achievements to push for renewed military escalation:
— making the armed forces more professional, allowing greater flexibility for interventions outside Europe, without recourse to draftees;

— acceleration of projects for the militarization of space, especially in the fields of communication and information, and in the development of anti-missile systems;

— adaptation of existing equipment — including nuclear weapons — to "police" operations in central Europe and the Third World;

— reinforcement of European cooperation in matters of arms production, military research, and at the strategic level.

The corollary of the inevitable increases in defense budgets is the vanishing of the "peace dividend." For France, one of the major nuclear powers on the continent, this means a shift in strategic orientation. Up to now the theory of deterrence, that is of "non-use," has been used to justify the burden of military spending. Post-Gulf War, President Mitterand admits openly that he plans to adapt the military machine for foreseeable future interventions. This may become a French version of "discriminate deter-rence."

These projects, in fact, are not new. For about two years, with the perception of a waning threat from the East, there has been increasing talk of "the threat from the South." Now politicians and military leaders want to take advantage of the state of public opinion for a more rapid and open implementation of these strategic plans.

Likewise the absence of the EEC as such in the Gulf War is presented as the result of the lack of an integrated European military force, due to older, imperialist, conceptions of power. Therefore the war has been the occa-sion for closer cooperation between European countries in military mat-ters, particularly within the framework of the Western European Union. In the Middle East, the coordination of the various European navies was under the control of the WEU. On August 27, the chiefs of staff of the nine members of WEU held an unprecedented meeting to set up this coordi-nated strategy. With instability continuing within Europe, the WEU ap-pears to many as a major element in the reinforcing of the European pillar of the Atlantic alliance.

Indeed, contrary to what is often believed, the goal is not to set up a European military power structure as a pole of resistance against the might of the United States. Washington and NATO not only gave the go-ahead for this reinforcement of WEU, they are actively encouraging it, so long as NATO remains the basis for security in Europe. This is the gist of President Bush's speech in Berlin, in which he defined the framework for what he termed the "new Atlanticism."

The WEU has a major advantage for the strategists in the Bush adminis-tration: it solidly binds the European Community to NATO, and so to the U.S. It is also less restricted than NATO in terms of areas of intervention, and, for example, the sizeable French military presence in Africa could provide a basis for such an operation. Such a pan-European orientation is very much in keeping with the concept of "burden sharing" forced upon the allies during the Gulf crisis by the White House. In all respects, the Gulf crisis has led to the rapid implementation of strategic plans defined by the Pentagon and NATO, which will lead to a global military redeployment.

Europe will play a key role in this new military order, thanks to its economic, military and political capacities.

From this point of view it is necessary to examine what will happen to the U.S. military presence in Western Europe. The withdrawal of several thousand troops and the redeployment of equipment to southern Europe, the Middle East and Southeast Asia, would not in fact mean American disengagement from the old continent.

Taking advantage of the swiftness of events, and relying on a measure of support, even if transient, in the aftermath of "victory," governments will be strongly tempted to introduce yet another round of increased military spending, and renewed doses of social austerity. If this new military build-up takes place, at the very moment that the Warsaw Pact is announcing its own dissolution, we shall be heading for an even more dangerous world. The war in the Gulf will prove to have been only a large scale exercise for future wars.

For the various groups and movements engaged in the anti-war struggle, there is a long road ahead. They can build on the actions and achievements of recent months. It will be essential to show that, even if they were unable to prevent the war, public opinion mobilized by the peace movement did exert pressure on governments, forcing them to take diplomatic initiatives; even if it was only to justify their military presence, and to be seen to have done everything in their power to prevent war. The power of the movement, and its persistence in the face of overwhelming odds, did contribute to the end of the conflict and to the ceasefire.

At the same time, as we have said, the movement will have to show that, despite its size, in the end it was not strong enough. This assessment calls for a sustained analysis of what must be achieved in order to ensure that this war will be the last.

Therefore one of the main challenges lies in the capacity of organized movements and coalitions to adapt their forms of action to the post-war situation, to expose the new perils, to shed light on the real meaning of the Gulf War, and to show the reality of the destruction in the Middle East, particularly the human devastation. They must show that war is never clean, and that it settles nothing — as can already be perceived. The Gulf War will have serious repercussions for the peoples of the region, for the Palestinians, for the Kurds, and even for the Israelis. On the economic level it will prove a disaster for the nations of the Third World. The scale of the ecological catastrophe is just beginning to become known, and can only get worse in the short to medium term.

In Europe, those in the anti-war movement can push for a refusal of alignment with the White House, and for a policy of peace in an unstable Europe. This will raise further questions on the meaning and content of a more integrated Europe.

All these strategies depend on stronger cooperation between the diverse movements struggling for peace, disarmament, social justice and environmentalism, both within Europe, but also between Europe and the

U.S. and with those forces struggling for peace and justice in the Third World.

The links are becoming increasingly apparent between a policy of domination and war, arms spending and the arms trade. The stakes are clear. They apply to the whole world: either the problems of development will be solved, in all their human, economic and ecological dimensions, which implies the eradication of the previous world order of domination and its corollary, a logic of war and militarization; or else, all these problems will get worse the world over, and the powerful, ever more powerful, will attempt to solve them by force, thereby solving nothing.

At this watershed in history, hope lies in the intervention of peoples and public opinion, and in their convergence at the international level. This is the experience acquired through recent events — the analysis of which must continue — starting from their particular and diverse conditions, by the peace movements of Europe.

# 27

## South Asia in the Wake of the Gulf War: The Pakistan Example

### Talat Rahman and Lyman Baker

The reaction of the people living in the Third World, euphemistically called the "developing countries," to the United States intervention in the Gulf was astonishingly uniform. This was not only true of Islamic countries like Indonesia, Bangladesh and Pakistan, but also of countries like India and the Philippines. In the five months that the Bush administration took to strengthen its position both militarily and politically vis-a-vis Iraq, the support for the people of Iraq and/or antagonism to the United States policy of bullying a Third World country only became stronger.

Interestingly enough, it was the people of these countries who took to the streets first and the leaders, mostly reluctantly, who followed later. It was not surprising then that the U.S. had to reduce its diplomatic staff in several of these countries. An analysis of this spontaneous response of the citizens of developing countries, particularly those with large Muslim populations, to the perceived threat of U.S. imperialism, would be a topic in itself. We, however, prefer to proceed slightly differently by focusing on the impact on one country, Pakistan. Much of what is said here could apply, with some adaptation, to any Islamic country.

There was, however, something quite special about Pakistan vis-a-vis the devastation and general crisis in the Gulf. Though not an Arab country, Pakistan was drawn into the Gulf debacle for many reasons: its strong link to Saudi Arabia, the presence of vast numbers of its nationals in the workforce of the Gulf countries, its geographical situation, its strong and ambitious military, its possible nuclear capacity, to name a few. The extent to which events of the first eight months of the crisis affected Pakistan was evident from the massive public demonstrations in the early days of the war, the nervousness of the ruling elite, and the debate and discussion emerging in the aftermath of the war.

Like Kuwait and several other states in the Gulf, Pakistan was created by its erstwhile British rulers. There were, of course, different reasons for carving these brand new countries out of the motherland — Pakistan out of India, and Kuwait out of Iraq. In the case of Pakistan the justification was a homeland for the Muslims in India who were perceived to be under threat from the Hindu majority. In the case of Kuwait it was to keep a small oligarchy loyal to the West in charge. In both cases, however, certain territories remained disputed — Kashmir between Pakistan and India, and the Rumaila oilfield between Kuwait and Iraq. The disputed territories have naturally led to instabilities in the respective regions, most recently the war in the Gulf and the intensified threat of war in the Indian subcontinent.

For many in the world it is a surprise that Pakistan — albeit only one-half of the original country — has survived 43 years. At its inception, Pakistan was comprised of two parts, East and West, separated by 1200 miles of Indian territory, by language and by cultural heritage. The partition of India was extremely bloody, and hostilities between the two countries have never completely ceased. India and Pakistan have fought three wars since their independence in 1947. The first two were over Kashmir (the land to the north-east of West Pakistan), whose situation was left unsettled by the departing colonial power. The last one, in 1971, ended in the dismemberment of Pakistan and the creation of Bangladesh out of what had been East Pakistan. About a million Bangladeshis lost their lives in the struggle for independence from the West Pakistanis, with whom they shared a common religion but by whom they felt oppressed and exploited. Today Pakistan is made up of four provinces, with Punjab comprising a giant share of land and resources and with separatist movements of varying strengths active in Sindh, Baluchistan and Sarhad. Separatist movements and communal riots between Hindus and Muslims and between Hindus and Sikhs also continue to take their toll on the population of India.

One might be tempted to suppose that it lies merely in the nature of countries comprised of peoples with several different languages and several different cultural heritages (however tightly linked through a common history) to be subjected to demands of separation by one ethnic group or another. But closer familiarity with particular instances reveals that it is policies of exploitation and discrimination that promote the break-up of nations along ethnic lines. In the case of the Indian subcontinent, both dismemberments (in 1947 and in 1971) can be traced to particular practices followed by the ruling parties. The "Divide and Rule" policy of the British Raj played such an important role in fueling the rivalries between Hindus and Muslims that by 1940 several Muslim leaders saw it as more to their advantage to press for a separate homeland for the Muslims than to struggle side by side with their Hindu compatriots for independence from the British. Their priority was instead the battle against domination and unequal treatment by Hindus of Muslims. Twenty-four years later it was Muslims in the two parts of Pakistan who were fighting each other (those in the eastern part with the help of India). The people of East Pakistan had had enough of the unequal treatment at the hands of the dominant groups from the western wing.

This brings us to the nature of the regimes in Pakistan, their ideological bases and their impact on the region. In brief: Pakistan has experienced two periods, each of 11 years' duration, of unadulterated military dictatorship, one 6-year period of civilian rule, and several shorter periods of civil or military rule. In 1991, a popularly elected government ruled in Islamabad. Nevertheless, the military remained strong and very much in control. The specter of threat of attack by India has always been used to divert attention from domestic issues in favor of building a strong military. The economic elite, for its part, has always chosen to ally itself with imperialism, to assure its own access to the markets of the West and a cut of the import trade from outside. Poverty, illiteracy, lack of access to health care, malnutrition — to cite some of the problems facing almost 80% of the country — have largely been ignored. Consequently, Pakistan — for whose creation many sacrifices were made by ordinary people in pursuit of a more egalitarian society — has yet to deliver the goods that were promised to its population at the outset. What one finds instead is a country with a weak infrastructure, but a strong military, and a people still searching for a system that will bring them not only material goods but also self-respect and pride. The latter two are all the more important when one appreciates that colonization has a lasting impact on the human psyche: that the "colonized mentality" — which is another term for feeling inferior and suppressed — is only made worse by alignment with imperialism.

The picture above is not a pleasant one, and one moreover that might cause one to wonder how such a country could be of any major importance to the West or to the oligarchies in the Arab world. Yet U.S. strategic interest in Pakistan emerged very early on. At its birth, Pakistan's leaders vowed to be democratic and non-aligned. But with the assassination in 1951 of Liaqat Ali Khan, the country's first prime minister, a major obstacle to U.S. involvement in Pakistan was removed. In 1952 Pakistan surrendered its neutrality when it became a member of SEATO (the South East Asia Treaty Organization); when it later joined CENTO (the Central Treaty Organization), it further cemented its allegiance to the United States. The 11 years of military rule (1958–1969) under General Ayub Khan saw further strengthening of ties with the West, particularly the United States. There was some cooling off while Zulfiqur Ali Bhutto (who was democratically elected) was Prime Minister (1972–1977). But the tides were reversed again, and overwhelmingly so, under the next military dictator, Zia ul Haq (1977–1988), whose support of the Afghan *Mujahideen* and whose offers of military bases to the U.S. silenced any criticism from the U.S. administration of his draconian domestic policy. The three governments following the fatal 1988 plane crash of Zia ul Haq have yet to show any independence from the United States.

What then is the basis for the United States' interest in Pakistan? Naturally, it has to do with Pakistan's position in the "old world order." Its proximity to the Soviet Union and China on the one hand and to the Middle East on the other was certainly a very important factor, one enhanced by the fact that Pakistan possessed a very strong and capable military — trained and equipped with the best available in Britain and the U.S., and eager for continued improvements along the same lines. This was, moreover, a military with a demonstrated willingness to crush domestic democratic movements and a proven ability to do so with relative ease. And it was quite willing to be employed as a mercenary force by other powers.

For their part, Pakistani leaders, in search of identity, found anti-communism to be an effective rhetoric, not only acceptable at the popular level, but serviceable in rationalizing alignment with the widely discredited imperial powers and with the rest of the Islamic world at the same time. (This predisposition was, to be sure, certainly reinforced by the fact that Moscow consistently showed a preference for India in its conflicts with Pakistan). Pakistan in any case did not have a strong national bourgeoisie: its elite could be easily bought.

Another answer to Pakistan's search for its identity lay in the Islamic world, particularly in the Arab world. But here, too, the link was far more than merely ideological. Like several other poor but relatively industrialized countries, Pakistan had what the thinly populated but oil-rich Arab countries needed — skilled labor, well-trained military personnel, and human resources in general. Beginning in the early 70s, Pakistanis began flocking in thousands to each of the newly formed or newly rich oil-producing countries. Very quickly human power became Pakistan's largest export, and revenues remitted by expatriate nationals became the largest source of hard currency for the country as a whole. This provided a solution to many problems: Pakistani leaders and politicians did not have to worry as much as they otherwise would about demands for social reforms and progressive changes at home, since an important component of the population likely to be frustrated by domestic conditions, and with the ready potential to organize for their rights, could focus their energies on obtaining jobs in the oil-rich countries instead of struggling for their rights at home. A visa to the Gulf states was the ticket to the betterment of the lives of millions in these poor countries. The irony, of course, is that in the Gulf countries these "guest workers" have no civil or political rights. They were paid far better than they could have imagined in their home country, but had no job security, no possibility of owning a home, let alone acquiring permanent residency. Yet, compared to what awaited them at home, theirs was a happy situation: they were the fortunate ones, living in glorified ghettos.

As for the newly wealthy Arabs, they were quite happy, too. Pakistanis (and others) were willing to do all the chores that their populace could not bring itself to stoop to. And these workers, skilled and unskilled, were willing to work on terms set exclusively by management: there was no question of threats from labor unions, no negotiations, no discussions of retirement benefits — and all subject to short-term (in fact, year-to-year) contracts. Pakistan even provided many recruits into the armed forces of many Gulf states, ready to be used against the indigenous forces if the occasion should ever arise. Back home, Pakistan provided the Gulf oligarchies with "holiday sites" to be used as sanctuaries if need be. These are colossal palaces built by the sheikhs and princes themselves for their private pleasure.

Obviously everything went wrong for the "guest workers" when Iraq invaded Kuwait on August 2, 1990. The sufferings of the citizens of a besieged country are bound to be terrible. But the impact upon Pakistani and other "guest workers" in Kuwait, and to a considerable extent in Iraq, was also catastrophic. And the poorer they were, the more they stood to lose what little they had. It was clear to them that once the established order in the country in which they were working had changed, they had no more status whatsoever. They had to leave, and faced a most uncertain future. Slowly they trickled back home, and the economic struggle they thought they had by-passed now lies ahead of them. There can be no question of the bitterness they felt towards the invasion.

Yet these reactive feelings soon became more complicated, and ultimately, underwent a drastic change. Once U.S. troops started landing in Saudi Arabia, only days after the invasion of Kuwait, these new refugees, together with most people in the Islamic world and in the Third World — at least judging from those who were allowed to express themselves — became fearful, ambivalent and, as the war deadline of January 15 approached, openly hostile towards the U.S. intervention. Once the war started, and as the relentless bombing brought unfathomable devastation to the very infrastructure of Iraqi society and to its population, the anger of the people in Pakistan continued to rise. There were several very obvious signs of the popular reaction to the barbaric acts of the Bush administration, and to the conduct of the West in general. With the start of the U.S. attack on Iraq, the popularity of Saddam Hussein rose overnight. In one day a million posters of Saddam Hussein (in prayer) were sold, much to the embarrassment of the government, which subsequently banned their sale.

What is striking here is that Pakistan had had relatively limited dealings with Iraq (in part because Iraq was perceived as pro-India and as more secular than Islamic). Until the Gulf crisis, Saddam Hussein was not a household name. On the contrary, Pakistanis have been very accustomed and even well disposed to the House of Saud and to the Sabah family. After all, these rulers had provided so much in aid to Pakistan, and employed and housed so many Pakistani workers and technocrats. Yet ordinary Pakistanis were quick to see the war as directed not at the liberation of Kuwait but at the destruction of Iraq — militarily and socially. In this respect, Pakistanis had no difficulty in identifying with the people of Iraq, and eventually even with Saddam Hussein himself. It was an amazing outpouring of anti-imperialist sentiment. Moreover, these huge demonstrations were spontaneous, supported initially only by some of the fundamentalist Islamic parties: the ruling Islami-Jamhoori-Itehad (IJI) and its chief opponent, the People's Party (PPP), were not quick to take advantage of the popular tide. In fact, the government had declared its anti-Iraqi, pro-allies stand, and Benazir Bhutto (PPP) had also publically toed the American line. The public support for Saddam Hussein and rage at the United States was so strong that the government had to issue a disclaimer about the role of

Pakistani troops stationed in Saudi Arabia: they were not to participate in any offensive against the Iraqi forces, but only to protect the holy sites in Mecca and Medina. The popular response to this scenario was the demand that troops should also be sent to Iraq to help protect the holy sites there. To calm the uproar, Prime Minister Nawaz Sharif agreed to and proceeded with a diplomatic tour of some of the principal countries in the Gulf (Turkey, Iran, Saudi Arabia), to present a proposal for peace. It was clear from the outset that this move was undertaken more for domestic consumption than as any real effort at finding peace in the midst of the Gulf War. Iraq, for its part, understandably refused to meet with the prime minister, for this reason, and because of the prime minister's anti-Iraqi remarks in his prior address to the nation.

It is worth pointing out that the decision to send troops to Saudi Arabia, at the latter's request, was taken by Pakistan's caretaker government installed in power by President Ishaq after he fired the popularly elected Prime Minister Bhutto on August 6, 1990 — four days after the Iraqi invasion of Kuwait. The commitment of troops to Saudi Arabia drew immediate controversy within the country, and aroused suspicions about the government's long-term interests in the Gulf region. It was rumored that Pakistani officials and the military were already bidding for a role in the security of the Gulf once American troops had left. For a mercenary army, this was indeed the right move lest other competitors in the region (Egypt, Syria, etc.) got a head-start.

Whether these deals were worked out or not remains to be seen. In early August 1990, the ousting of the Prime Minister subjected the nascent democracy to confusion and chaos. Under such circumstances, and with the threat of a war looming large, the opposition to sending troops to Saudi Arabia was eclipsed, and did not resurface till after the elections in November.

To anyone conversant with recent Pakistani politics, it is abundantly clear that all important decisions of the ruling elite must have the blessing of the military. The decision to send troops to Saudi Arabia could not have been an exception. The statements made by General Beg, the Chief of Armed Services, following the U.S. attack on Iraq, were thus very surprising. As if deliberately to embarrass the government, and as if to show the military's support for the masses, General Beg declared that Pakistani forces had been deployed on the wrong side. Of course, there was an immediate reaction from Saudi Arabia and Kuwait, and the general had to visit Riyadh to reassure the benefactors there of the loyalty of the Pakistani establishment.

As the war on Iraq continued, so did the protests and demonstrations in the major cities of Pakistan. Except for a very small group of fundamentalist Sunnis (Jamaat al-Hadis), the messages were openly pro-Iraq, and explicitly against the policies of the Pakistani administration. The protestors included even some close allies of Nawaz Sharif. There were calls to bring Pakistani troops back from Saudi Arabia. There were also demands to send troops to Iraq. About 205,000 volunteers applied for transit visas to Iraq (which were refused). The aim of this massive group of Pakistani civilians was not to bear arms on the side of Iraq but rather to relieve Iraqi citizens of non-military duties, so as to enable them to channel their efforts into military operations. There were also repeated demands to the government that in the event of an Israeli attack on Iraq, the Pakistani military should fight on the side of Iraq. There would be no such thing as neutrality in that case. In short, a clear message was sent to the Pakistani government: if you want to represent the people, change your policy towards the United States. It was the most overt display of anti-imperialism yet seen in a country where politicians of the two chief contending parties avoid exploiting such sentiments for fear of alienating their American sponsors.

There was also an immediate sense of solidarity with the Iraqi people. The common people of Pakistan, like their counterparts in many Third World countries, had no difficulty focusing their anger and their sorrow. They knew that Bush's "new world order" did not bode well for people like themselves. The years ahead looked worse than the Cold War days. The protection that they had received (sometimes unbeknownst to them) in the superpower rivalry was no longer there. In this unipolar world, the monopolizer of power was superior only in military might, and not in providing the world's poor with the basic necessities that they so badly needed. This superpower was committed to aggression at any cost to others. Today the people of Iraq were paying the price; tomorrow it would be another Third World country.

Now that Bush has achieved his goals in Iraq, the people of Pakistan await the United States' next move. They question whether the U.S. will transcend its hypocrisy and double standards and force Israel to give up its 24-year-old occupation of the West Bank and Gaza. They ask what can be the justification for providing aid to Israel to the tune of more than $11 million a day when it continues to violate dozens of UN resolutions that call for Israeli withdrawal from the occupied territories and for the self-determination of the Palestinian people?

These are of course ancient issues in the consciousness of the people of Pakistan. And the leadership has long been accustomed to paying lip service to the need to oppose Israeli expansionism. But given the stridency with which it responded to the occupation of Kuwait the leadership will increasingly discredit itself insofar as it has to explain to the masses why it continues to subordinate itself to a power that suspends that principle in an even more flagrant and long-standing case.

At the same time as these discussions are going on, there is a startling discussion in progress amongst the members of the Pakistani establishment — the military, the civilian bureaucracy and the politicians. This debate is over the alignment of Pakistan in the post-Gulf War world. And for the first time in the history of Pakistan the military is contemplating a stand independent of the United States. The Iranian government has already sent a high-level, 100-member delegation, which was well received in Islamabad. China has also reaffirmed its traditional cordial ties with Pakistan. To many in the establishment, the Iran-China deals seem more attractive than hanging on to the United States and its clients in the Middle East, particularly after the October 1990 decision by the U.S. Congress to halt aid to Pakistan on the grounds of its possible possession of nuclear weapons.

Pakistan's nuclear weapons development program is hardly a secret to the world. It is estimated that Pakistan is at least five years ahead of where Iraq was before the recent destruction of its facilities. This means that Pakistan may well be on the verge of possessing a workable bomb. Such a prospect may sound perilous to someone living in a Western country, but to most people in the Third World it is far less threatening than the idea of such weapons being monopolized by the industrialized countries. And why should Pakistan or Iraq not be allowed to have the bomb? Israel is further along than either of these two countries, possessing over 200 high-density nuclear bombs and a delivery system. And Israel's nuclear program has hardly been a hindrance to its receiving U.S. aid. On the contrary, U.S. aid to Israel — military, economic, diplomatic — has increased dramatically as Israel reached out for a nuclear bomb, much to the chagrin of its Arab neighbors. India exploded its first bomb in 1974, and its nuclear program continues unchecked by Western powers. So why target Pakistan, which has all along served as a faithful ally? The Pakistani establishment finds it unbelievable that the U.S. would treat it so shabbily and Israel so well. It is also painfully reminded that Iraq under Saddam Hussein was also in the U.S. camp, and almost as good an ally as Pakistan under Zia. Are there some parallels to be drawn? Naturally, the establishment, including the military, have to rethink the new developments and renegotiate some of the terms of its relationship with the one remaining superpower. Could it be that, with the eclipse of what was formerly the second superpower, the Pakistani establishment has outlived its utility to the U.S.?

While a breaking away from U.S. hegemony may seem attractive, many of the objective conditions that led to Pakistan's adopting its position within the "old world order" have not changed. The system of dependency that the rulers of Pakistan collaborated to build is not likely to be dispelled so easily. The agricultural, commercial and manufacturing elites are still addicted to markets in the West, to Western imports and to Western investment in Pakistan. They are in no better position than are their counterparts in Mexico to resist the policies of the IMF and the World Bank. Pakistan's military may draw scenarios in which the United States finds a pretext to eliminate its nuclear capability, but it cannot maintain or improve its current equipment without American and British parts. Moreover, it shows no signs of being willing to forego its habitual privileges in favor of redirection of massive spending from defense to infrastructure. It is difficult to imagine how either the Chinese or the Iranians have anything immediate to offer that could replace what these elites have derived from their alliance with imperialism.

Given the fact that, over the last 14 years, Pakistan has fallen more securely under the control of dependent elites, the destiny of the country to a large degree hinges on external factors. And indeed there have been some essential changes in this external complex of factors. The most striking of these is the disappearance of the Soviet resistance to imperialism. Another is the increasingly precarious condition of international capitalism itself. Ironically, it may be that together these two factors, which from one familiar perspective seem contrary, may work together to open the prospects for change within countries like Pakistan.

One open question concerns the degree to which it will remain politically feasible at home for the ruling elite of the United States to continue to divert scarcer resources to the projection of its own military power in the absence of the ideological justification of the Soviet threat. A related question concerns the willingness of the populations of Western countries, and chiefly of the United States, to continue to tolerate the proliferation of conventional arms in the Third World. One imagines that this will depend in part on the degree to which politicians can convince voters that continued militarization is an enhancement rather than a detriment to an ailing economy. To what degree will scaling back the arms industry be seen as necessarily a net threat to jobs and to the balance of trade? And to what degree will Third World military elites cease to be seen as a necessary evil (as a bulwark against the Evil Empire) and come to be seen as just evil — as nothing more than naked oppressors of their own peoples?

In any case, to the degree that the West is forced to adopt the political decision to curb arms exports, to that degree Third World military elites will be forcibly weaned from their dependence on U.S., French, British and German weaponry. One response might be to shift to a new dependency, on Soviet or Chinese suppliers (Iran would seem to have little to offer in this regard). But the prospect might also emerge of a redirection of local resources to the development of domestic infrastructure, provided that other sectors of these increasingly polarized societies were to find themselves in a more organized condition to demand such a shift.

Moreover, should the economy of the U.S. continue to deteriorate, its buying power will be considerably reduced. Such a development would be traumatic, in turn, for the European Community and Japan, but even more so for Third World countries like Mexico and Pakistan, which have become organized as support economies dependent on the three industrialized capitalist centers, as well as for the prospects of those formerly Eastern bloc countries aiming to compete with other suppliers of cheap labor in external markets. Under such conditions, the agricultural, commercial and manufacturing elites of countries like Pakistan would face economic ruin with a corresponding reduction of political clout. Profits from Western imports would shrink as the supply of foreign exchange evaporated along with exports.

Of course, the reaction of established economic elites to this prospect will, in the short run, be to try to stave off disaster by reducing expenditure on employment and housing. They will have to conspire with receptive elements of the military to suppress the predictable resistance of the overwhelming majority of the population of the country to these developments.

Whether these elites are able to accomplish the bloodbath that would be necessary to maintain themselves until capitalism pulled itself out of a new world depression, would depend not only on whether capitalism was able to accomplish this feat without the mobilization of a World War II-style command economy, but whether the popular forces were in a state of organization capable of preventing a *matanza* (massacre) like that in El Salvador in 1932. The point is that, if it is true that when the metropolis sneezes the dependencies catch pneumonia, it is also true that disorder can in such conditions open the way to progress.

Again, an opening could occur for turning inward — or for a regional economic pattern (China, Iran, even India) — and for the development of a national infrastructure designed to raise the basic standard of living of the population as a whole. We are not speaking of inevitabilities here, only of possibilities. That is, even if such an opening were to occur, it is by no means certain that the prospects it offered would be realized. An essential determinant would be the degree to which the majority of the population (including at least some elements of the armed forces) were conscious of the state of affairs and organized to act on the basis of it. One important contribution to this crucial necessity could be the role played by returning workers from oil-rich countries. Another is how prepared progressive elements in the country are to work towards this end as opportunities emerge.

What can be said with some assurance, however, is that if this opportunity were to be lost, the vast majority of the world's population is, for the indefinite future, going to suffer even more terribly than it has so far, both in terms of starvation, disease and enforced ignorance, but also in terms of the harsh measures that will be required to maintain the privilege of the elites in the midst of these horrors.

# PART SIX

Storm Watch:

Human Rights, the Environment,

the Aftermath

# 28

# Human Rights and the Gulf Crisis: The Verbal Strategy of George Bush

*Naseer Aruri*

The issue of human rights was raised by President George Bush as a major factor in his campaign against Saddam Hussein. It was employed in galvanizing public support for Bush's policies and determining the timetable for transition from sanctions against Iraq to the aerial bombardment and devastation of that country in January and February of 1991.

This essay will examine the manner by which inconclusive or contradictory intelligence reports were used by the United States President to fit his political agenda; the manner by which George Bush channeled particular legal principles and specific findings by established human rights organizations into his own political agenda. It will further examine the credibility of the human rights component of U.S. policy in the Gulf in light of Washington's attitude towards the violation of human rights in Iraq during the 1980s and towards abuses committed by America's so-called coalition partners and allies in the region.

## The Human Rights Climate in the Arab World[1]

The Arab world's human rights record has been broadly unfavorable since independence after World War II. Most Arab governments have been reluctant to cooperate with international human rights organizations; most have made it a criminal offense to disseminate information about human rights violations inside the country or abroad; most still have not ratified treaties such as the United Nations Human Rights Charter. The Arab governments are reluctant to admit international observers to their prisons or political trials; their responses to complaints raised by international human rights bodies range from procrastination to utter contempt.

Certain patterns of violations of human rights tend to characterize certain geographical or cultural clusters within the Arab world.

305

1. The Gulf/Peninsula region is particularly restrictive regarding rights of assembly, cultural freedoms, women's and workers' rights. Saudi Arabia tends to rank highest among the violators. Kuwait, by no means a citadel of enlightenment, ranks near the bottom.

2. Syria and Iraq, ruled by rival factions of the Ba'ath Party, are notorious in their treatment of political dissidents. Detention without charge and trial, torture and executions are among the most common violations committed in these countries.[2] Iraq adds to the list expulsion of undesirable nationals and repression of ethnic minorities.

3. The record of the Nile Valley countries displays an exceedingly high number of emergency regulations.[3]

4. The common denominator of violations in the Maghreb focuses on the crises of labor unions, limitations on political activity. Libya is somewhat unique in limiting all forms of expression, murdering dissidents and dealing ruthlessly with workers.

5. The most common victims of these violations across the Arab world are the Islamist and Marxist groups, and to a lesser extent some Arab nationalist parties. Ethnic minorities constitute a target in Iraq and Sudan.

6. Progress towards some form of pluralist existance and a more open society has been reported in Yemen, Jordan, Tunisia and Algeria.

## Human Rights Along the Divide: Iraq v. "Allies"

### Iraq

A comprehensive report on Iraq released by Middle East Watch six months before the invasion of Kuwait reveals a consistent pattern of gross violations of internationally recognized human rights, including detention, torture, disappearances, executions and suppression of substantive and procedural rights.[4] Torture techniques include hangings, beatings, burning and rape. Numerous people are reported to have died under torture including Kurdish children in the mid-1980s. The reports of Amnesty International and the Arab Organization for Human Rights corroborate this pattern of gross violations.

The conditions of human rights in Iraq are almost unique in terms of the rampant flagrant violations of civil and political rights even before the Iran-Iraq war of 1980. The rights of citizens are almost non-existent; even as a member of the ruling party one can always be subjected, without probable cause, to questioning, detention, disappearance, abusive treatment and torture. Many times, these violations include deprivation of life without due process and without a public accusation, hearing or trial. Such violations are practiced in an atmosphere of emergency regulations or decrees issued by the Revolutionary Command Council in violation of the state's commitments to its own constitution or international obligations.[5]

Any criticism of the political system or irreverence towards the head of state is considered a crime, outside the parameters of acceptable public discourse. The Iraqi Revolutionary Command Council, in November 1986, adopted an amendment to the Law of Punishments Number 111 of 1969 which imposes life sentences together with confiscation of property for publicly insulting the president of the republic, his designee, the Revolutionary Command Council, the Ba'ath Party, the National Assembly or the government. This sentence can be elevated to execution if the act carries the intention of incitement. The punishment for insulting a court or a government agency is a mere seven years.[6] In Iraq, most political prisoners, estimated in the thousands, are tried before special courts staffed by members of the executive branch, including the military. Pronouncements are final. Right to counsel is highly restricted in the Revolutionary Court of Baghdad, while completely absent in the special military court of Kirkuk, which deals mainly with the Kurdish population.[7]

Iraq had already been accused of horrendous crimes against the Kurds in March, August and September of 1988.

## *The Allies: Syria, Egypt and the Gulf Countries*

All but a few Arab countries have constitutions which prominently promote civil and political liberties and social justices. Some of them do not even have constitutions, such as Saudi Arabia, Qatar, Oman and the UAE. Many constitutions, however, effectively transfer the regulation of rights legislation and assign authorities extraordinary powers, thus rendering constitutional protection abstract and superfluous.

Some countries, such as Bahrain and Kuwait, have suspended the constitution; Kuwait's parliament was dissolved in 1976 and again in 1986. Emergency regulations have rendered constitutions inoperable in Syria, Iraq, and Egypt. Egypt offers a good example of a government in which laws have taken precedence over the constitution. The constitution in use today, adopted in September 1971 at the beginning of the Sadat era and known as the "permanent constitution," bestows sweeping powers upon the president of the republic. Article 47, for example, grants the president emergency powers to combat imminent challenges to public security or threats to "national security." Article 108 grants the president full legislative powers upon authorization by the People's Assembly.

President Hosni Mubarak reconfirmed Egypt's Emergency Law of 1938 in the aftermath of Sadat's assassination. When it is in force in full, the system can be said to border on totalitarianism. Preventive detention is one of more than a dozen special measures which this law permits. Under the Emergency Law, the president or his designees can order imprisonment as a "preventive" measure without formal accusation for a period of up to 30 days, renewable to six months. The president, moreover, has the power to approve or disapprove court verdicts in cases involving the emergency laws.[8]

Syria's constitution of January 31, 1972, similarly guarantees most individual basic liberties; yet these protections are subject to presidential edicts, military decrees and special laws.

The suspension of key provisions of the 1962 Kuwaiti constitution by the emir on June 2, 1986 enabled the government to rule by decree in accordance with Article 71. Among the casualties was Article 107, which mandates new elections within two months of the National Assembly's dissolution; otherwise, "the dissolved Assembly shall be restored to its full constitutional authority . . . [and] continue functioning until the new Assembly is elected." Thus with Article 107 suspended, the government was able to rid itself of any legislative scrutiny, and proceeded to ban or restrict speech, press and assembly.

Kuwait's press, considered rather free during much of Kuwait's independent period, is constrained by amendments to the Press Law adopted by the government after dissolution of the National Assembly on June 2, 1986 and the subsequent appointment of the Wise Men's Assembly (*majlis al-Hukama'a*) in its place. Accordingly the state can withdraw the license from a publication and close it for up to two years.[9] Newspapers were also subjected to prior censorship, which continued in 1990, with prison penalties of up to three years and fines of up to five thousand Kuwaiti dinars ($17,150).[10]

The government of Kuwait also infringed Article 44 of the Constitution, which grants individuals "the right to assemble without permit or prior notification." It also banned on January 9, 1990 any meeting that discusses "concrete national issues," including those of *Diwaniyyas*, the traditional Kuwaiti semi-public living rooms.[11]

These measures, however, emboldened the opposition, which in late 1989 began to demand the restoration of the Assembly and constitutional life. Operating under the "Constitutional Movement," *al-Harakah al-Dusturiyeh* (also known as pro-democracy forces), the opposition collected a 30,000 signature petition demanding the restoration of parliamentary life.[12] When the emir refused to receive the petition, their struggle picked up momentum and the *Diwaniyyas* emerged as a principal force for the opposition, which began to call for broad liberalization in the areas of suffrage, trade unions, women's rights, nationality and the substantive freedoms of speech, assembly, association and press.

The government countered by announcing on April 22, 1990 plans to form a 75-member "parliament" with 50 elected members and 25 chosen by the emir. When 26 former members of the Assembly expressed their intent on May 5 to boycott the elections the government arrested at least twelve prominent members of the opposition and began to impose its authority in all walks of life.[13]

Despite those restrictions, however, the Kuwaiti opposition at least exists and has been able to operate without political parties. In Syria, on the other hand, dissent is brutally suppressed and in Saudi Arabia and the rest of the Gulf Cooperation Council (GCC) member states, it is almost taboo. In addition to the ban which these dynasties maintain on basic political activities, the GCC made those bans applicable to all members by multilateral treaties.[14] Kuwait, where a constitution at least exists and where the press is among the freest in the Arab world, was particularly affected by these curtailments.

Judicial rules in practice in most of the Arab countries permit the authorities to circumvent the normal jurisdiction of the courts. Accused persons often find themselves facing military tribunals. Most of the countries in the anti-Iraq coalition give military courts jurisdiction over the police and over civilians accused of criminal offenses which somehow relate to the armed forces. Most of them have what is called a court of state security for trying prominent political prisoners. Punishments normally reserved for criminal acts are frequently imposed in cases where the authorities allege a threat to security.

The 1987 report of the Arab Organization for Human Rights (AOHR) shows that executions have increased dramatically in Syria after such star chamber proceedings, which provide no procedural protections. "The purpose of these trials," the report says, "is most likely to impose the death penalty, which is often carried out immediately and inside the prison where the trials are held."[15]

Kuwait and Bahrain also employ state security and special courts to suppress dissent. Bahrain enacted a law on December 12, 1984, appropriately called the Law of Speedy Justice; a trial may be held within 24 hours of the arrest; punishments of up to 10 years in prison have been imposed under this law.

Bahrain still retains the colonial-era Governmental Declaration Number 55 of 1956, under which police may use force of break up demonstrations. The Law of General Security for 1965 prohibits demonstrations, marches and the distribution of pamphlets critical of the government.

Bahrain's 1976 Law of Punishment, enacted after dissolution of the National Assembly which had criticized the 1974 Law of State Security, permits preventive detention. According to the Law of Punishment, anyone who offends the ruler is subject to the death penalty.

Migrant workers have almost no rights whatsoever in most of the Gulf countries, where they are deprived of the right to own immovable property or to claim residence for their immediate families. Migrant workers are subject to immediate deportations in these countries, as well as in Iraq.

Women's rights in the Gulf countries are abysmal. Men and women in parts of the Gulf region are still subject to stoning in cases of adultery. In Saudi Arabia, women are not equal with men before the law. Their participation in public life is severely curtailed and so is their freedom of movement, including the right to travel abroad and drive automobiles in the country.

The Arab Organization for Human Rights received a complaint from a woman in Oman who sought assistance from the central government against her father, who allegedly tried to force her to marry against her will. The vice-governor sent her to prison for one week, during which time she was allegedly tortured and was subsequently sentenced by a judge who himself beat her during the trial, according to her complaint.[16]

Corruption and nepotism are rampant throughout the Gulf where every regime belongs to a dynasty. Sharing some power with non-royalists from the merchant class is an occurrence of the past two decades. But even in Kuwait, which is less reactionary than other emirates, the top ten positions in the government are occupied by four brothers and six cousins, who also control the largest portion of the country's wealth. Members of the al-Sabah family invest in a broad spectrum of enterprises ranging from the world's financial markets and choice real estate in the U.S. and Europe to the smallest commercial activities in Kuwait such as supermarkets, video-rental shops, used car sales and even barber shops. When the government pledged to bail out investors during the crash of the Kuwait Stock Exchange, known as Souq al-Manakh, numerous millionaire al-Sabahs applied for compensation along with the commoners.

Throughout the Gulf and Saudi Arabia, alien residents from Arab countries and East Asian migrant workers cater to the citizens. They staff the lower and middle level positions in government bureaucracies, run the educational and healthcare systems, constitute the administrative and clerical apparatus of the private sector and do the menial and unskilled work. They are subjected to severe discrimination in jobs, pensions, medical care and access to public facilities including education. In Kuwait, for example, they are deprived of owning immovable property and of having their Kuwaiti-born offspring live with them unless the latter are granted work permits when they come of age.

Our brief survey of human rights and political freedoms with special focus on Iraq and its Arab protagonists, has shown serious problems. In fact, it may be said that this is a disaster area in terms of human rights. Irrespective of the type of government, republics, emirates, or kingdoms, and irrespective of ideological alignment or foreign policy orientation, whether aligned with the West in the anti-Iraq coalition or not, most Arab regimes fall short of the minimum international requirements for human rights.

### George Bush's Human Rights Arsenal

For reasons of their own, however, United States leaders and particularly President Bush decided to single out Iraqi violations in the aftermath of that country's invasion of Kuwait, and use it as a weapon in the confrontation with Saddam Hussein. What follows is an account of the methods through which George Bush utilized human rights to attack Iraq.

Bush asserted with frequent repetition, during the six month stand-off in the Gulf before he began the war, that the defense of human rights was a principal motivation for his determination to challenge the Iraqi occupation of Kuwait. He invoked legal principles and cited reports of human rights organizations on Iraq as evidence to support his position. It was a classic case of manipulation of the human rights movements and international law to advance his case against Saddam Hussein.

In a series of speeches on U.S. policy in the Gulf, between August 1990 and February 1991, George Bush charged the Iraqi government and President Saddam Hussein in particular of egregious violations of human rights and international law. Although his stand on Iraq's occupation was couched in moral terms, designed to supply the emotional fervor for his geo-strategic aims, he managed to appeal to the economic self-interest of the American public; the conflict was also over "jobs," "oil," and a "way of life."[17] Secretary of State James Baker went so far as to blame Saddam Hussein for threatening a recession, ignoring the fact that it had been ongoing in the U.S. for several months:

> But this is not about an increase in the price of a gallon of gas at the local service station . . . It is rather about a dictator who, acting alone and unchallenged, could strangle the global economic order, determining by fiat whether we all enter a recession or even the darkness of a depression.[18]

## Aggression Against Neighbors and Own Citizens

In a speech to employees at the Pentagon on August 15, 1990, George Bush decided to add his voice to those of the various international human rights organization which condemned the gassing of Kurds in 1988:

> Saddam has claimed that this is a holy war of Arab against infidel: this from the man who has used poison gas against the men, women, and children of his own country.[19]

Bush's very belated condemnation is a good example of how controversial and/or contradictory reports can be contorted to accommodate a political stance. To begin with, the intelligence reports on the gassing of Kurds have been rather inconclusive and also contradictory. In September 1988, the State Department leveled charges that Iraq had used chemical weapons against its Kurdish population. But according to a study published in 1990 by three authors on the staff of the U.S. Army War College in Pennsylvania, the situation was far more complex.[20]

The study revealed that both Iran and Iraq used chemical weapons in attacking the border city of Halabja, which each side mistakenly believed was being held by enemy troops. The study revealed that the Kurds had died of cyanide gas, possessed only by the Iranians: "It seemed likely that it was the Iranian bombardment that had actually killed the Kurds."[21] Moreover, Turkish physicians, who treated the Kurds for various ailments at that time, revealed that they were unable to verify claims of chemical attacks. The Army War College study also concluded that "having looked at all of the evidence that was available to us, we find it impossible to confirm the State Department's claim that gas was used in this instance [late August 1988]."[22]

But despite the inconclusive nature of this matter, the alleged use of gas by Iraq was to emerge as one of Bush's favorite themes, which assisted in mobilizing public support for a broad ideological campaign to conduct the war. He repeated it with monotonous frequency unmindful of the total indifference to these alleged abuses by the Reagan administration in which he served as vice-president and in which his Chairman of the Joint Chiefs of Staff, Colin Powell served as Reagan's national security advisor. Indeed his initial justification of the military deployment was based on this notion of aggression against neighbors and own citizens:

> Given the Iraqi government's history of aggression against its own citizens as well as its neighbors, to assume that Iraq will not attack again would be unwise

and unrealistic. And, therefore, after consulting with King Fahd, I sent Secretary of Defense Dick Cheney to discuss cooperative measures we could take. Following those meetings, the Saudi government requested our help. And I responded to that request by ordering U.S. air and ground forces to deploy to the Kingdom of Saudi Arabia.[23]

With regard to Bush's charge of aggression by Saddam Hussein against his own people, the Reagan-Bush administration not only remained mute in the face of the widespread reports of the gassing of Iraqi Kurds in 1988 but actually helped Iraq escape international condemnation. Together with certain Arab and Third World governments, it protected Iraq in the United Nations Human Rights Commission in 1989 from being branded as a "gross violator of internationally recognized human rights." That shield was also extended to Iraq by the Bush administration until only a few weeks prior to its August invasion of Kuwait. The Reagan-Bush administration had also protected Saddam Hussein's government in the U.S. Congress, where the Senate's success in imposing sanctions in September 1988 was reversed in the House, in which sanctions were scaled down before finally being allowed to die in conference committee. They were finally imposed *after* the Iraqi invasion of Kuwait in August 1990.

Columnist Mary McGrory calculated that the Reagan administration had issued fifteen statements on the question of poison gas, but that when Vice-President Bush spoke against its use, he never had any mention of Saddam Hussein or Iraq.[24] She found the explanation in the power of the oil companies, the farm lobby and an assortment of other beneficiaries from the trade with Iraq. And yet, the aggression theme continued to characterize Bush's approach to the conflict in the Gulf as one between good and evil. For example, he said at a news conference on August 22, 1990:

This is not a matter between Iraq and the United States of America. It is between Iraq and the entire world community. Arabs and non-Arabs alike, all the nations of the world lined up to oppose aggression.

### Plunder and Atrocities

The widespread reports of Iraqi atrocities and "plunder" of Kuwait supplied by human rights organizations and Kuwaiti exiles offered George Bush another justification for his endeavor towards an eventual crippling of Iraq's economic, military and political potential. Less than two weeks after the invasion of Kuwait, he said "the reports out of Kuwait tell a sordid story,"[25] and on October 1, he charged Iraq before the UN General Assembly of "crimes of abuse and destruction,"[26] again citing the record which he had previously managed to overlook:

But this outrageous disregard for basic human rights does not come as a total surprise. Thousands of Iraqis have been executed on political and religious grounds and even more through a genocidal poison-gas war against Iraq's own Kurdish villagers.[27]

None of the preceding findings and indictments, however, animated George Bush to the extent of making a direct correlation between human rights abuses and the timetable for transition from economic sanctions to military action. He admitted at an October 9 press conference that the "dismantling" of Kuwait as told to him by the Emir Jaber al-Sabah and the horrendous account by Amnesty International was making his "patience wear thin."[28] When asked to confirm whether his advisors said that the emir's stories about "dismantling" could affect the timetable for permitting sanctions to work, he replied:

> I am very much concerned, not just about this physical dismantling, but of the brutality that has now been written on by Amnesty International confirming some of the tales told us by the emir, of brutality and — oh, it's just unbelievable, some of the things at least he reflected. I mean people on a dialysis machine cut off, the machine sent to Baghdad; people in — babies in incubators heaved out of the incubators and the incubators themselves sent to Baghdad. Now, I don't know how many of these tales can be authenticated, but I do know when the emir was here he was speaking from his heart. And after that came the Amnesty International, who were debriefing many of the people at the border. And its sickening . . .[29]

## Bush, Incubators, and Amnesty International

The report by Amnesty International which President Bush was referring to was actually a press release dated October 2, 1990 in which Iraq was cited for abuses ranging from arbitrary arrest, extra-judicial executions, beatings, to torture and summary execution.[30] The incubators story was told to him by the emir and was not to appear in Amnesty International's literature until December 18 when an 82-page report was issued based on interviews with some 100 Kuwaitis who fled to Saudi Arabia and other Gulf states.[31]

Apparently George Bush found in Amnesty's work the kind of ammunition for his moral arsenal to humiliate Saddam Hussein and move towards his brave new world. He used the report in his encounters with church leaders who expressed opposition to war in the Gulf. Both the National Council of Churches and the Catholic Conference issued statements critical of Bush's policies.[32] The *Los Angeles Times* reported on December 22, 1990 that presiding Bishop Edmond Browning of the U.S. Episcopal Church who had visited Baghdad spoke of seeing on the President's desk "an Amnesty International report on atrocities committed by Iraqi forces in Kuwait." He said that Bush "cannot read the report without complete revulsion," and quoted Bush as asking "what is the moral response to this?" Bush used Amnesty's report also in a nationwide television interview with David Frost on January 2, 1991. He was quoted as saying that when he gave the report to his wife Barbara, "she read about two pages of it, and said I can't read anymore. But the torturing of a handicapped child . . . the shooting of young boys in front of their parents . . . women dragged out of their home and repeatedly raped."[33]

What is truly remarkable was the degree of passion with which Bush recited the litany of abuse, as well as his propensity to do it in exceptional detail. His rediscovery of the United Nations, which had been much maligned in the U.S. as a debating club for the Third World, paralleled another sudden discovery of human rights and Amnesty International, perhaps for the first time. Consider the following detail in the Frost interview:

> The tying of those that are being tortured to ceiling fans so they turn and turn. The killing of a Kuwaiti and leaving him hanging . . . from a crane and so others will see him. Electric shock to the . . . private parts of men and women . . . broken glass inserted in — jabbed into people. I mean, it — it is primeval. It's almost impossible to rationalize this behavior with the fact that this is 1990.[34]

This near obsession with a single Amnesty report, which the President cited at least half a dozen times, is again revealed in an account by Hugh Sidney in *Time* magazine. Bush is described as pointing "a long forefinger at a stack of papers in the center of his neat desk. It is Amnesty International's report." When asked about the possibility of compromising with Saddam Hussein, he says:

> I am absolutely convinced you can't . . . there is a question about moral purpose here, I really urge people to read this report. It's going to have a devastating effect.[35]

After urging his listeners and television viewers to read a 950-page book on Hitler's Death Head Regiment which inflicted brutalities in Poland during the 1930s he "lowers his voice so much it is hard to hear him. He looks again at the Amnesty International report. 'No question . . . you do not placate an aggressor . . . there is a lot of historical precedent . . .'"[36]

The abuses which stirred George Bush to express shock and sound an alarm are unfortunately common occurrences for the hundreds of thousands of human rights activists around the world. This is not to underestimate the suffering of the Kuwaiti people under occupation or to discount the brutal nature of the abuse inflicted upon them by Iraqi forces; it is a reflection on George Bush's own indifference to a general problem with which most heads of states tend to be familiar. Having served as the U.S. Ambassador to the United Nations and CIA chief prior to assuming the presidency, George Bush should have been aware of Amnesty International's annual reports, if not its special reports on torture and extra-judicial executions. Had he glanced over the latest report for 1989, he might have discovered horrendous crimes of torture in countries that joined his war against Iraq, such as Turkey, Syria, Egypt and Saudi Arabia.[36A]

Writing in *The Nation* (January 21, 1991), David Corn advised George Bush to look up Amnesty's *Torture in the Eighties* and share with his wife Barbara an eyewitness account of a married couple under interrogation in Turkey, "a favored partner" in the anti-Iraq alliance:

> A torturer would play with the genital organs of the wife, squeezing her breasts and caressing her hair while the husband watched. The reverse would be applied

to the husband. While his wife watched they would give electric shocks to his penis, hang him by his feet. They would threaten to rape his wife unless he would admit the accusations made against him.[37]

Corn goes on to mention other U.S. favorites in Latin America such as "Argentina (electric shocks, cigarette burns, water immersion), Chile (shock, rape, drugs, blows to the ears, drowning) and El Salvador (burning the flesh with sulfuric acid)."

Referring to Bush's interview with David Frost, the *Oakland Tribune* (January 12, 1991) commented on the President's shock with an equal shock:

> To our knowledge, this is the first time either Bush or his mentor, Ronald Reagan has even recognized Amnesty International in public. But anyone familiar with the organization knows that its reports cover not just Iraq, but scores of countries around the world where brutal regimes terrorize helpless citizens.[38]

The editorial goes on to describe the double standard and expose the futility of the Bush approach to human rights unless it becomes a salient feature of U.S. policy worldwide:

> But when countries that are our own "friends" are involved, we fall back on Jeanne Kirkpatrick's hypocritical formulation that "authoritarian" regimes are more tolerable than "totalitarian" ones. Until we can denounce rape as rape without regard to whether the perpetrators or victims are our friends or adversaries . . . Bush's denunciation of Iraq's atrocities will carry the hollow ring of hypocrisy.[39]

Bush also used the Amnesty report in an article which he directed to hundreds of university newspapers across the United States. The relevant portions read:

> Listen to what Amnesty International has documented . . . There is no horror that could make this a more obvious conflict of good v. evil . . . If we do not follow the dictates of our own moral compass and stand up for human life, then his lawlessness will threaten the peace and democracy of the emerging new world order we now see, this long dreamed of vision we've all worked towards for so long.[40]

The repetitious and imprudent appropriation of Amnesty's name over a period of more than three months by George Bush, in a relentless campaign to undermine all efforts to resolve the conflict diplomatically, not only irritated the organization, but began to generate questions about its credibility. Intellectual honesty became a focal point in a debate in which at least one other major human rights organization and columnist Alexander Cockburn became involved. Middle East Watch, which monitors human rights violations throughout the Middle East and North Africa and the most recent constituent of Human Rights Watch, questioned the accuracy of Amnesty International's findings. It suspected the Kuwaiti government in exile of "orchestrating exaggerated tales of horror for political gains."[41] And in December 1990 the organization's Executive Director Andrew

Whitley told *Time* magazine: "The situation is bad enough . . . there is no need to inflate the statistics."[42] Middle East Watch's argument with Amnesty was not over the substance and the nature of the abuse, but simply over the degree and numbers; Amnesty's report was thought to have been "overdrawn."

Alexander Cockburn, on the other hand, writing in the *Los Angeles Times* asserted that "the story of babies' mass murder is untrue."[43] Referring to the incubators story in Amnesty's report, which George Bush quoted with expressions such as "Good God . . . You wouldn't be able to believe it," Cockburn questioned whether it is "likely that any hospital in Kuwait would have so many (312) incubators." He added that "Los Angeles County, University of Southern California Medical Center, for example, has 13."[44] Cockburn also quoted Aziz Abu Hamad, a Saudi consultant for Middle East Watch as saying that "as yet no credible eyewitnesses or testimony have surfaced to sustain the charges of mass murder of babies in incubators."[45] A Red Crescent physician who was interviewed by Abu Hamad at the Taif Sheraton, headquarters of the Kuwaiti government-in-exile said that he buried 72 babies and did not know whether they were in incubators or what was the cause of their death. A more recent report by ABC News (15 March, 1991) sheds some additional light on the incubator controversy. Dr. Fayeza Youssef, head of the obstetrics unit at the maternity hospital in Kuwait City told an ABC reporter on *World News Tonight* the following: "Iraqi soldiers did not take the babies from their incubators. There were no nurses to take care of the babies so they died."[46] When the reporter asked another doctor, Mohamad Sanir Matar, whether the babies were taken out of the incubators and put on the floor to die, the latter replied: "I think that was just for propaganda." He further explained that when doctors and health personnel fled in fear, babies and other patients died in large numbers as a result. An ABC team visited the hospital nursery and found it filled with incubators that had been hidden by technicians to prevent any theft.[47]

By April 1991, the incubator episode began to assume more realistic dimensions. Both Middle East Watch and Amnesty International issued reports based on separate investigative missions conducted by each organization. Andrew Whitley, who led Middle East Watch's mission to Kuwait, told the *Washington Post* that extensive checks of Kuwait City hospitals showed that "no incubators were stolen, and no babies were taken out of incubators and allowed to die."[48]

At the same time, Aziz Abu Hamad said that Kuwait City's maternity hospital still has all of its more than 80 incubators, about two-thirds of the total in the country. He attributed the death of an unusual number of babies during the occupation to "lack of doctors, support staff and some medicines."[49]

Amnesty International updated its December 1990 report, which so fascinated George Bush, and issued a virtual retraction. The AI report of April 18, 1991 states:

On the highly publicized issue in the December report of the baby deaths, Amnesty International said that although its team was shown alleged mass graves of babies, it was not established how they had died and the team found no reliable evidence that Iraqi forces had caused the deaths of babies by removing them or ordering their removal from incubators.[50]

The organization acknowledged that doubt was cast on the credibility of its December 1990 report, causing it to recheck its information in early 1991:

> However, once we were actually in Kuwait and had visited hospitals and cemeteries and spoken to doctors at work, we found that the story did not stand up. . . . We take good care to check and update the information we publish and we are always ready to reissue corrections if previously published data is later shown not to stand up. In line with this policy, an update with corrections is being issued for our December 1990 report.[51]

Apparently, the source of the incubator story was the Kuwait Red Crescent Society. Again contradictory and inconclusive reports dealing with a highly sensitive subject such as children's death were utilized by George Bush to dramatize the righteous nature of his campaign against Iraq. But the fact that the incubators were hidden for safekeeping and a large number of babies were in fact buried led to speculation on the ABC program that the two were linked as evidence and a conclusion was drawn that the incubators must have been stolen.

Alexander Cockburn whose article was written long before the ABC report concluded it with biting criticism of Amnesty International:

> Human rights organizations should have higher standards than the yellow press; otherwise, they add to the lies that, in this crisis, are already shoulder deep, starting with Bush's early pledge that U.S. troops were going to the Gulf purely to defend Saudi Arabia . . . The incubator myth shows how quick we are to believe something when it grabs so savagely at our instincts.[52]

Amnesty International's irritation with the manner in which George Bush was exploiting its work to undermine the sanctions policy, which until the start of 1991 enjoyed the support of 7 out of 10 Democrats in the U.S. Congress, was expressed in a response to the same campus newspapers which received Bush's article. Executive Director John Healey left no doubt about Amnesty's assessment of the president's motivation:

> I hope the administration will soon learn that Amnesty members and other student activists can not be misled by opportunistic manipulation of the international human rights movement . . . We can teach our political leaders that people's human rights are not convenient issues for rhetorical arsenals.[53]

Given that the Reagan-Bush administration was tolerant of Iraqi abuses and that the Bush administration itself refused to conclude that Iraq had engaged in a consistent pattern of gross human rights violations, only two weeks prior to the August invasion, Healey wondered about the lack of "presidential indignation, for example, in 1989, when Amnesty released its findings about the torture of Iraqi children."[54] He also wondered about the lack of extending that indignation to "long-term 'friends,'" such as Saudi Arabia, Egypt and Israel, and "new-found 'friends,' such as the Syrian government."[55] Knowing that Bush's constant invocation of Amnesty was part of the verbal strategy to mobilize public opinion for war, Healey again warned against the exploitation of human rights by Bush:

> President Bush's selective indignation over Iraq's abuses in Kuwait undermines the norms of "human decency" he touts in his letter to campus newspapers . . . Exploiting human rights to justify violent confrontation is itself indecent.[56]

Such overwhelming preoccupation with human rights and the work of Amnesty International in particular by a president, whose own record has been badly tarnished in the mainstream human rights community, appeared unnatural, if not downright hypocritical. The Republican Senator from Oregon, Mark Hatfield, expressed his own misgivings about Bush's exploitation of Amnesty's work:

> But Mr. President, even the most brutal human rights violations of one nation do not justify an offensive strike against another nation. Indeed, it makes a mockery of the exceptional work done by organizations like Amnesty International to use their documentation of human rights abuses as a convenient justification for launching an attack that will very certainly cause even more suffering. When it comes right down to it, this is about oil . . . We must be honest about the real motivation behind our policy . . .[57]

The double standard was also raised by Congressman Stokes of Ohio during the January 12, 1990 debate on the use of force resolution:

> There is no question that the outrageous violations of human rights reported by Amnesty International defy all standards of human rights decency. But I have to wonder where was the outcry from the Administration when three United States servicemen were recently murdered in El Salvador . . . In Guatemala, China, Kenya and South Africa pervasive human rights violations have occurred and continue to occur . . . I venture to say that if Kuwait produced bananas, instead of oil, we would not have 400,000 American troops there today.[58]

### Human Rights and Geopolitics in the Middle East

The foregoing argues that despite the widespread abuse of human rights in the Middle East, President Bush has disengenuously singled out Iraq for moral reproach and ignored the violations of his regional allies and new friends, with whom he came to share a convergence of interest in the Gulf crisis. For example, Amnesty International, whose report on Kuwait Bush quoted so liberally, also issued critical reports and statements detailing the torture of hundreds of Yemenis by Saudi security forces, arrests of opponents of the Gulf War in Egypt and abuses committed by Kuwaiti forces against Palestinians, Yemenis and Sudanese.[59]

So blatantly vengeful were the actions of the martial law courts, as well as those of the Kuwaiti security forces and vigilantes, that human rights organizations and the U.S. mainstream media were almost unanimous in their condemnation. The pervasive torture, summary executions, disappearances, indiscriminate incarceration of people by the thousands, and the violation of the basic requirements of due process, did not even elicit a condemnation from George Bush. He simply expressed concern and urged Kuwait "to extend fair trials to everybody," and went out of his way to emphasize that Kuwaitis had been subjected to brutal treatment during the Iraqi occupation. He said that he "could understand that there's a lot of bitterness among those Kuwaitis who saw their country raped and pillaged in an unconscionable way."

This section will show how shifting alignments and convergences during the 1980s influenced the uses and abuses of human rights. That Iraq under Saddam Hussein was one of the worst violators of human rights is a given, and not even open to question. What is significant, however, was the utility which human rights acquired in geopolitics as much as the convenience which Saddam's invasion afforded George Bush. It is equally important that the campaign against Saddam Hussein was not initiated by George Bush. Long before Bush's moral arsenal was in place, Congress and the media launched their own campaign, which Bush picked up on only after the invasion of Kuwait. Previous to that, Bush and Congress had been at cross purposes in their assessment of Iraq's impact on America's geo-strategic interests in the Middle East. At the same time, America's Arab allies were lined up with Iraq in the face of the Congressional and media attacks. What happened to alter that equation?

As early as 1986, when the Reagan-Bush administration was tilting towards Iraq in its war against Iran for geopolitical reasons, Congress attempted to bar "indirect" U.S. aid, i.e. using its contributions to the World Bank to fund various undesirable countries, including Iraq. In 1988 the Senate Foreign Relations Committee sponsored a resolution (S2763) which urged that sanctions be imposed on Iraq affecting $800 million in guaranteed loans. The sanctions would also force the U.S. representatives in the World Bank and the IMF to vote against all loans to Iraq. These sanctions also barred sales to Iraq of any item subject to U.S. license. The bill, as Senator Clairborne Pell remarked, was to condemn Iraq for practicing "genocide" against the Kurds. To quote Senator Pell: "Iraq has undertaken a campaign to depopulate the Kurdish regions ... by depopulating all Kurdish villages in a large part of northern Iraq and by killing the civilian population." The bill passed in the Senate on September 9, 1988. The State Department called this bill "premature" and appealed to the House to tone down the legislation.

The House version of S2763 was HR5337, which was a milder version with limited sanctions but still authorizing the president to increase penalties in the future unless Iraq agreed to stop using chemical weapons. Immediate sanctions involved the banning of all exports of military and military-related equipment, as well as items such as computers and oil drilling equipment that were subject to U.S. government export controls. The House Foreign Affairs Committee approved the bill on September 22 and the House Ways and Means approved it the following day. The House also passed it on September 27 with a vote of 388–16.

On September 30, 1988, the Senate Foreign Relations Committee tried to force the House to accept a compromise. Sen. Pell and Sen. Helms proposed substantially weaker sanctions than those in the first bill but somewhat stronger than HR5337. This would have banned immediately the exports of military equipment and dual use technology, mandated U.S. votes against Iraq in international financial institutions and toughened the House measure making the president impose additional sanctions within 60 days unless he received assurances that Iraq would no longer use chemical weapons.

On October 7, the Senate Foreign Relations Committee, the House Foreign Affairs and other committees worked out a compromise. The plan against Iraq called for imposing immediate limited sanctions, a ban on exports of arms and high technology equipment, and required the president to impose more sanctions by the end of the year unless Iraq abandoned the use of chemical weapons. Broad Congressional support for the sanctions was made possible by a decision by Capitol Hill leaders to exempt U.S. agricultural goods. The original House and Senate bills opened the possibility of a ban on farm products to Iraq. Agricultural groups campaigned against that, recalling the damage to the farm economy caused by President Jimmy Carter's grain embargo on the USSR in protest at their attack on Afghanistan. Ultimately, the Iraq sanctions bill was buried under the weight of special interests and concerns.

In 1989, for the second year in a row, a last minute dispute in the Senate held up sanctions against countries that used chemical weapons. S195 would have imposed sanctions against any country that used chemical/ biological weapons in violation of international law; it would also require sanctions against foreign companies that helped those nations develop such weapons. The Foreign Relations Committee approved S195, but the Banking panel insisted that part of the bill belonged in its jurisdiction and demanded changes. Aides to the two panels failed to settle the dispute before adjournment in November. A Foreign Relations Committee spokesman said they would try again in 1990. HR3033, the counterpart to the Senate's bill, passed in the House on November 13, 1989 with Presidential support because greater discretion was given in the House's version in imposing sanctions than in the Senate's version. S195 received opposition from the Bush administration because it did not give the president broad enough discretion to determine when to impose sanctions and when to use other diplomatic means to protest the use or spread of chemical weapons overseas, and the effort died in conference committee. In the end the executive branch prevailed over the legislature, despite human rights and other domestic considerations. As expected, presidential supremacy in the conduct of foreign affairs was simply reaffirmed. The issue of human rights became a major element in what Iraq, the Arab League and the Gulf states perceived as a Western campaign to discredit Iraq shortly after the end of the Iran-Iraq war in the autumn of 1988. The discourse centered on Iraq's use of chemical weapons against Iran, poison-gas against the Kurds, the execution of an Iranian-born reporter for the

London *Observer* and alleged attempts to smuggle nuclear triggers into Iraq. The European and American media together with Western-based human rights organizations published numerous reports about Iraqi violations and the United States Congress joined in attempts to apply sanctions against Iraq. The issue of human rights became a central element in an anti-Iraqi campaign waged in the West from the latter part of 1988 onwards.

That the Iraqi stand against the Western campaign throughout the period September 1988 through August 2, 1990 received support from the Arab League and individual governments including Egypt, Jordan, Saudi Arabia, and most of the Gulf states was in itself significant. Iraqi assertions of its right to guard its security against people like journalist Farzad Bazoft, whom it executed on March 15, 1990, won the support of Saudi Arabia, Bahrain, Kuwait, and the Arab Cooperation Council (Iraq, Egypt, Yemen, and Jordan), among others. The campaign against Iraq assumed new and larger dimensions when the strongly denied accusations that Iraq was developing a nuclear capacity confirmed convictions in the Arab world that the U.S. and Israel were intent on reducing Iraq to manageable proportions. The storm against Bazoft's execution was followed by the electronic capacitators affair in which Iraq was accused of attempting to smuggle capacitators used to trigger nuclear explosions. By April 1990, the U.S. media had succeeded in making Saddam a household name and pariah. "Public Enemy Number 1" was the headline of a *Newsweek* story about Iraq's alleged efforts to buy parts for a nuclear bomb.[60] Illustrated with photographs of Saddam Hussein and his missiles, the story offered an account through the candid cameras of NBC of the alleged purchase and loading of nuclear capacitators and Kytron switches aboard an airplane in San Diego.

Not to be outdone, *U.S. News and World Report* (June 4, 1990) featured a cover story with a drawing of Saddam Hussein looking stern and devious. The caption read: "The Most Dangerous Man in the World."[61] The statistics, maps, weapons delivery tables and the gruesome effects of nerve gas are all illustrated in the story with a breadth and color that is intended to make the caption credible. An inside sub-title read: "With billions to spend and help from the U.S., the Soviet Union and Europe, Saddam Hussein is amassing a truly terrifying arsenal." The world came to know in February 1991 how really terrifying it was!

In another article in the *New York Times* (March 30, 1990) "Battles to Baghdad," William Safire wrote:

> From the Battles to Baghdad, the umbrellas of appeasement are unfurling . . . The State Department, which could not have been ignorant of Iraq's attempt to steal our nuclear secrets, has long sought to appease Saddam.[62]

The context for this "appeasement" was supposedly an order by Secretary of State James Baker requesting the U.S. Information Agency to have the Voice of America refrain from beaming messages that would anger Saddam Hussein. An example was a message saying "the rulers of these countries hold power by force and fear," which Hussein protested formally as a "call to revolution." It is, to say the least, ironic that appeasement and the 1930s became a dominant theme in the Bush administration's own campaign against Saddam Hussein five months after Safire used it against the administration.

Another headline in the *New York Times* (April 3, 1990) read "Iraq Can Deliver, U.S. Chemical Arms Experts Say." An insecure Saddam Hussein, fearing that the Western media campaign was a prelude to an Israeli invasion of Iraq made a threat to destroy "half of Israel," if that country attacked Iraq. Headlines were printed across front pages in the United State "Iraq Threatens Israel with Nerve Gas," or "with Chemical Weapons," leaving out the proviso, "if attacked by Israel."

CBS news correspondent Dan Raviv and Israeli journalist Yossi Melman co-authored articles on the Iraqi "threat," which appeared in the *New York Times*, *Boston Globe* and the *Washington Post* in April and May 1990, and made several television appearances. The *Boston Globe* article (May 27, 1990), which displayed a large photo of the Halabja victims in 1988 next to a picture of Saddam, carried the headline: "Iraq's Weapons Craze Threatens Middle East." The *Washington Post* headlined its detailed article: "Iraq's Arsenal of Horror." The *Wall Street Journal* (April 23, 1990) headlined "Iraq Buying Spree on Arms Bodes Ill for Its Neighbors." Jack Anderson and Dale Van Atta headlined: "Iraq, New Arab Powerhouse," and so on and so on, not to mention the cartoons, the television programs, and the radio talk shows, which certified Saddam Hussein as the new Hitler and made him the personification of all evil.

By the time U.S. Ambassador April Glaspie had the conversation with Saddam Hussein which he interpreted as a green light to invade Kuwait in late July, he had been so dehumanized and demonized that the use of the most violent measures against him and his people appeared to require little justification. That justification is what George Bush provided, using human rights, economic self-interest and patriotism, all wrapped in a package which he called "new world order." His rendition of the crisis and its projection as "naked aggression" and the "conflict of good v. evil," ensured that the American people would be saved from intellectual hardship and feelings of guilt over the consequences of the "high tech" war that was being planned. Six months of that rendition (August 1990–January 1991), in which human rights occupied a prominent space, reinforced and finalized the media spring campaign.

Almost from the very inception of the controversy in April 1990 broad segments of the Arab world perceived the matter in a broad strategic context. Iraq's military prowess, scientific advances in the areas of aerospace industry, chemical warfare, nuclear research and long-range missiles were seen as part of an Iraqi quest for mutual deterrence vis-a-vis Israel. These ambitions had been claimed by Egypt a quarter of a century earlier and the result was the 1967 defeat and the subsequent pacification of Egypt and its eventual separate peace with Israel at Camp David. Syria's quest for strategic parity had never materialized after its air force's costly encounter with Israel when the latter invaded Lebanon in 1982. It was subsequently laid to rest when the Soviet Union under Gorbachev repealed its commitment to help Syria check Israeli military supremacy in 1985. It was only natural that a third and more determined attempt by Iraq to neutralize Israel's regional hegemony would meet the same fate. America's determination to maintain and expand its dominion over the world's key resources would not be compromised by a Third World power.

The human rights factor proved to be an effective tool in Washington's arsenal at the service of *pax Americana*. It was a viable component of Bush's strategy towards reshaping the strategic landscape in the Middle East. The 1969 commitment of Richard Nixon would be upheld and reaffirmed: "Israel is to be guaranteed a margin of technological and military superiority over all her Arab neighbors combined." Saddam's challenge to that commitment was to cost Iraq not only its military and industrial infrastructure; it brought the greatest devastation since 1258. As for George Bush, generations of Arabs for a long time will remember him as the new Hulago.

## Notes

1. The information in this section is based on an earlier work by the author. "Disaster Area: Human Rights in the Arab World," *Middle East Report*, No. 149 (Nov.-Dec. 1987), pp. 7–16.
2. *Human Rights in the Arab Homeland* (Cairo: Arab Organization for Human Rights, 1987), pp. 73–84. This is the Triannual Report submitted to the General Assembly of AOHR in Khartoum on January 30, 1987. Hereafter, *AOHR Report*; see also Middle East Watch, *Human Rights In Syria* (New York, 1990).
3. See Amnesty International, "Torture In Egypt, 1981–83," *AI Index: MDE* 12/3/85, Oct. 23, 1985, p. 78. See also *AOHR Report*, pp. 32–43.
4. Middle East Watch, *Human Rights In Iraq* (New York, 1990).
5. *AOHR Report*, p. 78.
6. *AOHR Newsletter* #10 (July 1987), p. 1.
7. Naseer Aruri, "Disaster Area: Human Rights In the Arab World," *op. cit.*
8. *AOHR Report*, p. 33.
9. *AOHR Newsletter*, #3 (July 1986), p. 1.
10. *Human Rights In Iraq and Iraqi-Occupied Kuwait*. Testimony of Andrew Whitley, Middle East Watch before the House Foreign Affairs Committee, January 8, 1991, p. 9.
11. Ibid., p. 10.
12. Virginia Sherry, "Kuwait Before and After: What the Democratic Forces Want," *The Nation*, November 5, 1990, p. 526.
13. Ibid., p. 528.
14. Testimony of Andrew Whitley, *op. cit.*, p. 9.
15. *AOHR Report*, p. 73.
16. Ibid., p. 107.
17. *New York Times*, August 15, 1990.
18. *New York Times*, September 5, 1990.
19. *New York Times*, August 16, 1990.
20. Stephen C. Pelletiere, Douglas Johnson and Leif Rosenberger, *Iraqi Power and U.S. Security in the Middle East*. Carlisle Barracks, Pa.: Strategic Studies Institute, U.S. Army War College (U.S. Government Printing Office, 1990).
21. Ibid., p. 52; see also Knut Royce, "A Trail of Distortion Against Iraq: Bush Promotes Folklore About Enemy on Key Issues," *Newsday*, January 21, 1991.
22. Ibid.
23. *New York Times*, August 8, 1990.
24. *Boston Globe*, January 28, 1991.
25. *New York Times*, August 15, 1990.
26. *New York Times*, October 1, 1990.
27. Ibid.
28. *New York Times*, October 10, 1990.
29. Ibid.

30. "Iraqi Forces Killing and Torturing in Kuwait, Says Amnesty International Fact-Finding Teams." Washington D.C.: Amnesty International, Oct. 2, 1990.
31. Amnesty International, *Iraq/Occupied Kuwait: Human Rights Violations Since August 2, 1990* (New York, December 1990).
32. For a text of the National Council of Churches statement, see *New York Times*, November 16, 1990.
33. *Press-Telegram*, Long Beach, CA, Dec. 19, 1990.
34. A.P. dispatch in *Press-Telegram*, Long Beach, CA, Dec. 19, 1990; see also *The Nation*, January 21, 1991.
35. *Time*, Dec. 31, 1990.
36. Ibid.
36A Summary of AI Concerns During 1990 *op. cit.*
37. David Corn, *The Nation*, January 21, 1991.
38. *Oakland Tribune*, January 12, 1991.
39. Ibid.
40. George Bush, *Iraqi Leader Threatens Values Worth Fighting For*. Sent to over 450 college and university newspapers during the first week of January, 1991.
41. *Time*, December 31, 1990.
42. Ibid.
43. *Los Angeles Times*, January 17, 1991.
44. Ibid.
45. Ibid.
46. ABC *World News Tonight*, March 15, 1991. New York: Audience Relations, ABC.
47. Ibid.
48. William Branigan and Nora Bustany, "Groups Probe Iraqi Torture in Kuwait," *Washington Post*, April 1, 1991.
49. Ibid.
50. Amnesty International. "Kuwait: Amnesty International Calls on Emir to Intervene Over Continuing Torture and Killings." Press Release dated April 18, 1991. New York.
51. Ibid.
52. *Los Angeles Times*, January 17, 1991.
53. John G. Healey, *Amnesty International USA Response To President Bush's Letter To Campus Newspapers*. Jan. 15, 1991.
54. Ibid.
55. Ibid.
56. Ibid.
57. *Congressional Record*, January 12, 1991, p. S375.
58. Ibid., p. H287–288.
59. See for example, *Update on Amnesty International's Human Rights Concerns In Countries Involved in the Gulf Conflict*, 18 February, 1991. AI Index: NWS 11/06/90; *Egypt: Arrests of Opponents of the Gulf War*, 19 February, 1991. AI Index: MDE 12/06/90; *Saudi Arabia: Torture, Detention, and Arbitrary Arrests*. AI Index: MDE 23/09/90. See also, Virginia Sherry, "Purging Kuwait," *The Nation*, March 18, 1991, pp. 328–329; Robert Fisk, "Kuwait Palestinians Face Gunmen's Revenge," *The Independent* (London) March 4, 1991; William Branigan and Nora Boustany, "Rights Officials: Kuwaiti Soldiers Commit Abuses," *Washington Post*, March 18, 1991; Tim Kelsey, "Saddam Has Left, But the Horrors Are Not Finished," *The Independent*, March 3, 1991.
60. *Newsweek*, April 9, 1990, pp. 26–28.
61. *U.S. News and World Report*, June 4, 1990.
62. *New York Times*, March 30, 1990.

# 29

## For Generations to Come: The Environmental Catastrophe

*Penny Kemp*

The coalition forces have stopped fighting and Kuwait has been "liberated." The emir has been restored but the country has not. A new human nightmare has emerged. The specter of exploding oil wells, day indistinguishable from night, black rain, a massive oil spillage, thousands of tons of toxic chemicals released into the atmosphere, the tragic plight of the Kurdish and Iraqi peoples mean that the misery and suffering will linger on, perhaps for decades. It has been estimated that spending a day in Kuwait City is equivalent to smoking 250 cigarettes. Only now, is the world waking up to the terrible price being paid for engaging in military hostilities in the Gulf. The world's ecology is very fragile. Yet, eco-terrorism is not a new phenomenon. Since humankind has engaged in violent activity, damage to the environment has been a result and at times the planned strategy of the military. All wars bear ecological scars, from the activities of Genghis Khan who destroyed irrigation facilities in Mesopotamia in the thirteenth century to the Americans' use of defoliants during the Vietnam War in the mid-sixties. Even in peacetime, weapon testing in the South Pacific has led to wholesale destruction of the environment. Jonathon Porritt, a past Director of the British Friends of The Earth, evaluates war in the Gulf thus: "It is a bloody omelette that the allies have set out to make and a lot of ecological eggs will be broken."

In November 1990, at the Second World Climate Conference in Geneva, King Hussein of Jordan warned that war in the Gulf would encompass severe ecological consequences. He said: "I feel that we live in a time and a place in which we can no longer draw a clear line between political concerns, our environmental life base, and the prospects for future generations around the world. Nowhere is this more evident than in the Middle East, and at no other time in recent memory — indeed in my lifetime and yours — has the Middle East held the seeds of a potentially global catastrophe as it does today." He then went on to outline the potential ecological consequences of a battle that would take place on top of the single richest natural petroleum reservoir in the world, choosing to focus on the contribution to global warming any conflagration of the oil wells would bring. In highlighting only global warming, however, he gave the world an excuse to say he was over-stating the problem. Indeed, the British prime minister of the time, Margaret Thatcher, dismissed his warnings as unfounded and scaremongering. However, in drawing attention to the environmental effects of a war in the Gulf, the king gave the impetus for scientists to evaluate his warnings.

In early December, Tim Elioart, a Briton who has spent years researching desertification, began to explore the problems associated with an oil conflagration. He remembered the effects of the fire-storms at Dresden in the Second World War, where gales allowed air to feed the fire and as a consequence people were sucked into the flames. He was so concerned that he contacted a group of environmentalists in Britain who began to discuss the ecological problems associated with a war in the Gulf. This in turn led to a scientific symposium, which was held on January 2, 1991 at the Conway Hall, London.

It was decided to contact Jordan to ask for the research papers which led King Hussein to make his speech in Geneva. Instead of the documents supporting the speech, the king asked his chief scientific adviser, Dr. Abdullah Toukan, to attend the London symposium. Other eminent scientists, including Dr. Frank Barnaby, Dr. John Cox and Professor Joseph Rotblat, gathered with people from the oil industry, British MPs and invited observers including the ambassador of Iraq and representatives of other Middle Eastern countries. A large contingent of press arrived and by the evening the British Broadcasting Corporation was carrying the story as a major news item.

A battle over the world's largest producing oilfields inevitably brings problems. Before the invasion of August 2 by Iraqi forces, Kuwait was producing around two million barrels of oil per day from 365 operating wells. Kuwait has 743 wells which have estimated reserves of over 94 billion barrels as detailed in the table below. It is important to note that of the 365 operating wells, 343 wells are natural flow and only 22 are artificial lift (OPEC statistical yearbook, 1989). This means that in the majority of wells, when bombed or subjected to deliberate sabotage, oil would flow at a rate faster than normal production. Any conflagration of Kuwaiti oil wells could have a substantial effect on regional climatic conditions.

*Kuwait Crude Oil Production*
*Jan. 1990*

|  |  | Number of wells | |
| --- | --- | --- | --- |
|  | Depth (ft) | Producing | Total |
| Burgan (1938) | 4,800 | 210 | 393 |
| Ahmadi (1952) | 4,800 | 11 | 84 |

| | | | |
|---|---|---|---|
| Magwa (1951) | 4,800 | 71 | 113 |
| Raudhatain (1956) | 8,600 | 41 | 53 |
| Bahra (1956) | 8,500 | – | 2 |
| Sabriya (1957) | 8,300 | 9 | 44 |
| Minagish (1959) | 10,000 | 1 | 21 |
| Umm Gudair (1962) | 9,000 | 20 | 33 |
| Total | | 363 | 743 |

| | |
|---|---|
| Proven oil reserves: | 94,525 billion barrels |
| Gas reserves: | 48,600 billion cubic feet |
| Number of refineries | 4 |
| Refining crude capacity: | 819,000 barrels per day |

(Source, *Oil and Gas Journal*, December 1989)

The London symposium opened with Dr. Toukan raising the issue of the environmental costs of war, which he believed could outstrip all other costs, great though those would be. Ex-British Prime Minister Edward Heath had testified to a U.S. Congressional sub-committee in December that he believed Iraq had mined the Kuwaiti oilfields and would be prepared to blow them up. Dr. Toukan estimated that up to ten million barrels of oil could be burned per day as a consequence of the Iraqi action. Dr. John Cox was rather more conservative, putting the likely figure at three million barrels per day. Dr. Paul Crutzen from the Max Planck Institute, Mainz, where he is Director of Air Chemistry, went further by stating that over a hundred days the burning of ten million barrels of oil per day would produce a blanket of soot and smoke that would cover an area half the size of the northern hemisphere, producing major climatic effects. On January 5, he wrote: "In my opinion, the explosion and burning off of so many oil-wells could mean a global, certainly regional climatic and environmental catastrophe. It should be made clear to the leaders involved in the conflict what the consequences can be, so that such an act of madness will not take place." On February 22, news broke that over 190 oil-wells had been set alight. After the "liberation" of Kuwait, it was revealed that over 600 oil wells were ablaze with an estimated six million barrels of oil burning daily.

Soot is a major absorber of the sun's radiation, and leading atmospheric scientists have calculated that one gram of soot can block out two-thirds of the light falling over an area of eight to ten square metres. Two to four million barrels of oil burning per day (taking the more conservative estimate) would cause a plume of soot and smoke that would cover an area roughly equivalent to half the size of the United States. Weather conditions and wind currents in the area could cause the plume to travel thousands of miles, thus disrupting agricultural production in many parts of the globe. The most serious threat is that identified by chemical engineer Dr. John Cox, who believes the consequences so serious that the Indian monsoon could be shut down. The monsoon is in effect a giant sea breeze. It requires the air temperature above the Asian land mass to heat up faster than the surrounding oceanic air. As the hot air rises, it sucks in the cooler air from the ocean and as a result summer monsoons occur in India. A plume of smoke over the Indian sub-continent during the summer of 1991 could shut out the sunlight, thus reducing the temperature gradient and in turn cause the failure of the monsoon. The monsoon represents literally the difference between life or death for approximately a billion people who rely on the summer deluge for their agricultural production. Dr. Cox calculated that even a partial failure of the monsoon could kill more people than the combined total populations of Iraq, Kuwait and Saudi Arabia.

In effect what is produced by an oil conflagration is the same as the "nuclear winter" scenarios pioneered by American scientists Carl Sagan and Richard Turco. Turco told a British scientific journal that, "Gulf oil fires burning for one month could release 3 million tons of black smoke into the upper atmosphere, shading up to 100 million square kilometers, more than a fifth of the planet's surface."

Equally serious is the height the smoke could reach. When burning occurs naturally in forest fires smoke stays in the troposphere before returning to earth. Professor Crutzen, Drs. Cox and Turco believe that because of the peculiarities of the desert atmosphere and intensity of the fires smoke could reach the stratosphere. Dr. Toukan estimates that the heat from the fires could attain 400°C, and points out that in the sub-tropical region (between 25° to 35° North) there is a belt of strong wind in the upper levels (35,000 to 40,000 ft) reaching 200 knots (370km/hr) during the months November through March, which is called the sub-tropical jet stream. Richard Small, director of fire research at the Pacific-Sierra Research Corporation in the United States, confirms that fire intensity has a profound influence on smoke injection. More intense fires, such as those involving hydrocarbons, create convective currents strong enough for the smoke to penetrate easily into the upper atmosphere. Should smoke reach these heights it is possible that ozone depletion could occur, which would be catastrophic for plant and animal life. Dr. Cox states in his paper that: "Without the protection of stratospheric ozone, more UV light would reach the earth and many life forms would be endangered. Medical researchers have shown that percentage increases in UV light cause a proven pro rata increase in the incidence of cancers, cataracts and other medical complaints."

Another effect of burning oil-wells would be the production of acid rain due to the smoke eventually returning to earth with the rainfall. Kuwaiti crude oil contains 2.44% sulphur and 0.14% nitrogen. It has been estimated that daily sulphur dioxide and nitrous oxide emissions could be between 750 and 10,000 tons per day. The effect upon agriculture would be devastating. The Gulf region is not renown for its fertility, and acid rain on this scale would threaten what little food production already exists. Not only could it affect the Gulf, but any spreading of the plume of smoke could effect North Africa and the Indian sub-continent, where famine has already caused millions of deaths.

How easy would it be to put the fires out? The responses to this question have shown a remarkable degree of consensus from oil personnel and scientists alike. Basil Butler, managing director of British Petroleum and former chief engineer for Kuwait Petroleum Corporation, attended the symposium held in London and confirmed that fires from oil-wells could take up to a year to extinguish. He disagreed with Dr. Cox on the amount of smoke produced by such oil-wells, recalling that a fire at the Burgan field in 1964 burned with a 150 yard flame for over six weeks producing very little smoke. Upon further investigation by the scientists involved, it was found that the fire to which Butler referred was a gas fire, and since oil was not burning plumes of soot and smoke would not occur. Red Adair, interviewed by the *Independent* on January 3, 1991, stated: "It could take up to six weeks to bring each sabotaged Kuwaiti oil well under control." A parliamentary briefing to British MPs stated that if the fires could not be extinguished by the conventional method (i.e. by explosives in order to seal the well head) because they would be re-ignited by another fire in close proximity, the well would have to be sealed by a much longer and more laborious method. This would involve drilling diagonally a new well as close as possible to intercept the burning well within its underground reservoir. After the connection is made, fluids and/or cement are pumped in and flow into the uncontrolled well, gradually stopping the oil flow. This technique is time-consuming and expensive, and it might not be possible to attack as large number of fires simultaneously.

In understanding the effects of large fires upon climatic conditions, the only comparable scenarios we can look at are volcanic eruptions and forest fires. Krakatoa in the East Indies in 1883 caused a 20% reduction in the intensity of sunlight in France for several months. Benjamin Franklin writing from Paris in 1783 described the volcanic Mount Laki in Iceland as causing "a constant fog all over Europe and a great part of North America." Following the Indonesian Tambora volcano eruption in 1815, Europe and America experienced a year without summer, crops failed and many thousands died of starvation.

Major forest fires in Siberia in 1915 generated between twenty and forty million tons of smoke, depressing day-time temperatures by between 2 and 5°C over much of Siberia. In 1982 Alberta wildfires reduced average day-time temperatures in the north-central United States by 1.5°C to 4°C. In 1987 a series of large wildfires in southern Oregon and northern California reduced the normal day-time temperature by as much as 20°C by blocking out sunlight. Dr. Turco states: "The stable air over deserts also provides ideal conditions for fast cooling of land surfaces shaded from sunlight. You can see the effect every night in the desert, where temperatures fall further than in other environments."

British Minister for Energy, John Wakeham, was quick to dismiss the above scenario put forward by the scientists, stating that "suggestions of a global environmental disaster are entirely misplaced." An adviser in Wakeham's office was quick to point out that some members of Wakeham's staff did not agree with the minister's assessment and they would be grateful to have any data the scientists produced. Tam Dalyell, a British MP, released the disagreement to the press and Drs. Toukan and Barnaby, when questioned by the press, revealed the interesting information detailed below taken from tape recordings of a press conference on Saturday, January 5, 1991.

*Q. What do you feel about Mr. John Wakeham's comments in his statement?*

*Dr. Barnaby. I think one has to say that the British government has to keep the political pressure on Saddam Hussein, that's their job. It's our job as scientists to present what evidence there is, the best evidence, about the consequences of any action in the Gulf, so we are a bit at cross purposes. It's very difficult to know what the basis of this type of statement the minister made can be, because scientists do work on the basis of probabilities and what we are saying is that all of the effects we have mentioned have a probability of occurring. You can make judgements about the probability and the consequences of assessing them, but to deny that they are possible I think is absurd and I am sure that scientists in the Departments of Energy and Environment would not do that . . . What we are saying is that the effects we have mentioned are possible and even probable and that should be taken into account, because environmental costs should be taken into account when decisions are made about actions in the region. And it seems to me a very reasonable statement and I am rather surprised at the objection, although understanding it because clearly it is necessary from the government's point of view to keep up the political pressure.*

*Q. Do you think it's impossible for John Major to go against the advice of such a body?*

*Dr. Barnaby. Well from discussions we have had . . . with environmentalists, climatologists and so on across the world, I think I would be surprised if the scientists in the department would claim that the statements made by these people are not true. I think that as scientists they are bound to support scientific evidence presented by the world's best climatologists and so on.*

*Q. The minister says that the reserves underground will not be affected. What do you say to that?*

*Dr. Toukan. Well, certainly, you see Kuwait's reserves are something like 94 billion barrels. So yes, it would be a very small percentage of that, but if it burns in the atmosphere that would be catastrophic. And the point we are trying to make is that the battlefield is literally over the oilfield, so all the oil wells, the facilities, pipelines, storage areas, will all be within the vulnerable areas of any target, and all will be subject to destruction. And therefore if there is destruction of some of the wells and fires are lit, or the wells are mined, even if you take from the overall 750 wells and say 70 to 80% of them are put on fire, and then if you break the control valves, if you open up all the pipes and just let the natural flow of oil take its course, with the gushing out of the oil, you might have something like 10 million barrels a day — and over one year that's 3 or 4 billion barrels. Three or four billion as a percentage of 94 billion is nothing, so we are not saying that the proven oil reserves of the world will be depleted and the world will be left with no oil. No, we are talking about this small percentage, and what an impact it will have on the world, that's the way that we look at it.*

*Q. Now Mr. Wakeham said in his statement that very few of these oil wells will gush to the surface, the oil mainly comes up through being pumped to the surface.*

*and if the pumps are not working there is no problem. Do you disagree with that?*
*Dr. Toukan. Well, Dr. Barnaby and I just looked today, even to confirm, we looked at the OPEC statistical yearbook for 1989 — page 42. You can look at it and it tells you that out of the operating wells — there are something like 365 wells — 22 were of artificial lift and 343 were of natural flow. Now if my English is correct, artificial lift implies many techniques such as gas injection, etc. to produce the oil, and natural flow means under its own pressure, it just flows out.*
*Q. So he's got it wrong?*
*Dr. Toukan. You see none of us is an oil expert, we didn't go out and drill in these oilfields, nor did we go out and blow up an oilfield to see the consequences or the effect; but these are just pure scientific facts and figures that you apply basic physics and chemistry to, and using the references that one tries to get. And so we try to go to the source of those who would have the information, and the OPEC yearbook gave us the information as to the dispersion of the wells, the size of the fields, and the diameter of the pipelines, so we use that as a fundamental resource really.*

Wakeham was forced to modify his statements. It was admitted that the British Meteorological Office had been asked by the government to make an immediate assessment of the scientists' claims.

Their report, which appeared on January 14, was to confirm the scientists' claims by stating: "Close to Kuwait, the plume could cause a considerable reduction in daylight and day-time temperatures. . . . Downwind of Kuwait, the obscuration of sunlight might significantly reduce the surface temperature locally. This in turn could locally reduce the rainfall over parts of South East Asia during the period of the summer monsoon. . . . If the smoke reaches the ozone layer, the smoke particles and nitrogen oxides could lead to small reductions in ozone concentrations within the northern hemisphere." Dr. Richard Turco was approached at the same time by scientists from the Lawerence Livermore Laboratory in California, a government center for defense research, to collaborate on an investigation into the effects of fires in the Gulf. It must be noted here that it is apparent that neither the United States administration nor the British government had evaluated the likely environmental effects of war in the Gulf before they committed their troops into action.

To date the torching of hundreds of oil wells has produced thick black clouds of soot and smoke spanning over a thousand miles. By late March 1991, skiers reported that some two inches of black oily snow had fallen on the Himalayan slopes in Kashmir. Air pollution is causing respiratory problems, and doctors in both Kuwait and Iraq are seeing patients with breathing difficulties, boils, sore throats and diarrhea. A scientist from Kuwait's Institute for Scientific Research confirmed that the effects of the air pollution are carcinogenic, and along with other leading scientists and environmentalists has called for a mass evacuation of the area. Teams of fire-fighters have not proved as successful as Red Adair at first implied they might be.

## Oil Spillage

Scientists feared an oil spillage in the Gulf and to date we have seen the largest spill the world has ever known. At the second symposium, held in New York on January 11, Richard Golob from Cambridge, Massachusetts presented a comprehensive paper on the effects of oil spillage. Golob, who has undertaken numerous environmental consultation projects relating to oil pollution for many oil companies and inter-governmental organizations, has established the world's most comprehensive database on oil spill incidents from tankers, wells, pipelines and storage facilities.

"A series of well blow-outs could develop into the largest spill in history, quickly dwarfing that of the Exxon Valdez," he prophesied.

He pointed out that the Gulf is recognized as one of the most fragile eco-systems in the world and has not fully recovered from the environmental damage caused in the Iraq-Iran war. Its vulnerability and fragility has been recognized by international law and the region has Special Area Status under the IMO (International Maritime Organization) regulations. During the Iran-Iraq war, offshore well blow-outs in the Nowruz and Ardeshir fields caused oil to be washed along the coasts of Saudi Arabia, Bahrain, and Qatar and finally entered the territorial waters of the United Arab Emirates. The spillage caused desalination plants and industrial facilities to be temporarily shut down, fishing was disrupted and large numbers of sea turtles, sea snakes, porpoises and finfish died.

The United Nations Environment Program, Inter-Agency Consultations, held in Geneva on February 5-6, were unable to estimate the damage so far caused and the situation is currently being monitored by the Global Resources Information Database of UNEP, Geneva. The meeting recognized that the damage which has been and might be caused, could have serious consequences for a long time to come and could jeopardize appropriate development in the area.

To understand why, it is necessary to appreciate the special peculiarities of the Gulf sea. The Gulf is an almost entirely closed sea. It is roughly 600 miles long and 50 to 220 miles wide and any oil spill would remain trapped within the Gulf region before dissipating, and the currents would carry the oil around the Gulf coastline. The Gulf is also extremely shallow, with an average depth of about 110 feet, and even the deepest area near the Strait of Hormuz is only 325 feet deep. Many of the Gulf's renewable resources lie in waters whose depth is between five and ten yards. Coral reefs, mangroves and tidal flats are particularly sensitive to pollution. It is rich in marine life, producing over 120,000 tons of fish per year for human consumption. Although fishing is a multi-billion dollar industry in the area, it is also a subsistence activity for many people living along the Gulf coast. Any major spillage in the winter would disrupt the year's supply of shrimp, since the spawning season occurs in winter and spring. During the Nowruz well blow-outs in 1983, the spilled oil brought most commercial fishing operations in the Gulf to a halt and many of the dependent nations had to import fish from the Red Sea by air freight.

It is estimated that between one and two million birds winter in the Gulf and they would be at risk from any oil spillage. Spring brings increased numbers of birds who are passing through on their way north to their breeding grounds. Waders are the most important migrants, and Dr. Andrew Price from the Department of Biology at York University notes that: "evidence has now accumulated showing that inter-tidal flats function as vital feeding areas, or 'refuelling stations' for many migrating waders, and clearly play an essential role in the life cycle of these bird species." Dr. Price emphasized that the Gulf represents the breeding area for a large part of the world's tern population.

Green and hawksbill turtles are classified as endangered species in the International Union for Conservation of Nature and Natural Resources (ICUN) Red data book. Leatherback and loggerhead turtles are also encountered and use the offshore coral islands as their breeding grounds. Dugongs, the rather strange marine mammal, have an estimated population of between 3,500 and 7,500 and are classified as vulnerable in the ICUN Red data book. Whales, dolphins and sea-snakes also inhabit the sub-tropical waters. Any spilled oil would cause extensive damage to the many coral reefs, sand flats and seagrass beds along the southern Gulf.

Water is a precious and vital resource in the Gulf area and approximately 70 to 90% of the population rely on desalination plants for fresh supplies, since evidence shows declining ground water tables and reduction in surface water availability. The internal renewable water resource per capita in 1989 was under 2,000 cubic meters. Countries with under 2,000 cubic meters per person per year are considered to be chronically short of water. Therefore healthy marine environments are fundamental not only to marine eco-systems but to human populations as well. Any oil spillage naturally threatens desalination plants, power plants and industrial facilities, especially along the southern Gulf. Although booms are used to protect desalination plants, during the Nowruz spill the presence of spilled oil in the water intakes forced the temporary shutdown of several desalination facilities, including the plant at Al Khobar, Saudi Arabia, which produces five million gallons of water per day. Although the Saudi authorities had installed a barrier system of booms and nets, it failed to keep submerged tarballs from entering the water intake. The five knot current in the water intake caused the tarballs to entrain beneath the boom, and the current sucked so many jellyfish into the nets that the fabric began to tear.

Richard Golob comments: "Oil contaminated water would present serious problems to desalination plants using either multi-stage flash distillation or reverse osmosis. In multi-stage flash distillation plants, the volatile oil components would evaporate during the desalination process and pass into the drinking water product; they would also foul the heat transfer surfaces. In reverse osmosis facilities, even small concentrations of oil would cause irreversible damage to the reverse osmosis membranes."

It is vital to remember that the past fifty years have seen massive development in the Gulf region, as the proceeds of oil have been realized. All developed countries have been quick to take advantage of the region's rich oil resources, and as a result the area is already heavily polluted from human activity. In Saudi Arabia nearly 40% of the coast has been developed. Land reclamation, dredging, water pollution, air pollution, land filling and human recreation have all been very costly in environmental terms. Kuwait has the highest per capita income in the region and the results of human wealth on the area have not gone unnoticed. Beach tar levels were the highest recorded anywhere in the world before the invasion by Iraqi forces.

President Bush stated of Saddam Hussein's deliberate release of oil into Gulf waters: "It doesn't measure up to any military doctrine of any kind. It's kind of sick." Although we would all agree that the actions of President Saddam Hussein leave much to be desired, one can find military precedents for environmental damage on this scale, and other leaders should remember their indifference when scientists and environmentalists warned the world of the great environmental costs of war in the Gulf. No doubt we will see the green crocodile tears of those politicians who so fervently advocated a military solution, as some of the damage predicted comes into being.

As talk of a new world order emerges, it is evident that environmental considerations must be taken into account at the initial stages of conflict decision-making. The Scientific Task Force asserts that an environmental database would be a confidence building measure, and would take us nearer to that definitive environmental treaty that will put a stop to environmental carnage at the national, regional and international levels. Such a database could act as an international crisis management system in times of potential conflict and assist in damage assessment, monitoring and finding solutions.

Echoing the Prince of Wales, "If science has taught us anything in this matter, it is that the environment is full of uncertainty and it makes no sense to test it to destruction."

# 30

## Desert Sin: A Post-War Journey Through Iraq

*Louise Cainkar*

After the beginning of August 1990, when American troops were sent to the Gulf to counter the Iraqi occupation of Kuwait, our office — the Palestine Human Rights Information Center, International — was inundated with calls from individuals and groups seeking information on Kuwait, Iraq, the Gulf region, and the history of U.S. intervention in the area. We were unprepared, but had been solicited like other groups because our work on behalf of the human and national rights of the Palestinian people made us among the few Americans who knew anything about the Middle East and the Arabs.

As war in the Gulf became imminent, something that was sure to occur, our office proposed to initiate a new project called "Gulf War Aftermath," focusing on civilian casualties and economic disruptions caused by the war. During the last week of the war we received funding for this project from some Americans committed to the public's right to know what the U.S. government was doing in the region. I left for Jordan on March 2, 1991 and planned to visit Iraq and Kuwait. While I had an Iraqi visa prior to the war, I needed to obtain a Kuwaiti visa in Jordan. Despite various attempts, including a letter requesting Kuwaiti assistance in my efforts from the American Embassy in Jordan, and in the United States, through my senator and the Kuwaiti Embassy in Washington, the Kuwaitis refused to issue me a visa. As a result, the closest I came to an eyewitness view of the effect of the war on civilians in Kuwait was the presence of almost 200,000 recently-arrived Palestinians and Jordanians in Jordan who had fled Kuwait, and five Palestinians I met in the Red Crescent Hospital in Baghdad who had been escorted over the Kuwaiti border into the American occupation zone in Iraq by Kuwaiti forces, after being detained and tortured by them. Their bodies bore clear signs of torture — cigarette burns, welts and bruises.

Jordan itself was suffering economically as a result of the sanctions imposed on Iraq, which cost Jordan an immediate loss of 39% of its GDP and the loss of Kuwait as an export market and source of aid. The combination of both rendered 50,000 Jordanians jobless. An additional 56,000 families lost their remittance incomes from Kuwait, Iraq and other Gulf states. Jordan also bore the burden of sheltering and feeding more than one million war-related refugees. While most of the refugees had been repatriated to other countries by the time I arrived in March, some 200,000 of them were Jordanian citizens, arriving without money and with little prospect of finding work, adding more economic stress to this already bleak picture. Most of them wanted to return to Kuwait; it seemed unlikely that the Kuwaiti government would allow this to occur. Most were Palestinians, who were of course still being denied their right to return to their own country. Jordan was thus an economic and possibly a political time-bomb waiting to explode. According to the UNICEF report on Jordan issued in February 1991, the Gulf crisis "brought instant, widespread economic devastation, rising poverty, the threat of impending hunger, and hardship and health setbacks at the family level."[1] Little of this was highly visible when I was in Amman, but then Jordan looked like paradise compared to Iraq.

## Traveling in Iraq: Bombings and the Fuel Shortage

I left for Iraq on March 24 with a Jordanian Red Crescent Society convoy of relief goods purchased from donations collected by international non-governmental organizations. The Amman-based Gulf Peace Team, a voluntary organization comprised of individual experts and activists from around the world, was responsible for a significant part of this shipment and facilitated, along with the Jordanian Red Crescent Society, my initial and subsequent journeys. On the road between the Iraqi border and Baghdad I saw the first evidence of civilian war casualties — no less than 40 bombed out civilian cars and freight trucks and two buses laying on the side of the road, most of them between the border and the 200km road marker. The Jordanian authorities said 12 Jordanian truck drivers were killed on this road. In Baghdad I met a family that had tried to leave Iraq in the initial days of the war, found the border closed when they arrived, and were awakened while sleeping in the car, terrified by the sound of nearby bombing. They returned to Baghdad, deciding that if they were going to die, they might as well die in their homes. Nearly one month later, all female members of this family were killed in the Ameriyeh bomb shelter. According to accounts printed in The *New York Times*, the road was bombed and strafed by coalition forces, and occupants of vehicles were "fleeing for safety into the desert as warplanes screeched above them firing missiles and cannons."[2] As in the rest of Iraq, it is unknown how many civilians were killed on this road, which, except for small craters and cracked sections of pavement from exploding weaponry, was wider and in better condition than most U.S. Interstate highways.

About two hours driving distance from Baghdad, at the Hit/Ramadi interchange, we diverted off the main highway and took a two-lane road that passed through Ramadi and al-Falluja on the way to Baghdad. The highway's bridge over the Euphrates River had been blown up and, as I later saw, was passable only by small vehicles weaving in and out of gutted asphalt and concrete. The bridge on the road we were taking had also been bombed, but by the time we passed it was functioning with one lane open. This of course resulted in traffic jams, as one line of cars waited while another line passed in the opposite direction — even though traffic in Iraq was nowhere near its pre-war level due to the fuel shortage, accompanying rationing and high prices. On the other side of the bridge I saw the devastated section of the al-Falluja market hit by British bombs when they "missed" the bridge (which they subsequently hit). Although at street level the tightly connected concrete structures housed stores, above these interconnected rows of stores were three levels of apartments. Just after the bombing, the American press quoted the Iraqi authorities' figure of 100 civilian deaths from this bombing. Since I did not get out of our vehicle, I could not assess the accuracy of this figure.

The al-Falluja bridge was just the first of many bridges I saw in Iraq that had been blown up. My trip to Basra was considerably lengthened by difficulties in crossing over the Tigris and Euphrates and the Shatt al-Arab. All of the bridges between Kut and Basra had been destroyed by bombs, no doubt rendering travel to and from the south of Iraq impossible throughout the war, which inevitably aided in the starvation of Iraqi troops on the border, in the Basra area, and in Kuwait. In the aftermath of the war, along with severe fuel shortages, it hampered the movement of people and relief supplies. By the end of March when I visited the area, we were able to cross these sweeping bodies of water because craters had been filled in at a point where some of the bridge still stood (Amareh), or a temporary bridge had been erected on the base of the old one (Qurna), or, after a long detour on a sand road past burnt and overturned tanks and army trucks, a military pontoon bridge was in place, at the base of which young Iraqi children sold small packages of Ali Baba Iraqi dates (Shatt al-Arab/Basra). (The other main road from Baghdad to Basra passes through An Nasariya and the American occupation zone, which is why our driver did not take it.) The Iraqi authorities reported the destruction of 83 road bridges in Iraq by bombing.[3]

The main transportation problem in Iraq is not bridges, however, but the lack of fuel. Clearly, if all of Iraq's cars were on the roads, the delays at the crossable bridges would be miles long and Baghdad, where three of six bridges were completely unusable and where they used to say there were as many cars as people (4 million), would be one huge traffic jam.

In Iraq, fuel had been cheap and plentiful. Because of sanctions and the embargo on Iraqi exports, in force even after the occupation and war had ended, fuel was scarce and expensive. Fuel cost five Iraqi dinars (ID) per liter in Baghdad in March 1991 — at the official government rate of exchange this equalled $18 per liter. Before the Gulf crisis it had cost 90 fils/liter — a price increase of 5000% (1 ID = 1000 fils). Government rationing allowed each family 30 liters every 20 days. Fuel was also available in Baghdad on the black market, for those who could afford it. According to the Ahtisaari report on Iraq to the UN Secretary General (March 20, 1991), the minimum monthly wage in Iraq is 54 ID and the average civil servant's is 70 ID; doctors and professors I met made between 200 and 450 ID per month. Thus, a full tank of gas (12 gallons or 45 liters) would cost 270 IDs, or nearly four times the entire monthly salary of the average Iraqi civil servant. The fuel shortage was obviously severely limiting civilian travel, causing overcrowding on the limited public transport system (also affected by shortages), and rendering the transportation of food stuffs and commodities to regions of Iraq outside Baghdad extremely difficult. Every Iraqi vehicle I was in carried a siphoning hose; some also carried jerry cans of gasoline in their trunk. Although we had brought our own gasoline from Jordan, we often had to siphon it from one vehicle to another, depending upon which one we were using that day, and on trips outside of Baghdad, we carried our own full jerry cans.

In order to take a field trip from Kirkuk to Mosul (both in Iraqi Kurdistan) and then return to Baghdad, our team had to find a car and a driver. This was relatively easy since we possessed sufficient fuel to make the trip and get the driver, a medical doctor, back to Kirkuk. We filled his tank with gasoline and brought two jerry cans of 20 liters each. His car broke down about six miles outside of Kirkuk, as a result of a worn out and filthy gas filter, which highlighted another problem in Iraq affecting both civilians and public services, namely the lack of spare parts, another direct effect of the sanctions. When we gave up on repairing the problem, we had to hitchhike back to Kirkuk. The driver stayed with his car on this lonely road, near what we understood to be the only refinery in Iraq not bombed by coalition forces, because he knew if he left it there all of its parts would be gone when he came back. He would have to find someone to tow his car back to Kirkuk, a common sight on Iraqi roads, even among the military. We found a ride to the taxi stand in Kirkuk from the driver of a small pick-up truck in exchange for 20 liters of gasoline; without this, he said, he could only have taken us to the checkpoint outside of town. We told him he had to siphon it out of the car we had just filled up and abandoned on the road. When we reached the taxi stand in mid-afternoon, our main problem in getting a ride to Baghdad was convincing a driver that we had enough gasoline in Baghdad to get him back to Kirkuk. Coordinating drivers, vehicles and gasoline usually delayed each day's departure by at least one hour; and we were able to be efficient since we had fuel.

### Civilian Casualties: Unknown, but Most are Not Yet Dead

In Iraq, I quickly learned two things about assessing civilian war casualties. First, I learned that information about them was not centrally available. Iraq's top officials were preoccupied with military planning, intelligence, and re-planning after each essential facility, piece of equipment, or road was destroyed by bombing; war and the end of war; internal rebellions; and how to get essential services such as electricity restored, up to and through the time I was there. The next layer of officials had significant management and information problems due to the combination of sanctions and the destruction of Iraq's infrastructure, which had rendered centralized information gathering and central management of the country very difficult. Officials beneath them in the hierarchy, especially at the level of managers, directors and lower ranking government officials, were used to functioning in a fairly closed system that left them ill-prepared for responding to the sudden and immediate need of non-governmental organizations for aggregated and accurate statistical information. On a practical level, many types of data were not collected by institutions and government agencies because the immediacy of other problems obviously rendered data collection a secondary concern. For example, hospitals that received patients and corpses during the war were so busy coping with the lack of water, electricity and medicine, in addition to being short-staffed due to transport problems and fleeing personnel, that keeping a statistician or record-keeper on hand each day no doubt appeared frivolous at the time. On the individual level, the total destruction of the telephone and postal systems by coalition bombing meant that people often did not know whether their missing neighbors and relatives were dead or had left the area to flee the war. In Iraq, the unknown is what is most known.

The data collector must understand all these constraints and obstacles and try to discern among various levels of "informants" who in each situation is the best source of data and what their limitations might be. In addition to this, one had to learn to distinguish between destruction and deaths from the "big war," as I came to call it, and that resulting from the Shi'a and Kurdish rebellions and their suppression, not to mention old destruction from the Iran-Iraq war. All of these merge together at some point in the minds of Iraqis; they are all war-related and they all caused suffering to the people. This is especially the case concerning the rebellions and the army's efforts to put them down; most Iraqis I met saw this destruction as an integral part of the coalition war on Iraq — the rebellions were encouraged by Western powers to continue the destabilization of Iraq and to force the Iraqi government into more brutal encounters with its own people.

Second, I learned that perhaps unlike other wars the civilian casualties from this war had only just begun. Consequently, this by-product of war could not be analyzed in the same way as it had in prior wars. Decimation of the infrastructure of Iraq was the aim of coalition bombing, a goal achievable only with good intelligence and highly sophisticated technology and weaponry. It naturally follows that most of the civilian casualties of this war would result from this destruction, and not from direct hits on civilian areas. Similarly, it follows that analysis of the extent of civilian casualties requires consistent and possibly long-term follow-up, rather than one-time data collection. If one had traveled through Iraq, and especially Baghdad, without this awareness, expecting to see blown up buildings and assuming that the civilian deaths that had already occurred were the conclusion to the story of the war, the resulting impression would have reflected the use of the wrong analytical tools, not reality, and would have been highly inaccurate. Iraq was characterized by doom and gloom, but one could only sense this through osmosis — a slow, unconscious process of absorption. What was happening in Iraq in the aftermath of the war could not be imaged on a crisp photograph, nor was it easily articulated in the language we customarily use to describe war and its aftermath.

The successful achievement of the mission to destroy Iraq's infrastructure not only threw Iraq back at least 100 years, it forced every single Iraqi to search for a way to cope with the new circumstances of life: no electricity, no running water, reliance on contaminated water, food and fuel shortages, transportation problems, for many no work, no income and thus no food, unreliable or total lack of access to medical care and medicine, massive inflation, and a real severing of human relations as a result of the difficulties in communication both inside and outside the country. Iraq had been a highly developed, technologically sophisticated, and self-reliant country. After the war most Iraqis appeared to be in silent shock, trying to figure out how to accomplish the day's tasks — many struggled just to feed and clothe their families. Within a 45-day period they had gone from 1991 to the 19th century; the way things were done in January was not possible in March. We cannot underestimate the psychological and logistical toll of this on human beings, nor the human ability to survive despite these conditions. But biological contamination and famine are forces which no human can stop single-handedly, and which no society broken to pieces and without the proper tools to combat them can halt. This was Iraq.

Given this situation, assessment of civilian casualties that had already occurred and would occur in the future could only be accomplished through microscopic field work in different regions of the country, and within regions at the village and urban-neighborhood level. To assess civilian deaths caused directly by coalition bombing, one had to visit bombing sites, inquire from different sources how many were killed, total the numbers for these sites, inquire about other sites not seen, calculate a crude estimate, and add on a small figure to account for the unknown. To extrapolate to an entire country using this method is quite imprecise. Hospital visits were not very useful for obtaining a general picture of these types of deaths, because only a minority of the victims ever reached a hospital; those that did might be redundant to data collected on the site. Hospital visits were useful however for estimating post-war deaths and projecting future casualties resulting from the loss of the country's infrastructure, sanctions and the trade embargo. A general assessment of an area's employment rates and available goods and services — food, water, fuel, electricity and medical care, and their costs — was also essential to predicting future outcomes.

To begin accomplishing this rather large task, I made field visits to Baghdad, Karbala, Basra, Zubair — a town in the Basra region — and Kirkuk, part of Iraqi Kurdistan. I also visited eight hospitals in these various parts of the country. Obviously a thorough job would require far more time than I was able to spend in Iraq (about two and a half weeks in all), which renders this work more of a pilot study. Furthermore, as mentioned above, the final figure for civilian deaths was impossible to ascertain so soon after the end of the war. One could say with certainty only that the casualty figures would continue to rise exponentially unless conditions in Iraq were to change drastically very quickly. As the Iraqi Red Crescent Society's Dr. Ameed Abdul Hameed, who facilitated much of my field work in Iraq, told me: "You must stay at least until May; the real health catastrophe will begin as the temperatures start to rise."

## Civilian Deaths from Direct Bombing in Residential Areas

### Amariyeh

The first neighborhood I visited in Baghdad was Ameriyeh, the site of the Ameriyeh bomb shelter. The shelter is still standing, and viewed from some sides looks almost untouched. Its ten foot thick concrete sidewalls withstood the two bombs dropped by the U.S. military, which did not explode the building's structure but instead sealed all its exits and incinerated the people inside. Only the roof bore a large hole. At about 4:30am on February 13 the first bomb pierced through an air duct on top of the building; the civilians sleeping inside were startled awake, their blankets and bodies burning. They began running toward the exit doors. The second bomb came almost immediately afterwards, neatly dropped through the eyehole, and sealed the exit doors while fires raged inside. I met one of the few survivors of this bombing, who got trapped between the inner (concrete) and outer (metal bars) exit doors when the second bomb hit — burns were visible on her body, scars on her psyche. The only child of a divorced mother, she was orphaned when her mother perished in the shelter. Apart from her, I met only the families of the dead.

The neighborhood of Ameriyeh was characterized by black banners hanging on houses, listing the names of the victims from each family. Each person we met near the shelter had lost someone, most had lost every female and child in the family. One home behind the shelter was vacant — 15 family members had burnt to death in the shelter. Few houses were untouched by this tragedy and Ameriyeh had become primarily a neighborhood of men. Males over the age of 16, excluding old men, were prevented from entering the bomb shelter after the first few days of its use. The social chaos of having hundreds of young men and women sleeping in the same room did not suit Arab customs. Thus males were forbidden, a dictum reinforced by threats of immediate induction into the army if they tried to enter, I was told. In Ameriyeh, the people who were supposed to die if the neighborhood was bombed remained alive, and the people who were supposed to be protected from death were all dead. Many of those who remained alive would have preferred to be dead, as they had lost everything that had meaning to them; their wives, mothers, sisters and children.

It was still impossible to enter most of the shelter when I was there.

Civil defense crews were pumping out the water that was used to douse the raging fires inside. Hundreds of corpses remained trapped. Once the water was removed, chemicals were dispersed in an attempt to kill the fumes, bacteria, and insects that preyed on the bodies inside for more than a month. Flies the size of quarters were visible everywhere, and teachers at the neighboring school complained about them. Neighborhood residents said that at least 1,600 women and children were in the shelter when it was bombed, and that its capacity was 2,000. Less than 400 bodies were recovered on the first day after the bombing, all unrecognizable.

The Director of Yarmouk Surgical Teaching Hospital in Baghdad, Dr. Boghossian, told of how, when they learned of the shelter bombing, they prepared the hospital to be capable of handling 600 injured persons, expecting burn, and bone crush and fracture cases. Instead, they received lorries of corpses and about 30 burnt survivors.

*Residential Structures and Institutions*

I asked to see civilian areas hit by bombs in each part of Iraq I visited. The bombing of the Ameriyeh shelter clearly caused the largest number of civilian deaths in a single bombing incident. Other residential areas of Baghdad were also hit by coalition bombs. The Adhamiyeh neighborhood was struck by what residents assume to have been a British bomb on February 7 at 8:30pm. (In Baghdad, Iraqis assume that the British were inaccurate and the Americans on target; this is not the case in other parts of Iraq, where the bombing was either "imprecise" or random.) Residents say some forty civilians were killed when seven houses were destroyed and twelve others damaged in this area not far from the Adhamiyeh bridge, one of the six bridges linking the two sides of Baghdad straddling the Tigris River. The bridge was left standing. The home that directly took the bomb lost seven persons belonging to a Kurdish family. Their last tea pot was still standing amid the rubble. Apartments in the Sheikh Omar section of Baghdad, near a concentration of markets, office and government buildings were also destroyed by bombs. Initial Iraqi reports indicated sixteen deaths in this bombing. According to the Ahtisaari report, the Iraqi authorities estimated that 2,500 homes in Baghdad were destroyed or damaged beyond repair by coalition bombing.[4] If this was the case, I personally saw only a fraction of them.

All telecommunication and postal centers in Baghdad were hit by bombs, usually more than once. In the initial days of attacks on these centers, when a night staff still operated, most of the staff were killed, but we could not calculate a total number of these civilians. The al-Midan Post Office and Communication Center in Baghdad sits next to a 350 year old Armenian Catholic Church. Father Boudrian, pastor of the church, showed us the destroyed stained glass windows of this historic church. He said the neighboring Communication Center had been bombed on January 17, February 4, February 6, and February 14. Throughout Baghdad other government buildings were hit by bombs, often causing considerable damage to neighboring residential buildings; again, no confirmed count of deaths resulting from these attacks was available. I noticed while in Baghdad that glass windows stretching some six blocks outward from targeted buildings were destroyed.

A minimum estimate of known civilian deaths directly from bomb attacks in Baghdad would be about 1,800 based on what I saw and accepting the 1,600 figure for the Ameriyeh bomb shelter; the real figure could be at least 1,000 persons higher. If the figure of 2,500 homes destroyed in Baghdad is correct and only half of the inhabitants were in them at the time, this figure would increase by an additional 5,000 civilians, very conservatively assuming four persons per home. These figures do not include indirect but immediate deaths from bombing or deaths caused by coalition destruction of the country's infrastructure (see below). One case of a large number of physically indirect but immediate deaths occurred at Saddam Hussein Central Children's Hospital in the Mansour area of Baghdad. According to the Director, Dr. Qasim Ismael, some forty to fifty infants died at this hospital in the first days of the bombing as a result of the loss of electricity for incubators and the severe cold and lack of i.v. units in the basement, where mothers took their young children for safety. In the following days, nearly all patients evacuated this and all other Iraqi hospitals.

The southern Iraqi city of Basra and its surrounding district received the most bombs of any areas of Iraq I had seen. The bombing included communications centers, power plants, bridges, water treatment plants, water towers, a Pepsi bottling plant, shops, private establishments, and quite a few civilian residential areas. I personally visited five different sections of Basra where bombs had hit civilian homes; none appeared to be near obvious military targets, unless the Pepsi plant could be described as such. The dates of these bomb attacks ranged from January 18 through mid-February. Residents of the Ma'kel district of Basra say that some 400 civilians were killed there by bombing. In this district alone I saw three areas hit, each with from four to twelve destroyed houses. Hospital statistics for Basra city from the Ministry of Health show 681 civilian injury hospital admissions between January 17 and February 16, of whom 285 subsequently died. This of course reflects only a portion of civilians killed by bombs, as many never reach a hospital. While the Iraqi authorities reported less homes destroyed by bombs in Basra[5] than in Baghdad, this did not match the clearly more intensive and less precise nature of the bombing of Basra that I saw. This could reflect an underestimate of Basra due to poor communications between Baghdad and Basra, or an overestimate of Baghdad.

On the grounds of the Tahrir Teaching Hospital of Basra, abutting the Shatt al-Arab, is a large crater about twenty feet in diameter, a characteristic feature of places where coalition bombs landed on soil. Shrapnel from this bomb, which landed on January 26 at 7:30am, hit the sixth floor of the hospital and immediately killed four adult patients in the intensive care unit and one baby. Every window of the hospital was blown out, much of its medical equipment was rendered unusable, and many of the damaged ceilings collapsed when the hospital was jolted by further bombing in the area. All patients were evacuated from the hospital after the January 26 bombing, and it was still incapable of handling patients when I visited in late March. Based on these observations in Basra, which may have been limited, a very conservative estimate of civilian deaths directly from coalition bombing in Basra city would be 600.

The town of Zubair lies southwest of Basra, about halfway between Basra and the Kuwaiti border, and has a population of some 250,000. I saw three residential areas of Zubair and a school that had been hit by coalition bombs. One residential area was in the center of a thickly populated quarter where narrow streets cut through old homes attached to each other. Fifteen people were killed when a bomb destroyed six houses on January 18 at 10:30pm. The small number of victims can be accounted for by the fact that many people in this area fled the city at the beginning of the war. Doctors in Zubair estimate that about 200 civilians were killed in Zubair by coalition attacks. Other parts of the Basra district suffered similar hits on residential areas, rendering 1,500 a very conservative estimate of direct civilian deaths from bombing in this district.

My visit to Karbala, south of Baghdad, revealed the destruction of parts of Iraq wrought by the post-war rebellions and subsequent efforts on the part of the Iraqi government to crush them. Coalition bombing had touched little of Karbala, according to doctors there, but the center of town as well as al-Hussein Hospital were devastated by battles between Shi'a rebels and the Iraqi army. Residents said only that "thousands" were killed by the rebels and in the ensuing battles for control. Amareh in the south was also the site of rebellion and army/rebel battles. Since I merely passed through the town, I was only able to see that the main hospital, next to a bridge over the Tigris River, had been hit by a coalition bomb. Other parts of the southern tier of Iraq were hit by coalition bombs, but I was unable to visit them on my tight schedule. Press and eye-witness reports indicate that An-Nassariyeh was heavily hit and that on February 7 alone 150 civilians were killed; that 67 civilians died when a bridge over the Euphrates in Samawa was blown up; that a residential area of Hilla was "hard hit by bombs"; and that homes in the village of al-Haswa are bombed, resulting in 35–40 civilian deaths.[6]

I visited Kirkuk, a city in Iraqi Kurdistan, shortly after the Kurdish rebellion was crushed by the Iraqi army and around the time international attention became focused on the Kurdish refugees. Kirkuk showed far less destruction, from any source, than I had seen in either the south of Iraq or in Baghdad. According to doctors in Kirkuk, coalition bombing struck two residential neighborhoods in Kirkuk, killing a total of 72 civilians. Doctors at Kirkuk's Saddam Hussein General Hospital also reported that between 10 and 20 children and 80 adults died in the hospital during the war, some from bombing related injuries, some because power shortages made necessary medical equipment unusable, and some due to car accidents as people attempted to flee the city (this same phenomenon was reported by the director of Yarmouk Surgical Hospital in Baghdad). Reports from other parts of Iraqi Kurdistan note less coalition bombing in population centers than in other parts of Iraq, although the region's oil refineries were heavily attacked. Like other parts of Iraq in the aftermath of the rebellions, it was difficult for officials and medical personnel to focus only on civilian deaths that resulted directly from coalition bombing — the damage to the infrastructure, from which everyone suffered, the lack of water, food, electricity and fuel, and the damage wrought by the rebels and the army in putting them down, were at that time far more immediate.

Based on these field visits, where I observed damage from coalition bombings responsible for the deaths of a minimum of 2,700 civilians, and the eye-witness press reports for certain towns in the southern tier of Iraq I did not visit, we can account for a minimum of 3,100 civilians deaths as an immediate result of coalition bombing. The question then becomes, what part of the total do these represent? I believe they certainly represent no more than one sixth of the total and could represent as little as one fifteenth. This range could only be narrowed through follow-up site visits, which our office planned to undertake in the summer of 1991. Initially, I would conclude that a good estimate of the total number of Iraqi civilians immediately killed by coalition bombing is between 11,000 and 24,500.[7]

## Post-War Civilian Deaths: Biological Warfare and Impending Catastrophe

Post-war civilian deaths occurring as a direct result of the January–February 1991 coalition bombing of Iraq far outnumbered deaths occurring during the war. The primary target of coalition bombing was the Iraqi infrastructure; the loss of this infrastructure, especially in combination with sanctions and the embargo against Iraq which began in August 1990, resulted in extensive human losses from malnutrition and disease and threatened a health catastrophe once epidemic diseases began to spread across the population. The Iraqi medical system was unprepared to deal with the level of sickness among the population due to the lack of medicines and hospital supplies, compounded by shortages in electricity, uncontaminated water, and food, and was unable to take preventative steps for the same reasons. The final human toll of this war on the Iraqi population was impossible to assess before the long-term follow-up necessary for accurate data had taken place. In political terms this meant that the international community was likely to become aware of the extent of the loss of civilian life caused by the UN sanctioned war on Iraq long after popular interest in Iraq has faded. It would therefore be difficult for people to hold the participating countries responsible and to prevent further wars of this kind. In the initial post-war period, international attention was focused away from this slow process of delayed death, and support in the form of relief was abysmal. Politics and hunger were once again holding hands.

The infrastructure of Iraq existed primarily to support twentieth century civilian life. It provided Iraqis with clean running water, a sewage system, electricity, internal and external communication, food, fuel, transportation, health care, goods and services. Their daily lives were conducted, their possessions were manufactured, and their survival was structured around the assumption of this technology-based context. With all of this gone, everything was turned upside down. All 18 million Iraqis suffered in some way as a result of the war, not just those directly under the rubble of a bomb, and they will continue to suffer for a long time to come, most likely years. Tens of thousands will die if the conditions in Iraq are not quickly reversed. Such change is highly unlikely at the time of writing, especially with the embargo and sanctions still in place and the pitiful level of international relief.

The infrastructure was destroyed by the targeted bombing of the main turbines providing electrical power to different regions of Iraq, water purification plants and pumping stations, plants that produce chlorine and aluminum sulphites for water purification, oil refineries, oil storage facilities, seed, animal vaccine and other warehouses, and factories. In combination with sanctions and the embargo, which reduced available supplies of medicines, food, fuel, and spare parts before the war began, the health situation of the Iraqi people became a "slow-motion catastrophe" as Dr. Jack Geiger of Physicians for Human Rights put it.

By the end of April 1991 the primary health problems in Iraq were gastroenteritis, malnutrition, and dehydration. These problems resulted from the shortage of food, which reached near-famine conditions in certain areas, and the absence of potable water in most of Iraq. While all of these illnesses are normally treatable, the shortage of medicines, food and uncontaminated water throughout Iraq made them potentially lethal. Each children's hospital I visited in Iraq — in Baghdad, Basra and Kirkuk — reported 20–40 new admissions per day from these illnesses. The Director of Saddam Hussein Children's Hospital in Baghdad said that on average two children arrived there dead each day. All of these hospitals reported child mortality rates that were two to three times normal. In some areas doctors estimated that at best 10% of the population was able to reach a hospital due to the fuel shortage, which rendered transportation difficult and quite expensive. The poor state of the medical system and the difficulty and expense of transportation meant that many families held out on seeking medical care until the health of the sick person was in severe jeopardy. In the initial post-war period, at least 100 children died each day from these illnesses, probably many more. This equals a minimum of 6,000 Iraqi civilian deaths as a direct result of the war for the months of April and May. This figure excludes Kurdish refugees in the mountains of northern Iraq, whose status was being monitored by the U.S. government and international organizations. Dr. Richard Sandler of Rush-Presbyterian-St. Lukes Medical Center in Chicago said on April 16 that some 400 to 1,000 Kurds were dying each day during his visit in early April from food shortages and contaminated water. When the Kurds return to their towns and villages in northern Iraq they will find similar conditions, shared by the rest of the Iraqi people, especially those outside of Baghdad — contaminated water, food shortages and a crippled medical system — all caused or instigated by the army and governments who protected them in northern Iraq.

The food shortage in Iraq resulted largely from the sanctions imposed by the UN. Iraq imported 70% of its food prior to August 1990, when sanctions were imposed. After that date, the population had to live off existing pre-August stocks, minimal domestic production, and a small amount of international relief. During the war, some government food warehouses were bombed, as well as food production centers (the infant formula plant is one well-known example). Seed and animal vaccination warehouses and the only laboratory that produced animal vaccinations were also destroyed, thereby putting future domestic agricultural and livestock productivity in jeopardy. Harvesting the 1991 domestic crop faced serious obstacles due to the lack of water and power for irrigation, a shortage of fertilizers and pesticides, and the lack of fuel and spare parts for farm machinery.

According to the Ahtisaari Report, government stores of items such as flour, rice, powdered milk, sugar and tea were nearly depleted by mid-March 1991.[8] With government rations of these foods running out, Iraqis had to resort to market products, which were available only in scarce quantities in the south and the north and were increasingly difficult to find, even in the Baghdad area. Fresh vegetables, plentiful in Baghdad in March, were becoming scarce by mid-May. In fact, most Iraqis could not afford to purchase products on the market anyhow — scarcity drove their prices up to an unaffordable level. Some 90% of Iraqi industrial workers were unemployed at the beginning of May because of the destruction of factories and/or the shortage of fuel and electricity needed for production. Other employment sectors were also affected. At the same time, food products cost 20 to 60 times more than they did before August 1990. A tin of infant milk had cost 2 ID on the market; by April its price had risen to 60 ID. A kilo of rice had risen from 200 fils to 6 ID in Baghdad. Similarly, flour and sugar were 5–6 ID/ kilo (1 ID=$3: official government rate); a kilo of each of these three items would cost 17 ID, or the equivalent of one week's salary for the average civil servant. These three items alone and in these low quantities could not provide an Iraqi family with a healthy or adequate diet; adequate quantities and a balance of essential food items were out of reach for hundreds of thousands of Iraqi families. Transportation problems and a system of internal privilege further aggravated the food shortage, leaving sectors of the north and south of Iraq, and certain sub-groups within these sectors, facing near-famine conditions.

The scarcity of uncontaminated, piped water in most of Iraq was an outcome of both coalition bombing and sanctions. Some water treatment plants, pumping stations and holding towers were destroyed by coalition bombing. Others remained standing but had insufficient electrical power — due to the bombing of electrical power plants and stations — and a lack of chlorine, aluminum sulphate and other necessary chemicals — due to bombing of storage facilities and sanctions — to allow for water treatment and distribution. The use of standby generators proved difficult because of the fuel shortage — from the bombing of oil refineries and oil storage facilities — and many were non-functional due to the lack of spare parts. Where standby generators were functioning, concerns remained over their insufficient level of output and the absence of alternative generators should the operative one break down. Functioning generators needed to be brought from places where they were not essential to sites where they were needed, but identifying these sites, communicating this to a central authority, and transporting equipment from one area of the country to another remained difficult in post-war and post-rebellion Iraq.

Untreated sewage flowed directly into bodies of water that were the source of drinking water. Most of Baghdad had some running water by April, but in highly reduced quantities and at insufficient levels of purification, according to experts. The Ahtisaari Report noted that prior to the war Baghdad received 450 liters/person of clean water; in mid-March this figure stood at 30–40 liters/person in 70% of Baghdad. Purifying chemicals were added at inadequate levels due to a dwindling supply of chemicals, but were increased after the water authority received promises of aid from UNICEF and ICRC (International Committee of the Red Cross). The report also noted that tests of the water quality and its bacteriological content were not being performed due to the lack of necessary power, chemicals and reagents.[9] In April, people in Baghdad were still being told to boil their drinking water. Hospitals in Baghdad were using water brought in by truck or on-site water-treatment facilities donated by international organizations to provide clean water; hot water was still rare in Baghdad.

Except for hospitals, it was a rare experience to find running water in any other place I visited in Iraq. Where I found it, it was unsafe for drinking, and intermittent. The landscape of southern Iraq is characterized by rivers, streams and marshes. Water seemed to be almost everywhere, but it was contaminated. In the Basra area it was common to see people washing their clothes and collecting water for their home from these contaminated waterways. Some were cooling off by dunking themselves in the water, and this was before the air temperature really began to rise. In the north it was also common to find women washing clothes and filling containers with water from rivers and streams. The lack of clean, running water has resulted in abnormally high levels of diarrhea, dehydration, other gastrointestinal problems, and malnutrition among Iraqis, especially children, and a dramatic increase in the infant mortality rate.

But the real catastrophe from the lack of running, potable water was expected to begin in May, when temperatures start to soar up to 130 degrees Fahrenheit (54 degrees Celsius). The population's need for water soars with the temperature and the likelihood of drinking contaminated water increases, further poisoning and weakening the population. In addition, these hot temperatures provide fertile conditions for the growth of bacteria, resulting in the likely spread of epidemic diseases, such as cholera, typhoid, meningitis, and hepatitis. Cases of cholera and typhoid had been clinically diagnosed in most parts of Iraq by April. This is the "slow motion catastrophe" Dr. Geiger referred to.

The water crisis produced other health problems, as evident from visiting Iraqi hospitals. Most Iraqi homes had a small kerosene burner on which water was boiled and food was cooked. These burners were also necessary in institutions because there was insufficient fuel and electricity to run other types of stoves, whereas kerosene was more available. Should kerosene supplies run out, even cooking and boiling water would be impossible for many Iraqis. It was common to see children in hospital surgical wards suffering from burns over their entire body from knocking over the kerosene stoves. Doctors said they had almost nothing with which to treat these patients, and could not even consider the eventual skin grafts which would be necessary. An increasingly sick population was being thrust upon an effectively paralyzed medical system.

I visited hospital after hospital characterized by severe shortages of medicines, milk and food, short supplies of clean water, and variable levels of electricity — some had it nearly 24 hours per day while others had it for only a few hours per day and/or in certain areas only (depending upon the capacity and fuel supply for existing back-up generators). Many hospitals were not functional at all, either because all of the windows had been blown out and the structures had been damaged from direct or nearby coalition bomb hits, or because they had been pillaged and ransacked during the post-war internal rebellions, and damaged again by the Iraqi army trying to rout the rebels. The town of Zubair in the Basra district had no functioning medical system at all when I visited it in late March. The main hospital had been damaged beyond use by some combination of bombing, rebel destruction, and Iraqi army fire. All of the town's available outpatient clinics were without medicine. At the request of one of the local doctors, we transported a woman and her three daughters, the infant obviously at an advanced stage of malnutrition, to the Jumhouriyya hospital in Basra. The doctors I was with were not optimistic about the baby's prognosis. This family reported that it had not eaten a solid meal for over a week. This made me wonder how many other children would die because they simply had no access to medical care, and no available means of transport to obtain it.

Upon arriving at Jumhouriyya hospital in Basra, the same scene I was to see over and over again emerged — Iraqi women holding thin, bloated and malnourished children, fanning them from the ever increasing heat. Doctors said that because laboratory analyses were impossible, their diagnoses were based on a clinical assessment of symptoms. For example, everything appearing to affect mainly the gastrointestinal system was called gastroenteritis. It was impossible to confirm diseases such as cholera and typhoid. This shortcoming was common to all Iraqi hospitals I visited, although by May laboratory testing was possible in Baghdad and hospitals had been instructed to establish isolation wards for cholera cases.[10] Doctors reported that in cases of malnutrition, only the attached symptoms of diarrhea and dehydration could be dealt with in hospital; the malnutrition itself could not.

Patients were treated for a maximum of three days, during which doctors attempted to halt the diarrhea and dehydration, only to be returned home to the same conditions of contaminated water, shortages of food, and increasing heat which caused the problems in the first place.

All hospitals reported shortages of medicines and supplies. The most common shortages, appropriate to the hospitals' immediate medical needs, were: infant formula, milk powder, intravenous antibiotics and fluids for treating diarrhea and dehydration, and scalp vein needles for children. But the lists were far longer than this, signaling fairly depleted medical supplies in many hospitals. Doctors stressed that a consistent source of pure water and electricity was essential to the delivery of proper medical care and the lack of it was seriously hampering their effectiveness. The lack of sufficient power also rendered central heating and air conditioning impossible. Doctors worried about the capacity of the healthy, let alone the sick, to survive the extremely hot temperatures which characterize Iraq in the summer. Before the war, Iraq had communicable diseases under control due to a large scale vaccination program. In mid-April supplies of vaccines were virtually non-existent because of sanctions and infrastructure destruction — pre-war stocks of vaccines were destroyed from lack of refrigeration.

Because of all these problems, Iraqi hospitals had been admitting emergency cases only since the beginning of the war. Surgical interventions, or "cold cases" had to wait until the situation normalized, an unpredictable date. The main surgical hospital in Baghdad, the 700-bed Yarmouk Hospital, had just begun admitting some cancer malignancy cases at the end of March. Dr. Boghossian, director of the hospital, which was clearly in better shape than most of those in Iraq, said, "we dare not carry out non-emergency surgery under these conditions, and expose the patients to the great risks of infection that exist." During the war, although Yarmouk Hospital remained open, it was without any electricity for the last two weeks of January and for nearly one month had no water supply, until it was brought in by truck. It began powering itself with two generators, but still had to economize due to the fuel shortage. For the remainder of the war electricity was switched on only when and where it was needed for surgical intervention and to treat serious injuries. The fuel shortage also affected staffing for the hospitals. Yarmouk Hospital switched to a staff rotation system whereby each staff member would work continuous two to three day shifts and sleep at the hospital. In April hospital directors still had beds in their offices for overnight stays. They knew that the worst was yet to come for the Iraqi people and that the burden on crippled hospitals would only increase.

In sum, sanctions and war created a biological and health disaster in Iraq. The destruction of Iraq's infrastructure by coalition bombing and the imposition of sanctions transformed a relatively healthy population into a sick one, denied proper medical care and nutrition. Creating sickness and then preventing a return to health, the outcomes of the two-tiered offensive against Iraq, are so directly related that they suggest well-planned and intended goals. The image evoked is a straight line that leads from health to hunger to sickness and then to death, faster for some, slower for others. Civilian deaths from these causes, averaging at least 3,000 per month since the war ended, will far outnumber those that occurred during the war. These deaths, however, are not indirect by-products of the war; they are a direct result of the type of warfare used. Surgical precision destroyed the brain of Iraq and the body was left to die. A new level of inhumanity, brought about by the development of weapons of precision, has been achieved.

Shortly after returning from Iraq I saw an advertisement in the *New York Times* for the Northrop Corporation — "people making advanced technology work." Its selling point was the beauty and precision of the Stealth bomber, and more importantly that "stealth saves lives." This myth was flatly contradicted by at least 20–30,000 Iraqi civilians who had died by the end of May 1991 as a direct result of the war, whether crushed by structures collapsing from bombing, incinerated in a bomb shelter, or devastated by starvation and disease. Thousands of Iraqi civilians will continue to die each month until sanctions are lifted — a necessary condition for reconstruction of the infrastructure and replenishment of food and medicine — each one bearing further testimony to the proposition that U.S. bombers, stealth or otherwise, did not save lives. They only introduced a new kind of killing, one that is delayed and prolonged.

"(N)othing we had seen or read had quite prepared us for the *particular form of devastation* which has now befallen the country" began the Ahtisaari Report on Iraq to the UN Secretary General (emphasis added). Six months of dying can now result from ten days of killing, with the added benefit of little damage to residential structures. Death and suffering are less visible to the naked eye; feelings of responsibility can be minimized. A society in which such deceptive claims can be made with ease, reflecting popular assent to the military and government-fed depiction that the war against Iraq was quick and clean, and caused little civilian death, is a society which is in danger of relinquishing the last remnants of its democratic ideals. If the new war machines are alleged — and believed — to be people-safe, we must wonder how much easier each successive U.S. conquest will be to sell domestically.

There was little public challenge to the "clean war" image, because the mainstream media, at least in the United State, provided little information that would put this image in question. Few reports discussed post-war conditions in Iraq or the effects of war and sanctions on the Iraqi civilian population. Attention was instead riveted on the Iraqi Kurds, who at the instigation of the Bush administration led a post-war rebellion against the Iraqi government, only to be crushed by the Iraqi army and sent fleeing into the northern mountains. Their living conditions, suffering, and deaths from gastroenteritis, diarrhea, dehydration and malnutrition, were the topics of long daily news reports in April and May. As for the rest of the Iraqi population, they simply did not exist.

I was amazed upon return to the U.S. to hear Americans of different social classes and ethnic groups speak spontaneously and with such sympathy about the Kurdish people. (They were actually only speaking about Iraqi Kurds; the status of the rest of the Kurdish people was not conveyed in the information package.) I had never before witnessed such unanimity of compassion about any Middle Eastern people apart from Israelis. But like most Israelis, Kurds are not Arabs, which is part of the reason why they have proven useful for regional destabilization programs directed from the West. Western governmental and non-governmental relief efforts for the Kurdish people were massive, hundreds of charities took up collections for them, and a Kurd Aid concert took place in May 1991.

Given the one-sided character of the Western press coverage of post-bombing Iraq, it is not surprising that popular attention focused on the Kurds; the tragedy befalling that people, betrayed once again by Washington, was bitter. But what was ignored was the equally bitter plight facing the rest of Iraq's population, who were dying from the very same diseases the Kurds were, caused by impure water, inadequate food, etc.

Relief ships bound for Iraq were still impounded by U.S. forces in the Red Sea, months after the war had ended. While every post-war investigative report on Iraq called for immediate drastic relief efforts and loosening of sanctions in order to avert further catastrophe in Iraq, relief efforts remained minimal and sanctions remained largely in place. The total amount of food relief reaching Iraq between August 1990 and April 1991 equalled 10,000 metric tons, enough to provide one breakfast for each of the 18 million Iraqi people.

We were told repeatedly by George Bush and other political and military leaders of the coalition forces this war was not fought against the Iraqi people. The video tapes shown on the evening news of smart bombs homing in on buildings and bridges reinforced this impression. But it is difficult to see how the Iraqi people were not the intended victims of this campaign, which combined sanctions and infrastructure destruction, insisted on the continuation of sanctions well after the occupation of Kuwait and war had ended, obstructed relief efforts, and diverted popular sentiments to another set of victims — all of this with full knowledge that innocent civilians were dying each day in large numbers.[11] The questions to be asked are simple: who was left without clean water, food, and electricity, who could not obtain adequate health care, and who were dying since the war ended? Who suffered from inadequate relief and the continuation of sanctions? The answer is Iraqi civilians, mostly children. Was the strategy to starve the Iraqi population into rebellion in order to overthrow President Saddam Hussein?

Even months after the end of the war, on May 20, President Bush announced that sanctions would continue. "We don't want to lift these sanctions as long as Saddam Hussein is in power," he said. The consequences for the Iraqi population of this position remained of little concern to U.S. officials. Deputy national security adviser Robert Gates, nominated by Bush to head the Central Intelligence Agency, stated the day before Bush's comments that "Iraqis will pay the price while he [Saddam Hussein] is in power."[12]

The new world order is one in which the inhumanity of disease and starvation can be induced where they did not exist before, in a relatively short period of time, by the products of human creation. It is one in which entire populations can be rallied behind a lie, while at the same believing they live in a free and democratic society; where intelligent people can be convinced that wearing yellow ribbons and waving flags are more important than human life; and where children are intentionally left prey to disease and starvation while those unable to see with their own eyes are told that lives have been saved. Desert Shield and Desert Storm have culminated in Desert Sin.

## Afterword

I had traveled from Amman to Baghdad with an 18 year old Palestinian from Ameriyeh named Ghasssan Khader. Ghassan's mother and four sisters were killed in the Ameriyeh bomb shelter. Except for his father, a professor of soil chemistry at the University of Baghdad with no citizenship, the rest of the family were Jordanian citizens and the Jordanian Red Crescent was facilitating his travel to and from Iraq. He was carrying with him enlarged photos of his sisters (Ghana, 10, Ghaida, 14, Abir, 17, and Ghada, 21) and his 47 year old mother (Adiba), to hang in their memory in the home that now housed only he and his father. Ghassan had invited me to visit and one day I took a taxi to Ameriyeh hoping they were home, wondering on the way how I could walk through the neighborhood of Ameriyeh if they weren't.

When I arrived at Ghassan's house, he and his father were washing clothes (the Ameriyeh neighborhood had had some of its water restored by this time), something I was sure they had not done before. With no relatives in Iraq, these men were now on their own. Professor Mohammed Khader was born in a village near Ramle, became a refugee when the State of Israel was declared in 1948, lived first in the Gaza Strip and then in the West Bank, where he met his wife, a graduate of Beirut University from Beit Sahour and an elementary school teacher in Iraq. They had moved to Iraq from Libya, where Mohammed had received a Masters Degree in soil geology, because Adiba had asthma and could not tolerate the climate in Libya. "Now we have nothing," Mohammed told me, his will to live gone. He showed me photos of his daughters and wife and then their rooms, clothes and possessions. He said this was the first time he had been able to touch these items. The day after the bombing he had attempted to set his house on fire, with himself inside of it. A neighbor had stopped him.

The scene in Mohammed's home was so unbearably painful for me and for them that I could not adequately reconstruct it and knew I would remain scarred by this awful memory. I knew then that saying I was sorry was totally insufficient. I was surprised that despite my years of human rights work and all that I had seen before, I could only respond with tears. After the woman who survived the shelter happened by the house and joined us, my tears shifted to streams. I said only that I had opposed the war from the start. I wondered if the millions of Americans who supported this war, waving flags and yellow ribbons, would feel differently about it if they were sitting in this room. An Iraqi-American bringing relief supplies to the Iraqi people had told me at a truck stop near the Jordanian border town of Ruweished that many Americans had donated to their relief fund, thus showing that "America is a great country"; I begged to differ with him.

Professor Khader and his son Ghassan wanted to leave their home, Iraq and the Middle East — because the memories haunted them; they were tired of running from one tragedy to another. Mohammed told me he could not look or pass in the direction of the bomb shelter, just blocks from his home. He knew the burnt corpses of his family lay there. But Professor Khader had no passport and no citizenship; he had only an Egyptian travel document for Palestinian refugees, which even Egypt would not recognize. He could go nowhere. I promised to try and find someone who could help get him travel documents and a job to begin a new life in another country.

Was the bomb shelter a military target, a command and control center, as the American authorities initially alleged and American lay experts so quickly confirmed? Shortly after the bombing it was revealed by the American press that in fact the American military authorities bombed the shelter not because it was a command and control center but because they had received intelligence information that Saddam Hussein and his inner circle were sheltering inside. They were not. Residents of the neighborhood say that the 22 shelters in Baghdad had been closed to the public when the war first began. Some thought that the government may have been moving documents into them to prevent their destruction. When the Ameriyeh shelter opened to the public, which they said was in the second week of the war, it was used solely for civilians; some 20 military personnel were in it in the role of shelter supervisors and staff. They said that they listened to the Voice of America radio station, which informed them that only military targets would be hit. They had no reason even to consider that this bomb shelter would be the target of an attack; otherwise, their families would never have gone there. In any case, the high-tech American reconnaissance planes were certainly capable of ascertaining that this shelter was used by hundreds of civilians. That the American military authorities did not bother to do so leaves the ultimate responsibility in their hands.

## Notes

1. *Jordanian Children in the Eye of the Storm*, UNICEF, February, 1991.
2. "More Air Raids on Road to Jordan," Alan Cowell, *New York Times*, February 1, 1991.
3. *Report to the Secretary-General by Under-Secretary General for Administration Martti Ahtisaari*, United Nations (S/22366), March 20, 1991.
4. Ibid.
5. Ibid.
6. "Baghdadis who Fled Find No Safety From Bomb," (Reuters), *New York Times*, February 4, 1991.
7. These figures were arrived at as follows: $(1,500 \times 6) + 1,600$ (Ameriyeh) $= 10,600$, rounded to 11,000 to account for error, $(1,500 \times 15) + 1,600 = 24,100$, rounded to 24,500 to account for

error. I used the neighborhood residents' figure for the Ameriyeh shelter, assuming that neighborhood residents have no inherent interest in overestimating. The Iraqi government did not have an official figure for Ameriyeh; in any case, I avoided using any official government figures. Multiple sources confirmed 2,000 as the shelter capacity. Totals were rounded upwards to account for the lack of complete data for each site I visited.

8. *Report to the Secretary-General by Undersecretary General for Administration Martti Ahtisaari*, United Nations (S/22366), March 20, 1991.

9. Ibid.

10. *Report of the Special Mission to Iraq: Health Assessment Team*, Gulf Peace Team, April 30, 1991.

11. The WHO/UNICEF Special Mission to Iraq estimated that there were about 750,000 Iraqi children under one year of age and 3,600,000 under five years. They also estimated that there were some 750,000 pregnant Iraqi women (WHO: 91; 6). These groups are the most vulnerable to malnutrition, infection and disease. See *Special Mission to Iraq Team Report*, WHO/UNICEF, February 1991.

12. "Bush Links End of Trading Ban to Hussein Exit," Patrick E. Tyler, *New York Times*, May 21, 1991.

# Chronology

## 1869

Suez Canal and powered river transport open up Mesopotamia to international trade (SI).

## 1912

The Turkish Petroleum Company is formed (with British, Dutch and German participation) and acquires the concession to prospect for oil in the Ottoman provinces of Baghdad and Mosul (SI).

## 1914

**November** British troops land at Shatt al-Arab to protect the Anglo-Persian oil installations at Abadan (SI).

## 1916

Sykes-Picot Agreement is secretly signed by Britain and France, dividing the Middle East into spheres of influence after the fall of the Ottoman empire.

## 1917

**March** British capture Baghdad (SI).

## 1918

**October** Mudros Armistice. British capture Mosul.

## 1920

**April** In the San Remo Agreement the League of Nations awards Britain the mandate for Iraq (SI).
**June** Turkey accepts the Treaty of Sevres, which promises an independent Kurdistan, but it is never ratified (SI).
**July–October** Revolt in Iraq against British mandate (SI).

# 1921

British colonial commissioner Sir Percy Cox draws the lines on the map that demarcate the future Iraq from the future Jordan, Saudi Arabia and Kuwait; the agreement denies Iraq any significant access to the Persian Gulf. The sons of Hussein, the sharif of Mecca, Abdallah and Faisal, are made kings of Transjordan and Iraq respectively.

# 1929

Turkish Petroleum Company becomes a consortium of Anglo-Iranian, Shell, Mobil and Standard Oil, known as Iraq Petroleum Company, with British, Dutch, French and U.S. participation (SI).

# 1932

Iraq is granted formal independence as a state from the British. British air bases remain, however.

# 1936

**October** First military coup d'etat in Iraq, led by Bakr Sidqi (SI).

# 1946

**January–December** Kurdish republic of Mahabad (SI).

# 1951

Iraqi Ba'ath Party founded (SI).

# 1953

In Iran a CIA-backed coup overthrows the nationalist government of Prime Minister Mohammed Mossadegh, who had nationalized the Anglo-Iranian Oil Company, and installs the pro-Western Shah Reza Pahlevi monarchy.

# 1955

The Baghdad Pact is signed (SI).

# 1958

**July 14** A group of Communists, nationalists and Nasserists overthrows the British installed regime in Iraq, which ends U.S. attempts to incorporate Iraq into a pro-Western alliance structure.

# 1961

Britain grants Kuwait its formal independence on June 19. A week later Iraqi leader Qasim declares that Kuwait belongs to Iraq; British and Arab League troops are deployed in defense of Kuwait.

# 1 9 6 3

**February 8** Ba'ath nationalist coup d'etat. Ten thousand killed in one week. Nine months of bloodshed (SI).
**November** Military-nationalist coup d'etat ousts the Ba'athists (SI).

# 1 9 6 8

**July 17** Bloodless coup returns Iraq to Ba'athist control with Ahmad Hassan al-Bakr as president; Saddam Hussein becomes assistant secretary general of the party.

# 1 9 7 2

**June** Nationalization of Iraq Petroleum Company (SI).

# 1 9 7 5

**March 6** The Shah of Iran and Saddam Hussein, now vice-chairman of Iraq's Revolutionary Command Council, sign Algiers Accord that gives Iran territorial border concessions in return for Iran closing its border to and withdrawing aid from Kurdish guerillas who had mounted a large-scale rebellion in northern Iraq in 1974.

# 1 9 7 9

**February 11** Iranian Revolution ends reign of the Shah, a key U.S. military and economic ally in the Persian Gulf area, and an Islamic revolutionary regime led by Ayatollah Khomeini assumes power.
**March 26** Egypt and Israel sign formal peace treaty cementing the Camp David Accords signed in September 1978; Egypt is ostracized by the Arab League, which imposes diplomatic and economic sanctions on Egypt; Iraq begins to emerge as a power in the region.
**July 17** Iraq's President al-Bakr is forced to resign; Saddam Hussein assumes formal governmental power as president, secretary general of the Ba'ath party and chairman of the Revolutionary Command Council (RCC) and purges leading state and party officials.
**November 4** Iranian students occupy U.S. embassy in Tehran and seize documents and diplomats.
**November** Israeli Prime Minister Begin announces that Israel has given Iran military equipment and spare parts since the revolution (AFD, p. 359).
**November 20** Hundreds of well armed Islamist guerillas seize the Grand Mosque in Mecca and denounce the Saudi regime while demanding the establishment of an Islamic republic and the severing of all ties with the U.S..
**December 24** Soviet military intervenes in Afghanistan.

# 1 9 8 0

**January 23** President Carter issues the "Carter Doctrine" in State of the Union Address which asserts that any attempt by an outside power to gain control of the Persian Gulf region would be considered an assault on the vital interests of the U.S..
**April 26** President Carter orders abortive Desert 1 rescue attempt to free American hostages held in Iran.
**June** U.S. signs agreement with Oman which allows the U.S. military to use Masira island base in Arabian Sea and to rebuild airfields and storage facilities near the mouth of the Strait of Hormuz for possible U.S. military use and exercises (MER, 5/85 IA, p. 265).
**September 12** In Turkey a military led coup overthrows government and installs pro-U.S. dictatorship.
**September 22** Iraq invades Iran after months of reported border skirmishes, threats and accusations between the two governments.
**September 30** U.S. sends AWACS reconnaissance planes to Saudi Arabia.

# 1981

January 20  President Ronald Reagan is inaugurated on the same day as the fifty-two American hostages in Iran are released after 444 days in captivity.

January 31  France authorizes first deliveries of 60 Mirage F1 fighter planes to Iraq under pressure from French business lobby created for Iraqi military contracts (MER 9/87).

March  U.S. Secretary of State Alexander Haig discusses possibility of improved U.S.-Iraq relations in testimony to Senate foreign relations committee.

April  U.S. and Saudi Arabia sign $8.5 billion deal for Saudi purchase of 5 AWACS which includes provisions for U.S. "overbuilding" of Saudi air bases to accommodate possible U.S. military deployment (MER, 9/87). Sale is lobbied through Congress by (ret.) General Richard Secord and includes the terms for further Saudi paybacks in support of "Reagan Doctrine" in Central America, Afghanistan and Angola (ICC, p. 14).

April  U.S. Deputy Secretary of State Morris Draper is sent to Baghdad as part of Alexander Haig's attempt to promote a regional "strategic consensus."

June 7  Israeli air force destroys Iraqi nuclear facility at Osirak, Iraq.

July 18  Plane crash on Turkish-Soviet border is found loaded with U.S. and Israeli made weapons in transit from Israel to Iran (N, 6/20/87).

September  Iranian forces break Iraqi siege of Iranian city of Abadan and begin offensive to force Iraqi army out of Iran.

October 1  U.S. Rapid Deployment Force (RDF) in Persian Gulf is officially established to prepare for possible U.S. intervention in the Persian Gulf region (MER, 9/87).

October 6  Members of *Tanzim al-Jihad* (The Holy War Organization) assassinate Egyptian President Anwar Sadat.

November 30  U.S. Defense Secretary Weinberger and Israeli Defense Minister Sharon sign an official Memorandum of Understanding on "strategic cooperation" between the U.S. and Israel that is suspended when Israel officially annexes the Syrian Golan Heights in December.

# 1982

February  U.S. Defense Secretary obtains Saudi Arabian approval to form a joint Saudi-American Military Committee to facilitate military cooperation (LW, p. 78).

February  Syrian forces brutally put down a Muslim Brothers rebellion in Hama killing thousands and destroying much of the city.

March  U.S. removes Iraq from list of nations sponsoring international terrorism in order to exempt Iraq from American trade restrictions (IA, p. 263).

April  Egypt, with U.S. approval, agrees to supply Iraq with $1.5 billion worth of military equipment in exchange for Iraq's easing its boycott against Egypt, upgrading diplomatic ties and increasing economic interaction (CSM, April 14, 1982). Syria cuts off all Iraqi exports including Iraq Petroleum Company oil pipelines through Syria (IT, p. 8).

June 4  Israel invades Lebanon in what is called "Operation Peace for Galilee."

June 6  UN Security Council passes Resolution 509 demanding Israel withdraw all its military forces immediately and unconditionally to the internationally recognized borders of Lebanon.

July 13  Iran rejects UN Security Council Resolution 514 calling for a ceasefire in the Iran-Iraq war and withdrawal of both sides to international borders and launches its own offensive into Iraqi territory near Basra (LW, p. 289).

July 21  Israeli Ambassador to the U.S. Moshe Arens tells the *Boston Globe* that Israel had furnished arms to Iran "in coordination with practically the highest echelon of the American administration in order to [encourage] a conspiracy against Khomeini" (BG, 7/21/82).

August 25  President Saddam Hussein meets with U.S. Rep. Solarz and says he recognizes Israel's "need for a state of security" and says that "no Arab leader has now in his policies the so-called destruction of Israel or wiping it out of existence" and makes overtures to accept U.S. presence in the region (LW, p. 119).

October  U.S. Secretary of State George Schultz meets with Tariq Aziz in Paris to discuss Iraq-U.S. relations.

December  U.S. begins to extend Iraq agricultural credits for purchase of U.S. goods and furnishes Iraq with a $450 million low interest loan (IT, p. 96).

# 1983

**January 1** Pentagon creates U.S. Central Command (USCENTCOM) to encompass Persian Gulf Rapid Deployment Forces within a larger regional military command structure.

**January** USSR takes higher profile in arms deliveries to Iraq (worth about $2 billion) since it halted arms sales to Iraq a short time after the Iraqi invasion and its overtures to Iran had come to naught (IT, p. 95).

**February** Iran launches offensives in Iraq to capture the Basra-Baghdad road.

**October** France delivers to Iraq five Super-Etendard fighter aircraft capable of firing Exocet anti-ship missiles.

**October 23** Two truck bombs explode killing 319 U.S. and French soldiers in marine barracks in Beirut.

**October 25** U.S. invades Grenada.

**November 29** U.S. signs improved "strategic accord" with Israel which calls for combined U.S.-Israeli military planning and positioning of U.S. equipment in Israel as well as increased military and technological assistance to Israel (MER, 11/84).

# 1984

**January** U.S. State Department includes Iran on its list of countries sponsoring international terrorism.

**March 21** UN investigations confirm that Iraq is using chemical weapons against Iranian troops.

**April** Iraq escalates oil tanker war in Persian Gulf, Iran retaliates by hitting ships serving Saudi and Kuwaiti ports in lower Gulf in May; U.S. is rebuffed in offer to Saudi Arabia, Bahrain, and Oman to provide air cover to the Gulf states against possible Iranian attack in return for land basing rights (MER, 9/87).

**May** Iraqi President Saddam Hussein publicly confirms that Iraq had been receiving intelligence from U.S.-manned AWACS dispatched in Saudi Arabia (LW, p. 159).

**November** U.S. reestablishes full diplomatic relations with Iraq cut off by Iraq during 1967 Arab-Israeli war.

**December** Iraq ranks as the largest arms importer in the world, buying $7.7 billion worth in 1984 (MER, 9/87).

# 1985

**May 25** Kuwaiti emir survives assassination attempt.

**September** A major trade delegation led by the U.S. Commerce Department visits Baghdad to work out Iraqi-U.S. general trade agreement that includes progress towards agreements with U.S. Overseas Private Investment Corporation and discussions with U.S. Export-Import Bank on easing credit policies towards Iraq (IT, p. 52).

**September 13** Iran secretly receives 508 U.S. made Tow anti-tank missiles in a secret arms for hostages deal with the Reagan administration (LW, p. 217).

**October** OPEC meeting ends without an agreement on export quotas; Saudi Arabia soon drives down price of oil by flooding market with an extra 2.5 million barrels per day in an attempt to cripple Iranian economy and secure non-OPEC cooperation.

# 1986

**January 17** President Reagan secretly authorizes CIA purchase of 4,000 Tow missiles to be sold to Iran through Israeli intermediaries (LW, p. 217), the proceeds of which go through Israel to fund the anti-Sandinista contras in Nicaragua (ICC, p. 113).

**February** Iran launches Fao offensive in southern Iraq which threatens Kuwait.

**March** UN Security Council adopts report strongly condemning Iraqi use of chemical weapons.

**April 4** U.S. air force bombs cities in Libya killing 17 and injuring more than 100 people.

**April 22** U.S. law enforcement officers arrest Americans, Israelis and Europeans involved in two arms deals worth $2,380 million to Iran (LW, p. 292).

**May 25** American delegation led by Robert McFarlane secretly arrives in Tehran with spare Hawk missiles but fails to meet with high level Iranians (LW, p. 218).

**July** Kuwaiti rulers dissolve Kuwaiti parliament and implement crackdown on opposition activity.

**August** An agreement between Iran and Saudi Arabia within OPEC lifts oil prices and restricts output; this agreement reportedly followed a visit by Vice-President Bush in the spring who asked the Saudis to stabilize the higher price of oil for "national security interest" (WP, 11/5/86).

**October** Israeli technician Mordechai Vanunu reveals to the *Sunday Times* of London that Israel has extensive nuclear weapons program.

**November 3** *Al-Shiraa*, a Beirut based magazine, discloses that the U.S. secretly sold arms to Iran and that former U.S. National Security Advisor McFarlane had visited Tehran.

**November 13** President Reagan discloses parts of Iran-contra affair and publicly justifies U.S. arms sales to Iran citing acceptance of Iranian Revolution, need to end the Iran-Iraq war and concern for hostages in Lebanon.

# 1 9 8 7

**January** Iranian forces breach Iraqi defenses around Basra in Iraq in an assault that ends in February.

**March 2** USSR agrees to lease three of its oil tankers to Kuwait.

**March 7** U.S. responds to Kuwaiti request and provides naval escort for re-flagged tankers in the Gulf.

**May 17** Iraqi war plane fires Exocet missile at USS *Stark* killing 37 American sailors in what is reportedly an attempt to draw superpowers into the Iran-Iraq war (LW, p. 186).

**July 20** UN Security Council adopts Resolution 598 calling for a ceasefire between Iran and Iraq.

**July 22** U.S. implements tanker escort plan for Kuwaiti oil tankers bringing number of U.S. warships in and near the Gulf to 31 (MER, 9/87).

**August 26** U.S. signs a five-year economic and technical agreement with Iraq which is accompanied by $1 billion worth of food aid and Iraq soon becomes third largest export market for the U.S. in the Arab world (MER, 167, 24).

**October** U.S. warships destroy two Iranian oil platforms in retaliation for attacks on American-flagged tanker.

**December 9** Palestinian uprising (intifada) begins in the occupied territories of West Bank and Gaza.

# 1 9 8 8

**March** Iran launches an offensive in northern Iraq with the assistance of two Kurdish organizations and captures Kurdish city of Halabja on March 15. The next day Iraqi jets allegedly bomb Halabja with poison gas causing nearly 5,000 civilian deaths.

**April** U.S. and Israel sign 5-year Memorandum of Agreement on strategic, economic and military cooperation (MER, 6/90).

**April 16–18** Iraq recaptures Fao peninsula and uses chemical weapons.

**July 3** USS *Vincennes* shoots down an Iranian Air Bus killing all 290 people.

**August 20** UN-brokered ceasefire between Iran and Iraq ends eight year war.

**September 17** Iraq's Foreign Minister Aziz says Iraq will abide by international law outlawing the use of chemical weapons; on these grounds the U.S. State Department opposes Congressional attempts to put sanctions on Iraq.

**November 15** Palestine National Council (PNC) (in Algiers) issues declaration of independence for the state of Palestine.

**December** U.S. agrees to open up a "substantive dialogue" with the PLO.

# 1 9 8 9

**January** Iraq announces industrialization plans and a debt repayment schedule based on the $18 per barrel price just set by OPEC.

**March** Saudi Arabia and Iraq sign a non-aggression pact and military assistance treaty.

**May** Egypt is readmitted to the Arab League.

**August** FBI agents discover that Atlanta branch of Banca Nazionale del Lavoro (BNL) had made $3 billion in loans to Iraq that were possibly used to purchase military hardware between 1985 and 1989 (VV, 3/12/91).

**November 14** Brigadier al-Fahd, Kuwaiti security commander, meets with CIA Director Webster and it is speculated that they also discuss taking advantage of deteriorating economic conditions in Iraq to weaken its post-war power (VV, 3/5/91).

**November 30** North and South Yemen sign declaration of intent to unite into Republic of Yemen.

**December 5** Iraq reportedly launches first satellite-carrying rocket and claims to have developed new surface to surface missiles.
**December 20** U.S. invades Panama; on the same day the White House announces it will lift ban on loans to Iraq.

# 1990

**January 14** Israeli Prime Minister Shamir says that a "big Israel" is needed to absorb massive influx of Soviet Jews.
**January 16** U.S. Senator Dole calls for across the board 5% reduction in U.S. foreign aid to Israel, Turkey, Egypt, and Pakistan in order to free funds for use in Central America and Eastern Europe.
**January 28** French Defense Minister Chevenement meets with President Saddam Hussein to discuss French cooperation in Iraqi development and industrial projects, including Iraqi desire to manufacture French aircraft and missiles under license in Iraq (MEI, 2/10).
**February 6** OPEC calls for oil consuming nations to help oil producers finance expansion of output capacity due to expected increase in demand for oil because of declining output in USSR and U.S. and new demands from Eastern Europe and East Asia (WSJ 2/7).
**February 8** U.S. Gen. Norman Schwarzkopf tells Congress that Iraq is receiving a large amount of Soviet arms material from Eastern Europe.
**February 24** President Saddam Hussein warns leaders of Arab Cooperation Council (ACC) that the collapse of the Eastern bloc countries leaves no deterrent to U.S. forces in the Middle East and warns Arabs against designs of the U.S. (MER, 1/91; VV, 1/22/91) and reportedly informs King Hussein and President Mubarak that Kuwait and Saudi Arabia must forgive Iraq's $30 billion debts and provide new grants or face reprisals (VV, 1/22/91).
**February 27** Kuwaiti opposition forces hold militant demonstrations demanding elections and reconstitution of the parliament.
**March 3** U.S. President Bush states that U.S. policy advocating the cessation of settlements in the occupied territories also applies to East Jerusalem.
**March 15** Israeli minister Peres reports that Syria has suggested peace talks with Israel and demilitarization of the Golan Heights. Iraq's government hangs Iranian-born British reporter Farzad Bazoft after convicting him of espionage.
**March 22** Canadian ballistics expert Gerald Bull, who was publicly linked to providing Iraq with engineering assistance that may have aided Iraq's missile and "super gun" programs, is murdered in Brussels after reported warnings that Israeli Mossad wanted him killed (4/6, WP).
**March 24** In Libya, Egyptian President Mubarak and Syrian President Assad meet for first time since restoring diplomatic relations in December 1989.
**March 28** British officials arrest five people for attempting to smuggle U.S.-made electronic triggers to Iraq for what U.S. and British authorities suspect was the manufacture of a nuclear bomb.
**March 30** The *New York Times* cites a U.S. intelligence report confirming that Iraq had built six launchers for modified scud missiles in western Iraq within range of Tel Aviv and Damascus (3/30, NYT).
**April 1** President Saddam Hussein accuses U.S. and Britain of supplying Israel with political and diplomatic cover to possibly attack Iraq and declares that Iraq would retaliate against any Israeli nuclear attack with chemical weapons, while at the same time offering to destroy chemical and biological weapons if Israel agrees to destroy its non-conventional and nuclear weapons.
**April 6** U.S. oil inventory is reported to be its highest in two years (4/6, WSJ).
**April 9** U.S. Commerce Department cancels aerospace trade mission to Iraq.
**April 12** Delegation of U.S. Senators led by minority leader Robert Dole and minority whip Alan Simpson meet with President Saddam Hussein in Baghdad; Dole reportedly tells President Hussein that recent Voice of America broadcasts critical of Iraq did not properly reflect policy of the Bush administration (VV, 1/22/91).
**April 25** U.S. Secretary of State Baker gives testimony before Senate appropriations subcommittee defending U.S. policy with Iraq.
**April 26** U.S. Under-Secretary of State for Middle East Affairs Kelly testifies before House Foreign Affairs Subcommittee on "U.S.-Iraqi Relations."
**April 30** State Department releases report on terrorism and includes Iran, Syria, Libya and Peoples Republic of Yemen on the list of terrorist states.
**May 1** OPEC calls extraordinary meeting in Geneva.
**May 3** Iraqi Foreign Minister Tariq Aziz vehemently criticizes unnamed OPEC member-states for oil overproduction.
**May 20** Former Israeli reservist kills seven Palestinians and wounds 10 others in massacre at Rishon Lezion, Israel. Seven more Palestinians are killed and nearly 500 wounded in Israeli army crack-down within hours after the massacre.
**May 21** U.S. Department of Agriculture announces it will delay Iraqi request to purchase $500

million in commodities after learning of possible kickbacks and "irregularities" in Iraqi dealings.

**May 22** Republic of Yemen formally declared in ceremony uniting North and South Yemen.

**May 26** U.S. blocks plan by UN Security Council to send a UN team to investigate Israeli treatment of Palestinians, citing Israeli opposition (5/27, NYT).

**May 28** President Saddam Hussein blames other Arab countries, at an emergency Arab League summit in Baghdad held in order to discuss Soviet Jewish emigration to Israel, for waging an economic war against Iraq by overproducing oil and calls for a united front against foreign aggression, pooling of Arab resources and the need to match words with deeds.

**May 30** Palestine Liberation Front commando units under Abu al-Abbas attempt seaborne raid on Israeli beach in response for Rishon Lezion massacre of Palestinians; no Israelis are killed or injured.

**May 31** U.S. vetoes UN Security Council resolution (14–1) demanding that a Security Council mission be sent to occupied Palestinian territories to inquire about their conditions.

**June 1** Palestinian leaders from the occupied territories call on Arab leaders to initiate sanctions against the United States in response to U.S. veto at the UN.

**June 5** The *Washington Post* quotes Abdullah Hourani, a PLO Executive Committee member, as saying that the PLO was moving away from Egypt and closer to Iraq because Egypt was too dependent upon the U.S. to bring pressure upon it after more than a year of dialogue (6/5, WP).

**June 6** Pentagon announces plans for a $4 billion arms sale to Saudi Arabia.

**June 13** Secretary Baker criticizes Israeli intransigence on movement towards talks with Palestinians and tells Israel that they know the White House phone number and can call when they are ready to talk about peace.

**June 20** U.S. suspends its dialogue with the PLO because it did not properly condemn May 30 beach attack by Palestine Liberation Front.

**June 26** Iraqi President Hussein warns Kuwait and UAE to curb excess production and Iraqi Deputy Prime Minister Hammadi informs Kuwaiti officials that prices should be raised from $14 to $25 a barrel.

**June 28** In a *Wall Street Journal* interview, Iraqi President Hussein said that unless the United States blocked "aggressive policies by Israel" another Middle East war was "inevitable" (6/28, WSJ).

**July 3** Iraq and Iran hold their first direct contact since the end of the Iran-Iraq war in 1988.

**July 9** Saudi Arabia signs a $3 billion deal to buy M-1 battle tanks from U.S. which Congress approved in 1989.

**July 11** Iraq is unsuccessful at special meeting of OPEC in convincing other members of the cartel to raise oil prices and limit production.

**July 12** United Arab Emirates agrees to observe OPEC quota after two month delay. Oil prices surge after Saudi Arabia announces it will temporarily reduce its share of daily OPEC exports in order to bolster prices.

**July 14** Pentagon gives in to pressure and says it will no longer sell Iraq industrial furnaces because of their possible use in manufacturing missile parts.

**July 15** Kuwait agrees to observe OPEC quotas.

**July 16** Iraq sends Arab League a detailed list of grievances against Kuwait, accusing Kuwait of stealing $2.4 billion worth of oil from Rumaila oil field and reducing Iraq's oil income as part of an "imperialist-zionist plan" to weaken Iraq, and demands reimbursement (VV, 1/22/91; WP, 7/19); Kuwait enacts state of alert.

**July 17** President Saddam Hussein accuses certain Arab leaders in the Gulf of embarking upon a pro-American policy to bring down the price of oil which represents a "pointed dagger" thrust into Iraq's back and threatens use of force to make Kuwait and the United Arab Emirates stop oil overproduction (VV, 1/22/91).

**July 19** U.S. Secretary of Defense Cheney tells reporters during a press briefing that the U.S. was committed to militarily defending Kuwait if attacked; spokesperson Pete Williams later explains that Cheney had spoken with "some degree of liberty" (VV, 1/22/91). Kuwait rejects Iraqi accusation and accuses Iraq of drilling oil wells inside Kuwaiti territory. Kuwait calls off state of alert.

**July 20** Kuwait insinuates that Iraqi belligerence is aimed at pressuring Kuwait and other creditors to write off its billion-dollar war debts.

**July 21** Iraq accuses Kuwait of renouncing Arab option to resolve the crisis and of preparing the ground for foreign intervention in the Gulf. The emir of Kuwait receives Arab League Secretary General Chedli Klibi and the Saudi foreign minister.

**July 22** Kuwait urges Iraq to resolve their dispute through the Arab League. Iraqi Foreign Minister Tariq Aziz flies to Cairo. Baghdad press calls on Kuwaiti citizens to dissociate themselves from their government.

**July 23** Two Iraqi armored divisions are moved from their bases to positions on the Kuwait border. Egyptian President Mubarak and Jordanian King Hussein attempt to mediate between Iraq and Kuwait in Cairo; U.S. fleet in the Gulf is placed on alert.

**July 24** President Mubarak visits Baghdad, Kuwait and Saudi Arabia. Washington announces that U.S. navy warships and aircraft are holding a "short notice exercise" in the Gulf with the United Arab Emirates. Kuwait reinstates alert. State Department spokesperson Margaret Tutwiler responds to question about U.S.-Kuwaiti military agreements: "We do not have any defense treaties with Kuwait, and there are no special defense or security commitments to Kuwait."

**July 25** Iraq and Kuwait agree to meet in Saudi Arabia; President Mubarak says Iraqi President Saddam Hussein has assured him Iraq has no intention of attacking Kuwait or any other party (during negotiation period) and urges U.S. to avoid any move that would complicate a problem between "two Arab brothers and neighbors." U.S. ambassador to Iraq April Glaspie meets with President Saddam Hussein and tells him that the U.S. has "no opinion on Arab-Arab conflicts like your border disagreement with Kuwait" (MER, 2/91).

**July 26** OPEC ministers meet in Geneva where Iraq demands that the minimum price per barrel of crude be set at $25.

**July 27** U.S. Senate and House vote to impose limited economic sanctions against Iraq against Bush administration pressure. The 13 OPEC member states reach accord to end four years of low-priced oil and to set minimum price at $21 per barrel and production ceiling at 22.5 million barrels per day until the end of the year.

**July 28** CIA director Webster informs President Bush that Iraqi invasion is imminent but that Iraq is likely only to take disputed oil field and islands (VV, 1/22/91).

**July 29** Iraq announces postponement of meeting with Kuwait scheduled for this weekend in Saudi Arabia.

**July 30** Jordanian King Hussein flies to Baghdad and Kuwait for meetings.

**July 31** Iraq and Kuwait send delegations to Jeddah, Saudi Arabia, to negotiate their oil and border dispute. Nearly 100,000 Iraqi troops are reportedly massed on Kuwaiti border. Kuwait refuses to meet Iraqi request to lease Gulf islands of Warbah and Bubiyan or write off Iraq's debts and offers Iraq $500,000 in war reparations (VV, 3/5/91). Kuwaiti version insists that Kuwait had agreed to forgive Iraq's oil debts and lease Warbah Island but Iraq asked for Bubiyan (FT, 9/18). U.S. Under-Secretary of State Kelly asserts before House foreign affairs subcommittee that "We have no defense treaty relationship with any Gulf country. That is clear . . . We have not historically taken a position on border disputes."

**August 1** Iraq-Kuwait talks break down amid mutual acrimony; the land border between the two countries is closed.

**August 2** Iraqi army invades Kuwait. President Saddam Hussein announces that the Kuwaiti government has been overthrown and that a nine-member provisional military government of Kuwait has requested the invasion. UN Security Council passes Resolution 660 which demands an immediate Iraqi withdrawal; U.S. freezes Iraqi and Kuwaiti financial resources and calls for moratorium on all arms deliveries to Iraq. King Hussein and President Mubarak meet in Cairo and have phone conversations with President Bush, Hussein, King Fahd and President Saleh of Yemen. King Hussein receives 48 hours from President Bush to secure a commitment from Iraq to withdraw; Saddam Hussein says he will withdraw if the Arab League does not condemn him. Israel warns Iraq that it will not tolerate the movement of Iraqi troops into Jordan.

**August 3** USSR and U.S. issue joint statement calling for an unconditional Iraqi withdrawal and restoration of Kuwaiti sovereignty. U.S. dispatches naval forces to Gulf and asks Turkey and Saudi Arabia to close Iraqi oil pipelines running through their territory. Iraq's Revolutionary Command Council announces that Iraqi troops will begin withdrawing from Kuwait in two days provided there is no security threat to Kuwait and Iraq. King Hussein returns from meeting with President Hussein believing that he has secured a summit and possible Iraq withdrawal and tries to postpone resolution condemning Iraq. Saudi officials announce that Iraqi President Saddam Hussein, President Mubarak, King Hussein and King Fahd have agreed to meet in Jeddah summit on August 5. The summit is shifted to Cairo after the Arab League ministerial council meets there and under heavy pressure from President Mubarak condemns Iraqi invasion and calls for Iraqi withdrawal from Kuwait, but cautions against foreign intervention in any Arab country. Twelve countries vote to condemn; Algeria, Jordan and Yemen abstain; Palestine, the Sudan, and Mauritania vote "reservations"; Libya and Iraq vote against.

**August 4** The European Community freezes Iraqi and Kuwaiti assets and embargo is placed on Iraqi oil. U.S. reported to have dispatched special operations units (including Delta Force) to the Middle East. Saudi Arabia officially postpones Jeddah summit. Pentagon officials offer President Bush a list of options including U.S. air attacks against Iraq and U.S. officials report Iraqi troops moving towards Saudi border.

**August 5** Iraqi government claims that some invasion forces have begun pulling back in the initial phases of phased withdrawal. Jordan's King Hussein says that President Saddam Hussein has told him he would not invade Saudi Arabia and warns that foreign intervention will set back chances for peaceful resolution. A Palestinian-Libyan peace plan calls for Iraqi withdrawal and Kuwaiti compensation to Iraq. President Bush says he will not accept anything less than a total Iraqi withdrawal from Kuwait and mentions using U.S. military force against Iraq and warns Arab leaders not to appease Iraq. Saudi Arabia begins to mobilize military. President Saddam Hussein orders formation of 11 new army divisions.

**August 6** UN Security Council passes Resolution 661 calling for economic sanctions against Iraq. President Bush meets with British Prime Minister Thatcher and NATO Secretary-General Manfred

Woerner and plans launch of "Operation Desert Shield"; orders U.S. government agencies to draft plans for "destabilizing and eventually toppling" Iraqi President Saddam Hussein. President Bush sends Cheney to Saudi Arabia and White House declares that Iraq poses a "threat" to Saudi Arabia. Iraq says it has no designs on Saudi Arabia; sources say that Saudi officials themselves doubt Iraq is planning attack (WSJ, 9/6). U.S. agrees to deliver 44 F-4 fighter planes to Turkey, urges Eximbank to provide Turkey credit to finance military projects and the World Bank frees up suspended $1.4 million in loans to Turkey which then freezes Iraqi assets and sets in force sanctions against Iraq more severe than those requested by the Security Council.

**August 7** U.S. Defense Secretary Cheney meets with King Fahd who "invites" U.S. forces into Saudi Arabia. President Bush orders U.S. ground and naval forces to Saudi Arabia; nearly 50 warships from the U.S., USSR, Britain and France converge on the Persian Gulf. President Hussein sends message to President Mubarak saying that Iraq would withdraw troops according to a timetable and asks Mubarak to prevent a foreign intervention which would obstruct such a withdrawal. Yemeni President Saleh calls President Bush and insists that immediate imposition of the sanctions does not give time for Arab effort to end the crisis. King Fahd reportedly sends envoy to King Hussein telling Hussein that despite Fahd's invitation for U.S. troops, there was no truth to reports that Iraq planned to invade Saudi Arabia (NYT, 10/16). Bush administration rules out drawing on the U.S. 590 million barrel strategic oil reserve to stabilize oil prices. Israeli Defense Minister Moshe Arens says Israel will go to war if Iraq moves into Jordan.

**August 8** Iraq declares annexation of Kuwait. U.S. informs NATO members that Iraq is deploying chemical weapons and calls for "multinational" force to join it in the Gulf to defend Saudi Arabia. President Bush says that independence of Saudi Arabia is of "vital interest" to the U.S. and that a disruption of Saudi oil supply represents a threat to U.S. "economic independence." Key members of Congress urge President Bush to sell strategic oil reserve stocks to moderate the price of oil. The Soviet Union says it will only join a multinational UN force in the Gulf. President Mubarak officially refuses to send his army to Saudi Arabia to back U.S. forces and calls for an emergency Arab Summit, reportedly to put an "Arab face" on U.S. intervention (NYT, 9/10).

**August 9** UN Security Council Resolution 662 unanimously condemns Iraq's invasion of Kuwait and declares Iraqi annexation illegal. U.S. approaches Syria and Iran to join the "multinational" force. France sends naval forces to participate in UN-sanctioned embargo and not as part of U.S. ground forces in Saudi Arabia.

**August 10** Emergency Arab League Summit in Cairo narrowly passes (twelve of twenty-one countries vote in favor) the only resolution that was brought to vote which condemns Iraq's aggression against Kuwait, asserts Kuwaiti sovereignty and agrees to send troops to Saudi Arabia. The PLO is prevented from presenting its own resolution calling for the Summit to designate a committee of Arab Presidents and Kings to discuss all the issues of the Iraqi dispute with Kuwait. U.S. Under-Secretary of State for Middle East Affairs John Kelly meets in Damascus with President Assad to obtain Syrian support.

**August 11** British, Egyptian and Moroccan forces begin to arrive in Saudi Arabia. President Mubarak declares there is "no hope" of peacefully reversing Iraq's annexation of Kuwait. Thousands demonstrate in Jordan, Yemen and Mauritania against U.S. intervention and condemn Mubarak and Fahd as being controlled by the U.S.

**August 12** Iraq calls for a settlement linking withdrawal from Kuwait to withdrawal from other occupied Arab lands: Syria and Israel from Lebanon, Israel from the occupied territories it conquered in 1967 and proposes that U.S. troops in Saudi Arabia be replaced by Arab forces under UN flag. Bush administration unilaterally declares it will use force to enforce embargo against Iraq.

**August 13** U.S. demands that Jordan close Aqaba port on Red Sea to all Iraqi transport and goods. U.S. military officials declare that U.S. aircraft carrying soldiers and material are landing "practically every ten minutes" in Saudi Arabia. Thousands of Palestinians demonstrate in Israeli occupied territories against U.S. intervention. King Hussein meets in Baghdad with President Saddam Hussein.

**August 14** The five permanent UN Security Council members meet to discuss U.S. unilateral decision to enforce militarily the embargo of Iraq; the Soviet Union proposes that naval forces opposing Iraq be placed under a UN umbrella. Syrian troops begin arriving in Saudi Arabia. U.S. increases helicopters, tanks and missile batteries in Saudi Arabia.

**August 15** President Saddam Hussein calls for full implementation of Resolution 598 in a major overture to Iran, accepts Algiers Accord of 1975, and calls for Iraqi troops to evacuate from Iranian territory and for all Iranian and Iraqi prisoners of war to be repatriated. He then proposes that Iran and Iraq cooperate against foreign intervention. King Hussein meets in Washington D.C. with President Bush where U.S. aid to Jordan is made contingent upon Jordanian compliance with embargo. U.S. forces in Gulf reach an estimated 60,000 ground, naval and air force personnel. The *Washington Post* reports that U.S. has secretly approved more than $1 billion worth of advanced U.S. fighter planes and anti-tank missiles to Egypt; the Defense Department announces that future U.S. arms sales to pro-Western Arab and other Middle East states might not be made public.

**August 16** UN Secretary General Perez de Cuellar announces that authorization for use of force against Iraq requires separate UN resolution because military action to enforce embargo would breach UN charter. President Bush presses King Hussein to enforce UN embargo or face blockade while King Hussein insists that embargo does not preclude food and medical supplies. Iraq orders 6,500 British and American foreign nationals in Kuwait to assemble in Kuwaiti hotels. Iraqi opposition forces in Damascus agree to join forces to overthrow President Saddam Hussein and seek national elections in Iraq.

**August 17** U.S. Defense Secretary Cheney flies to Saudi Arabia to negotiate agreements under which U.S. will supply Saudi Arabia with the most sophisticated version of the F-15 fighter plane and drastically expand amount of U.S. military equipment in the kingdom. Jordan announces acceptance of UN resolution on the embargo.

**August 18** Iraq announces that citizens of "aggressive nations" in Iraq and Kuwait have been moved to strategic civilian and military facilities to serve as "human shields" to prevent a foreign attack; UN Security Council passes Resolution 664 calling for Iraq to release all detained foreign nationals. Iraq demands that food and medical supplies be exempted from embargo. Saudi Arabia says it will increase oil production by two million barrels per day regardless of other OPEC members.

**August 19** President Saddam Hussein offers to release foreign nationals if U.S. troops leave the region and lift the embargo and the sovereignty of Kuwait be treated as an Arab issue. U.S. and Britain dismiss Iraqi offer. The PLO calls for a solution that will "guarantee the integrity of Iraq, Kuwait, Saudi Arabia, the Gulf and the entire Arab region." Foreign ministers of Iran, Pakistan and Turkey condemn the occupation of Kuwait and call for "regional cooperation to prevent the presence of foreign forces." Israeli Foreign Minister David Levy demands that gas masks be immediately distributed to Israelis.

**August 20** United Arab Emirates accepts deployment of U.S. troops. Iran informs UN secretary general that it will abide by UN sanctions against Iraq. Saudi Arabia is unable to garner enough support for an emergency meeting of OPEC.

**August 21** UN Security Council refuses to authorize U.S. proposal for use of "limited military force" to sustain economic sanctions against Iraq. Foreign Minister Tariq Aziz in Amman, Jordan says that Iraq is ready to discuss wide range of issues with the U.S.. President Saddam Hussein sends an open letter to President Bush saying he is not hostile to "legitimate interests" of the West and that he is open to dialogue. Britain, France and the U.S. reject Iraqi offers so long as Iraq holds hostages and occupies Kuwait. France announces it will send ground forces to Saudi Arabia and the Emirates. The parliaments of Algeria and Jordan announce their support for Iraq against foreign military intervention.

**August 22** President Bush orders military reservists to active duty for an additional deployment of 50,000 U.S. troops to the Arabian Peninsula. King Hussein announces he will visit Iraq and other Arab countries in a final effort to end the conflict peaceably. The UN Security Council agrees to put together an aid package for Jordan to help it cope with complying with the embargo and the flood of refugees from Iraq. The U.S. ambassador in Cairo declares that the U.S. is studying the possibility of annulling part of Egypt's $50 billion debt, $13 of which is owed to the U.S. government.

**August 23** Iraqi proposal reportedly delivered to National Security Advisor Brent Scowcroft which calls for Iraqi withdrawal from Kuwait and release of all foreign nationals in return for lifting of sanctions, full Iraqi control of Rumaila oilfield, guaranteed access to the Gulf, and negotiations on an oil agreement to alleviate Iraq's financial problems; the White House rejects proposal as a "nonstarter" (ND, 8/29). Deposed al-Sabah family of Kuwait sets up government in exile in Saudi Arabia. PLO leader Yasir Arafat and high ranking officials attempt to mediate between Baghdad and Saudi Arabia.

**August 24** Soviet President Gorbachev appeals to President Saddam Hussein to abide by Security Council resolutions or the UN will be forced to take appropriate measures. Algeria and the PLO present President Hussein with a peace plan which includes withdrawal of Iraqi forces from all of Kuwait except for Bubiyan Island and an Arab League force to oversee Iraqi withdrawal and elections in Kuwait leading to negotiations over Iraqi grievances. Japan offers Turkey, Egypt and Jordan financial compensation for losses incurred during embargo. Israeli military reports that it does not have enough gas masks to accommodate Palestinians in the occupied territories.

**August 25** UN Security Council passes Resolution 665 authorizing the use of (primarily American) naval forces to enforce economic sanctions against Iraq, in major victory for Bush administration.

**August 26** UN Secretary General Perez de Cuellar begins attempt to mediate by meeting Foreign Minister Aziz in Jordan. U.S. reiterates that (i) Iraq must unconditionally withdraw from Kuwait, (ii) the al-Sabah family must be restored to power and (iii) all foreign nationals must be released before it will consider negotiating with Iraq. U.S. adds that forces will not leave the region until the free and uninterrupted flow of oil is assured and declares that its military posture is moving from defensive to offensive with the arrival of armored divisions. The International Red Cross claims that U.S. is in flagrant violation of the UN charter for withholding food and medicine in its embargo of Iraq.

**August 28** Iraq officially confirms its annexation of Kuwait as its 19th province. President Saddam Hussein announces he is ready to negotiate immediately and directly with President Bush and Prime Minister Thatcher and challenges the two to a televised debate. Egyptian President Mubarak and Syrian President Assad meet in Alexandria and agree to a unified view on the Gulf crisis. Saudi Arabia sets up separate command to coordinate Arab/Islamic troops and American troops. Saudi Arabia obtains commitment from President Bush to consult with King Fahd before launching a military action from Saudi territory.

**August 29** Iraq announces that detained foreign women and children may seek exit visas and leave the country; Iraqi ambassador to the U.S. says male hostages would be free to leave if the U.S. promises not to launch a military strike. OPEC ministers decide to increase temporarily crude production by four million barrels per day. President Bush approves $2.2 billion armaments sale to Saudi Arabia including F-15 fighters, M-60 tanks and Stinger missiles. French prime minister meets with PLO leader Arafat who presents his five point peace plan. Syrian forces are reported to have bloody clashes with demonstrators opposed to Syrian support for U.S. intervention.

**August 30** *New York Times* reports that Iraq has proposed several initiatives to the U.S. but that none were accepted because they did not include an unconditional Iraqi withdrawal. President Bush begins effort to obtain financing for American military deployment in the Gulf of up to $23 billion in aid for first year; Prime Minister Thatcher criticizes West European states for not supporting the U.S. as much as they should. President Bush indicates that Washington is considering annulling Egypt's $7.1 billion military debt to the U.S.. Only 13 out of 21 Arab foreign ministers attend Arab League meeting in Cairo. PLO spokesman Bassam Abu Sharif says PLO "cannot possibly support the usurpation by one Arab country of another" (NYT, 9/4).

**August 31** UN Secretary General Perez de Cuellar and Iraqi Foreign Minister Aziz begin two days of meetings in Jordan. Arab League resolutions rebuke Jordanian efforts to resolve crisis. As a trade-off for U.S. arms sales to Saudi Arabia, U.S. agrees to provide Israel with an advance of $1 billion in military equipment from U.S. bases in Europe.

**September 1** British Prime Minister Margaret Thatcher threatens that President Saddam Hussein and his supporters will be charged with war crimes when the crisis is over. Saudi Defense Minister Sultan says that U.S. forces would not be allowed to launch any action from Saudi soil that is not defensive.

**September 2** Iraq orders rationing of food supplies.

**September 3** Arab League Secretary-General Chedli Klibi resigns over Arab League handling of Gulf crisis. U.S. combat aircraft are deployed to bases in Oman, Qatar, Bahrain and UAE for the first time. Thousands of displaced refugees are stranded in Jordan.

**September 4** U.S. Secretary Baker calls for creation of U.S.-led NATO-style security structure in the Middle East. Bush administration begins asking economic allies to contribute at least $25 billion to defray costs of Gulf deployment (WP, LAT, 9/5).

**September 5** Bush administration offers to mount international effort to provide economic aid to USSR in return for USSR agreement to join forces in the Middle East. Secretary Baker says NATO-style security arrangement "would have to fit regional realities."

**September 6** Saudi Arabia announces it will cover virtually all of the hundreds of millions of dollars in monthly operating costs of U.S. forces and contribute several billion dollars to aid Middle East nations that have joined coalition against Iraq. U.S. troop build-up reaches 100,000.

**September 7** Secretary Baker meets with Kuwait's emir and announces Kuwait's intention to provide $5 billion during 1990 to U.S. and Gulf states' military and economic campaign against Iraq. Treasury Secretary Brady meets with Gulf leaders and says that contributions "should not only cover the costs of America's involvement in the Gulf, but may even produce a profit for the Treasury" (NYT, 9/8).

**September 8** Iraq's President Hussein sends open letter to Presidents Bush and Gorbachev restating his intention of holding on to Kuwait unless mediated by Arabs, not superpowers.

**September 9** Bush and Gorbachev meet in Helsinki and issue joint statement declaring unconditional support for economic and political sanctions against Iraq but President Gorbachev does not agree to use of force to resolve crisis in the Gulf.

**September 11** Clovis Maksoud, the Arab League envoy to the UN, resigns citing opposition to Iraq's invasion of Kuwait and to the foreign military build-up in the Gulf.

**September 12** Before U.S. Secretary Baker meets with President Assad, Syria announces it will deploy troops in Gulf and President Assad says that U.S. troops will leave Saudi Arabia when the crisis is over.

**September 13** UN Security Council Resolution 666 holds Iraq responsible for safety of foreign nationals and specifies guidelines for delivery of food and medical supplies. U.S. Secretary of State James Baker meets with Syrian President Hafez Assad.

**September 14** Japan agrees to double its contribution to funding military intervention in the Gulf to $2 billion and agrees to grant a soft loan worth another $2 billion to Turkey, Egypt and Jordan. U.S. officials report that Bush administration is planning to sell Saudi Arabia about $20 billion in sophisticated weaponry in what would be biggest U.S. arms sale in history (LAT, NYT, 9/15).

**September 16** UN Security Council Resolution 667 demands immediate Iraqi release of foreign nationals.

**September 17** U.S. Air Force Chief of Staff General Michael Dugan is fired by Defense Secretary Cheney for revealing U.S. plans for massive bombing against Baghdad that specifically targets President Saddam Hussein, military centers and power systems.

**September 19** White House backs off from plans to sell Saudi Arabia $20 billion in weaponry citing legislative support for only a fraction of total sale. Saudi Arabia cuts off Jordan's oil supply in retaliation for Jordan's refusal to join anti-Iraq coalition (VV, 1/5/91). King Hussein, King Hassan and President Benjedid meet in Rabat to search for Arab solution to crisis.

**September 23** President Saddam Hussein threatens to light Kuwaiti oilfields and attack Saudi Arabia and Israel if Iraq is pushed to its limit.

**September 24** French President Mitterand outlines four-stage proposal at the UN for Iraqi withdrawal: (i) Iraq signs declaration of intent to withdraw, (ii) UN supervises withdrawal, (iii) restoration of Kuwaiti sovereignty and democratic vote for government, (iv) dialogue on other outstanding Middle East issues and reduction of arms in region. UN Security Council Resolution 669 emphasizes that only special sanctions committee has power to permit food and medical supplies to Iraq or occupied Kuwait.

**September 25** USSR warns Iraq that it will face the use of force unless it withdraws. UN Security Council Resolution 670 expands economic embargo to include air traffic in or out of Iraq or occupied Kuwait. U.S. House appropriations committee shelves President Bush's request to cancel Egypt's military debt to U.S. because it was said to face certain defeat.

**September 26** President Bush scales back arms sale to Saudi Arabia to include only $7.5 billion of most important weaponry for immediate threat to Saudi Arabia. Bush also announces U.S. will sell 5 million barrels from U.S. strategic petroleum reserve to curb $40 dollar a barrel oil prices.

**October 2** U.S. Senate appropriations subcommittee approves administration proposal to forgive Egypt's $7 billion military debt.

**October 3** USSR begins diplomatic initiative to resolve crisis. Amnesty International issues report accusing Iraqi troops of carrying out torture and extrajudicial killings to crush resistance in Kuwait.

**October 5** Egyptian President Hosni Mubarak reveals that Iraq and Israel had engaged in secret exchanges in 1987 and 1989 (N, 2/25/91).

**October 7** Israeli military begins to hand out gas masks and chemical weapons defense kits; Palestinians in the occupied territories are told they will not be given kits but will have to purchase them; military refuses to provide masks for more than 1/10 of Palestinian population.

**October 8** Israeli forces kill at least 19 and wound more than 100 Palestinians at Haram al-Sharif compound in Jerusalem.

**October 9** Bush declares at a UN meeting that "I hope nobody questions our interest in seeing a solution to the Palestine question, to the implementation of the Security Council resolutions."

**October 11** UN Security Council members attempt to draft resolution on Haram al-Sharif killings that is acceptable to U.S.; majority ready to support resolution sponsored by non-aligned countries, but U.S. threatens veto.

**October 12** UN Security Council Resolution 672 condemns Israel for Haram al-Sharif killings and calls for a UN secretary general mission to occupied territories rather than Security Council mission.

**October 13** Kuwaiti exiles hold "Popular Kuwaiti Congress" of 1,200 and crown prince suggests that country's defunct parliament would be revived and free elections held once Kuwait is liberated from Iraq. Israeli cabinet says it will not cooperate with UN secretary general mission but will admit it into country.

**October 15** Syrian forces attack Lebanese General Aoun's forces and take over East Beirut.

**October 16** U.S. Secretary Baker says that Iraqi President Hussein had expressed interest in compromise settlement that would leave Iraq in control of Bubiyan Island and Rumaila oilfield but that Washington considers the terms unacceptable because it is a conditional withdrawal (LAT, 10/17).

**October 17** Amnesty International issues report on Egypt that details illegal detentions and torture.

**October 18** Arab League resolution unanimously condemns Israel for killings at Haram al-Sharif and deplores U.S. pro-Israel bias after rejecting more strongly worded PLO resolution 11–10.

**October 19** UN secretary general says he cannot send mission to Israel unless it agrees to cooperate.

**October 20** Defense Secretary Cheney states that UN-imposed embargo on Iraq and Kuwait is beginning to have serious impact on Iraqi economy and its ability to maintain troops in Kuwait (WP, 10/21).

**October 21** Saudi Arabia's Defense Minister Sultan tells press that Saudi Arabia would not oppose Iraq's withdrawal from Kuwait in exchange for possible territorial concessions from Kuwait (NYT, WP, 10/22).

**October 22** President Bush rejects anything less than a full withdrawal; King Fahd and Saudi Ambassador to the U.S. Prince Bandar assert that Sultan was not advocating territorial concessions to Iraq. U.S. Senate votes to give Israel at least $700 million worth of used weapons being withdrawn from Europe over and above annual military aid.

**October 24** Saudi Arabia, United Arab Emirates and Kuwait cancel Egypt's debts — Saudi Arabia, $4.2 billion; UAE, $2 billion; Kuwait, $1.5 billion. Qatar had earlier cancelled Egypt's $600 million debt. UN Security Council adopts Resolution 673 which condemns Israel for its refusal to accept UN secretary general mission to investigate Haram al-Sharif killings.

**October 25**  Bush administration decides to expand number of U.S. forces in the Gulf by as many as 100,000 more than originally planned 240,000. Israel rejects UN Security Council resolution and criticizes U.S. support for resolution.

**October 28**  President Gorbachev and President Mitterand meet in Paris to discuss ideas for ending Gulf crisis short of military conflict.

**October 29**  UN Security Council Resolution 674 condemns Iraqi mistreatment of Kuwaiti citizens and foreign hostages. *Los Angeles Times* reports that Bush administration will meet next week to discuss timetable for possible use of forces against Iraq at talks with U.S. allies in Europe and the Gulf (LAT, 10/30).

**October 30**  President Bush secretly approves a timetable for launching an air war against Iraq in mid-January and a large-scale ground offensive in February according to *New York Times* report of 3/3/91.

**November 1**  UN Secretary General de Cuellar suggest all signatories to the 1949 Fourth Geneva Convention on protecting civilians in wartime should meet to discuss possible measures against Israeli refusal to allow UN mission to occupied territories. Amnesty International reports that Saudi Arabia has detained and tortured hundreds of Yemenis over their country's stand in the Gulf crisis. World Bank officials say that more than 1.5 million people have been displaced by the Gulf crisis.

**November 3**  Secretary Baker leaves for Gulf and Europe to lay groundwork for new UN Security Council resolution authorizing use of force against Iraq and to ask anti-Iraq partners under what conditions they would support military action.

**November 4**  President Mitterand says that UN embargo against Iraq should be given more time because it is working.

**November 5**  Secretary Baker and King Fahd agree to framework for command and control of military forces in event of war. Twenty four of world's wealthiest nations joined together as Gulf Crisis Financial Coordination Group, pledge to give $13 billion in special aid to nations hurt worst by economic sanctions against Iraq — Egypt, Turkey, Jordan are to receive $10.5 billion by end of 1991 (NYT, 11/6).

**November 6**  U.S. Congressional elections. 47 women in Saudi Arabia drive their own cars in protest of driving restrictions on women.

**November 8**  President Bush sharply increases the number of U.S. troops by 200,000 to insure "offensive military option" if needed and raise number of troops in region to 430,000. Secretary Baker meets with then Soviet Foreign Minister Shevardnadze to discuss possible use of military force.

**November 9**  President Bush rejects call by Republican senators for special session of Congress to approve president's plan for additional military deployment to the Gulf. Defense Secretary Cheney cancels rotation of U.S. troops who will remain in Gulf for duration of crisis.

**November 10**  U.S. Congress demands President Bush seek authorization before use of force against Iraq. Prime Minister Thatcher declares that there is no need for UN resolution on using military force because forces already have authority.

**November 11**  Morocco's King Hassan proposes Arab summit to avert war in the Gulf. Iraq insists Palestine issue be on summit agenda.

**November 12**  Secretary of Defense Cheney authorizes the activation of 72,500 reservists.

**November 13**  Secretary Baker says that Iraq's invasion of Kuwait threatens "economic lifeline" of the West and that the U.S. intervention is justified to protect American jobs (WP, NYT, 11/14). President Saddam Hussein informs Chinese officials that he would like to negotiate as long as he is not humiliated.

**November 14**  Saudi Arabia says that Iraq must first leave Kuwait before an Arab Summit could convene.

**November 15**  Secretary Baker meets with more members of UN Security Council in Brussels to discuss possible resolution authorizing military action in Gulf. President Hussein tells ABC news he wants to negotiate peaceful settlement and refuses to withdraw from Kuwait as precondition for talks. President Mubarak and President Assad reject call for Arab Summit.

**November 16**  Secretary Baker rejects Soviet envoy's suggestion that a solution of the crisis can be linked to Palestinian-Israeli conflict.

**November 19**  Iraq calls up 60,000 military reservists and 100,000 new conscripts into Iraqi military and adds six new divisions to southern Iraq and Kuwait.

**November 20**  245 members of Congress file suit in Washington D.C. court to force President Bush to seek Congressional approval before he can launch a war against Iraq.

**November 22**  President Bush visits Saudi Arabia and justifies military build-up by saying that U.S. must prevent Iraq from developing nuclear weapons.

**November 23**  President Bush meets with Syrian President Assad in Geneva.

**November 27**  President Gorbachev expresses support for use of military force against Iraq.

**November 28**  UN Security Council passes Resolution 677 which condemns Iraq's actions within occupied Kuwait. It is reported that Gulf states offer nearly $6 billion in financial aid to USSR in consideration of its support during the crisis — Saudi Arabia $4 billion, UAE $1 billion and Kuwait $1 billion.

**November 29** UN Security Council passes Resolution 678 which authorizes the use of all necessary means against Iraq unless it withdraws by January 15.

**November 30** President Bush calls for talks with Iraq and invites exchange between Foreign Secretaries Baker and Aziz.

**December 1** President Saddam Hussein agrees to meetings with U.S. and demands linkage with other occupations.

**December 3** U.S. Secretary of Defense Cheney says that Iraq can survive sanctions.

**December 4** UN General Assembly passes Resolution 45/58 J which reaffirms the long-standing ban against military attacks on nuclear facilities 141–1; the U.S. votes against the resolution. Iraq's minister of health announces that 1,416 children under the age of 5 have died in the past four months as a result of embargo on food and medicine.

**December 5** CIA director Webster reports that trade embargo has dealt a "serious blow" to Iraq's economy. Israeli Foreign Minister Levy warns U.S. not to leave Iraqi military intact.

**December 6** President Saddam Hussein declares the release of all foreign hostages in Iraq.

**December 9** Jordan and Algeria begin new negotiations aimed at arranging meeting between President Saddam Hussein and King Fahd.

**December 10** Soviet foreign minister tells Secretary Baker that USSR will not deploy troops due to opposition in USSR.

**December 11** Israeli Prime Minister Shamir meets with President Bush for the first time since August 2 and Bush promises Shamir that there will be no linkage between Gulf crisis and Palestinian issue. U.S. says it will seek additional $4 billion in assistance for Turkey, Jordan and Egypt from Japan or European countries. It is reported that U.S. has received pledges of nearly $13.4 billion from 25 nations.

**December 13** U.S. rejects Iraqi proposal for January 12 meeting. Algerian president Benjedid meets with President Saddam Hussein to open dialogue between Iraq and Arab states.

**December 14** Saudi King Fahd refuses to receive respected mediator Algerian President Benjedid (reportedly under pressure from U.S.; MEI, 11/21) who is attempting to mediate between Iraq and Saudi Arabia.

**December 15** Iraq cancels Foreign Minister Aziz's visit to U.S. because U.S. does not accept Iraqi dates for Secretary Baker's visit to Baghdad. King Hussein unveils a peace plan which provides international conference as cover to implement UN resolutions; U.S. ignores plan.

**December 18** European Community rejects proposal to participate in talks with Tariq Aziz before U.S. meets with Iraq. Amnesty International issues report on Iraqi atrocities in Kuwait.

**December 19** Second in Command of Desert Shield tells press that U.S. forces will not be ready by January 15.

**December 20** Security Council Resolution 681 calls on Israel to observe Geneva Conventions in the occupied territories.

**December 21** Israeli ferry boat carrying U.S. naval crews capsizes in Haifa harbor drowning 21 U.S. navy crew.

**December 23** U.S. Secretary of Defense Cheney warns Iraq not to use chemical weapons because "the U.S. response would be absolutely overwhelming and it would be devastating."

**December 24** President Saddam Hussein says Israel will be the first target if Iraq is attacked. Iraq withdraws its ambassadors to major world capitals for a meeting in Baghdad.

**December 26** President Saddam Hussein says he is willing to participate in a serious and constructive dialogue. Secretary Cheney and Chief of Staff Powell inform President Bush after visit to the Gulf that U.S. forces will not be prepared for action by January 15.

**December 27** Major Iraqi opposition groups, including Kurds, Shi'a groups, pro-Syrian Ba'ath party and Communists sign Damascus Declaration which calls for overthrow of present Iraqi government.

# 1991

**January 2** U.S. officials disclose Iraqi offer to withdraw from Kuwait if U.S. pledges not to attack and foreign troops leave region and that there can be an agreement on Palestinian question and the banning of weapons of mass destruction in the region (ND, 1/3).

**January 3** President Bush offers Secretary Baker to meet with Iraq's Minister Aziz in Geneva.

**January 4** U.S. Congress announces it will debate U.S. position in the Gulf on January 10. U.S. and Saudi Arabia postpone $14 billion arms deal that was to be the follow up to the two earlier deals under heavy Israeli opposition.

**January 6** Saudi King Fahd says he would consider negotiations only after Iraqi withdrawal from Kuwait.

**January 8** President Bush sends a letter to Congress asking for a resolution of support similar to UN resolution.

**January 9** Secretary Baker and Minister Aziz hold talks in Geneva; Baker reiterates demands for unconditional Iraqi withdrawal.

**January 10** Nine news organizations and four journalists file a lawsuit in federal court in New York challenging Pentagon censorship and press restrictions imposed on reporting the conflict in the Gulf.

**January 12** U.S. Congress authorizes President Bush to use force against Iraq if Iraq does not withdraw by January 15 in close vote. Senate vote is 52–47; House is 250–183.

**January 13** UN Secretary General Perez de Cuellar flies to Baghdad for meetings with President Hussein.

**January 14** France proposes plan for Security Council call for a rapid Iraqi withdrawal from Kuwait along with agreement for future consideration of convening an international conference supported by Belgium, Germany, Spain, Italy, Algeria, Morocco, Tunisia and several non-aligned nations (Z, 2/91); U.S. immediately rejects proposal. Israeli Supreme Court rules that gas masks should be provided to all residents of the occupied territories; military says they have stock of only 170,000 for the 1.7 million Palestinians. A renegade bodyguard slays PLO second-in-command Saleh Khalaf and PLO security chief Hayel Abdel-Hamid in Tunis.

**January 15** UN-sanctioned deadline for Iraqi withdrawal from Kuwait. Israel imposes 24-hour-a-day curfew on occupied Gaza strip.

**January 16** U.S. launches massive air bombardment of Baghdad, Iraq and Kuwait.

**January 17** Israel imposes total 24-hour curfew on entire West Bank and Gaza. Iraq launches four scud missiles that land in Israel. U.S. bombers destroy Iraqi nuclear research center at Tuwaitha near Baghdad in contravention of UN Resolution 45/58 J.

**January 21** After meeting with U.S. Under-Secretary of State Eagleburger, Israeli Prime Minister Shamir declares that Israel will respond to Iraqi scud attacks at a "suitable time."

**January 22** Iraq launches scud missiles at Israel. It is reported that U.S. refused to provide Israeli air force with the codes necessary to avoid hostile encounters with U.S.-led coalition aircraft operating in Iraqi airspace (N, 2/18).

**January 23** U.S. and other forces announce they have flown more than 12,000 bombing missions over Iraq and Kuwait.

**January 25** Iraq launches seven scud missiles at Tel Aviv and Haifa and one at Riyadh, Saudi Arabia.

**January 26** Bush administration officials say that ground war is likely because air power alone will not drive Iraq out of Kuwait; new Soviet Foreign Minister Bessmertnykh increasingly worried that U.S. is exceeding UN mandate and cautions U.S. not to destroy Iraq. More than 200,000 protest against the war in Bonn and a Washington D.C. protest draws nearly 250,000. Four scud missiles are fired at Israel.

**January 27** Egyptian officials tell press conference that they are not in favor of destroying Iraq or overthrowing President Saddam Hussein.

**January 28** Prominent Israeli activists for Palestinian-Israeli peace, including many Peace Now members, hold news conference to declare their support for the war against Iraq and condemn anti-war movements outside Israel for being against the war.

**January 29** German leaders announce that they will provide a further $5.5 billion to the anti-Iraq coalition. French Defense Minister Chevenment resigns because he feels the U.S. aims in the war go beyond UN-sanctioned actions. U.S. reportedly cuts development aid to Yemen by 85% for not siding with the anti-Iraq coalition (NYT, 1/30). Israeli authorities arrest prominent Palestinian peace advocate Professor Sari Nusseibeh and accuse him of spying for Iraq but refuse to issue official legal charges.

**January 30** Bush administration backpedals on joint statement issued by Secretary Baker and USSR Foreign Minister Bessmertnykh that called for a ceasefire if Iraq were unequivocally to commit to leaving Kuwait and also that solving the Israeli-Palestinian conflict would be a priority after the conflict. Iraqi forces occupy Khafji, Saudi Arabia and engage U.S. troops in battle before being driven out with heavy casualties.

**January 31** The UN Security Council members, under strong pressure from the U.S. and Britain, resist an attempt to force public debate on a ceasefire for an Iraqi withdrawal in the Persian Gulf War (NYT 2/1). Iraqi scud missile lands in occupied West Bank and Israelis announce policy of no longer saying whether or not a Patriot missile has been used.

**February 3** Israeli cabinet votes to accept Rehavim Zeevi, leader of the right-wing Moledet party which advocates mass expulsion of Palestinians from territories occupied by Israel, as a new member of the government. 300,000 Moroccans demonstrate in Rabat against U.S. coalition bombing in the Gulf.

**February 4** Iran's President Rafsanjani offers to serve as a mediator between the U.S. and Iraq. U.S. battleships begin to fire on Iraq while B-52s bomb outskirts of Baghdad. Israeli Prime Minister Shamir warns against pressing Israel for international peace conference after conflict in first Knesset address since start of the war.

**February 5** Iraq announces suspension of all fuel sales after U.S. bombers destroy its refineries and distribution networks. Israeli curfew is loosened in some Palestinian towns for the first time since it was imposed on January 17. U.S.-led bombing missions against Iraq and Kuwait reportedly exceed 41,000 (MEI, 2/8).

**February 6** Baghdad radio reports civilian casualties of U.S. coalition bombing near 7,000.

**February 7** King Hussein makes speech on Jordanian national television supporting Iraq against

U.S. objectives in the war and the region saying that the real aim of Western powers is to "destroy Iraq and reorganize the area in a manner far more dangerous to our people than the Sykes-Picot agreement" (NYT, 2/7). Iraq reports that about 150 people, including 35 children were killed by bombing in southern city of Nairiya.

**February 8** Bush administration announces it will review U.S. aid to Jordan in light of King Hussein's speech.

**February 9** President Gorbachev warns in speech that U.S. is in danger of exceeding UN mandate by trying to destroy Iraq. UN Security Council announces it will finally meet but U.S. and British-led effort keeps meeting behind closed doors.

**February 10** It is reported that U.S. has received more than $50 billion in pledges to cover military costs: the major contributors were Saudi Arabia, $16.8 billion; Kuwait, $16 billion; Japan, $10.7 billion and Germany, $6.6 billion (NYT, 2/11).

**February 11** Defense Secretary Cheney informs President Bush that General Schwarzkopf asked for a "window" of dates to begin the ground war no earlier than February 21 (NYT 3/3).

**February 12** President Gorbachev sends special envoy Primakov to meet with President Hussein in Baghdad who says he would be willing to cooperate with the USSR to end the war.

**February 13** U.S. military bombs destroy Ameriyeh shelter in Baghdad killing over 1500 civilians.

**February 14** The first UN Security Council session since the war began meets in closed session and Yemen and Cuba circulate a ceasefire plan that will lead to an Iraqi withdrawal. Kuwait's interior minister announces formulation of "a comprehensive security plan" for first three months after liberation (N, 3/18).

**February 15** Iraq's Revolutionary Command Council announces that Iraq may be ready to accept Resolution 660 and mentions "withdrawal" for the first time; Bush denounces it as a "cruel hoax" and encourages the overthrow of Saddam Hussein.

**February 17** Foreign Minister Aziz arrives in Moscow to discuss peace proposal with President Gorbachev. French Foreign Minister Dumas says in interview that "we are on the eve or the pre-eve of the ground offensive." British bombers miss bridge near city of Falluja and kill nearly 150 civilians.

**February 18** Foreign Minister Aziz meets President Gorbachev in Moscow.

**February 19** Gorbachev announces a revised plan which includes a timetable for Iraqi withdrawal from Kuwait. Without disclosing its contents, President Bush says peace plan "falls well short of what would be required" and says that military campaign remains on schedule. Iran says it is convinced Iraq is sincerely interested in a withdrawal.

**February 20** U.S. and Britain say problem with Soviet plan is that it lacks a tight timetable for an immediate withdrawal. U.S. announces it will finally release $400 million in housing loan guarantees to Israel which had been held up for months.

**February 21** Soviet plan is accepted by Iraq and calls for a one-day ceasefire to allow Iraq to withdraw from Kuwait City in one week and from the entire country in 21 days. U.S. rejects conditions and demands its own conditions for Iraqi withdrawal from Kuwait City in four days, from Kuwait in one week, and that all mines be removed from Kuwait, while the air war would continue full-force during the entire process.

**February 22** President Bush gives Iraq an ultimatum to withdraw by noon, February 23 or face ground war, despite Iraqi acceptance of Soviet plan. It is reported that U.S.-led bombing missions fly record number of raids over Kuwait and southern Iraq.

**February 23** Soviet ambassador announces at UN that Iraqi Foreign Minister Aziz had agreed to U.S. demands; President Gorbachev phones President Bush to demand more time because agreement is close at hand. U.S. launches ground war against Kuwait and Iraq while UN Security Council was to discuss integrating U.S. and USSR proposals (G, 3/6). Pentagon announces press blackout.

**February 25** President Hussein announces Iraqi pullout of Kuwait; President Bush says that a ceasefire will only come after Iraq has "laid down its arms" and leaves military equipment behind; attack continues on Iraqis leaving Kuwait.

**February 26** Iraq says it will accept any terms; U.S. aircraft relentlessly bomb retreating Iraqi military as they retreat from Kuwait, killing and wounding up to 100,000 on the roads north to Basra. Three month martial law is imposed in Kuwait by royal decree; the Crown Prince will serve as military governor.

**February 27** President Bush announces that hostilities would be suspended as of midnight. U.S. corporations win massive contracts to rebuild Kuwait.

**March 2** Bush administration pushes through UN Security Council resolution which puts off ceasefire until all its conditions are met and bars UN observer forces until that time and refuses to lift the food embargo against Iraq (G, 3/13). Fighting breaks out in Iraqi cities between anti-government and pro-government troops.

**March 3** U.S. and Iraqi generals meet and Iraq accepts all terms; Saudi Arabia accepts long-term U.S. troop presence in kingdom. UN compromise plan exempts more food and humanitarian aid from Iraqi sanctions against U.S. pressure, but continues embargo. Kuwaiti forces begin crackdown on Palestinians.

**March 4** Fighting in Iraq spreads to nearly 12 cities. Kuwaiti crown prince arrives in Kuwait. Shi'a rebels reported to have seized Basra.

**March 5** Iraq releases all coalition POWs.

**March 6** Reports of widespread unrest among the Shi'a population in southern Iraq and the Kurds in the north. Baghdad expels all foreign journalists "temporarily." In his post-war address to Congress, President Bush stresses the need to find a solution to the Arab-Israeli conflict, based on UN Resolutions 242 and 338, and on the concept of "territories for peace" (NYT, 3/7/91).

**March 8** Secretary of State Baker begins the first of his post-war trips to the Middle East in search of a formula for regional peace.

**March 10** Ten Arab foreign ministers meet with Baker, and afterwards call for Israeli concessions on the occupied territories and a UN-sponsored peace conference.

**March 12** Baker meets with Israeli Prime Minister Shamir, and later with Palestinian leaders from the occupied territories.

**March 13** Iraq is reported to have deployed helicopter gunships and tanks against the rebel groups.

**March 14** Sheikh Jaber al-Ahmad al-Sabah, emir of Kuwait, returns to the country after seven months in exile, as reports circulate of the harassment and torture of Palestinians, Sudanese and other non-citizens by Kuwaitis.

**March 20** The Kuwaiti government resigns amid criticism of the slow pace of democratic reform. A U.S. plane shoots down an Iraqi fighter jet. Congress votes to eliminate all U.S. aid to Jordan, despite President Bush's objections.

**March 21** A UN study of conditions in post-war Iraq describes the situation as "near apocalyptic," saying the coalition bombing had relegated Iraq to a "pre-industrial age" (NYT, 3/22/91).

**March 23** Israeli Housing Minister Ariel Sharon calls for the annexation of the West Bank and Gaza Strip.

**March 26** White House spokesperson Marlin Fitzwater says: "We don't intend to involve ourselves in the internal affairs of Iraq," as pressure mounts for U.S. action to aid the rebels attempting to overthrow Saddam Hussein's government (NYT, 3/25/91).

**March 28** Baghdad claims to have re-captured the strategic city of Kirkuk from the Kurdish rebels, and to have completely crushed the Shi'a rebellion in the south of the country.

**April 1** Masud Barzani, leader of the Kurdish Democratic Party, calls for international support to prevent the "torture and genocide" of the Iraqi Kurdish population (NYT, 4/2/91).

**April 3** Sulaymaniye, the last major town still held by the Kurdish rebels, is recaptured by the Iraqi Army. UN Security Council adopts Resolution 687, laying down stringent conditions on Iraq for a permanent ceasefire in the Gulf War, including the payment of reparations to Kuwait; sanctions are not relaxed. The mass flight of hundreds of thousands of Kurdish refugees towards the Turkish and Iranian borders begins in northern Iraq.

**April 10** In a belated recognition of the need to aid Kurdish refugees, Washington orders Iraq to halt all military actions north of the 36th parallel.

**April 16** U.S. troops are deployed in northern Iraq, joining British and French forces already stationed there. Reports indicate that up to a thousand Kurds are dying every day from disease and starvation in the mountainous border region.

**April 19** An Amnesty International report is released, saying that scores of mainly Palestinian Arabs have been murdered and hundreds arrested and tortured in Kuwait since coalition troops entered the city in February (NYT, 4/20/91).

**April 20** Kuwait announces a new cabinet, in which all the key posts remain in the hands of the ruling al-Sabah family.

**April 24** Kurdish leaders conclude a first round of talks with Saddam Hussein in Baghdad, and announce an agreement "in principle" for an autonomous Kurdish region in northern Iraq (NYT, 4/25/91).

**April 26** Secretary Baker ends his third post-war trip to the Middle East, with little or nothing to show for it in terms of furthering the peace process.

**May 6** The final contingent of U.S. troops leaves southern Iraq, and is replaced by a 1,500-strong UN force operating in a demilitarized zone along the Iraq-Kuwait border.

**May 19** In Kuwait trials begin of alleged "collaborators" with the occupying Iraqi regime. A man is sentenced to fifteen years in jail for wearing a T-shirt with a picture of Saddam Hussein on it during the occupation (NYT, 5/20/91).

**May 20** President Bush says that he would oppose any relaxation of anti-Iraq sanctions until Saddam Hussein is removed from power.

**May 29** President Bush calls for restraint in the sale of arms to countries in the Middle East.

**May 30** Secretary of Defense Cheney announces plans to sell 25 F-15 fighter-bombers to Israel, along with $210 million in military aid for the development of the Israeli Arrow anti-missile missile system.

**June 2** The emir of Kuwait announces plans for general elections, to be held in October 1992. The Bush administration releases details of its analysis of the situation in post-war Iraq. Eighty per cent of the country's power supply is still out of action, and the civilian telecommunications system is described as "a total loss." Total repair bill is estimated by the CIA at $30 billion. High temperatures and a chronic lack of clean water, food and even basic medicines has created a "public health catastrophe," in which "tens of thousands" have already died since the war formally ended, and in which countless thousands more face death as summer approaches (NYT, 6/3/91).

**June 4** U.S. Defense Department, responding to a request under the Freedom of Information Act, releases its "tentative" estimates of Iraqi military casualties during the Gulf War: 100,000 killed and 300,000 wounded, (NYT, 6/5/91).

**July 18** Secretary of State Baker begins new round of shuttle diplomacy focusing on bringing Israel and the Palestinians to a peace conference.

**August 4** Israel agrees to participate in peace conference on condition that there is no involvement of the PLO or Palestinians from East Jerusalem. It also announces it has no intention of giving up any territory in a land for peace exchange. Palestinians tell Baker that they have the right to select their own delegation. They submit new questions to Baker to clarify the U.S. position.

**August 5** Baker holds press conference in Algiers claiming victory in peace conference plans. Hours later, Israeli settlers construct newest settlement outside of Hebron in occupied West Bank.

**August 10** Lebanese organizations holding Western hostages call for UN Secretary General to coordinate hostage negotiations. Briton John McCarthy is released in Lebanon, followed by American Edward Tracy three days later. New round of hostage-release negotiations is launched.

**August 15** UN Security Council votes to allow Iraq six months to sell limited amount of oil to finance civilian needs. Parallel resolutions divert 30% of oil earnings for war-related claims against Iraq.

# Chronology Source Abbreviations

AFD (*All Fall Down*, Gary Sick, Penguin, 1986, New York)
BG (*Boston Globe*, Boston)
CSM (*Christian Science Monitor*, Boston)
FT (*Financial Times*, London)
G (*Guardian*, New York)
IA (*Israel and the American National Interest*, Cheryl Rubenberg, University of Illinois Press, 1986, Champaign)
ICC (*The Iran-Contra Connection*, Marshall, Scott, Hunter; 1987, South End Press, Boston)
IT (*Iraq in Transition*, ed. Fred Axelgard, 1986, Westview, Boulder)
JPS (*Journal of Palestine Studies*, Washington D.C.)
LAT (*Los Angeles Times*, Los Angeles)
LW (*Longest War: The Iran-Iraq Military Conflict*, Dilip Hiro, 1991, Routledge, New York)
MEI (*Middle East International*, London)
MET (*Middle East Times*, Nicosia)
MEJ (*Middle East Journal*, Washington D.C.)
MER (*Middle East Report*, [MERIP], Washington D.C)
NYT (*New York Times*, New York)
N (*Nation*, New York)
RI (*Revolutionary Iran*, R.K. Ramazani, 1988, Johns Hopkins, Baltimore)
SI (*Saddam's Iraq: Revolution or Reaction?*, CARDRI, 1989, Zed Books, London)
WP (*Washington Post*, Washington D.C.)
VV (*Village Voice*, New York)
YA (*Yediot Ahranot*, Tel Aviv)
Z (*Z Magazine*, Boston)

# Glossary

*Abbasid*  ruling Arab dynasty from 750–1258; based in Baghdad but ruled over entire Arab world during Golden Age of Arab civilization.

*AIPAC*  American-Israel Public Affairs Committee; coordinates pro-Israeli political efforts and lobbies in Washington.

*Fatwa*  decision by Muslim authorities based on interpretations of the Qur'an.

*Hajj*  pilgrimage to Mecca required of every Muslim able to go once in her or his lifetime.

*Hamas*  Islamic organization in Gaza Strip and West Bank; challenges PLO's nationalism with religious-based opposition to Israel.

*Herut*  largest component party of right-wing Likud Bloc in Israeli parliament.

*Hulago*  Mongol leader who defeated Abbasid dynasty in 1258.

*Imara*  territory controlled by one individual or family group (emirate).

*Intifada*  Palestinian uprising that began in December 1987 to challenge Israel's occupation of the West Bank and Gaza Strip.

*Jihad*  holy war to defend Islam; sometimes refers to individual Muslim's struggle against evil.

*Madhab*  a system of thought or intellectual approach.

*Molodet*  extremist Israeli party; part of government formed in 1990. Advocates forced expulsion of Palestinians.

*Mustad'afun*  dependent; used to describe relationship of some Arab governments to Western powers.

*Savak*  notorious secret police during regime of Shah of Iran.

*Shari'a*  canonical law of Islam.

*Shi'a*  branch of Islam that split from Sunni majority over issue of Mohammad's successor.

*Sunni*  majority orthodox branch of Islam.

*Ulamma*  religious scholars.

*Umma*  community of believers in Islam.

# Appendices

## Appendix A-The UN Resolutions

*The full text of all the UN resolutions on the Gulf crisis, from 660—condemning the Iraqi invasion of Kuwait—through 687—which laid out the conditions for a permanent ceasefire.*

**Resolution 660**
*2 August 1990*

*The Security Council,*

*Alarmed by* the invasion of Kuwait on 2 August 1990 by the military forces of Iraq,

*Determining* that there exists a breach of international peace and security as regards the Iraqi invasion of Kuwait,

*Acting* under Articles 39 and 40 of the Charter of the United Nations,

1. *Condemns* the Iraqi invasion of Kuwait;

2. *Demands* that Iraq withdraw immediately and unconditionally all its forces to the positions in which they were located on 1 August 1990;

3. *Calls upon* Iraq and Kuwait to begin immediately intensive negotiations for the resolution of their differences and supports all efforts in this regard, and especially those of the League of Arab States;

4. *Decides* to meet again as necessary to consider further steps to ensure compliance with the present resolution.

**Resolution 661**
*6 August 1990*

*The Security Council,*

*Reaffirming its* resolution 660 (1990) of 2 August 1990,

*Deeply concerned* that that resolution has not been implemented and that the invasion by Iraq and Kuwait continues with further loss of human life and material destruction,

*Determined* to bring the invasion and occupation of Kuwait by Iraq to an end and to restore the sovereignty, independence and territorial integrity of Kuwait,

*Noting* that the legitimate Government of Kuwait has expressed its readiness to comply with resolution 660 (1990),

*Mindful* of its responsibilities under the Charter of the United Nations for the maintenance of international peace and security,

*Affirming* the inherent right of individual or collective self-defence, in response to the armed attack by Iraq against Kuwait, in accordance with Article 51 of the Charter,

*Acting* under Chapter VII of the Charter of the United Nations,

*1. Determines* that Iraq so far has failed to comply with paragraph 2 of resolution 660 (1990) and has usurped the authority of the legitimate Government of Kuwait;

*2. Decides*, as a consequence, to take the following measures to secure compliance of Iraq with paragraph 2 of resolution 660 (1990) and to restore the authority of the legitimate Government of Kuwait;

*3. Decides* that all States shall prevent:
*(a)* The import into their territories of all commodities and products originating in Iraq or Kuwait exported therefrom after the date of the present resolution;
*(b)* Any activities by their nationals or in their territories which would promote or are calculated to promote the export or transshipment of any commodities or products from Iraq or Kuwait; and any dealings by their nationals or their flag vessels or in their territories in any commodities or products originating in Iraq and Kuwait and exported therefrom after the date of the present resolution, including in particular any transfer of funds to Iraq or Kuwait for the purposes of such activities or dealings;
*(c)* The sale or supply by their nationals or from their territories or using their flag vessels of any commodities or products, including weapons or any other military equipment, whether or not originating in their territories but not including supplies intended strictly for medical purposes, and, in humanitarian circumstances, foodstuffs, to any person or body in Iraq or Kuwait or to any person or body for the purposes of any business carried on in or operated from Iraq or Kuwait, and any activities by their nationals or in their territories which promote or are calculated to promote such sale or supply of such commodities or products;

*4. Decides* that all States shall not make available to the Government of Iraq or to any commercial, industrial or public utility undertaking in Iraq or Kuwait, any funds or any other financial or economic resources and shall prevent their nationals and any persons within their territories from removing from their territories or otherwise making available to that Government or to any such undertaking any such funds or resources and from remitting any other funds to persons or bodies within Iraq or Kuwait, except payments exclusively for strictly medical or humanitarian purposes and, in humanitarian circumstances, foodstuffs;

*5. Calls upon* all States, including States nonmembers of the United Nations, to act strictly in accordance with the provisions of the present resolution notwithstanding any contract entered into or licence granted before the date of the present resolution;

*6. Decides* to establish, in accordance with rule 28 of the provisional rules of procedure of the Security Council, a Committee of the Security Council consisting of all the members of the Council, to undertake the following tasks and to report on its work to the Council with its observations and recommendations:
*(a)* To examine the reports on the progress of the implementation of the present resolution which will be submitted by the Secretary-General;
*(b)* To seek from all States further information regarding the action taken by them concerning the effective implementation of the provisions laid down in the present resolution;

*7. Calls upon* all states to co-operate fully with the Committee in the fulfilment of its task, including supplying such information as may be sought by the Committee in pursuance of the present resolution;

*8. Requests* the Secretary-General to provide all necessary assistance to the Committee and to make the necessary arrangements in the Secretariat for the purpose;

*9. Decides* that, notwithstanding paragraphs 4 through 8 above, nothing in the present resolution shall prohibit assistance to the legitimate Government of Kuwait, and calls upon all States:
*(a)* To take appropriate measures to protect assets of the legitimate Government of Kuwait and its agencies;
*(b)* Not to recognize any regime set up by the occupying Power;

*10. Requests* the Secretary-General to report to the Council on the progress of the implementation of the present resolution, the first report to be submitted within thirty days;

*11. Decides* to keep this item on its agenda and to continue its efforts to put an early end to the invasion by Iraq.

**Resolution 662**
*9 August 1990*

*The Security Council,*

*Recalling* its resolutions 660 (1990) and 661 (1990),

*Gravely alarmed* by the declaration by Iraq of a "comprehensive and eternal merger" with Kuwait,

*Demanding*, once again, that Iraq withdraw immediately and unconditionally all its forces to the positions in which they were located on 1 August 1990,

*Determined* to bring the occupation of Kuwait by Iraq to an end and to restore the sovereignty, independence and territorial integrity of Kuwait,

*Determined also* to restore the authority of the legitimate Government of Kuwait,

1. *Decides* that annexation of Kuwait by Iraq under any form and whatever pretext has no legal validity, and is considered null and void;

2. *Calls upon* all States, international. organizations and specialized agencies not to recognize that annexation, and to refrain from any action or dealing that might be interpreted as an indirect recognition of the annexation;

3. *Further demands* that Iraq rescind its actions purporting to annex Kuwait;

4. *Decides* to keep this item on its agenda and to continue its efforts to put an early end to the occupation.

**Resolution 664**
*18 August 1990*

*The Security Council,*

*Recalling* the Iraqi invasion and purported annexation of Kuwait and resolutions 660, 661, and 662,

*Deeply concerned* for the safety and well-being of third state nationals in Iraq and Kuwait,

*Recalling* the obligations of Iraq in this regard under international law,

*Welcoming* the efforts of the Secretary-General to pursue urgent consultations with the Government of Iraq following the concern and anxiety expressed by the members of the Council on 17 August 1990,

*Acting* under Chapter VII of the United Nations Charter,

1. *Demands* that Iraq permit and facilitate the immediate departure from Kuwait and Iraq of the nationals of third countries and grant immediate and continuing access of consular officials to such nationals;

2. *Further demands* that Iraq take no action to jeopardize the safety, security or health of such nationals;

3. *Reaffirms* its decision in resolution 662 (1990) that annexation of Kuwait by Iraq is null and void, and therefore demands that the government of Iraq rescind its orders for the closure of diplomatic and consular missions in Kuwait and the withdrawal of the immunity of their personnel, and refrain from any such actions in the future;

4. *Requests* the Secretary-General to report to the Council on compliance with this resolution at the earliest possible time.

**Resolution 665**
*25 August 1990*

*The Security Council,*

*Recalling* its resolutions 660 (1990), 661 (1990), 662 (1990) and 664 (1990) and demanding their full and immediate implementation,

*Having decided* in resolution 661 (1990) to impose economic sanctions under Chapter VII of the Charter of the United Nations,

*Determined* to bring an end to the occupation of Kuwait by Iraq which imperils the existence of a Member State and to restore the legitimate authority, and the sovereignty, independence and territorial integrity of Kuwait which requires the speedy implementation of the above resolutions,

*Deploring* the loss of innocent life stemming from the Iraqi invasion of Kuwait and determined to prevent further such losses,

*Gravely alarmed* that Iraq continues to refuse to comply with resolutions 660 (1990), 661 (1990), 662 (1990) and 664 (1990) and in particular at the conduct of the Government of Iraq in using Iraqi flag vessels to export oil,

1. *Calls upon* those Member States cooperating with the Government of Kuwait which are deploying maritime forces to the area to use such measures commensurate to the specific circumstances as may be necessary under the authority of the Security Council to halt all inward and outward maritime shipping in order to inspect and verify their cargoes and destinations and to ensure strict implementation of the provisions related to such shipping laid down in resolution 661 (1990);

2. *Invites* Member States accordingly to co-operate as may be necessary to ensure compliance with the provisions of resolution 661 (1990) with maximum use of political and diplomatic measures, in accordance with paragraph 1 above;

3. *Requests* all States to provide in accordance with the Charter such assistance as may be required by the States referred to in paragraph 1 of this resolution;

4. *Further requests* the States concerned to coordinate their actions in pursuit of the above paragraphs of this resolution using as appropriate mechanisms of the Military Staff Committee and after consultation with the Secretary-General to submit reports to the Security Council and its Committee established under resolution 661 (1990) to facilitate the monitoring of the implementation of this resolution;

5. *Decides* to remain actively seized of the matter.

**Resolution 666**
*13 September 1990*

*The Security Council,*

*Recalling* its resolution 661 (1990), paragraphs 3 (c) and 4 of which apply, except in humanitarian circumstances, to foodstuffs,

*Recognizing* that circumstances may arise in which it will be necessary for foodstuffs to be supplied to the civilian population in Iraq or Kuwait in order to relieve human suffering,

*Noting* that in this respect the Committee established under paragraph 6 of that resolution has received communications from several Member States,

*Emphasizing* that it is for the Security Council, alone or acting through the Committee, to determine whether humanitarian circumstances have arisen,

*Deeply concerned* that Iraq has failed to comply with its obligations under Security Council resolution 664 (1990) in respect of the safety and well-being of third State nationals, and reaffirming that Iraq retains full responsibility in this regard under international humanitarian law including, where applicable, the Fourth Geneva Convention,

*Acting* under Chapter VII of the Charter of the United Nations,

1. *Decides* that in order to make the necessary determination whether or not for the purposes of paragraph 3 (c) and paragraph 4 of resolution 661 (1990) humanitarian circumstances have arisen, the Committee shall keep the situation regarding foodstuffs in Iraq and Kuwait under constant review;

2. *Expects* Iraq to comply with its obligations under Security Council resolution 664 (1990) in respect of third State nationals and reaffirms that Iraq remains fully responsible for their safety and well-being in accordance with international humanitarian law including, where applicable, the Fourth Geneva Convention;

3. *Requests*, for the purposes of paragraphs 1 and 2 of this resolution, that the Secretary-General seek urgently, and on a continuing basis, information from relevant United Nations and other appropriate humanitarian agencies and all other sources on the availability of food in Iraq and Kuwait, such information to be communicated by the Secretary-General to the Committee regularly;

4. *Requests further* that in seeking and supplying such information particular attention will be paid to such categories of persons who might suffer specially, such as children under 15 years of age, expectant mothers, maternity cases, the sick and the elderly;

5. *Decides* that if the Committee, after receiving the reports from the Secretary-General, determines that circumstances have arisen in which there is an urgent humanitarian need to supply foodstuffs to Iraq or Kuwait in order to relieve human suffering, it will report promptly to the Council its decision as to how such need should be met;

6. *Directs* the Committee that in formulating its decisions it should bear in mind that foodstuffs should be provided through the United Nations in co-operation with the International Committee of the Red Cross or other appropriate humanitarian agencies and distributed by them or under their supervision in order to ensure that they reach the intended beneficiaries;

7. *Requests* the Secretary-General to use his good offices to facilitate the delivery and distribution of foodstuffs to Kuwait and Iraq in accordance with the provisions of this and other relevant resolutions;

8. *Recalls* that resolution 661 (1990) does not apply to supplies intended strictly for medical purposes, but in this connection recommends that medical supplies should be exported under the strict supervision of the Government of the exporting State or by appropriate humanitarian agencies.

**Resolution 667**
*16 September 1990*

*The Security Council,*

*Reaffirming* its resolutions 660 (1990), 661 (1990), 662 (1990), 664 (1990), 665 (1990) and 666 (1990),

*Recalling* the Vienna Conventions of 18 April 1961 on diplomatic relations and of 24 April 1963 on consular relations, to both of which Iraq is a party,

*Considering* that the decision of Iraq to order the closure of diplomatic and consular missions in Kuwait and to withdraw the immunity and privileges of these missions and their personnel is contrary to the decisions of the Security Council, the international Conventions mentioned above and international law,

*Deeply concerned* that Iraq, notwithstanding the decisions of the Security Council and the provisions of the Conventions mentioned above, has committed acts of violence against diplomatic missions and their personnel in Kuwait,

*Outraged* at recent violations by Iraq of diplomatic premises in Kuwait and at the abduction of personnel enjoying diplomatic immunity and foreign nationals who were present in these premises,

*Considering* that the above actions by Iraq constitute aggressive acts and a flagrant violation of its international obligations which strike at the root of the conduct of international relations in accordance with the Charter of the United Nations,

*Recalling* that Iraq is fully responsible for any use of violence against foreign nationals or against any diplomatic or consular mission in Kuwait or its personnel,

*Determined* to ensure respect for its decisions and for Article 25 of the Charter of the United Nations,

*Further considering* that the grave nature of Iraq's actions, which constitute a new escalation of its violations of international law, obliges the Council not only to express its immediate reaction but also to consult urgently to take further concrete measures to ensure Iraq's compliance with the Council's resolutions,

*Acting* under Chapter VII of the Charter of the United Nations,

1. *Strongly condemns* aggressive acts perpetrated by Iraq against diplomatic premises and personnel in Kuwait, including the abduction of foreign nationals who were present in those premises;

2. *Demands* the immediate release of those foreign nationals as well as all nationals mentioned in resolution 664 (1990);

3. *Further demands* that Iraq immediately and fully comply with its international obligations under resolutions 660 (1990), 662 (1990) and 664 (1990) of the Security Council, the Vienna Conventions on diplomatic and consular relations and international law;

4. *Further demands* that Iraq immediately protect the safety and well-being of diplomatic and consular personnel and premises in Kuwait and in Iraq and take no action to hinder the diplomatic and consular missions in the performance of their functions, including access to their nationals and the protection to their person and interests;

5. *Reminds* all States that they are obliged to observe strictly resolutions 661 (1990), 662 (1990), 664 (1990), 665 (1990) and 666 (1990);

6. *Decides* to consult urgently to take further concrete measures as soon as possible, under Chapter VII of the Charter, in response to Iraq's continued violation of the Charter, of resolutions of the Council and of international law.

**Resolution 669**
*24 September 1990*

*The Security Council,*

*Recalling* its resolution 661 (1990) of 6 August 1990,

*Recalling also* Article 50 of the Charter of the United Nations,

*Conscious* of the fact that an increasing number of requests for assistance have been received under the provisions of Article 50 of the Charter of the United Nations,

*Entrusts* the Committee established under resolution 661 (1990) concerning the situation between Iraq and Kuwait with the task of examining requests for assistance under the provisions of Article 50 of the Charter of the United Nations and making recommendations to the President of the Security Council for appropriate action.

**Resolution 670**
*25 September 1990*

*The Security Council,*

*Reaffirming* its resolutions 660 (1990), 661 (1990), 662 (1990), 664 (1990), 665 (1990), 666 (1990), and 667 (1990),

*Condemning* Iraq's continued occupation of Kuwait, its failure to rescind its actions and end its purported annexation and its holding of third State nationals against their will, in flagrant violation of resolutions 660 (1990), 662 (1990), 664 (1990) and 667 (1990) and of international humanitarian law,

*Condemning further* the treatment by Iraqi forces of Kuwaiti nationals, including measures to force them to leave their own country and mistreatment of persons and property in Kuwait in violation of international law,

*Noting with grave concern* the persistent attempts to evade the measures laid down in resolution 661 (1990),

*Further noting* that a number of States have limited the number of Iraqi diplomatic and consular officials in their countries and that others are planning to do so,

*Determined* to ensure by all necessary means the strict and complete application of the measures laid down in resolution 661 (1990),

*Determined* to ensure respect for its decisions and the provisions of Articles 25 and 48 of the Charter of the United Nations,

*Affirming* that any acts of the Government of Iraq which are contrary to the abovementioned resolutions or to Articles 25 or 48 of the Charter of the United Nations, such as Decree No. 377 of the Revolution Command Council of Iraq of 16 September 1990, are null and void,

*Reaffirming* its determination to ensure compliance with Security Council resolutions by maximum use of political and diplomatic means,

*Welcoming* the Secretary-General's use of his good offices to advance a peaceful solution based on the relevant Security Council resolutions and noting with appreciation his continuing efforts to this end,

*Underlining* to the Government of Iraq that its continued failure to comply with the terms of resolutions 660 (1990), 661 (1990), 662 (1990), 664 (1990), 666 (1990) and 667 (1990) could lead to further serious action by the Council under the Charter of the United Nations, including under Chapter VII,

*Recalling* the provisions of Article 103 of the Charter of the United Nations,

*Acting* under Chapter VII of the Charter of the United Nations,

1. *Calls upon* all States to carry out their obligations to ensure strict and complete compliance with resolution 661 (1990) and in particular paragraphs 3, 4 and 5 thereof;

2. *Confirms* that resolution 661 (1990) applies to all means of transport, including aircraft;

3. *Decides* that all States, notwithstanding the existence of any rights or obligations conferred or imposed by any international agreement or any contract entered into or any licence or permit granted before the date of the present resolution, shall deny permission to any aircraft to take off from their territory if the aircraft would carry any cargo to or from Iraq or Kuwait other than food in humanitarian circumstances, subject to authorization by the Council or the Committee established by resolution 661 (1990) and in accordance with resolution 666 (1990) or supplies intended strictly for medical purposes or solely for UNIIMOG [The United Nations Iran-Iraq Military Observer Group];

4. *Decides further* that all States shall deny permission to any aircraft destined to land in Iraq or Kuwait, whatever its State of registration, to overfly its territory unless:

(*a*) The aircraft lands at an airfield designated by that State outside Iraq or Kuwait in order to permit its inspection to ensure that there is no cargo on board in violation of resolution 661 (1990) or the present resolution, and for this purpose the aircraft may be detained for as long as necessary; or
(*b*) the particular flight has been approved by the Committee established by resolution 661 (1990); or
(*c*) The flight is certified by the United Nations as solely for the purposes of UNIIMOG;

5. *Decides* that each State shall take all necessary measures to ensure that any aircraft registered in its territory or operated by an operator who has his principal place of business or permanent residence in its territory complies with the provisions of resolution 661 (1990) and the present resolution;

6. *Decides further* that all States shall notify in a timely fashion the Committee established by resolution 661 (1990) of any flight between its territory and Iraq or Kuwait to which the requirement to land in paragraph 4 above does not apply, and the purpose for such a flight;

7. *Calls upon* all States to co-operate in taking such measures as may be necessary, consistent with international law, including the Chicago Convention, to ensure the effective implementation of the provisions of resolution 661 (1990) or the present resolution;

8. *Calls upon* all States to detain any ships of Iraqi registry which enter their ports and which are being or have been used in violation of resolution 661 (1990), or to deny such ships entrance to their ports except in circumstances recognized under international law as necessary to safeguard human life;

9. *Reminds* all States of their obligations under resolution 661 (1990) with regard to the freezing of Iraqi assets, and the protection of the assets of the legitimate Government of Kuwait and its agencies, located within their territory and to report to the Committee established under resolution 661 (1990) regarding those assets;

10. *Calls upon* all States to provide to the Committee established by resolution 661 (1990) information regarding the action taken by them to implement the provisions laid down in the present resolution;

11. *Affirms* that the United Nations Organization, the specialized agencies and other international organizations in the United Nations system are required to take such measures as may be necessary to give effect to the terms of resolution 661 (1990) and this resolution;

12. *Decides* to consider, in the event of evasion of the provisions of resolution 661 (1990) or of the present resolution by a State or its nationals or through its territory, measures directed at the State in question to prevent such evasion;

13. *Reaffirms* that the Fourth Geneva Convention applies to Kuwait and that as a High Contracting Party to the Convention Iraq is bound to comply fully with all its terms and in particular is liable under the Convention in respect of the grave breaches committed by it, as are individuals who commit or order the commission of grave breaches.

**Resolution 674**
*29 October 1990*

*The Security Council,*

*Recalling* its resolutions 660 (1990), 661 (1990), 662 (1990), 664 (1990), 665 (1990), 666 (1990), 667 (1990) and 670 (1990),

*Stressing* the urgent need for the immediate and unconditional withdrawal of all Iraqi forces from Kuwait, for the restoration of Kuwait's sovereignty, independence and territorial integrity and of the authority of its legitimate government,

*Condemning* the actions by the Iraqi authorities and occupying forces to take third-State nationals hostage and to mistreat and oppress Kuwaiti and third-State nationals, and the other actions reported to the Security Council, such as the destruction of Kuwaiti demographic records, the forced departure of Kuwaitis, the relocation of population in Kuwait and the unlawful destruction and seizure of public and private property in Kuwait, including hospital supplies and equipment, in violation of the decisions of the Council, the Charter of the United Nations, the Fourth Geneva Convention, the Vienna Conventions on Diplomatic and Consular Relations and international law,

*Expressing* grave alarm over the situation of nationals of third States in Kuwait and Iraq, including the personnel of the diplomatic and consular missions of such States,

*Reaffirming* that the Fourth Geneva Convention applies to Kuwait and that as a High Contracting Party to the Convention Iraq is bound to comply fully with all its terms and in particular is liable under the Convention in respect of the grave breaches committed by it, as are individuals who commit or order the commission of grave breaches,

*Recalling* the efforts of the Secretary-General concerning the safety and well-being of third-State nationals in Iraq and Kuwait,

*Deeply concerned* at the economic cost and at the loss and suffering caused to individuals in Kuwait and Iraq as a result of the invasion and occupation of Kuwait by Iraq,

*Acting* under Chapter VII of the Charter of the United Nations,

*Reaffirming* the goal of the international community of maintaining international peace and security by seeking to resolve international disputes and conflicts through peaceful means,

*Recalling* the important role that the United Nations and its Secretary-General have played in the peaceful solution of disputes and conflicts in conformity with the provisions of the Charter,

*Alarmed* by the dangers of the present crisis caused by the Iraqi invasion and occupation in Kuwait, which directly threaten international peace and security, and seeking to avoid any further worsening of the situation,

*Calling upon* Iraq to comply with the relevant resolutions of the Security Council, in particular its resolutions 660 (1990), 662 (1990) and 664 (1990),

*Reaffirming* its determination to ensure compliance by Iraq with the Security Council resolutions by maximum use of political and diplomatic means,

1. *Demands* that the Iraqi authorities and occupying forces immediately cease and desist from taking third-State nationals hostage, mistreating and oppressing Kuwaiti and third-State nationals and any other actions, such as those reported to the Security Council and described above, that violate the decisions of this Council, the Charter of the United Nations, the Fourth Geneva Convention, the Vienna Conventions on Diplomatic and Consular Relations and international law;

2. *Invites* States to collate substantiated information in their possession or submitted to them on the grave breaches by Iraq as per paragraph 1 above and to make this information available to the Security Council;

3. *Reaffirms* its demand that Iraq immediately fulfil its obligations to third-State nationals in Kuwait and Iraq, including the personnel of diplomatic and consular missions, under the Charter, the Fourth Geneva Convention, the Vienna Conventions on Diplomatic and Consular Relations, general principles of international law and the relevant resolutions of the Council;

4. *Also reaffirms* its demand that Iraq permit and facilitate the immediate departure from Kuwait and Iraq of those third-State nationals, including diplomatic and consular personnel, who wish to leave;

5. *Demands* that Iraq ensure the immediate access to food, water and basic services necessary to the protection and well-being of Kuwaiti nationals and of nationals of third States in Kuwait and Iraq, including the personnel of diplomatic and consular missions in Kuwait;

6. *Reaffirms* its demand that Iraq immediately protect the safety and well-being of diplomatic and consular personnel and premises in Kuwait and in Iraq, take no action to hinder these diplomatic and consular missions in the performance of their functions, including access to their nationals and the protection of their person and interests and rescind its orders for the closure of diplomatic and consular missions in Kuwait and the withdrawal of the immunity of their personnel;

7. *Requests* the Secretary-General, in the context of the continued exercise of his good offices concerning the safety and well-being of third-State nationals in Iraq and Kuwait, to seek to achieve the objectives of paragraphs 4, 5 and 6 above and in particular the provision of food, water and basic services to Kuwaiti nationals and to the diplomatic and consular missions in Kuwait and the evacuation of third-State nationals;

8. *Reminds* Iraq that under international law it is liable for any loss, damage or injury arising in regard to Kuwait and third States, and their nationals and corporations, as a result of the invasion and illegal occupation of Kuwait by Iraq;

9. *Invites* States to collect relevant information regarding their claims, and those of their nationals and corporations, for restitution or financial compensation by Iraq with a view to such arrangements as may be established in accordance with international law;

10. *Requires* that Iraq comply with the provisions of the present resolution and its previous resolutions, failing which the Security Council will need to take further measures under the Charter;

11. *Decides* to remain actively and permanently seized of the matter until Kuwait has regained its independence and peace has been restored in conformity with the relevant resolutions of the Security Council.

*12. Reposes* its trust in the Secretary-General to make available his good offices and, as he considers appropriate, to pursue them and to undertake diplomatic efforts in order to reach a peaceful solution to the crisis caused by the Iraqi invasion and occupation of Kuwait on the basis of Security Council resolutions 660 (1990), 662 (1990) and 664 (1990), and calls upon all States, both those in the region and others, to pursue on this basis their efforts to this end, in conformity with the Charter, in order to improve the situation and restore peace, security and stability;

*13. Requests* the Secretary-General to report to the Security Council on the results of his good offices and diplomatic efforts.

**Resolution 677**
*28 November 1990*

*The Security Council,*

*Recalling* its resolutions 660 (1990) of 2 August 1990, 662 (1990) of 9 August 1990 and 674 (1990) of 29 October 1990,

*Reiterating its concern* for the suffering caused to individuals in Kuwait as a result of the invasion and occupation of Kuwait by Iraq,

*Gravely concerned* at the ongoing attempt by Iraq to alter the demographic composition of the population of Kuwait and to destroy the civil records maintained by the legitimate Government of Kuwait,

*Acting* under Chapter VII of the Charter of the United Nations,

*1. Condemns* the attempts by Iraq to alter the demographic composition of the population of Kuwait and to destroy the civil records maintained by the legitimate Government of Kuwait;

*2. Mandates* the Secretary-General to take custody of a copy of the population register of Kuwait, the authenticity of which has been certified by the legitimate Government of Kuwait and which covers the registration of the population up to 1 August 1990;

*3. Requests* the Secretary-General to establish, in co-operation with the legitimate Government of Kuwait, an Order of Rules and Regulations governing access to and use of the said copy of the population register.

**Resolution 678**
*29 November 1990*

*The Security Council,*

*Recalling and reaffirming* its resolutions 660 (1990) of 2 August 1990, 661 (1990) of 6 August 1990, 662 (1990) of 9 August 1990, 664 (1990) of 18 August 1990, 665 (1990) of 25 August 1990, 666 (1990) of 13 September 1990, 667 (1990) of 16 September 1990, 669 (1990) of 24 September 1990, 670 (1990) of 25 September 1990, 674 (1990) of 29 October 1990 and 677 (1990) of 28 November 1990,

*Noting that,* despite all efforts by the United Nations, Iraq refuses to comply with its obligation to implement resolution 660 (1990) and the above-mentioned subsequent relevant resolutions, in flagrant contempt of the Security Council,

*Mindful* of its duties and responsibilities under the Charter of the United Nations for the maintenance and preservation of international peace and security,

*Determined* to secure full compliance with its decisions,

*Acting* under Chapter VII of the Charter,

*1. Demands* that Iraq comply fully with resolution 660 (1990) and all subsequent relevant resolutions, and decides, while maintaining all its decisions, to allow Iraq one final opportunity, as a pause of goodwill, to do so;

2. *Authorizes* Member States co-operating with the Government of Kuwait, unless Iraq on or before 15 January 1991 fully implements, as set forth in paragraph 1 above, the foregoing resolutions, to use all necessary means to uphold and implement resolution 660 (1990) and all subsequent relevant resolutions and to restore international peace and security in the area;

3. *Requests* all States to provide appropriate support for the acitons undertaken in pursuance of paragraph 2 of the present resolution;

4. *Requests* the States concerned to keep the Security Council regularly informed on the progress of actions undertaken pursuant to paragraphs 2 and 3 of the present resolution;

5. *Decides* to remain seized of the matter.

### Resolution 687
3 April 1991

*The Security Council,*

*Recalling* its resolutions 660 (1990) of 2 August 1990, 661 (1990) of 6 August 1990, 662 (1990) of 9 August 1990, 664 (1990) of 18 August 1990, 665 (1990) of 25 August 1990, 666 (1990) of 13 September 1990, 667 (1990) of 16 September 1990, 669 (1990) of 24 September 1990, 670 (1990) of 25 September 1990, 674 (1990) of 29 October 1990, 677 (1990) of 28 November 1990, 678 (1990) of 29 November 1990 and 686 (1991) of 2 March 1991,

*Welcoming* the restoration to Kuwait of its sovereignty, independence and territorial integrity and the return of its legitimate Government,

*Affirming* the commitment of all Member States to the sovereignty, territorial integrity and political independence of Kuwait and Iraq, and noting the intention expressed by the Member States cooperating with Kuwait under paragraph 2 of resolution 678 (1990) to bring their military presence in Iraq to an end as soon as possible consistent with paragraph 8 of resolution 686 (1991),

*Reaffirming* the need to be assured of Iraq's peaceful intentions in the light of its unlawful invasion and occupation of Kuwait,

*Taking note* of the letter sent by the Minister for Foreign Affairs of Iraq on 27 February 1991[1] and those sent pursuant to resolution 686 (1991),[2]

*Noting* that Iraq and Kuwait, as independent sovereign States, signed at Baghdad on 4 October 1963 "Agreed Minutes Between the State of Kuwait and the Republic of Iraq Regarding the Restoration of Friendly Relations, Recognition and Related Matters", thereby recognizing formally the boundary between Iraq and Kuwait and the allocation of islands, which were registered with the United Nations in accordance with Article 102 of the Charter of the United Nations and in which Iraq recognized the independence and complete sovereignty of the State of Kuwait within its borders as specified and accepted in the letter of the Prime Minister of Iraq dated 21 July 1932, and as accepted by the Ruler of Kuwait in his letter dated 10 August 1932,

*Conscious* of the need for demarcation of the said boundary,

*Conscious also* of the statements by Iraq threatening to use weapons in violation of its obligations under the Geneva Protocol for the Prohibition of the Use in War of Asphyxiating, Poisonous or Other Gases, and of Bacteriological Methods of Warfare, signed at Geneva on 17 June 1925,[3] and of its prior use of chemical weapons and affirming that grave consequences would follow any further use by Iraq of such weapons,

*Recalling* that Iraq has subscribed to the Declaration adopted by all States participating in the Conference of States Parties to the 1925 Geneva Protocol and Other Interested States, held in Paris from 7 to 11 January 1989, establishing the objective of universal elimination of chemical and biological weapons,

1. S/22275, annex.
2. S/22273, S/22276, S/22320, S/22321 and S/22330.
3. League of Nations, *Treaty Series*, vol XCIV (1929), No. 2138.

*Recalling also* that Iraq has signed the Convention on the Prohibition of the Development, Production and Stockpiling of Bacteriological (Biological) and Toxin Weapons and on Their Destruction, of 10 April 1972,[4]

*Noting* the importance of Iraq ratifying this Convention,

*Noting* moreover the importance of all States adhering to this Convention and encouraging its forthcoming Review Conference to reinforce the authority, efficiency and universal scope of the convention,

*Stressing the importance* of an early conclusion by the Conference on Disarmament of its work on a Convention on the Universal Prohibition of Chemical Weapons and of universal adherence thereto,

*Aware* of the use by Iraq of ballistic missiles in unprovoked attacks and therefore of the need to take specific measures in regard to such missiles located in Iraq,

*Concerned* by the reports in the hands of Member States that Iraq has attempted to acquire materials for a nuclear-weapons programme contrary to its obligations under the Treaty on the Non-Proliferation of Nuclear Weapons of 1 July 1968,[5]

*Recalling* the objective of the establishment of a nuclear-weapons-free zone in the region of the Middle East,

*Conscious* of the threat that all weapons of mass destruction pose to peace and security in the area and of the need to work towards the establishment in the Middle East of a zone free of such weapons,

*Conscious also* of the objective of achieving balanced and comprehensive control of armaments in the region,

*Conscious further* of the importance of achieving the objectives noted above using all available means, including a dialogue among the States of the region,

*Noting* that resolution 686 (1991) marked the lifting of the measures imposed by resolution 661 (1990) in so far as they applied to Kuwait,

*Noting* that despite the progress being made in fulfilling the obligations of resolution 686 (1991), many Kuwaiti and third country nationals are still not accounted for and property remains unreturned,

*Recalling* the International Convention against the Taking of Hostages,[6] opened for signature at New York on 18 December 1979, which categorizes all acts of taking hostages as manifestations of international terrorism,

*Deploring* threats made by Iraq during the recent conflict to make use of terrorism against targets outside Iraq and the taking of hostages by Iraq,

*Taking note* with grave concern of the reports of the Secretary-General of 20 March 1991[7] and 28 March 1991,[8] and conscious of the necessity to meet urgently the humanitarian needs in Kuwait and Iraq,

*Bearing in mind* its objective of restoring international peace and security in the area as set out in recent resolutions of the Security Council,

*Conscious* of the need to take the following measures acting under Chapter VII of the Charter,

1. *Affirms* all thirteen resolutions noted above, except as expressly changed below to achieve the goals of this resolution, including a formal cease-fire;

---

4. General Assembly resolution 2826 (XXVI), annex.
5. General Assembly resolution 2373 (XXII).
6. General Assembly resolution 34/146.
7. S/22366.
8. S/22409.

A

2. *Demands* that Iraq and Kuwait respect the inviolability of the international boundary and the allocation of islands set out in the "Agreed Minutes Between the State of Kuwait and the Republic of Iraq Regarding the Restoration of Friendly Relations, Recognition and Related Matters", signed by them in the exercise of their sovereignty at Baghdad on 4 October 1963 and registered with the United Nations and published by the United Nations in document 7063, United Nations, *Treaty Series*, 1964;

3. *Calls upon* the Secretary-General to lend his assistance to make arrangements with Iraq and Kuwait to demarcate the boundary between Iraq and Kuwait, drawing on appropriate material, including the map transmitted by Security Council document S/22412 and to report back to the Security Council within one month;

4. *Decides* to guarantee the inviolability of the above-mentioned international boundary and to take as appropriate all necessary measures to that end in accordance with the Charter of the United Nations;

B

5. *Requests* the Secretary-General, after consulting with Iraq and Kuwait, to submit within three days to the Security Council for its approval a plan for the immediate deployment of a United Nations observer unit to monitor the Khor Abdullah and a demilitarized zone, which is hereby established, extending ten kilometres into Iraq and five kilometres into Kuwait from the boundary referred to in the "Agreed Minutes Between the State of Kuwait and the Republic of Iraq Regarding the Restoration of Friendly Relations, Recognition and Related Matters" of 4 October 1963; to deter violations of the boundary through its presence in and surveillance of the demilitarized zone; to observe any hostile or potentially hostile action mounted from the territory of one State to the other; and for the Secretary-General to report regularly to the Security Council on the operations of the unit, and immediately if there are serious violations of the zone or potential threats to peace;

6. *Notes* that as soon as the Secretary-General notifies the Security Council of the completion of the deployment of the United Nations observer unit, the conditions will be established for the Member States cooperating with Kuwait in accordance with resolution 678 (1990) to bring their military presence in Iraq to an end consistent with resolution 686 (1991);

C

7. *Invites* Iraq to reaffirm unconditionally its obligations under the Geneva Protocol for the Prohibition of the Use in War of Asphyxiating, Poisonous or Other Gases, and of Bacteriological Methods of Warfare, signed at Geneva on 17 June 1925, and to ratify the Convention on the Prohibition of the Development, Production and Stockpiling of Bacteriological (Biological) and Toxin Weapons and on Their Destruction, of 10 April 1972;

8. *Decides* that Iraq shall unconditionally accept the destruction, removal, or rendering harmless, under international supervision, of:
(a) All chemical and biological weapons and all stocks of agents and all related subsystems and components and all research, development, support and manufacturing facilities;
(b) All ballistic missiles with a range greater than 150 kilometres and related major parts, and repair and production facilities;

9. *Decides*, for the implementation of paragraph 8 above, the following;
(a) Iraq shall submit to the Secretary-General, within fifteen days of the adoption of the present resolution, a declaration of the locations, amounts and types of all items specified in paragraph 8 and agree to urgent, on-site inspection as specified below;
(b) The Secretary-General, in consultation with the appropriate Governments and, where appropriate, with the Director-General of the World Health Organization, within forty-five days of the passage of the present resolution, shall develop, and submit to the Council for approval, a plan calling for the completion of the following acts within forty-five days of such approval:

(i) The forming of a Special Commission, which shall carry out immediate on-site inspection of Iraq's biological, chemical and missile capabilities, based on Iraq's declarations and the designation of any additional locations by the Special Commission itself;
(ii) The yielding by Iraq of possession to the Special Commission for destruction, removal or rendering harmless, taking into account the requirements of public safety, of all items specified under paragraph 8 (a) above, including items at the additional locations designated by the

Special Commission under paragraph 9 (b) (i) above and the destruction by Iraq, under the supervision of the Special Commission, of all its missile capabilities, including launchers, as specified under paragraph 8 (b) above;

(iii) The provision by the Special Commission of the assistance and cooperation to the Director-General of the International Atomic Energy Agency required in paragraphs 12 and 13 below;

10. *Decides* that Iraq shall unconditionally undertake not to use, develop, construct or acquire any of the items specified in paragraphs 8 and 9 above and requests the Secretary-General, in consultation with the Special Commission, to develop a plan for the future ongoing monitoring and verification of Iraq's compliance with this paragraph, to be submitted to the Security Council for approval within one hundred and twenty days of the passage of this resolution;

11. *Invites* Iraq to reaffirm unconditionally its obligations under the Treaty on the Non-Proliferation of Nuclear Weapons of 1 July 1968;

12. *Decides* that Iraq shall unconditionally agree not to acquire or develop nuclear weapons or nuclear-weapons-usable material or any subsystems or components or any research, development, support or manufacturing facilities related to the above; to submit to the Secretary-General and the Director-General of the International Atomic Energy Agency within fifteen days of the adoption of the present resolution a declaration of the locations, amounts, and types of all items specified above; to place all of its nuclear-weapons-usable materials under the exclusive control, for custody and removal, of the International Atomic Energy Agency, with the assistance and cooperation of the Special Commission as provided for in the plan of the Secretary-General discussed in paragraph 9 (b) above; to accept, in accordance with the arrangements provided for in paragraph 13 below, urgent on-site inspection and the destruction, removal or rendering harmless as appropriate of all items specified above; and to accept the plan discussed in paragraph 13 below for the future ongoing monitoring and verification of its compliance with these undertakings;

13. *Requests* the Director-General of the International Atomic Energy Agency, through the Secretary-General, with the assistance and cooperation of the Special Commission as provided for in the plan of the Secretary-General in paragraph 9 (b) above, to carry out immediate on-site inspection of Iraq's nuclear capabilities based on Iraq's declarations and the designation of any additional locations by the Special Commission; to develop a plan for submission to the Security Council within forty-five days calling for the destruction, removal, or rendering harmless as appropriate of all items listed in paragraph 12 above; to carry out the plan within forty-five days following approval by the Security Council; and to develop a plan, taking into account the rights and obligations of Iraq under the Treaty on the Non-Proliferation of Nuclear Weapons of 1 July 1968, for the future ongoing monitoring and verification of Iraq's compliance with paragraph 12 above, including an inventory of all nuclear material in Iraq subject to the Agency's verification and inspections of the International Atomic Energy Agency to confirm that the Agency's safeguards cover all relevant nuclear activities in Iraq, to be submitted to the Security Council for approval within one hundred and twenty days of the passage of the present resolution;

14. *Takes note* that the actions to be taken by Iraq in paragraphs 8, 9, 10, 11, 12 and 13 of the present resolution represent steps towards the goal of establishing in the Middle East a zone free from weapons of mass destruction and all missiles for their delivery and the objective of a global ban on chemical weapons;

D

15. *Requests* the Secretary-General to report to the Security Council on the steps taken to facilitate the return of all Kuwaiti property seized by Iraq, including a list of any property that Kuwait claims has not been returned or which has not been returned intact;

E

16. *Reaffirms* that Iraq, without prejudice to the debts and obligations of Iraq arising prior to 2 August 1990, which will be addressed through the normal mechanisms, is liable under international law for any direct loss, damage, including environmental damage and the depletion of natural resources, or injury to foreign Governments, nationals and corporations, as a result of Iraq's unlawful invasion and occupation of Kuwait;

17. *Decides* that all Iraqi statements made since 2 August 1990 repudiating its foreign debt are null and void, and demands that Iraq adhere scrupulously to all of its obligations concerning servicing and repayment of its foreign debt;

18. *Decides also* to create a fund to pay compensation for claims that fall within paragraph 16 above and to establish a Commission that will administer the fund;

19. *Directs* the Secretary-General to develop and present to the Security Council for decision, no later than thirty days following the adoption of the present resolution, recommendations for the fund to meet the requirement for the payment of claims established in accordance with paragraph 18 above and for a programme to implement the decisions in paragraphs 16, 17 and 18 above, including; administration of the fund; mechanisms for determining the appropriate level of Iraq's contribution to the fund based on a percentage of the value of the exports of petroleum and petroleum products from Iraq not to exceed a figure to be suggested to the Council by the Secretary-General, taking into account the requirements of the people of Iraq, Iraq's payment capacity as assessed in conjunction with the international financial institutions taking into consideration external debt service, and the needs of the Iraqi economy; arrangements for ensuring that payments are made to the fund; the process by which funds will be allocated and claims paid; appropriate procedures for evaluating losses, listing claims and verifying their validity and resolving disputed claims in respect of Iraq's liability as specified in paragraph 16 above; and the composition of the Commission designated above;

F

20. *Decides*, effective immediately, that the prohibitions against the sale or supply to Iraq of commodities or products, other than medicine and health supplies, and prohibitions against financial transactions related thereto contained in resolution 661 (1990) shall not apply to foodstuffs notified to the Security Council Committee established by resolution 661 (1990) concerning the situation between Iraq and Kuwait or, with the approval of that Committee, under the simplified and accelerated "no-objection" procedure, to materials and supplies for essential civilian needs as identified in the report of the Secretary-General dated 20 March 1991,[9] and in any further findings of humanitarian need by the Committee;

21. *Decides* that the Security Council shall review the provisions of paragraph 20 above every sixty days in the light of the policies and practices of the Government of Iraq, including the implementation of all relevant resolutions of the Security Council, for the purpose of determining whether to reduce or lift the prohibitions referred to therein;

22. *Decides* that upon the approval by the Security Council of the programme called for in paragraph 19 above and upon Council agreement that Iraq has completed all actions contemplated in paragraphs 8, 9, 10, 11, 12 and 13 above, the prohibitions against the import of commodities and products originating in Iraq and the prohibitions against financial transactions related thereto contained in resolution 661 (1990) shall have no further force or effect;

23. *Decides* that, pending action by the Security Council under paragraph 22 above, the Security Council Committee established by resolution 661 (1990) shall be empowered to approve, when required to assure adequate financial resources on the part of Iraq to carry out the activities under paragraph 20 above, exceptions to the prohibition against the import of commodities and products originating in Iraq;

24. *Decides* that, in accordance with resolution 661 (1990) and subsequent related resolutions and until a further decision is taken by the Security Council, all States shall continue to prevent the sale or supply, or the promotion or facilitation of such sale or supply, to Iraq by their nationals, or from their territories or using their flag vessels or aircraft, of:
(a) Arms and related *matériel* of all types, specifically including the sale or transfer through other means of all forms of conventional military equipment, including for paramilitary forces, and spare parts and components and their means of production, for such equipment;
(b) Items specified and defined in paragraphs 8 and 12 above not otherwise covered above;
(c) Technology under licensing or other transfer arrangements used in the production, utilization or stockpiling of items specified in subparagraphs (a) and (b) above;
(d) Personnel or materials for training or technical support services relating to the design, development, manufacture, use, maintenance or support of items specified in subparagraphs (a) and (b) above;

25. *Calls upon* all States and international organizations to act strictly in accordance with paragraph 24 above, notwithstanding the existence of any contracts, agreements, licences or any other arrangements;

9. S/22366.

26. *Requests* the Secretary-General, in consultation with appropriate Governments, to develop within sixty days, for the approval of the Security Council, guidelines to facilitate full international implementation of paragraphs 24 and 25 above and paragraph 27 below, and to make them available to all States and to establish a procedure for updating these guidelines periodically;

27. *Calls upon* all States to maintain such national controls and procedures and to take such other actions consistent with the guidelines to be established by the Security Council under paragraph 26 above as may be necessary to ensure compliance with the terms of paragraph 24 above, and calls upon international organizations to take all appropriate steps to assist in ensuring such full compliance;

28. *Agrees* to review its decisions in paragraphs 22, 23, 24 and 25 above, except for the items specified and defined in paragraphs 8 and 12 above, on a regular basis and in any case one hundred and twenty days following passage of the present resolution, taking into account Iraq's compliance with the resolution and general progress towards the control of armaments in the region;

29. *Decides* that all States, including Iraq, shall take the necessary measures to ensure that no claim shall lie at the instance of the Government of Iraq, or of any person or body in Iraq, or of any person claiming through or for the benefit of any such person or body, in connection with any contract or other transaction where its performance was affected by reason of the measures taken by the Security Council in resolution 661 (1990) and related resolutions;

G

30. *Decides* that, in furtherance of its commitment to facilitate the repatriation of all Kuwaiti and third country nationals, Iraq shall extend all necessary cooperation to the International Committee of the Red Cross, providing lists of such persons, facilitating the access of the International Committee of the Red Cross to all such persons wherever located or detained and facilitating the search by the International Committee of the Red Cross for those Kuwaiti and third country nationals still unaccounted for;

31. *Invites* the International Committee of the Red Cross to keep the Secretary-General apprised as appropriate of all activities undertaken in connection with facilitating the repatriation or return of all Kuwaiti and third country nationals or their remains present in Iraq on or after 2 August 1990;

H

32. *Requires* Iraq to inform the Security Council that it will not commit or support any act of international terrorism or allow any organization directed towards commission of such acts to operate within its territory and to condemn unequivocally and renounce all acts, methods and practices of terrorism;

I

33. *Declares* that, upon official notification by Iraq to the Secretary-General and to the Security Council of its acceptance of the provisions above, a formal cease-fire is effective between Iraq and Kuwait and the Member States cooperating with Kuwait in accordance with resolution 678 (1990);

34. *Decides* to remain seized of the matter and to take such further steps as may be required for the implementation of the present resolution and to secure peace and security in the area.

# Appendix B—The Glaspie-Hussein Transcript

*On July 25, 1990, U.S. Ambassador to Iraq, April Glaspie, met the Iraqi president and the foreign minister, Tariq Aziz. This is the full text of that meeting, as released by the Iraqi government. At the time the U.S. State Department described the Iraqi transcript as "essentially correct," but the document sparked controversy due to Ambassador Glaspie's assurance to Saddam Hussein that "we have no opinion on the Arab-Arab conflicts, such as your border disagreement with Kuwait." When Glaspie finally spoke on the subject, on March 20, 1991, she claimed that the Iraqi version was heavily edited in order to tone down her warnings to Iraq not to use force. The State Department, however, continued to refuse to release Glaspie's own report of the meeting.*
**Saddam Hussein** I have summoned you today to hold comprehensive political discussions with you. This is a message to President Bush:

You know that we did not have relations with the U.S. until 1984 and you know the circumstances and reasons which caused them to be severed. The decision to establish relations with the U.S. were taken in 1980 during the two months prior to the war between us and Iran.

When the war started, and to avoid misinterpretation, we postponed the establishment of relations hoping that the war would end soon.

But because the war lasted for a long time, and to emphasize the fact that we are a nonaligned country, it was important to re-establish relations with the U.S. And we chose to do this in 1984.

It is natural to say that the U.S. is not like Britain, for example, with the latter's historic relations with Middle Eastern countries, including Iraq. In addition, there were no relations between Iraq and the U.S. between 1967 and 1984. One can conclude it would be difficult for the U.S. to have a full understanding of many matters in Iraq. When relations were re-established we hoped for a better understanding and for better cooperation because we too do not understand the background of many American decisions.

We dealt with each other during the war and we had dealings on various levels. The most important of those levels were with the foreign ministers.

We had hoped for a better common understanding and a better chance of cooperation to benefit both our peoples and the rest of the Arab nations.

But these better relations have suffered from various rifts. The worst of these was in 1986, only two years after establishing relations, with what was known as Irangate, which happened during the year that Iran occupied the Fao peninsula.

It was natural then to say that old relations and complexity of interests could absorb many mistakes. But when interests are limited and relations are not that old, then there isn't a deep understanding and mistakes could leave a negative effect. Sometimes the effect of an error can be larger than the error itself.

Despite all of that, we accepted the apology, via his envoy, of the American president regarding Irangate, and we wiped the slate clean. And we shouldn't unearth the past except when new events remind us that old mistakes were not just a matter of coincidence.

Our suspicions increased after we liberated the Fao peninsula. The media began to involve itself in our politics. And our suspicions began to surface anew, because we began to question whether the U.S. felt uneasy with the outcome of the war when we liberated our land.

It was clear to us that certain parties in the United States — and I don't say the president himself — but certain parties who had links with the intelligence community and with the State Department — and I don't say the secretary of state himself — I say that these parties did not like the fact that we liberated our land. Some parties began to prepare studies entitled, "Who will succeed Saddam Hussein?" They began to contact Gulf states to make them fear Iraq, to persuade them not to give Iraq economic aid. And we have evidence of these activities.

Iraq came out of the war burdened with a $40 billion debt, excluding the aid given by Arab states, some of whom consider that too to be a debt although they knew — and you knew too — that without Iraq they would not have had these sums and the future of the region would have been entirely different.

We began to face the policy of the drop in the price of oil. Then we saw the United States, which always talks of democracy but which has no time for the other point of view. Then the media campaign against Saddam Hussein was started by the official American media. The United States thought that the situation in Iraq was like Poland or Romania or Czechoslovakia. We were disturbed by this campaign but we were not disturbed too much because we had hoped that, in a few months, those who are decisionmakers in America would have a chance to find the facts and see whether this media campaign had had any effect on the lives of Iraqis. We had hoped that soon the American authorities would make the correct decision regarding their relations with Iraq. Those with good relations can sometimes afford to disagree.

But when planned and deliberate policy forces the price of oil down without good commercial reasons, then that means another war against Iraq. Because military war kills people by bleeding them, and economic war kills their humanity by depriving them of their chance to have a good standard of living. As you know, we gave rivers of blood in a war that lasted eight years, but we did not lose our humanity. Iraqis have a right to live proudly. We do not accept that anyone could injure Iraqi pride or the Iraqi right to have high standards of living.

Kuwait and the UAE were at the front of this policy aimed at lowering Iraq's position and depriving its people of higher economic standards. And you know that our relations with the Emirates and Kuwait had been good. On top of all that, while we were busy at war, the state of Kuwait began to expand at the expense of our territory.

You may say this is propaganda, but I would direct you to one document, the Military Patrol Line, which is the borderline endorsed by the Arab League in 1961 for military patrols not to cross the Iraq-Kuwait border.

But go and look for yourselves. You will see the Kuwaiti border patrols, the Kuwaiti farms, the Kuwaiti oil installations — all built as closely as possible to this line to establish that land as Kuwaiti territory.

Since then, the Kuwaiti government has been stable while the Iraqi government has undergone many changes. Even after 1968 and for ten years afterwards, we were too busy with our own problems. First in the north, then the 1973 war, and other problems. Then came the war with Iran which started ten years ago.

We believe that the United States must understand that people who live in luxury and economic security can reach an understanding with the United States on what are legitimate joint interests. But the starved and the economically deprived cannot reach the same understanding.

We do not accept threats from anyone because we do not threaten anyone. But we say clearly that we hope that the U.S. will not entertain too many illusions and will seek new friends rather than increase the number of its enemies.

I have read the American statements speaking of friends in the area. Of course, it is the right of everyone to choose their friends. We can have no objections. But you know you are not the ones who protected your friends during the war with Iran. I assure you, had the Iranians overrun the region, the American troops would not have stopped them, except by the use of nuclear weapons.

I do not belittle you. But I hold this view by looking at the geography and nature of American society into account. Yours is a society which cannot accept 10,000 dead in one battle.

You know that Iran agreed to the ceasefire not because the United States had bombed one of the oil platforms after the liberation of the Fao. Is this Iraq's reward for its role in securing the stability of the region and for protecting it from an unknown flood?

So what can it mean when America says it will now protect its friends? It can only mean prejudice against Iraq. This stance plus maneuvers and statements which have been made has encouraged the UAE and Kuwait to disregard Iraqi rights.

I say to you clearly that Iraq's rights, which are mentioned in the memorandum, we will take one by one. That might not happen now or after a month or after one year, but we will take it all. We are not the kind of people who will relinquish their rights. There is no historic right, or legitimacy, or need, for the UAE and Kuwait to deprive us of our rights. If they are needy, we too are needy.

The United States must have a better understanding of the situation and declare who it wants to have relations with and who its enemies are. But it should not make enemies simply because others have different points of view regarding the Arab-Israeli conflict.

We clearly understand America's statement that it wants an easy flow of oil. We understand America saying that it seeks friendship with the states in the region, and to encourage their joint interests. But we cannot understand the attempt to encourage some parties to harm Iraq's interests.

The United States wants to secure the flow of oil. This is understandable and known. But it must not deploy methods which the United States says it disapproves of — flexing muscles and pressure.

If you use pressure, we will deploy pressure and force. We know that you can harm us although we do not threaten you. But we too can harm you. Everyone can cause harm according to their ability and their size. We cannot come all the way to you in the United States, but individual Arabs may reach you.

You can come to Iraq with aircraft and missiles but do not push us to the point where we cease to care. And when we feel that you want to injure our pride and take away the Iraqis' chance of a high standard of living, then we will cease to care and death will be the choice for us. Then we would not care if you fired 100 missiles for each missile we fired. Because without pride life would have no value.

It is not reasonable to ask our people to bleed rivers of blood for eight years then to tell them, "Now you have to accept aggression from Kuwait, the UAE or from the U.S. or from Israel."

We do not put all these countries in the same boat. First, we are hurt and upset that such disagreement is taking place between us and Kuwait and the UAE. The solution must be found within an Arab framework and through direct bilateral relations. We do not place America among the enemies. We place it where we want our friends to be and we try to be friends. But repeated American statements last year made it apparent that America did not regard us as friends. Well the Americans are free.

When we seek friendship we want pride, liberty and our right to choose.

We want to deal according to our status as we deal with the others according to their status.

We consider the others' interests while we look after our own. And we expect the others to consider our interests while they are dealing with their own. What does it mean when the Zionist war minister is summoned to the United States now? What do they mean, these fiery statements coming out of Israel during the past few days and the talk of war being expected now more than at any other time?

We don't want war because we know what war means. But do not push us to consider war as the only solution to live proudly and to provide our people with a good living.

We know that the United States has nuclear weapons. But we are determined either to live as proud men, or we all die. We do not believe that there is one single honest man on earth who would not understand what I mean.

We do not ask you to solve our problems. I said that our Arab problems will be solved amongst ourselves. But do not encourage anyone to take action which is greater than their status permits.

I do not believe that anyone would lose by making friends with Iraq. In my opinion, the American president has not made mistakes regarding the Arabs, although his decision to freeze dialogue with the PLO was wrong. But it appears that this decision was made to appease the Zionist lobby or as a piece of strategy to cool the Zionist anger, before trying again. I hope that our latter conclusion is the correct one. But we will carry on saying it was the wrong decision.

You are appeasing the usurper in so many ways — economically, politically and militarily as well as in the media. When will the time come when, for every three appeasements to the usurper, you praise the Arabs just once?

When will humanity find its real chance to seek a just American solution that would balance the human rights of two hundred million human beings with the rights of three million Jews? We want friendship, but we are not running for it. We reject harm by anybody. If we are faced with harm, we will resist. This is our right, whether the harm comes from America or the UAE or Kuwait or from Israel. But I do not put all these states on the same level. Israel stole the Arab land, supported by the U.S. But the UAE and Kuwait do not support Israel. Anyway, they are Arabs. But when they try to weaken Iraq, then they are helping the enemy. And then Iraq has the right to defend itself.

In 1974, I met with Idriss, the son of Mullah Mustafa Barzani [the late Kurdish leader]. He sat in the same seat as you are sitting now. He came asking me to postpone implementation of autonomy in Iraqi Kurdistan, which was agreed on March 11, 1970. My reply was: we are determined to fulfil our obligation. You also have to stick to your agreement. When I sensed that Barzani had evil intention, I said to him: give my regards to your father and tell him that Saddam Hussein says the following. I explained to him the balance of power with figures exactly the way I explained to the Iranians in my open letters to them during the war. I finished this conversation with the result summarized in one sentence: if we fight, we shall win. Do you know why? I explained all the reasons to him, plus one political reason — you [the Kurds in 1974] depended on our disagreement with the shah of Iran [Kurds were financed by Iran]. The root of the Iranian conflict is their claim of half of the Shatt al-Arab waterway. If we could keep the whole of Iraq with Shatt al-Arab, we will make no concessions. But if forced to choose between half of Shatt al-Arab or the whole of Iraq, then we will give the Shatt al-Arab away, to keep the whole of Iraq in the shape we wish it to be.

We hope that you are not going to push events to make us bear this wisdom in mind in our relations with Iran. After that [meeting with Barzani's son], we gave half of Shatt al-Arab away [1975 Algeria agreement]. And Barzani died and was buried outside Iraq and he lost his war.

[At this point, Saddam Hussein ends his message to Bush, and turns to Ambassador Glaspie]

We hope we are not pushed into this. All that lies between relations with Iran is Shatt al-Arab. When we are faced with a choice between Iraq living proudly and Shatt al-Arab then we will negotiate using the wisdom we spoke of in 1975. In the way Barzani lost his historic chance, others will lose their chance too.

With regards to President Bush, I hope the president will read this himself and will not leave it in the hands of a gang in the State Department. I exclude the secretary of state and Kelly because I know him and I exchanged views with him.

**April Glaspie** I thank you, Mr. President, and it is a great pleasure for a diplomat to meet and talk directly with the president. I clearly understand your message. We studied history at school. They taught us to say freedom or death. I think you know well that we as a people have our experience with the colonialists.

Mr. President, you mentioned many things during this meeting which I cannot comment on on behalf of my Government. But with your permission, I will comment on two points. You spoke of friendship and I believe it was clear from the letters sent by our president to you on the occasion of your national day that he emphasizes —

**Hussein** He was kind and his expressions met with our regard and respect.

**Glaspie** As you know, he directed the United States administration to reject the suggestion of implementing trade sanctions.

**Hussein** (smiling) There is nothing left for us to buy from America. Only wheat. Because every time we want to buy something, they say it is forbidden. I am afraid that one day you will say, "You are going to make gunpowder out of wheat."

**Glaspie** I have a direct instruction from the president to seek better relations with Iraq.

**Hussein** But how? We too have this desire. But matters are running contrary to this desire.

**Glaspie** This is less likely to happen the more we talk. For example, you mentioned the issue of the article published by the American Information Agency and that was sad. And a formal apology was presented.

**Hussein** Your stance is generous. We are Arabs. It is enough for us that someone says, "I am sorry, I made a mistake." Then we carry on. But the media campaign continued. And it is full of stories. If the stories were true, no one would get upset. But we understand from its continuation that there is a determination [to harm relations].

**Glaspie** I saw the Diane Sawyer program on ABC. And what happened in that program was cheap and unjust. And this is a real picture of what happens in the American media — even to American politicians themselves. These are the methods the Western media employs. I am pleased that you add your voice to the diplomats who stand up to the media. Because your appearance in the media, even for five minutes, would help us to make the American people understand Iraq. This would increase mutual understanding. If the American president had control of the media, his job would be much easier.

Mr. President, not only do I want to say that President Bush wanted better and deeper relations with Iraq, but he also wants an Iraqi contribution to peace and prosperity in the Middle East. President Bush is an intelligent man. He is not going to declare an economic war against Iraq.

You are right. It is true what you say that we do not want higher prices for oil. But I would ask you to examine the possibility of not charging too high a price for oil.

**Hussein** We do not want too high prices for oil. And I remind you that in 1974 I gave Tariq Aziz the idea for an article he wrote which criticized the policy of keeping oil prices high. It was the first Arab article which expressed this view.

**Tariq Aziz** Our policy in OPEC opposes sudden jumps in oil prices.

**Hussein** Twenty-five dollars a barrel is not a high price.

**Glaspie** We have many Americans who would like to see the price go above $25 because they come from oil-producing states.

**Hussein** The price at one stage had dropped to $12 a barrel and a reduction in the modest Iraqi budget of $6 billion to $7 billion is a disaster.

**Glaspie** I think I understand this. I have lived here for years. I admire your extraordinary efforts to rebuild your country. I know you need funds. We understand that and our opinion is that you should have the opportunity to rebuild your country. But we have no opinion on the Arab-Arab conflicts, like your border disagreement with Kuwait.

I was in the American embassy in Kuwait during the late 60s. The instruction we had during this period was that we should express no opinion on this issue and that the issue is not associated with America. James Baker has directed our official spokesmen to emphasize this instruction. We hope you can solve this problem using any suitable methods via Klibi or via President Mubarak. All that we hope is that these issues are solved quickly. With regard to all of this, can I ask you to see how the issue appears to us?

My assessment after twenty-five years' service in this area is that your objective must have strong backing from your Arab brothers. I now speak of oil. But you, Mr. President, have fought through a horrific and painful war. Frankly, we can only see that you have deployed massive troops in the south. Normally that would not be any of our business. But when this happens in the context of what you said on your national day, then when we read the details in the two letters of the foreign minister, then when we see the Iraqi point of view that the measures taken by the UAE and Kuwait is, in the final analysis, parallel to military aggression against Iraq, then it would be reasonable for me to be concerned. And for this reason, I received an instruction to ask you, in the spirit of friendship — not in the spirit of confrontation — regarding your intentions.

I simply describe the concern of my government. And I do not mean that the situation is a simple situation. But our concern is a simple one.

**Hussein** We do not ask people not to be concerned when peace is at issue. This is a noble human feeling which we all feel. It is natural for you as a superpower to be concerned. But what we ask is not to express your concern in a way that would make an aggressor believe that he is getting support for his aggression.

We want to find a just solution which will give us our rights but not deprive others of their rights. But at the same time, we want the others to know that our patience is running out regarding their action, which is harming even the milk our children drink, and the pensions of the widow who lost her husband during the war, and the pensions of the orphans who lost their parents.

As a country, we have the right to prosper. We lost so many opportunities, and the others should value the Iraqi role in their protection. Even this Iraqi [the president points to the interpreter] feels bitter like all other Iraqis. We are not aggressors but we do not accept aggression either. We sent them envoys and handwritten letters. We tried everything. We asked the Servant of the Two Shrines — King Fahd — to hold a four-member summit, but he suggested a meeting between the oil ministers. We agreed. And as you know, the meeting took place in Jidda. They reached an agreement which did not express what we wanted, but we agreed.

Only two days after the meeting, the Kuwaiti oil minister made a statement that contradicted the agreement. We also discussed the issue during the Baghdad summit. I told the Arab kings and presidents that some brothers are fighting an economic war against us. And that not all wars use weapons and we regard this kind of war as a military action against us. Because if the capability of our army is lowered then, if Iran renewed the war, it could achieve goals which it could not achieve before. And if we lowered the standard of our defenses, then this could encourage Israel to attack us. I said that before the Arab kings and presidents. Only I did not mention Kuwait and UAE by name, because they were my guests.

Before this, I had sent them envoys reminding them that our war had included their defense. Therefore the aid they gave us should not be regarded as a debt. We did no more than the United States would have done against someone who attacked its interests.

I talked about the same thing with a number of other Arab states. I explained the situation to brother King Fahd a few times, by sending envoys and on the telephone. I talked with brother King Hussein and with Sheikh Zaid after the conclusion of the summit. I walked with the sheikh to the plane when he was leaving Mosul. He told me, "Just wait until I get home." But after he had reached his destination, the statements that came from there were very bad — not from him, but from his minister of oil.

Also after the Jidda agreement, we received some intelligence that they were talking of sticking to the agreement for two months only. Then they would change their policy. Now tell us, if the American president found himself in this situation, what would he do? I said it was very difficult for me to talk about these issues in public. But we must tell the Iraqi people who face economic difficulties who was responsible for that . . .

**Glaspie** I spent four beautiful years in Egypt.

**Hussein** The Egyptian people are kind and good and ancient. The oil people are supposed to help the Egyptian people, but they are mean beyond belief. It is painful to admit it, but some of them are disliked by Arabs because of their greed.

**Glaspie** Mr. President, it would be helpful if you could give us an assessment of the effort made by your Arab brothers and whether they have achieved anything.

**Hussein** On this subject, we agreed with President Mubarak that the prime minister of Kuwait would meet with the deputy chairman of the Revolution Command Council in Saudi Arabia, because the Saudis initiated contact with us, aided by President Mubarak's efforts. He just telephoned me a short while ago to say the Kuwaitis have agreed to that suggestion.

**Glaspie** Congratulations.

**Hussein** A protocol meeting will be held in Saudi Arabia. Then the meeting will be transferred to Baghdad for deeper discussion directly between Kuwait and Iraq. We hope we will reach some result. We hope that the long-term view and the real interests will overcome Kuwaiti greed.

**Glaspie** May I ask you when you expect Sheikh Saad to come to Baghdad?

**Hussein** I suppose it would be on Saturday or Monday at the latest. I told brother Mubarak that the agreement should be in Baghdad Saturday or Sunday. You know that brother Mubarak's visits have always been a good omen.

**Glaspie** This is good news. Congratulations.

**Hussein** Brother President Mubarak told me they were scared. They said troops were only twenty kilometers north of the Arab League line. I said to him that regardless of what is there, whether they are police, border guards or army, and regardless of how many are there, and what they are doing, assure the Kuwaitis and give them our word that we are not going to do anything until we meet with them. When we meet and when we see that there is hope, then nothing will happen. But if we are unable to find a solution, then it will be natural that Iraq will not accept death, even though wisdom is above everything else. There you have good news.

**Aziz** This is a journalistic exclusive.

**Glaspie** I am planning to go to the United States next Monday. I hope I will meet with President Bush in Washington next week. I thought to postpone my trip because of the difficulties we are facing. But now I will fly on Monday.

# Appendix C — The Ahtisaari Report*

*These are excerpts of the Report of the United Nations Mission to Assess Humanitarian Needs in Iraq, led by Martti Ahtisaari, Under-Secretary General for Administration and Management. The UN mission spent the period March 10–17, 1991 in Iraq. The report made headlines because of its assessment of conditions in post-war Iraq as "near-apocalyptic." Following its publication, and that of detailed studies of conditions in Iraq by the Gulf Peace Team and a group from Harvard University in April and May 1991 respectively, criticism mounted of the Bush administration's policy of continued sanctions against post-war Iraq, and pressure grew for them to be lifted.*

... I and the members of my mission were fully conversant with media reports regarding the situation in Iraq and ... with the recent WHO/UNICEF report on water, sanitary and health conditions in the Greater Baghdad area ... [N]othing that we had seen or read had quite prepared us for the particular form of devastation which has now befallen the country. The recent conflict has wrought near-apocalyptic results upon the economic infrastructure of what had been, until January 1991, a rather highly urbanized and mechanized society. Now, most means of modern life support have been destroyed or rendered tenuous. Iraq has, for some time to come, been relegated to a pre-industrial age, but with all the disabilities of post-industrial dependency on an intensive use of energy and technology.

... [M]y report to you ... seeks with as much exactitude as possible to convey the extent of needs in the primary areas of humanitarian concern: for safe water and sanitation, basic health and medical support; for food; for shelter; and for the logistical means to make such support actually available. Underlying each analysis is the inexorable reality that, as a result of war, virtually all previously viable sources of fuel and power (apart from a limited number of mobile generators) are now, essentially, defunct. The far-reaching implications of this energy and communications vacuum as regards urgent humanitarian support are of crucial significance for the nature and effectiveness of the international response.

These conditions, together with recent civil unrest ... mean that the authorities are as yet scarcely able even to measure the dimensions of the calamity, much less respond to its consequences, because they cannot obtain full and accurate data. ... Most employees are simply unable to come to work. Both the authorities and the trade unions estimate that approximately 90 per cent of industrial workers have been reduced to inactivity and will be deprived of income as of the end of March. Government departments have at present only marginal attendance. Prior to recent events, Iraq was importing about 70 per cent of its food needs. Now, owing to the fuel shortage, the inability to import and the virtual breakdown of the distribution system, the flow of food through the private sector has been reduced to a trickle, with costs accelerating upwards. Many food prices are already beyond the purchasing reach of most Iraqi families ...

### Food and Agriculture

... Food is currently made available to the population both through government allocation and rations, and through the market. The Ministry of Trade's monthly allocation to the population of staple food items fell from 343,000 tons in September 1990 to 182,000 tons, when rationing was introduced, and was further reduced to 135,000 tons in January 1991 (39 per cent of the pre-sanctions level). ... [A]ll evidence indicates that flour is now at a critically low level, and that supplies of sugar, rice, tea, vegetable, oil, powdered milk and pulses are currently at critically low levels or have been exhausted. Distribution of powdered milk, for instance, is now reserved exclusively for sick children on medical prescription.

Livestock farming has been seriously affected by sanctions because many feed products were imported. The sole laboratory producing veterinary vaccines was destroyed during the conflict ... all stocks of vaccine were stated to have been destroyed in the same sequence of bombardments on this centre, which was an FAO [Food and Agriculture Organization of the UN] project.

The country has had a particular dependence upon foreign vegetable seeds, and the mission was able to inspect destroyed seed warehouses. ... [R]elevant agricultural authorities informed the mission that all stocks of potatoes and vegetable seeds had been exhausted ...

This year's grain harvest in June is seriously compromised for a number of reasons, including failure of irrigation/drainage (no power for pumps, lack of spare parts); lack of pesticides and fertilizers (previously imported); and lack of fuel and spare parts for the highly-mechanized and fuel-dependent harvesting machines. Should this harvest fail, or be far below average, as is very likely barring a rapid change in the situation, widespread starvation conditions become a real possibility.

The official programme for the support of socially dependent groups of the population (the elderly, disabled, mothers and children, hospital patients, orphans, refugees, etc.) is affected by the overall grave deficiencies in the food situation.

The mission had the opportunity to conduct independent research relating to household costs and living standards in Baghdad. Such standards have declined rapidly in the last months, while food and the fuel prices have climbed dramatically.... Interviews with private wholesale food distributors revealed that their stocks are near depletion.... The government-initiated rationing system was designed to provide families with a fraction of their basic necessities at prices comparable to those prevailing before August.... [I]ndependent surveys in several diverse areas of Baghdad showed that many families cannot draw their full rations, since the distribution centres are often depleted and they have great difficulty in travelling to other centres. The quality of food distributed has itself deteriorated to the point of causing health problems. Most families also reported that they could not meet their needs through the private markets.... The price of most basic necessities has increased by 1,000 per cent or more. For example, flour is now 5–6 dinars per kilogram (and seemingly still rising); rice has risen to 6 dinars per kilogram ... and whole milk to 10 dinars. In contrast to this hyperinflation, many incomes have collapsed. Many employees cannot draw salaries, the banking system has in large measure closed down and withdrawals are limited to 100 dinars per month. The minimum monthly wage was 54 dinars and the average monthly salary of a civil servant was 70 dinars. In short, most families lack access to adequate rations....

The mission recommends that ... sanctions in respect of food supplies should be immediately removed, as should those relating to the import of agricultural equipment and supplies. The urgent supply of basic commodities to safeguard vulnerable groups is strongly recommended, and the provision of major quantities of the following staples for the general population: milk, wheat flour, rice, sugar, vegetable oil and tea. These are required to meet minimum general requirements until the next harvest....

The mission observes that, without a restoration of energy supplies to the agricultural production and distribution sectors, implementation of many of the above recommendations would be to little effect. Drastic international measures across the whole agricultural spectrum are most urgent.

### Water, Sanitation and Health

As regards water, prior to the crisis Baghdad received about 450 litres per person supplied by seven treatments stations purifying water from the Tigris river. The rest of the country had about 200–250 litres per person per day, purified and supplied by 238 central water-treatment stations and 1,134 smaller water projects. All stations operated on electric power....

With the destruction of power plants, oil refineries, main oil storage facilities and water-related chemical plants, all electrically operated installations have ceased to function. Diesel-operated generators were reduced to operating on a limited basis, their functioning affected by lack of fuel, lack of maintenance, lack of spare parts and non-attendance of workers. The supply of water in Baghdad dropped to less than 10 litres per day but has now recovered to approximately 30–40 litres in about 70 percent of the area (less than 10 percent of the overall previous use).... [I]n Baghdad, untreated sewage has now to be dumped directly into the river — which is the source of the water supply — and all drinking-water plants there and throughout the rest of the country are using river water with high sewage contamination.... While the water authority has warned that water must be boiled, there is little fuel to do this, and what exists is diminishing....

Only limited information is available ... [on] the remainder of the country.... In those areas where there are no generators, or generators have broken down, or the fuel supply is exhausted, the population draws its water directly from polluted rivers and trenches. This is widely apparent in rural areas, where women and children can be seen washing and filling water receptacles....

... A further major problem, now imminent, is the climate, Iraq has long and extremely hot summers, the temperature often reaching 50 degrees Celsius. This has two main implications: (a) the quantity of water must be increased ...; and (b) the heat will accelerate the incubation of bacteria.... [O]verall sanitary circumstances ... have already led to a fourfold increase in diarrheal disease incidence among children under five years of age....

As regards sanitation ... rapidly rising temperatures will soon accentuate an existing crisis. Heaps of garbage are spread in the urban areas and collection is poor to non-existent.... Incinerators are in general not working.... Iraqi rivers are heavily polluted by raw sewage.... Pools of sewage lie in the streets and villages. Health hazards will build in the weeks to come.

... [T]he mission found that health conditions in Baghdad and throughout the country remain precarious. A major factor is the water and sanitation situation described above. Additionally, the total lack of telephone communication and drastically reduced transport capability pose other problems to the health system since basic information on communicable diseases cannot be collected and disseminated, and essential drugs, vaccines and medical supplies cannot be distributed efficiently....

There is an urgent need to establish a national surveillance and reporting capacity for communicable diseases.... Communications, functional laboratories, including necessary chemicals and reagents, and transport and power resources are essential to provide for this emergency humanitarian need.... The mission concluded that a catastrophe could be faced at any time if conditions do not change....

**Refugees and Other Vulnerable Groups**
Conditions described above affect the whole population of Iraq and, most especially, low-income groups. The mission paid particular attention to the plight of especially vulnerable groups, whether Iraqi or non-Iraqi. Thus, it found that care for orphans, the elderly and the handicapped had been in many instances disrupted, with residents of institutions having had to be moved and regouped at various locations. It recommends the urgent implementation of a humanitarian programme aimed at enabling some 25 orphanages and 71 other social welfare centres to resume their normal activities. . . .

As regards the displaced and the homeless, the authorities themselves have not yet been able fully to assess the impact of the recent hostilities. They have, however, calculated that approximately 9,000 homes were destroyed or damaged beyond repair during the hostilities, of which 2,500 were in Baghdad and 1,900 were in Basrah. This has created a new homeless potential total of 72,000 persons. Official help is now hampered by the conditions described throughout this report and, especially, a virtual halt in the production of local building materials and the impossibility to import. The input of essential materials should be permitted.

**Logistics: Transportation, Communications and Energy**
. . . At present, Iraq's sole available surface transport link with the outside world is via Amman to Aqaba [Jordan]. (It has been reported that a bridge has recently been destroyed on the Iskenderun/ Mersin road to Iraq from Turkey; and the ports of Basrah and Umm Qasr are currently out of use; nor has there for some years been any direct cargo traffic to Iraq via the Syrian Arab Republic.) Internal transportation by road is now severely affected by a lack of spare parts and tyres and, above all, by a lack of fuel. . . . The mission was informed that a total of 83 road bridges had been destroyed. . . .

. . . [T]he mission was informed that all internal and external telephone systems had been destroyed, with the exception of a limited local exchange in one town. . . . Communication in Iraq is now on a person-to-person basis, as mail services have also disintegrated.

The role of energy in Iraq is especially important because of the level of urbanization (approximately 72 per cent of the population lives in towns), its industrialization, and its prolonged, very hot, summers. . . . Bombardment has paralyzed oil and electricity sectors almost entirely. . . . There have, officially, been virtually no sales of gasoline to private users since February. The mission was told that the only petrol, oil and lubricants products now available are heating oil (rationed to 60 litres per month, per family) and liquefied petroleum gas (LPG), which is rationed to one cylinder per month, per family. . . . [S]tocks of these two products are close to exhaustion. . . . Initial inspections are said to show that necessary repairs to begin power generation and oil refining at minimal levels may take anywhere from 4 to 13 months. Minimal survival level to undertake humanitarian activities would require approximately 25 per cent of pre-war civilian domestic fuel consumption. Its absence . . . may have calamitous consequences for food, water supply and for sanitation; and therefore for health conditions. It seems inescapable that these fuel imports must take place urgently. . . .

**Observations**
. . . I, together with all my colleagues, am convinced that there needs to be a major mobilization and movement of resources to deal with aspects of this deep crisis in the fields of agriculture and food, water, sanitation and health. . . . [I]t will be difficult, if not impossible, to remedy these immediate humanitarian needs without dealing with the underlying need for energy, on an equally urgent basis. . . . It is unmistakable that the Iraqi people may soon face a further imminent catastrophe, which could include epidemic and famine, if massive life-supporting needs are not rapidly met. The long summer, with its often 45 or even 50 degree temperatures (113–122 degrees Fahrenheit), is only weeks away. Time is short.

* Excerpts of the Ahtisaari Report were prepared by Martha Wenger and appeared in *Middle East Report* issue number 170.

# Bibliography

## Middle East History and General

Asali, K. J., *Jerusalem in History*, New York: Olive Branch Press/Interlink, 1990.

Berque, Jacques, *Arab Rebirth: Pain and Ecstasy*, New York and London: Saqi Books, 1983.

Chomsky, Noam, *Pirates and Emperors: International Terrorism in the Real World*, Brattleboro: Amana, 1986.

Choueiri, Youssef M., *Arab History and the Nation-State: A Study in Modern Arab Historiography 1820–1980*, London: Routledge, 1989.

Draper, Theodore, *A Very Thin Line: The Iran-Contra Affairs*, New York: Farrar, Straus & Giroux, 1991.

Flavin, Christopher and Nicholas Lenssen, *Beyond the Petroleum Age: Designing a Solar Economy*, Washington, D.C.: Worldwatch Institute, 1990.

Freedman, Robert O. (ed.), *The Middle East from the Iran-Contra Affair to the Intifada*, Syracuse: Syracuse University Press, 1991.

Friedman, Thomas L., *From Beirut to Jerusalem*, New York: Farrar, Straus & Giroux, 1989.

Fromkin, David, *A Peace to End All Peace: The Fall of the Ottoman Empire and the Creation of the Modern Middle East*, New York: Avon Books, 1990.

Golan, Galia, *Soviet Policies in the Middle East: From World War Two to Gorbachev*, Cambridge: Cambridge University Press, 1991.

Gresh, Alain and Dominique Vidal, *A to Z of the Middle East*, London: Zed Books, 1990.

Halliday, Fred, *The Threat from the East?*, Harmondsworth: Penguin, 1982.

Hourani, Albert, *The Emergence of the Modern Middle East*, Los Angeles and Berkeley: University of California Press, 1981.

Hourani, Albert, *Europe and the Middle East*, Los Angeles and Berkeley: University of California Press, 1980.

Hourani, Albert, *A History of the Arab Peoples*, Cambridge, Mass.: Harvard University Press, 1991.

Issawi, Charles, *An Economic History of the Middle East and North Africa*, New York: Columbia University Press, 1982.

Khalidi, Walid, *The Gulf Crisis: Origins and Consequences*, Washington, D.C.: Institute of Palestine Studies, 1991.

Khamsin (ed.), *Forbidden Agendas: Intolerance and Defiance in the Middle East*, New York and London: Saqi Books, 1984.

Khouri, Rami, *Lines in the Sand: The Roots of Arab Anger and the Future of the Middle East*, New York: Lawrence Hill, 1991.

Lamb, David, *The Arabs: Journeys Beyond the Mirage*, New York: Random House, 1987.

Maalouf, Amin, *The Crusades Through Arab Eyes*, New York: Schocken, 1987.

Mansfield, Peter, *A History of the Middle East*, New York: Viking, 1991.

Middle East Report, *Crisis in the Gulf*, resource packet, Washington, D.C.: 1990.

Mostyn, Trevor (ed.), *The Cambridge Encyclopedia of the Middle East and North Africa*, New York: Cambridge University Press, 1988.

Nore, Petter and Terisa Turner, *Oil and the Class Struggle*, London: Zed Books, 1980.

Ridgeway, James (ed.), *The March to War*, New York: Four Walls Eight Windows, 1991.

Rumaihi, Muhammad, *Beyond Oil: Unity and Development in the Gulf*, New York and London: Saqi Books, 1986.

Said, Edward W., *Covering Islam: How the Media and the Experts Determine How We See the Rest of the World*, New York: Pantheon, 1981.

Said, Edward W., *Orientalism*, New York: Pantheon, 1978.

Sifry, Micah L. and Christopher Cerf (eds.), *The Gulf War Reader: History, Documents, Opinions*, New York: Times Books, 1991.

Stork, Joe, *Middle East Oil and the Energy Crisis*, New York: Monthly Review Press, 1975.

Woodward, Bob, *The Commanders*, New York: Simon & Schuster, 1991.

Yergin, Daniel, *The Prize: The Epic Quest for Oil, Money and Power*, New York: Simon & Schuster, 1991.

# Iraq

Atiyyah, Ghassan, *Iraq 1908–1921: A Political Study*, Beirut: Arab Institute for Research and Publishing, 1973.

CARDRI (Campaign Against Repression and for Democratic Rights in Iraq), *Saddam's Iraq: Revolution or Reaction?*, revised edn., London: Zed Books, 1989.

Gabbay, Ronay, *Communism and Agrarian Reform in Iraq*, London: Croom Helm, 1978.

Helms, Christine Moss, *Iraq: Eastern Flank of the Arab World*, Washington, D.C.: The Brookings Institute, 1984.

Hussein, Adil, *Iraq: The Eternal Fire*, London: Third World Centre for Research and Publishing, 1981.

Hussein, Saddam, *Khandaq am Khandaqani* (One Trench or Two Trenches?), Baghdad, n. p., 1977.

Hussein, Saddam, *Saddam Hussein on Current Events in Iraq*, London: Longman, 1977.

Khadduri, Majid, *Independent Iraq 1932–1958: A Study in Iraqi Politics*, 2nd revised edn., London: Oxford University Press, 1960.

Khadduri, Majid, *Republican Iraq: A Study in Iraqi Politics Since the Revolution of 1958*, London: Oxford University Press, 1969.

Khadduri, Majid, *Socialist Iraq: A Study in Iraqi Politics Since 1968*, Washington, D.C.: Middle East Institute, 1978.

al-Khalil, Samir, *The Republic of Fear*, New York: Pantheon, 1990.

Kienle, Eberhard, *Ba'th v. Ba'th: The Conflict Between Syria and Iraq 1958–1989*, London: I. B. Tauris, 1990.

Marr, Phebe, *The Modern History of Iraq*, Boulder, Co.: Westview Press, 1985.

Matar, Fuad, *Saddam Hussein: A Biography*, revised edn., London: Highlight, 1990.

Mejcher, Helmut, *The Imperial Quest for Oil: Iraq 1910–1928*, London: Ithaca Press, 1976.

Middle East Watch, *Human Rights in Iraq*, New Haven: Yale University Press, 1990.

Miller, Judith and Laurie Mylroie, *Saddam Hussein and the Crisis in the Gulf*, New York: Times Books, 1990.

Niblock, Tim (ed.), *Iraq: The Contemporary State*, London: Croom Helm, 1982.

Roux, Georges, *Ancient Iraq*, 2nd edn., London and New York: Penguin Books, 1980.

Sluglett, Peter, *Britain in Iraq 1914–1932*, London: Ithaca Press, 1976.

Sluglett, Peter and Marion Farouk-Sluglett, *Iraq Since 1958: From Revolution to Dictatorship*, revised edn., London: I. B. Tauris, 1990.

## Palestine, Israel, the Arab-Israeli Conflict

Bennis, Phyllis and Neal Cassidy, *From Stones to Statehood: The Palestinian Uprising*, New York: Olive Branch Press/Interlink, 1990.

Cobban, Helena, *The Palestine Liberation Organization: People, Power and Politics*, Cambridge: Cambridge University Press, 1984.

Flapan, Simha, *The Birth of Israel: Myths and Realities*, New York: Pantheon, 1987.

Goldstein, Eric, *The Israeli Army and the Intifada, Policies that Contribute to the Killings: A Middle East Watch Report*, New York: Human Rights Watch, 1990.

Gowers, Andrew and Tony Walker, *Behind the Myth: Yasser Arafat and the Palestinian Revolution*, New York: Olive Branch Press/Interlink, 1991.

Gresh, Alain, *The PLO: The Struggle Within*, London: Zed Books, 1988.

Hadawi, Sami, *Bitter Harvest: A Modern History of Palestine*, 4th revised edn., New York: Olive Branch Press/Interlink, 1991.

Harkabi, Yehoshafat, *Israel's Fateful Hour*, New York: Harper & Row, 1988.

Khamsin (ed.), *Palestine: Profile of an Occupation*, London: Zed Books, 1989.

Lockman, Zachary and Joel Beinin (eds.), *Intifada: The Palestinian Uprising Against Israeli Occupation*, Boston: South End Press, 1989.

Langer, Felicia, *An Age of Stone*, London: Quartet, 1988.

McDowall, David, *Palestine and Israel: The Uprising and Beyond*, Los Angeles and Berkeley: University of California Press, 1989.

Rodinson, Maxime, *Cult, Ghetto and State: The Persistence of the Jewish Question*, New York and London: Saqi Books, 1983.

Said, Edward W., *After the Last Sky: Palestinian Lives*, New York: Pantheon, 1986.

Said, Edward W. and Christopher Hitchens (eds.), *Blaming the Victims: Spurious Scholarship and the Palestinian Question*, London and New York: Verso, 1988.

Said, Edward W., *The Question of Palestine*, New York: Times Books, 1979.

Shehadeh, Raja, *The Third Way: A Journal of Life in the West Bank*, London: Quartet, 1982.

Shipler, David K., *Arab and Jew: Wounded Spirits in a Promised Land*, New York: Times Books, 1986.

Swirski, Shlomo, *Israel: The Oriental Majority*, London: Zed Books, 1989.

# Iran, the Iran-Iraq War, the Gulf States

Abdulghani, Jasmin M., *Iraq and Iran: The Years of Crisis*, Baltimore: The Johns Hopkins University Press, 1984.

Abdullah, Muhammad Morsy, *The United Arab Emirates: A Modern History*, New York: Barnes & Noble, 1978.

al-Alkim, Hassan Hamdan, *The Foreign Policy of the United Arab Emirates*, London and New York: Saqi Books, 1989.

Amnesty International, *Iran: Violations of Human Rights 1987–1990*, New York, 1990.

Assiri, Abdul Reda, *Kuwait's Foreign Policy*, Boulder, Co.: Westview Press, 1990.

Chubin, Shahram, and Charles Tripp, *Iran and Iraq at War*, 2nd edn., London: I. B. Tauris, 1989.

Cottrell, Alvin J. (ed.), *The Persian Gulf States: A General Survey*, Baltimore: The Johns Hopkins University Press, 1980.

Crystal, Jill, *Oil and Politics in the Gulf: Rulers and Merchants in Kuwait and Qatar*, Cambridge: Cambridge University Press, 1990.

Halliday, Fred, *Arabia Without Sultans*, London: Penguin, 1974.

Hiro, Dilip, *The Longest War: The Iran-Iraq Military Conflict*, New York: Routledge, 1991.

Hiro, Dilip, *Iran Under the Ayatollahs*, London: Routledge & Kegal Paul, 1985.

Holden, David and Richard Johns, *The House of Saud: The Rise and Fall of the Most Powerful Dynasty in the Arab World*, New York: Holt, Rinehart & Winston, 1981.

Hunter, Shireen T., *Iran and the World: Continuity in a Revolutionary Decade*, Bloomington: Indiana University Press, 1990.

Khadduri, Majid, *The Gulf War: The Origins and Implications of the Iran-Iraq Conflict*, New York: Oxford University Press, 1988.

Ismael, T. Y., *Iraq and Iran: Roots of Conflict*, Syracuse: Syracuse University Press, 1982.

Keddie, Nikki R., *Roots of Revolution: An Interpretive History of Modern Iran*, New Haven: Yale University Press, 1981.

Lacey, Robert, *The Kingdom: Arabia and the House of Sa'ud*, New York: Harcourt Brace Jovanovich, 1981.

Mofid, Kamran, *The Economic Consequences of the Gulf War*, London: Routledge, 1990.

Mottahedeh, Roy, *The Mantle of the Prophet*, New York: Pantheon, 1985.

Nonneman, Gerd, *Iraq, the Gulf States and the War: A Changing Relationship 1980–1986 and Beyond*, London: Ithaca Press, 1986.

Quandt, William, *Saudi Arabia in the 1980s*, Washington, D.C.: The Brookings Institute, 1981.

Rahnema, Ali and Farhad Nomani, *The Secular Miracle: Religion, Politics and Economic Policy in Iran*, London: Zed Books, 1990.

Safran, Nadav, *Saudi Arabia: The Ceaseless Quest for Security*, Cambridge, Mass.: Harvard University Press, 1985.

Shawcross, William, *The Shah's Last Ride*, New York: Simon & Schuster, 1988.

Wright, Robin, *In the Name of God: The Khomeini Decade*, New York: Simon & Schuster, 1989.

Zahlan, Rosemarie Said, *The Making of the Modern Gulf States*, London: Unwin Hyman, 1989.

## The U.S. and the Middle East

Bates, Greg (ed.), *Mobilizing Democracy: Changing the U.S. Role in the Middle East*, Monroe, Maine: Common Courage Press, 1991.

Chomsky, Noam, *The Fateful Triangle: The United States, Israel and the Palestinians*, Boston: South End Press, 1983.

Curtiss, Richard, *Stealth PACs: How Israel's American Lobby Seeks to Control U.S. Middle East Policy*, Washington, D.C.: American Educational Trust, 1990.

Findlay, Paul, *They Dare to Speak Out*, Westport, Ct.: Lawrence Hill, 1985.

Green, Stephen, *Living by the Sword: America and Israel in the Middle East*, Brattleboro: Amana, 1988.

James, Bill, *The Eagle and the Lion: The Tragedy of American-Iranian Relations*, New Haven: Yale University Press, 1988.

McNaugher, Thomas L., *Arms and Oil: U.S. Military Strategy and the Persian Gulf*, Washington, D.C.: The Brookings Institute, 1985.

Quandt, William, *Camp David: Peacemaking and Politics*, Washington, D.C., The Brookings Institute, 1986.

Sick, Gary, *All Fall Down: America's Tragic Encounter with Iran*, New York: Random House, 1985.

Tivnan, Edward, *The Lobby: Jewish Political Power and American Foreign Policy*, New York: Simon & Schuster, 1987.

Woodward, Bob, *Veil: The Secret Wars of the CIA 1981–1987*, New York: Simon & Schuster, 1989.

## Islam

Boulares, Habib, *Islam: The Fear and the Hope*, London: Zed Books, 1990.

Cole, Juan R. I. and Nikki R. Keddie (eds.), *Shi'ism and Social Protest*, New Haven: Yale University Press, 1986.

Glasse, Cyril, *The Concise Encyclopedia of Islam*, San Francisco: Harper & Row, 1989.

Haddad, Yvonne Yazbeck, Byron Haines and Ellison Findley (eds.), *The Islamic Impact*, Syracuse: Syracuse University Press, 1984.

Hiro, Dilip, *Holy Wars: The Rise of Islamic Fundamentalism*, New York: Routledge, 1989.

Khuri, Fuad, *Imams and Emirs: State, Religion and Sects in Islam*, London: Saqi Books, 1990.

Mortimer, Edward, *Faith and Power: The Politics of Islam*, New York: Random House, 1982.

Wright, Robin, *Sacred Rage: The Wrath of Militant Islam*, New York: Simon & Schuster, 1985.

# Kurdistan

Chaliand, Gerard (ed.), *People Without a Country: The Kurds and Kurdistan*, revised edn., New York: Olive Branch Press/Interlink, 1991.

Eagleton, William, Jr., *The Kurdish Republic of Mahabad*, London: Oxford University Press, 1963.

Ghareeb, Edmond, *The Kurdish Question in Iraq*, Syracuse: Syracuse University Press, 1981.

Jawad, Sa'ad, *Iraq and the Kurdish Question 1958–1970*, London: Ithaca Press, 1981.

Laizer, Sheri, *Into Kurdistan: Frontiers Under Fire*, London: Zed Books, 1991.

# Egypt, Jordan, Syria, Lebanon

Amnesty International, *Egypt: Recent Human Rights Violations Under the State of Emergency*, New York, October 1990.

Baker, Raymond W., *Sadat and After: Struggles for Egypt's Political Soul*, London: I. B. Tauris, 1990.

Fisk, Robert, *Pity the Nation*, New York: Atheneum, 1990.

Giannou, Chris, *Besieged: A Doctor's Story of Life and Death in Beirut*, New York: Olive Branch Press/Interlink, 1991.

Gubser, Peter, *Jordan: Crossroads of Middle Eastern Events*, London: Croom Helm, 1983.

Holt, P. M., *Egypt and the Fertile Crescent 1516–1922: A Political History*, London: Longman, 1966.

Lawyers Committee for Human Rights, *Torture in Egypt in 1989: A Report by the Egyptian Organization for Human Rights*, New York, 1990.

Paul, James A., *Human Rights in Syria: A Middle East Watch Report*, New York: Human Rights Watch, 1990.

Petran, Tabitha, *The Struggle Over Lebanon*, New York: Monthly Review Press, 1987.

Salibi, Kamal, *A House of Many Mansions: The History of Lebanon Reconsidered*, London: I. B. Tauris, 1988.

Seale, Patrick, *Asad: The Struggle for the Middle East*, Los Angeles and Berkeley: University of California Press, 1989.

Tripp, Charles and Roger Owens (eds.), *Egypt Under Mubarak*, New York and London: Routledge, 1989.

Waterbury, John, *The Egypt of Nasser and Sadat*, Princeton: Princeton University Press, 1983.

# Articles

Abdalla, Ahmed, "Mubarak's Gamble," *Middle East Report*, January-February 1991.

Ahmad, Eqbal, "Nightmare Victory?" *Mother Jones*, March–April 1991.

Bahbah, Bishara, "The Gulf Crisis: An Israeli Heyday," *Washington Report on Middle East Affairs*, November 1990.

Ball, George, "How to Resolve the Crisis," *New York Review of Books*, December 6, 1990.

Baram, Amazia, "The Ruling Political Elite in Ba'thi Iraq 1968–1986," *International Journal of Middle East Studies*, 21, 1989.

Barhoum, Khalil, "The Gulf War and After: Perception versus Reality," *Middle East International*, April 19, 1991.

Berman, Paul, "The Gulf and the Left," *Village Voice*, October 23, 1990.

Borosage, Robert, "The Peace Movement: Countering Bush's Gambit in the Gulf," *The Nation*, September 24, 1990.

Brown, Michael E., "The Nationalization of the Iraq Petroleum Company," *International Journal of Middle East Studies*, 10 (1979).

Caesar, Judith, "Saudi Dissent: Rumblings Under the Throne," *The Nation*, December 17, 1990.

Childers, Erskine B., "The Use and Abuse of the UN in the Gulf Crisis," *Middle East Report*, March-April 1991.

Chomsky, Noam, "Nefarious Aggression," *Z Magazine*, October 1990.

Cockburn, Alexander, "The Press and the 'Just War,'" *The Nation*, February 18, 1991.

Ehkeshami, Anonshiravan, "Iran Rides out the Storm in the Gulf," *Middle East International*, March 8, 1991.

Emery, Michael, "How the U.S. Avoided Peace," *Village Voice*, March 5, 1991.

Fagan, Shannon, "The Wasteland: Environmental Devastation in the Wake of the Gulf War," *In These Times*, March 27–April 2, 1991.

Farouk-Sluglett, Marion, Peter Sluglett and Joe Stork, "Not Quite Armageddon: The Impact of the (Gulf) War on Iraq," *MERIP Reports*, 125–126, July–September, 1984.

Ferguson, Thomas, "The War's Inevitable Fifth Horseman," *New York Times*, February 3, 1991.

Gasperini, William, "Kuwaitis Battle for Their Psyches," *In These Times*, March 27–April 2, 1991.

Gitlin, Todd, "Towards a Difficult Peace Movement," *Village Voice*, February 19, 1991.

Hiro, Dilip, "Chronicle of the Gulf War," *MERIP Reports*, 125–126, July–September 1984.

Hitchens, Christopher, "Realpolitik in the Gulf: A Game Gone Tilt," *Harpers*, January 1991.

Indiana, Gary, "Victory Life: Notes on the Postwar Culture of Resentment," *Village Voice*, June 11, 1991.

Kinsley, Susan, "The Kurds: Persecuted Throughout the Region," *Human Rights Watch*, Winter 1991.

Klare, Michael T., "Fueling the Fire: How We Armed the Middle East," *Bulletin of the Atomic Scientists*, January-February 1991.

Klare, Michael T., "An InterNation Story: High-Death Weapons of the Gulf War," *The Nation*, June 3, 1991.

McCarthy, Colman, "The Coward's Air War," *Washington Post*, February 17, 1991.

MacShane, Denis, "Gulf Migrant Labor: Working in Virtual Slavery," *The Nation*, March 18, 1991.

Molnar, Alex, "If My Marine Son Is Killed . . .," *New York Times*, August 23, 1990.

Parry, Robert, "Did Saddam Want a Deal: The Peace Feeler That Was," *The Nation*, April 15, 1991.

Payton, Brenda, "The Black Antiwar Movement: Looking for a Post-Gulf Role," *The Nation*, July 1, 1991.

Pfaff, William, "Islam and the West," *The New Yorker*, January 28, 1991.

Pool, David, "From Elite to Class! The Transformation of Iraqi Leadership 1920–1939," *International Journal of Middle East Studies*, 12;3, November 1980.

Sadowski, Yahya, "Arab Economies After the Gulf War," *Middle East Report*, May-June 1991.

Said, Edward W., "A Plan for Palestinian Self-Determination," *Washington Post*, March 17, 1991.

Schanberg, Sydney H., "Censoring for Political Security," *Washington Journalism Review*, March 1991.

Schlesinger, Arthur, Jr., "White Slaves in the Persian Gulf," *Wall Street Journal*, January 7, 1991.

Schofield, Richard, "The Iraq-Kuwait Boundary: A Problem Outstanding," *Middle East International*, April 19, 1991.

Sherry, Virginia, "Kuwait Before — and After?" *The Nation*, November 9, 1991.

Sid-Ahmed, Mohamed, "The Gulf Crisis and the New World Order," *Middle East Report*, January-February 1991.

Sifry, Micah L., "Iraq, 1958 to the Present: America, Oil and Intervention," *The Nation*, March 11, 1991.

Stork, Joe and Martha Wenger, "The U.S. in the Persian Gulf: From Rapid Deployment to Massive Deployment," *Middle East Report*, January-February, 1991.

Trebay, Guy, "Life After Wartime: Surreal Snapshots from Kuwait," *Village Voice*, June 25, 1991.

Vine, Peter, "The Ecological Disaster in the Gulf," *Middle East International*, April 5, 1991.

Viorst, Milton, "The House of Hashem," *The New Yorker*, January 7, 1991.

Waas, Murray, "What Washington Gave Saddam for Christmas," *Village Voice*, December 18, 1990.

# Index

408